Multi-Party Elections in Africa

Multi-Party Elections in Africa

Edited by
Michael Cowen
& Liisa Laakso

James Currey
OXFORD

palgrave
NEW YORK

Multi-Party Elections in Africa

James Currey Ltd
73 Botley Road
Oxford OX2 0BS

© James Currey Ltd 2002
First published 2002
1 2 3 4 5 06 05 04 03 02

British Library Cataloguing in Publication Data
Multi-party elections in Africa
1. Elections – Africa, Sub-Saharan – History
I. Cowen, Michael II. Laakso, Liisa
324.9'67'0329

ISBN 0–85255–844–9 (James Currey Cloth)
ISBN 0–85255–843–0 (James Currey Paper)

First published in the United States by
PALGRAVE, 175 Fifth Avenue, New York, NY 10010
Companies and representatives throughout the world, PALGRAVE is the new
global imprint of St. Martin's Press LLC Scholarly and Reference Division and
Palgrave Publishers Ltd. (formerly Macmillan Press Ltd).

Library of Congress Cataloging-in-Publication Data

Multi-party elections in Africa/edited by Michael Cowen & Liisa Laakso.
    p. cm.
  Includes bibliographical references and index
  ISBN 0-312-29486-7
  1. Elections–Africa, Sub-Saharan. 2. Africa, Sub-Saharan–Politics and
government–1960- I. Cowen, Michael. II. Laakso, Liisa.

JQ1879.A5 M85 2001
324.967–dc21   2001036824

Typeset by Saxon Graphics Ltd, Derby
Printed and bound in Great Britain by
Woolnough, Irthlingborough

Contents

Preface

This collection of election studies was based upon a research project that covered elections in 14 of the roughly 40 sub-Saharan countries which have experienced multi-party elections during the 1990s. The list of countries was drawn up randomly to the extent that it was based on the area of expertise of a selected number of researchers who are based at, or have connections with, the Helsinki University Institute of Development Studies. To this extent, the volume of studies is mainly confined to anglophone Africa. However, while there is no coverage of francophone Africa and despite the omission of some cases such as South Africa, the collection of studies is enriched by the inclusion of countries, such as Ethiopia, Guinea-Bissau and the Sudan, which are often neglected in the study of elections in Africa.

In each case, the analysis concentrated on the most recent electoral experience before or during the project period, from late 1996 to the end of 1998. While all those involved in the project have a general interest in elections, they come from different academic disciplines, and have studied different aspects and different kinds of elections. One of the main aims of the project was to adopt a historical approach by looking at electoral experiences of the colonial and one-party periods as well as multi-party elections during the 1990s. For the majority of the cases in this collection, the recent multi-party experience has included two sets of general elections, thereby enabling some conclusions to be drawn about possible trajectories of multi-party politics.

Given the background to, and aims of, the project, a range of electoral experiences – parliamentary, presidential, by- or local elections – appears in the case studies. Thus, for example, general or *national* elections were covered for Ethiopia (1995), Ghana (1996), Kenya (1997), Sudan (1996), Tanzania (1995), Zambia (1995), and Zimbabwe (1995). *Local* or by-elections were covered for Malawi (1997), Namibia (1998) and Nigeria (1997). Some of these, together with other case studies, such as Botswana, Lesotho and Swaziland and Guinea Bissau, have provided an opportunity of looking in detail at more than one set of elections. However, a *local* approach was also used for some cases. Thus, the Tanzania study is based on comparisons between two borderland case studies; the Kenya and Zambia cases use both a local and national approach; and the Malawi case consists of a single but significant urban by-election.

Since neither the project nor this volume, upon which it is based, was intended to be 'the entire study' of elections in Africa, no over-arching framework was imposed upon the studies as a whole. Nevertheless, contributors were well aware that one aim of the project was to provide an understanding of electoral factors, issues or themes that have often been ignored during the course of previous election studies in Africa. Foremost among these themes are the economic background and implications of elections, differences between rural and urban areas and the experiences and expectations of political party leaderships in relation to different local electorates. These factors often play a large place in election studies generally and there is no reason why they should be absent from African elections. Further, other neglected issues, such as religion and gender, were also brought to the fore, as in the respective cases of the Sudan and Ethiopia. While no one case study can be expected to include all the above-mentioned factors, issues or themes, they do appear across the case studies taken as a whole.

Locality, in particular, emerged as one very significant electoral theme. Although there was some conjecture about the significance of locality as an issue or factor that should be taken into account for the explanation of the electoral process, the extent to which 'the local', whether rural or urban, appears recurrently as an electoral theme was not anticipated at the onset of the project. Some of the case studies, together with the introduction, elaborate on the significance of locality and show that it is not to be simply conflated with the well-trodden issues of communality, especially those of the ethnic or 'tribal' as sources of political identity. Moreover, the local is not to be regarded as some enclosed, distinct arena of political virtue that is separate from 'high politics' at the national level. Rather, the changing relation between the local and the national, especially within a global frame of reference, is better understood as a powerful political force that stems from locally expressed desires for economic and social improvement – what is popularly known as 'development'. A change in the political party ruling over state power does not in itself necessarily make improvement possible but the question of why candidates and their parties win and lose elections owes much to local development politics.

Incumbent ruling parties, for virtually all the cases included in this particular volume, have been able to come to terms with multi-party politics during the 1990s and have learned how to electorally retain power. Opposition parties, on the other side of the same coin, have found it difficult to win multi-party elections. Apart from other well-known issues that arise from the administrative manipulation of the electoral process as a whole, thereby preventing a level playing field for 'free and fair' contests, locality is a factor that explains why elections do not easily result in the transfer of government. An understanding of where the playing field of electoral politics is located matters as much as the degree to which it is level.

The first workshop of the project, concentrating on the aims of the project and some methodological issues, was held at the Institute of Development Studies (IDS), Helsinki, 19–21 December 1996. Drafts for the chapters that appear in this collection were presented and were discussed in the final workshop at Kellokoski, 10–12 June 1998. Both workshops were valuable events in themselves and did much to extend our understanding of electoral processes in Africa.

The project was mainly funded by the Academy of Finland. Supplementary funding, largely for travel, especially from Africa to the second workshop, was provided by the Nordic Africa Institute in Uppsala, Sweden and the Finnish Department of International Development Cooperation (Kyo, or better known as Finnida). Kyo also provided the subsidy that will enable this book to reach libraries and readers in Africa.

We are indebted to those who assisted in both the project and the preparation of the manuscript for publication. Riina Yrjölä was an exceptionally assiduous research assistant during the earlier stages of the project. Simo Virtanen enabled us to carry out the data analysis of political business cycles. Liisa Koski, Terttu Turunen and Riikka Saar made materials available through their respective libraries, those of Helsinki University's main library, the Faculty of Social Sciences library and that of IDS. Ellen Mustonen, Maj-Lis Lehtinen, Lari Kangas, Eva-Marita Rinne and Katja Hirvonen all assisted in the administration of the project and its workshops. Together with Lari Kangas who also assisted in preparing the manuscript, Lalli Metsola proved to be an astute and conscientious editorial assistant during the last stages of the project as a whole.

Last, but not least, we are grateful to Clare and James Currey who showed how they were committed to publishing the results of the project by participating to the full in the Kellokoski workshop. Douglas Johnson has sympathetically guided the production of this book through to fruition.

Michael Cowen & Liisa Laakso

Notes on Contributors

Anthony Kwesi Aubynn has been a research student at the University of Tampere and a researcher at the Institute of Development Studies, University of Helsinki. He is presently working in Ghana. He has a special interest in the politics of the environment.

Michael Cowen worked at the Institute of Development Studies, Helsinki, where he had been invited to fill the first professorial post; he was on an extended leave of absence from the Department of Economics at London Guildhall University. Cowen made an enormous contribution to the Institute of Development Studies in Helsinki, establishing new BA and PhD programmes and initiating and leading several research projects. Before his premature death in February 2000, he was only able to complete one of them, *Elections in Africa,* whose results are presented in this volume. With R.W. Shenton he had two extensive manuscripts in preparation (on Fabian colonialism and on the fiction of community). Cowen is the author (with R.W. Shenton) of *Doctrines of Development* (1996) and (with Scott MacWilliam) *Indigenous Capital in Kenya* (1996).

Atta El-Battahani teaches politics at the University of Khartoum. He has researched for many years on the political economy of the Sudan and written many papers within this area of work. He has been a visiting research fellow at the Institute of Development Studies, Helsinki.

Harri Englund, a social anthropologist, is the Finnish researcher at the Nordic Africa Institute in Uppsala, Sweden. He has carried out extensive ethnographic fieldwork in both rural and urban areas of Malawi. His doctoral thesis, for Manchester University where he has also been a research fellow, is entitled *Brother Against Brother: The Moral Economy of War and Displacement in the Malawi-Mozambique Border* (1995) and is about to be published.

Jeremy Gould is a researcher at the Institute of Development Studies, Helsinki. He has had substantial experience of fieldwork in northern Zambia. Among other publications, based on a wide area of research, he is the author of *Localising Modernity: Action, Interests and Association in Rural Zambia* (1997) which was presented as his doctoral thesis.

Karuti Kanyinga is a research fellow at the Institute for Development Studies, University of Nairobi. He has researched on the political economy of Kenya and has recently completed his doctoral dissertation, *Struggles of Access to Land*, for Roskilde University, Denmark.

Liisa Laakso teaches politics at the University of Helsinki. She has researched and published widely on politics in Africa, including editing (with Adebeyo Olukoshi) *Challenges to the Nation State in Africa* (1996). Her doctoral research has been on the state and politics in Zimbabwe.

Michael Neocosmos teaches sociology and development studies at the University of Botswana. He has also taught at the Universities of Lesotho and Swaziland while researching for many years on the political economy of Southern Africa. His published writings include *The Agrarian Question in Southern Africa and 'Accumulation from Below'* (1993).

Sanna Ojalammi-Wamai has been a research student in geography at the University of Helsinki and has carried out fieldwork among the Maasai of Tanzania. She presently works in the Finnish Department of International Development Cooperation.

Adebayo Olukoshi is a professorial researcher at the Nordic Africa Institute, Uppsala. He has researched extensively on both Structural Adjustment Policy and politics in Africa with a special interest in Nigeria. As well as many other writings, he has edited (with Henock Kifle and Lennart Wohlgemuth) *A New Partnership for African Development* (1997) and *The Politics of Opposition in Contemporary Africa* (1998).

Tuulikki Pietilä is a researcher in social anthropology at the University of Helsinki. She has recently completed her doctoral thesis, *Gossip, Markets and Gender: The Dialogical Construction of Morality in Kilimanjaro*, as well as writing other articles based on her fieldwork in northern Tanzania.

Eva Poluha is a social anthropologist at the University of Stockholm. She has had a lengthy experience of fieldwork in Ethiopia. She has written *Central Planning and Local Reality* (1989) in addition to other articles on state-peasant relations and democracy in Ethiopia.

Lars Rudebeck, as an active member of the Seminar for Development Studies, teaches politics at the University of Uppsala. He has researched for very many years on Guinea Bissau. Among his extensive publications on political change and democracy, he has edited *When Democracy Makes Sense* (1992) and (with Olle Törnquist) *Democratisation in the Third World* (1996).

Iina Soiri is a researcher in politics at the Institute of Development Studies, Helsinki. She has written (with Pekka Peltola) *Finland and National Liberation in Southern Africa* (1999). While her doctoral work has been based upon this area of research, she has also researched and written on the politics of decentralisation, especially in Mozambique.

Simo Virtanen, having previously taught at Rutgers University and the University of New Hampshire, is an adjunct lecturer at Helsinki University's Renvall Institute. His writings include a 1992 doctoral thesis from SUNY, State University of New York at Stony Brook, *Group conflict and racial prejudice as sources of white opposition to policies assisting black Americans,* and articles in the *Journal of Politics* and the *Journal of Personality and Social Psychology.*

1

Elections & Election Studies in Africa[1]

MICHAEL COWEN & LIISA LAAKSO

That more than thirty sub-Saharan African states have introduced multi-party electoral systems since 1990 has led many to think that there is something intrinsically new about the process of competitive electoral politics in Africa. Yet in Africa, as elsewhere in the world, electoral competition has a relatively long history. Local elections, as in some former British colonies, were conducted on the basis of universal franchise from the 1920s while it was during the period of the interregnum, between the colonial period and independence from the late 1950s to the one-party period of the 1970s and 1980s, that multi-party national elections were conducted for most of the countries under review here.

While a competitive electoral process cannot in itself be equated with democracy, it is a cardinal precept of liberal democratic theory and practice. According to its own precepts, liberal democracy involves free and fair electoral competition which includes the possibility of criticising government's decision-making, of offering alternatives, thereby enabling *choice* to be made between one set of decisions and another and, more generally, holding politicians accountable for their decisions. As such, the actual form and content of the electoral process is one aspect by which one can gauge the extent to which liberal democracy is realised. Accordingly, as elsewhere in the world, a detailed analysis of elections is part of an understanding of the possibilities and constraints of democratisation in Africa.

Whatever the extent to which a competitive electoral process might indicate the actual realisation of liberal democracy, the process stems also from other trajectories of political practice. However free and fair, the purpose of elections might not simply serve to conform with the precepts of liberal democracy but rather serve the state and the ruling élite. An electoral process, by this account, provides the means to manage regime change thereby pre-empting a possible prospect of violent change through revolution or the coup d'état, whether managed by military or civilian forces. In this case, there is no guarantee that the new political regime will act to a degree that can be judged to be more liberal than the one which it has replaced. From a liberal standpoint, that of Fareed Zakaria (1997, 30), the 'tendency for a democratic government to believe it has absolute sovereignty (that is power) can result in the centralisation of authority, often by extraconstitutional means and with grim results'.

Thus, it is possible to distinguish two standard theoretical approaches to elections in modern states. A vital element of the first approach implies what Dennis Cohen (1983, 80–3) has called the theoretical perspective of *voter choice*, while the second approach concerning the function of the elections for the state and its rulers refers to *the legitimation of state authority* (see Hermet *et al.* eds. 1978). While emphasis put on voter choice in the electoral processes implies an understanding that democratic practice is governed by an inherent uncertainty of outcomes, the function of elections in legitimating state authority is guided by some intent that outcomes should be

---

[1]An earlier version of this article was published in *the Journal of Modern African Studies* 35(4) 1997, 717–744. We are grateful for advice from Erkki Berndtson, David Kimble and Scott MacWilliam.

predictable (see Przeworski 1985 and 1988). But as will become evident in the cases studied in this collection, this distinction between voter choice and legitimation is analytical only, made for the purpose of distinguishing between two logical sources of political authority.

In practice it might seem obvious that all national elections are organised in order to gain legitimacy for state authority, if not internally, then certainly internationally, especially during the 1990s. Simultaneously, however, the main issue at hand during the period of elections under review here, namely the demand that elections should be 'free and fair', and peaceful, carried with it the conviction that voters can be provided with an effective choice. Opposition parties and international agencies, whether official or not, made this demand recurrently upon the assumption that effective choice was necessary to dislodge ruling regimes from state power. While state authorities may claim that elections are important in that 'voting is a duty of a citizen', voters may exercise their right to choose by deciding not to vote, as a refusal to recognise the legitimacy of a given ruling regime. Nowhere is the voters' consciousness of the functionality of the elections for state authority as revealing as it is in countries where the legitimacy of that authority is put into question by voters' apathy, so rampant throughout large parts of Africa, especially towards the end of the 1990s. Nevertheless, as Harri Englund, has argued in the case of Malawi, and what Anthony Aubynn suggests for the Ghana 1992 and 1996 elections, it is also possible that the electorate exercises the right to choose, as much due to its fear of violence and general social instability that would follow from elections as to awarding legitimacy to a ruling party which wins elections. In other words, for the modicum of a peaceful life, voters accommodate themselves to what they regard as illegitimate forms of state authority.

By the same token, the electoral process also serves the more general purpose of reproducing state authority. For an electorate to legitimate state authority, popular assent – it is generally assumed – is conferred upon one particular party (or coalition) which forms the government of a ruling regime. As Michael Neocosmos shows for his Southern African cases by referring to the 1994 elections in South Africa, elections resting upon precepts of liberal democracy presuppose that voters be mobilised solely through the means of a political party. Voting brings an individual person into the political arena by stripping the individual of any personality to make 'the vote' both abstract from the person of any particular voter and equivalent to all other votes. It is the political party which acts to give voice to a particular set of votes so that democracy can be claimed to be representative of an associated interest in society rather than a mere aggregate of individual votes which have no recognisable social condition of existence. Yet, in organising votes through the form of a party organisation, Neocosmos shows that the purpose of elections also acts to disorganise other, and more spontaneous, forms of political mobilisation. Elections, thereby, can be politically demobilising.

Yet, Atta El-Battahani shows in his case study of the Sudan why and how the Islamic Party, which has effectively ruled the country during the 1990s, has acted to create a plethora of civic associations, including the re-invention of 'traditional' institutions, to justify its dismantling of a preceding liberal democratic apparatus of parliamentary representation. In this case, the formal justification for bringing state power closer to 'the people', on the grounds that multi-party politics had led to economic and political decay in the Sudan, has been actually accompanied by a re-centralisation of state power, as shown by the 1996 elections. For this case, the attempt to reproduce state authority by politically mobilising associations from above has made elections effectively redundant, on the grounds of either legitimation or voters' choice, for a country that has had a relatively rich history, in its Northern part, of multi-party elections since the early 1950s.

It is against this background that it is possible to assess the extent to which elections during the multi-party period have embedded liberal democratic practices in Africa. When Africa is treated as an exceptional case of political practice, it is often the case that cultural sources of identity are claimed as the reason why African countries are considered to be ill-fitted for democracy. Much, both in defence of, and against, multi-party electoral politics, has been written about forms of regional, ethnic and religious political mobilisation (see, for example, Diamond et al. eds. 1988). However, from the standpoint of representative democracy, it is not the politicisation of these identities which is significant as such but, rather, the particular secular interests that are given expression through them. The commonplace assertion that distinct policies, or ideological beliefs, seem to be absent from formal party programmes, in Africa as well as the rest of the world, does not mean that there is no content of interests in political mobilisation. Thus, any attempt to understand the meaning of multi-party elections in Africa requires that the theoretical framework for election studies should be extended beyond the electoral process itself. In addition to historical and institutional perspectives, a political economy approach is useful for also countering prevailing impressions that there is something essential about the African experience that makes it essentially different from the rest of the world.

The colonial period

Elections during the colonial period were of two kinds. First, unofficials were elected to the Legislative Councils (Legco), under the most restrictive of franchises. Bounded by race and other prescriptive sources of exclusion, Legco became a forum for arguments with colonial administrations over policy (see for example Wight 1946). Second, and this involves a now almost-forgotten history for some British colonies, elections were held for Local Native Councils (LNCs), and their successor local governing bodies, according to the precept of universal franchise. Thus, to take Kenya as an example, the first elections of unofficial representatives to Legco in 1920, relatively long after the Legislative Council was established in 1907, was followed soon after, in 1923, by the first elected LNCs within the then African 'reserves'. Although the LNCs were confined to local jurisdictions, and were therefore in themselves a cause of early nationalist resentment, elected representatives were trusted with decisions over local resources, especially for education. Councils, thereby, also became sites of political contest. Four decades before universal franchise came to be the basis of national elections in Kenya, as part of the transition to political independence, a generation and more of African politicos had been well versed in the art and craft of electoral politics.

Elections to the colonial legislatures served to endorse the political presence of European settlers or *colons* within colonial territories. In the extreme cases, that of Southern Rhodesia and South Africa, referenda and elections played no small part in making the territories independent of British colonial administration. Thus, the first legislative elections in Rhodesia (1899), and the first referendum (1922), made the territory first the fiefdom of the British South African Company (BSAC) according to a Royal Charter and then, a white-dominated self-governing colony with both as an alternative to colonial rule from London. The general point is that it was political mobilisation by, and of, the settlers that forced an electoral process upon the territory in question. In the Rhodesian case, elections served as an attempt by the BSAC to make settlers more politically responsible. To presage what has happened during the 1990s in Zimbabwe, turnout was markedly low during the first elections, thereby suggesting that the degree of effective mobilisation was a failure.

The electoral process, with its franchise qualifications, was the main constitutional means by which the African majority was excluded from legislative and executive power. It was also the source of the nationalist demand for majority rule, 'one man, one vote', as it was then called with limited gender consciousness, especially in the post-1945 years. African nationalist renewal also played no small part in determining the degree to which Africans, and 'non-whites', were included in voters' registers for electoral participation.

By way of sharp contrast in South Africa, the twentieth-century experience was one of increased exclusion from voters' registers. Whereas in the Cape Colony, a common qualification had applied to all male subjects regardless of colour, the vote was rigidly confined to whites in the Transvaal and the Orange River Colony. After Union in 1910, these pre-Union rights were affirmed alongside the simultaneous award of power to the white-dominated National Parliament to prescribe voting qualifications. In 1930, the vote was extended to European women. To overcome the anomaly that all males in the Cape and Natal had to meet a stipulated qualification, stipulation was removed for all white voters in 1931. This kind of de-qualification reduced the relative electoral voting power of non-whites. A separate system for the representation of Africans was established in 1936, resulting in the removal of Cape Africans from the common roll. Cape coloureds were removed from the common roll in 1956. (Heard 1974.)

For most British colonies, however, it was the post-war norm for frequent constitutional demands to be about voting qualifications. Local pressures, stemming from the attempt to confront nationalist organisations, succeeded in bringing an increasing number of Africans onto the electoral rolls, although each Legco was still dominated by nominated unofficials and senior colonial administrators. Francophone colonies worked differently in that a small number of officially 'assimilated' Africans were able to vote for a *député* to the French *assemblée nationale*, as in the *communes* of Senegal after 1848 (Hayward 1987, 1). Such constitutional patterns of inclusion and exclusion of voters and candidates during the colonial period should be kept in mind when looking at the sources of exclusion, largely linked to nationality and ethnicity, in the post-independent and multi-party years.

Historical couplings of limited and universal franchises at territorial and local levels, as evidenced above, were also accompanied in some colonies by an acknowledgement that paramount chiefs could play a valuable role in local, provincial, and even central government. Mahmood Mamdani has claimed that it was the 'decentralised despotism' of colonial administration for Africans that marked off a conception of community separate from that of civil society. A number of officials and settlers claimed that African political culture involved its own source of accountability and that a 'Western' if not 'European' conception of political participation through the electoral process was alien to Africans. Mamdani (1996, 80) quoted from Sir Donald Cameron, Governor of Tanganyika, who argued in 1925 that it was a British colonial duty 'to do everything to develop the native on lines which will not Westernise him and turn him into a bad imitation of a European'. Others since then, especially during the 1980s, have queried the supposed merits of a Western-designed electoral system, not least since it might be feasible to create a more workable form of African political accountability.

Questions about the significance of the pre-colonial inheritance have frequently been raised. For example, Tom Young, in his introduction to the proceedings of a conference on 'Elections in Africa' (1991),[2] has asked:

> How important is the pre-colonial, i.e. non-Western inheritance of notions of responsibility of the governors to the governed through some mechanism (however formalised or not) of choice of the former by the latter? It is argued by some scholars that in certain cases this is of some importance whereas other literature suggests that attachment to the ideals of electoral democracy is only to be found amongst Western-educated elites and then only when it suits their particular purposes.

Young was referring to another collection edited by Fred Hayward. Hayward seemed to have gone further than his collaborators in claiming that there was 'an extensive tradition of election of leaders in many African societies prior to colonialism'. But by defining an election to mean 'the act or process of choosing between individuals to fill an office', then, as he also readily admits, 'both participation in such elections and the range of choice was often very limited' (Hayward 1987, 5).

Whatever the extent to which there was consultation and discussion among the ruled in the selection of the rulers, we should note the following. First, that 'decentralised despotism' was as much colonial invention as a pre-colonial inheritance. Second, even when Mamdani's thesis can be questioned, as in the account of elected local councils, it was as much the office as the person of the chief which was contested by the ranks of elected representatives to local councils. Following from both these points, there is no doubt that the aspirations of African nationalists for elections based on universal suffrage were directed at securing a change of government. This is a far cry from what has been interpreted to be the inheritance of pre-colonial tradition.

Interregnum elections: transitions to political independence

The first elections based on universal suffrage, and normally without restrictions on candidature and party, were held during the last stages of decolonisation in the late 1950s and before the formal date of independence. Apart from heralding freedoms of association, assembly and the media, these multi-party contests in what might be called 'interregnum' were hotly fought and full of political interest. Since the elections would decide who were to form the first post-colonial

---

[2]The proceedings of this SOAS conference were later published in *Africa* 63(3) 1993, 299–418. Also, see below for a further reference to this collection of election studies.

regimes, they could also be interpreted as the means whereby the transition to a new system of government and administration was to be achieved. However, it is sufficient to say here that in many, if not all, of the first majority-rule elections, it was the more 'radical' rather than the more 'conservative' parties that were most electorally favoured, mainly since the latter were perceived to be amenable to a perpetuation of the old colonial regime.

The interregnum elections were also interesting on political science grounds. For the first time, political systems in Africa were subject to a form of enquiry that differed markedly from earlier studies, invariably deriving from anthropological method and presuppositions. The new studies used concepts, which were understood to be universally applicable, and from a perspective which attempted to regard Africa as part of the modern world. In part, this liberal endeavour reflected the earlier emergence of area (including African) studies in the United States after World War II, which immediately drew upon the latest methodology, theorems and expertise of practitioners in all the social sciences, political science among them.

Election studies were part of this trend. In Britain, where the American science of politics had been eschewed in favour of modern political history (see Kimble 1963), a different tack was followed. Nevertheless, the new discipline of 'political development' emerged, girding its loins in the first substantive studies of African elections during the interregnum. W.J.M. MacKenzie and Kenneth Robinson edited, in 1960, a collection of *Five Elections in Africa*. In the late colonial world of Africa, they declared,

> there is seldom any native tradition of unified government that can be revived, each new state must create its own tradition of political authority. What ideological basis is available except that of free elections under a wide franchise? This is the principle accepted by the West as the true pattern of sovereignty within the state; those seeking independence aspire to it; Western opinion (in so far as the West is anxious to facilitate transition) thinks of new states as legitimate only if they are framed in this Western image [...] Elections are, accordingly, an important device in facilitating the transfer of power: they provide a basis for a new legitimacy acceptable in theory both to the 'colonialists' and to their 'nationalist' opponents. (Mackenzie and Robinson 1960, 1)

Election studies, MacKenzie and Robinson concluded, were 'an important entry into an extremely complex and diverse subject, that of political development in non-Western countries under Western influence'. In other words, they served as the means for replacing one regime by another and this was, in part, a matter of Western influence. However, given that the contributors were writing about elections that had taken place in 1956–7, the nationalist component of the equation was not then easily identified. What Tom Young referred to much later as the 'particular purposes' of 'Western-educated elites' – their interest in elections as a means for legitimating power – had not then been systematically researched (see Coleman 1958).

The Nuffield surveys of British elections since 1945 help to explain why much of the MacKenzie and Robinson collection in 1960 was an analysis of the institutional arrangements that had been made for voting to take place in four African countries, namely Nigeria, Western Region, May 1956 (Phillip Whittaker), and Eastern Region, March 1957 (J. A. Price); Senegal, Territorial Assembly, March 1957 (Robinson); Kenya, March 1957 (Geoffrey Engholm); and Sierra Leone, May 1957 (D. J. R. Scott). Three more comprehensive studies deserve to be mentioned here: *The Nigerian Federal Election of 1959: politics and administration in a developing political system* (1963) by K. W. J. Post; *The Kenyatta Election: Kenya, 1960–1961* (1961) by George Bennett and Carl G. Rosberg, who explained the course of events leading to the negotiated end of colonialism, including what may be regarded as the initial interregnum contest in East Africa; and *African Political Parties* (1961) by Thomas Hodgkin, the British socialist in Ghana.

Whether by way of modern political history or the Nuffield methodology, involving a systematic analysis of the opinions and behaviour of voters, the British-influenced electoral studies of West and East African territories during the interregnum marked the advent of 'political development' which served to establish the potential for institutions to thrive upon the basis of self-government. An integral part of this institution-building was the movement for education in democracy. Thus for example, in the Gold Coast during the run-up to independent Ghana, the University's Department of Extra-Mural Studies organised adult education courses and conferences which were designed to provide an interested public, including aspirant politicians, with the wherewithal to actively participate in the electoral process (see Kimble 1953; and Titmus and Steele 1995, ch. 5). But when 'development' came to be questioned, as the Hayward collection shows for the 1980s, much of the earlier interest in institutions was also eclipsed.

Election studies in new nations

The classic in 1960s American science of politics literature, the collection edited by Gabriel Almond and James S. Coleman *The Politics of the Developing Areas* (including Coleman's 1959 article 'The Politics of sub-Saharan Africa') was already published in 1960, but it was not until the interregnum ended and the era of new nations began, especially in West Africa, that the behaviouralist approach gathered pace in Africa. Coleman and Rosberg's *Political Parties and National Integration in Tropical Africa* and Ruth Morgenthau's *Political Parties in French-Speaking West Africa* both appeared in 1964. In the same year, a collection of essays, *Independent Black Africa*, edited by William Hanna, appeared to signal the rapid maturing of British-originated 'political development' and its semi-detached relation to the American science of politics. This collection included Dennis Austin's article on elections in Ghana titled 'Elections in an African Rural Area', Ruth Morgenthau's 'Single-Party Systems in West Africa', and David Apter's theoretically important 'Some Reflections on the Role of a Political Opposition in New Nations' to which we will turn below.

As stated in Almond and Coleman's collection, this behaviouralist approach was based on the analytical elements of 'political structure', 'party system', 'political role', 'leadership', 'political culture', 'mobilisation', 'political socialisation' and 'functions'. Typically then the rapid political change towards one-party rule by African political regimes was interpreted in this framework as an expression of the traditions, political culture and the multi-ethnic character of African societies. When one-party rule appeared functional to social scientists, they were more often than not impelled towards non-critical analysis by their optimism for the democratising potential of new national state order. Optimism for democracy was evident in Immanuel Wallerstein's *Africa: The Politics of Independence* (1961) and, differently, in Ruth Morgenthau's works. The latter, however, made a distinction between 'mass' and 'patron' parties. According to Morgenthau, 'single patron-party states' were 'moving towards military dictatorship' whereas 'the mass party states rest on popular consent, strengthen procedures and institutions on a scale essential for accomplishing the tasks of the modern democratic state, reflect egalitarian values and leave room for the expression of opposition' (Morgenthau 1964, 437, 443).

Aristide Zolberg, in his *Creating Political Order: The Party-States of West Africa* (1966), analysed in detail the institutional aspects of one-party state formation. This was to be one of the major exceptions, during the later 1960s, to the rule which Young (1991, 1) had later castigated as the 'liberal timidity' which prescribed 'Western political arrangements' for parts of the world other than Africa. When paying attention, for example, to governmental manipulation of the electoral processes in West Africa, Zolberg was far more critical than most of the other academic commentators.

David Apter's writings on Ghana provide a good example of the difficulties which behaviouralists faced in presenting an unambiguous analysis of the possibilities of liberal democracy in Africa. In his 1955 *Gold Coast in Transition*, Apter discussed the role of the leadership and the mass party in facilitating the creation of new political norms and new political relationships which might be compatible with tenets of parliamentary democracy. He was much more concerned about the weakening of charisma, the 'integrative integer' as a regulative source of legitimation for state authority, than about a trend towards authoritarian political development. In the second edition Apter concluded that Ghana was 'for all intents and purposes, a one-party democracy'[3] although he had noted the authoritarian tendencies in the ruling party and the fact that the transformation to a parliamentary democracy had not been as successful as he had earlier expected.

Colin Leys (1969, 5) wrote of Apter:[4]

---

[3]Apter 1959, xiii quoted in Zolberg 1966, 3, 5.
[4]Leys was referring to Apter 1968.

It is doubtful if anyone of intelligence is now pursuing either field research or theory building with the same unreserved commitment to the original behavioral ideals that infused, say, Apter's early work on Ghana or even his much later work on modernisation.

Leys welcomed the import of the American science 'at its best' to Britain, and thereby through to Africa, as an antidote to the unthinking kind of institutional approach to politics. Leys himself was rapidly about to turn 'political development' into 'underdevelopment', the kind of theorising about politics which produced the final reaction against behaviouralism and structural-function-alism (see Leys 1975). By the 1970s, and given the one-party regimes that by then existed throughout most of Africa, the earlier academic interest in elections had waned.

However, by the time he had written the above-mentioned 1962 article, 'Some Reflections on the Role of a Political Opposition in New Nations', Apter turned towards a critical analysis of state repression of political opposition. He concluded that 'few examples of a successful post-independence multi-party system can be found among new nations except Israel and Nigeria' (Apter 1964, 459). This was because of the importance of opposition for a democratic process. Theoretically, his analysis was eloquently built on liberal assumptions about the role of the 'middle' for Western democracy, suggesting that,

> one of the practical rules of politics which works out in normally functioning democracies is that *when there is open party competition and free elections, both parties, government and opposition, seek the support of the large middle spectrum of voters* [...] Hence the importance of free party competition – *it does not divide where all political parties are responsible – but instead exerts a constant pull on the parties drawing them together.* It neutralizes the extremists. Thus party competition is basically not divisive, as is commonly thought, but most often unifying instead.[5]

Apter continued:

> The forms of disunity which characterize governments in new nations are thus often premature. Equally, an opposition which fears and mistrusts the government of the day helps to magnify the fears of a majority party leadership that the opposition, in its efforts to achieve power, is out to destroy all. In those first years of self-government both sides need to recognize how absolutely necessary each is to the other (Apter 1964, 470–471).

Leaving aside the obvious flaws in Apter's analysis of 'normally functioning democracies', which regularly experience exceptionalism or extremism of various kinds due to the opening of a political vacuum when the traditional left or right moves towards the centre, his idea of the 'middle spectrum of voters' deserves a closer look. The thesis here, much explored in the rest of the world but too little in Africa, is about an account of understanding of democratisation as a consequence of the emergence and growth of a middle class. It is what the middle class, rather than *bourgeoisie* as class of capital, might mean in Africa, during different periods of growth of state employment and retrenchment, which is a significant factor. Another factor is the economic and political weight of the middle class with respect to both classes of capital and labour. Again, periods of wage-labour formation and, as more recently, the relative decimation of wage labour forces throughout Africa, and the rapid expansion of self-employment, are likely to tell much of the 'middle' in politics.

Behaviouralism came to bed down as the modernisation school. Given so much optimism towards social and economic development, it is not surprising that the study of modernisation became increasingly popular in the search to establish a correlation between this process and liberal democracy. Although this correlation has been difficult to challenge through empirical research alone,[6] the historical and logical explanation for the association is anything but resolved

---

[5]Emphasis in original.
[6]For instance, Seymor Martin Lipset (1959) compared economic development and democracy in European and Latin American states. Indeed, over 30 years later, another American scholar qualified Lipset's basic argument by using the UNDP Human Development Index and showing that economic development promotes democracy to the extent that it leads to higher levels of 'human well-being' (Diamond 1992).

(see Rueschmeyer *et al.* 1992). Behaviouralists understood the 'modern' as represented, for example, by urbanisation, western education, commercialisation of land and labour and seculari-sation. People were to be socially ordered not through traditional identities but according 'to specific interests requiring new modes of expression consonant with secular authority structure and appropriate to a modern territorial society' (Coleman 1960, 325).

The emergence and expansion of middle classes seemed to be essential for the modernisation project. Liberal economic policy was seen as a vital ingredient in the quest for guaranteeing the economic independence of a class which, while committed to property and social order, would form a counterbalance to the exercise of state power. Without a relatively large and prosperous class, independent of state largesse for its well-being, it was supposed that liberal democracy could not survive. This same kind of argument became popular much later, largely in connection with the Structural Adjustment Programmes (SAPs) in Africa. For instance in the case of Nigeria, Larry Diamond has made the following claim:

> any basis for [...] peaceful, democratic politics [...] will require the development of a real bour-geoisie – both grande and petite, agricultural and industrial – that will not depend on the state for its survival, and hence that will be able to view the electoral struggle with some degree of detachment. (Diamond 1988, 85.)

For our purposes here, it is sufficient to note that modernisation theory gave grounds for postu-lating much confusion between, for instance, prerequisites for commercial, agricultural and indus-trial development, ordered well-being and acquisitive accumulation, planned education expansion and the provision of relatively attractive jobs. Imbalances between sides of these equations, as in the normal course of capitalist development, together with sets of unexpected outcomes of economic and other policy decisions, played havoc with what might have been intended to be the proper course of political development in Africa from an optimistic perspective of the end of the interregnum. In short, by the late 1960s, it was no longer possible to postulate the existence of a middle class that would be independent of the state. By the late 1970s, for most cases under review here, it was equally difficult to ignore the extent to which the middle classes had been suppressed as an agency of the kind of development that had been earlier envisaged.[7] Nor, for that matter, was it possible to seriously entertain the conception that one-party democracy represented some ideal for political development.

Samuel Huntington had warned that a relentless stress on modernisation in the post-colonial world would result in political decay. In making distinctions between modernisation and modernity, modernisation and westernisation, and economic and political development, Huntington came to lay stress on the prerequisites for the institutionalisation of politics. Before deciding to discard the concept of political development in favour of stressing the relationship between participation and order, Huntington (1965; 1971) argued that the political aspects of development were as much about decay as progress and should be regarded as being intended to create governing institutions which express a public interest in state order. His emphasis upon the meaning of development as one which must incorporate an understanding of decay and destruction is a rare exception to the general thrust of post-1945 development theory. To this extent, it is logical for Huntington to turn to classical political theory, especially that of Plato and Aristotle, and to claim that this theory 'is a far less misleading guide to what has taken place in Ghana and other new states than many things written today' (Huntington 1965, 416).[8]

---

[7] Of the countries in this collection, Kenya might have seemed to be an exception but much hinges on the period under review, as is shown in the case study. In other cases, the qualifier of a 'state' or 'bureaucratic bour-geoisie' was there to make this kind of middle class distinct from the 'real bourgeoisie' that was meant to be linked to the development of liberal democratic practices. For this general point, as well as a view of the Zimbabwe case, see Taylor (1999).

[8] It is also instructive to note that Huntington dubbed the failure to distinguish between intent to develop and the 'actual tendency' of change as 'Webbism', a particular British Fabian inclination of paying optimistic and sympathetic regard to the Stalinist experience of Soviet development, especially from the late 1920s: Webbism 'is the tendency to ascribe to a political system qualities which are assumed to be its ultimate goals rather than qualities which actually characterize its processes and functions' (Huntington 1965, 391).

Some of Huntington's conservative-realist criticism of modernisation theory predated those critiques coming from the radical left in that his theory had been founded on a critical view of the universality, linearity and irreversability of progress. Huntington argued that the 'optimism of retroactive progress', which might have explained the past emergence of liberal democratic practice in the West, was now being extrapolated, without logical justification, as precepts for the rest of the world. Modernisation theory 'rationalised change abroad and the status quo at home', especially of the United States. The dominant theory of the 1950s complacently 'left blank the future of modernity', while the non-modern, unjustifiably equated with non-western polities and societies, was regarded as 'tradition', the 'mutually-exclusive' residual of the modern (Huntington 1971, 364–6). Post-colonial, one-party state regimes, for Huntington, were a consequence of the 'corruption' of political institutions which had developed earlier. The decay of democratic practices had to be explained, contrary to the postulates of modernisation theory, by the imposition of institutions whose scope, complexity, adaptability and coherence could not contain the forces of political mobilisation and participation which had been unleashed during the late colonial and interregnum periods (Huntington 1965, 394–403).

According to Huntington, all 'actual societies are transitional or mixed' between traditional and modern ideal-types (1971, 366). Although dubiously assuming that 'the psychological and cultural characteristics of peoples differ markedly and with them their abilities at developing political institutions' (1965, 417), he found it necessary to ask how 'traditional political institutions' might be adapted 'to accommodate the social forces unleashed by mobilisation' (*ibid.*, 422). Where traditional institutions had collapsed or 'are weak or non-existent', then 'strong party organisation is the only long-run alternative to the instability of a corrupt or praetorian or mass society' (*ibid.*, 425). Huntington's criterion for instability was the propensity of a state to be subject to a military coup since political independence. Further, those countries with many parties were only slightly less prone to instability than those with none:

> The weak institutionalisation of parties in the multiparty system makes that system extremely fragile. The step from many parties to no parties and from no parties to many parties is an easy one. In their institutional weaknesses, the no-party system and the multiparty system resemble each other (*ibid.*, 427).

The point to emphasise here is that elections since 1990 have generally been multi-party, and that the strategies of many African governing regimes have been directed precisely at making opposition parties as institutionally weak as possible.

Election studies during the one-party period

In his 1983 survey article, Cohen identified four approaches for the study of elections. The *Nuffield* approach, Cohen explained, treated each election as a major political event in itself. Aggregate data was used to focus on the issues and mechanics of the campaign and 'the political history of the constituencies, parties and candidates'. For more recent elections, questions of voting along lines mainly determined by class had also come to the fore. The drawback, identified by Cohen, was that the approach paid too much attention to 'the centre of the political system and corresponding neglect of the political periphery', put bias upon the urban against the rural and reified the rhetoric of party political leaderships. On the other hand, the *case-study approach*, which relied upon intensive investigation of a single village, town, district or area, often meant, according to Cohen, that 'the connection between this local arena and the greater political system' was not thrown into relief. Given the cost and complex organisation of the *sample-survey*, as pioneered in Africa by the University of Botswana, Lesotho and Swaziland in its study of the 1974 election in Botswana (Parson 1975), this academic approach has probably been assimilated into the exit-poll, often conducted by commercial firms and/or broadcasting organisations, when voters' preferences are correlated with income, class, gender, racial and other background variables.

Cohen clearly favoured the *system* approach, which presupposed a 'primary concern for the impact of the election on the political system, rather than for the explanation of the electoral event itself'. He felt that the collaborative study undertaken by Lionel Cliffe (ed.), *One-Party Democracy: the 1965 Tanzania general elections*, was a good example of an analysis that rests upon 'structural-functional categories of systems theory'. It is of interest to note here that Cliffe's endeavour was to justify a perspective on socialist democracy, whereas the behaviouralist theories favoured by social scientists in North America were intended to prescribe the validity of representative politics according to liberal norms. Yet, Cohen's account of Cliffe's collection on Tanzania remarked that its conclusions revolved 'around the impact of the election on political recruitment, interest articulation, political socialisation, the role of Parliament, and the role of the ruling party'. Not for the first time, the cross-over between liberal and socialist endeavours for Africa was caught up in the conceptual confusion between behaviouralism and structural-functionalism but played out against a background where any prospect of liberal representative democracy was fast receding for most of Africa.

It may be possible to argue that our understanding of African politics was not helped as much as expected by this perspective, not because of what was included within its conceptual framework, but because of what was more or less excluded from it. The 'state', 'representation', 'citizenship', 'public power' and 'private accumulation' were all missed as concepts for the analysis of regime change. While attempting to be as scientific as possible, on positivist grounds, by avoiding the normative and legal orientation of the continental European tradition of *Staatenlehre* or the criticism of Marxism and political economy approach, the theory ended up by giving a sociological treatment to political processes. This is one reason, among others, which explains the extent to which the trend towards authoritarianism was not foreseen, and why the American science of politics, together with the 'discipline' of political development, lost its relevance for Africa when it seemed that one-party politics was either the source of disillusion or the arena of non-politics.

Botswana, where the sample-survey method was pioneered as mentioned above, was one case where multi-party elections continued after the interregnum. Other cases that had also appeared to buck the post-colonial trend towards the installation of one-party state regimes and elections included Senegal and Mauritius. Another case was Sierra Leone, typified as an authoritarian state during the 1970s (Allen 1997) but which Martin Kilson (1966, 289) had suggested, before the 1967 military coup, 'has been almost unique in maintaining a fair measure of the democratic polity it inherited from colonial rule' and which Kilson rather forlornly hoped 'can persist in this'. More generally, virtually all these cases conformed to what John Holm (1988) reflected upon for Botswana when he wrote that the 'mass of the population' had little faith in the electoral system as 'a means of controlling its leaders'. Multi-party elections in Botswana, as elsewhere, have been a limited means of democratic representation when, as Neocosmos shows in his case study for this collection, the electoral process is subsumed by non-electoral sources of political authority.[9]

By the 1970s, and given the extent of one-party regimes throughout most of Africa, the earlier academic interest in elections had waned. Meanwhile, the behaviouralist approach was being challenged on a number of fronts, notably by the increasing popularity of theories about

---

[9]What was common to these 'exceptional cases' was the extent to which multi-party politics was built around 'traditional' forms of political association and authority. Holm (1988) suggested that if the ruling BDP party were to be defeated at the polls, 'it could abolish elections while continuing to operate by' a '*kgotla* style' of Tswana communal discussion 'and succeed in convincing the population that a government by consent was operating'. Holm (1974, 1986 and 1988) has written extensively on elections in Botswana, as has Polhemus (1983). For Senegal, O'Brien (1978, 187–188) commented that the post-colonial state can best be pictured as a 'bizarre but effective confusion of the traditions of the French *municipalité* and the Muslim *zawiya*' (brotherhoods). For other overviews of Senegal from the standpoint of the 1970s, see Zuccarelli (1970); and Schumacher (1975). Kilson's seminal work on Sierra Leone paid attention to the continuing role played by chiefs 'as the sole legitimate representatives of traditional values (especially as they relate to personal or group allegiances to authority) in the eyes of most people'. The new nationalist élite, especially of the Sierra Leone People's Party, 'normally accommodated its political organisation, methods and policies to the strategic position held by Chiefs in local society' (Kilson 1966, 67). In addition to Allen (1977) for Sierra Leone, also see Cartwright (1970 and 1972); Fisher (1969) and Hayward (1972).

For general overviews of Mauritius, perhaps the only exceptional case in Africa from the point of view of one-party period and its associated authoritarianism, see Brautigam (1999); and Dommen (1999). Multi-party elections in Mauritius invariably resulted in coalition governments.

'dependency' which offered a neo-Marxist explanation about what was happening in Africa. For an increasing number of African scholars, there was growing interest in the links between the evident economic crisis, the authoritarianism of one-party regimes and the armed conflicts of the continent. With few exceptions, the political was subserved by the economic and where the political was given emphasis, it was the agrarian and politics in the countryside which loomed large. Later, from the early 1980s, the politics of difference entered the fray, to contest the universalist and economistic presuppositions of both modernisation and dependency theorising. Gender, post-modernism and discourse analysis brought the 'particular' to the agenda of large chunks of academic research.

Although the different perspective of what has become known as the 'new institutional economics' emerged to look at government, policy and the analysis of phenomena, such as interest group formation, rent-seeking, corruption and clientelism (see for example Chabal ed. 1986), electoral processes were seldom found important enough to be studied in detail. Apart from speculation, as mentioned above, as to whether pre-colonial political systems were democratic or not, the conditions for democracy in Africa raised little interest. As Hayward pointed out, 'the interest in and enthusiasm for elections became less frequent, the one-party state or military regime became the norm, and the utility of the electoral process itself was called into question' (Hayward 1987, 1). Theorising beyond any particular country or case study of an election was exceptionally rare.

After the MacKenzie studies of the interregnum elections, the above-mentioned Hayward's collection *Elections in Independent Africa* (1987) and Ruth Berins Collier's *Regimes in Tropical Africa* (1982) remain the most complete sets of studies on elections in Africa, following a *longitudinal comparative* approach. In her study, Collier tried to explain the formation of different types of authoritarian regimes in the post-independence period by different heritages of the introduction of electoral politics in Africa, looking especially at the differences between ex-British and ex-French colonies. We know of another unpublished 1991 collection of seven country studies, *Elections in Africa*, which arose out of a conference at SOAS in London. Some other occasional studies of elections during the one-party period are also worth noting. Of particular interest are Naomi Chazan's 1979 article on elections between 1974 and 1978, 'African Voters at the Polls', and Cohen's 1983 article 'Elections and Election Studies in Africa'.

Although not restricted to Africa alone the theoretically ambitious collection, *Elections Without Choice* (Hermet *et al.* eds. 1978) sponsored by IPSA's Committee on Political Sociology, included three cases from Africa: Jean-François Bayart's article on Cameroun, Joel Barkan's and John Okumu's on Kenya and Denis Martin's on Tanzania. The collection focused on the experience of the period when, as the editors pointed out, only one-third of all countries in the world could be classified as liberal democracies while, for the other two-thirds, elections were held regularly but their significance was unexplored.

Virtually all the above-mentioned studies were aware of the distinction, as we mentioned at the start of this section, between a focus upon the function of elections for the state and its rulers, namely the question of the legitimation of state authority, and the theoretical perspective of voter choice. The question was how to bring the two perspectives together. Interestingly enough, the perspective of legitimation, favoured by the IPSA collection, and that of voter choice were coupled by bringing the concept of competitive politics inside the one-party electoral structure. Instead of the period being regarded as that of non-politics, it is better presented as that of 'suppressed politics'. Thus, one result of the studies carried out during the 1970s and 1980s was the creation of typologies of elections according to their 'competitiveness'.

Much was made in the literature of the electoral facts, that election after election removed as many as one-half of incumbent MPs, and that this number would often include at least one-quarter of government ministers. Although the voters could not change the regime, it was argued that the electoral process was competitive because voters had a choice between candidates in most constituencies, and the turnout was relatively high. Hayward (1987, 16), for instance, claimed that voters could and did 'punish politicians' they did 'not like':

> In Kenya, Tanzania, Nigeria and Sierra Leone, surprisingly large numbers of incumbents have been defeated by voters unhappy with their performance. Such results occur in both one-party states and in highly competitive systems.

Given the impression that there is some historical continuum between the one- and multi-party periods, three points arise. First of all, the choices made by voters have often been explained by reference to ethnicity, including that in urban areas, where voters have punished politicians they did not want on communitarian grounds. This impression goes back to the information presented by Post about the aforementioned 1959 Nigerian federal election, where it was the 'new men', of new property and the salariat, rather than the 'traditional' authority figures of 'rival kin-based communities', who 'acted as opinion makers in shaping the community decision' (see Cohen 1983, 81). All the evidence during the one-party period bears out Post's proposition.

Thus, secondly, voters 'punished' those that other politicians wanted them to punish. Given that the administration of the electoral process was generally in the hands of provincial or regional officials, albeit often directed and/or supervised from the Office of the President, there is evidence that voting was viewed as a strategic aspect of political management by the central organs of state power. Often, the sanctions inflicted on those seeking to be elected were as much intra- as inter-ethnic.

Third, and connected to the above, those defeated in their attempts to be (re)elected were considered not to have played their expected role as regards 'development'. Where a central regime has an effective monopoly over the nation's resources, it becomes a serious matter for any group or organisation to be cast as 'anti-development', especially in the countryside. The electoral process coerced politicians to play a role in what has been called 'development project politics', the means by which schools, clinics and other projects were funded according to the demand of political faction as much as the imperative of rationally administered welfare need.

The new wave

It was the hope of the various reform movements that appeared in most African countries from the late 1980s that authoritarian one-party regimes were to be succeeded by 'the restoration of democracy' or 'multi-party democracy', the platforms from which the first opposition parties were mostly launched to contest the elections of the early 1990s. Simultaneously, from the stand-point of international donor agencies, political liberalisation was regarded as a condition of economic liberalisation for improved economic performance, growth and development. This second continent-wide transition towards liberal democracy has raised at least as much interest among political scientists as independence did. To a large extent, the recent 'wave' of research has concentrated on the struggles for multi-party politics, the way that this was introduced and the external and internal pressures behind the transitions. Observations have also been made on the need to define and measure the conditions which are prerequisites for democratisation.

Some comparative studies have recently been published on the 'great diversity', as John Wiseman has put it, of the new electoral experience of the 1990s. These studies have included Wiseman's 'Early post-democratization elections in Africa' (1992) in addition to Richard Sandbrook's 'Transitions Without Consolidation' (1996). As noted above, Tom Young edited a collection of four election studies for Côte d'Ivoire, Botswana, Kenya and Nigeria. Entitled 'Understanding Elections in Africa' (1993), it appeared as a special issue of *Africa*.[10] Young's collection was followed, most importantly, by Michael Bratton's and Nicolas van de Walle's book *Democratic Experiments in Africa* (1997).

From our standpoint of stressing the historical continuities and discontinuities from the inter-regnum and after, one finding of Bratton and van de Walle is especially interesting. Experiences of continuing struggles for democratic reform, involving political competition, seem to be more conducive for bedding down a process of democratisation than participation in elections. Regimes that have arranged elections without effective competition, irrespective of the degree of electoral participation, seem to have been less successful in advancing liberal democracy than those that had developed some traditions of political competition. In other words, it is easier for incumbent state regimes to democratise by expanding participation than by introducing competition (Bratton and van de Walle 1997, 140–147). However, in contrast to Bratton and van de Walle, who interpret

---

[10]See note 2 above.

their findings within the general framework of characterising non-competitive regimes as 'neopatrimonial', we suggest that the explanation for democratic discontinuities is more likely to lie in the experience of elections as a means to accommodate and/or legitimate and reproduce state authority.

While Bratton and van de Walle certainly claim that institutions do matter for the democratic process, Sandbrook compared the first post-transition elections in six cases by paying closer attention to the arrangements of the elections, to the organisation of the parties and to the performance of the mass media during the election campaign. It was the design of his study, in confining his coverage to the first transitional elections without taking a historical approach, which prevented him from drawing very definite conclusions about the consolidation of liberal democracy in this set of countries. Likewise, Wiseman's earlier comparative study, along similar lines and based on seven cases, tentatively concluded:

> The victory of opposition parties in four out of the seven states is a matter of consequence in the development of post-independence politics in Africa although one must be careful of not assigning importance only to elections in which the opposition win. All the parties whether still ruling, newly ruling, still opposition, or newly opposition must be regarded as being in a fluid state (Wiseman 1992, 290).

When speculating on why fluidity was so significant for political practice, Wiseman then emphasised the capacities of both ruling and opposition parties to manage their coalitions as the vital aspect of recurrent electoral struggle. His final shot was: 'At very least Africa has now become more interesting for psephologists!' (*ibid.*, 290). Perhaps, but more than psephology is at stake in an attempt to draw more definitive conclusions from the new wave of elections in Africa.

Other recent collections which tend to go beyond election studies include Marina Ottaway's (ed.) *Democracy in Africa: the Hard Road Ahead* (1997), Richard Joseph's (ed.) *State, Conflict, and Democracy in Africa* (1999) and Adebayo Olukoshi's (ed.) *The Politics of Opposition in Contemporary Africa* (1998). Two other collections, going well beyond Africa, are also worth mentioning: *Consolidating the Third Wave Democracies* edited by Larry Diamond, Marc F. Plattner, Yun-han Chu and Hung-mao Tien (1998) and *Postconflict Elections, Democratization & International Assistance* edited by Krishna Kumar (1998). Examples of work paying immense detail to particular elections include the study of the 1994 elections in Mozambique by Brazão Mazula (ed.) and that of the 1992 elections in Kenya by David Throup and Charles Hornsby.

The main question that arises in all the above-mentioned work is the extent to which elections during the multi-party period have made a difference to political rule in Africa. There is little doubt that for many countries, multi-party elections have been about more than a contest between two or more political parties that offered the basis for a choice on the part of an individual voter. During the 1990s, elections were to serve as a means of change in regime to make a transition away from 'corruption' as a systematic form of government. Elections were meant to be the means for establishing 'governance'. As an alternative to violent change, through a coup or revolution, elections were to legitimate a change in regime and make a new regime, through successive elections, an accountable one. Together with the Kenya case, the studies of multi-party elections in Malawi and Zambia show that, in themselves, elections do not guarantee this desired outcome.

Likewise, electoral politics in Nigeria during the 1990s provides an extreme but not necessarily an exceptional case. As argued by Adebayo Olukoshi in his chapter, the whole intention of the successive military regimes' 'democratic transition' project in Nigeria, in spite of its ideological illegitimacy, and gross failure to sustain political and economic stability, was to provide a number of local and national elections for entrenching military rule. Therefore, the administration of electoral processes was doomed to be arbitrary. Yet, even more importantly, elections took place through increasing state repression of civil and political liberties, since they only served to evoke opposition to military rule.

However, in most other African states as part of electoral competition but extending beyond the electoral process, the political transition, involving extra-parliamentary struggles, has created conditions for a degree of freedom of speech and association that might have seemed to be utopian, for most of the cases here, during the 1970s and 1980s. It is not surprising that electorates seem to have treasured these liberal aspects of democratisation, including the opening up of public space for criticism of the incumbent regimes, much more than the fact of regularly held elections. Lars Rudebeck highlights this point for Guinea-Bissau. Tuulikki Pietilä, for the case of Chagga voters in Tanzania, shows that even where the choice between different political parties was meaningful, elections were valued not so much due to the prospect that an opposition party might gain state power but because the actual experience of politics became 'visible' by voting for an opposition party. While there have been cases in which gains, for relatively free political expression and activity, that were won in the early 1990s have been reversed – as in Zambia – reversals have been contested through sets of institutions, including the media, which have come to form the political basis of 'the civil society'. In other cases, such as Kenya and Ghana, it has been the prelude to elections when electoral and political reform have been progressively furthered. In the Sudan, the most obvious case here, reversals have led to an intensification of general political conflict and war. It is this aspect of multi-party politics, the gains made in political freedoms, that suggests a 'democratic break' between the one- and multi-party periods.

Multi-party elections and democratisation reconsidered

Most significantly, the studies presented here show that incumbent regimes, whose ruling parties won the first multi-party elections during the 1990s, have learned to live with multi-party politics.[11] Alternatively, to put it the other way around, opposition parties have found it difficult to win parliamentary and presidential elections after the 'consolidation' of the new 'wave of democracy' in Africa. There was no case in which opposition parties won a general election or significantly gained at other elections studied as part of this project. This finding contrasts with the fact that the first multi-party elections, at the beginning of the 1990s, changed the ruling party in almost half of the more than thirty one-party regimes (Bratton & van de Walle 1997, 7). What has to be explained, therefore, is why opposition parties find it difficult to win second and successive rounds of multi-party elections.[12]

Some recent multi-party elections have been as closely and keenly fought as the first multi-party elections of the 1990s. Others have been marked by voter apathy. Therefore, most elections of the 1990s can be distinguished three-fold:

Relatively competitive elections: This category includes cases which experienced at least a moderate degree of party competition arising out of some reasonable expectation that the ruling party could be dislodged from power. These elections show a relatively high rate of turnout. Opposition parties, either singly or taken together, win a substantial proportion of the popular vote and at least one-third of seats in parliament. From the selected case studies, closely-fought elections in this category include Botswana (1994), Ghana (1992 and 1996), Kenya (1992 and 1997), Tanzania (1995), Nigeria (1993), Malawi (1994) and Guinea-Bissau (1994).

Landslide elections: Elections are keenly contested with high voter turnout, one party wins a very high proportion of the popular vote and, as in the extreme case (Lesotho, 1993 and 1998), also wins all the parliamentary seats on offer. One result of this category of elections is that the lack of parliamentary opposition returns the country to effective one-party rule and voter apathy. Other cases in this category include Zambia (1991 and 1997).

Elections with marked voter apathy: Voters' apathy, it should be stressed, amounts as much to a refusal to vote as to any general uninterest in politics or the electoral process as a whole. Generally, apathy accompanies 'elections without choice' because, for one reason or another, the majority of the registered, or potential, electorate do not expect that any given election or set of elections will lead to a change in the ruling party, the governing regime and/or their own life expe-

---

[11]Bratton and Posner (1999, 381) make the same point when they argue that during the course of the 1990s, 'leaders became more adept at accommodating the emerging global consensus about the desirability of competitive elections, while at the same time learning to manage and manipulate these events to their own ends'.
[12]While it may be naive to imagine that practices of liberal democracy presuppose that elections should normally be won by opposition parties, the concept has often been operationalised through measuring the extent to which opposition parties do win elections. See, for example, Dahl 1989; and Vanhanen 1984.

riences following any such change. Case studies include Ethiopia (1995) Namibia (1998), Zambia (1995), Sudan (1996), Swaziland (1993) and Zimbabwe (1995).

This third category may also involve a distinction between:

a. The manipulation of electoral instruments by ruling parties, on administrative and legal grounds, to an extent which makes either nominal or real party political competition impossible (Sudan, Swaziland, Zambia, Zimbabwe).

And:

b. The tendency for the electorate to discount any regime change without the need for extensive manipulation on the part of the ruling party (Namibia). Or, contrariwise, as in the case of Ethiopia, where the experience of political competition has been extremely brief even though participation during the previous regime was compulsory and ostensibly very high.

In this Ethiopian case, Bratton and van de Walle's general finding about the difficulties entailed in measuring democratisation seem to ring true. Yet, in grasping the reasons for why apathy takes root, and by the same token, the potential for political change, Eva Poluha's case shows that understanding the most 'oppressed' of voters, rural women, requires a level of analysis that goes beyond the political system and incorporates the question of gender in socialisation and livelihood strategies.

Experiences of the post-1990 multi-party period in Africa may be going through roughly similar phases of electoral participation to what broadly happened after the interregnum and at the onset of the one-party period. After the enthusiastic flush of the first multi-party elections, cases of massive voter apathy became apparent, thereby undermining attempts to present elections as the source of state and governmental authority.

According to Diamond – who has been criticised by Balefi Tsie, for example – democracy 'demands that citizens care about politics but not too much'.[13] Diamond's view accords well with the early findings of the behavioural school which contradicted the normative assumptions of liberal democratic theory. Berelson, Lazarfeld and McPhee (1954, 313–314), after their pioneering work on voting behaviour in the United States, based on a case study on the presidential elections of 1948, concluded that the 'underlying paradox is an assumption that, if something is a political virtue (like interest in the election), then everyone should have it; that there is such a thing as "the" typical citizen on whom uniform requirements can be imposed'. They continued:

> The tendency of classic democratic literature to work with an image of 'the' voter was never justified… How could a mass democracy work if all the people were deeply involved in politics?… Extreme interest goes with extreme partisanship and might culminate in rigid fanaticism that could destroy democratic processes if generalized throughout the community. Low affect toward the election – not caring much – underlies the resolution of many political problems… Low interest provides manoeuvring room for political shifts necessary for a complex society in a period of rapid change.

In short, the behaviouralists paid attention to empirically evident political apathy in the United States and to the simultaneous functioning of its political system. Instead of constituting an anomaly or a problem, apathy came to be interpreted as a guarantor of political stability.

Huntington, from his conservative-realist bearings, brought the same approach to the onset of the post-colonial world. 'In contrast to the theory of representative government', Huntington (1965, 414) suggested, under 'the procedural concept of government',

> government institutions derive their legitimacy and authority not from the extent to which they represent the interests of the people or of any other group, but from the extent to which they have distinct interests of their own apart from all other groups.

---

[13]Diamond in L. Diamond and Marc F. Plattner (eds.) (1993) *The Global Resurgence of Democracy*, Baltimore: Johns Hopkins University Press, 103 (quoted by Tsie 1996, 5).

Huntington's earlier work, as might be expected, paid little attention to elections as the means by which legitimation might be secured. When he did refer to voting, the general impression was that mass voting was a cause of political decay rather than development.

Behaviouralist advocacy of apathy, both as pragmatism and the fear of democracy as popular power, was motivated and highly coloured by twentieth-century experiences of fascism and communism in Europe. However, Huntington's reading of communism, especially in East Asia in the 1970s, was one that valued Communist Party organisation as a model for withstanding political decay. Furthermore, he extended and generalised the earlier fear of 'mass society'[14] into the post-colonial world which, in the main, had not gone through the same experiences of mass society. Therefore, a Huntington law of voting was proposed:

> Sharp increases in voting and other forms of political participation can have deleterious effects on political institutions. In Latin America since the 1930s, increases in voting and increases in political instability have gone hand in hand (*ibid.*, 407).

Nor was the cause of the problem the preponderance of 'the illiterates', as Huntington called the relatively uneducated, in the mass of any given voting population. Rather, 'limited political participation by illiterates may well, as in India, be less dangerous to political institutions than participation by literates', whose greater aspirations for well-being imposed 'more demands on government' (*ibid.*, 420). Apathy, therefore, generally served as a positive function for political development by reducing the overload on public institutions and thereby securing the institutional capacities for state order.

In his account of prerequisites for state order, Huntington took the unabashed view that a distinct political interest could function to express the public interest through élite political leadership. Early American behaviouralism from the science of politics in America also referred to an élitist understanding of politics: 'The classical requirements [of the virtues of citizen] are more appropriate for the opinion leaders in the society' (Berelson *et al.* 1954, 322–323). For Africa, as Post had pointed out, opinion leaders were most often the 'new men', possibly of the incipient class of capital whose distinct interest was in private accumulation as much as in the political expression of a public interest, and who faced, during the ensuing decades for most of Africa, periodic exclusions from state power and opportunities to express opinions.[15] The 'new men' were also frequently of the 'middle', probably facing too much uncertainty to become deeply involved in politics in contemporary Africa.

What has to be explained today is why incumbent regimes win multi-party elections and why there has been variation in electoral participation both across country cases and, for any one case, variation between one election and another. Among the factors that have been deployed to explain how and why voters vote, and for and against whom, it is the institutional framework for, and the political economy behind, more recent elections that are given emphasis in this overview. The communality of politics also enters into how multi-party elections can be understood.

The significance of institutions

An electoral observation and monitoring industry has grown up around multi-party elections in Africa. Each general election in most of the cases under review has resulted in a plethora of reports on electoral practices. We probably now have more detail about the conduct of elections in Africa than for any other continent.

On the one hand, monitoring has had an effect on electoral conduct in that it is the most open aspect of the electoral process, that of voting itself, which has become less subject to malpractice

---

[14]Huntington (1965) made much of William Kornhauser (1959) *The Politics of Mass Society*, New York: Glencoe Press.

[15]For the instructive case of Kenya, see Cowen and MacWilliam 1996. Robert Bates (1999) has recently focused on the middle classes as a determining issue of democracy, an issue which we pursue further below. As is often the case in this kind of literature, there is some confusion due to the conflation between the middle classes, as intermediate strata between capital and labour, and the bourgeoisie as a class of capital.

than the preceding, and less monitored, stages of the electoral process.[16] On the other hand, as malpractice has been pushed further back within the process as a whole, it becomes increasingly difficult to distinguish between general administrative, constitutional and legal practices and those directed towards electoral conduct. Thus, for example, the delimitation of constituency boundaries is often linked to presidential decrees creating administrative districts; the registration of voters to the administrative issue of identification cards; the regulation of candidates' eligibility to stand for office to legal contest in courts; the conduct of election campaigning to administrative practice and regulation ranging from policing to regime control of the media as well as other focal points in civil society, such as trade unions and universities. In all these cases, what counts specifically as the administration of elections is difficult to determine.

Given the extent of the reach and range of the administrative, and its attachment to the political, electoral reform is necessarily based on political reform. Yet, political reform arises as both a cause and effect of the potential of elections to produce a change in both the ruling party of government and that of a state regime. This explains why heightened political struggle and conflict has often appeared in the prelude to elections and subsists in many of the cases during inter-electoral periods as whole. Political struggle, ranging from bloody direct action on the streets to arcane legal niceties in courts, has invariably involved the struggle for institutions with the aim of arriving at a constitutional settlement which, for opposition parties, makes it more likely that incumbent regimes can be defeated at the polls.

A minimal account of the post-1990 election studies, especially as evidenced by the Sandbrook study, indicates the extent to which the conjuncture of the second transition has drawn research back to the method of the interregnum, especially in the attention given to the institutional forms of the electoral process. As we pointed out above, while the concept of competitive politics provided one way of coupling the perspectives of legitimation and voter choice during the one-party era, the multi-party era only amplifies the point that bringing institutions back requires going beyond the electoral law and its implementation. Issues arising out of political contest over the administration of the electoral process highlight the constraints inhibiting even the *potential* of voter choice during the course of elections in acting to check the exercise of state power by incumbent governing regimes.

According to a fundamental principle of modern liberal democratic theory, government is recognised as one part of an interactive relationship with the electorate and not the authoritative subject of state power whose sole political object is to use the electoral process as a source of dictatorship over the people as a whole. Or, as Adam Przeworski (1988, 64) put it, democracy may work only if 'relevant political forces can find institutions that would provide reasonable guarantees that their interests would not be affected in a highly adverse manner in the course of democratic competition'.[17]

Institutional manipulation of the electoral process, including the economic manipulation of the electorate, normally arises when voters cannot be trusted to vote as intended by incumbent state regimes. A paradox is that voters must be assumed to be obedient for elections to conform to the liberal precept that electoral law and rules be agreed in advance. Obedient voters would not have to be institutionally manipulated but the fear of a disobedient electorate makes government manipulate elections, with the rules of the game either not made or changed during the course of the process itself.

Insofar as the theoretical perspective of the interregnum is to be recaptured, it is the universalism of institutional validation which interests us most. There is nothing intrinsically African, or

---

[16]The same point has been made by Bratton and Posner (1999, 404) who claim that elections in the 1990s, with few exceptions, 'confirm that polling procedures and vote counting are not the principal sources of electoral malpractice in Africa'. Rather, 'vote buying' and 'political intimidation', happening before polling day, make reports of election observers and monitors 'increasingly distinguish between the growing efficiency and effectiveness of polling administration, on the one hand, and persistent problems with election rules or campaign conduct, on the other'.

[17]As also quoted by Leftwich (1993, 615–616) who reinforces this point. The question of what constitutes a 'political force' and 'interests' of a group, especially in the form of a political party, is very problematic. There may well be a difference between theorising about social democracy and liberal democracy in relation to voter choice, but the point about uncertainty of outcomes, as mentioned above, is at the core of liberal democratic dilemmas of politics.

black African, that might suggest that universal norms of free and fair elections are invalid for Africa. Critiques of electoral practices, such as the official invention of parties, ballot rigging, gerrymandering of constituencies, and state intimidation are the legacies of the past, and continue to be pressed, throughout all regions of the world. Constitutional reform continues to be advocated in countries such as Britain, the original home of electoral practice for much of former British colonial Africa, according to the same principle that reform is advocated in Africa itself.

As we saw above, claims continue to be made that western-style practices are irrelevant for Africa, or that Africans should participate in forms of traditional democracy rather than European and American inventions of representative democracy. It is striking, however, that these claims have been made most forcibly by established sources of state authority, whether by colonial administrations or post-colonial state dictatorial regimes in Africa.

Apart from the case already mentioned of the 1996 elections in the Sudan, two examples suffice here. We referred earlier to the tendency, apparent during the one- and multi-party periods, for the effective disenfranchisement of populations through an unfair electoral process. There has been little that is black African about effective exclusion through electoral practice. For white South Africa elections, held during the apartheid years between 1948 and 1970, an average of 24 seats out of 150 were unopposed for each election; for 1961, as many as 67 seats were unopposed (Heard 1974). The second example comes from Kenya during the Moi presidency. During 1986, at the height of one of his self-created political crises, Daniel arap Moi contended that western-style elections were western, imperialist fictions for Africa. Africans in Kenya, he declared, should stand proudly and openly in line behind the candidate of their choice during the course of voting at all levels of elections.

Moi's proposal was widely ridiculed, not least because it meant that state security officials would see precisely who voted for whom, and may not have permanently entered into general electoral practice in Kenya. But the proposal typifies the argument of the perspective that institutional arrangements are the major means by which incumbent African regimes try to influence the outcome of the elections. Furthermore, and in spite of international attention paid to human rights, various forms of coercion continue to be used to determine the outcome of election results.

If this is so, the obvious question to ask is why roughly one-half, or more, of incumbent governments were electorally defeated during the first wave of post-1990 elections. Part of the reason, we suggest, is that there is variation, not merely in why and how parties and other political groups are organised, but in the art and craft of institutional arrangement, management, and manipulation. The other part of a plausible explanation for the variation is economic. Whether for the interregnum, the one- or multi-party period, electoral studies in Africa have paid little or no attention to the economic background of the electoral process.

Political economy

It has been 'uncommon' for relatively liberal multi-party democracies to subsist under continuous rule by one and the same party. Uncommon cases, such as Japan or Sweden, have been explained by relatively successful economic progress and development and state support for an industrial export policy alongside the simultaneous incorporation of working classes into the structure of the state through the direct or indirect expansion of welfare services. (See, for example, Pempel ed. 1990).

None of these conditions have applied in virtually all the African cases under review here. One exception, as Neocosmos shows for Botswana, only proves the general rule. Ruling parties have stayed in power during a period of general economic regress, without an industrial policy, and with the retraction of provision of the minimum of welfare services for wageworkers who have formed a declining proportion of the economically active population in most African countries.

Relatively liberal multi-party democracies attempt to manipulate the business or trade cycle of economic activity in such a way that the peak of a cycle appears in the prelude to an election and its trough during the electoral aftermath. Following from the above, two conditions are required to make the political business cycle necessary and operative. The first is that the incorporation of wage-working classes into the structure of the state and/or the ability of ruling parties to rule is that the state regime possesses a policy for improving the standard of life for its national constituents. Secondly, there must be an institutional apparatus of government which has the capacity to put the policy into practice. Again, neither of these conditions is to be found in the African cases under review.

While wage-workers increasingly form a minority of the economically active population, the power of organised labour through trade unions to systematically inform policy has decreased through time. Strikes, especially in the public sector, and over money wage demands, have featured strongly as part of election preludes and their aftermath. However, while trade unions were able to take advantage of impending elections to press their case, industrial action of this kind was a response to a governmental failure of policy to match real wage flows with those of the electoral cycle. If policy was put to work during the early post-colonial period, then it was effectively extinguished by the later 1970s. In many ways, policy, including the capacity for government, was decimated before the advent of Structural Adjustment Policy (SAP) which appeared as an externally informed substitute for it.

African state regimes, it is often said, 'rule' rather than 'govern'. SAP appeared alongside the claim, becoming increasingly strident from the late 1980s, that 'good *governance*' carries with it a presupposition that democratic practice is necessary for good economic performance, rather than the assumption that 'good *government*' should be regarded as a principled end in itself. If governance was intended to make African regimes govern for the end of an economic purpose, then, economic means were deployed in the generally successful attempt to win multi-party elections. However, these means rested upon institutional procedures for ruling rather than governing states.

Instead of institutional manipulation of the economy for a political purpose, and what can be regarded as 'institutional bribery', it is evident that some state regimes attempt to throw money at electorates during the electoral period. Regimes are then forced to deflate economies during electoral aftermaths when countering the effects of a politically motivated pre-election injection of money liquidity. In some cases, ruling parties are involved in elaborate scams to make (relatively) large amounts of money available for funding election campaigns. Such scams are made necessary during International Monetary Fund (IMF) surveillance of monetary policy as part of SAP. Like other electoral practices, when scams associated with one election have highlighted the corrupt propensities of regimes, they provoke the suspension of IMF and other donor grant and loan finance during a subsequent election. As a result, ruling parties may face an election when the economy is destabilised, thereby making it more necessary for non-institutional forms of bribery to be used electorally by ruling parties.

Bribery, normally involving the payment of cash to individual voters, has been seen as an integral part of elections during both the one- and multi-party periods. Incidental evidence, coupled with the above, suggests that the incidence of bribery has increased during the multi-party period with payments made by both agents of ruling and opposition parties. Yet, there is no systematic evidence to show that bribery *in itself* makes individuals vote for candidates from whom they have received payments. It is more likely to be the case that bribery works when it is accompanied by other factors, especially that of a class interest and the kind of political logic which is discussed below.

A political interest in a party, and especially a ruling party, often carries with it a private, individual interest in the primary accumulation of capital. Competition to accumulate capital is therefore also an integral part of political party competition. It is common for individuals and particular economic interest groups to fund political party campaigns in the endeavour to maximise a competitive advantage that a ruling party might confer through one or other policy. However, the kind of economic interest which has often been found to be at play during the multi-party period is more profound than that of individual or group pressure. When the primary accumulation of capital serves as the medium through which capitalist classes are formed, then it is the ground, and not merely the form, of policy that is called into question. Since elections threaten the possibility of continued rule, the leaderships of ruling parties, who subsist on the basis of an economic interest in primary accumulation, have a powerful and uncommon incentive for winning elections.

The fact that governments may not use the full range of institutional or administrative weapons, which are potentially available to coerce the electoral process, does not mean that electoral management and manipulation are absent. On the contrary, it is a well known fact that the governments of relatively advanced liberal democracies do manipulate the electoral process. However, instead of manipulating institutional arrangements for elections, governments manipulate the economy in an attempt to secure re-election. They do so through creating what have come to be called political business cycles.[18]

Conventional wisdom has it that, since the globalisation of capital proceeds apace, national governments may be less able to manipulate the economic cycle, an immanent aspect of capitalism, to make the amplitude of peaks and troughs in the economic cycle correspond to electoral periods. Broadly and simply speaking, the normal intention of governments is to ensure that the trough in the economic cycle happens after an election and that the peak of the cycle corresponds to the date of a forthcoming election. From an electoral point of view, the macroeconomic aggregate of real disposable income is the target which the government attempts to manage and manipulate. Even given globalisation, national government capacities for labour market regulation, including social welfare benefits, are a powerful instrument which can be employed to promote an immediate and transient period of relative well-being.

We know of only one systematic study which has examined and found evidence of political business cycles in the post-colonial world. Schuknecht (1996) studied the outcomes of fiscal policies in 35 countries through a profile of years before and after electoral years over the 1970–1992 period. As such, his study was biased, for our purpose here, because so few African states were formal multi-party states during the period under review. This study was also IMF-driven and clearly conscious about the political imperatives which might have made countries counteract SAP, especially during the 1980s. As virtually all African countries have gone through SAP experiences, involving the enforced reduction in government expenditures, the question is to examine, and possibly estimate, the extent to which any evidence of political business cycles has been suppressed by IMF conditionality as part of SAP.

One activity of the project associated with this book was to examine whether there is evidence for political business cycles at work in Africa. The *Appendix* to this volume sets out the methods that were used to test for political business cycles and the results from the analysis. Across the twelve countries from the cases under review, there is little or no secure statistical evidence that there has been an operative political business cycle for the period 1967–97 taken as a whole. Given the above-mentioned conditions for the cycle to operate, and that this period contains the experiences of both multi- and one-party politics and elections, the results are generally intuitive. However, the results also show that multi-party elections could possibly have had some impact upon the year-on-year change and the trend of the measured macroeconomic variables that entered into the analysis. Estimated impacts of elections upon economic variables for the later 1990–97 period tended to be more significant than for either the earlier 'one-party' period, 1967–89, or that of the full period taken as a whole. One variable, that of deficit financing for government spending, was statistically significant for the multi-party period.

Further, the results show some minimal evidence that the governments tended to manipulate money supply aggregates (especially M2) during electoral years for multi-party elections. Although less significant than other measured variables, there is also some evidence that domestic credit expansion, through bank lending, was evident for the 1967–1997 period as a whole. These results are also reasonably intuitive. While not all incumbent regimes may have the will and/or capacity to throw money at potential electorates, the extent to which one or more may do so is likely to be captured, however slightly, in this simplest kind of analysis. Furthermore, the abrupt expansion and then retraction of liquidity in an economy, is often associated with the direct bribery of voters and other forms of economic manipulation to secure an electoral purpose.

No African election study can be seriously complete without an analysis of bribery of voters. In earlier years, and probably including the interregnum, voters' own accounts of elections stressed, with much humour, the memory of elections as personal boom-time occasions. Candidates and their agents gave handouts, of money and in kind, to voters. In later years, the evidence is that the

---

[18]The concept of *political business cycle* was probably launched by Michael Kalecki in his article on political aspects of full employment (Kalechi 1943). See also Frey ed. 1997; Lewis-Beck 1990; Nordhaus 1975; Tufte 1978; Willett ed. 1989.

issue of money, including that to finance handouts in kind, especially foodstuffs and beverages, had become highly organised and complex, involving the conversion of a substantial part of a country's foreign exchange reserve into an election fund. As such, the analysis of political business cycles should include monetary as well as fiscal policy. There is evidence, with the Kenya 1992 election as an exemplary case, of quasi-official monetary creation on a scale that had major inflationary consequences for the economy after the election. Other recent evidence includes profligate borrowing by the Tanzanian government during the prelude to the 1995 election and an upsurge in general government spending in Ghana that seemed to have been directed towards the 1996 elections (Young 1999, 33–34).

Generally, a body of economic theory, and the political economy that accompanies it, argues that voters' expectations of the economic outcomes nullify governmental policy intentions. This argument, associated most obviously with the radical right's conviction that state manipulation of the economy is intrinsically corrupt, is that the political business cycle has no effect because voters come to understand the cycle itself. Election-induced increases in government expenditure, and money-printing, before elections is paid for through increased taxation, and inflation, after the election. In other words, voters come to distrust government intentions because they anticipate that a period of enforced ill-being is likely to follow transitory well-being before and during the election period. Insofar as the radical and liberal left has joined the original critique, a general picture has been painted of manipulation that undermines trust in government. Trust in government is one of the convictions of liberal democratic doctrine.

Voters may counter governmental irresponsibility by opting for their own source of responsibility. An ingredient of the African voter's account of elections is to say: 'I willingly took money from him but I deliberately voted against him'. It is difficult to disentangle the reactions to manipulation from the feedback effects that follow when reactions are incorporated into governmental intentions themselves. All we can suppose is that electoral practice, both institutional and political economy-wise, changes because the state is forced to reform practice due to social and political pressure. One powerful force of pressure is class voting.

We know, for example, from European experiences during the nineteenth and early twentieth centuries, that the extension of the franchise, and electoral reform generally, was connected to the emergence of classes of industrial labour. Much of the experience of political and social reform was mediated through the middle classes who took up different stances towards what was called 'the social question'. Middle classes acted politically both to represent their particular interests and in contest, for and against, the cause of political and social reform. Electoral practice was a vital part of dispute over the general question of reform.

It is not surprising, therefore, and as mentioned above, to find critiques of theories that emphasise the middle class as the motivating, rather than a mediating, force of electoral reform. Dietrich Rueschmeyer, for instance, has argued powerfully against the behaviouralist perspective, so closely associated with modernisation theorising, and the emphasis that is put on middle class behaviour. Rueschmeyer has argued that the correlation between development and liberal democracy followed from the way in which 'industrialization transformed society in a fashion that empowered subordinate classes and made it difficult to politically exclude them' (Rueschmeyer *et al.* 1992, vii). The relatively long history of struggle to secure effective general elections, as we suggested above, was about means to secure the co-optation of subordinate classes so that discontent would be ameliorated without revolutionary ruptures in the economy and society generally.

One striking historical fact about the present conjuncture of post-1990 political reform in Africa is that it has happened during a period when economic experience has generally been of non- and de-industrialisation. Instead of facing an emerging industrial class of labour, the prospect for governmental agencies, both national and international, has been one of mass unemployment. Indeed, the emergence of mass non-wage self-employment, so necessary for subsistence and livelihoods, has been assumed to be an ideal of economic and social organisation, a doctrinal virtue of development, and presented positively in much of the discourse on development.

As part of this same conjuncture between the economic and the political, the current emphasis on the ideal of civil society in the current literature on Africa has repeated the older liberal ideal of the 'middle class' (see Harbeson *et al.* 1994). In particular, perspectives of legitimating state authority and voter choice can be plausibly connected by presenting and re-presenting the ideal of rational voting, by individual voters, who are able to decide rationally because they are also supposed to be autonomous economic agents who secure their own livelihoods in self-employed enterprise.

However, we know that the majority of the African voters do not belong to the middle class or civic organisations interacting autonomously with the state. Nor is it clear that the ideal of the middle class, acting in pursuit of particular interests, and in the cause of reform, carries conviction during the current conjuncture when professionals and the intermediate strata of society are perforce so committed to private accumulation and acquisition.

Communality, locality and representative democracy

For virtually all the cases under review, the majority of electoral constituencies are rural. Since the African countryside has been largely administered according to regions, which are identified by 'tribal' and/or 'clan' *territories*, communal politics have loomed large in some elections. This is especially so where there is contest, as on the grounds mentioned above, over the borderlands between territories or for those which have not been demarcated administratively according to 'non-tribal' identities or criteria.

Communal politics often inform the logic of political association through changing the basis of groupings upon which political parties contest elections. Yet, as discussed below, it is as much in the negative as the positive, that electoral contests are fought. Votes are cast for parties that express a communal interest against one or other of those parties which are supposed to represent a communal threat, posed as that of 'tribal domination' or 'tribal discrimination'.

Electoral politics is as much about the negative as the positive reasons that voters cast their votes. Voters vote as much against parties as for them. Insofar as voters are expected to vote against ruling parties, they also vote against opposition parties that they expect to have a substantial chance of winning elections. Furthermore, it is the fear of regime change following an election, which contributes to the reasons why voters vote for incumbent ruling parties. Fear does not merely rest on policy and/or ideological differences between parties but on the general political environment that may include a past experience of political violence. In particular, it is the fear of generalised political violence, associated with communal phenomena, ranging from that of ethnicity to religion, which can be embedded in electoral opinion. In addition, it is the fear that bodies of voters might expect relative economic loss in relation to their perception of present living standards – however much their actual standard of living might have deteriorated – which can also make voters incline towards voting against opposition parties.

Some cases of *relatively competitive elections,* such as Kenya and Ghana, show how the counterbalancing of negative electoral forces has been made to work in favour of ruling parties. Communality, especially that of 'tribe', was made more emphatic as freed-up public political expression accompanied the advent of multi-party elections. However, in spite of this, the question of communality cannot be conflated with that of locality. For example, while it is possible to agree with Richard Joseph's conception of 'virtual democracy' insofar as he argues that the experience of multi-party elections has been one in which the process of democratisation has been manipulated 'by those enjoying governmental and social power', we also need to question the emphasis that he puts upon 'competition among communities' as the form of this manipulation (Joseph 1997, 366–367).[19] As well as that of the Sudan and Zambia, the Kenya case also shows that much of what goes by the name of the communal is not to be conflated with local political representation at work, with elections serving to force representatives to make economic development possible. It is often within different localities of the same region that electoral contests have been keenly and closely fought over the 'politics of development'.

Locality is an issue that crops up time and again during the course of the case studies in this collection. What is significant here is that locality means more than the bounded location of territorial space, the province or region, to be regarded as 'a container', within which votes are amassed by one party on 'tribal' grounds, with the container used as the political unit for

---

[19]'Pluralist and competitive democracy in Africa has tended to take the form of competition among communities rather than individuals, parties, and administrative subunits' (Joseph 1997, 366).

contesting national elections. Locality also means more than the locale or particular arena in which different parties contest elections on local issues. For our purpose here, the issue of locality also involves change in the scale of both location and locale in relation to other centres of political power, especially the change in the impact of central government upon different localities.[20] This issue involves more than changes in both the boundaries of territorial locations for electoral purposes and/or the extent to which the boundaries of 'containers' are changed due to the interest of both ruling and opposition parties in widening the basis of their electoral support while narrowing that of their opponents.

One important issue at hand here is that the growing absence of government, and central governmental provision of infrastructure and welfare services, has increased the pressure from below and upon electoral candidates to prove their capacities for delivering development to the locality in question. Likewise, when landslide elections appear across all the constituencies of a particular region, the reason is also akin to the politics of development. In this case, it is the winning political party of a region which, whether in state power or not, is expected to make it possible for state resources to be delivered for development.

A related issue of locality is that of the political impacts of rapid urbanisation. In many of the cases under review in this collection of studies, ranging from Zimbabwe to Kenya, there is evidence of electoral under-representation of urban populations. Partly, the reason is due to malapportionment of urban constituencies on politically manipulative grounds. Another reason is a reluctance or inability among the urban poor to register for voting. Whatever the reason, urban constituencies often show below actual average turnout ratios for any one election and this factor plays an important part in *elections with marked voter apathy*.[21] Yet, under-representation in voting power may be matched by over-representation in political influence, especially by the intermediate stratum of the so-called middle classes, including the state salariat, professionals and students. This is the social stratum which carries the cause for political and electoral reform but does not have the voting power to translate the cause into electoral results.

Multi-party elections came to Africa in the 1990s along with relatively rapid political and economic liberalisation. Given the extent of political repression during the one-party period, open political opposition to ruling party regimes has also been of a short duration. Thus, whether in state power or in opposition, political parties have yet to create forms of internal political practice which are adequate for externally formal norms of liberal democracy. For many of the cases here, with Malawi of special note, political liberalisation has not meant the dismantling of patrimonial power structures, so suggestive of corrupt and authoritarian regimes, but has merely provided a new kind of platform for previous one-party practices to continue within a formal multi-party framework.

The general tendency for ruling political parties to stay in power during the multi-party period also means that those opposition parties that do not disintegrate after elections spend long periods of time in opposition. In coping politically with the consequences of losing elections, it might be that opposition parties are also faced with the necessity of creating forms of political practice which are less authoritarian than what has prevailed hitherto. During the late colonial interregnum, as for the period of the 'second liberation' during the late 1980s at the onset of the new wave of multi-party politics, political parties were either mass or liberation movements with leaderships who expected veneration from their followers as a matter of course while they awaited an imminent transfer of power to themselves. After a decade of multi-party elections, and without the

---

[20]The literature on issues of locality is now extensive, partly due to the phenomenon of globalisation and new approaches towards international relations, and for which 'territory' has always been a major question. See, for example, Taylor (1994). It should be noted that the question of the change in the scale of locality also has arisen by way of transnational relations, often embodied by international NGOs that attempt to operate locally and beyond the reach of state power and the central government administration in the territories in which they operate. Agnew (1987, 5–6) has defined the difference between *location, locale* and *sense of place;* see also Agnew and Duncan (1989); Agnew and Corbridge (1995); and Cox (1997). We are indebted to Maaria Seppänen for our introduction to issues of locality.

[21]As the Zimbabwe case shows, while official ratios of registered voters to eligible voting populations might be relatively high in urban areas, it is the actual turnout rate to vote that can be very low.

experience of expecting a sudden succession to state power, leaders of opposition parties are facing a new experience of politics. It may not be clear what this new experience will bring but, if and when opposition parties do win elections in the future, it could mean that their behaviour in government is also likely to be different from practices of the past.

Conclusions

As we outlined above, incumbent government regimes might seek legitimation via elections without effective choice. Elections are organised and voters make choices as to whether to register or not and, in contested constituencies, whether to vote or not. Although nominal choice has been presented, the governing regime can, through institutional engineering, manipulation and bribery, effectively frustrate the opposition. This institutional manipulation of elections disorganises opposition parties and/or leads to election boycotts which deprives some voters of any choice at all. Obvious questions then arise about whether it is the state rather than the governing regime which is the source of legitimating authority and whether it is the electorate or some other source of authority, such as the donor 'community', which is the reason why elections have been organised according to liberal democratic precepts.

Against this background, it might be useful to view the post-1990 experience as containing two countervailing forces of democratisation which, on historical grounds at any rate, cannot easily be separated from each other. The first is that of the renewal of political freedoms, those of public and private opinion, including the 'freedom to insult' political figures of authority; of association and assembly; of freedom from arbitrary arrest, detention and torture; and of the freedom to organise politically. The gains in these freedoms might be relative and uneven but they have been hard won and are generally popular. Multi-party elections have been introduced as part of the same process, namely of renewing freedoms of political expression. Yet, the extent of mass voter apathy, also relative and uneven, means that the second force of democratisation, that of prevailing multi-party democracy, may be nothing other than an extreme form of an élite democracy, sometimes called an elective dictatorship. Elite democracy, it can reasonably be argued, has been foisted upon reluctant non-elective dictatorships by economically dominant classes who have been excluded from state power: professionals and middle classes, international donors and financial institutions. The result is that this second force counteracts the first in making the electoral process a possibly unpopular form of political expression.

One influential view of the post-1990 experience, as expressed most clearly by Fareed Zakaria (1997, 23), has referred to the 'growing unease at the rapid spread of multi-party elections across south-central Europe, Asia, Africa and Latin America, perhaps because of what happens *after* the elections'. According to this view, the new democratic wave of multi-party elections has been accompanied by constitutional illiberalism. Instead of, say, a Western European or North American progressive conjunction of an elective democracy with constitutional liberalism, the new wave has revealed a disjuncture between a compulsion for an elective process of government together with official disregard of the rule of law, civil rights and the protection of individual liberties.

'Constitutional liberalism', Zakaria (*ibid.*, 30) writes, 'is about the limitation of power, democracy about its accumulation and use.' Yet, if any general conclusion is to be drawn from this collection of studies for Africa, it is the opposite to that of Zakaria: while electoral democracy remains still-born because voters do not exercise effective choice, there has been a progressive advance in the exercise of liberal rights during the 1990s and after decades of authoritarian rule in Africa. Furthermore, this advance in constitutional liberalism has not necessarily resulted from the motive force of 'government's goals', as Zakaria (*ibid.*, 25) would have it on normative grounds. Rather, gains in exercising liberal rights have been the outcomes, as mentioned above, of often violent struggles for political reforms that have accompanied multi-party elections in Africa. Moreover, these gains have been valued by people as ends in themselves, rather than as an instrumental outcome of political conditionality, namely the attempt of international agencies to enforce political reform as a condition for 'good governance' and free-market economic reforms that are also espoused by Zakaria. What might be called the *conditionality of the political,* the political conditions that secure liberal freedoms as ends in themselves, has often been eclipsed by an unremitting focus upon political conditionality.

Much has been made of the extent to which political conditionality, and especially that the advent of multi-party democracy be a condition for international aid and finance, has been viewed as the means to coerce African state regimes into 'good governance' (see, for example, Leftwich 1993; Williams and Young 1994; Moore 1996). Thus, a major 1989 World Bank report argued that 'political legitimacy and consensus are a *precondition* for sustainable development'.[22] According to this premise, post-1990 elections have been a means to secure legitimation. Furthermore, as Williams and Young (1994, 87, 91) point out, 'good governance is concerned with *civil society*'. Insofar as political participation is to be furthered in the gamut of associations, from NGOs to trade unions, where '*mentalities*'[23] can be changed, then political expression is not meant to be directed towards state institutions directly.

Leftwich (1993, 619–620) has pointed out that 'from a developmental point of view, the general but simplistic appeal for better "governance" as a condition of development is virtuous but naive':

> For an independent and competent administration is not simply a product of 'institution building' or improved training, but of *politics*. And if the politics do not give rise to the kind of state which can generate, sustain and protect an effective and independent capacity for governance, then there will be no positive developmental consequences.

Leftwich's appeal for a strong, developmental state, which acts politically to empower the poor for development (*ibid.*, 621), is muddied by the fact that the same case for empowerment and participation is advocated by liberal proponents of 'good governance'. Contest between the developmental and liberal cases for empowerment and participation, ostensibly about mentalities, is highly political. It is a contest over the question of who are to be the trustees[24] of the people for development and, for either side of the contest, legitimation of authority is the key. However, from the electoral perspective, the conjunction of democracy and development is doubly problematic for the liberal case and its precept of voter choice. If apathy is needed for the functioning of good governance, including political order, then liberal democracy can only function, devoid of effective voter choice, as no more than the legitimation of good governance.

Voter choice is more than an abstract axiom for, and of, liberal democracy, but the means whereby the modern individual-self is potentially able to make demands on the state by forcing a change in the meeting of need, not least by change in tax-and-spend policies. When no effective choice is to be had, when state institutions either do not provide for, or withdraw from, the meeting of need, then voter choice becomes redundant as an electoral perspective. Time will tell whether legitimation alone serves as a functioning perspective for the elections of the new wave of democratisation in Africa. However, in conclusion, it is worth going back to the early days of the one-party period when one influential prospective view was then taken of the future trajectory of politics in Africa.

Nearly three decades ago, Goran Hydén and Colin Leys surveyed the 1969 and 1970 one-party elections in Kenya and Tanzania. They concluded that the elections 'were deliberately structured to ensure that they could not have a very far-reaching impact on the character of the regime' and merely 'served to *register* the prevailing state of political consciousness rather than to act as an independent influence on it'. More significant than the elections themselves, the authors continued, were the consequences, if any, of the elections and 'the long-run experience' of which the electoral contest was a part. Among the long-run consequences for Kenya, to take one of their

---

[22]World Bank (1989), *Sub-Saharan Africa: From Crisis to Sustainable Growth*, Washington, D.C.: World Bank, 60 (emphasis added as quoted in Williams and Young 1994, 86).

[23]Williams and Young (1994, 97) quoted, with emphasis added, from P. Landall-Mills, 'Governance, Civil Society and Empowerment in Sub-Saharan Africa', unpublished paper presented at the Annual Conference of the Society for the Advancement of Socio-Economics 1992. Moore (1996) also refers to a paper by Pierre Landall-Mills (1992) 'Governance, Cultural Change and Empowerment', *Journal of Modern African Studies* 30(4), 543–567. Peter Landall-Mills, a World Bank guru, claimed, in the unpublished paper, that 'the benefits of a participatory approach is not simply the immediate advantage of a project better tailored to the clients' needs, but also the impulse it gives to the long term process of *changing mentalities*'.

[24]For social, colonial and post-colonial trusteeship, see Cowen and Shenton 1996.

examples, Hydén and Leys mentioned the possibilities of 'pressure for freedom of party competition' and 'a shift towards a more policy-orientated or ideological conception of politics'(Hydén & Leys 1972, 419–420). What is significant here is that the first of the above consequences, multi-party competition through elections, has arrived without the kind of shift in the content of politics that was postulated as a possibility for the long term. Our explanations for the major findings of this project may also play a part in addressing the question of why multi-party elections have not produced policy-orientated politics for most cases under review. Insofar as Hydén and Leys understood the earlier politics to be that of clientelism and based overwhelmingly on 'clan and locality cleavages' (*ibid.*, 401), then it must also be concluded here that the basis of those cleavages has shifted, by being brought into the trajectories of multi-party politics. In doing so, the politics of communality takes different shapes and forms from what was suggested for the early one-party period. Secondly, policy-orientated and ideological conceptions of politics owe much to the particular economic conditions for liberal democracy that we mentioned above. It is not only that those conditions are mainly absent from the African cases here but that, during the same period under review, that of the 1990s, politics in liberal democracies are often also said to be bereft of policy and ideological contest.

Hydén and Leys also conveniently raised the purpose of election studies. They contested the claim of Bill MacKenzie and Kenneth Robinson (1960): 'No human observer can ever grasp the whole life of a political system in action, but more can be learnt in the space of about three months during an election than in any other comparable period' (quoted in Hydén and Leys 1972, 391). It is during an election that the various strands of politics come together like 'an intricate knot' and the researcher tries to untie it. In contesting this claim, at the onset of the one-party period, Hydén and Leys proposed that election studies with this purpose in mind could only matter for elections that mattered. And to understand if and why elections mattered as sources of substantial political action, it would be necessary to bring 'a broadly conceived socio-economic analysis' into the picture as well (*ibid.*, 420). It is to this end that this book has been directed.

2

The Politics of National Elections in Botswana, Lesotho & Swaziland
Towards a Comparative Analysis

MICHAEL NEOCOSMOS

Introduction

If we are to start from the assumption that we wish to understand elections in Africa, then it seems a truism that this understanding can only be achieved if elections are situated within a historical, socio-economic and political context. The question is rather about the way in which this context is analysed and the manner in which elections are situated within it. I have argued, in an earlier paper (Neocosmos 1997), that the electoral context should involve a historical dimension and should stress the importance of an analysis of the form of state. For the countries of Botswana, Lesotho and Swaziland (BLS), state formation has evidently differed both according to the three countries' different political systems and in the fact that the state ruled the countryside and the town in different ways.

I wish to move further in this chapter by suggesting that elections and the struggles surrounding them must be understood within a political context which stresses not simply the different forms of state, but more broadly, the different forms of politics under which various forms of state can be subsumed. The reasons are that politics in general cannot be reduced to the form of the state and that, in contemporary Africa, there is evidence of a limited form of politics which subsists outside the state. In short, what is often assumed to be the dominant form of politics, usually a state form of politics, is not the only way of conducting political activity. At different times, to a greater or lesser extent, alternative forms of politics have been and are in evidence.

Alternative forms of politics are particularly apparent when the central state is on the verge of semi-collapse and people have to conduct political activity in a manner which draws on their popular history and experience. Alongside other cases, the recent examples of Kinshasa, during the final years of the Mobutu regime, and the South African urban townships of the 1980s come readily to mind. Elections do take place under these conditions but may fulfill somewhat different functions to those held under the sway of a dominant central state. If we are to make sense of elections therefore, we need to have some kind of understanding not only of historical process, and of the 'mode of rule', but also of what can be called the 'mode of resistance'. Even in those cases where there is no obviously organised alternative politics, the relations between the state and (civil) society are structured in such a way as to make such alternatives more or less (im)possible. The existence and trajectory of popular social movements, along with the political identities associated with them, are arguably regulated by the broader relations between state and civil society (Neocosmos and Selinyane 1998).

The question, for example, of what explains the difference between relatively high levels of electoral participation and electoral apathy can only be asked within a context of state-society relations. Apathy often suggests both an explicit rejection of a particular government together with an implicit rejection of the state itself (such as in Zimbabwe) and a rejection of politics, as such, through such phrases as 'all politics is corrupt', 'politics is a dirty business' and 'politics is only for the powerful and/or rich'. Yet, while apathy implies a rejection of a particular form of state-dominated politics, it does not refer to alternative forms of politics which remain unevaluated. The dominance of forms of state politics is often connected to the undermining and limiting of alternative forms of politics by the state and is thus itself a product of state–society relations.

Thus, this question of apathy versus participation, which is such a problem for the liberal-democratic model, as Cowen and Laakso (1997a; 1997b) note, is highly influenced by relations between the state and society more broadly. Here, I wish to put particular stress upon the importance of analysing the manner in which alternative forms of politics from within civil society are dealt with by the state. I address the questions of whether alternative forms of politics are limited or completely stifled and, if they are stifled, how alternative politics are effectively suppressed One way of limiting or stifling the alternatives is by the state control of elections which largely serves the function of incorporating people into state-monopolised politics. If Good (1997, 253) is correct to note that 'liberal or representative democracy is a phenomenon of this century which expresses not the fulfilment of democratic aspirations but their deflection, containment, and limitation', then the issue of the dominance of state politics is very important in understanding elections.

Therefore, the representational and legitimation functions of elections, as discussed by Cowen and Laakso (1997a; 1997b) in their review of election studies in Africa, are closely related to, and need to be supplemented by, another function which may be termed the limitation function of elections. The example of African nationalist politics in South Africa, as I have argued elsewhere (Neocosmos 1998), shows a transition between a popular form of politics and a state-dominated politics during the decade between 1984 and 1994. State-dominated politics was consummated in an election and electoral politics which not only legitimised the new government and state but also allowed the whole population a voice in choosing its national political representatives for the first time. But this particular process of electoral politics also undermined popular militancy and aspirations and incorporated them, especially after 1989, into a state-dominated politics. This was a process which demobilised the people, took away their ability to control their own organisations directly, made their representatives unaccountable, and generally gave rise to a new state and political elite which substituted itself for popular organisations and practices.

Elections are more likely to fulfil the limitation function in the Africa of the 1990s when the alternative mode of containing and limiting popular alternatives through simple authoritarianism is not quite as dominant as it was in the post-independence period. For Southern Africa, as for other African countries, the authoritarian option is limited by external as well as by growing internal pressures. While elections serve to legitimise the state in the eyes of powerful international or regional interests, they often restrict popular aspirations to a particular mode of politics which does not necessarily conform to, or fulfil, popular aspirations. Rather, elections deflect, contain and limit alternative politics to insignificant enclaves which are easily controllable or isolated. In sum therefore, the state in Africa (although not exclusively in Africa), tends to limit democracy and it can do so partly through the medium of elections.

However, while the example of South Africa shows how state politics contains and limits alternative forms of politics, state politics also has to be reproduced. It is by no means assured of a once and for all victory over alternative forms of popular democratic politics. Nor is the state, whether liberal-democratic or authoritarian, automatically isolated from democratic pressures exerted from sites within civil society. As part of the process of reproduction of state power, therefore, the state has a tendency to exclude popular democratic forms of politics, to restrict democratic prescriptions to itself and monopolise forms of representation. Liberal democracy assumes that the state monopolises representation when politics are equated with the state and the state with politics (Wamba-dia-Wamba 1995). If the statement by Larry Diamond (as cited by Balefi Tsie) that liberal democracy 'demands that citizens care about democracy but not too much' expresses the contradictory flaw of liberal democratic models of multi-party democracy (Cowen and Laakso 1997a; 1997b), it also expresses the threat posed to such models by different forms of politics where citizens care fully about democracy. To care is never 'too much' but rather forms the basis for the continued defence and extension of democracy by the people through regular democratic prescriptions on the state.

The following case studies will address the three issues of legitimation, representation and limitation in analysing the context of elections in the BLS countries. In doing so for each country, albeit to an uneven extent, particular attention will be paid to the historical context, to rural-urban differences and to different forms of politics including forms of state politics, in the country concerned. The three countries' similar colonial and historical experiences as peripheral suppliers of migrant labour to, and as tribal reserves of, the South Africa economy are part of this common historical context. There is another source of commonality for the BLS countries although it may not have a had a direct bearing on their political forms (Neocosmos 1997). Despite indications of major changes, especially in Botswana, the importance of the rural areas is still crucial for the government of each state since the majority of the population in the three countries is still rural based. The forms of state control in the rural areas have their roots in the colonial and immediate post-colonial periods, thereby making a comparative historical analysis paramount.

Of the three countries, only Lesotho was engaged in an election during the study period (1995–1998). The struggle for multi-party elections in Swaziland continues while elections are due in Botswana during 1999. However, the BLS make it possible to compare cases where elections have been episodic (Lesotho), with those which have taken place regularly since independence (Botswana), in contrast to Swaziland, where multi-party elections have yet to appear.

Swaziland and the struggle for multi-party elections

The way in which the struggle for multi-party elections is taking place in Swaziland reveals much about elections in Africa generally. Although it is fruitless to speculate about the final outcome of this struggle, its terrain and political context suggest that the issues of representation and legitimation are central to the debate about multi-party politics, while the question of the defusing and limiting of general popular-democratic aspirations is crucial for the state's thinking and strategy.

The historical background

The historical context of the struggle for multi-party elections is significant in Swaziland because the issues are basically about a decree, which King Sobhuza enacted in 1973. This decree, which bans all political parties, is still in force.

At independence, Swaziland emerged with a 'traditional' monarchy which was soon to transform itself into an absolute monarchy. The chieftaincy retained all its supposed 'traditional' powers, including those of mobilising tribute labour, holding courts, punishing offenders, allocating and withdrawing land from cultivation and calling on armed force to coerce the peasantry to provide unpaid labour, cash or produce for state, chieftaincy, or an individual chief's needs. Also, chiefs played an administrative role as well as a central role in rural development. These awesome powers are still in force today, leading to what I have called the 'institutionalised plunder' of the rural population (Neocosmos 1987).

The effects of institutionalised plunder are primarily the reproduction of state power in the rural areas and secondly the enabling of accumulation 'from above' to take place. The 'traditionalism' of the state, although primarily a rural phenomenon, is not exclusively so. Every Swazi citizen is in theory the subject of a chief and every citizen has to pay allegiance to a chief in order to acquire Swazi citizenship. As we shall see, the current electoral process is heavily dominated by a form of 'traditionalism', around which contemporary democratic struggles are being waged.

The dominance of the chieftaincy in post-colonial Swaziland is explained by the outcome of the struggles, during the colonial period, between the colonial state, the chieftaincy and the rising *petit bourgeoisie*. A number of general, as well as specific, factors contributed to chiefly dominance. First, the influence of missionaries on Swazi pre-colonial and colonial history was minimal, especially in that the authority and powers of the chieftaincy were not undermined by religious teachings. Also, there were no missionary schools and hence no mission-educated middle class in Swaziland which could form a challenge to 'tradition' until the eve of independence.

Second, and connected to the first, was the lack of independent commoner organisations during the colonial period which could challenge the domination of the Swaziland National Council by the chiefs and provide a focus for national grievances.[1] The *petit bourgeois* parties formed on the eve of independence were thus too inexperienced to be able to mount an effective challenge

---

[1] In actual fact, a Progressive Association was formed in 1929, but it was largely ineffectual and had to be formed with the help of the Resident Commissioner. It was never able to mount an effective challenge to the aristocracy. See Levin 1993, ch. 4.

against the colonial state and the chieftaincy. As a result, the *petit bourgeoisie* found itself ill prepared at independence to challenge the chieftaincy for control of the country. Therefore, colonial history principally revolved around the struggles between the colonial state and the chieftaincy, mainly over the form of the state in the run up to independence. A secondary struggle between the chieftaincy and settler interests revolved around the control of Swazi labour. However, settler interests never really developed as a force opposed to the colonial state and at independence they threw their lot behind the aristocracy and King Sobhuza.

Central to earlier Swazi colonial history, and to the struggle between the colonial state and the chieftaincy, was the Swaziland land partition of 1911. As in other colonies where reserves were created, Swaziland was divided into three parts. In one part, land was a commodity and held through title deed. 'Title deed land' was owned by settlers and concessionaires. On another part, 'Swazi Nation Land (SNL)' was 'owned by the Swazi Nation' or rather 'held by the King in trust for the Nation', subject to customary law rather than that of contract, upon which the overwhelming majority of Swazi population lived as peasants. Finally, there was 'Crown Land', most of which reverted to SNL at independence.

Although initially attempting to resist the land partition, the Swazi aristocracy soon discovered that, under the conditions of colonial Swaziland, it was control over labour rather than that of land which reproduced their position within the political economy (Crush 1987). As a quid pro quo for the partition, the chieftaincy was able to prevent colonial authority from interfering with SNL. As long as the colonial authorities received taxes, they were not interested in what forms of (mis)rule existed on SNL. Those colonial officials who did raise objections could easily be reminded of the nationalist grievances of the chieftaincy over the history of land partition and of the fact that, without their cooperation, colonial rule might not be such a trouble-free process, especially given the strong control of the chieftaincy over the population. The attempts by colonial authorities to privatise land in different ways were always successfully resisted by the chieftaincy (Neocosmos 1987).

The only challenges to the 'tribal nationalism' of the aristocracy, for leadership of the nationalist struggle in Swaziland during the colonial period, developed during the immediate pre-independence period. Challenges came the small working-class, mainly concentrated in mining, and the urban *petit bourgeoisie*. Working class action took the form of a series of strikes in 1963 initially over pay but, in the circumstances of decolonisation, they had a strong nationalist content (Levin 1993, ch. 4). The strikes were crushed by use of military force.

Political parties were only formed during the 1960s, when the main *petit bourgeois* party eventually emerged (in 1963) with a radical populist nationalist programme as the NNLC (Ngwane National Liberatory Congress). Clearly, the urban *petit bourgeoisie* did not feel that the 'traditional' institutions of the chieftaincy represented its interests. The NNLC, although able to bring together support from the working class as well as from a section of the well-to-do peasantry, was never able to contest the powers of the traditionalist aristocracy who organised themselves into a political party at the eve of independence.

The constitution with which Swaziland emerged at independence was an 'adapted' Westminster model. It was 'adapted' in the sense that the King was not a constitutional monarch but emerged with significant powers such as the power to nominate a fifth of the lower house and a half of the upper house of Parliament. At the same time, the constitution guaranteed the rights of movement, association and assembly as well as freedom of speech. At the elections of 1972, the NNLC, weakened by splits, won only 3 of the 24 elected seats, while the King's party won the rest. The chieftaincy's control over the peasantry, as the majority of the population, was the major instrument of victory since peasants were regularly threatened with expulsion from their land, meaning total impoverishment, if they did not vote for the aristocracy's party.

Levin (1993) argued that despite the 1972 victory, the parliamentary system had placed too many obstacles in the way of Sobhuza's absolutist and repressive tendencies. In any case, Sobhuza had only reluctantly agreed to accept multi-partyism anyway (Kowet 1978, 150). It does seem that the constitution did allow for the voice of an organised opposition to be heard, but under 'traditional' rule, as devised by the chieftaincy, there was little room for anything but absolutism. Whatever the reason, the *petit bourgeois* party of the NNLC and the trade unions seemed to have acquired the ability to frighten Sobhuza into abrogating the constitution (during 1973), banning all political parties and instituting a state of emergency with its notorious power of 60 day detention, renewable at will. Henceforth all powers were to be vested in the King 'in council' and the country to be ruled by decree. As we shall see, these provisions have remained in force until very recently.

Before ending this historical background, it is necessary to sketch the workings of two institutions of royal autocracy in Swaziland. The first is a peculiarly Swazi economic institution, Tibiyo Taka Ngwane, which is ostensibly one of two public corporations owned by the 'Swazi Nation' but in fact run as the King's and ruling aristocracy's personal enterprise, alongside the other, Tisuka Taka Ngwane. The Tibiyo corporation has entered into joint deals with TNCs to exploit national resources and has been the main source of capital accumulation by the ruling aristocratic oligarchy since independence (Levin 1986). While Tibiyo now operates in public and publishes an annual report and accounts, Tisuka still operates in secret.[2]

More important for our current purposes are the *tinkhundla* political institutions which were given a prominent role under the constitution of 1978. These are basically 40 'traditional' local authorities which comprise a number of chieftaincies and are headed by an appointee of the King. They are also the vehicles for 'election' to parliament. What happens is that each *inkhundla* elects members of an electoral college which then elects the 40 members of the House of Assembly.

Voting in *tinkhundla* amounts to candidates being announced in the morning with voters then walking through the gate next to which the candidate of their choice is standing.[3] The two with the highest votes then become members of the electoral college which both nominate and elect the members of the House of Assembly. Between the two processes, the candidates' suitability is determined by an electoral committee comprising the King's seven nominees. Once nominations have been approved by the committee, elections in the College are by secret ballot (Levin 1986). As we shall also see, this system of elections has been slightly revamped under pressure from the organised opposition.

The post-colonial state in Swaziland, having been so heavily pivoted on the person of the King, entered a major crisis when Sobhuza died in 1982. His death was followed by a long period of palace intrigues until the young King Mswati III was crowned in 1986. Corruption and intrigue did not stop after the ascension to power of the new king, but rather became a central feature of the Swazi state after this period.

The struggle for multi-party elections: late 1980s–1998

The struggle for multi-party elections can be divided in two phases: from the late 1980s (the beginning of mass agitation for multi-partyism) to 1993 (the date of the 'elections') and the second from 1993 onwards. The next 'election' is due in October 1998.

Phase 1: late 1980s–1993
Dissatisfaction among members of the urban classes during the 1980s along with the influence of the democratic struggles in South Africa, such as those of the United Democratic Front (UDF), led to the formation of the People's United Democratic Movement (PUDEMO). PUDEMO has recently – especially after 1990 and the unbanning of the ANC in South Africa – been able to transform the political debate in Swaziland and put the issue of democracy on the agenda. PUDEMO was able to clearly express the grievances of large sections of the Swazi population coherently and to exploit skilfully the mistakes of the state in its attempt to charge PUDEMO leaders with high treason in 1990, and when this failed, to attempt to gag them by using the 60-day detention method. The use of the weapon of the hunger strike was very effective in releasing international pressure, which in the current more liberal political conjuncture in Southern Africa, was successful in restricting the more repressive actions of the Swazi State.

Political space was gradually won by PUDEMO to organise and criticise the government in the independent press and, gradually, a number of civil society organisations were formed which have collectively come to form an unofficial opposition. These have included the Swaziland Youth Congress (SWAYOCO) and the Human Rights Association of Swaziland (HUMARAS). By

---

[2]*Economist Intelligence Unit Quarterly report on Botswana, Lesotho and Swaziland*, 1st quarter 1997.
[3]Swaziland has the dubious honour of having invented this 'tradition' of voters queuing behind candidates which was used with much fanfare by the Nigerian and Kenyan states at different times in their history.

1992, PUDEMO made a public decision to 'unban itself'. A number of opposition organisations surfaced, including the NNLC.

Much of the pressure exerted by PUDEMO and other popular organisations has been directed at arguing for multi-party democracy and a scrapping of the *tinkhundla* system. Pressure from a number of quarters succeeded in forcing the King to agree to a constitutional review in 1991. This review was entrusted to a committee of royal supporters which became known as the Vusela committee which canvassed people's views from each *inkhundla*. Despite intimidation, canvassing enabled opposition to the system to be voiced. It seems that the *tinkhundla* system was overwhelmingly rejected in the exercise (Levin 1993, ch. 8).

Another review commission, soon dubbed Vusela 2, was decreed by the King to study the submissions of the earlier committee and report to the King. Although an attempt was also made to co-opt members of the opposition (PUDEMO's organising secretary and the president of HUMARAS) onto the committee, both HUMARAS and PUDEMO rejected the commission as a waste of money and resources. Among the recommendations of Vusela 2 made public in October 1992, was a revamping of the *tinkhundla* system whereby MPs would be elected in two stages, first at the level of the chiefdom and then at the level of the *inkhundla* where direct elections to parliament would be held by secret ballot. It also recommended that the number of *tinkhundla* be increased to 50 and that chiefs become salaried officials.[4] Unsurprisingly, PUDEMO and the democratic opposition as a whole rejected the recommendations as they fell far short of multi-party democracy. The state nevertheless went ahead with those recommendations regarding the changed electoral system and inaugurated an electoral education committee, Vusela 3, to 'educate' the country about the new system and to prepare the population for the elections due to be held before July 1993.

During the run up to the elections which eventually took place in three stages (registration: June–July; primary elections: September; final elections: October), two periods are distinguishable. The first period lasted for the first three months of 1993 when the opposition was very active in challenging the absence of multi-party elections in the country. From the end of March to the holding of the elections, the opposition felt the strain of very repressive measures and was effectively silenced. The elections were conducted in the absence of any political debate.

From a detailed analysis of the press over the first three months of 1993, it appears that the major area of struggle between the state and the opposition during this period, concerned the Vusela 3 exercise. For the state, the strategy was clearly an attempt to create propaganda and gather support for the revamped *tinkhundla* system, while at the same time defusing protest through delaying change towards multi-partyism. It also sought to legitimise the system by calling for the use of international observers at its *tinkhundla* elections.[5]

The strategy of the opposition, led by PUDEMO, was to call for a boycott of the elections and for a referendum on multi-partyism. At the same time, PUDEMO, SWAYOCO and other opposition organisations, used the education exercise as a platform to criticise the repressive nature of the state of emergency, the 60 day detention system, and the arbitrariness of the chieftaincy. Even the need for a constitutional monarchy was publicly mentioned. This creative use of political space managed to largely undermine the state's strategy. Later meetings were held in chiefs' kraals rather than in *tinkhundla* centres to intimidate the opposition. The police as well as vigilantes were also used for this purpose, but without much success.[6] At the same time the turnout at Vusela meetings has often been low, indicating a lack of interest by the population.[7]

Yet the opposition has had impact on wider democratic struggles within the country as the oppressed generally acquired greater confidence in challenging the state. For example, farmers

---

[4]See also *Swazi Observer* 24 September 1993, special election supplement.
[5]*Swazi Observer* 8 February and PUDEMO's response in *Times of Swaziland* 15 February. This call by the state was largely unsuccessful as it turned out. Although some foreign governments did provide funds for the election, no official observers were provided. For example, the EU provided R1 million but refused to send observers. This seems to have been the extent of Western governments' protest at the sham elections which eventually took place.
[6]*Times of Swaziland* 7 March and 11 March 1993; *Swazi News* 13 March 1993.
[7]*Swazi Observer* 29 January 1993; *Times of Swaziland* 15 March 1993.

began to complain publicly about the Central Cooperative Union, a state organ, which they wanted to be scrapped; wildcat strikes increased; government corruption started to be exposed in newspapers and the police were regularly forced to justify their arbitrary actions through the media; the opposition, though with less success, attempted to pursue a campaign for free education.[8] Generally, people have been talking openly and giving an impression of political vibrancy never before experienced in the country.[9]

At the same time, the state continued with its arbitrary actions such as the evictions of squatters, and the destruction of people's homes built without the chief's permission, but these events are now regularly reported in the media.[10] The state scored its big 'success' when PUDEMO attempted to take the struggle into the countryside. Previously PUDEMO had attacked the chiefs' use of unpaid labour. Now, it attempted to help peasants with weeding their fields. However, the opposition's ability to operate in rural areas was heavily circumscribed. PUDEMO members were attacked by mobs organised by chiefs while, at the end of March, police were out in force and arrested 60 PUDEMO members including most of its leaders at an attempted rally in a rural area. No attempt was made to arrest the local thugs who attacked PUDEMO members and who had been organised by the local chief (a prince and ex-prime minister).[11]

PUDEMO was effectively silenced after this episode because its leadership was prohibited, effectively according to sections 12 and 13 of the 'King's Proclamation of 1973', the famous decree which banned the Westminster constitution and all political activity in the country.[12] At the same time, while the notorious 60-day detention without trial law was repealed on September 27, all other repressive laws remained on the statute book including those which restricted freedoms of assembly, expression and association. For the duration of the elections, all public meetings were banned.[13] Candidates, whose parties were banned, could not campaign publicly. One newspaper reported: 'The Chief Electoral Officer, Mr Robert Thwala has confirmed that campaigning for nomination in the coming elections is not allowed. He did not explain why.'[14] By all accounts, the state generally explained so little that there was extreme confusion over both the registration process and actual voting. There was particular confusion over registration as voters were supposed to register, following state 'tradition', 'under' a chief, so that in many instances where chieftaincy disputes had not been resolved, people did not know under which chief to register. The relative lack of interest in registration was so widespread that the authorities had to extend the registration period twice.[15] After initially claiming that 400,000 voters had registered, the authorities admitted that, in total, only 283,700 people had registered, 80 per cent of eligible voters.[16]

The turnout at the actual elections was so low that it largely invalidated the whole exercise and confirmed support for PUDEMO's call for a boycott. The authorities never released the figures for the turnout but newspapers, civil society organisations and the political opposition made their own approximations. The total number of votes polled by victorious candidates was only 38,882, leading one analyst to surmise that the total number of voters did not exceed 100,000, an estimated

---

[8]*Times of Swaziland* 18 January and 20 January 1993; *Swazi Observer* 21 January 1993.

[9]*Times of Swaziland* 27 January, 2 February and 12 March 1993.

[10]*Swazi Observer* 25 February; *Times of Swaziland* 28 February 1993.

[11]See *inter alia, Times of Swaziland* 19, 22 and 23 March 1993; *Swazi Observer* 22 and 24 March 1993. The fact that this particular chief was eventually rewarded by the King with a seat in the Upper Chamber (the Senate) can leave us in little doubt that he was acting with official support at the time. *Times of Swaziland* 19 March and 3 November 1993.

[12]*Times of Swaziland* 23 March, 9 June and 29 July 1993; *Swazi Observer* 28 July 1993.

[13]On the repeal of the sixty-day law, see *inter alia Swazi Observer* 28 and 29 September 1993; on the banning of public meetings see *Swazi News* 12 June 1993. Western governments had made it plain through the academic Larry Diamond who had been visiting Swaziland that donors would pull out if the sixty-day detention law was not repealed; see *Swazi Observer* 29 July 1993. The Swazi government obviously enacted the minimum level of democratic legislation to satisfy its patrons.

[14]*Times of Swaziland* 1 July 1993.

[15]See especially *Times of Swaziland* 14 and 15 June 1993 on the slow registration process, *Times of Swaziland* 17 June 1993 *inter alia* on chieftaincy disputes and *Times of Swaziland* 20 June 1993 and *Swazi Observer* 1 July 1993 for the extension of the registration period.

[16]*Economist Intelligence Unit* 3rd Quarter 1993, 43.

rate of 35 per cent. In one constituency of the capital where 11,000 registered, less than 2,000 votes were recorded.[17] HUMARAS estimated the turnout at 15 per cent of the registered voters, while PUDEMO maintained that only 13 per cent voted.[18]

There was also evidence of voter intimidation by the chiefs, especially since the percentage of participating voters was higher in the rural than urban areas. One renowned commentator stated that 'one lesson which has emerged clearly after the recent nomination process is that electoral power lies in the rural areas'.[19] The intimidation of voters by chiefs varied from the creation of special squads to expel PUDEMO supporters from their areas to more subtle forms of pressure. Thinly veiled allegations of intimidation by chiefs were made by civil servants as well as journalists but nothing, for example, was done to investigate allegations of forced registration.[20] One ex-MP commented rhetorically:

> How are the people going to reject those candidates who would have been nominated by their chiefs? What guarantee is there that people will not be victimised by those chiefs whose nominees they would have rejected?[21]

On the other hand, a journalist maintained that the best way for candidates to win was 'to get chummy with your area's chief'. He added: 'who can have the guts to accuse a chief of receiving bribes? Who can accuse a loyal subject of having bribed a chief?' It was therefore not surprising when HUMARAS reported that 'there was a lot of voter intimidation (sic) by chiefs and *tindvuna* (headmen) to persuade voters to vote for certain candidates'.[22]

Clearly, by all available evidence, the elections in Swaziland were a travesty of democracy. Yet, the Western powers, led by the United States, declared these to be free and fair, leading the opposition to describe the foreign policy of that country as 'inconsistent'.[23] Nevertheless, given the low turnout, the people of Swaziland did not need the assessment of the West to decide on the nature of the elections. They voted to stay away.

Phase 2: 1993–1998

During the second period of the struggle for multi-party elections, the opposition became more dominated by civil society organisations and less by political parties. Concurrently, regional powers, through the Southern African Development Community (SADC), attempted to influence the Swazi state to engage in serious democratisation. The strategy of the state was to appoint more and more commissions, thereby delaying decisions while bribing and co-opting a significant proportion of the middle class into the state's structures by easing access to public salaries and perks, thereby contributing to a revenue crisis. A general stalemate developed between civil society and the state with the latter still firmly in control of the transition process. The Swazi state seems to be totally committed to the *tinkhundla* system. This is simply an indication of the continued dominance of the royalty and chieftaincy within the state whose strategy is to seek to divide the opposition and to manage the process of transition until it can work out a system whereby the current beneficiaries of the status quo lose out as little as possible. It has simultaneously clamped down hard on the poor and dangled carrots in front of those with aspirations to join the state. Repression plus co-optation so far has seemed to have succeeded. While the *tinkhundla* are still firmly ensconced as the basis of the representative institutions within the state structure, reports about their corruption and wastage of resources abound. A report in the *Times of Swaziland*, (09/02/1995) for example, noted that salaries and allowances of top officials, namely chiefs, in the *tinkhundla* amounted to R8m per year while it was said that they simply duplicated the duties of MPs and were paid for doing very little (in 1995, the US$ was equivalent to Rand

[17]*Times of Swaziland* 21 October 1993.
[18]*Times of Swaziland* 7 November and 5 December 1993.
[19]*Times of Swaziland* 12 September 1993.
[20]*Times of Swaziland* 9 June, 13, 19 and 23 July 1993; *Swazi News* 10 July 1993.
[21]*Times of Swaziland* 25 July 1993, 3.
[22]*Times of Swaziland* 7 November 1993.
[23]*Times of Swaziland* 11 November 1993.

3.7). It has been reported that even some rural communities have begun to complain openly about the system.[24]

At the apex of the 'traditional' structure and the country at large is the King, the absolute monarch who both rules by decree and plays a mediation role in conflict. Thus, the King has at various times intervened on behalf of University of Swaziland students in their struggles with the university administration and praised workers but has also dismissed labour and opposition leaders as 'foreigners'.[25] Likewise, he has berated international pressure as interference in Swaziland's internal affairs while also placating it by setting up yet another commission of enquiry into constitutional matters. Generally, the King has found it increasingly difficult to claim a position 'above politics', where he can be a genuine representative of the nation, since his political partiality is becoming more obvious to all, as shown by refusing to repeal the 1973 decree banning political parties.[26] On the other hand, the opposition organisations are showing extreme reluctance to criticise the King directly and often let him off the hook. As well as his massive personal fortune, the King and his relatives are paid just under R5m annually as part of the 'Royal Emoluments and Civil List'.[27]

Like the 1989–93 period described earlier, the repression of opposition political activity continues at the same time that some state institutions have been forced to become more accountable. The courts, for example, have shown some measure of independence from government as government cases against democracy activists do not automatically win.[28] Another example has been the attempt to clamp down on the press through the attempted introduction of a draconian piece of legislation – the Media Control Bill – which was basically intended to prevent the publication of articles critical of the government. The bill has drawn strong criticism both locally and regionally where one of the points made was that the decision to enact such legislation undermined the current Constitutional Review Commission (CRC) initiative.[29]

The number of Vuselas, as also mentioned for the earlier phase, has proliferated. Although these government commissions give the impression of consultation, their hearings generally take place in Tinkhundla Centres under the control of the chiefs and the 'traditionalists'. These commissions, of course, only make recommendations and the King is at liberty to ignore them if he so wishes. Although there has been growing criticism of the Vuselas, as evidenced by the letter pages of the press, they serve to rebut external pressures for democratic change which are exerted by international donors and regional power brokers such as South Africa and Zimbabwe.[30] In addition, as well as buying time in frustrating the internal opposition, the commissions co-opt some of the middle classes into the state strategy as earlier indicated.)[31]

Operations of the Constitutional Review Commission (CRC) can be used to illustrate the work of commissions in general. First, it seems that the King was not too keen on the idea of having a national commission, representative of a majority of 'stakeholders' in the country, to report on the writing of the first constitution for Swaziland. A written constitution would necessarily have to make recommendations on limits to the King's powers, multi-party democracy and human rights. Apparently, the King tried to circumvent the whole idea by reviving the British colonial invention of the Swazi National Council (SNC), the unrepresentative institution which in other British colonies was more accurately referred to as the Native Advisory Council. This council was 're-invented' as a forgotten aspect of 'tradition' and was duly packed with the King's men, including 6 princes and 4 chiefs among its 19 members, while its duties were said to be advisory to the King on constitutional reform and other 'traditional' issues such as the question of resolution of chieftaincy boundary disputes. By 1998, 2 years after its relaunch, it was reported that no chieftaincy disputes had been resolved by the SNC.[32]

[24]For example *Times of Swaziland* 7 June and 5 July 1995 and 30 December 1996.
[25]*Times of Swaziland* 7 February 1995 and 29 January 1996.
[26]*Times of Swaziland* 4 November 1995, 2 February and 25 March 1997.
[27]*Times of Swaziland* 9 March and 13 April 1995.
[28]*Times of Swaziland* 24 January, 26 April, 2 and 4 July and 3 September 1995.
[29]*Economist Intelligence Unit* 4th quarter 1997.
[30]See for example *Times of Swaziland* 14 and 18 August 1995 for a typical letter and a report on Mandela's advice to King Mswati.
[31]The population is 938 000, a mid-1996 estimate according to the *Economist Intelligence Unit*.
[32]*Times of Swaziland* 26 February 1998.

The CRC was finally set up in July 1996 after the presidents of South Africa, Zimbabwe, Mozambique and Botswana had put pressure on the acting prime minister at a meeting in Maputo in the same month, called to discuss Swaziland.[33] By April 1997, the commission had not yet commenced its work since its terms of reference had only just been finalised, and its budget had not yet been completed. The CRC had spent its time mainly discussing commissioners' salaries and benefits. Government had requested R45m from foreign donors to fund its work over a two year period. After it was announced that the CRC's mandate would be extended by another two years, the members of the democratic opposition, who were present in their personal capacities, started to withdraw. Its deputy chairman withdrew and then rejoined after a time.[34] During November 1996, it was announced that the 30 members of the commission would each be paid R18,000 per month[35] while the chairman, his deputy and secretary received R20,000 and R19,000 respectively, excluding perks. The CRC proved to be a boon for the businessmen and professionals who comprised the members of the commission, while the civil servants seconded to it received higher pay, all during a period when hospitals had to downsize their operations due to funding shortages.[36] By March 1998, it was reported that R15m had been spent during the first year's work of the CRC. During September 1997, the King told the 52nd General Assembly of the UN that 'all is well with the CRC'.[37]

It was finally reported that the new constitution would only be brought into effect after the five year term of the current parliament expired in October 1998.[38] Members of the opposition and civil society organisations criticised the CRC exercise for being designed to enshrine the status quo, while foreign ambassadors apparently pressured the opposition to stay with the process.[39]

The spending of so much of public funds on simple bribery has not been without nefarious effects. At the end of 1997, provisional estimates showed an overall budget deficit of just under R217m in 1996/97 and forecast an increase in the deficit of over R96m for 1997/98.[40] Donors have expressed concern at the proportion of the budget devoted to recurrent expenditure, notably on personnel. The IMF delegation, in an interview after its annual consultative meeting with the government during 1996, had earlier stated that 'present spending levels must be cut as soon as possible. The cost of the civil service remains a major contributing factor to the deficit, and the cost of civil service salaries is high compared with other countries in the region.'[41] Despite this warning, the 'gravy train' of corruption has extended throughout the government. In early 1997, the Minister of Finance was forced to resign because of his seeming determination to restructure the government-owned Swazibank which was owed millions by princes, members of parliament, cabinet ministers and others among the elite.[42] At the same time, a commission of inquiry into a debt recovery programme from peasants in 1990 revealed that bank employees made an 'immense fortune' from seizing farmers' property. The property seized was by all accounts 'in monetary terms far higher than the loans owned' and was aimed at 'illiterate farmers'.[43]

It had also been noted – in an earlier article in the *Times* – that ultimately ministers, permanent secretaries, ambassadors, the Attorney General and the Director of Public Prosecutions in particular, could only really be removed on the orders of the King (19 July 1996). It is worth adding that Tisuka Taka Ngwane, one of the two royal corporations mentioned above, was

[33]*Economist Intelligence Unit* 3rd quarter 1996.

[34]*Economist Intelligence Unit* 1st and 2nd quarter 1997; *Times of Swaziland* 27 September 1997.

[35]*Times of Swaziland* 4 November 1996.

[36]*Times of Swaziland* 12 January 1998.

[37]*Swazi News* 27 September 1997. The CRC had spent 15 million rand on 'administrative expenditure, the extension and construction of the Nkhanini Conference Room, additional offices and the moving of the Royal Filling Station and construction of a security brick wall around the premises' (*Swazi Observer* 24 March 1998). The total budget for the same year was 20 million rand of which 13.7 million was government money and the rest donor funds. *Ibid.*

[38]*Swazi Observer* 25 February 1998.

[39]*Economist Intelligence Unit* 4th quarter 1996.

[40]*Economist Intelligence Unit* 4th quarter 1997.

[41]*Economist Intelligence Unit* 4th quarter 1996.

[42]*Economist Intelligence Unit* 1st quarter 1997.

[43]*Times of Swaziland* 29 May and 31 July 1997.

reported as acting as a 'royal bank' paying the personal debts of princes and princesses to government ministries.[44] It was later shown that parliament and the cabinet were in fact accountable to chiefs and the King's advisers and that the Prime Minister was powerless.[45] It is impossible therefore to escape the conclusion that it is extreme power and complete lack of accountability which in Swaziland lies at the basis of state corruption.

Moving now from the level of the state to that of civil society, it is apparent that, during the period in question, a number of groups within society have taken direct action to protest both against state arbitrary actions and for better conditions. These have included civil servants, teachers, school children, university students and their parents, workers in trade unions and hawkers. To these must be added PUDEMO and a revived NNLC. Undoubtedly the most powerful of the civil society organisations have been the trade unions since they have recruited among sugar plantation workers and pulp workers in particular. Generally, these actions and strikes have involved both 'economic' and 'political' issues and it is thus sometimes difficult to disentangle them. The single most important and recurring demand of the opposition is the lifting of the state of emergency and the unbanning of political parties, which means revoking the 1973 decree, thereby leading to multi-party elections.

The constant harassment of political parties by police is founded on the notion of the 'rule of law', however oppressive that law may be.[46] Evidently this shows the limits of legal and semi-legal political activity by political parties which have unbanned themselves but which find it extremely difficult to operate. As a result, the opposition movement has helped in building and in organising a trade union movement which has organised workers in the most important sectors of the country such as sugar and wood pulp. Trade union action erupted in 1996 and 1997 and, after a series of actions, the Swaziland Federation of Trade Unions embarked on a mass stay away on 3 February 1997, lasting for a month and proving to be the longest strike in the history of Swaziland. Grievances included the repeal of the 1973 proclamation, the establishment of a representative and legitimate constitutional forum, the introduction of a national minimum wage and the right to strike for all workers (Dlamini and Levin 1997). The strike was called off after it became clear that business had suffered severely. That this strike ended in stalemate is indicative of the relations between the progressive forces of civil society and the state.

Generally, while urban civil society has been in turmoil throughout this period and has put pressure on the government to introduce multi-party elections, the state is still very much in control of the transition process. The state has still not caved in on repealing the 1973 decree – a demand which has mass support – although if it were to do so, according to some commentators, it would deflate the radicalism of the 'progressive forces'.[47] The problem for the state is that the issue of the repeal of the 1973 decree is as bound up with 'tradition' as it is with the guarantee of chiefly power over the state as a whole. Repeal is perceived as threatening the whole edifice of the Swazi state as constructed by Sobhuza in the post-independence period. While it is clear that the 'traditionalists' would probably win an election if 'free and fair' elections were to be held tomorrow, since they fully control the rural peasantry, to do so would be to lose the total control over the state which they possess at present . It would be to admit that the peasants are to be represented by one political party with control in rural areas in which two thirds of the population live. This undoubtedly would mean a certain loss of power by the chiefs.

Until popular organisation begins to embrace the peasantry and move to a position where it is able to link broad demands for democratisation with the concrete grievances of the majority, it seems that the state will always be slightly ahead of the urban opposition. Unfortunately it is clear that the opposition is largely populist in its rhetoric and has ignored the rural areas in particular. It is apparent that an urban-based discourse on 'rights', as Mamdani (1996) has argued, is not one which can easily appeal to the peasantry. Instead, the rural areas operate within a discourse on 'tradition'. The debate over 'tradition' is one which systematically characterises the transition

---

[44]*Times of Swaziland* 25 November 1996.

[45]*Times of Swaziland* 17 April 1997.

[46]See *Times of Swaziland* 13 September 1996 where a delegation of PUDEMO leaders is told by the Prime Minister that 'the rule of law should be maintained at all costs'.

[47]*Economist Intelligence Unit* 1st quarter 1997.

process and although it is clearly and easily undermined in the press, 'tradition' has different reso- nances in the rural areas.[48] It is not difficult for rural people to understand that the current tradition of the chiefs and *tinkhundla* is oppressive. The opposition needs to take 'tradition' seriously, to show the peasantry that it is possible to transform such tradition in a democratic direction and in order for the political balance to be tilted in favour of democratic change.

The state is continuing to deflate the opposition by playing for time. While this does not legit- imize the state in the eyes of the urban population and the rural working class, it is sufficient to deflect foreign political pressure and criticism.[49] The main problem is that the strategy pursued by the state is extremely costly and ultimately it is in the economic sphere that the battle for elections and democracy is likely to be won or lost. The ultimate danger to the state comes from the International Financial Institutions (IFIs), as its strategy is leading it to over-borrow in order to placate internal opposition and international opinion, and to co-opt more and more members of the middle class to its form of politics.

The main economic indicators for Swaziland do not look good with average Gross Domestic product (GDP) growth rates of less than 3 per cent for 1995/96. Trade and current account deficits continue to widen as a result of continuing low prices for major exports and increased state expen- diture. While the government has adopted an internal adjustment programme which started in 1995/96, ostensibly to restrain expenditure and to seek additional sources of revenue, this has not had the desired effects so far. Although, as I have noted, the fiscal deficit has worsened in recent years, it has not yet reached the IMF's critical level of 5 per cent of GDP which would mean an imposed Structural Adjustment Programme.[50]

According to economic analysts, one of Swaziland's main areas of 'comparative advantage' is low labour costs, which have to be maintained in order to increase the declining level of Foreign Direct Investment (FDI) since sanctions busters who had set up shop in Swaziland have returned to South Africa.[51] It should be evident that this comparative advantage is maintained simply because of the highly repressive nature of the Swazi 'traditional' state. With the introduction of democracy, especially if this democracy were to be far reaching, it would be unlikely that the people of Swaziland would be content with starvation wages and appalling living conditions. It remains to be seen whether the contradictions in the political economy will be resolved in favour of the long suffering people of the country.

Lesotho: elections, crises and continuity

The 1998 elections in Lesotho were the second since the liberal democratic model of represen- tation was restored to the country. The intervening period since the elections of 1993 has osten- sibly been one of crises at both the economic and political levels. However, despite these apparent crises, the same political organisation (although under different names) scored an overwhelming victory on both occasions. If this is to be explained, we need to go beyond the obvious discontinu- ities and crises to an analysis of the continuity of the political process in the rural areas of Lesotho.

It is arguably the case that the character of post-colonial politics in Lesotho was largely deter- mined during the colonial period, for it was during this period that the main class forces as well as state practices and forms of rule were brought to fruition. In this, Lesotho is certainly no exception to the rest of Africa (Neocosmos 1997). The shape of the political arena in the post-colonial period is largely the outcome of struggles between the colonial state, 'traditional' authorities (chiefs) and the rising *petit bourgeoisie*. For a time, the middle-peasantry also managed to secure a position on the political scene, but this was of short duration. Again this is not particularly exceptional. What were unique to Lesotho were the specific conditions and particular outcomes of these struggles.

---

[48]See for example *Times of Swaziland* 9 January and 17 and 19 February 1995.
[49]The Swazi state has also attempted to muzzle the *Times* newspaper through the enactment of legislation. This has provoked reaction from local as well as regional interest groups (including SADC) and so far the proposed Media Control Bill has not been made into law. (*Economist Intelligence Unit* 4th quarter 1997.)
[50]*Economist Intelligence Unit*, various issues.
[51]*Ibid.*

The historical background

Lesotho was constituted as a labour reserve economy in the period following the 1890s. It was during this period in particular that the burgeoning 'peasant road' to the development of capitalist agriculture in South Africa was cut short by the 'alliance of maize and gold'. White maize farmers, wishing to undercut competition from African peasant producers and mining capital in need of labour, secured the destruction of the 'peasant road' through an array of extra-economic state measures. The most notorious of these measures was the Land Act of 1913 which destroyed black peasant land ownership outside puny ethnically defined 'reserves'. By the 1930s, Lesotho had changed from being the 'granary of Southern Africa' to a net importer of maize (Murray 1981). Increasingly, the peasantry in Lesotho was only able to reproduce itself through some link to wage-labour in South Africa, especially in the mines.

There was no creation of reserves in Lesotho, but after the loss of its best land to the Orange 'Free' State, Lesotho itself became a reserve too poor to offer any inducements to would-be settlers. The colonial state, the chieftaincy and the European traders competed to extract resources from the worker-peasantry and to send labour to the mines from which chiefs, as elsewhere throughout the region, received capitation fees.

While the history of the peasantry during the colonial period was one of proletarianisation and exploitation by extra-economic coercion, that of the chieftaincy was one of systematic loss of its 'traditional' powers.[52] At the close of the colonial period, the chieftaincy had lost its powers to mobilise tribute labour and to preside over 'traditional' courts. Chiefs had become gazetted and paid state officials; the position of the 'paramount chief' was that of a constitutional monarch. The gradual loss of powers by the chiefs in Lesotho was due to successful struggles waged against them 'from above', firstly by missionaries and, later, by the colonial state itself, and from below by relatively successful commoner organisations of the rising urban *petit bourgeoisie* and the rural poor, mainly under middle-peasant leadership. In addition, the proliferation of chiefs in Lesotho led to divisions among them, especially that between 'principal' and 'minor' chiefs.

The most interesting aspect of these struggles was the nature and role of the two main organisations of civil society during the colonial period, namely the Basutoland Progressive Association (BPA) and the Lekhotla La Bafo (LLB) (Council of Commoners). It is due to these two organisations that the powers of the chieftaincy were substantially reduced since the colonial state on its own had little incentive to do so.

The BPA was founded in 1907 by Protestant mission-educated members of the urban *petit bourgeoisie*, such as teachers, evangelists, newspapers editors, petty traders and clerical employees of the colonial state. It was founded after the establishment of Basutoland National Council (the consultative forum which the colonial state set up as in other colonies). The BPA saw its role as expressing the interests of the educated elite *vis-à-vis* the 'traditional' authority of chiefs within the forum of the Council. The BPA believed in progress through evolutionary change and was respectful of colonial authority. It argued for a reduction of chiefly power and for a greater role for the educated elite in the economic and political affairs of the territory (Rugege 1993).

The LLB was a much more radical organisation which largely represented the interests of the rural peasants and semi-proletarians. Its ideology was radical nationalist and critical of the new élite. It was highly critical of the malpractices of the chiefs and the latter's association with the colonial state, but was always supportive of the chieftaincy as such. The LLB failed to mobilise the rural poor in any meaningful way. Therefore, its actions were limited to bombarding the authorities with eloquent complaints regarding the injustices of colonial rule, the subversive influence of the missionaries, the exploitative practices of traders and the malpractices and abuses of power of chiefs. Such procedures were obviously possible only because Lesotho was a highly literate society by colonial standards and possessed a vibrant press. In addition to peasants and semi-proletarians, the membership of the LLB also included petty traders, hawkers, labour agents, shop clerks and evangelists of the new African churches with whose anti-missionary positions the LLB closely identified (*ibid.*; Edgar 1988). The LLB was thus largely a peasant movement which, like others of its kind on the continent during this period, combined both ethnic and national characteristics.

---

[52]For a history of the chieftaincy in Lesotho, see Rugege 1993.

The LLB was regarded by the colonial state as a subversive organisation, especially when it started publishing its attacks in the Communist Party press of South Africa. Despite its links with organisations such as the ANC and CPSA, the ideology of the LLB remained largely circumscribed by its peasant material base. Its main success lay in expressing and raising the nationalist consciousness of the population and reducing the powers of the chiefs, while it has been seen as the ideological precursor of nationalist political parties (Bardill and Cobbe 1985, 32). Together, the BPA and the LLB were largely successful in weakening the position of the chieftaincy in Lesotho through the pressures which they exercised on the colonial state.

Nevertheless, while chiefs in Lesotho, during the post-colonial period, have not possessed the powers of their Swazi counterparts, for example, who can still call on tribute labour, they have, by virtue of their office, the ability to engage in a wide variety of 'unofficial transactions', from requesting bribes for official business to claiming the right to sell stray stock to augment their income (Perry 1983). Chiefs also have formed, until recently, the main state institution through which development projects operate and hence can have access to choice material 'pickings' as well as having the capacity to mobilise community labour and funds. They are also central, by virtue of their ability to secure access to state resources, to the reproduction of patron-client relations which undermine the development of democratic participation in politics. Political parties up until 1994 attempted to supplant chiefs' authority by monopolising more 'modern' institutions such as Village Development Committees, but without the same success or legitimacy. After 1994, as we shall see, the Basutoland Congress Party (BCP) has shown itself able to channel funds through MPs and to effectively by-pass chiefs.

During the 1950s, the political role of the LLB was taken over by the Basutoland African Congress (BAC), which now was much more able to mobilise the population behind a national project than was possible in the inter-war period. At the same time, the popular political content of the LLB was transformed and replaced by statist politics as the BAC took over the mantle of nationalism and gave it a statist content. The BAC was the first political party to be formed, in 1952 under the leadership of Ntsu Mokhehle. In 1957, the BAC merged with the LLB, and in 1959 it changed its name to the Basutoland Congress Party (BCP) in preparation for the 1960 elections. Nevertheless, the resilience of political parties in Lesotho, especially that of the BCP in the countryside and despite intense repression in the post-colonial period, is partly due to the long history of national protest inaugurated by the LLB.

In social composition, the leadership of the BCP was similar to that of the BPA, although its ideology was much closer to that of the LLB. The main influences on this ideology were, initially, pan-Africanism and African Socialism. When the Pan-African Congress (PAC) and ANC split in South Africa, the BCP aligned itself with the PAC. The BCP was able to mobilise support successfully in both urban and rural areas and to link up with both the cooperative movement and organised labour in towns. It engaged in systematic verbal attacks on the colonial government, white traders, Catholic missionaries and chiefs (Bardill and Cobbe 1985). The extremism of the BCP provoked a reaction among a number of supporters who broke away to form rival organisations. The most important was the Basutoland National Party which took more 'moderate' positions, such as close cooperation with South Africa, an important role for the chiefs and white traders after independence, along with a rabid anti-communism. The party was originally founded by minor chiefs and Catholic teachers under the leadership of Leabua Jonathan, who appealed to precisely those whom the BCP had attacked. The BNP was less able to appeal to the poorer classes of the country because of its lack of the populism mastered by the BCP.

The last of the political parties worth mentioning was the Marema-Tlou Freedom Party (MFP) which was formed in 1963 as a result of a merger between two smaller parties. Insofar as it had any distinctive appeal, this organisation was monarchist and representative of the interests of the principal chiefs. It was particularly concerned to support the monarchy from the attacks of the BCP and the palace manoeuvres of Jonathan, as well as to secure, for the new King Moshoeshoe II, an executive role in the future independence constitution of the country (*ibid.*).

The first general elections in 1965 under a Westminster-type constitution were won by the BNP with 41.6 per cent of the votes and 31 out of 60 seats. According to Bardill and Cobbe (*op.cit.*), the BCP had been internally divided, was short of funds and experienced difficulty in canvassing in the rural areas because of opposition by chiefs. The BNP, on the other hand. experienced no such difficulties since it was funded by white traders, Catholics and the South African government.

Moreover, the virulent anti-communist scaremongering propagated by the BNP and by the Catholic church succeeded in frightening a large proportion of the electorate.

Lesotho became formally independent in 1966 but a few weeks before independence a number of repressive measures were passed which gave the BNP government sweeping powers over the declaration of a state of emergency, the holding of public meetings, censorship and the proscription of 'unlawful' organisations (*ibid.*, 39).The first Jonathan government was characterised by a steady move towards authoritarianism; the abolition of district councils where the opposition had support; curtailment of the powers of the King; cancelling the holding of by-elections; and staffing the higher echelons of the civil service by South Africans. The opposition was still at this point able to operate but was subjected by the government to a systematic campaign of criticism.

Lesotho's first post-independence elections took place in January 1970. The results were never officially released but reliable estimates gave the BCP 50 per cent of the vote and 36 seats, while the BNP had 42 per cent of the vote and 23 seats (Table 2.1). The victory of the BCP has been explained by the neglect of mountain areas by the BNP and the moderation of the BCP platform on the issues of the chieftaincy and South Africa (Bardill and Cobbe *op. cit.*, 130). To these explanations, we must be add the monopolisation of business ventures by foreigners and the exclusion of potential local businessmen from access to government resources and institutions.

Having been assured by the British police commanders that the repressive apparatus would remain loyal, Jonathan suspended the constitution, arrested opposition leaders, banned opposition publications and imposed a curfew. The King was sent into exile and sittings of the High Court were suspended. Hundreds of people died in the months following the coup as resistance was harshly suppressed and by the middle of 1970, the state had asserted its control by extreme repression, the use of force and intimidation. Britain decided to withhold diplomatic recognition and aid but soon relented after Jonathan showed signs of entering into reconciliation talks with the main opposition parties. Recognition and aid were restored in June 1970 and other donors followed suit. This led Jonathan to abandon the talks and to go it alone.[53]

Increased repression enabled the regime to coerce the opposition into passivity. Eventually released from prison, BCP leaders became more and more frustrated with the lack of political space and in desperation switched to a violent confrontation during early 1974 when police stations were attacked to seize weapons for an uprising against the regime. These attacks were easily foiled and the regime launched a counter-offensive in which several hundred BCP supporters were detained and tortured while the BCP leadership fled into exile.

The regime's reliance on force was accompanied by attempts to centralise authority and to expel opposition supporters from the state apparatus. Thus, roughly around 700 civil servants were dismissed in the months following the coup and their positions were filled by BNP supporters. Village and district development committees were increasingly restricted to members of the ruling party. Compliant civil society organisations, such as cooperatives, women's groups and trade unions, were brought into the state fold through patronage. Those organisations which were less compliant were harassed. At the same time, the regime attempted to split the opposition by co-opting some leaders of small parties and a minority faction of the BCP into government.

The regime's attempts at securing its rule over a disaffected population were linked in some ways to Jonathan's complete turnabout in foreign policy the 1970s, especially in his break with apartheid South Africa; he refused to recognise the 'independent' Bantustans, more support was provided to the South African liberation movements and hospitality was provided to ANC refugees and cadres. In addition, Lesotho opened diplomatic relations with a number of state-socialist countries. This turnabout had several advantages for the Jonathan regime: it undercut the BCP's hitherto monopoly of anti-South African rhetoric; it deflected attention from pressing domestic problems; it led to a dramatic increase in foreign assistance and support, thus enabling the state to be much more ambitious in its economic development plans than it had been hitherto. On the negative side, this policy alienated Catholic support, and that of the chieftaincy which saw its powers of land allocation withdrawn and given to land allocation committees through the Land Act of 1979.

---

[53]For a detailed 'blow by blow' discussion of the coup, see Khaketla 1971.

It was after this shift, in 1979, that the BCP's armed wing, the Lesotho Liberation Army (LLA), started launching attacks on infrastructural targets in Lesotho from South Africa and with South African support. By 1986, the problems within the Lesotho state had reached crisis proportions and after a short South African blockade of Lesotho's borders, a military coup under Major General Justin Lekhanya was undertaken which finally saw the demise of the Jonathan government. All political activity was banned under Order No 4, but the military, no doubt under external pressure, promised to return the government to civilian rule by 1992. Political exiles returned in 1989 and the LLA was largely disbanded in 1988. In the interim, power was vested in a military council while plans were set up to create a 100 member constituent assembly which was inaugurated in 1990.[54] Members of this assembly were never elected but came from both civilian and military sources. Army representatives were the dominant force.

The struggle between the King and the military council over their respective powers came to a head and the King was first sent into exile and finally dethroned in favour of his son Letsie III during 1990. Lekhanya was removed from office by disaffected military leaders in April 1991 and on May 10, Order No 4, which had banned all political activity, was repealed and political parties were allowed to organise. The proposed elections were still set for June 1992. In the event, because of the slowness of voter registration and the delimitation of constituencies, the elections were postponed several times before they finally took place during March 1993.

The urgency of holding elections was brought home in May 1991 when riots, directed mainly against Asian traders, erupted in Lesotho's urban centres, beginning with Maseru, the capital. In all, 34 people were killed, 66 injured and 425 arrested within a week.[55] The basis of popular discontent appeared to be government policies which gave the appearance of favouring foreign businesses which often dominated the commercial sector in urban centres (Tangri 1993). Also, many workers felt discriminated against and exploited by foreign employers in connivance with local state agents who seemed to be open to bribery by these self-same foreign business interests. The riots expressed the frustrations and impotence of the masses of the urban population in the face of mounting unemployment and perceived corruption in government circles, combined with over-exploitation by foreign commercial interests. Riots were the only possible response, given the absence of avenues for the expression of popular anger, grievances and frustrations. They ended as suddenly as they had begun.

In the run up to the elections, 12 political parties were registered including the traditional parties, the BCP, BNP and MFP, but there seemed to be few ideological differences among them.[56] There was no real political debate and no campaign posters appeared in the main towns. None of the following issues were debated: the disastrous effects of the drought, which caused untold misery in the rural areas, the retrenchment of miners from South Africa, human rights and the endemic corruption in government.[57] The appeals of the BCP leadership to the voters were rather based on the fact that they were deprived of their rightful opportunity to control state power in 1970. The fact that this approach worked owed more to the experiences of oppression and corruption under the Jonathan and military regimes than to any innate BCP loyalty among the majority of the population. Evidently, loyalty was a prime issue among BCP families but it did not affect the majority of the population. Rather, the most frequent utterance was that government had been so disastrous since 1970 that the BCP deserved to be given a chance. Also common was the view that the current leader of the BNP, who was widely believed to have been engaged in corrupt practices, was also a major liability to his party. During the weeks before the elections, rumours of coups and LLA intervention had circulated but none materialised despite the well known BNP sympathies of the armed forces.

Whatever the reasons, the results confirmed what many suspected, namely the massive support for the BCP in the country. The turnout was calculated at an average 72 per cent throughout the country and the BCP won all 65 constituencies with just under 75 per cent of the vote. The election was declared free and fair by all international observers. Support for the BCP was therefore not

[54]See *Economist Intelligence Unit* 2nd quarter 1990 and 1st quarter 1991.
[55]*Economist Intelligence Unit* 3rd quarter 1991.
[56]*Mirror* 24 March 1993.
[57]See inter alia *Mirror* 15 January, 20 February and 24 March 1993.

confined to its traditional support base in the rural areas but was nationwide. Nevertheless, in the Maseru constituencies, the turnout at 65 per cent, was slightly lower, confirming an impressionistic poll by a local newspaper which discovered significant disaffection among the urban youth.[58]

Table 2.1: General election results in Lesotho 1965, 1970, 1993 and 1998.

		LCD	BCP	BNP	MFP	OTHER	TOTAL
1965	votes	—	103,050	108,162	42,837	5,776	239,825
	% of votes	—	39.67	41.60	16.50	2.23	100.00
	seats	—	25	31	4	0	60
1970	votes	—	152,907	129,434	22,279	1,909	306,529
	% of votes	—	49.80	42.20	7.30	0.52	100.00
	seats	—	36	23	1	0	60
1993	votes	—	398,355	120,686	7,650	6,287	532,978
	% of votes	—	74.70	22.60	1.40	1.20	100.00
	seats	—	65	0	0	0	65
1998	votes						
	% of votes	61.00	TOTAL OPPOSITION VOTES			39.00	100.00
	seats	78	0	1	0	1 by election	80

Source: Bardill and Cobbe (1985, 37, 160) for 1965 and 1970; Southall (1995, 42) for 1993, Langa Commission (1998) for 1998.

The election also showed the complete contempt of the electorate for the monarchy and for the antics of the royal family leading up to the election since the MFP won only 1.5 per cent of the vote.[59] The chiefs clearly lost power at the national level, but the outcome of the power struggle at the local level in the rural areas was then still undetermined. Central to the BCP's massive election victory was its ability to maintain its support in the rural areas over twenty years. While this was made possible by the general opposition to the BNP's obvious oppression of the peasantry, it was also helped in no small measure by the BCP's support among Basotho mineworkers in South Africa, among whom it was able to canvass for material support over the years.[60]

Economic and political crises, 1993–1998

Both economic and political crises affected Lesotho in the period between the 1993 and 1998 elections. It is the ongoing crisis of poverty for the majority of its citizens, under conditions of very little surplus creation, which lies at the root of Lesotho's economic and political problems as well as explaining the landslide victory of the Lesotho Congress for Democracy (LCD) at the May 1998 elections. At the same time, it is the sectarian form of politics, the fact that entering the state is a matter of survival for the winning section of the political elite, which accounts for the life and death struggle and the collapse of the state in the crisis immediately following the election process.

The labour reserve nature of Lesotho's economy is well known and need not be elaborated here. For our purposes, this has had two important consequences during the late 1980s and 1990s. First, at an increasing rate since 1987, local labour and mechanisation have substituted for 'foreign' migrant labour in South Africa, thereby diminishing the traditional source of Basotho wage labour employment. Recent data suggests that the number of Basotho employed in the South African gold mines in 1997 was nearly 90,000, roughly a one-third reduction since 1991.[61] However, while fewer Basotho workers are employed in South Africa, money wages have increased so that official and unofficial remittances, upon which the Lesotho government depended for revenue, have not

---

[58]*Mirror* 26 February 1993.

[59]See for example *Mirror* 22 January and 26 February 1993; *Lesotho Today* 4–10 March 1993.

[60]This support was, in the 1980s, challenged by the organisation of South African miners in the National Union of Mineworkers (NUM) which eventually took a pro-African National Congress position. However, for miners, there seems to be no necessary contradiction between supporting the BCP in Lesotho and the NUM in South Africa.

[61]*Economist Intelligence Unit* 3rd quarter 1996 and 1st quarter 1997.

declined as much as that of employment and have even increased during the very recent past.[62] This means in effect that the 'élite' status of migrant labour in the Lesotho countryside has increased at the same time that unemployment has put pressure upon the rural economy.

While the government has been very sensitive to the effects on the economy caused by the decline in remittances – amounting to nearly one-third of of GNP in 1984 – the crisis of social reproduction and survival in the rural areas of Lesotho is not really reflected in the relatively buoyant formal economic indicators since the crisis has mainly affected the rural 'informal' economy. As the Economist Intelligence Unit put it in 1997, data 'indicate that Lesotho has enjoyed impressive economic growth in the early 1990s and that the short term prospects remain favourable'.[63] The real GDP growth rate for 1994/95 was 12 per cent, but from an extremely low base.[64] This increase reflected the impact of the multi-billion dollar Lesotho Highlands Water Project, which was complemented by improved performances in manufacturing, both due to increased investment in textile manufacturing by Asian businesses and a good harvest.

Since 1989, the state has been following a structural adjustment programme which has also had deleterious effects on levels of employment and social conditions more generally. Government subsidies have been withdrawn and wages depressed.[65] A 1991 study showed that poverty was 'extensive' and that it was 'much more common in the mountain and other remote rural areas than in urban areas, district headquarters and lowland villages' (Gay et al. 1991, 87). Another contemporary source indicated that poverty affected about 66 per cent of all households in the country (Gustafsson and Makonnen 1991, 17).

Recent news reports which use Lesotho as an example of 'African economic resurgence' seem to consist largely of wishful thinking by international organisations, masking the terrible conditions in the countryside where a preponderance of 80 per cent (in 1991) of the population live and survive to a great extent outside the formal economy. An indication of this was the popularity of 'Food for Work' projects during the 1980s and early 1990s where female labour were paid a meagre pittance for working in constructing infrastructure such as roads. There has been no significant investment by the state in small-scale agriculture and, more generally, rural petty-commodity production since independence (Johnston 1996).

The crisis of reproduction for the majority of rural inhabitants of Lesotho has not been replicated in the urban areas to the same degree. It is here in fact that the political crises have been unfolding since 1993 at an alarming rate, often leading to farcical results. Lesotho's political elite is very small but very active and is extremely sectarian in its approach to politics as the economic and political survival of each of its sections depends on it achieving access to state resources and keeping other sections out. The BCP government has done very little to alleviate the suffering of its population since it came to power and has been primarily concerned to satisfy the demands of international donors and the IFIs rather than those of its rural population. In fact when it did address the plight of its poorest citizens, this was as a result of World Bank intervention as we shall see below.

The continuous series of political crises affecting the Mokhehle government since its election, were related to the inability of both government and opposition forces to attempt to overcome their differences in the national interest. The extreme sectarianism, around which most – if not all – official state politics operates, is usually indicative of ethnic or regional divisions in African politics. These are however of minor significance in Lesotho. The sectarianism and complete lack of discipline characteristic of Lesotho politics is evident in the following summary account of a number of crises, also showing that since assuming office, it became apparent that the BCP government had absolutely no vision or plan for the country. This seems true of all the major parties which are not distinguishable on ideological grounds.

The immediate aftermath of the 1993 elections witnessed unrest among the military as two factions fought out artillery duels over the hills surrounding Maseru. This crisis was basically

---

[62]*Economist Intelligence Unit* 2nd quarter 1997.

[63]*Ibid*.

[64]GDP per capita in 1995 was $428 for Lesotho as compared to $2,594 for Botswana, $1,300 for Swaziland, $2,046 for Namibia and $3,224 for South Africa.

[65]For a discussion of SAP and political economy more generally in Lesotho, see Lundhal and Petersson 1991; Petersson 1991; Neocosmos 1993; and Selinyane 1993.

precipitated by a scramble for pay increases as the government's first act on achieving power was to increase the salaries of parliamentarians (all BCP) and ministers by 300 per cent and 100 per cent respectively.[66] Not only did senior army officers feel that they should have access to the state trough along with that section of the political elite in power, but their position was insecure in that it was expected that they might be retrenched following their possible replacement by ex-LLA officers. Contemplating a coup, the military split on the question of who should replace the government and this ended up in chaos and artillery fights between different factions, both of which were opposed to the government (Matlosa 1995, 125). In appearing unable to control events, the BCP government was saved by regional pressure brought to bear by SADC leaders and then, after the South African elections of April 1994, by Mandela in particular. The army was bought off with a 66 per cent pay increase while civil servants were to receive 10 per cent. It then became the turn of the police to go on strike. They received a 42 per cent salary increase (*ibid.*, 130).

The government appointed a commission of enquiry into the events surrounding the military, together with a commission to investigate King Moshoeshoe II's wish to return to the throne, a ploy which was supported by his son from the throne. The royal commission's terms of reference were opposed by the King who saw them as critical of the monarchy, and this precipitated an alliance between royalty, the army and the opposition BNP which erupted in a royal coup in August of the same year. King Letsie III suspended the government and the constitution and arrogated to himself all legislative powers. Opposition to the coup was not long in coming and the Lesotho Congress of NGOs (LCN) was able to mobilise support for a total stay-away which completely shut down the country. South African and broader regional pressure, combined with local protest at the overthrow of a legitimately elected government, forced Letsie to come to terms with Mokhehle. An agreement was signed in August 1995 returning the democratically elected government to power, Moshoeshoe to the throne as a constitutional monarch with no involvement in politics, and the return of the military to barracks as a neutral politically independent force (*ibid.*, 137). The officers involved in the rebellion were eventually granted amnesty. The LCN was unable to sustain a committed defence of the elected government through stay-aways so that, ultimately, the government's main support against a coup by its own armed forces was the regional power of South Africa.[67]

During September 1995, a six-day national forum was held to discuss national democratic issues as per the agreement reached in August 1995. The government refused to bring other interests into a broader alliance, and the forum was powerless to force it to do so. The main decision arrived at was to institute an independent electoral commission for the 1998 elections. King Moshoeshoe died in a car crash in January 1996. Now, his son succeeded to the throne legally. Nevertheless, the differences which had been apparent within the ruling BCP came to a head. Two main factions vied for control of the organisation: Mokhehle's faction – dominant among the leadership of the BCP – representing the older members of the organisation who had been in exile and the opposition 'pressure group' which was somewhat more radical, based on younger members who had borne the brunt of Jonathan's repression at home. Although not based on any policy differences, the conflict seemed to turn around which faction would be in control of the succession to the ailing prime minister.

The March 1996 elections at the BCP party conference returned Mokhehle's faction to power but the opposition faction contested the results in court, accusing the Prime Minister, six ministers and 24 other party officials of contravening the party constitution.[68] By November, the High Court had declared in the opposition's favour. A new National Executive Committee (NEC) was elected in January 1997 which was dominated by the opposition but these elections were also invalidated by the High Court in February. The court ordered new elections but the confusion was increased by the fact that the Prime Minister and his supporters were expelled from the conference during February, a decision then confirmed by the NEC of the BCP, while the government issued a

---

[66]See Matlosa 1995. Matlosa provides a blow by blow account and analysis of the crisis.
[67]This reliance by government on a foreign military became vividly apparent in the post 1998 elections crisis see postscript below.
[68]*Economist Intelligence Unit* 3rd quarter 1996.

statement that Mokhehle remained leader of the BCP. In mid-March, Mokhehle announced his decision to retire from politics prior to the 1998 elections on the grounds of ill-health and old age. In April the High Court ruled that Mokhehle was to remain interim leader until the election.[69]

Violent clashes between supporters of the two factions of the BCP during June 1997 led to two deaths in the south-east of the country. Mokhehle and a majority of 42 MPs crossed the floor of the House to join a newly-created Lesotho Congress for Democracy (LCD). The balance of 22 MPs (one was an independent) remained in the BCP which refused to accept the status of official opposition. They argued that Mokhehle should have resigned from his position as Prime Minister and held new elections. The LCD argued that the constitution was not contravened as it had the support of a majority of MPs. Protest marches to the palace to demand the resignation of the government had no effect.[70]

Throughout all this confusion, the 'governance' of the country was compromised but the state's ability to rule was not. What did add to the confusion and seemed to threaten the state's ability to rule was when a small group of police officers, who had been resisting arrest for their involvement in the shooting of three officers in October 1995, seized control of the police headquarters and police college in Maseru during February 1997 with support from a small number of colleagues. The rebellious police dismissed senior officers and appointed their own police commissioner. A strike by supporters of the mutineers within the force resulted in the closure of police stations. This coup seems to have been a simple rebellion by junior officers and the lower ranks against the police leadership's involvement in political deals and due also to a fear of reprisals after a number of police officers had earlier refused an order to shoot at striking teachers. They were unable to get support from the population and in February 1997, after failed attempts to get them to surrender, the army was mobilised and swiftly regained control. More than 100 police officers were arrested. The various confidence-building measures such as the granting of amnesty to officers involved in the rebellion seemed to have succeeded in ensuring the army's loyalty to the government. There was labour unrest in September 1996, and clashes between the police and workers at the Lesotho Highlands Water Project (LHWP), after 2000 workers were dismissed for breach of contract. Violent action by the police resulted in four dead. Similar events occurred in early 1998 as women workers at a textile plant in Maseru were shot by the police for protesting, among other things, against management racism.

The government had to face pervasive opposition during its tenure of office simply because of the absence of avenues for the expression of grievances which often revolved around issues of pay and conditions linked to what was seen, with justification, as political favouritism in appointments to jobs. The absence of an opposition in parliament also helped to exacerbate the often violent street protest by armed protesters. The crisis was acerbated by the political sectarianism and immaturity characteristic of politics in Lesotho, where the ground for debate quickly disappears as interest groups take up extreme positions due to a small 'national cake' which lends the struggle for power and the ability to access state resources by factions of the elite, a life or death character.

The continuous crisis made the simple administration of the country ('governance') rather difficult, but it also seemed to suggest indeterminacy when the 23 May 1998 election was held. Most 'commentators' and 'experts' gave the three main parties the same chance of winning. Although the opposition thought it would be able to harness the resentment against Mokhehle's BCP and LCD, the outgoing ruling party won another landslide victory taking all of the 80 constituencies apart from two, one of which the BNP narrowly won and another where a by-election had to be fought. The question is how this landslide victory is to be explained, especially under conditions declared 'free and fair' by foreign observers?[71] Clearly, the raising of the salaries of the civil servants by 10 per cent one week before the election helped, yet it cannot account for such a landslide, neither can the apparent incompetence of the Independent Electoral Commission or the apparent election rigging as this could not have been extensive enough to substantially alter the results. The importance of the allegations of rigging is that the opposition parties chose to

---

[69]*Economist Intelligence Unit*, various issues.

[70]*Ibid.*

[71]Of course the apparent fairness at the polls does not preclude fraud before the voting process, for example at registration. This, however, was in no way unique to this particular election.

believe them and, as just under 40 per cent of the electorate was not represented in parliament because of the 'first past the post' electoral system, a major crisis ensued as we shall see. Paradoxically, I will argue here that the best explanation for this LCD victory is to be found in economic hardship and access (or lack of it) to economic rewards through political power and patronage. But in order to explain the victory, we must move from the constant crisis of Maseru politics to the continuity and apparent calm of the countryside.

Political control in the rural areas

Basically, the LCD won the 1998 elections because of the 'first past the post' electoral system, and because it exercised control over the rural areas, control which the party was able to inherit from the BCP through its system of patronage, and which made the rural population dependent on BCP (and later LCD) MPs for access to development funds. In ignoring the rural context, most urban-based analysts found themselves expressing surprise at the election results.

According to Selinyane (n.d., 26), the BCP in government, in contrast to the BNP and the military regime which had exercised control over the worker-peasantry primarily via the chiefs, had attempted to undermine the chieftaincy and to rule over the countryside directly through its own party structures. Three measures were taken after the BCP assumed office. First, little was done for a whole year regarding the re-election of members of the Village Development Councils (VDCs) whose term had expired in 1993, thus enabling local BCP activists gradually to take over the functions traditionally performed by the councils. These functions included the identification of households requiring drought relief food aid, the taking over and politicising of the distribution of food aid, and the general administration of village projects. Second, the Development Councils Act was amended to provide for election by secret ballot rather than by queuing behind candidates at the same time as the chiefs were removed as ex-officio chairpersons of VDCs. Third, the levels of fines imposed by chiefs for stock trespassing on reserved communal lands was reduced from 60 to 6 rand during 1995. The chiefs frustrated the elections of the new councils through a series of court cases, and by attempting to chase away electoral officials. Elections had to be conducted under heavy police presence in many areas. Also, chiefs refused to hand over offices and other equipment to the VDCs for their use. However, the chieftaincy has not managed to unite and has been substantially sidelined (*ibid.*).

In addition to a sidelining of the chiefs, the shift of power and control in favour of the BCP government was achieved through access to funds from the LHWP and providing them to constituency MPs for disbursement, thereby bypassing the administrative infrastructure of districts and civil servants. In fact, the idea first came from the World Bank which persuaded the military government in 1992 to set up a specific fund to handle all revenue from the LHWP. This fund, called the Lesotho Highlands Water Revenue Fund, established three main accounts one of which was a development fund – the Lesotho Highlands Water Development Fund (LHWDF). The World Bank, it seemed, was becoming quite sensitive to reports (including its own) which emphasised the negative consequences of the huge project. One report estimated that the livelihood of 20,000 people would be affected in the first phase of the project (until 1998), and that the living standards and health of the majority of the affected people would be worsened, including insufficient provision of water and sanitation to communities and schools.[72] The establishment of the LHWDF was specifically designed to provide development assistance to the poorest communities and hence help to deflect existing and potential criticism from the LHWP. As one team of World Bank consultants put it, a compelling 'argument for the use of a special fund is that it can provide a direct and visible link between the often controversial LHWP and local community development' (Lesotho Highlands Water Revenue Fund 1996, 2–3).

Financial disbursements from the Development Fund began in February 1995 following a government decision in 1994 that they should be made through constituencies.[73] Since the Bank wanted fast action, initial disbursements were made in a rush while the Fund's management adopted an 'informal and flexible approach' (*ibid.*, 8). To cite from the above consultancy report, 'members of parliament currently function as promoters and monitors of the Fund's activities in

---

[72]See the report in *World Rivers Review* 10(1), May 1995.
[73]Interview with Ministry of Planning official, 18 January 1996.

their respective constituencies' while the VDC 'acts as the Fund's day-to-day management unit' (*ibid.*, 9). In practice, some MPs called meetings of the community where their needs were discussed but, in the majority of the constituencies, party branch committees made the decisions on which projects were needed. When there was a conflict between the local party and the MP, it was the latter who prevailed and appointed his own committee to administer projects.[74]

The kinds of projects proposed were basically the standard infrastructural projects common in rural Lesotho, such as roads, footbridges and small dams, whose main purpose was to provide employment for a very poor population at money wages lower than the statutory minimum. These civil infrastructural projects, known derogatively by the people as *fato-fato* (literally 'scratch scratch' which mimics the actions of a chicken) have brought quick money to the village and have provided a useful counter to unemployment. They have done so by providing MPs with extreme power and patronage, and there is evidence that in the early days of the project, MPs came up with any scheme as long as it 'brought bread' to the village (Selinyane n.d., 40). Selinyane cites a number of cases where villages have made complaints and protested that several of the projects funded did not meet community needs at all (*ibid.*, 40–42). He concludes:

> In this landscape the real beneficiaries of the fato-fato tend to be the ruling party politicians and their rural elite allies who make a big catch of these projects. Because the scheme operates outside of government channels, it does not use heavy plant vehicles or other machinery regularly used by government departments. Rather the MPs enter into hire contracts with the private operators of this equipment, vehicles and machinery in the villages and towns. The expenses for these contractual arrangements are paid out of the Fund allocations for each constituency. This is made easy by the fact that the budgets for the constituencies are open-ended. There is no ceiling to the amount that can be allocated a constituency for a particular type of project. The elasticity of the budgets is justified by stating that fato-fato is a learning and experimentation process where the costs and needs of the works cannot always be foreseen. (*ibid.*, 43)

The majority of MPs belonged to the LCD when it broke away from the BCP. Unsurprisingly, given their undemocratic control over the rural areas, MPs were followed by their party committees and village supporters Those constituencies with MPS who remained loyal to the BCP soon understood that development funds would dry up if they stuck to their original MPs, so they had little difficulty in switching support to the LCD at the election. The popularity of Mokhehle as an individual clearly also had a role to play in this.

The fact that the constituencies were increased from 65 in 1993 to 80 for the 1998 election also gave more members of the political elite access to the resources of the Development Fund. Royalties from water sales are projected to increase rapidly, from an expected R69m in 1998 to R242 million by the year 2003. On top of these sums must be added revenues from taxes and the Southern African Customs Union (SACU), amounting to an expected additional R56m for the Development Fund by 2003, the date of the next election (Lesotho Highlands Water Revenue Fund 1996, 4–5, 8). While through *fato-fato* and its control over the rural areas, the LCD was able to win the elections, the extreme sectarianism of the political elite was to account for the post-election crisis and the collapse of state authority.

Postscript: the 1998 post-election political crisis
The fact that around 40 per cent of the voting population was unrepresented in parliament (see Langa Commission 1998, iv) due to the 'first past the post' electoral system operating to give the LCD an easy win, led the opposition parties to refuse to accept the result and to claim that irregularities in the elections were such as to invalidate it. A number of opposition protestors camped outside the King's palace over several months demanding that the King annul the results and call new elections. The government's inability to remove the protesters and the King's inaction served merely to inflame the situation as rumours of irregularities circulated. The government's refusal to talk to the opposition and the ability of the latter parties to secure support among civil servants and

---

[74]Interview with Ministry of Planning official, 18 January 1996.

the lower ranks of the military still opposed to the LCD, led to instability in the country. Regular strikes by civil servants and rumours of a coup showed, by September, that while the government had won the elections it had not been able to secure its legitimacy among a substantial sector of the population. An independent commission of inquiry (Langa Commission) into the elections was set up under the auspices of SADC and it reported that while there had indeed been irregularities in the elections, these were largely the result of the problems faced by the Independent Electoral Commission and there was no evidence that any one party had benefited as a result (Langa Commission 1998, iv). The report of the commission arrived too late to legitimise the government and it was itself contested.[75]

In fear of completely losing its ability to govern and under what seemed like an imminent coup by junior ranks who had mutinied, the LCD government finally called upon the only source of power it could count on: foreign intervention. South African troops backed by troops from Botswana entered Lesotho on 22 September at dawn in order to restore law and order. Undertaken as a SADC initiative, the mission soon degenerated into standard 'rape, looting and pillage' as the South African troops were not trained in peace keeping. Despite the fact that they were called for by the LCD government, their unannounced arrival gave the operation the character of an 'invasion' and it was seen as such by the majority of the population of the country.[76] The government thereby lost any remaining legitimacy it may still have had, and both the junior ranks of the army and the population as a whole resisted what they saw as an illegitimate invasion by a foreign country. Looters, partly spontaneously and partly incited by opposition politicians, targeted foreign-owned businesses and soon the commercial centre of the capital and that of other towns were burned to the ground. Whatever small commercial economy Lesotho had was largely destroyed, and pockets of armed soldiers vowed to resist in the mountains against the 'foreign invaders'.

By December during the author's short visit, the town had still not returned to normal and there was generally no law and order after dark. Gangs of marauding BNP-aligned youths, particularly incensed after their leader died of cancer in December, were capable of attacking and killing stray people (particularly foreigners) on sight. Currently an interim/transitional administration is running the country and new elections are due to be held in early 2000. To add insult to injury, the people of Lesotho were told that they would have to foot the bill for the 'intervention' in their own country.[77]

How is this disaster to be explained – a disaster which led to the complete collapse of the state and the destruction of the commercial sector of Lesotho's economy? Clearly the reasons for what was basically a South African military intervention under conditions where the justification for this was not wholly convincing, are to be answered through an analysis of the development of militaristic thinking within South Africa itself and are beyond the scope of this paper. On the other hand, it is a crisis of election politics in Lesotho which lies at the heart of the issue. Contrary to common newspaper reports, this crisis was not brought about by any rigging, for the latter was in no way exceptional nor sufficient to produce a landslide result.[78]

Rather, this is a crisis brought about by the character of the political elite in the country who have adhered to a 'winner take all' position over the years since independence, simply because an entry into the state has meant economic survival and the continuation of patronage relations of power, in a situation where the 'national cake' has not been considered large enough for the whole elite. It is this political sectarianism which lies at the root of the crisis. It can be formulated as the inability of a political elite to form itself into a class around a common political state project and a unifying or common ideology. The lack of formation of a (basically united) ruling class able to interpellate and mobilise a nation is what lies at the basis of this intra-political elite sectarianism. 'Development', the project around which ruling classes were formed in the rest of post-colonial Africa, was never a unifying project in Lesotho precisely because only the political supporters of

---

[75]There were reports that it had been doctored as a result of South African political intervention (*Mail and Guardian* 25 September–1 October 1998).

[76]*Mail and Guardian* 14(40), 9–15 October 1998.

[77]*Business Day* 9 October 1998.

[78]See the Langa Report (Langa Commission 1998, iii) for why systematic widespread fraud would have been rather impossible to achieve to the benefit of one organisation.

the BNP benefited when it was in power, while only those of the BCP benefited when it achieved power. Arguably, the only ideology in Lesotho with some claim to being unifying has been an opposition to South Africa which has been seen historically (with justification) as a bully neighbour, and a related (largely unjustifiable) national chauvinism, apparent mainly among the elite and aspiring elite, whereby all the ills of the country are ascribed to foreigners. Indeed there were few voices in Lesotho to be heard supporting the South African 'intervention' with the exception of the government and the top ranks of the military. Unless some way is found whereby the various factions of the elite can achieve some kind of agreement and reconciliation for the benefit of the nation, or unless that elite itself is pushed aside by other forces, the economic and political crises which the country has been facing since independence are unlikely to be overcome despite its much vaunted recent adoption of liberal-democratic norms.

Elections in Botswana: the historical background

Unlike Swaziland and Lesotho, and virtually all other countries in Africa, Botswana has held regular elections since independence in 1966. The question is whether the success of this exceptional case of a liberal democratic project in Africa, often advertised as a shining 'paragon of virtue', is more apparent than real. The answer partly lies in the economic sphere since, in recent years, Botswana has experienced higher growth rates than the so-called Asian 'tigers'.[79] Yet, along with rapid growth, regular parliamentary elections have returned one party, the Botswana Democratic Party (BDP) into government since independence. At the same time, Botswana has also experienced massive inequalities within its population and the systematic oppression of minority 'nationalities'.[80] Inequality and oppression are both related to the form of state rule which extends back historically to the colonial period.

Some specific features of Tswana societies were entrenched during the colonial period, including the perpetuation of a number of powerful states, a highly stratified social structure, the domination and exploitation of minority nationalities and a significant degree of relatively independent capital accumulation. However, only a very small proportion of the huge land mass of the country, roughly five per cent, was alienated to settlers. (Opschoor 1980, 12.) By the mid-nineteenth century, various Tswana-speaking nationalities had developed sophisticated state structures which were founded on a highly stratified social system, itself more elaborate than the simple distinction between aristocrats and commoners characteristic of the Swazi and Sotho peoples. In the Tswana case, four strata made up the social structure: the aristocracy and rich commoners; ordinary commoners; foreigners, most of whom lived outside the capital; and serfs, most of whom were members of specific ethnic groups (Hitchcock 1985).

The Tswana states were administratively divided into wards, some of which were made up of ethnic minorities that had been accepted into the nation. Wards were placed under the authority of their own traditional headmen, thus initiating an effective system of indigenous 'indirect rule'. This administrative system was most developed among the Bangwato, the most powerful nationality. The kings also bound commoners directly to them through the loaning of cattle, thus bypassing possible aristocratic contenders for power. Commoners were grouped in wards and allocated land 'but it was not only the land that was allocated to tribesmen but also the people who lived on the land' (*ibid.*, 100). As the Bangwato, for example, expanded into the semi-arid zones of the Kalahari, San speakers, who had only developed relatively weak states, were conquered and dispossessed of their cattle and

---

[79]Botswana's GDP has grown at an annual rate of 14.5 per cent between 1966 and 1980 while per-capita GDP grew at an annual rate of about 4.5 per cent between 1965 and 1985 outperforming the Asian NICs, see for example *Sunday Times* (South Africa) 24 October 1993 and the analysis in Mhone 1993.

[80]Botswana has some of the worst figures on income and wealth distribution in the world, and there is evidence that such disparities are growing. During 1985/86 for example the gap between the highest and the lowest 20 per cent of income earners was reported as 23.6:1 (comparable figures for Brazil were 26:1). This inequality is particularly acute in rural areas, thus one recent study commented that 'income inequality is high in rural Botswana even by the standards of least developed countries' (Colclough and Fallon 1983, 137). For detailed analyses see *ibid.* and Good 1993.

eventually enslaved/enserfed (Wilmsen 1989). Their servile labour was then considered as a simple appurtenance of the land and allocated with it to new settlers on the 'sandveld'. Slaves provided tribute to the aristocracy and more importantly for our purpose here, free labour for the commoners to whom they were attached.[81] Labour in cattle rearing was expended in return for 'clothing, food, and sometimes other goods such as tobacco' (Hitchcock 1985, 100). The King also appointed overseers who supervised tribute collection and, as the population grew, also governors of districts who held similar functions including presiding over court cases and settling disputes (*ibid.*, 101).

This state system amounted to a sophisticated system of control and extraction of surplus labour from the population. Arguably, the system also enabled the distribution of surplus labour, and access to land, to a wider group than the aristocracy. Moreover, unlike in the case of other nationalities in the region, the state provided the basis for an alliance between aristocrats and powerful commoners who both had a stake in the system. The state system was largely frozen during the colonial period of 'indirect rule' since British colonial power found in Tswana 'law and custom' a state structure which matched in its own interests. Like elsewhere in the region, chiefs' powers over their people were increased during the colonial period, for example through rule-making and the decreasing relevance of the (male) popular assembly, the *kgotla*, as a democratic forum, although chiefs were subjected to the control of the colonial High Commissioner and his representatives.

As long as British colonial authority received tax revenue, it was not overwhelmingly concerned with too close a scrutiny of state arbitrariness, the use of state powers for personal gain or indeed the prevalence of slave relations on Kalahari 'cattle posts'.[82] Taxes were received to an extent such that between 1911 and 1956, the Bechuanaland Protectorate revenue matched or exceeded expenditure, while 'most of the costs of administration were being carried by the tribal governments' (Parsons 1977, 130). The basis of this relative wealth, when compared to Lesotho and Swaziland, and hence of the alliance between the chiefs and the colonial state, was an extensive cattle industry and involvement in lucrative trade from which both benefited, profiting from providing cattle to the British South Africa Company and from the colonisation of the Rhodesias. The drain of labour to the South African mines only became significant during the twentieth century when there is evidence that part of migrant labour was replaced by San slave labour at home (Parsons, *op. cit.*).[83]

This process of accumulation, together with taxation by the colonial state, created a substantial and exceptional degree of differentiation among the colonised. Elsewhere in southern Africa, colonial domination had tended to homogenise the colonised population. While accumulation only benefited a minority, and many had therefore to migrate to South Africa in order to acquire funds for the hut tax, among much else, both accumulation and migration was made possible largely because of a readily available pool of slave-like labour. As it has been said,

> the only peoples available to be hired in any numbers (in rural areas – MN) were Basarwa and Bakgalagadi; in large measure this is why they are to be found on almost every cattle post ... today, rather than only on those of the wealthy. Ethnic minorities, San-speakers in particular, played a critical role in providing a second tier labour pool, thereby releasing for labour migration Tswana men who would otherwise have been indispensable for immediate household production (Wilmsen 1989, 287).

---

[81]In the 1980s, San speakers made up 77 per cent of the population of the Western Sandveld of the Ngwato (Central) District of 3,500 people (Hitchcock 1985, 90). In the words of Miers and Crowder (1988, 177): 'Malata (slaves – MN) ... formed a fully controlled, and partly transferable, hereditary labour force, performing the most menial tasks in return for the barest necessities of life, and in hard times even these sometimes were not forthcoming. Their treatment depended on the wealth and compassion of their masters, who considered them their property.'

[82]For a very informative discussion of the latter case, see Miers and Crowder (1988) from which the following quote of a Tswana aristocrat in 1926 is taken: 'The Masarwa (San – MN) are slaves. They can be killed. It is no crime, they are like cattle. They have no liberty. If they run away their masters can bring them back and do what they like in the way of punishment. They are never paid. If the Masarwa live in the veld, and I want any to work for me, I go out and take any I want.'

[83]In 1911, Khama abolished the payment of tribute by San clients, but whether or not such reforms were effective is questionable. In any case it was the provision of free labour rather than tribute in kind which was crucial for accumulation purposes. See Hitchcock and Holm (1993, 311).

The 1920s and 1930s, in addition to witnessing the setting-up of 'indirect rule', saw the development of borehole technology. This meant that the Western Sandveld could begin to be opened-up to cattle grazing on a larger scale. Borehole drilling developed to a large extent after the early 1950s. At the same time,

> there is evidence that at the very time of these British enquiries of the 1920s and 1930s (into slavery – MN), Ngwato cattle owners were using cases brought to the dikgotla and other legal means to deprive the Basarwa of stock systematically and to dispossess those who had any control over land and, most crucial, over sources of water (Miers and Crowder 1988, 195).

While surface water could not be monopolised privately under Tswana 'law and custom', where water was obtained through the expenditure of 'capital' and labour, such as in well digging, people essentially acquired private rights over it and were thus able to gain de facto control of the surrounding grazing area. In this way, wealthy cattle owners obtained preferential rights over grazing land since only the relative few could afford to sink boreholes. Such was the beginning of the large-scale use of communal land for private accumulation which has been typical of the post-colonial period (Hitchcock 1985).

The effects of the consequent differentiation, accumulation plus impoverishment, became evident at independence when the 1967–68 Agricultural Census was published. It showed that 13 per cent of the rural population in Botswana survived on foraging without access to crops or cattle; that a further 31 per cent possessed no cattle at all; and that among the remaining 56 per cent who did own cattle, 12 per cent owned 60 per cent of the cattle (Parsons 1977, 135). In sum, accumulation for a few had resulted in the impoverishment of many during the colonial period itself. Unsurprisingly, it was these wealthy 'cattle accumulators' who were to inherit the state at independence.

Colonial authorities, especially in the 1950s, provided infrastructural development for the cattle industry and thereby supported the cattle accumulators. Furthermore, the accumulators received the support of chiefs on whom they were dependent for the allocation of borehole sites. Unlike Lesotho, for example, there was little economic or political antagonism between a rising bourgeoisie and the chiefs during the colonial period. It was the alliance between cattlemen and chiefs which lay behind the formation of the Botswana Democratic Party (BDP), the subsequent ruling party, in 1962. Seretse Khama, the BDP leader, was both heir to the Bangwato throne as well as a wealthy cattle owner in his own right. Many cattle accumulators were drawn from the aristocracy as well as from civil servants, such as teachers, policemen, and clerks who had succeeded in investing their salaries in cattle and syndicate boreholes (Tsie 1993, 36).

The BDP was formed with British support in response to the successes of the Botswana People's Party (BPP), adhering to a radical pan-Africanist ideology which was also stridently anti-colonial and anti-chief. The BPP articulated the views of the poor migrants and the intellectuals who were opposed to the arbitrariness and abuse of power by chiefs, such as the use of tribal funds for Seretse Khama's education, to the chiefs' cooperation with the colonial authorities, as in the African Advisory Council where commoners were excluded, and to colonialism more generally. BPP supporters were refused permission by chiefs to hold meetings in rural areas. Chiefs were easily able to 'persuade' rural people to vote BDP through their obvious control over the population. The BPP was also labelled 'communist' while the BDP was supported, financially and otherwise, by the colonial power, more importantly, and was acceptable to the Republic of South Africa (Kowet 1978, 153–6; Parson 1984, 29–33; Moamogwe 1982). Under such conditions it is not surprising that the BDP was to win the 1965 elections leading to independence, while the BPP's support was overwhelmingly in urban areas (Moamogwe op.cit., 16). At independence, the country became a presidential republic, a fact which clearly points to the relative weakness of the chieftaincy in the country's constitution.

Having achieved power, the 'cattle barons', who controlled the BDP, wasted no time in cutting the chieftaincy down to size. The first elected district councils were set up, followed by the Chieftainship Act of 1965 which vested the powers of recognition, appointment, deposition and suspension of chiefs in the president. At the same time, the Act confirmed many of the chiefs' existing powers, such as the right to preside over 'traditional' courts, the power to allocate land and the right to convene meetings (Parson op.cit., 43). Many of these powers were removed in later years. The allocation of land became vested in Land Boards in 1970, regimental (tribute) labour for public works was abolished and most of the staff and administrative assets of the chiefs were transferred to the councils (*ibid.*). Although the judicial functions of chiefs were curtailed and restricted to cases of customary law, they were given powers to increase the penalty for stock theft to up to four years imprisonment or a fine of P4,000. It is reasonably apparent from the above that these measures restricted the chiefs' ability to curtail the use of communal land for private accumulation. As Kowet recognises, 'the new elite class ... was now armed with a legal machinery through which they could easily challenge the chiefs, and claim large tracts of land for themselves. The majority of the peasant population, however, was indifferent to the new reform' (*op.cit.*, 194). As a quid pro quo, the chiefs were 'compensated' through the creation of a national House of Chiefs which was given advisory powers on matters affecting 'traditional' custom. Members of the House were paid salaries in addition to their emoluments as government-appointed chiefs.

Land Boards are composed of the chief (as an ex officio non-voting member) plus a nominee, two elected members, and two members appointed by the Ministry of Local Government, Lands and Housing (*ibid.*, 193). However, in practice, the BDP has so far managed to control the Boards largely through clientage and not without some bending of the rules.[84] At the same time, worker-peasants have to petition the Land Board through the local headman, chief or Village Development Committee on which the chief is a powerful figure, so that chiefs still retain some indirect control over land allocation, especially where the poor are concerned (Hitchcock 1980, 10). At independence, the cattle barons were able, through the government and party which they dominated, to restrict the powers of the chieftaincy which affected their ability to accumulate. Equally, the cattlemen maintained, and even increased, the powers of the chieftaincy over the majority of the rural population.

During the 1970s, the government continued to provide conditions for capital accumulation for the large 'cattle barons'. Schemes were now found to privatise large areas of communal grazing land for the cattle industry whose market was guaranteed by European Community quotas. Requests for new boreholes began to increase during the 1970s while, in 1975, the state embarked on a major programme of land reform and livestock development. Under the Tribal Grazing Lands Policy (TGLP), communal land was to be transformed into private leasehold tenure, and large livestock owners were to be removed from overgrazed communal areas to new grazing areas on the *sandveld*. The outcomes were more privatisation of land, increased accumulation by the minority of cattlemen, more inequality as land and water resources became monopolised by the few, and dispossession of the San's land to which they they had never been able to claim title (Hitchcock 1980; 1985; Good 1992; Hitchcock and Holm 1993).

The right of San peoples to foraging areas was not recognised since, in official discourse, they neither constitute a 'tribe' nor have 'traditional' leaders (Hitchcock and Holm *op.cit.*, 317–22). In general, rural inequality is extreme by any standards and access to cattle in particular is highly skewed. San speakers are the poorest.[85] Recent data on income poverty suggest that the percentage of those defined as poor or very poor declined from nearly 60 per cent of the population in 1985/86 to 47 per cent in 1993/94. While this shows a substantial decline in absolute poverty, numbers classified poor still amount to just under half of the total population. Rural households and female households were more likely to be among the poor (Botswana Institute for Development Policy Analysis 1996, 12; Jefferis 1997). Good and Molutsi note that:

---

[84]See *Mmegi* 46, 18–24 November 1994. See also reports concerning the land scandal in 1992 where ministers (the Vice-President and Minister of Local Government and Lands who was also chairman of the BDP, as well as the Minister of Agriculture at the time who was also secretary general of the BDP) were shown to have abused their powers and influenced a land board allocating land in a peri-urban area to allocate land to themselves. See for example *Economist Intelligence Unit country report* 1992, 24.

[85]It was reported recently that the UNDP inequality index ranked Botswana the country with the most skewed income distribution in the world (*Mail and Guardian* 14–20 October 1994, 21). Data from the 1980s shows between 45 and 54 per cent of rural households did not own any cattle and that 70 per cent of these were female-headed. At the other end of the distribution, nearly 80 per cent of cattle farms had less than 40 head per farm, while roughly 6 per cent had more than a hundred head per farm, amounting to nearly 40 per cent of all cattle holdings, while 15 per cent of all farm households accounted for three-quarters of the national herd (ILO/SATEP 1987, *Unemployment Challenge: Prospects for Employment Generation through Diversification of the Economy*, 74. Cited in Mhone 1993, 41).

as in the past, the starkness of the dichotomy of wealth and power with poverty and weakness is a structural element in the political economy of relatively wealthy Botswana, manipulated and often maintained, often in nuanced terms, sometimes ostensibly, by government policy (Good and Molutsi, 1997, 7).

While arable agriculture in Botswana had been systematically starved of funds in the 1970s, as the state geared its resources towards funding cattle husbandry (Holm 1982), when faced with severe drought during the 1980s, the state was successful in instigating a drought relief programme which meant that no-one starved. From 1985 to 1990, peasants were paid to plough, thereby earning the capability to buy food. However, the effect of these subsidies was to permit the larger and wealthier farmers to 'dramatically enlarge their farms while at the same time, many smaller, particularly resource-poor farmers, were unable to take full advantage of the programmes' (Solway 1994, 475). It is clear from the literature that development programmes in Botswana have tended to increase inequality dramatically although they have provided some basic benefits for the poorest as a cushion against complete destitution, hence the reduction in poverty noted above. Moreover, as in other countries of the region, one of the effects of top-down, bureaucratic, or statist development practice has been to reproduce state power in the rural areas.[86] During the run-up to the 1994 elections, the hitherto relatively clean image of the government, as one which kept 'rent-seeking' to a minimum, had been tarnished by press reports of regular scandals involving major state parastatals and high ranking government officials.[87]

The main source of this corruption seems to be the new breed of politicians and high ranking civil servants (BDP supporting) who find themselves excluded from the cattle business and who have sought alternative areas of accumulation such as real estate and financial investments. A survey of the Democracy Project at the University of Botswana found that 70 per cent of permanent secretaries did not own cattle and have preferred to support urban-oriented policies which encourage local business outside agriculture and retailing. They held shares in parastatals, investment trusts and commercial banks (Molutsi 1989, 111). Molutsi argues that it is this bureaucracy which constitutes the new ruling class in Botswana. Whatever the merits of this argument, it appears that a major conflict exists within the ruling BDP between the cattlemen on the one hand and the urban-based 'yuppies' who are not keen on continuing beef subsidies at the expense of other lucrative investments on the other (Cokorinos 1993, 11).[88]

Revelations of corruption, unemployment and housing shortages in towns have all helped gather support for the Botswana National Front (BNF) opposition, starting out as a 'Marxist-Socialist-oriented' party but which then took a more populist/social democratic position.[89] The

---

[86]For a detailed argument on this point concerning Lesotho, see Ferguson 1990. For limited arguments on Swaziland, see Neocosmos 1987, 111–114.

[87]Apart from the example of the two ministers and the Land Board previously mentioned, some of the more notorious scandals have involved the Botswana Housing Corporation (*Economist Intelligence Unit* 1st quarter 1993) and the National Development Bank to which high-ranking government officials (including the President) owed a total of over P2 million in loans which were never repaid (*Mail and Guardian* 14–20 October 1994). Before the 1993 elections, it was reported after the Auditor General had submitted his report for the financial year ending March 1993, that millions of Pula remained unaccounted for. See *Botswana Gazette* 21 September 1994 and *Midweek Sun* 21 September 1994. The Director of the Directorate of Corruption and Economic Crime was quoted as saying that: 'the problems of corruption and economic crime are much more widespread and serious than the public are generally aware of' (*Mmegi* 11(37), 16–22 September 1994).

[88]This division is potentially much more threatening to the political system in the future than any 'ethnic' division. The main (political) 'ethnic' divide is between the Bakalanga minority and the eight Tswana-speaking 'principal tribes'. Bakalanga recognise that they are an integral part of the nation but want their language, customs and tradition to be officially recognised (Mhone 1993). So far San speakers have not been able to provide evidence of clear political organisation, although there are signs that this could be changing. See Good 1993; Hitchcock and Holm 1993.

[89]See the interview with Kenneth Koma, the long-time party leader of the BNF in *Southern African Political and Economic Monthly* 6(12), 1993. Originally, although the BNF saw itself as a Marxist party 'of the working class' it saw no problem in alliances with 'corrupt feudal elements' (i.e. chiefs) because workers had 'tribal connections'. It seems that this line was taken because a powerful chief had deserted the BDP for the BNF with all his followers. See Parson 1984, 33, 54.

first-past-the-post electoral system has hidden the fact that the BNF has increased its support in urban areas, especially since 1989. Botswana, during the 1990s, has experienced very rapid rural-urban migration. Gaborone is often stated to be the fastest growing town in Africa. From various data sources, and although the total population is still small at 1.5m, it is estimated that the proportion of population living in urban areas has increased from less than one-quarter to nearly one-half between 1991 and 1997 (World Bank 1991, 294).[90] It has not, therefore, surprised observers that the BNF increased its representation in parliament from 3 to 13 seats at the 1994 elections.

Electoral support for the BNF has overwhelmingly come from the urban and peri-urban areas to which most of its campaigning slogans and tactics had been addressed. The main issues which it raised during the campaign were of primary concern to urban residents. Issues included the setting up of an independent electoral commission rather than one controlled by the BDP government, votes for migrants to South Africa and a reduction of the minimum voting age from 21 to 18 years. These last two issues, along with proportional representation, would have given the party more seats in parliament. As mentioned above, the BDP manages to retain control over the rural areas and the chiefs still get people out to vote for it in large numbers. Generally, opposition political parties have seemed unable, over the years, to confront the actual socio-economic conditions of the population and prefer to repeat populist slogans often somewhat divorced from reality (Good 1992, 94).

Popular organisations of civil society in Botswana are usually described as rather weak and have found their activities circumscribed by the state (Holm and Molutsi 1990). Insofar as trade unions are concerned, committee members are legally proscribed from being full-time officials, and labour legislation makes official strikes largely impossible. Labour unrest is therefore easily declared illegal and easily quashed. Also, public sector unions are proscribed *de facto* (Molutsi 1989, 6). Their position was made more difficult by a high unemployment rate, reported to have been 21 per cent in 1994.[91] Statutory minimum wage rates were in the range of P1.23 to P1.45 per hour in 1996, but actual wages paid are commonly below that figure.[92] The vigorous independent press is subject to constant threats by the government while women's organisations have been undermined by the state (Molutsi 1989).

The 1994 elections and after

There is an obvious answer to the question of who will win the elections in 1999. The results are really a foregone conclusion, mainly because of the splitting-up of the opposition BNF. Nevertheless before this issue is outlined, there are some broad general points which need to be made about general elections in Botswana.

Despite the high level of poverty in Botswana, it is true to say that even poor people have bene-fited in some measure from the general 'social democratic' orientation of the government. Much has been done in making state-provided goods and services available, especially in rural areas, by increasing access to education (secondary education is now also free), access to health care, water and roads to a population which was extremely poor at the time of independence. In other words, some of the surplus has been spread around as and when the government could afford to do so, while at the same time some of this 'spreading' did take place in periods immediately preceding elections. It would have been surprising had it been otherwise.

At the same time, as already noted, 'the modern politicians have drastically reduced the chiefs' powers since independence, yet used the residual authority of the traditional leaders as part of the institutional process of development' (Stevens and Speed 1977, 382). This has meant that elected District Councils, VDCs and Land Boards have substituted for chiefly power and have allowed a broader constituency to have a say in local politics while the corresponding ethnic mobilisation, which can only be effective with chiefly support, has been minimised.

---

[90]*Economist Intelligence Unit* Basic Data 1996/1997. The explanation for the staggering increase probably lies in the fact that a more encompassing definition of urban boundaries is now used by government statisticians (personal communication by statistician at the University of Botswana).
[91]See *Midweek Sun* 19 October 1994, 14.
[92]*Economist Intelligence Unit* Basic Data 1996/1997

There is evidence that rural people are clearly aware of the benefits which they have received and that this has contributed in no small measure to the BDP's regular victories at the polls. It is important to note that the 1994 elections took place during a downturn in the economy. The 1999 elections will definitely take place at a time when the economy is buoyant. The EIU forecast for 1998–99 is that growth in GDP should be 'robust over the next few years driven by diamond exports, government spending and construction', while the forecast for GDP growth for 1998 is 7.3 per cent.[93] Government spending will undoubtedly reflect this fact as the election date approaches. Although the opposition BNF may have benefited from the economic downturn in 1994, this is not likely to happen this time around.

Table 2.2: Botswana parliamentary elections 1965–1994: Number of seats and percentage of votes by Party

YEAR	BDP		BNF		OTHER	
	Seats	Votes %	Seats	Votes %	Seats	Votes %
1965	28	80.4	–	–	3	19.4
1969	24	68.6	3	13.4	4	17.8
1974	27	76.6	2	11.5	3	11.3
1979	29	75.5	2	13.1	2	11.3
1984	28	85.3	5	11.8	1	3.0
1989	31	65.0	3	27.7	0	7.3
1994	27	53.1	13	37.7	0	9.2

Source: Reports to the Minister of Presidential Affairs and Public Administration on general elections.

A referendum on constitutional reform was held in October 1997. The turnout was very low at 17 per cent, largely because all parties had come to an agreement to support the proposed changes, including reducing the minimum voting age to 18, instituting an Independent Electoral Commission in time for the next elections and establishing voting rights for Botswana residents abroad. As a result, the wind was taken out of the sails of the BNF which had advocated these changes since 1994. Two other reform issues, which were not included in the referendum, restricted the president's term of office to ten years and provided for the automatic succession of the vice-president, subject to confirmation by the National Assembly, on the death or resignation of the president. In fact, President Masire retired in March 1998 with a huge 'golden handshake' and Festus Mogae became president soon after.[94] The only issue supported by the opposition. but not included in the reform package, was the election of the president by universal suffrage rather than by members of parliament. Many of these liberalising measures can be seen as the result of the greater pressures for openness, participation and equality which led up to the 1994 election (Good 1996).

Although the victory of the BDP at the polls in 1999 seems assured, two other developments will have medium to long-term effects. The first, as mentioned above, is rapid urbanisation which means that different forms of political rule and social control are necessary. For example, 'traditional leaders' can no longer be used as vehicles for mobilising votes (Molutsi 1998). The other is the evidence for lower registration figures and turnout at the polls as voters become disaffected and cynical with a liberal democratic system which regularly churns out the same people into power. For example, it has been noted that although the turnout at the polls for the 1994 elections was a respectable 77 per cent, the proportion of those registered for the 1994 election was only 62 per cent as opposed to 72 per cent in 1989 (Wiseman and Charlton 1995, 327). The BDP won the election with 53 per cent of the vote (see Table 2.2) but with a much smaller proportion of those entitled to vote.

This problem could be exacerbated at the next election as voter cynicism could be increased by the lack of a viable alternative. While the opposition BNF had seemed to have such an opportunity in posing a successful challenge to the BDP, it has been riven by internal conflicts to such an

---

[93]*Economist Intelligence Unit* 4th quarter 1997.
[94]*Mmegi* 6–12 March 1998.

extent that its splitting-up seems imminent. During January 1998, two groups in the party were publicly accusing each other of 'indiscipline' and the breaching of party procedures.[95] One faction, calling itself the 'Concerned Group', also included the longstanding president of the party Kenneth Koma; another consisted of the members of the Central Committee of the party. Over the Easter weekend, open dissension and violence erupted between the two factions at a party congress in Palapye where Koma was expelled as party leader. Two factions claimed to be the genuine BNF. The majority of the MPs sided with the Central Committee and informed the speaker of the House of Assembly that Koma was no longer the leader of the opposition.[96] They eventually formed themselves into a new party the BCP (Botswana Congress Party), while Koma and his immediate supporters have remained in the BNF. It has been reported that they have been seeking to unite with the small United Action Party (UAP).[97]

The split in the BNF seems to have involved a number of issues which included both the replacement of a leadership which was viewed by some (the Central Committee) as out of touch, as well as a fear by many (the 'Concerned Group') that they would not be selected as parliamentary candidates and hence not have access to state resources, salaries and perks. In this confused state of affairs, it was factions within the leadership which were fighting for dominance, while the rank and file and the electorate were simply ignored. One trade unionist was quoted as saying:

> Anyone can realise that the people who we have elected are now fighting for power. It is like they have forgotten that we elected them to serve us. They seem now to have forgotten about the electorate.[98]

Evidently, while this BNF split can only help the BDP win power, it undermines the liberal democratic process, increasing cynicism among voters. The people of Botswana clearly deserve better, but then some of these issues are not simply a problem for the BNF alone but are endemic to political parties as organisations whose operations are authoritarian, forming mini-states in their structures and procedures. This question cannot solely be addressed from within political parties themselves, but has also to be addressed from outside such organisations, by social movements in civil society.

Conclusion: comparing Swaziland, Lesotho and Botswana

I have attempted to situate elections in Botswana in a framework which has stressed the importance of both history and the rural areas in an understanding of the political context of elections in the BLS countries. At the same time, I have tried to stress the importance of what reproduces a specific form of politics – state politics – in the struggle for and operation of national elections in the BLS countries. Whether one attempts to understand the politics of national elections in Botswana or Lesotho, or indeed the politics surrounding the struggle for multi-party elections in Swaziland, one is struck by a number of characteristics which they exhibit in common.

It is control over the rural areas which enables the dominant power to either resist demands for democratic rights as in Swaziland, or to retain state power as in Lesotho and Botswana. The importance of the rural areas is crucial for the reproduction of state power. Rural areas have largely been ignored by modern civil society organisations which have been overwhelmingly urban-based and have operated within a discourse on rights rather than one on tradition (Mamdani 1996).

There is a large gulf between the two discourses of rights and tradition. The history and context of rural politics has been different to that of urban society (*ibid.*). Historically, it has been the outcome of struggles in, or about, rural interests which have enabled the emergence of liberal democratic modes of politics, as in Botswana, or stifled it completely, as in Swaziland. In

---

[95]*Mmegi* 30 January–5 February 1998.
[96]*Mmegi* 12–23 April 1998.
[97]*Mmegi* 13–19 November 1998.
[98]*Botswana Guardian* 8 May 1998.

Botswana, the chiefs were removed from a position of power by an alliance of a rising commoner elite and a modernising 'paramount chieftaincy' during the post-independence period. This process was a continuation of a Tswana (particularly Bangwato) 'tradition' whereby monarchs had ruled by using patronage to tie commoners to the state power. There was no real opposition to Botswana becoming a republic at independence. In Swaziland, on the other hand, the powers of the chieftaincy were increased during the post-colonial period through the banning of political parties, the bedrock of liberal democracy. Hence, the monarchy was able to retain absolute powers and undermine any potential opposition through the rule of an oppressive 'tradition'. These struggles fashioned the framework for electoral politics in both countries.

In Lesotho, it has also been the struggle, dating back to the colonial period, surrounding rural power which largely accounts for the overwhelming victory of the LCD at the polls in 1998. The fact that the LCD subsequently lost its legitimacy does not negate this observation, for the winning of elections and the gaining of popular legitimacy cannot be simply equated in Lesotho (as elsewhere in Africa) as the legitimation function of elections is not simply given in any one instance. Popular organisations of civil society played a prominent part in undermining the powers of the chieftaincy during the colonial period. The BCP/LCD is the inheritor of this tradition, and one which in another context could be called 'radical republican', although the form of this struggle was neither a mass struggle nor a revolutionary democratic one. There have been no popularly elected committees dominated by the masses of the people contesting the powers of the chieftaincy, as happened, for example, in Pondoland in South Africa during the 1960s.

Generally, in all the above-mentioned historical struggles between commoners, chiefs, the colonial state and 'modernising elites', the 'masses' have rarely been involved in struggles for leadership positions. Rather, these struggles have generally involved politicians, those ruling classes in the making, without allowing for the development of different forms of democratic politics, as happened in South Africa of the 1980s (Neocosmos 1998). This means that, in the absence of new forms of politics, no way is found around the contradictions of state political forms. In Swaziland, for example, the issue of the legitimacy of the state, and the legitimation function of elections, is limited by the opposition between a discourse based on rights, that is the right to vote, and a discourse of tradition, based on need to vote. Urban civil society organisations, together with international donors and power brokers, argue that the Swazi tradition of the chiefs is undemocratic; the Swazi monarchists argue that it is a question of tradition and not rights which are 'foreign' inspired . The parameters of the debate have not been challenged by a popular perspective which could question both the oppressive notion of existing 'tradition' (and argue the point that tradition is itself not simply given in an inherited form but transformable) and the limitations of a Western liberal conception of individual rights. The issue, therefore, revolves around one form or another of state politics, not popular politics which is excluded both in discourse and in practice.

In Lesotho the politics of elections, like all politics, are quite straightforwardly manipulative and sectarian, as the political elite – and would-be elite – fight for a seat at the state trough of money and resources. There is a dominant 'winner takes all' conception of politics whereby whoever dominates meetings, or has access to power or funds, dominates outright, rewarding friends and leaving adversaries out in the cold. It is this crude manipulative nature of a political elite, obvious to all, which is the main threat to the legitimation function of elections the fragility of which was so clearly illustrated by the Lesotho case in 1998. In Botswana, there is a more 'mature' and far less 'infantile' form of politics. Issues, which are debated both in society and academia, revolve around questions asking the extent to which the state fulfils the criteria of a genuine liberal democracy. While the state discourse in Botswana is characterised by the dominance of a discourse of rights over a discourse of tradition so to speak, it is the exact opposite in Swaziland. At the same time, in Botswana, there is evidence of extreme sectarianism among the opposition which finds itself under pressure to obtain access to salaries and benefits for its dominant members. Even in Botswana, the threat to the legitimation function of elections does not lurk far below the surface of liberal democratic politics.

Both the state and electoral politics in all three countries exclude popular alternatives and politics. The parameters of discourse and practice make it clear that state politics is to be the exclusive form of politics in each country. Whether the question is about traditionalism in Swaziland, sectarianism in Lesotho or liberal democracy in Botswana, there is little room for direct popular participation, for people debating what kind of politics is appropriate for them or what kind of politics may overcome apathy. In Swaziland, popular democratic aspirations are limited by both state action, restricting broader political participation to state commissions of various kinds, and by the opposition which operates in a populist mode and is not able to link up national demands for elections with local 'grass roots' concerns. In Lesotho, where jobs are exchanged for electoral support, the poor are used as simple election fodder with a cynicism clear to all. Single party dominance in Botswana since independence has excluded questions about alternatives to both the ruling party and party politics as such. Party politics is state politics. This is part of the reason why national elections in the BLS offer little opening to alternative forms of democracy and politics.

3

Beyond the Silence of Women in Ethiopian Politics[1]

EVA POLUHA

Background

In Ethiopia, as in many African and other countries, women's participation as voters and candidates in elections is lower than that of men. Because participation is often discussed in general, broad terms, designating the whole population, the absence of women often goes unnoticed. This is yet another aspect of the general neglect of women as political actors in much of Africa. There are few studies where the authors pose the question as to why African women are absent and what should be done to engage them in politics. Rarer still are studies which depict or analyse the connection between elections, political activities and women. The behaviour of those who vote and run for office is on the agenda, rather than of those who do not vote or do not present themselves as candidates.

Some research on women in Africa has been carried out, however. Thus, Chazan (1982) shows both non-formal political participation and Staudt (1986), Tripp (1994), Ardener and Burman (1995) and Rosander (1997) discuss the wider social, economic and political ramifications of women's groups and networks. But in spite of the many organisational and networking activities carried out by women, Rosander, in an anthology of women's organisations in West Africa, comes to the rather sad conclusion that 'the women's informal and formal associations are not spaces for change but mirrors of the prevailing power structure of the society' (Rosander 1997, 29). Somewhat more positively, Hirschmann (1991) suggests that we unpack the state and lay bare the various levels to which women of different categories have access. Hirschmann shows that women in Malawi mostly find themselves behind but sometimes also on the political scene, though more often in local contexts than in national political ones.

Still, the question of why women have been so little focused upon as potential political actors in Africa remains. There seems to be a parallel between the lack of information available on African women and what was earlier the case regarding European and North American women. According to Jones (1988), research on women in the West has gone through three different phases. The first lasted well into the 1960s and focused on the invisibility of women; women's behaviour was depicted as deviant from that of 'political man'. In the second phase, female researchers criticised the earlier tendency to exclude women. Instead they started to bring forward new knowledge about women's political activities. This was the period of 'limited visibility'. During the third phase, women have been made visible in political science. Through a redefinition of various concepts like politics and power, the political system itself, which tends to exclude women as a category, has also been questioned.

Some writers have viewed the exclusion of women from politics as a 'group versus individual rights' debate. Phillips (1993), for example points out that liberal democrats usually argue in

[1] I want to thank Judith Narrowe, Mona Rosendahl and Jónínà Einarsdottir for very useful comments on various drafts of this article.

support of the individual's right and capacity to make her/his own choices. Implicit in their reasoning is that people as individuals have the right to elect their own representatives. The argument is that when these representatives come together in democratic institutions, they can transcend their parochial or group concerns and engage in the needs of the larger community. Although this argument may have some validity, the view has been much contested by feminists and members of minority and aboriginal groups. Their point is that, however democratically elected various political fora are, existing gender or minority groups are rarely proportionally represented in politics. The recent debate consequently gives greater emphasis to how political representation can be equalised, both with regard to women and minority groups (see for example Phillips *ibid.*; Young 1989).

Anthropologists' attempts to understand the exclusion of women from political fora have followed a somewhat different track. For almost a century an implicit distinction has been made between the domestic and the politico/jural domains – a dichotomy which was explicitly elaborated upon by Fortes (1969, in Collier and Yanagisako 1987). The effect, according to Collier and Yanagisako (1987, 4), was that 'the domestic/politico-jural dichotomy thus assumes a "domestic" sphere dedicated to sexuality and childrearing, associated primarily with women, and a "public" sphere of legal rules and legitimate authority, associated primarily with men.' The fact that women were responsible for child care and emotionally engaged in their offspring and the home was given as an explanation for their subjugation (Rosaldo 1974). A parallel distinction was made between nature and culture, where women, due to their reproductive capacity, were associated with nature and therefore given little symbolic value, while men were associated with culture and highly valued since they had the responsibility to re-model and control the 'savage' nature (Ortner 1974; Ortner and Whitehead 1981). These views were criticised for their tendency to generalise about gender systems from all over the world when these in themselves vary and the forms of women's subjugation differ. Indeed, in many societies no distinction is made between the domestic and the public. There was also an acknowledgement that the tendency to identify a distinction between spheres is a Western conceptualisation of society. According to Comaroff (1987) this distinction between the private and the public appears throughout Western social theory as well as in Western folk models. One effect of the distinction between the 'private' and the 'public' in the social sciences seems to be that explanations for what happens in the political arena are not sought within the so-called 'private' sphere. Thus, conditions under which children grow, relations between husband and wife and the norms and values regulating these become peripheral or uninteresting to a social science understanding of public affairs.

In this article, I shall examine participation in Ethiopian politics, particularly elections, from a gender point of view. Instead of focusing on where women are, as proposed by Hirschmann (1991), the question which has framed my approach is why so few women are involved in politics in Ethiopia. My emphasis is on what prevents women's participation in politics rather than on what promotes it. I look first at the structural framework provided by the Ethiopian state as a window to examine the state's attitude toward political participation in both women and men. It is a descriptive assessment of the general political climate in Ethiopia over the past forty years. The second part focuses on the socialisation process as it can be experienced in a parish in Gojjam. This other window on Ethiopian reality reveals some of the ways in which people organise their lives and the norms and values upon which they, to a large extent, seem to agree. My argument is that there is a relationship between gender socialisation during childhood and individuals' subsequent activities as political persons and adults. Childhood experience is a neglected field in political research and knowledge of the ways in which children acquire cultural competence has not been considered important for an understanding of adult political behaviour. Here I discuss male–female interactions, decision-making and values regarding labour, *cathexis* or sexual/love relations, economy and power, as proposed by Connel (1987). The purpose is to show that what happens in the home has a great impact on the way men and women conduct their public selves; and conversely, the way they conduct their common or public activities has repercussions on life in the household. The last part of this article deals with some of the implications of the first two sections and discusses possible opportunities for change.

Election history

The first Ethiopian constitution was promulgated in 1931. The document had the 1889 Meiji Constitution of Japan as its major source of inspiration and shows many similarities to it. Both constitutions were conceived of as gifts from a benevolent Emperor to his people; both were also explicit in that the power of the Emperor was absolute. Thus, even the additional rights bestowed on the Ethiopian subjects by Emperor Haile Selassie could be abrogated at his will (Paul and Clapham 1972, 336–339).

There seems to be some agreement as to why emperor Haile Selassie promulgated a constitution within a year of his coronation. Not only was the Emperor 'progressive' and wanted to use the constitution to modernise his country; it was also a means to centralise governmental power and reduce the influence of the nobility, especially in the provinces. In addition, the constitution was important to gain international prestige and show that 'the government of Ethiopia is constitutional' – especially in view of fascist Italy's rather overt designs for different parts of Ethiopia (Markakis 1975, 271).

With the 1931 Constitution, a parliament with two deliberative chambers was instituted. The members of the Senate were appointed by the Emperor himself, from the nobility and local chiefs, and the members of the Chamber of Deputies were chosen by the nobility and local chiefs. No universal elections were involved.

In 1955, the Ethiopian Constitution was revised. In its new form, there were many provisions for greater influence for individuals and democratic institutions such as an independent judiciary, as well as an acceptance of many of the human rights adopted by the United Nations. Nevertheless, the supreme power of the Emperor was retained in the new Constitution. The reasons for making the changes seem, again, to have been to strengthen central control of the provinces and to make a good impression on the international community. Eritrea had been federated with Ethiopia and had a constitution which more resembled those of Western countries thus forcing Ethiopia to modernise its constitution according to the same pattern (Paul and Clapham 1972; Nuescheler 1978; Keller 1988).

The most radical change in the Revised Constitution was the introduction of universal suffrage. The members of the Senate were still to be appointed by the Emperor but the members of the Chamber of Deputies were to be elected through direct elections with secret ballot. There was to be no discrimination between Ethiopian subjects. Candidates for the Chamber of Deputies had to be 25 years of age, have a property worth 1,000 Birr[2] and immovable property worth 2,000 Birr (Haile 1979, 30). According to Markakis (1975, 281), they also had to deposit the sum of 250 Birr when presenting their candidacy.[3] There were also qualifications of residency which were strictly upheld, ensuring that the Chamber represented the entire country (Clapham 1969, 413). The term of office for deputies was 4 years and for senators 6 years.

The first election in the history of Ethiopia was held in 1957. Subsequent elections under the Emperor took place in 1961, 1965, 1969 and 1973. No political parties were allowed; the candidates competed on personal grounds. Each constituency consisted of 200,000 eligible voters and the number of Deputies to be elected was 210. The number was increased to 250 in 1961. According to figures presented by Markakis (1975, 279–287), the number of registered voters between 1957 and 1969 increased from 3.7 to 5.2 million and the number of votes increased from 2.5 to 3.4 million adults, corresponding approximately to the population increase.[4] Yet despite campaigns and educational material sent to the provinces – in 1968, provincial officials even resorted to various intimidations to make people register – few people voted.

On the other hand, the number of candidates presenting themselves grew steadily, from about 600 in 1957 to 1,500 in 1969. In the first election, the majority were former government employees and teachers though as many as 26 per cent of the Deputies were from the aristocracy. In the different elections between 1957 and 1969, from 33 to 38 of the Deputies were Muslims.

---

[2]1,000 Birr equalled US$400 and was the approximate monthly salary of a government minister.
[3]According to Keller 1988, 87, candidates had to own 850 Birr in land in the constituency or possess 1,700 Birr in moveable property. Since several authors give the same information as Haile (1979) and Markakis (1975) I shall, in the following, stick to their figures.
[4]There were only estimates of the total population.

In 1966, a bill was introduced to permit some local participation in the provincial administration in the form of an elected council at the *awraja* or district level. The bill would also permit some shift of financial responsibility to local government units. This attempt to shift some power from the central government to local governments met with strong opposition from some groups in Parliament and the bill was never passed (Markakis 1975, 315; Cohen and Koehn 1980, 53).

In 1974 a change of regime stopped any further attempts at parliamentary change. It was not a peaceful, constitutional transition of power from one party to the next, but a military *coup d'état*. This violent take-over of the government was not new in Ethiopian history; state power has repeatedly been captured by armed warlords. However, the coup in 1974 was directed by the military and supported by civilians and sought an end to feudal relations of property and power. By May 1975, a land reform law was passed which proclaimed all rural lands as public property. The peasants became responsible for the redistribution of land. To this end, elections of peasant representatives were carried out in the rural areas. Elections to Urban Dwellers Associations were simultaneously carried out in the towns. These initial elections were open to most adults, except previous big landowners and rich businessmen, who had been deprived of land and/or private property, according to the proclamation. The new government, the 'Derg', did not want to rely on the old administration to carry out the elections and the land reform but made use of university teachers and students. Through launching a 'National Development Through Cooperation Campaign', the latter were able to assist the peasants both in carrying out elections and in implementing the land reform.

In the first election in 1975, people were asked to suggest candidates whom they really trusted to carry out the reform properly and therefore to give the names of respected heads of households as candidates. In Bahar Dar for example, where I lived at the time, the names and pictures of candidates, together with information about what they were doing, were put up on the doors of the *kebbele* (Urban Dwellers' Association) office, to facilitate the elections. The procedure was the same for Women's Associations and Youth Associations. From my own experiences and comments from friends and interviews, these elections were free. Everyone was new to the procedure and wanted to make it democratic, in the most basic sense of the word, namely to let the population decide who their representatives would be. I worked as a teacher in Bahar Dar at the time and I was pointed out as a possible candidate for the Women's Association committee by some women in my *kebbele*. They had no photograph of me but described what I was doing on a piece of paper. In the election, I got the second highest number of votes. From what some women later told me, I was wanted as a cashier. They explained the very logical reason why: both I and my husband had jobs that gave us an income, so if any money disappeared from the association, they expected me to be able to pay it back. The other representatives of my Women's Association were elected for just as obvious reasons, namely that their neighbours knew and trusted them as candidates. They had been able to observe them at work and in their homes with their families and neighbours. They knew what kind of people they were.

By 1977/78, however, the situation had changed: representatives of the central government tried to select more of the candidates and to run the Associations. In 1979, a Commission for Organising the Party of the Working People of Ethiopia, COPWE, was established which vested all powers and duties in chairman Mengistu Haile Mariam. As an institution, the COPWE was closely modelled on the centralist, top-down communist parties of Eastern Europe: the COPWE leadership exhibited a very strong need to control officials, COPWE's own members and people at lower levels all over the country. In the third *kebbele* election in 1981, all candidates were thus carefully screened by COPWE. Similarly, the first national election including the nominating procedure in 1987 was, according to Clapham (1988, 95), 'stage managed': 'in all but fifteen of the 702 contested seats for which voting figures are available, the first-placed candidate won...' (*ibid.*). This practice continued until 1991. Democracy defined as choice between individuals, even if not between parties, thus became a very short experience in the time of the Derg. People were forced to vote or they would be penalised, but they had no choice since the candidates had been decided upon beforehand.

In May 1991, the guerrilla forces that had fought the Derg took control of the government and Mengistu Haile Mariam fled. The most well organised and powerful of these groups was the Tigre People's Liberation Front. Now renamed as the Ethiopian People's Revolutionary Democratic Front (EPRDF), it came to coordinate the other groups. In July 1991, the EPRDF convened a conference to discuss the formation of a transitional government. Representation was quite widespread, although some groups who had fought the Derg but were in exile, were not allowed to attend. Together the representatives who were present agreed on a Transitional Period Charter. According to the Charter, the country should be run by a Transitional government until a new Constitution had been ratified and representatives elected according to the new Constitution. The Introduction of the Charter reiterates the Universal Declaration of Human Rights, stating that these are rights 'that Ethiopian people have not enjoyed at any previous time in their history' ('Transitional Period Charter of Ethiopia' 1991). As was pointed out earlier, these rights had also been enunciated in the 1955 Constitution of Emperor Haile Selassie.

In June 1992, less than a year after the establishment of the Transitional government, the first elections were held. They were district and regional elections and were to be the first free, multi-party, genuinely democratic elections in Ethiopia. Shortly before election day, however, the major parties complained that their candidates were being harassed and even arrested and that it was impossible for them to carry out an election campaign. According to them, their only choice was to withdraw from the elections. If not, their participation could be interpreted as a legitimation of the elections, which they considered undemocratic. Different observer groups concurred with this view, saying that these elections were more formal than real. There was only a single party, the EPRDF, on the stage and not even a choice of candidates. (Norwegian Observer Group 1992; Ottaway 1993; 1994; 1995; Human Rights Watch 1994; Pausewang 1994)[5]

The next elections, carried out by the Transitional government in 1994, were for a Constituent Assembly which would discuss, amend and ratify the new Constitution. This election was again boycotted by the major opposition groups in Ethiopia, for the same reasons mentioned earlier, namely harassment and arrest of candidates and supporters. Again the EPRDF with its various coalitions took an overwhelming majority of the seats. Abbink mentions that 'in the countryside the psychological dominance of pro-EPRDF candidates, as well as the pressure to "vote correctly" was again such that one could perhaps not really speak of fully free and fair elections' (Abbink 1995, 158). EPRDF won all the seats in the Oromia and Amhara regions and took a total of 484 out of 548 seats.

The May 1995 elections implied an end to the Transitional government and an implementation of the new Constitution, which had been ratified by the Constitutional Assembly. These elections were thought by the international community to give an important indication of the status of democracy in Ethiopia and a number of international observers followed what was happening. The Ethiopian government therefore had to present a convincing image to impress outsiders with its willingness to act democratically. Thus, when the major opposition parties again stated that they could not campaign for their candidates, since their supporters were harassed and offices closed down, the US government called representatives of both the EPRDF and the opposition groups to Washington to mediate between them. Both went, but to little avail since the parties could not agree on what would be 'democratic' and 'fair' methods for conducting the elections. Again the major opposition parties decided to abstain from participation.

In the 1995 election, 545 representatives were elected to what was now called the Federal Parliament, since Ethiopia according to the new constitution had become a Federal Republic. The EPRDF and its affiliated parties together with 'individual' candidates who were directly or indirectly supported by the EPRDF power structure took all the seats. The only exceptions were one representative for an independent party in the town of Dessie and two individual candidates in Addis Abeba, who were known to many city-dwellers as being really independent of EPRDF. The 1995 election thus again became a one-party event.

The essentially undemocratic nature of this election was remarked upon by a Donor Election Unit with representatives from major Western powers, who followed the elections all over the country. In their report they point out that 'elections, however, are about choice. For the reasons stated in this report, the ability of the Ethiopian people to use the ballot effectively to choose their leaders is still limited. Until alternative political organisations participate, however, such choices will remain restricted.' (Donor Election Unit 1995, 53.) Similar comments are made by other observers. According to Tronvoll and Aadland (1995) the elections were 'neither fair,

---

[5]See also Harbeson 1998 for a discussion of the wider ramifications of the 1992 elections.

free, nor impartial'. Aspen (1995, v) concludes that 'the rural electors in Northern Shäwa do not seem to trust the democratic process which was initiated by the transitional government and EPRDF'.[6]

These observations concur with my study of three regions during the 1995 elections (Poluha 1995 and 1997); all over the country there was great pressure put on peasants and people in smaller towns – they had to vote or they would somehow be punished later. From people's experiences with the last three governments, they knew that such a threat was real. They might be denied land, when land is redistributed; they might not get a job or further education when school is finished; and they might be imprisoned and killed (Poluha forthcoming). Clearly, a high voter turnout in these circumstances does not mean that the population is actively supporting the government but rather that they have a vivid understanding of the possible repercussions of abstention.[7]

To sum up, we can say that Ethiopian experiences with democratic elections have been very brief. Successive Ethiopian governments and their various officials from the reign of Haile Selassie to the present today, have prevented women and men from exercising or even testing what it is to have a choice between candidates. Parties were prohibited in the time of the Emperor. During the Derg, one party, the Workers Party of Ethiopia, developed and controlled all activities. Since 1991, opposition parties have been formally allowed, but are not free to act if they represent an alternative to the politics of the EPRDF. A small group within the EPRDF controls the state apparatus and uses it to increase their influence. At the same time, members of the EPRDF use the party to offer jobs and career opportunities to those who follow their lead. Patron-client relations are widespread, implying that local representatives – who prevent other parties and groups from coming forward – are not necessarily trying to fulfil the ambitions of the Prime Minister Meles Zenawi, but are primarily strengthening their own power positions.

Gender and politics

Even if, during the last forty years, neither men nor women have been encouraged to participate actively in Ethiopian politics, except to vote for already selected candidates, the question remains whether women's and men's participation in the elections has been equally affected by the various governments. To answer this, a review of the election data from a gender perspective is necessary.

For the parliamentary elections from 1957 until today, gender disaggregated data on voter behaviour are lacking. Since, however, both the Derg and the EPRDF governments force people to vote, voter behaviour in itself might not say much about female involvement in politics. Instead, we can look at the proportion of female representatives to try to understand whether there have been any important changes during the last 40 years. In the reign of Haile Selassie and the first parliamentary elections in 1957, two women were elected, corresponding to 1 per cent of the Deputies. In 1965, two or 0.8 per cent were women. In 1969, five or 2 per cent were women and in 1973, eight Deputies or 3 per cent were women.

During the reign of the Derg, there was no significant change at the national level and according to Clapham (1988) there is no evidence of any improvement since the revolution. In the table below, the absence of women becomes quite conspicuous, with only 2.5 per cent of the Central Committee of the Working Party of Ethiopia being women. The only women Clapham could find at lower levels had Amhara/Tigrean names; there were none with a Muslim name and only a few with recognisably Oromo names (*ibid.*, 139).

---

[6]Compare also Amnesty International 1995 and Ethiopian Human Rights Council 1995.
[7]The only opinion diverging from this description of the 1995 elections – apart from those of the government and its supporters – comes from the journalist Colin Legum, who in one of his Third World Reports (24 May 1995) hails the 1995 elections as the triumph of democratic elections. He says that according to the Organisation of African Unity (OAU) and Western embassies, the elections were free and fair. However, he does not present any references about the sources for these views.

Table 3.1: Composition of the Central Committee of the WPE, September 1984

	Full member	Alternates	Total	Per cent
Male	135	60	195	97.5
Female	1	4	5	2.5
Total	136	64	200	100

Source: Clapham 1988, 85, Table 1.

During the EPRDF government, not much has changed with regard to female representation in higher bodies. Below are all the percentages from the 1995 elections, from which detailed data have been obtained for the national level down to the *kebbele* level.

Table 3.2: Percentage of women elected in the 1995 elections, including ethnic group

	Tigray	Amhara	Oromia
National Council of People's Representatives	5	0.7	1.7
Regional Councils	18	5	3
Woreda	22	14	2
Kebbele	17	22	18

Source: National Electoral Board of Ethiopia 1996; Nigussie 1998.

No women were elected to the Council of Representatives from the other regions. With the exception of the Hadiya area where four women out of a total of 19 (21 per cent) were elected, no other women were elected to the Regional Councils.

What is interesting about the figures presented above is that there seems to be a trend that the lower the level of the institution, the more women find their way into politics through it (also noted by Hirschmann 1991, above). This is especially valid for the Amhara region, from where the case study is taken. There are some exceptions even to this. Thus, the *Kebbeles* in Tigray had relatively few women representatives and there were also few in the *woreda*s in Oromia. The importance of the relatively higher number of elected women at the lower levels is difficult to assess, as no comparable data are available from previous years. Nevertheless, the fact that the number is higher shows that, especially in the Amhara region, women's participation in politics at the *kebbele* level is quite substantial with 22 per cent of the elected representatives women.

In 1995, 13 women were elected to the highest institution in Ethiopia, the Federal Council of Representatives. This figure corresponds to only 2 per cent of the representatives, the same as that elected in Haile Selassie's reign. From the point of view of elections at the national level, there has thus been no significant change in the number of women parliamentarians since 1957. Whether this means that the non-participatory climate in Ethiopian politics has affected women to an equal degree with men is more difficult to say. It is, however, obvious from the election data that increased participation of women in national politics has not been promoted during the last forty years. Instead, male dominance has remained at the same level as before.

Constitution and laws

We can also look for an explanation of the differential behaviour of men and women in how they are treated under the laws of the country. In a workshop paper entitled 'Women and the Ethiopian Legal System', Rahel Alemayehu (1992) reviews the Ethiopian constitutions and formal laws in order to identify existing guarantees against sex discrimination. She finds that the 1955 Revised Constitution, the 1987 Constitution of the People's Democratic Republic of Ethiopia and the 1991 Transitional Charter with the universal declaration of Human Rights all acknowledge the equality of the sexes before the law. She then goes on to look at major laws concerning the Family, Labour and the Land Nationalisation Proclamation, to see how they treat relations between men and women. With respect to Family Law, Rahel Alemayehu focuses on the Civil Code of 1960 where she finds many examples of differential treatment between men and women. Some examples she mentions are: a child's name shall be chosen by his father; the family on the paternal side should act as guardian of a child if there is no father and mother; the marriage age for men is 18 years while for women it is 15 years; the husband is the head of the family and the wife owes him obedience; the husband chooses the common residence; the husband should guide the wife's conduct and administer their property (*ibid.*).

In an earlier study, Daniel Haile (1979) points out that the Fetha Negast, a customary law applying to Christians, gives marriageable age as 20 for men and 12 for women, while the Sharia, or Muslim law, gives the minimum age as 12 for boys and 9 for girls. Daniel Haile comments that 'all of them set a lower age for women than for men ... it is easy to see that once a man marries a woman younger than himself, he assumes a paternal relation to his wife by virtue of his maturity and experience in life' (*ibid.*, 4).

With regard to employment laws, Rahel Alemayehu (1992) finds that these explicitly prohibit discrimination. Still, she says that in practice women are differentially treated since they are usually found in low-paid and less-skilled jobs (*ibid.*, 36). Here, it is important to note, however, that very little research has been carried out on gender issues in the distribution of work and salaries within the industrial and service sectors. According to what is known, Ethiopia does not differ from other countries in the world, where women in general have lower-paid jobs and occupy very few managerial positions, although the degree of disparity may of course vary from country to country.

Looking at the Proclamation providing for the public ownership of rural lands, Rahel Alemayehu finds no sex discrimination pertaining to either the acquisition or administration of land. But because the peasant associations distribute land in the name of the husband, women are excluded from membership in the association. Rahel Alemayehu's finding is substantiated by Clapham, who points out that in 1982 only 13 per cent of the associations' membership were women. Two of the highest percentages were in Tigray (32 per cent) and Eritrea (27 per cent), a fact that he attributes to 'the death or absence of men due to civil war' (Clapham 1988, 160).

In general, neither old nor new constitutions discriminate against women in Ethiopia. Similarly, the Employment Law states that women should be equally treated. Family law, on the other hand, still contains many paragraphs where women are treated as inferior to men. The Proclamation on land ownership is, moreover, a clear example of a law which seems to be neutral but which, when interpreted locally, leads to men being favoured over women. As men, traditionally, are seen as the heads of households, land is registered in their names and not in that of their wives, depriving women of this security. Practice has in this way a strong impact on the interpretation of laws, a fact that may require that laws become much more specific in order not to discriminate against women.

To improve the situation of women, in 1993 the Prime Minister's Office of the Transitional government of Ethiopia issued a national policy on Ethiopian women. Very similar to that of the Derg, the policy recognises that there is discrimination of women in many areas and that this must be combated by organising women. Although the present government has not, as yet, organised women at the local level, the intention is to establish Women's Affairs Bureaus in all regions in order to create conditions conducive to the speeding up of equality between men and women. Despite the policy, there is very little evidence of it having had any impact on the hiring policies of government offices. Thus, according to a survey by the Addis Abeba Administration in 1996, only 28 per cent of the government employees are women. Most of those employed were secretaries. Only 7 per cent of the higher level government officials were women.[8]

The neutrality of laws are often not enough to promote women's involvement due to traditional norms and practices. To understand how values, dispositions and norms develop, how they can be experienced and what effects they may have on the political landscape, we shall next take a closer look at everyday life in a local community. Of special interest will be practices relating to gender socialisation – how females are guided into womanhood and males into manhood and how this might relate to subsequent political activity.

Growing up in Ashena

In this section, I shall give a brief description of life in a parish called Ashena[9] in north-western Ethiopia. Ashena is in the centre of Gojjam, which is also the heartland of Coptic Christian

---

[8] *Addis Tribune* 3 July 1998.
[9] This is a pseudonym, see also Poluha 1989.

Ethiopia. Christianity has been the state religion in Ethiopia since the end of the fourth century and people in Ashena are strong adherents of the Coptic Church. The centre of the parish is the church, where the inhabitants meet every Sunday to celebrate mass. After mass, they break the fast together and eat and drink from supplies brought in turn by individual member households. This is also a time to discuss affairs of the church, necessary restorations, and how to protect it against thieves. Most adult households participate in these Sunday meetings and only a few very poor families remain outside the congregation. In 1980, the parish covered about 800 hectares on which a total of about 350 households lived. Today, the borders have been redrawn and the number of households has increased manifold.

The Ashena population consists of self-subsistent farmers who mainly cultivate cereals, four to five different crops a year. What people do not produce themselves they buy from the market, selling their own crops or some smaller animals to be able to pay. The main residential unit in Ashena is the household. It consists of husband, wife and their children. Sometimes a mother- or father-in-law, and often a daughter-in-law or grandchild, will for a period of their lives be part of the household. Members of the household produce what they need and farm labour is seldom contracted from the outside. The cooking is also done for all the members together. In brief, the Ashena household is at once a residential unit, a production unit and a consumption unit.

People in Ashena live in kin-based neighbourhoods. Settlement is patri-viri-local, meaning that a newly married couple first settles with the husband's parents and then moves to a house of their own, close to the husband's parents, after a couple of years. In this way, fathers, sons and grandsons will provide the social core for a kin-based settlement group. With few exceptions, women move to their husbands' homes when they marry.

Children in Ashena are thought to be the most beautiful gift from God. Sons, however, have higher status than daughters. Until they are four to five, both girls and boys stay at home and help their mother. When at play, boys are left alone unless disturbingly noisy while girls are admonished to be silent, stay close to their mother and help her. Already around the age of five, girls start learning gender-specific tasks; they fetch water, clean crops and cook. In time they learn to spin and make baskets. Boys start plowing, the main male task, when they are between twelve and fourteen. In general, boys are free to play, fight and roam around without too much responsibility for many more years than their sisters. While boys experience public places and watch how adults behave outside, girls are expected to stay inside the house, be obedient, work and take responsibility when their mothers are away. Girls thus get little exposure to space away from home, but learn to fear public places as arenas where they do not know how to act. While boys are encouraged to be outspoken, forward, even a little aggressive, girls are expected to be taciturn and withdrawn.

When girls are about six or seven and boys a couple of years older their parents will arrange for their marriage. Marriage is of central importance to life in Ashena and is thought of as a natural condition of life, something that parents have to provide for sons and daughters. Marriage does not mean reaching adulthood, boys and girls are considered to be adults only when they have a child.

A first marriage is the first for both the boy and the girl and rarely do young girls marry mature or elderly men as their first husband. At this young age, the couple has no sexual relationship. The girl is brought to stay with her young husband and his parents for shorter or longer periods. She does not know anyone there, but is brought along to learn the ways of the family; how food is cooked, where water is fetched and how they treat each other. In order not to be alone, she sleeps with her young husband's mother or sisters and returns to her home when her parents call for her. Since the place is new to her, she will not venture far outside the house and everybody expects her to stay close to the home.

When a boy and girl marry, their parents try to give them the opportunity to support themselves, through providing them with oxen to plow the land. The parents make it a point that the girl and the boy are equally economically endowed for the marriage. That husband and wife should be economically equal when they marry, particularly with regard to animals, is an explicit goal in Ashena and Gojjam, though unusual in the rest of the country. Thus, it is the woman herself and not her husband, brother or father who controls the animals. In addition to this, before the land reform in 1975, an Ashena woman had usufructuary rights in land from her parents, just like her brothers. She still has such rights but it is more difficult for her to make claims on land today, when land is distributed to households and each household is represented by the husband.

Although parents take so much care in finding a proper marriage partner for their children, the marriage bond is not very strong. Divorce is common, used by both young husbands, wives and their respective parents. There is no stigma attached to a divorcee, whether male or female. This, combined with the fact that women are economically independent and have the right to leave their husbands, seems to facilitate divorce. Girls may ask for it, when they get homesick away from their parents, and boys can try to find some acceptable cause to call the marriage off when they are disappointed in the looks or behaviour of their brides. Divorce is thus a very real option, open to both boys and girls when they want to alter their marriage status. Once children have been born to a marriage, however, divorce is less frequent. Elders usually recommend that a couple try to mend their marriage, once they have children. If not for themselves, it is at least thought to be better for the child.

Boys and girls begin an active sexual relationship when the girl is between twelve and fifteen and the boy between sixteen and twenty. This is thought of as a natural result of their growing together and is not celebrated with any special ritual or commented upon by the family. Often a girl becomes pregnant before she has even experienced her first menstruation. She may know so little about what is happening in her body, her mother-in-law may have to tell her that she is expecting a baby.

Labour, economy and status

The labour inputs of men and women necessary for the reproduction of the household and the farm are strictly gender defined. Women see to the maintenance of the household members and the house. They store, cook, tend to the young, old and sick. They produce many of the household utensils and assist in farm work. Men build the house and work on the farm. Plowing the soil is considered to be the most important male task. Women's work is time-consuming with many tasks needing to be carried out simultaneously. Men's work, on the other hand, is mostly required during peak seasons when they can do one thing at a time like plow or harvest, which can be very tiring but also allows for concentration. Women's work is mostly around and inside the house, while men's work is in the fields.

When discussing work with women and men and what ideas they had about their own as well as their partner's work, I found that their thoughts were, at first, in many respects similar. Both men and women initially said that men's work was very hard, especially plowing; both said that women do not work much, they are at home. When I asked them if there is no work that women do at home, they agreed that of course there is 'women's work'. It is very light, said the men. The women themselves, however, once they started to reflect upon their own work, said that their work was very hard and tiring. Cooking they found especially troublesome because their eyes suffered from all the smoke. When asked to compare their own input with that of their husbands, most women answered that they work as hard as their husbands. They also thought that their work was as essential to the well-being of the family as that of their husbands. Some said that they even worked harder while a few found that their husbands' work was tougher than their own. Men thought that work was what they did in the fields. They complained of having to plow in rain and scorching sun. That was work. They even had to stay out in the night sometimes with the oxen, which was cold and tough, especially when it rained. Women, on the other hand, spent all day inside their nice homes. The only work women did, which several of the men admitted seemed a bit tough, was to give birth. That was a topic never mentioned by women as work, to them it was part of life.

The fact that work is gender defined makes it possible for women and men themselves to decide when and how to carry out their respective tasks. There are limits to women's freedom, however, and some men do interfere with the work of their wives telling them what to do and when, a cause for much female irritation. And, if a woman makes mistakes in her work or shows some bad judgement, her husband always has the right to correct her. If a man makes a mistake, however, no wife will comment upon it.

Economic decisions are concerned with what to plant and what to re-invest, what to consume and what to sell. In general, husbands decide on these issues and the overall financial responsibility is theirs, according to both themselves and their wives. Thus, they make the decisions about what to plant, although they often discuss with their wives if they need something extra for, say, a planned celebration. Men know about the quality of the fields, which crops are suitable and in which order they should be planted. What to re-invest is also the man's decision, since it is his task to know which seeds best suit the soil and which animals to breed. Women decide about food consumption, how the resources shall be redistributed within the household. They know how much food and drink is required for the family and expected guests and try to relate this to what they have in the stores. When it is a question of eating meat, which usually means buying some from the market, the husband will make the decision, but in consultation with his wife.

Many husbands and wives discuss important sales in the market, especially when a big animal or a large amount of grain needs to be sold to pay for fertiliser or improved seeds, earlier taken on credit. For the small market sales, women themselves choose something to sell – some crop, eggs, or a chicken – to buy whatever is needed for the house. However, if husband and wife are not on good terms, or the husband does not respect the wife, he will make these decisions on his own. Nobody will find any fault with that. But when there is 'peace in the house' (*beselam sinoro*), an oft-repeated statement and a condition most women yearn for, husband and wife discuss what to sell and buy together. When I interviewed individual women and men as well as groups of men and women about decision-making practices, it was much more common for women to say that their husbands decided, while men said that they discussed the issues with their wives. The ideal for both women and men, but more important for women, thus seems to be that husband and wife should discuss and agree about what to do. Reality is, however, often far from this ideal.

One of the most important values mentioned by adults when discussing what they try to teach their children, is that they must show respect to older people. Another basic requirement is that children must learn their gender-defined tasks; such knowledge is considered necessary for their survival. What is less often discussed is how parents teach their children to use space (Ardener 1993). People in Ashena have rules for how to use space in the house, the compound and in public places. In the house, men and boys sit on the benches, in rows according to age and status, while women and girls stay close to the fire and cook. When playing in the compound, girls are often told to go inside to help their mother while boys may be told to go and look after the cattle. While girls' and women's work keeps them in the home, that of boys and men makes them go out of both home and compound. Boys are encouraged to experience outer space, to be a bit forward, while girls are expected to 'stay in' spatially and be shy and subdued in their behaviour. Thus, the use of space articulates the norms of social organisation: boys assisting their mothers with girls' tasks are pointed out, laughed at and asked in a negative tone 'are you a woman?', while girls who try a male task are encouraged and praised for what they are doing.

Thus, we can say that the experiences girls and boys have of growing up in Ashena and the observations they make of their environment are that both are valuable but those of boys more so than girls. Boys are expected to take initiatives and speak up, while girls' knowledge is mainly valued in relation to how it promotes their chances for a good marriage. Girls are encouraged, even exhorted, to stay behind. Their work input is given little value and they are not encouraged to have independent views on economic decisions. The overall status order in the household, in terms of social respect, power and influence, thus enhances the position of men. Growing up in such an environment has implications for boys and girls and how they view themselves and each other when young and later as adults and for how they will behave in different contexts, private and public.

Local public arenas

There are two types of organisations in Ashena which constitute public arenas in the sense that individuals meet in order to discuss and also decide on issues of common concern. They are what people call the 'private' (*yegil*) and the 'governmental' (*yemengist*) organisations (Poluha forthcoming). 'Private' organisations are those which Ashena peasants have organised themselves, mainly for matters of spiritual and economic survival. The largest is the *Senbete*, the parish organisation to which almost every adult belongs to protect the church and its compound. There is also a burial organisation, the *Idir* which is smaller than the *Senbete*. The *Idir* is a mutual self-help organisation where all members assist each other in case of death and sometimes also during a prolonged illness. Everybody in Ashena belongs to an *Idir*: 'to be without it is to be without a family', they say. The third 'private' organisation is the *Mahaber*, a much smaller social organisation with religious connotations, which consists of some 10 to 20 members. The *Mahaber* meets once a month, on the same religious saint's day, when the *Mahaber* members enjoy sharing food and drink. They also try to help each other when someone is sick or needs assistance.

Ashena peasants are also organised by state officials for purposes of the state in 'governmental' organisations. When first created, the purpose of these organisations was to encourage the participation and self-administration of the peasants. Indeed, in 1975, the Peasant Associations were established to carry through the land reform, and the Ashena Women's Association was very active and encouraged women to meet and discuss issues of common concern. Slowly, however, more and more tasks were put on these associations, charging them, among other things, with the responsibility for the collection of taxes and other dues to the state. As time went on, meetings became more of a formality and although Peasant Associations still have their duties to fulfil, the Women's Associations have ceased to exist.

The leaders in both 'private' and 'governmental' organisations are usually elders, mostly men advanced in age. There are very few women whom both men and women consider to be elders. The male elders have gained respect from their neighbours because they are stable and peaceful. An important criterion is their impartiality, essential to make peace between contestants. The issue of accountability is what primarily distinguishes leaders in the 'private' and the 'governmental' organisations. In 'private' organisations, relations between members are horizontal and leaders are accountable to the 'electorate'. In contrast to these, 'governmental' organisations are vertical and everybody is accountable to those above him, making the organisations strictly hierarchical.

Speaking in public, in both 'private' and 'governmental' meetings, one finds almost exclusively men. Younger men usually only watch and listen to their elders and do not participate until mature enough. Yet all the time they learn how to behave in public arenas. They are also fully aware that when mature enough, they will have the right to act and to speak up. Women, even when present, are silent and on the periphery of the group, attentive but not expected to have an opinion. Thus, men exchange ideas and make decisions. Men define which are the issues of common concern and which are private, thereby establishing what should be given priority and what should be put aside. The whole agenda of the parish with the religious organisations and the peasant association is thus defined by men.

Women's behaviour in public space is very much a repetition of their behaviour in and around the house. Physically they keep to the outskirts of most gatherings where men are present. They do not move about or make themselves conspicuous. They very seldom let their voices be heard or speak up in a meeting. Instead one finds them talking to each other in subdued voices. There seems to be nothing in their up-bringing to encourage them to be active politically or socially.

Actually, women in the countryside in today's Ethiopia seldom meet, especially not as a group. The previous Women's Associations that once encouraged them to participate, turned into a means to exploit and control them. The women were happy to close the associations down so they would no longer have to pay a monthly fee to an organisation from which they gained no advantage. Thus, while men still have their formal and informal institutions and continue to see each other, discuss and decide on various issues, women no longer meet as a group. Sisters-in-law see each other socially now and then, but women's main social contact is with their husbands when they come home from the fields, meetings or town. Thus in spite of the fact that they often influence their husbands concerning family affairs, there are no structures, formal or informal, for them to express themselves as a collectivity. Because they no longer meet each other, peasant women know little about what other women think about different issues or what experiences they have. As individuals, they have no real group to which they can refer. Therefore, they mostly express what they think or feel as their own personal feelings or refer to other individual women for something they have said or done. One can thus hear men use the expression 'we peasants here in Ashena think the government...', while women say 'I feel that it is very hard for me...' In this way, women have not been able to develop a shared conceptualisation of their common experiences and therefore find it difficult to speak in general terms. The lack of common regular meetings also results in a lack of knowledge about what is happening, both in the local society and at the regional and national levels.

The only exception to the subdued women in the countryside that I have seen, so far, are the few women who have gained the respect of men and women together. These women are often elderly, no longer child-bearing and have often been widowed for some time. From my observations in Ashena, older women have, due to their age, gained a lot of self-confidence. They know what life is about, they have experienced the responsibilities of child-rearing and of managing a household. They have observed what happens in the community and know about power struggles and the ambitions of individuals and groups. Age itself makes them senior to almost all women who could comment on their behaviour and to most men who have any position. Such men may be their own children, nephews or the children of neighbours. The women have seen them grow up and know their character, strengths and weaknesses. As widows, these women have learnt to take responsibility for all activities in the house as well as on the farm. They have had to administrate the household themselves, marry their children and often assist sons and daughters-in-law with advice. To attribute older women's freedom to their sexlessness (for example Ardener 1993; Hastrup 1993) thus seems to completely miss the point of their strength.[10] These women may be vulnerable if they are poor or have none to assist them to plow, that is if they have not given birth to any son or brought up a child. But the same goes for a man who is growing old and who cannot farm himself. It rather seems as if these older widowed women have at last regained some of the strength and freedom they could have had earlier in life had their self-confidence not been so threatened during childhood.

There is in general, however, quite a strong awareness among women that men lead better lives than women. On a recent visit to Ashena, I asked individual women and groups of women the same question: 'What would you like to be, if you were allowed to be reborn, a woman or a man?' Their eyes started shining just thinking the thought. With one exception, they all answered, 'a man'. 'Why?', I asked. 'I would like him to try the work I do every day, that he thinks is so easy,' said one. 'I want to show him how it is to be ordered about, and what it is to be a woman; at least for a couple of weeks, so that he might understand,' said another. Others agreed that only experience could teach men how tough it is to be a woman. I put the same question to a couple of well-educated women in Addis Abeba and I got the same answer. The men in Ashena also gave me the same answer, namely that they would never like to be reborn as women, 'that would be dreadful'. They wanted to stay as men. Clearly, both men and women are aware of the lower status of women. But as the women expressed it, men would never really know what it is to be a woman unless they were forced to experience it.

The fact that rural women in Ethiopia lack structures to create a common consciousness is, it seems to me, one explanation for their invisibility in elections and political activities. The lack of formal as well as informal women's organisations has made it difficult for them to become conscious that the inhibiting cultural and structural conditions they encounter and the problems they have met with, are experiences they share with many others. When they were able to exchange ideas about things they did not like, as they did in the Women's Associations in the beginning of the Derg, women all over Ethiopia started to question the beatings by husbands. They put forward demands to the Peasant Associations to punish husbands who beat their wives (Poluha 1994). When the Associations were transformed into tools of control for the government, the women also lost a forum to identify these issues as problems and to actively participate in social life. This important relationship between active participation and self-consciousness is discussed by Gaventa (1987, 40ff) who, referring to a number of studies, shows that a very close connection exists between participation and consciousness. Consciousness promotes participation and participation, in turn, broadens and deepens consciousness.

---

[10]There is a tendency in anthropological and other studies (in the Swedish media I have even heard it mentioned as a social fact), to attribute older women's freedom to their sexlessness. Men are no longer threatened by their sexuality thus women can act independently (Ardener 1993). Hastrup divides the course of a woman's life into three stages. The first stage is that of the unspecified, yet creative virgin. The second that of the sexually specified, childbearing woman and the last a return to unspecificity, of widowhood and an old woman's impotence; a time when she is 'completely lacking in sexuality and devoid of creativity' (Hastrup 1993, 44). In my experience, having reached menopause is not the reason why these women act the way they do. It seems as if the whole discussion and interpretation of women's lives again implies looking at them from a male perspective and perceiving them as the passive victims of male relatives.

The 1995 elections in Ashena

The 1995 June elections were held to select representatives to the regional council and parliament. No women candidates were presented in Ashena. People were not very interested in the elections and when the last day for registration approached, very few had registered. Then, political cadres went out to say that everybody had to register, otherwise they would not be able to get any land when the redistribution was to take place. They also said that youngsters from the age of 14 should register themselves as 18, and get a voting card or they would not be given any land. The cadres even went to people's homes to distribute voting cards.

On election day, the polling station opened at 6 a.m. Many went to vote before the church service started at seven. Some also went during the service, which lasted for several hours. Those who went often took the voting cards of others in their family so that they would not all have to queue. The voting itself, as I overheard people talk about it, implied that the electors told the voters to sign for a special candidate through indicating his symbol.

One lady who sat with lots of other women, away from the men in the churchyard said in a loud voice: 'I took three people's (voting) cards, my mother's, my sister's and my own and went voting before coming here.' Somebody asked her: 'Could you really vote for three people?' Then someone else intervened: 'No, that is not possible'. Then the initial lady's voice became louder and she said: 'They told me to sign three times for the sickle (each candidate and party was represented by a symbol, like a sickle, bee etc. on the election cards) and then one time for the bee.' The others asked what she meant by that but she ignored their questions and continued: 'So I asked why I should only sign once for the bee and then they said that is enough. They got angry with me for asking. So I just said alright and left. But I wanted to ask them why I should sign three times for one person and only one time for another. But I knew that I would not get a good answer from them so I just left.' Others in the churchyard talked of similar experiences. Someone had taken five people's cards and gone to sign without any problem. A young 17-year old boy, who also had voted, was rather upset but for a somewhat different reason. He told us of his experiences, saying: 'When I came many were waiting for their turn, queuing. I did not want to wait so I approached the soldiers by the door and when the next name was called I said "yes" and went in and gave my card. They put a mark on my hand so I would not be able to go to another polling station. Then they said: "Come and sign here". So I asked them: "Can I not choose myself?" Then all of them looked angrily at me and one of them said: "You just sign!" I felt I had better sign so I did and went out.' Later the young man again and again repeated to himself: 'Why was I not allowed to choose myself; why did I register to vote if I am not even allowed to choose myself?'

In the later local elections, no women were elected as representatives to the Peasant Association. Some 8 per cent of those elected to the *woreda* or district were women. All of them came from Dangla town; no one came from the rural areas.

Women's political participation and opportunities for change

Does the fact that the economy, norms and traditions do not seem to have altered much over the generations in Ashena make ideas of change impossible and prevent women's participation in politics for generations to come? This is not what I am contending here.

I think it is important to recognise that human beings are to a great degree formed through the interactions they have in the society where they grow up. Individuals watch and observe the behaviour of others. They listen to gossip, myths, songs and historical tales told and retold from generation to generation and incorporate relevant parts into their own experiences. Together, the experiences and ideas that each individual has of her/his world and of her/ himself provide a rationale for how persons should behave and why. Some of these experiences are conscious and easier to change while others are unconscious. The latter, discussed by Bourdieu (1990) as *habitus*, and expressed as customs and habits often reflecting norms and values which are taken for granted and not reflected upon or questioned. This unawareness makes them difficult to change. Connerton (1989) discussing the continuity of mores, norms and values in the form of collective memory, identifies an inertia in social structures which is important to understand when we study social change.

Experiences are, however, heterogeneous and different role models exist. Those knowledgeable about Ethiopian history – which includes many in the rural areas – know that strong women of especially noble heritage have acted forcefully both at home and in the public arena. Empress Illeni, for example, defended the Christian empire from Muslim aggressors in the fifteenth century Empress Seblä Wängel and Empress Taitu headed their own armies against foreign attacks in the sixteenth and nineteenth centuries respectively. Such women are often alluded to in talks about strong women.

Change, of course, is always in process and, depending on the individuals and context, new circumstances are used by people to change their lives. Thus, when Womens' Associations were introduced during the Derg, women all over the country came to know each other, to exchange personal experiences and to support each other. They also learned about how to cooperate, to identify common needs and to collect money and to engage in activities that could be beneficial to them as women. Some women made greater use of their Association than others. Many were completely uninterested in the activities and disliked having to attend meetings. In spite of all these different reactions, it was obvious in the early years of the Derg that changes were taking place. Laws were passed requiring women's participation, even making men responsible for their implementation. Their effect could be heard in the ways that women expressed themselves and one could even observe it in the way some women walked. This was made possible because structures were created, public arenas opened and laws enacted that enabled and encouraged women to meet and also because the Peasant Associations were told to support them.

Individuals also change their lives, depending on the context in which they find themselves and the experiences they have gone through. There are always new issues to consider, new decisions to be made and new people to encounter. To illustrate this last point and to show that change is possible, even if difficult, I want to end with the story of Bisemash, a 12-year-old girl from Ashena, who devised her own strategy to change her fate.

Bisemash was married when she was nine years old. She herself wanted to go to school, but her stepfather thought it better for her to be married together with his other child. Although Bisemash was only his step-daughter, he gave her two cattle, thus generously treating her to the same marriage endowment as he gave to his own child. Her mother knew she wanted to go to school, but realised that her husband had decided upon the marriage and did not try to dissuade him.

Bisemash has been going between her in-laws' house and her mother's for three years now. 'My in-laws are all right', she says, but she still wants to go to school like her younger sisters. She has now come to a crucial point in life because her husband wants them to build a house of their own and move out of his parents' house. This means that they will also start having sexual relations and Bisemash can soon become pregnant. That would mean an end to all her dreams of going to school. So, in October 1996, Bisemash told me, my assistant Tiruye and her mother that she had devised a plan so that she would not have to go back to her husband's place.

> Now I take care of most of the work in our house to help my mother who is sick, that is why I was called home, anyway. I also take the cattle out grazing during my spare time because my father has nobody to look after them. I shall continue like this to help my father in order to make myself indispensable to him. I shall then find some shepherd who can look after our cattle. Then I shall tell my father, 'look you need me at home. Let me stay at home and I shall continue to help my mother with the house while I go to school.' By that time he will be so dependent on me that he will have to say yes and I can start school next year.

'Do you think it will take a full year to convince your father?' I asked, 'Don't you think it is possible to start school already by the spring term?' 'No,' she told me, and her mother agreed, 'you see it is like this: now all the shepherds are busy. They have yearly contracts until February with the people who employed them. So I shall find out who would be interested to come to us in February and arrange something with him, but that will be too late for school, so I shall have to wait for another year until I start. But when you come back next year, you will find me in school', she concluded.

I have not been able to go back there yet.

4

Behind the Transparent Ballot Box
The Significance of the 1990s Elections in Ghana

ANTHONY KWESI AUBYNN

Introduction

Ghana has taken part in two main national level elections in the 1990s, a period generally referred to as 'the second wave of democratisation in Africa.' The first election, which ended eleven years of military rule, was held in November 1992. The result of the 1992 elections, which were won by the incumbent Provisional National Defence Council's party, the National Democratic Congress (NDC), was strongly disputed by the opposition parties. The second major presidential and parliamentary elections, which were held on 7 December 1996, have attracted much international acclamation. These have been trumpeted as 'pace setters' and a 'symbol of true democracy' by world leaders such as the then British Prime Minister John Major, United States President Bill Clinton as well as other political analysts. There was a huge voter turnout (78 per cent) during the elections and the opposition parties made a quick declaration of acceptance of the elections. Leaders and supporters across the entire political spectrum of Ghana attended the inauguration of the ensuing Fifth Republic, which was nothing short of an opulent display of pomp and pageantry. All this seemed to neatly signify a positive political involvement of Ghanaians and a clear trajectory towards democratic consolidation. It also provided sense of an apparent unanimity and consensus about the 'rupturous' and 'highly significant' nature of the 1996 elections in the country's democratisation process.

This chapter examines the 1996 elections in Ghana and assesses their significance within the context of the post-1990 wave of democratisation in Africa. My central aim is to go beyond the ballot box and examine and explain the undercurrent issues and processes that underlined the 1996 electoral contestations in Ghana. Although the outcome of both the 1992 and 1996 elections did not result in a change of government, they have understandably generated significant interest in academia as well as the world especially from the point of view of consolidation of democracy in Africa, where the prospect of substantive democracy has been extremely narrow. The decisive question is whether the 1990s elections are different, in terms of content and significance, from the previously held elections and whether they reflect an advance in liberal democracy. I will contend that, although certain elements of institutional changes such as the introduction of transparent ballot boxes, the use of voter ID cards and the very actuality of elections, rather than the *coup d'état*, as the conduit for the peaceful transition from one republic to another, may be unprecedented in the post independence history of Ghana, the entire process may not represent the significant advance in democracy that it seemed to portend.

I am very grateful to Dr Amos Anyimado of the Department of Political Science, University of Ghana and all participants of the Internet Conference held on this subject in March 1996 for their useful comments on the draft.

The data used in this chapter are a combination of primary data collected during the fieldwork and other relevant secondary sources both in Ghana and abroad.[1] In particular, primary data for the 1996 elections are based on fieldwork I undertook during November and December 1996 to coincide with the presidential and parliamentary elections. In all, 146 electorates were randomly selected from electoral areas in the Western, Greater Accra and Central regions in the distribution as indicated in Table 4.1 below.

Table 4.1: Sample interviewed

Area	Male	Female	Total
Takoradi	10	12	22
Half Assini	8	6	14
Tarkwa	10	10	20
Essiama	8	8	16
Damang	15	15	30
Accra-New Town	10	10	20
Swedru Villages	12	12	24
Total	73	73	146

Although the basis for the selection of the sample was arbitrary, consideration was given to two guiding principles: that the sample should include a fairly equal number of both sexes, and that there should be representation from big cities (Takoradi and Accra), medium towns (Tarkwa, Half Assini and Essiama), and small villages such as Damang and the Swedru cluster of villages. The ages of the people interviewed ranged between 18 and 85. The idea behind the interview was to gain a deeper insight into the main issues that influenced voters' voting decisions. This served to complement the rich secondarysource data as well as observation of the general discourse in the country within the period of elections.[2]

The chapter is divided into seven sections. Section 1 takes a brief historical look at elections in Ghana while section 2 examines the organisational environment that provided the framework of choice. Section 3 examines the participating parties and in section 4 the results of the 1992 and 1996 elections are presented and discussed, while sections 5 and 6 look at how strategic issues and undercurrents such as budgets and regional and ethnic differences were manipulated and exploited during the elections. Section 6 in particular gleans the key reasons behind voters' choice of candidates and parties. The main conclusions of the chapter are presented in section 7.

It is instructive for at least three reasons, to focus on the 1996 presidential and parliamentary elections within a comparative framework of past elections in Ghana. Firstly, the last two elections (1992 and 1996) represent a landmark in the country's post-independence history in which, for the first time, elections, instead of a military *coup d'etat*, have been held consecutively to usher in

---

[1]The fieldwork provided a unique opportunity to observe the campaign process, follow the local discourses through the news media, local newspapers, magazines, radio and TV, and informal discussion in local forms of transport, clubs and markets. The fieldwork was assisted by Ms Beatrix Allah-Mensah, a lecturer at the Department of Political Science, University of Ghana, Ms Dorothy Eluah Ayim, a final year BA student from the University of Science and Technology, Kumasi, and Mr John E. Ocrane, a high school teacher and graduate from the University of Ghana.

[2]During the Election Day, interviews were conducted in the form of an in-depth exit poll in five of the sampled areas – Accra New Town, Damang, Takoradi, Half Assini and Tarkwa. Almost the same questions were posed to all the respondents. Questions asked centred around voters' choice of candidates and parties and why; major issues that influenced voters' decisions; possible change of voting pattern between 1992 and 1996; and voters' expectations from candidates and the future of democracy in Ghana. However, each interviewer was required to probe deeper into voters' political interests, aspirations and economic background to elicit voters' impressions about the election process, the main reasons for their choice of party and candidate, and also to ascertain the correctness of voters' responses. It was practically impossible for the assistant to travel to Essiama after conducting interviews at Takoradi and Half Assini the same day, so interviews in Essiama were conducted the following day (8 December 1996). However, I do not expect the one day difference to significantly affect the voters' responses since a greater part of election results were not yet known.

another republic. Against both internal and external pressures for good governance and multi-party democracy, Ghana held its first multi-party presidential and parliamentary elections in November and December 1992, respectively, after eleven years of military authoritarianism, and a return to constitutional rule. The results of the presidential election, which was won by Jerry Rawlings, were contested by the four main opposition parties, the New Patriotic Party (NPP), the Peoples' Convention Party (PCP), the Peoples' Heritage Party (PHP), and the People's National Convention (PNC), which later boycotted the parliamentary elections. They particularly accused the ruling Provisional National Defence Council (PNDC), of which Rawlings was the incumbent leader, of massive rigging in favour of its offspring party, the National Democratic Congress (NDC), through, among other things, strategic timing of the polls and other institutional manipulations (New Patriotic Party 1993; Jeffries and Thomas 1993; Oquaye 1995). On the contrary, in the 1996 elections both the parliamentary and presidential polls were held on the same day, 7 December 1996, with the active and keen participation of all the key opposition parties. It needs to be elucidated how the different timings of the two elections affected the results and what other institutional changes or improvements and compromises were made, over the three years before the 1996 elections, to re-attract the opposition to the electoral contest.

Secondly, Ghana's transition to independence was powered by two main political forces: The United Gold Coast Convention (UGCC) – United Party (UP) and the Convention Peoples Party (CPP). Since 1957, Ghana's party politics have been 'traditionalised', 'iconised' and organised around the main ideologues of these two parties – as the *Danquah-Busiah* and *Nkrumah* traditions, representing the UGCC-UP and the CPP, respectively. Ideologically, the Nkrumahist CPP has a leftist-Marxist inclination while the UGCC/UP tradition has a centre-right conservative ideology. However, in 1992 the dominance of these political traditions in Ghana's party political arena was broken, following the triumphant entry of what may be described as a *third force* or the *Rawlings tradition*. The questions are what are the implications of this 'third force' in the democratic politics of Ghana and what political constituency does the Rawlings tradition represent?

Finally, both the 1992 and 1996 elections were held under a neo-liberal political economy regime defined by the World Bank and the IMF-designed Structural Adjustment Programme (SAP). The SAP regime represented a significant shift, from the state-centric control of economic activities which characterised almost all previous political regimes, to the private sector. In Ghana, as elsewhere in Africa, it also occasioned a gradual redefinition of state-citizen relations and thereby possibly affected the outcome of the elections (Oquaye 1995; Chazan 1987; Jeffries and Thomas 1993). One interest of this study is how political economy issues were exploited during the election and the extent to which the elections can be seen as a referendum on the broad acceptance or otherwise of the SAP (Hart 1995; Green 1995).

Definition and a brief history of elections in Ghana

Over 25 years ago, Robert Dahl (1971) argued that for any democracy to flourish, the broad citizenry must not only wield the power to select its governors, but must have the ability and opportunity to choose between multiple alternative governors. It is in so doing that the governor may act with consent, legitimacy and responsibility. Elections are placed at the core of the process of democratisation everywhere, not least in Ghana, in order to give substance to these democratisation precepts.

Fred Hayward (1987, 5) defined elections simply as the 'act or process of choosing between individuals to fill an office'. Although Hayward considers participation and range of choice as important ingredients in elections, such a definition sees election as episodic and instrumental and hardly unearths the conjuncture of forces that produce the 'episode.' Yet, as Richard Rose and Ian McAllister (1990, 1) rightly argue, elections cannot be reduced to a simple choice between two parties or candidates vying to fill an office in either a state apparatus or private organisation. For Naomi Chazan (1987), elections are an indispensable index of state legitimacy and not only the basis for the identification of specific sources of regime support. She notes that 'elections [in themselves] are not good substitutes for the institutionalisation of participation or the entrenchment of notion of public accountability'. Thus, in liberal democracy, elections are significant only insofar as they serve as a source of public legitimation of power and make office holders accountable to the power giver, the voter. In other words, a truly free and fair election is the process through which the will of the people is expressed within a constitutionally stipulated period. In theory, then, elections provide the terrain *for participation and contestation* of the broad citizenship in recruiting and legitimating the authority of their rulers (Cohen 1983; Dahl 1971; Remmer 1996; Hornsby and Throup 1992).

To fully grasp the significance of elections in Ghana it is imperative to study these within the broad framework of institutional provisioning, political economy and the particularities and differences in voting patterns. In his highly influential book, *Politics in Ghana 1946–1960,* Dennis Austin remarked that 'in the central Ashanti region, African self-government, a highly developed order of political achievement, existed for more than two centuries before British rule was imposed at the end of the nineteenth century' (Austin 1964: 3). Furthermore, writers such as Kofi Agovi (1991), Fred Hayward (1987), and Patrick Chabal (1995) reckon that elections and other principles, which provide legitimacy and the means of political accountability, were present in the African traditional political systems and that colonialism destroyed these systems. The kind of picture that the above descriptions paint of pre-colonial elections and political participation might be a romanticised celebration of tradition.[3] Nevertheless, they make a point that elections and democracy in Ghana have been part of a historical process, which dates back to the pre-colonial era.

Modern elections, within the context of liberal democracy in Ghana, began during the late colonial period. Ghana, which pioneered sub-Saharan Africa's movement for independence from colonial rule, became the first territory to adopt multi-party elections, which led into independence. Elections of different kinds were held during both the colonial and post-colonial periods. In 1946, the colonial government of Ghana (then the Gold Coast) opened a fresh chapter in the country's history of modern democracy when the Legislative Council was enlarged to include a limited number of elected representatives. From this period on, until independence in 1957, a series of elections, with varying degrees of territorial restrictions and enfranchisement, were held in Ghana (Austin 1964; Chazan 1987).

In 1954, the British colonial government called an election, which was essentially to determine the precise complexion of government prior to the transfer of power. Kwame Nkrumah, who had broken away from the then dominant UGCC nationalist movement to form the CPP, led his party to win 55 per cent of the votes, and subsequently became the first African leader of government business, the equivalent of a prime minister in the Gold Coast colony.[4] Table 4.2 shows the participation in elections between 1956 and 1979. In 1956, an election that ushered Ghana into full self-government was held to select representatives to the 107-seat national assembly. The 1956 elections sought to shape not only national institutions, but also to do so through political competition and free choice.

Table 4.2: Participation in parliamentary and presidential elections in Ghana, 1956–79

Election Year	Estimated Electorate	Percentage of registered voters	Actual voters	Percentage turnout
1956	2 450 224	65	697 257	48
1960	2 450 224	65	1 141 085	78
1969	3 160 194	75	1 493 371	63
1979L	5 600 000	87	1 774 433	38
1979P	5 600 000	84	1 804 402	39

L: Parliamentary elections including the first round presidential polls; P: Second round presidential elections.

Source: Adapted from Chazan 1987, 82.

As both Naomi Chazan and Denis Austin separately reckon, a mass anti-colonial party, the CPP, with its urban, youthful, populist, and minority ethnic composition, was pitted against a loose

---

[3]Although there was a minimal electoral process in some parts of the pre-colonial *Akan* areas in Ghana, there was only limited mass participation and scarcely any choice.

[4]Naomi Chazan (1988, 95) footnotes that Nkrumah and the CPP actually won close to 70% of the votes if other CPP candidates who stood as independents are taken into account.

rural-based constellation of elitist, entrepreneurial, traditional and professional interest groups focused around the National Liberation Movement (NLM), an offshoot of the UGCC (Chazan 1988, 95–96; Austin 1964). The distinct ideological orientation of the two main parties created a pattern of intra-elite conflict that was to endure for years to come. In the 1956 elections, slightly less than half the registered voters, who comprised only 30 per cent of the entire population of voting age (21 years and above), went to the polls. The CPP won 54 per cent of the popular votes and amassed 71 out of the 104 parliamentary seats.

Since Ghana gained independence its political fortunes have vacillated between elected government and military rule. That is, short spells of elected civilian rule have been followed by long spells of military rule through coups and counter-coups, leading to the continuous production of political 'continuities' and 'discontinuities'. Ghana has taken part in five fully-fledged elections, held in 1960, 1969, 1979, 1992 and 1996; and three plebiscites.[5] Apart from the 1969 election which, like the 1954 and 1956 elections, was designed on the Westminster parliamentary model, the remaining elections have been based on the American-type presidential elections in which the president is elected separately from parliament. The 1960 election was, however, a special case. It was a referendum-cum-presidential election. Nkrumah presented a new republican constitution for approval by the people, while at the same time presenting himself as presidential candidate. The republican constitution won a resounding approval, and consequently elevated Kwame Nkrumah to the position of president of the republic.[6]

Nkrumah and the CPP government was overthrown on 24 February 1966 by a military junta, which later came to be known as the National Liberation Council (NLC), ushering Ghana into its first military rule. True to its promised temporary nature, after three years of military rule, the NLC organised a parliamentary election in 1969, which marked the beginning of a second republic.[7] The competition was a reincarnation of old UGCC-UP and CPP political rivalry. These parties re-emerged, respectively, as Progress Party (PP) led by K.A. Busiah and the National Alliance of Liberals (NAL) led by K.A. Gbedema, a CPP stalwart who had fallen out with its founder in the early 1960s (Awoonor 1990, 219). As expected, Busiah and the PP won a decisive victory of 105 of the 140 seats with a voter turnout of 63 per cent of registered voters, which represented 75 per cent of the eligible voters.

In 1972, the Progress Party government was, in turn, overthrown by another military junta led by Col. I.K. Acheampong, barely two years after coming to power. The National Redemption Council (NRC), later to be called the Supreme Military Council (SMC 1 and II), ruled the country for over six years. After six years of military misrule and tussles over the future of democracy in Ghana, including an unsuccessful attempt to introduce what would have been a novel military-cum-civilian form of government in the country in the form of a union government, the SMC II government initiated a return to civilian rule. In August 1978, the SMC II government began a process that would culminate in presidential and parliamentary elections in July 1979. In spite of yet another military intervention by the Armed Forces Revolutionary Council (AFRC) led by Flt. Lt. Jerry John Rawlings, the date and the overall process of the elections were not interrupted. Nearly two dozens of parties resurfaced with the lifting of the ban on party politics. However, in the run up to the elections, the traditional UGCC-UP and CPP rivalry re-emerged under different banners. The UGCC-UP was re-born into a Popular Front Party (PFP) with its rural-elitist background and ethnically Akan dominance. The CPP, on the other hand, 'reincarnated' in the form of the People's National Party (PNP) with a more urban-populist base and a wider ethnic appeal. As

---

[5]The first plebiscite was held in 1964 to seek the approval to make Ghana a one-party state; the second in March 1978 to run Ghana into a non-party Union Government system; and the third in 1992 approved of the draft constitution for the Fourth Republic.

[6]The ulterior motive behind Nkrumah's push towards a republican state was to eliminate opposition to establish a firmer grip on the reigns of government. Hence, the amount of opposition was carefully circumscribed. J.B. Danquah, the leader of the NLM contested the move but was largely ineffective at the polls.

[7]The NLC's retreat to barracks may not be entirely voluntary. It could as easily be due to increasing pressure by a growing number of sections of the Ghanaian public such as students, trade unions and other ethnic groups, which had culminated in a series of strikes and demonstrations in the country. See Awoonor (1990) and Chazan (1988) for more on this issue.

many as 10 candidates, including 4 independent candidates, participated in the presidential contest. In addition to the PFP and the PNP, four other parties, namely, Action Congress Party (ACP), Social Democratic Force (SDF), United National Convention (UNC), and the Third Force Party (TF) took part in the parliamentary elections which produced a voter turnout of only 38 per cent of the registered electorate. The PNP, led by Hilla Limann, won both the presidential and parliamentary elections with 71 of the total of 140 seats.

Of great interest is the fact that almost all the major elections in Ghana have been conducted mainly to usher in a regime change: from colonial rule to self-determination (1956 elections), from multi-party to one-party regime (1964) and from military to civilian rule (1969, 1979 and 1992). Similarly, while party acronyms have been replaced with bewildering alacrity and new leaders have surfaced, the campaign methods, electioneering style, voting pattern and the general electoral procedure in the above elections have exhibited remarkable commonalties (see Austin 1964; Chazan 1987 and 1988; Jeffries 1980; Awoonor 1990). Only the 1996 election could be said to assess legitimacy and renew accountability, and in that sense represent a departure from past practice.

Towards the 1996 elections: institutional process and the framework of choice

In this section, I describe and examine the institutional and organisational process which foreshadowed and provided the framework of choice during the 1996 elections. Procedural issues such as the making of constitutions and the establishment of electoral commissions are very important in elections in Ghana since they have always served as a harbinger for most national elections. With the exception of the 1960 and 1996 elections, all the post-independence national elections in Ghana have followed the same procedural rituals: the establishment of a constitutional assembly to draft and discuss a new constitution, the reorganisation of the electoral commissions, referendum to approve or reject the draft constitution, the unbarring of party politics, the formation and registration of parties and candidates, the regulation of campaigns and then the actual elections. However, as I show below, the institutional process, which provided the framework of choice in the 1992 elections, was different from previous experiences.

In mid-1990, the PNDC government established the District Assemblies with two-thirds elected members. Whatever the extent of its intentions towards participation in local policies, local level democracy seemed to be the directed democracy of the military dictatorship. While the direction of democracy at the base level seemed clear, it was still unknown what would be the nature of the 'superstructure' at the national level. The PNDC government by its own name, 'provisional', acknowledged the temporary nature of the regime. The introduction of district level elections and the establishment of the National Commission for Democracy (NCD) during 1990 were, perhaps, an indication that the PNDC government was not totally unmindful of the need for some form of democracy at the national level. Yet, they were persistently unclear of what form it should take. Rawlings, in person, and the PNDC government, in general, were ambivalent towards multi-party elections especially since the president often associated multi-party democracy with elitism. However, during July 1990, the government entrusted the NCD with the responsibility of collecting and collating views on the kind of democracy which was to be made suitable for Ghanaians. NCD was anything but independent since its chairman, Justice D.F. Annan, was a member of the ruling government.[8] Nonetheless, the conduct of its activities was relatively open. Regional and district seminars were organised with open participation, including the participation of the well-organised main democracy movement, Movement for Freedom and Justice (Shellington 1992, 169–172; Jeffries and Thomas 1993, 334–337). The NCD's final report indicated the overwhelming desire of Ghanaians for multi-party elections (National Commission for Democracy 1991).

In spite of the NCD's report, the eventual acceptance of the challenge for multi-party elections by the PNDC can only be described as grudging. It took some direct and indirect pressure from

---

[8] Mr D.F. Annan has been the Speaker of Parliament since the return of civilian rule in 1992.

both external sources such as Western governments, IMF and the World Bank, and internal democracy movements such as the Movement for Freedom and Justice (MFJ), and perhaps indicates the government's own desire to legitimise to some extent the military government by committing itself to the idea of multi-party elections. (Aubynn 1993; Oquaye 1995; Ninsin 1991; Gibbon *et al.* 1992).[9] Thus, the eventual realisation of multi-party elections in Ghana is rooted in not only internal political dynamics but also external forces and conditionalities.

The next major phase was the establishment of a constitution-making body.[10] The 1992 process departed from the previous pattern of setting up a Constituent Assembly by establishing a Consultative Assembly. These two bodies cannot be assumed to be a mere change in nomenclature. Unlike the Constituent Assemblies, the Consultative Assembly consisted of 117 members elected by the District Assemblies, 121 members elected from 62 established organisations and corporate groups and 22 members appointed by the government.[11] The 1991 Consultative Assembly was relatively broad-based, more representative and represented a departure from the elitist character of its predecessors. For example, its membership included hitherto inconceivably recognised groups such as hairdressers, butchers, farmers and fishermen, among other 'traditional' groups such as lawyers and academics. Nevertheless, it did not ensure an improvement in the quality of the democratisation process. In fact, its effectiveness and ability to carry out a balanced debate was dubious. Firstly, the District Assemblies from which the majority of the members of the Consultative Assembly came were entirely pro-government and this was in addition to the 22 members who were handpicked by the government. The 62 corporate bodies from which the 121 members were elected were chosen arbitrarily. Secondly, out of the 260 members of the Consultative Assembly, only 25 were women. This constituted a serious perpetuation of the past imbalance in gender representation especially since women constituted slightly more than half of Ghana's population and formed 50 per cent of the electorate during both the 1992 and 1996 elections. Thirdly, the newly 'enfranchised' hitherto marginalised groups, such as butchers and drivers, might not have had the requisite legal knowledge to articulate and comprehend the technical complexities of constitution writing. In effect, while the 1990s Consultative Assembly expanded its scope of participation, it lacked the necessary balance of political forces in the country since effective opposition views were virtually absent.[12] It was therefore an effectively 'toothless bulldog' since the process was largely controlled by the government. Moreover, rather than restructuring the state and its powers to be more useful to the needs of its citizens, the constitution, which eventually came out without much public debate, concentrated on perpetuating the old constitutional structure of the state.

During the second half of 1991, an Interim National Electoral Commission (INEC) was established to oversee all state elections in the country. In terms of structure, INEC was slightly different from the 1969 and 1979 commissions which were, in each case, headed by a sole commissioner responsible only to the Constitution in the performance of its duties. INEC was a four-man commission, chaired by Justice J. Ofori-Boateng, two deputies, Dr Afari-Gyan and Nana Oduro Numapau and one other member, appointed by the PNDC government under PNDC Law 271 and 278. The major tasks of INEC included the delimitation of constituencies and the compilation of a voters' register. For the purpose of the 1992 elections, INEC expanded the existing electoral constituencies from 140 to 200, ostensibly to reflect the increasing population

---

[9]The World Bank, for instance, had by 1989 insisted on 'good governance' as a conditionality for continued disbursement of loans to its recipients including Ghana. The Bank argued that 'political legitimacy and consensus are a precondition for sustainable development' (World Bank 1989, 60). The central role of external factors in ensuring a substantive move towards multi-party democracy accentuates the increasing leverage of external forces over questions of local political legitimacy.

[10]During 1991, the licences of most of the banned newspapers, such as the *Catholic Standard* and the *Ghanaian Chronicle*, were returned. In fact, many private newspapers began to proliferate, particularly in Accra.

[11]*West Africa* 18–24 November 1991.

[12]Jeffries and Thomas maintain, however, that the Consultative Assembly contained 'many opposition sympathisers' (1993, 337). My view is that drawing up an effective constitution requires more than sporadic and unorganised 'sympathisers' of alternative views. A well-balanced representation is absolutely important.

and the changed regional structures.[13] The 1996 elections were not prefaced by the rituals that preceded the 1969, 1979, and 1992 elections. Two issues, regarding the electoral process, are of interest. Firstly, with the coming into force of the 1992 constitution in January 1992, INEC become a permanent institution with constitutional backing.[14] Thus, the 1996 election was guided by an established constitution which also gave more extensive and explicit responsibilities to the electoral commission than the 1969 and 1979 Constitutions. The range of functions of the NEC was expanded to include financial and internal management detail of political parties and public education on the electoral process and its purpose (Ghana 1992, Article 45). Secondly, the principle of the independence of the electoral commission was also enshrined in the Constitution, which, in turn, provided a hope of electoral impartiality and free and fair elections. An evaluation of the operations of NEC during the 1996 elections will require a separate and more determined study. However, it is important to make a brief comment on the conditions of the operations of NEC since it has implications for the commission's ability to discharge its duties impartially.

It is fair to begin my comment with the appointment of members of NEC. As I have indicated above, members of INEC were appointed by the then PNDC whose Chairman, Jerry Rawlings, had, as an open secret, ambitions to contest in the presidential elections. The PNDC itself was to sponsor a political party to compete in the parliamentary elections (Kumado 1993, 48–50). Under the 1992 Constitution, NEC was appointed by the President, albeit with the advice of the Council of State. However, at least two of NEC's most important current members, its chairman, Dr Kwadwo Afari-Gyan and David Kanga were members of INEC and effectively owe their positions to the president. Under this procedure of appointment, it was highly unlikely that NEC would be totally free from governmental control. Furthermore, with the expansion in the range of responsibilities of NEC as already indicated above, one would have expected that it would be matched by logistical and financial support. Yet, as Boateng (1996, 55) observes, these responsibilities were hardly matched by financial, material and manpower resources. The financial and logistical disabilities of NEC compelled it to rely upon other organisations like the Non-Formal Education Unit (NFEU) and the National Commission for Civic Education (NCCE), the leadership of which could hardly be described as non-partisan.[15] Thus, although the 1992 constitution created an electoral machinery with more clear-cut responsibilities, its independence and effectiveness were highly circumscribed, especially given the processes of appointment of its members and the logistical, financial and human resource limitations.[16]

One important novelty introduced in the 1996 electoral process was the provision of voter-ID cards and transparent ballot boxes. This was possibly in direct response to opposition complaints during the 1992 elections. The main reason for the opposition boycott of the 1992 parliamentary polls centred upon the lack of transparency in the voting process. Accusations backed by some evidence were made about impersonation and the pre-stuffing of ballot boxes with ballot papers (New Patriotic Party 1992; Oquaye 1995). These malpractices, if they happened, were thought to have been made possible by the use of non-transparent ballot boxes located in a secluded cage.[17]

To forestall the recurrence of this situation and to recapture the badly-bruised confidence of the people in the electoral process, many corrective steps were taken by the NEC for the 1996 elections, important among which were the following: the voters' register was reopened in 1995 for

---

[13]The population had grown from about 12 million since the last elections in 1979, to about 16 million in 1992. The PNDC government during the second half of the 1980s had created new administrative regions such as (the splitting of the Upper region into) Upper East and Upper West regions as well as 45 new administrative districts.

[14]Subsequently, its name changed from an 'interim' to a National Electoral Commissioner (NEC).

[15]The Director of NFEU, Mr Mettle-Nunoo, for example, was a member of the NDC party who appeared on radio and TV programmes on behalf of NDC during the 1996 election campaigns. He was elected to the Executive Committee of the NDC during the party's recent congress at Sekondi in December 1998. Similarly, the deputy director of the NCCE, Dr J.E Oppong was a former minister in the PNDC government and was likely to be sympathetic to the NDC.

[16]A member of NEC, Mr Kanga, alluded to some of these drawbacks in a post-election interview on the national TV programme, Talking Point on 16 December 1996.

[17]Process of voting in the 1992 elections was that, after a ballot paper was issued to a duly registered voter, he/she cast the ballot into an opaque ballot box placed in a covered cage erected in the open space.

public inspection; all parties were provided with a copy of the list of registered voters; voter-ID cards – with photographs for urban voters and without photographs for voters in rural areas – were issued; transparent ballot boxes were provided at the polls; and above all, voting was done in the open. These changes apparently regained confidence in the electoral process of both ordinary people and the suspicious elite. A survey conducted by the NCCE, barely a month before the elections, indicated 95 per cent public confidence in the electoral procedures.[18] My own survey, involving 40 people randomly selected in Accra one week before the elections, produced the same result. I asked whether the respondents thought it was possible to rig the impending elections. About 80 per cent of respondents answered that it was highly impossible for the elections to be rigged. The remaining 20 per cent were sceptical. They generally maintained that, although the procedural changes were good, 'anything could happen'. Similarly, in a radio interview monitored in Accra, Mr Obetsebi Lamptey, the director of publicity of the NPP, admitted that 'we have at this time no problem with the NEC'.[19] The representatives of other parties who were on the show expressed similar beliefs. The procedural changes described above reactivated the confidence of the people in the elections and gave credibility to the process which may explain the relatively high degree of enthusiasm and, as we will see later, voter turnout during the elections.[20]

Participating parties: nature and organisational environment

The seven main parties registered to contest in the 1992 parliamentary elections included NCP, NDC, PHP, PNC, Egle Party (EP), NIP and NPP. All the parties laid claim to being either Danquah-Busiahist or Nkrumahist. There was no challenge to the NPP's claim to be the sole descendant of the Danquah-Busia tradition. Its leadership was made up former activists and ministers of the Busiah government such as Dr K. Safo-Adu, J.H. Mensah and J.A. Kufuor. During the 1992 elections, it chose an internationally respected historian and retired university professor, Albert. Adu Boahen, as its presidential candidate. As will become apparent below, although the NPP maintained the traditional middle-cum-intellectual-class, Asante-dominated membership of UGCC-UP tradition, it had lost its rural base. Instead, its frontiers of support had shifted into the urban centres.[21]

There was a proliferation of parties that claimed to be 'true Nkrumahist'. Prominent among them were the NIP, PNC, NCP, PHC and, to a greater extent, the NDC (although only implicitly). The popularity of Kwame Nkrumah as the founding father of the nation made association with him a very important electoral vote catcher, and thus accounted for the proliferation of parties which used Nkrumah's name. The NIP had the largest concentration of the CPP 'old guard' politicians' headed by 76 year-old long-time ally and minister of Kwame Nkrumah's CPP regime, Kojo Botsio (Jeffries and Thomas 1993, 343). Kwabena Darko, a religious and successful poultry businessman, was chosen as the party's presidential candidate. His selection was most probably to appeal to the increasingly large number of the evangelical Christian voters and to demonstrate his practical economic managerial skill through his success in the poultry business.

The PNC faction was made up of those who supported the last civilian president of the Third Republic, Hilla Limann, and who believed that since the Third Republic, ruled by the pro-CPP Peoples National Party (PNP), was illegitimately overthrown, it was necessary to reorganise the CPP around its immediate previous leader. The third faction, the PHP, grew out of a grouping of younger, more seriously policy-minded Nkrumahists, who were reluctant to accept domination by, or even too close an association with, the 'old guard' politicians. It had as its leader, a retired United Nations field commander, Lt Gen E. A. Erskine, whose distinguished military career was

---

[18]*Ghanaian Times* 4 November 1996.

[19]*Joy FM* 29 November 1996.

[20]It needs to be noted that the improvement in the electoral procedure did not necessarily stop electoral frauds. Some impersonations were detected during the 1996 elections. The local newspapers (*The Daily Graphic, Ghanaian Chronicle*, and *Free Press*) also frequently reported the buying of voter ID cards from voters who were thought to be potential voters for another party.

[21]One possible reason for this change is the increasing (P)NDC party's influence in the rural areas of Ghana through its rural development project and the hurting impact of SAP in the urban area.

thought to be a formidable asset to challenge another retired (and lower-ranked) military man, J.J. Rawlings, during the presidential contest.

The NCP faction was a mixture of old CPP senior activists and youth cadres who were more prepared to do business with Rawlings, while maintaining their party independence. Interestingly, the founding leadership of the party included many PNDC members or ministers. The leadership included a former minister of the Nkrumah regime, Kweku Boateng, and a number of leading members of the PNDC such as Ato Austin, Captain Kojo Tsikata, Ebo Tawiah, Dr Kofi Awoonor and John Tettegah. The inclusion of a large number of the PNDC cadres in the leadership of NCP created suspicion among other Nkrumahist groups that the government had strategically created this party in order to infiltrate and split the ranks of the Nkrumahists. This suspicion seem to be credible, particularly given the fact that the NCP party later formed an electoral alliance with the government's NDC party.[22] Again, targeting the Nkrumahist group was strategically important to the success of the ruling party in the elections because, arguably, given the fact that the CPP and its related party have won all but one previous national level elections, they were likely to have the largest following, and any division in their ranks would be of strategic interest to any competing party, particularly a new party such as the NDC.

The NDC party is believed to have been formed by some key members of the incumbent PNDC government including Obed Asamoah, the Secretary for Foreign Affairs, Alhaji Idrissu Mahama, Secretary for Defence, and the first lady, Nana Konadu Agyman-Rawlings.[23] The leading members of the NDC included both former Nkrumahist and Danquah-Busiahists who Jeffries and Thomas (1993, 347) describe as 'centrist-pragmatist'. The party's initials, NDC, were probably well-crafted to resemble the P(NDC), ostensibly to remind the electorate of its association with the PNDC which had been in power for eleven years and which had been associated with certain developments such as the construction of roads and electricity, particularly in the rural areas. As was to be expected, the party chose the incumbent head of state, Rawlings, as its presidential candidate. The NDC drew its membership from the numerous 'revolutionary' organisations such as the Committee for the Defence of the Revolution (CDRs), June Fourth Movement (JFM) and the 31st December Women's Movement, most of which were created by the government throughout the country. Since most of the activists in these organisations were young (mostly between 18 and 35 years) low income class, less-educated people such as drivers and 'truck pushers', the NDC drew most of its popular support from the grass roots. In addition, by being the government party, it expected support from farmers and other rural voters who were believed to be the major beneficiaries of the government policies. In effect, the NDC was the incumbent government's own party and expected to draw its support from the numerous organisations set up by the government across the length and breadth of the country and from the perceived beneficiaries of the government's economic policies, the rural farmers.

The principal strategy of all the parties in the presidential contest during both the 1992 and 1996 elections was to form an electoral alliance. The EP and NCP formed an alliance with the NDC to sponsor one presidential candidate, J.J. Rawlings.[24] The NCP, which was a relatively stronger party among the Nkrumahist factions, agreed under the alliance that its presidential candidate, K.N. Arkaah, would be the running mate of Rawlings. On the other hand, the remaining four opposition parties, NPP, NIP, PHP and PNC, would go it alone in the first round in the hope of forming an alliance in the event that no presidential candidate emerged with an absolute majority of over 50 per cent during the first round. The opposition parties' main strategic target was not the NDC party per se, but its presidential candidate J.J. Rawlings, who was thought to be the main orbit around which the party revolved. The idea was that once Rawlings was defeated, the 'order' of the traditional Danquah-Busiah – Nkrumahist political competition would be returned since the NDC party itself would have collapsed.[25]

---

[22]The NCP's presidential candidate later became Rawlings' running mate.

[23]*Africa Confidential* 21 June 1996.

[24]This alliance was called the Progressive Alliance. The Egle Party would not originally field a separate presidential candidate but preferred that Rawlings stood on the Egle rather than NDC party ticket. The NCP on the other hand reached a decision to form an alliance with the NDC at its party convention on 18 September 1992.

[25]All the alliance agreements during 1992, both within the government party and the opposition, did not include the parliamentary elections. Each party in the alliances presented its own parliamentary candidates irrespective of the outcome of the presidential votes.

In 1996, the key issue of alliance formation remained a critical electoral strategy for both the government and the opposition parties, although the mode of the alliances changed considerably, especially for the opposition parties. The governing NDC party lost one of its previous partners, the NCP, due to a feud between President Rawlings and Vice-President Arkaah of the NCP which culminated in physical exchanges between the two during a cabinet meeting on 28 December 1995.[26] The NDC sought a replacement with the low key, coastal-based Democratic People's Party (DPP), apparently formed by the NDC party. The DPP later played the role of propaganda *par excellence* for the Rawlings campaign by running media advertisements, and sometimes negative campaigns (I will return to the campaign issue later). On the other hand, for the NCP, the abro-gation of alliance with the NDC led to the division of the party into splinter groups with some members joining the NDC while others joined Vice-President Arkaah, who merged with other Nkrumahist parties such as the NIP and PHP to form another party, the Peoples Convention Party (PCP), in a frantic effort to revive and unite the CPP tradition.[27] The combined Nkrumahist group, on 7 June 1996, chose Vice-President Arkaah as its presidential candidate.

Perhaps the most interesting set of alliances was that between hitherto bitter political adver-saries, the Nkrumahist PCP and the Danquah/Busiahist NPP. After two years of discussions, the PCP and the NPP formed an effective electoral alliance at the beginning of September 1996 under the name of the Great Alliance. The 1996 opposition alliance was very different from the 1992 'attempted' alliance. The Great Alliance fielded a single presidential candidate, provided by the relatively more popular NPP with a PCP running mate, right from the first round of the elections. Similarly, unlike the 1992 case, which was limited only to the presidential elections, the 1996 alliance was extended to parliamentary candidates. That is, to avoid the splitting of votes, the alliance presented joint parliamentary candidates in the constituencies in the ratio of 112 to 86 for the NPP and PCP respectively. The chief rationale for what can be described as a 'marriage of inconvenience' or, in the words of the *Africa Confidential* newspaper, 'a streak of cold-blooded rationality',[28] was summed up to me by a leading member of the NPP in Accra: 'it is better for two enemies to unite to fight a common enemy. We can begin hostility again after the common enemy has been eliminated.' In the description of this informant, the common enemy was Rawlings and the NDC, who needed to be defeated during the election battles. However, the alliance between the two former political antagonists was not smooth sailing as the initial lack of consensus that characterised the idea of alliance formation continued to haunt the Great Alliance. Some key members, notably Da Rocha, the deputy national chairman of the NPP, and Asuma Banda, the PCP national chairman, questioned the viability of alliance as a political strategy and constantly spoke against it.[29]

In a nutshell, the different forms of alliances produced three major political groupings during the 1996 elections, as against five in 1992, as follows: The Great Alliance presented an Oxford-educated lawyer and long time politician, J.A. Kuffuor of the NPP, as their joint candidate with the incumbent vice-president K.N. Arkaah (PCP) as his running-mate; the Progressive Alliance (NDC with EP and DPP) sponsored the incumbent president, J.J. Rawlings and a University of Ghana law professor, John Atta-Mills as the presidential candidate and running-mate respectively; the PNC, on the other hand, had a medical doctor, E.N. Mahama as its presidential candidate with Mrs Adeline Mate, a Deputy Minister of Health during the Third Republic, as his running mate. Evidently, the PNC was the only party without alliance and which had a woman in the presidential

---

[26]This duel was widely reported by both local and foreign news media such as the BBC, *West Africa* and *Africa Confidential*.

[27]The name of the party, the People's Convention Party was a re-arranged name of the old Convention People's Party. The notable exception was Limann's PNC party, another Nkrumahist faction which won the 1979 election as the Nkrumahist PNP and which refused to join the all-Nkrumahist unification on account of its strong belief that its leader, ex-President Limann, should be the legitimate leader of any reformed Nkrumahist party.

[28]*Africa Confidential* 21 June 1996.

[29]Lack of unity was clear. In less than two weeks to the elections there were still differences in the distribution of parliamentary constituencies among the members of the alliance. In the Ayawaso Central constituency, for instance, two candidates within the alliance, Kwesi Pratt (PCP) and I.C. Quaye (NPP) contested against each other, contrary to the alliance agreement.

contest. Also, with the exception of Rawlings, all the presidential candidates did not take part in the 1992 elections, which meant that Rawlings could draw on his campaign experiences during the previous election campaigns. None of them, however, was entirely new to politics.[30]

Surprisingly, with the exception of the NDC, none of the parties seemed to have any coherent, readily available document on policy and programmes.[31] The only way to gather the main policy objectives of the parties was through fragments of public interviews and pronouncements during campaigns. For all the three parties, there was hardly any difference between the aims and policies. All parties had 'development' as the main objective. While the NDC's aim was 'development and progress', its strongest rival, the NPP, had 'development in freedom' as its main aim. The NPP proposed to pursue development while ensuring freedom and human rights, against what was seen as authoritarian development by the incumbent government. Apart from the PNC, which aimed to re-nationalise some privatised state companies, virtually all the parties offered free market policies, including the SAP from which the incumbent government had gained its name. The main issue for the parties was not *what* kind of alternative development ideology was to be pursued, but *how* the existing policies could be better implemented.

In the absence of real issues, the campaign was reduced to sloganeering, 'logoism', provocative insults, and sometimes, violence. Differences were clear in party logos, symbols and cliches. Rawlings and the NDC party had as their symbol the umbrella, with green, red, white and black as their colours. The NPP's symbol was the elephant with blue, white and red colours, while the PNC had the coconut as its symbol with party colours of red, green and white. Party logos were everywhere: on caps, T-shirts, flags and cloths. All the parties had cliches and slogans, often more than one. In fact, the two main contending slogans, well known in both urban and rural areas, were *eshi* for the NPP party (a word from a Ghanaian language, Ga, which literally means 'it's boiling'), and *eheidzo* ('it's cooled') for the NDC.[32] The PNC party whose slogan was in English – 'two direct, two sure' – did not seem to catch on very well with voters. The NDC slogan meant that it was the 'reigning' party in control while the NPP predicted that the ruling party's days were over. The NPP often boasted of the strength and might of the elephant and how the latter would 'destroy' the tiny umbrella during the elections and protect Ghanaians. The NDC, on the other hand, presented the umbrella under which all Ghanaians, old and young, poor and rich, would gather under its care, and pointed to the destructiveness of the elephant.[33] It was observed during my interviews that most local people knew the parties only by their slogans and symbols.

The NDC emphasised the stable economic and political achievements of the (P) NDC in the previous 15 years, while the NPP and other opposition parties stressed the negative impact of the economic policies and the 'nervous' political stability of the period, and promised better economic prospects. During the 1992 elections, the NDC was able to capture a local 'phrase', *obiara ba nye,* (translated as 'no one's child is perfect') as a slogan portraying some of the drawbacks of the PNDC administration and to acknowledge the fallibility of any government, including the PNDC. This phrase won the NDC some public sympathy and introduced doubt about the ability of the opposition to deliver on their promises or to do better than the incumbent government.[34] In short, the NDC's campaign theme in 1992 can be summed up as 'the devil you know is better than the angel you don't know'.

---

[30]Kufuor, for example, is an old-time politician, a deputy minister in the Busiah government and a Minister for Local Government in the early part of the Rawlings' PNDC government and contested in his party's presidential primaries during the 1992 elections.

[31]I visited the NPP headquarters on 5 December 1996 (two days before the elections) and was told by the party's General secretary, Agyenim Boateng, that the NPP had a policy document but because of its alliance with another party it was not possible to make the document public or campaign on it. The NDC's policy document was no more than the Economic Recovery Programme framework. See also *New Africa* 15 November 1996, for the NDC party manifesto.

[32]The shout of any of these clichés often elicited immediate response from a supporter of an opposing party.

[33]There was a frequently run TV documentary about the 1992 elections in which the running mate of Rawlings, Ekow Arkaah, at a rally in the central region showed how the elephant could easily destroy their farms.

[34]It was widely believed that P.V. Obeng, the *de facto* second in command in the PNDC government, introduced the catchphrase (though a common Ghanaian saying) into the election politics.

During 1996, the NPP captured the initiative in constructing the new electioneering phraseology: *hwe w'asitena mu na to aba pa* ('examine your living conditions and vote wisely'). Somehow, this slogan became popular and provocative and to some extent, brought political economy to the core of the 1996 campaign. The NDC claimed that the provision of roads, electricity and drinking water in the villages and the general availability of the essential commodities, especially imported consumer goods, were indications of improved living standards for which they were responsible. On the other hand, the opposition alliance sought to question the distributional impact of the government's economic policies on the broad mass of the people by emphasising price hikes, poverty and unemployment. 'Rawlings has tarred roads, but that is not what development is about. Development is about bringing jobs, drinking water, schools and health facilities to the people,' said Kwabena Baffuor, a former Minister and now leading member of the PCP.[35] At a campaign rally in Tamale in Northern Ghana, Kufuor, the NPP presidential candidate said, 'my message is simple: check your living conditions for the past 15 years of the Rawlings rule and vote wisely'.[36] However, the use of economic issues during the campaign was cosmetic because neither party ventured into the critical issues such as how to solve problems of poverty, unemployment, interest rates, and inflation, thereby underlining the absence of real choice for the voter.

Campaign style and rhetoric, as well as the public appearances of the main candidates, are particularly interesting, although often less studied. During both the 1992 and 1996 campaigns, all the presidential candidates appeared in simple cloth in contrast to their normal suits and smart shoes. Rawlings usually wore the *batakari,* a traditional smock from the northern region of Ghana, with a muffler of the NDC green, white, red and black colours around his neck, or a white loose smock with NDC party logo – the umbrella – and a muffler around the neck. Similarly, the NPP candidates wore a loose smock made of the party symbol – the elephant – and blue and white colours and the party's neck-scarf. The campaign dressing style was tailored to hit a common chord with the ordinary Ghanaians, at least during the campaign period. By wearing the northern smock, Rawlings, in particular, sought to give expression to the Northern tradition which in the post-Nkrumah past had gained less attraction for the elite in Ghana, in general, and southerners in particular.

All the parties used the cults of past personalities: Kwame Nkrumah, for the Nkrumahist groups (PCP and PNC); J.B. Danquah and Kofi Busiah for the NPP. They promised to continue with the works of their respective icons. Even the NDC, which did not openly adopt any of these iconic images, often implicitly claimed to be Nkrumahist by frequently comparing some its development programmes with that of Nkrumah. For example, at the NDC party's national congress held in September 1996 at Sunyani in mid-north Ghana, one of the party stalwarts, Local Government minister Kwamena Ahwoi, said: 'We have said we will light up the whole country. The opposition call it electricity politics. We call it making Osagyefo Dr Kwame Nkrumah's dream come true'.[37]

Therefore, two main points can be emphasised from the foregoing sections. First, the contending parties during both the 1992 and 1996 elections were not particularly distinct in terms of their political programmes, and hence emphasis was placed on slogans and heckling. To some extent, the symbols and slogans could be seen as the only significant way of explaining the elections to the less formally educated, for example, for whom the whole process was practically meaningless in their daily lives but whose votes were indispensable for any party with a chance of winning the elections. Nevertheless, sloganising indicates the extent of the political elite's manipulation of voters by their pretentious attitudes at rally grounds. Second, the role of personality cult of past icons seemed to have permeated the campaign politics of all the parties. Hence, for the voter, there was no real choice between policy alternatives (this may be one explanatory factor for the victory of Rawlings and the NDC party).

The different timing of the 1992 and 1996 election dates is interesting for its possible strategic implications for the incumbency. In 1996, both the parliamentary and presidential elections were

[35]*Reuters* 14 November 1996.

[36]*Daily Graphic* 4 November 1996.

[37]*West Africa* 16–22 September 1996. The Democratic Peoples Party (DPP), an ally of the NDC, ran a twice weekly full page campaign advert in the *Daily Graphic* titled 'who is a true Nkrumahist' in which it compared the works and achievements of the present government with that of Nkrumah, thus claiming that the government was doing exactly what Nkrumah envisioned for Ghana.

slated for the same day, contrary to the 1992 elections when the parliamentary polls took place a week after the presidential elections. Voting was originally scheduled for Tuesday, 10 December 1996. However, during the first week in August 1996, the NEC changed that date to Saturday 7 December with the argument that the inauguration of the next republic should coincide with the date of the coming into force of the Constitution (7 January). The above explanation given by the NEC touches on the Constitution and may require some legal competence to interpret it, a competence which this writer lacks. However, my reading of that specific provision (PNDCL 282) does not suggest any constitutional bonding for the Fifth Republic to be inaugurated exactly on 7 January. Besides, if that date were so important, it would be totally absurd that a competent electoral commission would have overlooked it when setting the date for national elections, until less than six months to the election. Thus, beneath the legal facade is the following possible reason. Higher voter turnout, particularly in the rural areas, was likely to benefit the government's NDC party,[38] and since Tuesday was a working day, it was likely to affect turnout as most farmers would probably ignore the elections and go to their farms. Hence, the date was changed to Saturday to coincide with national farmers' day off.

In the case of the 1992 elections, the different timing of the presidential and parliamentary votes was probably orchestrated to give a definite advantage to Rawlings himself. Jeffries and Thomas (1993) are probably right to argue that the time-lag was designed to help divorce Rawlings from the increasingly unpopular PNDC. Rawlings enjoyed a fair amount of popularity especially in the rural areas and the northern parts of the country. He was associated with the provision of lights and good roads to certain remote parts of the country (see also Jeffries 1991). However, it seems that if Rawlings wanted his party in parliament in order to facilitate his rule, then such a move could have been a miscalculated risk. This is because, judging from the previous voting patterns, such as in 1979, and as it showed up in the 1996 elections, voters were less likely to differentiate between Rawlings and his party. By separating him from the party, voters could have punished the 'unpopular' P(NDC) parliamentarians once they had voted for their 'favourite' candidate to be the president. At any rate, the 1992 parliamentary elections were virtually an in-house game played among members of the same team. The point, however, is that even though it is not so clear how much electoral benefit the incumbent government gained, and conversely how much the opposition parties lost, from the timing of both the 1992 and 1996 elections, it seems clear that the dates were set with the intention of giving an advantage to the governing party.

Election results: continuity and discontinuity

About 53 per cent of Ghana's estimated 17 million population registered for the 1996 elections. The bulk of the registered electorate (70 per cent) was between the ages of 18 and 39. The gender ratio of the electorate was even, that is, 50 per cent apiece. Similarly, in 1992, INEC reported that more than half (8.3 million) of Ghana's estimated 14–15 million population had registered to vote during the impending elections. On both occasions the opposition parties suspected an over-bloating of the electoral register which, they argued, would facilitate double-voting in favour of the ruling government, and they initially challenged the authenticity of the result. Even though the opposition could not sustain their challenge, apparently for lack of precise and up-to-date population data, the basis for their suspicion was valid. During all past national elections in the country (1954–1979), registered voters have been less than 40 per cent of the population. For example, during the 1969 elections only 2.4 million out of the country's 8.4 million population (about one-quarter) registered. Therefore, it seemed dubious that more than half the population would have attained the voting age during the 1992 elections, let alone registered. Nevertheless, it needs to be said that population issues in Ghana, as in many other developing countries, are tricky as they are normally based on best guesses or estimates, which are often some distance from reality. The same lack of precision extends to estimates of voting population, particularly with regard to those who qualify under the current eligible voting age. Hence, there has always been the potential of over-bloating the voting number. As it later turned out, this was one of the issues which underlay the opposition boycott during the 1992 parliamentary elections (New Patriotic Party 1992).

---

[38]It is commonly known in Ghana that the NDC had a strong rural support base. See also *Africa Confidential* 13 December 1996; *New African* November 1996; *West Africa* 23–29 September 1996.

According to the NEC, 780 candidates registered to contest for the 200 parliamentary seats in the 1996 elections. Of this figure, 725 represented political parties while the remaining 55 were independents, up from 5 in 1992. The NDC fielded candidates for all the constituencies while the NPP and PCP fielded 174 and 98 respectively. During the 1996 elections there were 57 women candidates, most of whom stood on the NDC ticket as against 23 during 1992.

Tables 4.3 and 4.4 show a regional breakdown of the presidential elections of 1996 and 1992 respectively.[39] As can be observed from Tables 4.2 and 4.3, Jerry Rawlings, the incumbent in both elections, standing on the ticket of the NDC and its Progressive Alliance, won with a comfortable margin of nearly 60 and 58 per cent of votes in the 1992 and 1996 polls respectively. The strongest challengers in both elections were the NPP presidential candidates, Albert Adu Boahen in 1992, and John Kuffuor in 1996. They lost on both occasions by winning only 30 per cent and 40 per cent of the votes respectively. In the 1996 parliamentary election, the NDC won 134 seats, representing 66 per cent of the total number of 200 parliamentarians, while the combined opposition won 66 seats (34 per cent). All except 17 of the parliamentarians were male. This meant that women's representation in parliament increased by just one MP from the 1992 number.

In 1992, parliamentary elections were contested only by the NDC and its allies, the EP and the NCP, who won 198 of the 200 parliamentary seats. The remaining two seats went to independent candidates. About 12 per cent (23 seats) of the parliamentary seats were uncontested.

Table 4.3: Regional distribution of the 1992 presidential election results

| Region | Percentage of votes received by candidate | | | | |
	Boahen (NPP)	Rawlings (NDC)	Darko (NIP)	Erskine (PHP)	Limann (PNC)
Western	23	61	6	2	9
G.Accra	37	53	4	1	4
Ashanti	61	33	4	1	3
B.Ahafo	30	62	2	1	5
Volta	1	94	1	1	2
Eastern	39	57	2	1	2
Central	26	67	4	2	2
U.East	11	54	1	2	33
U.West	9	51	2	1	37
Northern	16	63	2	8	33
Total average	25	60	3	2	13

Source: National Electoral Commission of Ghana, December 1996.

Table 4.4: The 1996 presidential elections by regions[40]

| Region | Turnout, per cent | | Candidate | |
| | | Kufuor | Rawlings | Mahama |
			Percentage share of vote	
Western	75	41	57	2
G.Accra	78	43	64	3
Ashanti	80	66	33	2
B.Ahafo	72	36	62	2
Volta	82	5	95	1
Eastern	81	45	54	1
Central	74	43	56	1
U.East	80	17	69	14
U.West	76	11	75	14
Northern	74	6	62	6
Total average	77	31	63	4

Source: National Electoral Commission of Ghana, December 1996.

[39]Since the 1992 parliamentary election was virtually a one-party contest, it does not make sense reproducing the detailed results here, although the differential turnouts between the parliamentary and presidential elections will be used to highlight the ethnic dimension of the elections.

[40]A look at the distribution of votes per region (Tables 4.3 and 4.4), suggests that the NDC won in all but one (the Ashanti) of the ten regions in Ghana during both the 1992 and 1996 presidential elections.

It is important to look at the voter turnout at the elections in order to gauge the level of mobilisation and participation. Admittedly, this is not an adequate barometer to measure actual participation, as it does not show the qualifications of those who actually voted, for example, authenticity of age and the conditions under which voters voted.[41] Nevertheless, turnout will give a rough indication of the conditions under which the elections took place.

The voter turnout during the 1996 presidential and parliamentary elections was nearly 78 per cent of the registered voters, evenly distributed across the regions. The region with the least turnout, the Northern region, produced as high as 74 per cent of registered voters during the polling day. The overall voter turnout was remarkable, particularly given the low turnouts since 1960 as shown in Figure 4.1. In 1996, the turnout in the presidential elections showed a rise of about 30 per cent from the 1992 turnout, which was 48 per cent, while parliamentary votes showed an increase of about 50 per cent. In the regions, the turnout increase in the inter-election periods ranged from 28 to 32 per cent. The notable exception was the Volta region whose 20 per cent change was less dramatic compared to the rest. This was simply because the region's turnout in the previous 1992 election (61 per cent) was about 15 per cent higher than other regions and therefore it could not have risen as much as other regions in 1996. The generally high voter turnout during the 1996 elections can be attributed to two major reasons: a) more vigorous campaigns and stiffer party competition; b) and more importantly, a relatively more credible and transparent electoral procedure, described earlier in this chapter, set in place for the 1996 elections which increased voters' confidence in the electoral process. The increased turnout thus meant that Ghanaians wanted democracy and, given a credible process and open party competition, they were willing to participate and stake a hold in the governance of the country.

Another noticeable issue was the difference in voting pattern between the Volta and Ashanti regions. During the 1996 elections, the Volta region showed a significantly high turnout of 81 per cent. About 95 per cent of the region's votes went in favour of Rawlings with only 5 per cent for Kuffuor, the opposition alliance candidate.[42] Conversely, the NPP candidate won 65 per cent of the

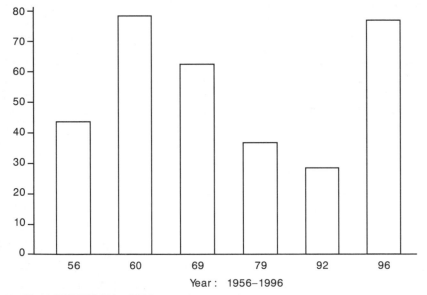

Source: Chazan 1987; NEC 1992 and 1996.

Figure 4.1: Voter turnout in parliamentary elections in Ghana, 1956–1996

---

[41]For example *The Ghanaian Chronicle* (11–12 December 1996) claimed to have observed foreigners (Malians to be precise) and a mad woman vote in Accra.

[42]Edward Mahama, the PNC candidate, received almost nothing (0.7 per cent).

votes in the Ashanti region, a significant rise from his 40 per cent average across the regions while Rawlings lost in that region with only half (32 per cent) of the 60 per cent average votes he won in all the regions.

The 1996 presidential election result in these two regions seems to be an exact replication of the 1992 results. The 61 per cent turnout in the Volta region was about 15 per cent higher than the regional average. Rawlings won almost the same percentage of votes from the regions in 1996 as he did in 1992. Again, the Volta region had an exceptionally high turnout and there was a conspicuous gulf in voting pattern between the Ashanti and the Volta regions. The reason for the sharp differences in voting pattern between the two regions, to which I will return later below, may be ethnic. However, this repetitive voting pattern opens up a can of worms especially regarding the continued tenability of the allegation by the NPP of vote rigging by the (P)NDC government during the 1992 elections.[43] Even though the pattern of vote distribution, in itself, is not a proxy for establishing whether the election was clean, it is difficult to believe that the results could have been constructed under the relatively transparent voting system of the 1996 election.

A superficial look at the results indicates that Rawlings' support dropped by an insignificant amount of 1.2 per cent from 1992 to 1996, while the opposition candidate gained a significant 9 per cent in the later elections. Three possible explanations can be offered. Firstly, it may reflect an improvement in the campaign strategy of the opposition party; secondly, judging from the result of the parliamentary elections, part of the 9 per cent may have been gained from NPP's alliance with PCP for the presidential contest. As we will recall from the previous sections, NPP did not form an alliance with any party in 1992. Finally, the NPP and its allies in the Great Alliance may also have benefited from the substantial voter turnout and fewer party contestants during the 1996 election, which could have split the votes for the alliance.[44] What difference did the 1996 parliament make in terms of composition and possible contribution to the course of democracy in Ghana? Table 4.5 shows the distribution of parliamentary seats according to party. To the extent that parliament included a respectable number of opposition members in parliament, 1996 presented a different picture from the 1992 one. As indicated earlier, three main parties actively participated in both presidential and parliamentary elections. However, the NDC effectively control both the male-dominated legislative and executive arms of government.

Table 4.5: The 1996 parliament: MPs by party

	NDC	NPP	PCP	PNC	Total
Number of seats	134	60	5	1	200

Source: National Electoral Commission.

Yet, it may be a wrong judgement to think that the opposition membership of parliament, representing about 66 MPs (34 per cent), represents a weak parliament as in the previous case. Most of the opposition parliamentarians are relatively experienced politicians and highly educated professionals, mostly lawyers (this is not to say the NDC members are any less qualified or experienced). Given the strong political distance between the NPP and the NDC, it does not seem realistic to think that the former will be bought over by the latter. Moreover, unlike the previous parliament, there is a popular confidence among Ghanaians that parliament with few opposition members is worth more than parliament with none.[45]

In terms of the membership of the parliament, it can hardly be said that it represents continuity with the past. Rather, parliament was made up of many new but inexperienced members, who

---

[43]A re-visit to the debate would be interesting. However, it is beyond the scope of this chapter to go into this See Oquaye (1995) and Jeffries and Thomas (1993) for a lively debate.

[44]As indicated earlier, two of the competing parties during the 1992 elections, NIP and PHP had merged into the PCP.

[45]The view of Mr Kofi Asaah, a teacher at Damang, summarises the popular opinion about the new parliament: 'We knew it was very unlikely to beat Rawlings and the NDC. The only name every school child knows is Rawlings. The people know Rawlings too much. But as long as there are some opposition parliamentarians, things are not going to be easy for the government as it was in the last four years'. Interview, 10 December 1996, Damang.

probably won their seat for lack of serious competition. More than 60 per cent of the 1992 parliamentarians were in parliament for the first time. While the injections of 'new blood' in parliament could represent new ideas and new ways of doing governmental business, the popular fear among Ghanaians was that, given their monolithic party affiliation (NDC and allies) coupled with a preponderance of inexperienced parliamentarians, the 1992 parliament could only pass for a rubber-stamp for the government and an entrenchment of business-as-usual. Whether or not later events will justify this fear is yet to be ascertained. There was a popular concern among my informants that the few experienced parliamentarians dominated parliamentary discussions while their own inexperience and inability to express themselves intimidated the majority.[46] It seems that this assertion was arguably based on the extent of newspaper and radio coverage the MP received. The less media coverage an MP had, the more the public seemed to deem him/her as ineffective.[47] This confidence gap notwithstanding, there were many people, usually not particularly friendly with the government, who were surprised at the depth of some of the parliamentary debate.[48]

With the exception of the vice-President and the Ministers of Education and the Environment, all the 19 cabinet members were a carry-over from the previous military (PNDC) regime. About 90 per cent of all key positions, from the presidency to ministerial levels of the government, were held by the same office holders during the military regime or were activist in one or the other of the many revolutionary groups formed by the regime, notably the CDR.[49] In effect, the multi-party elections were essentially trivialised, and, rather than creating a multi-party state, the 1992 parliamentary elections created a *de facto* one-party state. As common descriptor in Ghana puts it, 'the PNDC government only removed the 'P' out of the acronym of (P)NDC.' It is therefore true that after 11 years of PNDC rule, the return of (P)NDC government represented an element of continuity rather than change.[50]

In any case, the extent of domination by the NDC in both the parliamentary and executive wings of government is, perhaps, not unusual for Ghana's civilian political regimes. Kwame Nkrumah's CPP dominated parliament between 1954 and 1966 with a majority of between 70 and 100 per cent. Similarly, the 1969 elections gave K.A. Busiah's Progressive Party (PP) a nearly 90 per cent majority in parliament. The key exception was the 1979 election, when Hilla Limann's Peoples National Party (PNP) won with a slim majority of 51 per cent in parliament.[51] Thus, though the NDC's dominance in parliament may seem troubling for effective balanced governance, the trend is just a repetition of history. At any rate, this is no less democratic than the Conservative Party's dominance for nearly two decades of the British parliament and the Democratic Party's domination of the American Congress for forty years.

Another issue of great importance in these elections is the rural-urban voting pattern. Most analysts expected or even believed that the results of the two elections would produce a rural-

---

[46]Informal discussions the author held with some educated Ghanaians in Accra underlined the general lack of confidence by some members of the public in the 1992 parliament. A female student of the University of Science and Technology made the following remark about a parliamentarian while listening to a radio interview on Greater Accra Radio on 4 December 1996: 'Listen to his English. Most of them cannot even speak English properly, how can they participate in any serious debate?'. Proceedings of parliament are conducted in English. However, there is no provision in the 1992 constitution, which restricts the use of local language. In practice, it is considered stigmatic for a parliamentarian not to be able to speak English.

[47]This rumour spread so much that the Speaker of Parliament, Justice D.F. Annan had to debunk it at a public forum held by parliament in November 1996 by saying that every parliamentarian played an active role in the house.

[48]Most of them were university graduates, some of whom were critics of the government.

[49]The CDRs were specially created by the PNDC to be the vanguard of the revolution at the grass root level. Other groups included the June Fourth Movement (JFM), Democratic Youth League of Ghana (DYLG), 31 December Women's Movement (31 DWM) and National Mobilisation Programme (NMP).

[50]This is not to suggest that continuity is necessarily evil, especially if the majority of the people want it. In my view, it is wrong to equate democracy with change and to bemoan continuity as inherently suspicious. However, the people must genuinely want such continuity.

[51]One possible reason in the significant difference in the 1979 case is that the 1979 election was the only post-independence election without effective incumbency support. In 1969, the PP arguably drew quite a lot from the incumbent government of the NLC which had overthrown Nkrumah and disbanded the CPP. Likewise, during the 1992 elections, the NDC gained incumbency support by being offspring of the then ruling PNDC.

urban dichotomy. Superficially, the two elections did produce a rural-urban bifurcation as Rawlings cleanly swept the rural votes and lost the urban polls to the opposition. Increasingly, most analysts appear to pin down this voting pattern on the differential impact of the Ghana government's economic policies (Hart 1995; Green 1995; Bawumia 1997). This widely held view is based on the assumption that the rural areas in Ghana have benefited immensely from SAP policies because prices of cocoa and other cash crops have seen significant increases under the SAP regime. Besides, in pursuing the SAP, the government did not cease to make public capital out of rural development projects, including improvement in drinking water, and the construction of roads and electrification (Tabatabai 1986; Herbst 1993; Ewusi 1987). Contrariwise, urban dwellers are reported to have borne the brunt of the SAP through retrenchments and high prices, particularly following the removal of subsidies and the devaluation of the currency (Herbst 1993; Ninsin 1991; Mikel 1989). According to Gwen Mikell (1989) the implementation of the SAP since 1983 represented a U-turn in economic policy whose effect alienated the urban working class and students, on whom Rawlings initially drew for his support. Low rates of income coupled with the reduction of state employment, according to proponents, have created massive urban disaffection with Rawlings and the NDC. The logical antecedent from the foregoing thought is that rural voters would, and indeed did, render their appreciation to their benefactor, the government, by voting to maintain it in power not only to protect their economic fortune but also to enhance it. On the other hand, urban voters voted for the opposition to lash at the government and to protest against their dwindling economic fortune. However, as I explain below, the rural–urban pattern may not represent a clear pattern of 'reward' and 'punishment' by the rural and urban voters respectively of government economic policy.

To illustrate this point I have selected the results of the parliamentary election in constituencies within the capital cities of the 10 regions: Accra, Koforidua, Sekondi-Takoradi, Kumasi, Ho, Tamale, Bolgatanga, Wa, Sunyani and Cape Coast (Table 4.6) as representative urban constituencies.[52] The remaining parts of each region were treated as rural.

Table 4.6: Urban constituencies and parliamentary seats by party

Urban area	NDC	NPP-PCP	PNC	Total
Sekondi/T'di	0	3	0	3
Accra	4	4	0	8
Kumasi	0	4	0	4
Sunyani	0	2	0	2
Ho	3	0	0	3
Koforidua	0	1	0	1
Cape Coast	0	1	0	1
Bolgatanga	1	0	0	1
Wa	2	0	0	2
Tamale	0	1	0	1
Total:	10	16	0	26

Source: Computed from National Electoral Commission election results.

It is evident from Table 4.6 that the opposition alliance, NPP and PCP, showed stronger in the urban areas, winning 16 seats or 60 per cent of the 26 urban constituencies. Conversely, Rawlings and the NDC won about 75 per cent of what may be considered as the rural votes. The opposition support within the urban constituencies derives largely from the working class, particularly the

---

[52]Apart from the regional capitals, there was no non-controversial definition of what constituted rural and urban constituencies. For example, Tarkwa is a fairly large town and a district capital in south-western Ghana. It has a population of about 25,000 people and a fairly well developed infrastructure such as hospitals, roads, electricity and pipe-bome water. But, as an electoral constituency, it includes other typical villages such as Nsuaem and Boboobo, which have populations of less than 2000 people and lack almost all the infrastructure identified with Tarkwa. Indeed, the highly aggregated nature of available data on the 1996 election results makes it problematic to say anything substantial about the urban-rural voting pattern.

trade unions which remained largely hostile to the government,[53] and the intellectuals – including university lecturers and students – as well as the unemployed secondary school leavers, mostly rural–urban emigrants. The NDC, on the other hand, built its urban support mainly around the former CDRs and the market women (particularly in Accra) through the 31 December Women's Movement (31 DWM) under the leadership of the First lady, Nana Konadu Agyeman Rawlings.

In my opinion, the difference of about 20 per cent in the urban votes between the NDC and the opposition alliance was not significant enough to constitute a clear dichotomy. Furthermore, as the winning party, the NDC won fairly good percentages of votes and seats in both urban and rural constituencies, and the opposition parties, particularly NPP and PCP, also won respectable numbers of seats in some rural constituencies. For example, with the exception of 5 constituencies, the NPP won all seats, including 23 rural constituencies, in the Ashanti Region. Thus, empirical evidence from the voting pattern in the 1996 elections does not unambiguously support a clear-cut rural–urban dichotomy, although some gyration in the voting pattern may suggest so.

Even though Rawlings and the NDC won comfortably in the rural areas, it seems to me that the reasons often assumed for the possible rural support were exaggerated and problematic. The widely-held argument (for example Bawumia 1998; Herbst 1993; Mikell 1989) that the SAP policies have largely benefited the producers of cash crops such as cocoa is true but only to some extent. True, the price of cocoa and other cash crops, the production of which is rural-based, have increased five-fold since 1984. Yet, income gains for farmers appear only slowly since most of the cash crops have relatively long gestation periods. For example, it takes seven years for a cocoa tree to yield a crop (ISSER 1994, 47; Herbst 1993, 82–83). Besides, only a minority of farmers would have benefited from the price improvements given that only a minority of farmers are in the cash crop sector. In fact, the terms of trade shifted against non-cash crops. The food sector, which is populated by the majority of farmers, still continues to suffer from the increased cost of inputs, price slumps and storage problems. As the World Bank concedes, 'the benefit of growth accompanying the Economic Recovery Programme may not have been enjoyed by many outside of cocoa production' (World Bank 1993, 31). It is also a fact accepted by the government and the World Bank that the majority of the poor in Ghana are domiciled in the rural areas and that people in the rural areas are still, absolutely, poorer now than they were in the mid-1970s (World Bank 1995; Herbst 1993; ISSER 1992–96). Therefore, the impact of increased cocoa prices could have been narrower than often estimated and it is contradictory that the SAP policy package, whose implementation is believed to have exacerbated rural poverty, would at the same time generate a political constituency for the government.

In the next section, I discuss the 'real issues' and undercurrents that provided the basis for the outcome of the 1996 elections. I argue on two key fronts: firstly, I contend that the severity of poverty in both urban and rural Ghana has made most Ghanaian voters susceptible to various economic manipulations; secondly, the pre-election fear among Ghanaians that the outcome of the election could lead to chaos and violence similar to the then prevailing situation in Liberia significantly influenced the choice of voters. As it will become apparent, the incumbency took full advantage of this collection of uncertainties by generating various schemes that would transform and harness them into electoral votes, in favour of the NDC party.

Pork-barrelling and other undercurrents

To understand how economic policies were used during the elections, it is imperative to understand the socio-economic situation of the country that foreshadowed the elections. Ghana, like most countries in Africa, experienced accelerated economic decline during the 1970s and early 1980s. From the mid-1970s to 1983 when the Provisional National Defence Council (PNDC) government began to implement neo-liberal political economy policies within the framework of Structural Adjustment Programme, Ghana's GDP growth declined to an annual average rate of minus 3 per cent. Income per capita was a little over US$300. Indeed the state of the economy

---

prior to the implementation of the SAP could, at the best, be described as miserable.

Admittedly, however, the tides began to turn from the mid-1980s when SAP policies started to impact on the economy. In terms of general macroeconomic stability, there is little dispute that the SAP has made a significant impact on the economy. Ghana experienced a remarkable macroeconomic turn-around after a decade of stagnation. Real GDP has grown at a consistent average rate of about 5 per cent between 1984 and 1995 compared to the decline of 3 per cent per annum during the preceding period of 1976–83. Gross fixed capital formation which had fallen from 12 per cent of GNP in 1970 to 3 per cent in 1982, picked up to 6 per cent in 1984 and 9 per cent by 1986. By 1994, Gross Domestic Investment was about 12 per cent of GDP. Inflation rates have been reduced from the triple-digit (around 120 per cent) during 1980–83, to double-digit, although they have yet to reach the 4 per cent rate recorded in 1970 (Leith 1996, 6).

However, much as the implementation of the SAP generally improved the economy, poverty has still been rife, especially in rural areas of the country (World Bank 1995, 207–208; Sandbrook 1996; Hutchful 1995; Cornia *et al.* 1988). Ghana's current income per capita of US$430 is still lower than in 1970 (US$450). Although real income per capita has grown at a rate of 3 per cent between 1984 and 1989 compared to a decline of 4 per cent in the decade before adjustment, measured in terms of standard of living, the level of real per capita income in Ghana was only two-thirds its level in 1980 and about one-third its level in 1970 (Ewusi 1987, 54–60; ISSER 1992).[54] Poverty is widespread with massive urban unemployment following the retrenchment exercise that followed from the SAP policies. The institution of health and user-fees in the social service sector and the persistent depreciation of the Ghanaian currency (the *cedis*), all products of the SAP, have served to increase the cost of living, particularly for those in the formal sector and depending on fixed income. The gradual neo-patrimonialisation of the state has also seen the steady return of *Kalabule*,[55] a social cancer that prevailed in the 1970s and against which Rawlings claimed to have launched his revolution (Dzorgbo 1998, 248–9). These negativities of the SAP's impact have made many voters susceptible to various economic manipulations, such as bribery through subtle means such as fiscal deficit and direct handing out of 'gifts' in cash or kind.

Evidence from the 1992 elections in Ghana suggests a clear attempt by the government to 'buy' votes through the fiscal box. Ghana's fiscal balance had, since 1986, shown a sustained surplus, albeit at an irregular rate, until 1992 (ISSER 1994, 9; World Bank 1995, 207). Figure 4.2 shows the fiscal balance as a percentage of GDP between 1989 and 1996. In 1992, the budget moved from a surplus of 2 per cent of GDP to a deficit of 5 per cent in 1991. Although the government's surplus had been declining since 1988, it is inconceivable that it would have incurred a deficit of that extent had 1992 not been an election year. Two facts about the intentionality of the government regarding the 1992 fiscal deficit are noteworthy. Firstly, the deficit occurred just three months before the 1992 elections when the government increased civil service wages by 80 per cent (World Bank 1995).[56] Secondly, immediately after the elections strong corrective measures were adopted to reduce the deficit by nearly 50 per cent to 2.1 per cent of GDP in 1993 and to a surplus of 1 per cent in 1994. Thus, given the timing of the deficit and the rapidity of its correction, there is little doubt that the (P)NDC government made a fat pork-barrel appropriation in order to

---

[54]The situation was better for cocoa farmers whose incomes rose as a result of increase in real producer prices. Herbst (1993) argues, however, that the impact of the improved cocoa prices may be minimal since it takes about 6 years for a new cocoa plant to mature. I agree with him. But in addition, it is well known that only less than half the Ghanaian farming populace is into cocoa farming. Therefore, the impact of increased cocoa prices could have been narrower than often estimated.

[55]Many journalistic and impressionistic accounts maintain that a new form of patron–client relationship has emerged in which government contracts, particularly for road-building, have gone only to NDC party supporters and government officials who demand kickbacks and political favours. *Kalabule* is a term in Ghana coined to describe the illicit and corrupt business behaviour often based on profiteering and cronyism. General Acheampong's SMC regime in the 1970s is often described as the period when corruption and *kalabuleism* in Ghana reached its apogee. This social cancer is now believed to be creeping back into the country as a result of the prevailing economic hardships.

[56]The president of the World Bank, J. Wolfensohn, corroborated this point when he blamed Ghana's 1992 budget deficit and the subsequent inflation on the imperatives of Ghana's 1992 elections (*Reuters* 12 February 1997).

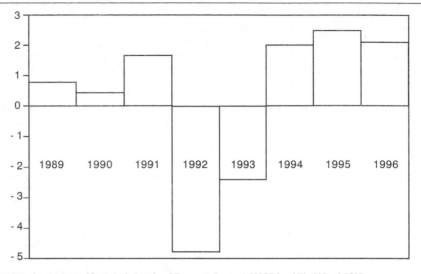

Source: *Based on Institute of Statistical, Social and Economic Research 1995/96 and World Bank 1995.*

Figure 4.2: Fiscal balance, 1989–1996

boost its own electoral fortunes. It is worthwhile noting that evidence from two previous elections in 1969 and 1979 does not unequivocally support the fiscal deficit thesis that governments increase budget deficits during election periods ostensibly to buy votes as suggested by Schuknecht (1994). During both periods, the extent of the fiscal deficit actually fell. During the 1969 election period, for example, the deficit fell from 7 per cent during the previous year to 3 per cent.

With regard to the 1996 elections, the government did not expand the deficit as it did in 1992, probably realising the negative macroeconomic consequences of deficit financing during the previous elections, coupled with warnings from the World Bank.[57] Indeed, as can be seen in Figure 4.2, the 1996 budget showed a modest surplus of about 2 per cent. Nevertheless, manipulation of the fiscal deficit policy was only one of the many incumbency advantages exploited by the government. For example, the government increased the price of cocoa just two months before the elections, a move that has been described by *Africa Confidential* (1 November 1996) as a 'shrewd vote-winning move'. Dee Roberts (1996) has catalogued a number of incumbency advantages in political economy exploited by the NDC during the 1996 elections. Her study observed two examples of practical political economy manipulation: a) development project delivery and b) direct bribery through the distribution of gifts, such as cash, T-shirts, and cutlasses. In 1996, the NDC government, running on its record of investing in rural areas, pumped 81 billion cedis (US$47 million) into the district assemblies as against the 56 billion cedis in the previous year. The effectively pro-NDC district assemblies would apparently use this fund in ultimate consolidation of NDC support at the rural and grassroots levels. Moreover, during the inter-election period many rural and urban development projects such as the repairing of old roads and construction of new roads, water, and electricity were either begun or those which had been left unattended for many years, were reactivated. In the run up to the election, the President went on a whirlwind tour of commissioning new, old, and according to some suspicions, even non-starter projects (Roberts 1996). In some cases, as in some parts of the Nzima districts, electric poles were presented and wiring promised after the elections. Similarly, it was difficult to separate state office holders from their positions as party candidates vying in an election. Access to presidential heli-

---

[57]One of the major consequences of budget deficits is inflation. The government's deficit policy in 1992 fired a high inflationary rate from around 18 per cent in 1991 to about 70 per cent in 1994. The IMF urged the government to keep inflation down to about 25 per cent in 1996. See *West Africa* 11–17 November 1996, 4124.

copters and other official vehicles, in the mask of performing official duties, made it possible for the NDC to penetrate many remote areas, which would have been impossible for the opposition parties given the weakness of their logistical resources.[58] It has been reported that 200 brand new Toyota 4-wheel drive vehicles were distributed to all NDC constituencies.[59] While the government had a definite electoral advantage in appearing to be caring, the opposition had nothing practical to demonstrate to the electorate, thereby accentuating the unevenness of the field of political competition. The opposition had a weak financial base not only because their support came from individual business people but because they were constrained by a constitutional clause that limited individual contributions to one million cedis a year (Dzorgbo 1998). Yet, opposition parties were able to show how some of the projects had been abandoned after the 1992 elections. In a taxi cab at Takoradi, a middle-aged woman pointed at construction work going on around the Takoradi market and commented:

> This road had been like that for the past three years. Nothing had been done. How come all of a sudden the bulldozers are here trying to make heaven on earth? We saw that in 1992 and we are not going to sit down this time (Interview, 2 December 1996, Takoradi).

While the development project vote-buying game was played exclusively by the incumbent party, the same cannot be said of the direct use of cash and gifts in enticing voters. All the major parties used direct inducements, although the NDC was able to use state resources to give more. Rumours of buying voters' ID cards were common over the two months before the elections. For example, during September 1996, some NDC activists in the Shama constituency in the Western region were alleged to have collected voters' ID cards from certain individuals under the pretext of offering jobs and loans.[60] The information about which party bought ID cards depended on which vehicle of the highly-polarised media was reporting on the incidents.[61] It was also common, especially in Accra and other big cities, to hear of the payment of cash and distribution of T-shirts to entice people to the rally grounds. Yet, it was also common for voters to conveniently take inducements irrespective of which candidate or party they intended to vote for. An apprentice mechanic said in Takoradi:

> I have all the parties' T-shirts. I have attended all the big rallies. I took 5000 cedis and a T-shirt from the NDC man, 3000 from NPP and just a T-shirt from Mahama's people [PNC]. I think it's good fun. All the politicians are the same. At least after the elections my brother can use the T-shirts to play football. Only God knows whom I will vote for at the ballot day. In fact I myself don't know yet (Interview).

---

[58]The opposition parties rightly complained about the issue of over-exploitation of incumbency advantage during the 1992 elections. However, in the 1996 election, the complaint was rather meek and feeble. Three reasons may account for why the complaints could not be sustained: a) the parties were over-confident about their support base; b) there was probably the feeling of hopelessness that even if they exerted much energy confronting the incumbent on the above question, there would be no change; c) the opposition parties grappled with their own moral uncertainty as to whether they would have done less if they were in power. For example during the 1992 elections period, a former president of Ghana and a presidential candidate of the PNC, Dr Hilla Limann, conceded in an interview that he would have done the same thing if he were in power *(West Africa* 16–22 November 1992, 1962; see also Jeffries and Thomas 1993, 339).

[59]I could not confirm whether the vehicles were paid for by the government or the NDC party itself. However, newspaper reports after the elections seem to suggest that most of the NDC campaign vehicles were official vehicles which were immediately repainted after the elections. See for instance *New Africa* November 1996; *The Independent* January 1997.

[60]*West Africa* 16–22 September 1996. There were newspaper reports about the arrest of culprits. See various issues of *Free Press, Ghanaian Chronicle, The Democrat, The Independent* and *Daily Graphic* between September and December 1996.

[61]The liberalised media in Ghana was quite polarised. The state media, *Daily Graphic, Ghanaian Times, and Ghana Television,* as well as a few private newspapers like the *Democrat* and *Horizon* were in many respects pro-government NDC. On the other hand, almost all the main private newspapers *Free Press, The Stateman* and *Ghanaian Chronicle* were openly biased against the government. The FM radio stations, which were mainly urban-based, were fairly balanced, by my own assessment.

The above attitude was not uncommon. One could see, in taxicabs, passenger trucks, and on the doors of shops and malls, posters of all the parties, although it was not possible to tell whether gifts had been received from all parties. Thus, a series of political and economic manipulations unsurprisingly were carried out by politicians, particularly the incumbency, to win the hearts and minds of voters during both the 1992 and 96 elections. The discussions so far may carry an impression that the voter was completely choiceless and only subject to external manipulations. In the following section, I will discuss how voters internalised the political economy environment of the day, including the influence of ethnicity, in forming their choices. In other words, some answers are provided to the questions of why people voted for Rawlings (and the NDC) against Kufuor (and the opposition alliance) and vice versa. Particular attention is paid to differences in rural–urban perception.

Why vote Rawlings or Kufuor?

To gain a deeper insight into the reasons for voters' choice, the respondents in my sample were asked to give the 'most important' reasons why they voted for Rawlings and the NDC or the opposition.

Table 4.7: Reasons for voting for Rawlings and the NDC

Reason	Percentage of respondents	
	Urban	Rural
Improvements in economy	22	35
Political stability	26	20
Fear of violence	34	20
Lack of confidence in opposition	13	25
The sake of change	5	–
Total	100	100

Several reasons accounted for the choice of Rawlings and the NDC by both the rural and urban voters, the most important of which are summarised in Table 4.7.[62] For rural voters, the economy was the single most important issue that influenced their choice of the NDC as evidenced by 35 per cent of the respondents. Availability of essential commodities such as soap, sugar and milk in the market, as well as increases in cocoa prices were the key economic reasons for voting for the government, although almost all respondents within this category were quick to point out that higher prices made it difficult for them to purchase the available essential goods. 'But at least you can see the things in the market. So if you have your money you can always buy what you want, unlike 15 years ago where there was neither money nor the goods,' said a 42-year-old primary school teacher (Interview, 7 December 1996, Takoradi). For the urban voters in Accra and Takoradi, the economic situation was not as important (22 per cent) as it was for their rural counterparts.

It was also clear that for the bulk of pro-Rawlings/NDC voters in both rural (65 per cent) and urban (73 per cent) areas, the real issues that combined to influence their choices were the need for political stability, the fear of violence if the NDC lost, and the lack of confidence that any substantial change would occur in their lives if the opposition came to power. The last factor seemed to be of particular importance to the rural voters which also seemed to reflect their conception of electoral democracy: 'a good thing that brought nothing'. A 60-year-old woman at Damang told me 'it is important for me to vote because it is my right, but I know this brings me no profit. I don't expect any change, no matter who gets there.'[63] For the majority of the urban voters, a combination of fear of political instability (26 per cent) and the impact of violence if one party would not accept the results (34 per cent), underlined their reasons for voting Rawlings. The

---

[62]The urban respondents were from Takoradi and Accra.
[63]The field assistants, who visited two other rural areas around Esiama, Half Assini and Swedru, reported the same lack of belief that whoever came into power could bring any significant change in their lives.

respondents believed that post-election violence could be initiated by either the Great Alliance parties (NPP and PCP) or the NDC and its Progressive Alliance parties (EP and DPP).[64] However, they perceived Rawlings and the NDC as being more capable of causing or/and controlling violence than the opposition parties. This was probably because, as the government party, the NDC controlled the state coercive apparatus including paramilitary commando groups.[65]

The fear of possible violence begun to build up in the cities already two months before the election and had, by three weeks before the elections, developed into a conflicting sense of enthusiasm and tension. The tension in the country during the run up to the elections can be partly explained by the fact that 1996 was the first serious electoral contest since 1979 and therefore generated concern about what might happen after the elections and how individuals intended to settle scores with their rivals. This concern was exacerbated by what became a near-credible rumour in Accra and other urban areas such as Kumasi, Cape Coast and Sekondi-Takoradi that the losing parties might not accept the results of the elections and might resort to violence which could lead to civil war.[66] The already heightened political tension was fuelled by the use of insults and abusive language and scare-mongering by the politicians during the campaign. The NDC (and the Progressive Alliance) candidates referred to the parties at the other side of the aisle as 'punks', 'nation wreckers' and 'thieves'. The opposition parties, particularly the NPP, on the other hand, described the NDC as 'murderers', 'rascals' and 'deceivers'. For example, during a campaign rally at Sekondi, one of the major cities in southern Ghana, Rawlings was alleged to have said the following: 'If we make a mistake and lose power, there is no way we can get it back again. Perhaps we can only get it through another June 4 … If June 4 repeats itself 10 times, I will do what I did then 10 times over.'[67] Such a pronouncement created the fear that Rawlings would 'come back' through a *coup d'état* if he lost the elections and this heightened the tension. An extract from a state-owned newspaper report sums up the situation:

> The Trade Union Congress (TUC) yesterday expressed concern about the recent spate of political violence and tension in parts of the country creating uncertainty around the forthcoming elections … Mr. Christian Appiali-Agyei, Secretary-general of the TUC, asked the politicians who trade insults as their instrument of politicking, to desist from that to save the country from 'the difficult social situation and strife that can follow electoral violence'.[68]

This negative intercourse between members of the political elite during both election periods cannot be described as just political heckling reminiscent of party campaigns in Britain and the USA, because it often led to violent clashes among party supporters.[69] For example, on the weekend of the 26–27 October 1996, there were violent clashes between NDC and NPP supporters at Tamale in the North and Kibi in the mid-East in which at least 20 people were severely beaten and seriously wounded.[70] Similarly, on 30 November 1996, barely 7 days before the elections, a group of NPP supporters attacked the NDC party office in Kumasi during a rally by the former and killed at least one person. Therefore, it is likely that many voters voted for Rawlings/NDC to avoid violence or to ensure peace and stability in the country.

---

[64]The PNC was generally seen to be too weak to be harmful.

[65]It was commonly believed by people in Accra and Kumasi that the NDC had an organised group of people called the *machomen* (physically built and trained young men) who were capable of causing violence in the event that the NDC lost the elections.

[66]The rumours became widespread and attracted the concern of organised groups like religious bodies and trade unions. Most of the religious groups devoted the last two weeks before the elections to prayer and fasting to forestall the widely perceived post-election violent situation.

[67]*The Ghanaian Chronicle* 18 November 1996. The same story was filed by the *Independent* and the *Free Press*. 4 June 1979 was Rawlings' first appearance on Ghana's political scene through a military take-over.

[68]*The Ghanaian Times* 5 November 1996.

[69]Both the private and public news media regularly reported clashes between opposing political parties and related deaths. See for instance the October to December 1996 issues of the *Daily Graphic, The Ghanaian Times, The Statesman, Free Press, The Ghanaian Chronicle, The Independent* and the *Ghana Review International*.

[70]*West Africa* 4–10 November 1996; *Africa Confidential* 1 November 1996.

The question then can be turned thus: why vote for Kufuor and the opposition? Table 4.8 summarises the reasons why some voters voted for the opposition (presumably against the government).

Table 4.8: Reasons for voting for Kufuor and the opposition

Reason	Percentage of respondents	
	Urban	Rural
Improvements in economy	35	20
Political stability	5	15
Fear of violence	10	20
Lack of confidence in government	15	10
The sake of change	35	35
Total	100	100

Unsurprisingly, 35 per cent of the sampled urban voters were highly dissatisfied with the economic situation under Rawlings. They were not particularly impressed with the government's economic achievements because of high unemployment (30 per cent of labour force) and the high prices of essential goods. Among both urban and rural voters, opinions were divided as to whether the opposition parties could improve the economy. Fifty-five per cent believed that the economy would improve under the opposition while 45 per cent were not sure. This, in effect, meant that most of the opposition voters wanted a change. There were 35 per cent apiece of both urban and rural pro-opposition voters who explicitly said they voted for the opposition for 'the sake of change'. Nearly 80 per cent of all respondents recognised the contribution of Rawlings in repairing the economy and especially his contribution in evacuating Ghanaian emigrants from Nigeria and the Ivory Coast in 1982 and 1995 respectively.[71] However, they thought that, somehow, a change would be better: 'He has tried his best, he should let somebody else come and try', was a common explanation given by respondents in this category.

Finally, evidence from our survey suggests a firm consideration that voting, by both rural and urban voters, was a duty and right which they must exercise. It was also evident that for the younger generation of 18–25 years, in both rural and urban areas, it was the campaigning funfair, the distribution of T-shirts and cash, the convivial feeling at party rallies, jingles, and blaring music that interested them. It needs to be said that there was no post-election violence as was widely feared, probably because of the relatively transparent voting process including 4000 trained non-partisan monitors both from home and abroad which gave credence to the outcome of the elections. In addition, unlike the 1992 elections, the unsuccessful candidates in the elections publicly conceded defeat shortly after the results were released and congratulated the victor. I now turn to the ethnic undercurrents that influenced the outcome of the elections.

The main ethnic groups in Ghana are nominally Akan (44 per cent), Moshi-Dagomba (16 per cent), Ewe (13 per cent) and Ga-Adangbe (8 per cent) (World Factbook 1995). Within the Akan group there are component cleavages such as the Wassa, Fanti and Asanti. Ethnic conflicts in Ghana have been relatively restrained although, from time to time, multi-party politics in the country has excited and sensitised ethnic consciousness (Austin 1964; Chazan 1987; 1988; Herbst 1993). The 1996 elections, like all previous ones, re-ignited and intensified the Asanti-Ewe political feud whose history lay beyond the Rawlings era.[72] Rawlings, the presidential candidate

---

[71]Between 1981 and 1982, over 1 million Ghanaians were expelled from Nigeria by the Nigerian government. Also, in 1995 many Ghanaians living in Côte d'Ivoire had to leave the country because of attacks by local citizens. The source of these attacks was believed to have emanated from a soccer match between the two countries. The recurrence of the issue of evacuation of Ghanaians as far back as the early 1980s was interesting because it indicated that voters did not only consider immediate issues, but also considered past relevant issues in their calculation of who to vote for.

[72]The two important undercurrents to the revival of political distaste among the Asantis and Ewes are the execution of three former heads of state of Akan ethnicity (two Asantis and an Akwapim) in 1979 and what has been perceived as the marginalisation of the Asantis in Ghana's politics.

for the NDC is an ethnic Ewe from the Volta region while both Kufuor and Boahen, the presidential candidates for the opposition parties during the 1996 and 1992 elections, respectively, are ethnic Asantis from the Ashanti, one of Ghana's 10 administrative regions. As can be inferred from Table 4.4, Rawlings won 95 per cent (690,421) of the votes and his NDC party swept all 19 seats in the predominantly Ewe Volta Region. In contrast, Rawlings and his NDC party gained only 32 per cent of votes, and won only 5 out of the 33 seats in the Ashanti Region which is about 98 per cent Asanti by ethnic composition. Kufuor and the NPP won nearly 66 per cent of the votes and 27 of the total 33 seats in the region. It is highly unlikely that these two ethnic entities voted for the respective parties because they preferred the policies of one party to the other. Clearly, the Asantis and the Ewes largely voted on the basis of their ethnic configurations. That is, Asanti voters did not vote for an Ewe candidate and vice versa. From the point of view of past elections in the country, both the 1996 and 1992 results *per se* are not very enlightening since no Asanti-based parties of the UGCC-UP tradition have ever won in the ethnically Ewe regions. The issue is the widening extent of the Ewe-Asanti political bifurcation. To provide a full explanatory background will require a separate study. Instead, I will give here only a brief background to this major factor that shaped the Ewe-Asanti voting pattern.

The Asantis long ruled many of the neighbouring ethnic groups until 1900 when their rule was destroyed by the invading armies of the British empire. Today, the Asantis are associated with commercial prosperity. The Ewes, roughly 13 per cent of Ghana's population, are poor and have sought wealth largely through the state's institutions, notably the army. It has been claimed that since his inception into power in 1981, Rawlings' inner circle has been dominated by Ewes with military backgrounds.[73] In 1989, Albert Adu Boahen, who later became the 1992 presidential candidate of the Ashanti-based NPP, argued in a J.B. Danquah Memorial lecture:

> Whether Rawlings is aware of this or not, this situation [all top government positions being held by Ewes] is giving an unfortunate impression that the country is being ruled by the single ethnic group [Ewe], and this impression is causing, …anger and irritation (Boahen 1989, 53).

Whether or not this allegation is empirically valid, it seemed to have struck a chord with a large number of the Akan population during the campaign and so much so that the Ewe hegemony thesis was apparently accepted by many without question (Aryee 1996). The NPP itself seemed to have been formed as a counter-group to stop what it perceived as an increasing Ewe domination in the politics of Ghana. Hence, for the Ewes, it was important to turn out massively and to vote overwhelmingly for their ethnic compatriot to protect and maintain the *status quo*. For the Asantis, a vote for Rawlings and the NDC would only perpetuate their marginalisation in the political arena, and it was important for them to close their ranks and vote *against* the Rawlings regime.

However, ethnic voting did not happen in all other areas. In the Upper West and Upper East regions, which were not so central in Asanti-Ewe ethnic politics, Rawlings and his party won all 20 seats. Even in the predominantly Akan constituencies in central and southern Ghana, voting was fairly well distributed among the parties. As can be seen in Table 4.9, out of a total of 101 ethnically Akan constituencies which I identified, Rawlings, and the NDC party won about 52 per cent while the opposition alliance won 48 per cent.[74] As I have indicated already, even in the opposition heartland of the Ashanti region, Rawlings and the NDC won a respectable number of votes and gained some 5 seats in the parliamentary polls. Thus, the 1996 election deepened the ethnic divide between the Asantis and Ewes.

However, to a large extent, many voters, as in the Akan constituencies, ignored narrow ethnic considerations. It is not possible to conclude, as it was widely believed, that ethnicity necessarily subverted the extent of participation and the legitimacy of Rawlings and the NDC. While voters may have voted for Rawlings and the NDC party for various reasons, the question of ethnicity, nonetheless, still remains a potential factor. In a multi-ethnic country like Ghana, politicised

---

[73]Boahen 1989; *Africa Research Bulletin* 33 (12) 1996.
[74]The identification was based on available ethnic maps and other literature sources as well as my own knowledge of the country.

ethnicity seems to be one of the hazards of liberal democracy. The potential for ethnicity being ignited and exploited during multi-party campaigns to boost the electoral fortunes of politicians is real.

Table 4.9: Distribution of votes in the Akan constituencies by parties

Region	Number of constituencies by party Total	NDC	NPP/PCP
Western	19	12	7
Central	15	13	2
Ashanti	33	5	28
Eastern	21	10	11
Volta[75]	2	2	0
Brong Ahafo	21	17	4
Total Akan	101	59	52

Conclusions

I have described in some detail and within a certain degree of historical context the two major presidential and parliamentary elections held in the 1990s and provided a comparative framework within which the period of the second wave of democratisation in Ghana can be seen. I have further underlined the extent of advancement towards liberal democracy that the elections within this period have sought to achieve. This study arrives at the following conclusions:

• The elections held during the period under consideration have been significant both in process and content. The 1996 elections in particular represented a break with the past where transfer of political power had always been mediated by military adventurism into politics. Thus, the simple actuality of elections, for the first time since independence, as the only legitimate means of transferring political power or renewing a mandate in Ghana makes the 1996 elections a landmark in the country's political history and an advance in its search for liberal democracy.

• The 1996 election brought in its trail some institutional changes such as inter-party review of the voters' register, voter-ID cards, the transparent ballot box and the open/outdoor voting system that enriched the external quality of the electoral process. Furthermore, the 1992 constitution within whose framework the 1996 election was conducted, provided for an independent electoral commission with a wide range of clear-cut functions. These new changes combined to raise voters' confidence in the electoral process which, in turn, led to a very significant increase in the level of participation. Besides, the presence of a large number (over 4000) of both foreign and local observers, whose verdict was an unanimous declaration of the 1996 election as 'free, fair and credible', gave credibility to Ghana's election process. This was contrary to the situation in 1992 when the election results were widely believed to have been rigged.

• Nevertheless, the improvement in the institutional environment per se, did not ensure a process of fair elections. One setback was the composition of the Electoral Commission whose appointment was entirely controlled by the President. Coupled with this, the expansion of the responsibility of the NEC did not go with concomitant commitment of adequate logistical resources, which thus impaired the ability of the commission to discharge its duties without partiality.

• On the election itself, pork-barrelling and fear of civil war played an effective role in the voting process. The incumbent NDC party that won on both occasions had an undue electoral advantage over its opposition competitors. There was not only unbridled exploitation of state resources by the NDC, like many an incumbent government party, but it effectively employed

---

[75]There are Akan enclaves in the predominantly Ewe Volta region which made up two electoral constituencies, the Akan and Biakoye constituencies.

pork-barrelling politics. As I have noted earlier in this chapter, during the 1992 elections the incumbent (P)NDC government manipulated the fiscal budget to calm dissent and, invariably, to buy votes. Handing out cash and other kinds of gifts were used by all contesting parties to win votes. Also in both 1996 and 1992, election dates were fixed in a subtle way to give a definite advantage to the incumbent party.

- Moreover, inter-elite rivalry galvanised into expectations of post-elections violence and created a tense fear among the electorate. This tense pre-election environment appears to have been strategically orchestrated by the politicians and at the end of it all, played a very important role in voters' decisions as to which party to vote for during the 1996 election. Apparently, many voters voted for J.J. Rawlings, and the NDC, not necessarily because of a passionate loyal attachment to them or any fervid approval of their economic policy but because, in addition to voters' lack of confidence in the opposition parties in bringing about change in their lives, they feared violence if Rawlings and the NDC lost the elections.
- Both the 1996 and the 1992 elections deepened the *Ewe-Asanti*, highly politicised, ethnic tension. It was clear from the elections that an Ewe did not vote for an *Asanti* candidate and vice versa, no matter how good the policy intentions of the candidate would have been. Although the election results, *per se*, do not allow for a sweeping conclusion of widespread ethnic tension during the elections, ethnic differences were tacitly employed during the campaigns and still have the potential of being manipulated by political parties for electoral gain, with possible negative consequences.
- Will there be a Rawlings-third force tradition? It seems to me that J.J. Rawlings will success-fully establish a third force tradition as a significant challenge to the UGCC/UP-Danquah-Busiah and the Nkrumahists/CPP traditions. One noticeable implication of Rawlings' political longevity is that it has brought the Ghanaian state under his personal rule with a key imperative of perpetuating NDC hegemony. This conscious 'project' appears to be possible in the face of the absence of ideological differences between all three political forces in the country and weak, ill-organised competing parties. In the absence of ideology, the NDC seems to have become the melting pot for politicians within the political margins of centre-right Danquah-Busiahs and the leftist Nkrumahist political factions. The NDC leadership is made up of former Nkrumahists and Danquah-Busiahist and employs socialist rhetoric to implement centre-right economic policies. With hindsight from Ghana's political historical environment, one could say that this approach might be appealing to a growing number of pragmatist politicians, espe-cially with the death of ideology. Similarly, judging from the party organisation and performance during both the 1992 and 1996 elections, it seems that the Nkrumahist group appears to be too feeble and fragmented and it will be extremely difficult to bridge this division to make the party the formidable and winsome political force of former years. The relatively well-organised Danquah-Busiah group, which has a low track record of winning elections (won only in 1969), did not offer enough, in relation to the incumbent, to make regime change likely. Formation of the opposition alliance did not prove to be a viable strategic alternative as it was hampered by internal bickering and strong differences. Finally, having been at the centre of Ghana's political scene for nearly 18 years, Rawlings was arguably the most well-known personality in Ghana particularly by the youth. One could rightly argue that Kwame Nkrumah and Kofi Busiah are indisputably the most important national heroes in the country. Nevertheless, most young voters (between the ages of 18 and 35 years) who form about 70 per cent of the electorate did not see or remember them. Hence, for the current generation, Rawlings is the leader they are familiar with. Therefore, a Rawlings-third force tradition is likely to emerge with the possibility of this engulfing the Nkrumahist groups in particular.

5

Multi-Party Elections in Guinea-Bissau

LARS RUDEBECK

Framework of analysis

Elections, democracy and democratisation in Africa and elsewhere

The editors of this volume emphasise in a background paper that while 'a competitive electoral process cannot in itself be equated with democracy, free and fair electoral competition is a cardinal precept of liberal democracy'. Thus, 'as elsewhere in the world, a detailed analysis of elections is part of an understanding of the possibilities and constraints of democratisation in Africa' (Cowen and Laakso 1997a, 2). They also recommend a political economy approach to such analysis, applied within a historical perspective, in order to 'counter prevailing impressions that there is something essential about the African experience, which makes it essentially different from the rest of the world' (*ibid.*, 3).

The present chapter on the electoral experiences of Guinea-Bissau has been written in that spirit, with reference to my own formulations on the subject in a recent essay on the respective roles of constitutionalism and popular sovereignty/autonomy in democratisation (see Rudebeck 1996a, 219–221; revised in Rudebeck 1998a, 208–211).[1] Democracy, I point out, is often conceptualised either as a form of rule characterised by *universal suffrage, regular elections and basic civil rights* or as *political equality in actual practice.* Modern political scientists push mostly in the former direction, while ordinary citizens all over the world, in thinking and talking about democracy, seem most often to favour the latter type of interpretation.

There are in principle two ways of overcoming the indicated dilemma: either one relegates issues assumed by many to be essential to democracy, such as social justice and equality in society at large, to the realm of hypothetical empirical prerequisites, conceptually disconnected from democracy 'as such'; or one holds that democracy can be meaningfully conceptualised only *in the context of its own realisation.*[2]

My own striving is to conceptualise *constitutional issues* and *issues of popular sovereignty/ autonomy* as *two distinct but linked dimensions of actually existing democracy and ongoing processes of democratisation.* By viewing democracy simultaneously as institutional norms and relations of power, culture as well as socio-economic structure, I thus follow the second of the two ways indicated.

---

[1] I am pursuing work on the conceptual problems involved, particularly with regard to popular sovereignty/autonomy. See Rudebeck (2000). This will thus not be dealt with in depth here.

[2] Samuel Huntington (1991), for instance, argues skilfully, in the established vein, for the first position. Robert Dahl (1982 and 1989), a living classic in political science, may be characterised as wavering creatively between the two types of positions. Amartya Sen (1981) and David Held (1995) offer theoretically significant examples of the second position. The notion of democracy's 'context of realisation', used by me, draws upon Held's 'conditions of realisation' and 'entrenchment' (Held 1995, 159 ff).

Context of discussion and theoretical issues

The historical context is that of the democratisations occurring in various parts of the world during the 1980s and 1990s, with more specific empirical reference to Africa. The key issue raised is that of the consolidation/sustainability or not of the newly introduced democratic systems. This is an analytical issue and, at the same time, a query about ongoing history. As a significant starting point for the analysis, the following empirical generalisation is offered:

In order for democracy as a form of rule to become sustainable, it appears that constitutionalism would have to be supplemented with a measure of popular sovereignty/autonomy going beyond the mere introduction of universal suffrage.

The notion of *constitutionalism*, or *rule of law*, underlying this formulation is rather conventional. It means *the institutionalisation of government, administration and judiciary, as well as of the rights of organisation, expression and property, into regular and predictable forms.*

The rule of law can be either democratic or non-democratic but it is difficult to see how a democratic version of rule could be conceptualised without universal suffrage. Thus we get *democratic constitutionalism* – synonymous with the established political-science definition of democracy which can be formulated as follows:

Rule based on universal suffrage, regular elections, legal guarantees for free discussion and opposition for everybody, the legally recognised right to associate and organise freely, and institutional safeguards against the arbitrary exercise of power.

Popular sovereignty/autonomy, on the other hand, is defined in a wider, more sociological sense as:

Shared power, viewed in terms of actual and effective participation in the making of decisions on matters of common concern and significance. This is about the larger political system as well as daily social life, economic production, places of living and work, and local decision-making.

Constitutionalism and popular sovereignty/autonomy, as defined above, are two crucial aspects of democracy to be distinguished in the historical processes leading up to actually existing democracy in today's world. The relative timing of the historical emergence of the two aspects of democracy differs significantly between, on the one hand, the 'western' democratisations of the past and, on the other hand, recent democratisations. Generally speaking, the former were characterised by a measure of popular sovereignty/autonomy imposing itself more or less gradually upon established constitutionalism. The latter democratisations, on the contrary, have been marked predominantly by the introduction of the constitutional aspect through a combination of external pressure and internal democratic demands raised in the middle and urbanised strata of society, while popular sovereignty/autonomy, beyond democratic constitutionalism as such, has so far been weak or sometimes even absent. Democratic consolidation, therefore, often seems to be a slow process in many recent African cases of democratisation.

The theoretical theme of the two aspects of democratisation and actually existing democracy when linked to the issue of democratic sustainability, will provide my framework for the analysis of national elections in Guinea-Bissau. In viewing democracy and its absence simultaneously as institutional norms and relations of power, I will hopefully be able to grasp the societal significance of the Guinea-Bissau elections in a theoretically meaningful way.

From late colonialism to the beginning of the end of the single-party system

The final years of colonialism in Portuguese Guinea were dominated by the futile efforts of the Portuguese army to defeat the guerrilla fighters of the *Partido Africano da Independência da Guiné e Cabo Verde* (PAIGC). The uprising began in 1963 and ended in 1974 with the full recognition by Portugal of Guinea-Bissau as a sovereign and independent state (see Rudebeck 1974). Interestingly, I shall show, the colonial regime organised its last election in 1973. This was after the PAIGC, in a different but simultaneous historical time, had in 1972 organised their first elections in the approximately two-thirds of the country then controlled by the anti-colonial movement.

Until the first democratic, multi-party, parliamentary and presidential elections were held in Guinea-Bissau in 1994, there had been two clearly distinguishable periods in the post-colonial politico-economic history of the country. The first period ran from independence in 1974 until around 1982. It was marked by one-party rule and attempts at socialist-inspired planning (Rudebeck 1979). The second period, after 1982, was that of liberalisation. From 1990 onwards, it also included the beginnings of democratisation and subsequent institutionalisation of democratic constitutionalism. But, until 1990, liberalisation had only touched upon the economy and not the political system. Under the umbrella of established one-party rule, the economy had been structurally adjusted according to World Bank and IMF prescriptions.

Moreover, it is now possible to see 1990 as the starting point of a third period, that of democratisation, in the midst of which Guinea-Bissau still finds itself. During this third period, economic liberalisation has continued but it has been supplemented with political liberalisation and its transformation into democratisation. The 1994 election confirmed the process. The 1998 civil and regional war in Guinea-Bissau interrupted the process but possibly only temporarily.[3] Before the war, a second round of multi-party elections was being planned for late 1998 or early 1999. Such elections may still take place, although in a new political context of challenge to authoritarian and corrupt practices.

So far, we can only speculate about the durability of the democratic constitutional system in Guinea-Bissau. In any case, and whatever the ultimate outcome of the 1998 war, the year 1994 marks an important turning point. The institutionalisation of a system with many parties and a government subjected to scrutiny by a legally recognised opposition was begun. After Portuguese colonialism, followed by 20 years of single-party independence, this was completely new in the political history of the country.

The following three main periods may be distinguished for the history of independent Guinea-Bissau:

1. Socialist inspired state planning and single-party rule   1974–1982
2. Economic liberalisation and single-party rule   1982–1990
3. Political liberalisation and democratisation   1990–1994
   under continued economic liberalisation   and after[4]

This periodisation helps us to see some but not all significant turning-points. The Guinean sociologist Raúl Mendes Fernandes (1994a and 1994b), for example, has pointed out that the divide between the first two periods hides the increasing political centralisation to the office of the President during the second period, while it does not say anything about the class dynamics in society. Cultural developments, furthermore, become only indirectly visible through this kind of periodisation.[5]

In spite of limitations, the division into three periods of Guinea-Bissau's history as a juridically sovereign state is still useful for the purposes of focusing upon the mutual interplay between the character of the political system and that of official development policies. The late-colonial, pre-independence years naturally constitute a period of their own, as will be seen from my presentation of data on the structure of the late-colonial state and the last election held in Portuguese Guinea under its regime. History, however, neither ended nor began with political independence, although it did shift political and economic tracks.

The late-colonial state in Portuguese Guinea and its 1973 non-party election

The first Portuguese settlers on the islands of Cape Verde received their charter from the Portuguese Crown in 1466, 'allowing them to have a judiciary and a revenue department, giving them absolute rights over the Africans, and granting them exclusive licence to trade on the adjacent mainland' (Rodney 1970, 72).[6] From then on, until 1974, Portugal tried in various ways

---

[3]See the section 'War in 1998/99 and new elections' at the end of this chapter.
[4]Although interrupted by the mid-1998 war, as mentioned.
[5]Some aficionados of Guinea-Bissau's modern history may also object to why the *coup d'état* of 14 November 1980 is not seen to work at the beginning of a new distinct period. As I show below, there are good reasons for regarding 1982, and not 1980, as marking the beginning of the second period.
[6]Contemporary Portuguese document cited by Rodney.

to exercise state authority over mainland Guinea and the islands of Cape Verde (see Rudebeck 1974, 19–20).[7] Constitutional designations shifted back and forth between colony, overseas province, overseas territory, autonomous region. Sometimes there was a complete absence of any special designation distinguishing between overseas territories and Portugal itself. The principles of decentralisation and centralisation were variously emphasised.

Under the fascist *Estado Novo* (New State) of prime minister António de Oliveira Salazar, centralisation was the goal of the colonial administration (see Frochot 1942). The constitutional indication of centralisation was the Colonial Act of 1930, which adopted the term 'colony'. Although the term 'overseas province' was introduced instead in 1951 when the Colonial Act was abolished, the centralising emphasis on 'political unity' and 'administrative differentiation', corresponding to a 'common spirit of nationality' which was assumed to exist all through the territories, continued as strong as ever even after the 1951 constitutional revision (Abshire and Samuels 1969, 137; Cabral 1970; Caetano 1970).

Such, in brief, were the abstract principles according to which Portugal claimed to rule in Africa until 25 April 1974, when the *Estado Novo* was toppled by the same armed forces who were ordered to defend it but who rejected in the end their futile task.

In *Guiné* of the nineteen-fifties, the application of these principles meant that the Portuguese Governor ruled practically alone. He was ordinarily a high military officer, appointed by the cabinet (*Conselho de Ministros*) in Lisbon, upon the nomination of the head of the Ministry of Overseas Affairs (Portugal 1972). It was only in 1963, after the armed insurrection by PAIGC had started, that a weak Legislative Council was installed in Bissau (see Nuscheler and Ziemer 1978, 850–851).[8] A minority of its members were elected by the tiny fraction of the population able to meet the literacy and tax payment requirements for being registered as a voter. In Portuguese Guinea at the time, this meant in practice that the electorate consisted of only a few thousand people.[9] The majority of the members of the Council were nominated by various authorities and professional groupings (Portugal 1963). This composition of the Council ensured that most measures proposed by the Governor to the Council were given a rubber stamp. Although constitutional, this clearly had nothing to do with democracy, neither by intention nor function.

In 1972, the Legislative Council was renamed the Legislative Assembly; the total number of elected members was increased to 17, 5 of whom were to be elected by direct suffrage (Portuguese Guinea 1972, Article 19). At the end of March 1973, elections for this new Legislative Assembly were held in Portuguese Guinea, including the election by direct suffrage of 5 deputies. Although the number of voters registered for the election was only 7,824, this was high in comparison with the number of inhabitants held to have been literate in the 1950s.[10] Yet the number of registered voters was *less than 3 per cent* of the adult population of the territory, reflecting both the fact that more than half of the territory was largely under PAIGC control and the exceptionally restricted suffrage.[11] Of

---

[7]The following information on historical background draws upon Rudebeck 1974.

[8]See Nuscheler and Ziemer for a few further details on the constitutional and institutional set-up of Portuguese Guinea of the 1950s and 1960s.

[9]United Nations (1963), table 2, gives a population figure for 1960 of 544,184 inhabitants, which may well be underestimated but is the only figure we have besides a round PAIGC estimate of 800,000 (Conférence des Organisations Nationales des Colonies Portugaises 1970, 10). The latter may well have been more realistic than the UN figure for the populations as a whole, but is nevertheless unrealistic when applied to only one of the two zones into which the country was divided at the time by the war. According to the 1950 census held by the Portuguese, 99.7% of the 'non-assimilated' population and 45.1 of the 'assimilated' population had been classified as illiterate (UNESCO 1958, 885). As the 'assimilated' were said to have been 0.39% of the total in 1950 (i. a. Duffy 1962, 10), it is easily seen that very few individuals could possibly have qualified as voters for the Legislative Council in 1963. According to *Marchés Tropicaux* (6 April 1973), the number of voters in 1973, reported to be 7,824, was 'practically the double' of the number having voted in a 1969 election for the Council.

[10]Cf. Note 9.

[11]Population of voting age roughly estimated as 45 % of 544,184 (1950 census) = 244,883. Although this is based on the 1950 census figures, it is still more realistic than any higher figure would have been, considering that the colonial government in 1973 did not control the whole territory.

those registered, 89.4 per cent (i.e. 6,995 individuals) were reported actually to have voted. Table 5.1 sums up available key data.

Table 5.1: Participation in 1973 elections, Portuguese Guinea

Number of registered voters	Number actually voting	Approx. part of total adult population (%)
7,824	6,995	2.9

Source: *Marchés Tropicaux* 6 April 1973, reproduced in *Facts and Reports* 3(9) 1973, 2, which refers in turn to official Portuguese sources.

The colonial Legislative Assembly election of 1973 offered an extreme illustration of the fact that constitutionalism as such may well be combined with the absolute absence of any semblance of democracy and popular sovereignty/autonomy. In the historical context of Africa's overall decolonisation from the late 1950s and onwards, this was an untenable combination which had also provoked an armed struggle for the decolonisation and liberation of then Portuguese Guinea, beginning in 1963.

The 1972 single-party elections in PAIGC-controlled areas

As early as between August and October 1972 – before the 1973 colonial election[12] – PAIGC carried through the election of 273 regional councillors for eleven regional councils, in the approximately two-thirds of the territory the liberation movement claimed to control at that time. In a second step, the councillors met in their respective regions to elect among themselves 91 of the 120 deputies of the National Assembly. The remaining 29 were designated by the party leadership to represent the regions still controlled by the Portuguese colonial regime. On 24 September 1973, the newly constituted National Assembly met in the region of Boé, in the eastern part of the country, to proclaim the *de jure* existence of Guinea-Bissau as a 'sovereign, republican, democratic, anti-colonialist, and anti-imperialist state' within the same borders as '"Portuguese" Guinea'.[13]

Since the 1972 election was a wartime operation, the voting took six weeks to carry out. Ballot papers were carried on foot to polling stations all over the country and military precautions had to be taken in organising the actual voting. This was a complex and carefully executed operation, the details of which have been described elsewhere (see Rudebeck 1974, 149–174).

There were 15 regions, but in 4, including the capital city of Bissau, the Portuguese were still in control and thus actual elections took place in only eleven regions. Councillors for the 4 Portuguese-controlled regions were designated by 'the party'. In each of the 22 regional and sub-regional electoral districts, the voters, all Guinean citizens over 17 years of age, were presented with a single list of candidates whose number varied from 6 to 21.[14] The candidates had been sorted out in discussions among PAIGC activists and then presented for discussion and approval at general meetings in the villages. The election campaign went on from early January until late August 1972.

An equal number (100,000) of *yes*/SIM (white) and *no*/NÃO (grey) ballot papers had been printed in neighbouring Guinée-Conakry and distributed in the PAIGC-controlled areas of the country. Most of these were actually used by the voters, as shown by the overall final result as published by PAIGC shown in Table 5.2:

---

[12]The reason for describing the 1973 colonial election before describing the 1972 PAIGC election is that I want to conclude the colonial political period before moving on to the post-colonial one.

[13]According to the solemn 'Proclamação do Estado da Guiné-Bissau', 1973, published by PAIGC (1973c).

[14]All the technical details are presented in PAIGC (1973b). Most of the electoral districts were sectors within the regions, but in 1972 a few districts were entire regions.

Table 5.2: Distribution of votes between *yes* and *no* in elections held in PAIGC-controlled Guinea-Bissau in 1972

	Number of votes	%
yes	75,163	97.0
no	2,352	3.0
total	77,515	100.0

Source: PAIGC 1973b, 3.

The 1972 elections were constitutional in the sense of being carried through according to rules prescribed in systematically constructed documents of a constitutional character. They also appear to have met the universal-suffrage requirement for democratic elections reasonably well, although the wartime character of the operation most likely precluded absolute universality. Very roughly calculated, the number of votes amounted to approximately 32 per cent of the population of voting age.[15] Considering that at the time PAIGC controlled at most two-thirds of the territory excluding the urban areas, that figure in itself does not say much in either direction about the level of participation.

On two grounds, however, the 1972 PAIGC elections did not meet normal democratic standards. The first was about the relative position of the elected organs (Regional Councils and National Assembly) *vis-à-vis* the party. The second was about the lack of choice linked to the fact that these were single-party and single-list elections.

In theory, PAIGC adhered strictly, in 1972, to the communist-inspired principle of party supremacy over the state. This can be seen in all authoritative party documents of the time, including the Constitution adopted for the state by the National Assembly on September 1973. Article 4 remained unchanged until May 1991:

> Power in Guinea is exercised by the toiling masses in close association with the *Partido Africano da Independência da Guiné e Cabo Verde* (PAIGC), which is the leading political force of society (PAIGC 1973a, Article 4).

There was no question at the time of challenging party supremacy. However, as long as the PAIGC leadership was closely dependent upon popular support in order to fight the colonial regime, the anti-democratic potential of the political and organisational principles of party supremacy and 'democratic centralism' was balanced by practical requirements and thus did not, yet, become dominant in actual practice.

Something similar can be said about the way nominations for the single-party lists were carried out according to the principle of 'democratic centralism'. It is quite probable that the party lists, in the conditions of the PAIGC-controlled areas of 1972, were fairly representative. On the other hand, it is also clear that the only way of defeating such a list would have been for the majority of voters of an entire electoral district to vote against it. This did not occur. The lowest percentages of *yes*-votes were registered in the eastern parts of the country, where PAIGC was also known to have less support than in the north and in the south. But the variations were small: from 95 per cent voting 'Yes' in the east to 98 per cent in the south. It is perhaps more interesting that there were six villages in the entire country where the majority of the voters rejected the list, although this did not have any effect at the level of the electoral district as a whole. In one northern village, the list was even reported to have been rejected by 100 per cent of the voters, for the simple reason that one of the candidates was unacceptable to that village (PAIGC 1973b, 4).

We might conclude, so far, that by applying carefully worked out rules under difficult circumstances, the PAIGC-organised 1972 election in *Guiné* was at least as constitutional as the rival Portuguese election held in 1973. In contrast to the latter, and despite the limitations shown above, it was also marked by a measure of popular sovereignty/autonomy. This is difficult to measure in

---

[15]Population of voting age roughly estimated as 45% of 544,184 (1950 census) = 244,883. Although this is based on the 1950 census figures, it is still more realistic than any higher figure would have been, considering that PAIGC in 1972 did not control the whole territory.

any other sense than by reference to the relatively wide suffrage employed, a fact which alone does not guarantee any popular sovereignty. However, my own research at the time of that historical turning-point, drawing upon direct observation, interviews and documents, led me to conclude, cautiously, that 'by themselves choosing, for the first time, people to represent them above the local level, the inhabitants of liberated Guinea-Bissau have been made to link, in their own minds, their own concrete interests to questions of more than local significance' (Rudebeck 1974, 174).

Even after 25 years of hindsight, I would still maintain that the 1972 elections were a serious contribution to potentially democratic institution-building. As we shall see, however, the project was undermined in subsequent economic and political developments.

Socialist-inspired state planning and single-party rule 1974–1982

As the anti-colonial liberation movement PAIGC took over state power from the Portuguese after independence in 1974, it found itself in a difficult position. The state treasury was empty, but expectations were massive. 'Everything' had to be done at once. According to the socialist-inspired ideology and programmes that had grown through the liberation struggle, development would now continue in the name of the people, modernising agriculture under the leadership of the state and the party in order to create a real economic surplus. This surplus would then be invested in infrastructure, education, and health, as well as some import-substituting industrialisation based on the country's own raw materials. International aid was necessary but only in order to supplement the people's own efforts.

This change required a political structure through which the people's developmental needs could be expressed and formulated into legitimate and realistic decisions, binding for and upon all citizens. As for many other African countries at the time, the solution was a one-party state. The liberation movement kept its name, PAIGC, but was transformed into the state party of two separate and sovereign states: Guinea-Bissau on the West African mainland and Cape Verde encompassing a group of islands 800 kilometres away in the Atlantic ocean. The party was meant to function as the necessary link between the people(s) and the leaderships of the two separate states.[16] According to the proclaimed ideology, internal discussion was to be free and open. It was claimed that a multi-party system would generate futile divisions and make development that much more difficult.

Most of all this went astray in Guinea-Bissau, and it happened quite quickly, as in many other countries at the time with similar historical backgrounds and political orientations (see Rudebeck 1982; 1991; 1992). The great majority of the Guinean people are peasant farmers. There was no spontaneous acceptance to be expected from peasants for the new state's planning and control ambitions. In Bissau, the capital city, conditions of life deteriorated rather than improved in spite of state subsidies for the staple food, rice. Such subsidies and state-controlled prices in turn made rural deliveries to the city relatively unremunerative for the farmers. Smuggling to the neighbouring countries was a more rewarding alternative. Imports of rice grew rapidly and became a heavy burden on the balance of payments. Despite developmentalist motives and motivations, state policies on the whole were not favourable for the majority of the people and could not be justified according to democratic means. The expected national surplus did not materialise. In its place, foreign aid rapidly outgrew all other potential sources of state revenue to become largely the dominant form of financing the state budget (see Rudebeck 1986; cf. also Gleijeses 1997).[17]

In the short run, the wielders of state power became more dependent upon aid donors than their own people for keeping their power. Social and political discontent grew and so did political repression within the framework of the only political party permitted. The system of popular rule which had been budding in the areas controlled by the liberation movement during the armed struggle for independence was now undermined. It withered fast.

---

[16]As a matter of fact, the party union was mostly a formality from the very beginning of Cape Verdean independence in 1975, less than a year after that of Guinea-Bissau. As we shall soon see, the party union was dissolved completely after the *coup d'état* of 14 November 1980 in Guinea-Bissau.

[17]Swedish and other Scandinavian aid was highly important. See Rudebeck 1986; cf. also Gleijeses 1997.

In the end contradictions could no longer be controlled but exploded into a coup on 14 November 1980 (see Rudebeck 1982).[18] The former Prime Minister and legendary guerrilla fighter, João Bernardo 'Nino' Vieira, took the lead and turned himself into President. The President deposed was Luis Cabral, younger brother of Amilcar Cabral, the historic leader of the liberation struggle, who had been murdered before independence in 1973. Although the new regime proclaimed a more popularly oriented line with more emphasis upon agriculture, very little changed in practice. Most of the members of the government remained, although in new posts. No democratisation of political life occurred.

When the economy began to be liberalised a few years later, this had nothing to do with 'Nino's' coup against the regime of Luis Cabral. The most important cause was the fact that state policies during the first years of independence had driven Guinea-Bissau into aid dependence and economic stagnation. Therefore, the leadership had no resources to prevent the rising demands for structural adjustment beginning to be heard from the powerful donors of aid and financial credits.

However, the events of November 1980 did lead to the breaking up of the party union with the neighbouring state of Cape Verde in the Atlantic. This was partly because the coup had had an 'ethnic' edge which was turned against the many Cape-Verdeans holding leading posts in Bissau, due in major part to the fact of their higher formal education, in turn an historical effect of the differences between the two countries stemming from Portuguese colonial educational policies. Luis Cabral himself was unjustly counted as a 'Cape Verdean', although born in Guinea-Bissau and having lived most of his life there.[19] After the coup, the Cape Verdean branch of PAIGC broke away, in January 1981, from the original movement and formed their own governmental party PAICV (*Partido Africano da Independência de Cabo Verde*) for their island state. Both PAIGC and PAICV claimed to be the legitimate political heirs to the heritage of Amilcar Cabral.

The 1976 single-party elections

The elections for Regional Councils and the National Assembly which were held in Guinea-Bissau over three days 19–21 December 1976 can most easily be described as a peacetime replication of the 1972 elections held in the then liberated areas. The same political principles and constitutional rules were applied, although now adapted to the new conditions of peace.[20]

The election campaign started at the beginning of December. All regions were visited by leading members of the party and the government. Discussions were lively. Most of the party-proposed candidates were approved. Some were discarded and replaced after popular consultation. At the end of this process, there were 475 nominated candidates, distributed between 36 sectorial lists offered to the voters for their acceptance or rejection in each one of the 36 sectors. The 'sectors' in this case were thus identical with sub-regional electoral districts or constituencies. All citizens who had reached the age of 18 were entitled to vote.

When all votes had been counted, it was established that 193,167 citizens had voted. Roughly calculated, this should have been about 55 per cent of the population of voting age.[21] Although 81

---

[18]See Rudebeck 1982 for an analysis of the 1980 coup and its aftermath.

[19]Many families have branches in both countries. See an interesting article by the Guinean social scientist Carlos Cardoso in the Bissau daily *Banobero* 17 March 1995. Cardoso refers primarily to political discussions and conflicts in the Guinea-Bissau of the 1990s, but what he writes is equally relevant to 1980 (this author's translation): 'Arguments of a racist type and fights over political power perhaps do not concern the masses but rather two opposed groups within what could be called the Guinean elite. One group was constituted earlier than the other. It is of straight Cape Verdean origin. The other group is Guinean and can perhaps be seen as stemming from the so-called *grumetes* and the Portuguese-Guinean elite that has emerged later.' (*Grumetes* were African 'ship's boys' who from the 17th century and onwards assisted Portuguese traders along the Guinean coast and who together with these are at the origin of today's Portuguese-West African creole culture in Guinea-Bissau.)

[20]The 1976 elections were reported in detail in the official newspaper *Nô Pintcha* ('Forward' in Guinean creole), 257–266, 4–28 December 1976.

[21]Population of voting age is roughly estimated here as 45% of 767,739 (1979 census) = 345,478. In estimating the population of voting age for the subsequent elections, I use rough extrapolations from the 1979 census up to the official estimate of 1.1 million inhabitants in 1995.

per cent of the latter had voted in favour of the single lists proposed to them, there were considerable regional variations in the vote. Support for PAIGC was strong in the former liberated areas, but in the eastern parts of the country (Bafatá and Gabú regions) where the Portuguese had been very influential until the very end, there were many hesitant voters. In 3 eastern sectors, the lists gained less than half of the votes; in one sector only 15 per cent was won. It was announced that the elections would be repeated in those sectors – with revised single lists. The regional results are shown in Table 5.3 below.

Table 5.3: Results of 1976 elections, by regions and for all Guinea-Bissau

Region	Number of votes	yes (%)
Bafatá	24,119	51.0
Bissau, region	18,098	95.6
Bolama-Bijagos	6,855	95.4
Buba	13,266	92.5
Cacheu	36,182	93.3
Gabú	23,130	55.7
Oio	33,493	84.5
Tombali	14,847	86.4
Bissau, city	23,227	84.0
Total	193,167	80.5

Source: Figures reported in *Nô Pintcha* 28 December 1976.

As in 1972, the 1976 regional elections functioned as indirect elections for the National Assembly. The most important task of the newly-elected regional councillors was to meet in their respective regions to elect, among themselves, 150 members or deputies for the National Assembly, an increase of 30 members when compared with the first assembly. When the deputies met later, in March 1977, their initial task was to elect the only candidate presented, the party leader Luis Cabral, to be the President of the Republic.

These were thus clearly party-controlled elections in which the political leadership did not put their positions at stake but did their best to have those positions willingly confirmed by the majority of the citizens of the newly sovereign state. Constitutional rules, first made by the leaders and then confirmed by the PAIGC-controlled National Assembly, were followed. On election day, the only choice offered to the voters was between a confirming *yes* and a demonstrative *no*, the latter without apparent or evident consequence. The preceding nomination procedure had been an occasion for the leadership to present their policies and candidates and to have them discussed to some extent by interested citizens.

The necessarily limited extent to which popular sovereignty/autonomy was involved or not in this can not be judged merely by studying the actual election, since the concept of sovereignty/autonomy also covers the everyday exercise of power in society. Some circumscribed citizen autonomy may nevertheless be assumed to have been exercised in these single-party, single-list elections. It seems probable, for example, that the 5,653 votes of *no* counted in the sector of Cossé, Bafatá region, against no more than 1,021 votes of *yes*,[22] did serve as a reminder to the national leadership that their power was not unconditional.

Economic liberalisation and single-party rule 1982–1990

With an increasingly negative balance of payments, growing dependence on foreign aid, insignificant economic growth, and no improvement after the coup of November 1980, Guinea-Bissau was an obvious target in the early 1980s for the structural adjustment programmes of the World Bank and the International Monetary Fund (IMF). The first agreement with the Guinean government on a programme of economic stabilisation came in 1983. Since 1987, structural adjustment has permeated life and development in Guinea-Bissau, placing the country under the firm tutelage of the World Bank, the IMF and other donors.

---

[22]*Nô Pintcha* 28 December 1976.

Through the reforms that have been implemented, the economy of Guinea-Bissau has gradually been liberalised and opened up to the world market. Typical and well-known effects of structural adjustment include the following: the trimming of the state apparatus; privatisations of state companies; credits to large farmers with links to the state; growing agricultural exports; problems with teachers' salaries; better supplies of goods in the markets; rising prices for basic goods; more difficult access to child and health care for the poor; social tensions in both rural and urban areas; growing unemployment in the capital city; less inflation (see for instance UNICEF 1988; Imbali 1993; Aguilar and Stenman 1996). During the major part of the 1980s, there was no *political* liberalisation corresponding to the *economic* liberalisation taking place, either in Guinea-Bissau or in most other African countries. It was rather the other way around, since the analysts of the World Bank feared that too much democracy would make it difficult to enforce savings in public budgets and retrenchments of various kinds, against the wills of the majority in the countries concerned. Structural adjustment policies failed in sheer economic terms in many countries, *inter alia* because undemocratic state power had economic interests of its own and liberalisation, precisely for that reason, was very far from complete. After such failures and influenced also by the democratisation of Eastern Europe, the dominant analysis began to change. Structural adjustment, it was now maintained, would need a human face in order to work better. This required its legitimation through 'good governance' and democratisation, including human rights. In a widely acclaimed 1989 report, the World Bank claimed that what was required for Africa in order to overcome its developmental crisis was 'a systematic effort to build a pluralistic institutional structure, a determination to respect the rule of law, and vigorous protection of the freedom of the press and human rights'.[23]

External pressure was supplemented with growing internal demands for democratisation, not least from public employees and from others working for salaries and wages who were hit hard by structural adjustment policies. Non-governmental organisations (NGOs) of various kinds, students, intellectuals and other groups pushed in the same direction. Ultimately, a wave of democratisation also began to sweep over Africa at the end of the 1980s (see Huntington 1991).

The 1984 single-party elections

According to the constitution, regional/national elections should have been held in Guinea-Bissau in 1980, within four years of 1976. But due to the emergency created by the *coup d'état* of November 1980, the elections were postponed for over three years and did not take place until 31 March 1984. After the coup, the country was governed by a Revolutionary Council led by the President and created by presidential decree (Rudebeck 1982). The 1984 elections and the adoption of a new constitution by the new National Assembly were thus presented as a return to constitutional legality, after a period of upheavals.[24]

By way of systematic organisation the people were mobilised from above to deliver their votes. There are no indications that this was an election of great concern to the people. The reported turnout of voters in the whole country (excluding the coast and island region of Bolama-Bijagós)[25] was lower than in 1976. At a rough calculation, only about 48 per cent of the population of voting age went to the polls in 1976, despite the efforts of party and state officials to exhort them to participate.[26] Table 5.4 gives the reported results.

---

[23]World Bank 1989, 61. During the 1990s this view has come to mark the analyses put forth by dominant donors of aid and credits, resulting in more or less open 'democratic conditionality' – i. e. demands for democratic political reforms as a condition for aid. A publication by the 'Development Assistance Committee' (DAC) of the OECD entitled *Participatory Development and Good Governance* is characteristic. Here, the close linkages between 'good governance', 'participatory development', human rights, and democratisation are emphasised (OECD 1995, 6 ff.). See also World Bank 1997.

[24]Speech by the president, reported in *No Pintcha* 19 May 1984. Also note the title of a 74-page party publication published in May 1984: 'Our constitution establishes the Republic of Guinea-Bissau as a state where the rule of law reigns.' ('*A nossa constituição estabelece a República da Guiné-Bissau como um estado de direito*' [PAIGC 1984].)

[25]Not yet counted when the figures available were printed in *Nô Pintcha* 4 April 1984.

[26]Population of voting age is roughly estimated here as 45% of 850,000 = 382,500. When calculating the participation rate for 1984, the absence of voters from Bolama-Bijagós in 1984 was compensated for by using the 1976 participation figure for that region.

Table 5.4: Results of 1984 elections, by region and for all Guinea-Bissau

Region	Number of votes	yes (%)
Bafatá	38,107	97.1
Bissau	28,583	95.9
Biombo	12,438	98.9
Bolama-Bijagos	–	–
Cacheu	21,066	96.2
Gabú	27,366	93.8
Oio	26,463	97.5
Quínará	8,708	97.7
Tombali	15,538	96.5
Total	178,538	96.5

Source: Figures reported in *Nô Pintcha* 4 April 1984.

It is striking in comparison with 1976 that there is no regional variation for this election. In 1984, the percentage of *yes*-voters was uniformly between 94 and 97 per cent, countrywide, which tends to support the impression of that year's single-party, single-list election as quite a top-steered, low-popular-interest event.

The 1989 single-party elections

The last in the series of single-party elections were held on 1 June 1989, less than two years before the constitution was changed to allow for the free formation of political parties. Like in 1984, there was a relatively low level of involvement in the 1989 elections.[27] The authorities reported having managed to get 221,723 citizens to deliver their ballot papers, which amounts roughly to 49 per cent of the population of voting age, i. e. less than half and as low as in 1984.[28]

There were 473 regional councillors elected, whose most important task was to elect 150 National Assembly deputies among themselves. In 1989, 96.52 per cent of the votes cast were counted in favour of the single lists for regional councillors presented in each sector.[29]

Data on the composition of the corps of councillors who were elected showed that approximately 60 per cent were newcomers, and 30 per cent were women, while 40 per cent were peasants and the remainder workers, intellectuals and party cadres. Among the 150 councillors later elected by their peers to be parliamentarians, there were 30 women, equivalent to 20 per cent of the total.[30]

Table 5.5: Result of 1989 elections, all Guinea-Bissau

Number of votes	yes (%)	Approximate participation (%)
221,723	96.5	49

Source: *Africa Research Bulletin* 26(6) 1989, 9309; *Marchés Tropicaux* 9 June 1989, 1595.

Thus, in 1989, on the eve of a new period of its political history, Guinea-Bissau still maintained single-party constitutionalism combined, as indicated by the voting data, with a relatively low level of popular sovereignty/autonomy within its political system.[31]

---

[27]The data for the 1989 election are found in *Africa Research Bulletin* 26(6) 1989, 9309, and *Marchés Tropicaux* 9 June 1989, 1595.

[28]Population of voting age is roughly estimated here as 45% of 1,000 000 = 450,500.

[29]The single list presented in each sector contained the names only of candidates for that particular sector. This procedure was the same in all of the four single-party elections held from 1972 to 1989.

[30]These sociological data are found in *Africa Research Bulletin* 26(6) 1989, 9309; *Marchés Tropicaux* 9 June 1989, 1595; and Sweden (no date, probably 1993).

[31]Claims with regard to popular sovereignty/autonomy obviously cannot be based on voting data alone but would have to be supplemented with other kinds of data. See Rudebeck 1991; 1996b; 1997b; and 1998a, both for analyses of such data and for further references.

The interpretation suggested both by the 1989 and the 1984 elections is that elements of popular sovereignty/autonomy, as encouraged through the anti-colonial liberation struggle, had not been underpinned with *democratic* constitutionalist practice in the post-colonial period. Sovereignty and autonomy had gradually therefore been undermined and largely lost. As coming events would clearly show, the single-party system itself had also been undermined through these developments.

Political liberalisation and democratisation under continued economic liberalisation from 1990 onwards

Liberalisation and democratisation reached Guinea-Bissau relatively late, since, despite all else, social contradictions were less acute there than in many other African countries. On the other hand, the PAIGC-regime was well entrenched, particularly in the rural areas, where there was hardly any organised opposition to be found. Surely, there was much discontent with the hard and unjust conditions of life, but most found it hard to conceive of any political alternative to 'Nino' as president and PAIGC as 'the' political regime. Instead, there was a tendency to escape into traditional, 'ethnic' ideas and hopes, even dreams and illusions, away from the problems and difficulties of modernisation (Rudebeck 1988; 1991; 1992). In the short run, this posed no threat to the political regime, because space was opened for political leaders to play upon people's fears and worries in order to safeguard their own positions of power. But from around 1990, the pressure for democratisation became stronger, both from within the country and from outside (Rudebeck 1996; 1997a; 1997b).[32]

During the early nineties, there were many younger PAIGC members with high positions in the state who demanded political liberalisation in addition to market reforms of the economy. Even outside the PAIGC, intermediate strata who wanted to organise themselves freely grew more confident. These groups included merchants, other entrepreneurs, public employees, and intellectuals such as journalists and others. Discontent brewed among teachers, for example, over deteriorating conditions of work and salaries which could not provide subsistence. Demands for freedom of the press and respect for human and civic rights were raised with increasing fervour, particularly in the capital city. The regime was also strongly aware of foreign donors' insistent expectations of democratic reforms. No organised opposition emerged, however, from the majority of the people living in the rural areas.

One of the first clear signals of democratisation coming from the regime itself was registered in the middle of August 1990, during an important speech delivered by the president in the old one-party National Assembly. The message from above was that the issues of multi-partyism and liberalisation of trade and labour union legislation were now under serious consideration.[33] A process had been set in motion that from now on would be moving largely under its own momentum.

The formation of political parties was constitutionally legalised in May 1991 by deleting from Article 4 of the Constitution the former reference to PAIGC as 'the leading political force of society'. Instead, the new version of Article 4 passed by the National Assembly guaranteed the right to form political parties according to the rules of the Constitution and ordinary law.[34] A

---

[32]Rudebeck 1996; 1997a; and 1997b.

[33]Abstract of President's speech, August 1990, in Sweden 1990.

[34]*Boletim Oficial* 18, 9 May 1991, 'Constitutional Law no. 1/91', Article 4, p. 3; as well as general law for political parties, 'Guinea: Bissau: Law no. 2/91', pp. 17–22. On 26 February 1993, the constitution was again revised. Now it came to include also the constitutionally protected right to 'form associations': *Boletim Oficial* 8, 26 February 1993, 'Constitutional Law no. 1/93', Article 44 D, p. 9. This states: '1. The citizens have the right to form associations, freely and without any kind of prior permission, as long as these do not aim to foster violence and their aims do not violate the laws. 2. The associations fulfill their aims freely without the intervention of public authorities. They cannot be dissolved or forbidden except in cases foreseen by the law and then by judicial decision. 3. Armed associations of a military kind, militarised or para-military, are not allowed. Nor are associations allowed that work in favour of racism and tribalism.' (Author's translations.)

constitutional guarantee for the freedom of the press was also formulated and supplemented in October the same year with a special press law.[35]

The tone of radio and television coverage grew more open. Independent newspapers began to appear. The teachers founded their own trade union, *Sindicato Nacional dos Professores* (SINAPROF), in connection with a major strike in 1991 against the failure to pay their salaries. Ever since then, SINAPROF has been very active in various ways. Guinean Non-Governmental Organisations (NGOs) were formed in growing numbers, including the *Liga Guineense dos Direitos Humanos* (LGDH), an independent Guinean human-rights organisation. By the mid-1990s there were over 30 Guinean voluntary organisations. Some of these had worked closely with the PAIGC even before their legalisation but most were new. In addition there were over 70 foreign NGOs in 1995, gaining from now being able to cooperate with organisations that were not directly linked to the state and the dominant party.

A multi-party system emerges

Political parties now also began to enter the stage where the drama of democratisation was enacted. During the first years of the 1990s, and in spite of the new constitutional rules, the old regime tried its best to resist party formation, among other things by delaying registration procedures and by police violence. The first legal opposition party, *Frente Democrática* (FD), was able to be registered as early as 18 November 1991 under the leadership of Aristides Menezes, former personal friend of the president as well as former member of the government and the director of the state bank from 1988 to 1990. This party had no other political profile other than pluralism and modernisation.[36] When FD was founded, Menezes was a successful businessman. He died in early 1994, before the election of that year.

The registration of the other parties did not seriously begin until 1992 and 1993. But when the first multi-party elections in the history of Guinea-Bissau were finally held on 3 July 1994, there were 13 legally registered political parties in the race for seats in the National Assembly. As for the presidential election, 8 candidates representing different parties had been registered.

The political parties of Guinea-Bissau cannot be distinguished from each other merely by studying their party programmes and platforms. Their catch-words and slogans are almost identical. Both PAIGC and the opposition parties assure their voters that they stand for democracy, justice and human rights as well as for a market economy with social responsibility.

FD, the first legal opposition party, was neither the largest nor the oldest. While the oldest was *Frente da Libertação Nacional da Guiné* (FLING), the two largest were *Resistência da Guiné-Bissau – Movimento Bâ-Fatá* (RGB/MB) and *Partido da Renovação Social* (PRS).

FLING was founded as early as in 1962, in Dakar, the capital of neighbouring Senegal, as a coalition of ethnic groupings which aimed to be a non-socialist alternative to the liberation movement PAIGC. It failed to gain any ground inside the country during the anti-colonial struggle and was repressed by the PAIGC-regime during the first years of independence. With democratisation, FLING has again been in a position to work openly. However, the party's following is limited, as shown by its very modest success in the 1994 election where it won only one seat and 2 per cent of the total number of votes.

RGB/MB is another originally exiled party. It was formally established in 1986 in Portugal, where it grew to become strong among political opponents to the authoritarian PAIGC-regime. This party does present a serious challenge to the government, as shown by its electoral score of 16 per cent of the votes in the 1994 election. From an ideological point of view, RGB/MB may be characterised as centre-liberal-populist with a possibly somewhat conservative and partially Christian touch.[37]

---

[35]*Boletim Oficial* 18, 9 May 1991, 'Constitutional Law no. 1/91', Article 44 A, p. 4; *Boletim Oficial* 39, 3 October 1991, 'Law no. 4/91', 3–11.

[36]In an interview on 3 December 1991, the leader's spokesman described the party to me as 'centre-social-democratic'.

[37]Because of the ideological vagueness of the parties, these kinds of characterisations are extremely difficult to make. In the case of PRGB/MB, the streak of Christian, conservative populism emerges mostly in printed materials from the Portuguese exile of the 1980s. More recent materials tend towards a social-liberal and even social-democratic direction, as emphasised by the leader of the party's parliamentary group, Helder Vaz, when interviewed by the author on 27 March 1996. In the interview Helder Vaz claimed, too, that the present leadership of the party comprises a larger number of Muslims than Christians.

The other major opposition party, PRS, was built up in the early 1990s, inside the country during the first years of democratisation. Its followers are found mainly among the unemployed youth of Bissau and the Balanta people in the rural areas. The Balanta are one of the two largest ethnic groups in Guinea-Bissau encompassing about one quarter of the population. The leader of the party is Koumba Yalá, a former PAIGC ideologist with a considerable personal political pull and a profile of populist, radical bent. He came second in the presidential election with 22 per cent of the votes, winning him the chance of a second round against president 'Nino'. This turned into an unexpected political thriller, where the president eventually kept his position by a 52/48 victory over Koumba Yalá. In the capital city, for example, the president was defeated by his much younger rival.[38]

Six small parties managed to form a coalition under the name of *União para Mudança*, Union for Change (UM), which after the election was transformed into a party.[39] They were all very small, their membership and voters largely made up of educated people, salaried employees, wage-earners and businessmen, ranging ideologically from left to centre and including also an ecological tendency. Together they scored just over 10 per cent of the popular vote in the parliamentary election.[40]

Three parties took part in the election without gaining any seats whatsoever in the National Assembly. These were *Partido da Convergência Democrática* (PCD); *Partido Unido Social Democrata* (PUSD); and *Fórum Cívico Guineense/Social Democracia* (FCG/SD). The most successful of the three was PCD, which won over 4 per cent of the votes rather equally distributed over the country. PCD seems to have lost out mainly against UM in competing for the votes of 'modern' businessmen and traders.

PUSD was a one-man movement, run by the former Prime and Foreign Minister Victor Saúde Maria, ousted by 'Nino' during the 1980s. Saúde Maria himself won a little over 2 per cent of the votes in the first round of the presidential election, which was also the vote his party gained in the parliamentary election. Since the election, he seems to have disappeared from public life.

The smallest party taking part in the 1994 election was FCG/SD, which was founded in connection with the election. In the parliamentary race this party scored only 494 votes – all received in the capital city. The party leader, Antonieta Rosa Gomes, a Brazilian-trained lawyer, presented herself as a candidate for the presidency as well, with a somewhat better result, winning close to 2 per cent or, in absolute numbers, 5,509 votes. She was the only woman candidate for the highest post of the country. Her political profile was decidedly liberal. She declared her intention to run also in the next election, intending then to be better prepared than in 1994.[41]

Of the parties discussed above only PAIGC, the old ruling party, and RGB/MB have a political and organisational presence in more or less the whole country. PRS is found in several but not all parts. The others are much more unevenly present.

---

[38]In the capital city of Bissau, Koumba Yalá, according to the final count (see Table 5.8), scored 52% of the votes against 46 for president 'Nino', while 2% were either blank or invalid votes.

[39]One of the six, LIPE (*Liga Guineense de Protecção e Desenvolvimento Ecológico*), did not join when the new party was formed in April 1995. In the National Assembly it has, however, worked with UM.

[40]Each one of the six parties making up UM does have a history of its own. The president of FDS (*Frente Democrática Social*), for example, is Rafael Barbosa, who belonged to the group of people around Amílcar Cabral who founded PAIGC in Bissau in 1956. In an interview with me on 11 December 1991, he said that he had founded a socialist party in Bissau as early as in 1948. During the anti-colonial war he was captured by the Portuguese and gradually alienated from PAIGC. In 1977, he was even condemned to death by the PAIGC-regime for treason but pardoned and released after the November 1980 coup. In 1991, he founded FDS which he describes as a social-democratic party.

The predecessor of PRD (*Partido Democrático do Progresso*) was a group of PAIGC members who came to play an historical part in the democratisation process by sending a petition to the PAIGC leadership during the autumn of 1991, demanding the rapid democratisation of the political system. This group was originally made up of the 121 persons who had signed the petition. Hence they were called the *Carta dos 121*. As democratisation did not proceed as rapidly as they wished, they broke away from PAIGC and formed their own party PRD under the leadership of a former Minister of Health, João da Costa, who had been jailed after the 1980 coup. João da Costa was elected president of the new party, UM, in April 1995.

The other four parties of the UM coalition were FD, mentioned above as the first legally recognised opposition party in 1991; LIPE, mentioned in note 12 above; MUDe (*Movimento para a Unidade e Democracia*); and PDP (*Partido Democrático do Progresso*).

[41]Articles by Rosa Gomes in *Nô Pintcha* 10 March 1995; *Banobero* 17 March 1995.

The emergence of the new party system was closely linked to the preparations for the first multi-party elections. These preparations were in part chaotic. The date of the elections was confirmed and then changed several times, from the autumn of 1993 until 3 July 1994. On the surface, the problem was presented as one to do with the registration of voters and the aid money used to do the necessary work of the national election commission CNE (*Comissão Nacional das Eleições*). But there were also tactical considerations involved, due to the different actors' perceptions of what date would be most suitable for his or her particular interest. Not least important was the fact that President 'Nino' himself seemed to have been interested in having the election take place fairly rapidly, once the decision had been made.

Note on the politicisation of social and cultural divisions in society

As already mentioned, 'socialism' in the first round of post-colonialism and then liberalisation had cruelly betrayed the common man's and woman's hopes and expectations for a more decent life in Guinea-Bissau, thus creating the basis for a kind of escape into traditional culture and ethnicity. The *Kiang-iang* movement among the Balanta people in the 1980s is an example of this. This movement could, very briefly, be characterised as expressing a kind of ethnic-traditionalist, religious populism in a 'modern' situation (see *inter alia* Callewaert 1994; 1995).[42]

There is also a certain correlation to be observed in many countries and situations between economic liberalisation and the politicisation of ethnic contradictions. This may seem paradoxical, as liberalisation is often seen as 'modern', while 'ethnicity' is held to be 'traditional'. On second thoughts, however, the connection is easily understandable, as economic liberalisation often results in the breakdown of both modern and traditional networks of social protection, in turn causing traditional culture to appear as a source of safety and security. This kind of mechanism has worked itself out with varying intensity in several very different parts of the world toward the end of the twentieth century, not least in post-1989 Eastern Europe and in many Muslim countries.

In spite of all this, political life and political divisions in multi-party Guinea-Bissau cannot be said to be particularly strongly marked by 'tribalism' or ethnicity. None of the new political parties presented itself openly as an 'ethnic' party, although it was obvious that the PRS of Koumba Yalá was quite strongly rooted among the Balanta people. Instead, the pre-election political debate was heavily marked by accusations against the old regime of corruption, mismanagement and repression. The main demand raised by the opposition was that an end must be put to all this. The president and the members of the old regime claimed that no one but they themselves had the competence required for carrying out the necessary reforms.

Multi-party elections in 1994

Two different elections were held in the summer of 1994. The *presidential election* required two rounds, one held simultaneously with the *parliamentary election* on 3 July, and the final one held on 7 August. International observers, who were present only on the first occasion, and local public opinion agreed that, on the whole, the elections had been fair and regular.[43] These elections will be studied here both at national and village level.

---

[42]The historian Inger Callewaert has studied *Kiang-iang* – since the 1980s.

[43]The following analyses of the outcome of the 1994 elections are based on data found both in the published and in the internal, unpublished, materials of the National Electoral Commission (National Election Commission 1994a; 1994b), verified by the UNDP observer (UNDP Election Co-ordinator 1994) and supported by international observers, as well as the full reports published in 1994 by the independent Guinean journal *Correio Guiné-Bissau*, Bissau, in particular the issues of 30 July 1994 (special issue giving a full account of the parliamentary and first round of the presidential elections 3 July 1994) and 19 August 1994 (same for the second round of the presidential election 7 August 1994). The differences between the two sources – *Correio Guiné-Bissau* and the National Electoral Commission – are insignificant, although the internal materials of the commission go further into local details. The following account draws heavily on Rudebeck 1996b; 1997a and 1997b.

The national level

At the national level, the old ruling party, PAIGC, won 38 per cent of the votes in the parliamentary election. Due to the workings of the proportional system of representation, favouring the largest party in each constituency, this gave the PAIGC 62 of the 100 seats at stake, while the various opposition parties together only received 38 seats, although their combined share of the votes was about equal to that of the PAIGC.[44] The outcome is a situation with 6 parties represented in parliament and 4 remaining outside.

The presidential election, in the final round, turned out to be dramatic as already told. The former President, João Bernardo 'Nino' Vieira, was challenged by 7 other candidates in the first round. With 40 per cent he came out first, but as he got less than half of the total vote, a second round was required by the constitution, so that 'Nino' had to face the opponent who had come second in the first round: namely Koumba Yalá, a former PAIGC activist. In the parliamentary election, Koumba Yalá's party, PRS, had received only 12 parliamentary seats out of 100. Yet, in the second round of the presidential election, Koumba Yalá came very close to victory. In the final count he received 48 per cent of the approved votes versus 52 per cent for the incumbent president.

Table 5.6 shows how the votes and parliamentary seats were distributed in the National Assembly election, while Tables 5.7 and 5.8 give the distribution of votes in the two rounds of presidential elections.

Table 5.6: Parliamentary election results, 3 July 1994

	Seats in ANP	Percentage of votes (total 355,992 votes)	
PAIGC	62	37.9	37.9
RGB/MB	19	16.2	
PRS	12	8.4	
UM with LIPE	6	10.3	
FLING	1	2.1	37.0
unrepres. parties	–	6.8	
blank votes	–	14.8	
invalid votes	–	3.5	25.1
Total	100	100	100

Sources: Published and unpublished materials of the National Election Commission and special issue on the election of *Correio Guiné-Bissau* (30 July 1994) based on the officially available materials of the National Election Commission.

Table 5.7: Presidential election results, first round, 3 July 1994

	Percentage of votes (total 357,682 votes)
'Nino' Vieira (PAIGC)	39.9
Koumba Yalá (PRS)	18.9
Domingos Fernandes Gomes (RGB/MB)	15.1
Carlos Domingos Gomes (PCD)	4.4
François Kankoila Mendy (FLING)	2.4
Bubacar Djaló (UM/LIPE)	2.4
Victor Saúde Maria (PUSD)	1.8
Antonieta Rosa Gomes (FCG/SD)	1.8
blank votes	10.8
invalid votes	2.9
Total	100

Source: Unpublished materials of the National Election Commission.

[44]The specific method used in this case was the so-called 'd'Hondt method', named after a Belgian jurist who devised it during the late nineteenth century. By this method, each time a party has been allotted a seat, the number of votes received by that party is divided by the number of seats received + 1, before comparing, for the distribution of the next seat at stake, with the numbers received by the remaining parties. If there are many parties in the run, of which one is clearly larger than the others, this means that the largest party often gets both the first and either the second or the third seat (sometimes both) in any given constituency.

Table 5.8: Presidential election results, second round, August 7 1994, by regions and all Guinea-Bissau[45]

Regions	Percentage and total number of votes				
	'Nino'	Koumba Yalá	Blank	Invalid	Votes
Tombali	41.2	54.5	3.1	1.3	23,075
Quinara	55.7	39.8	3.3	1.2	15,247
Oio	`35.7	58.1	4.7	1.5	54,820
Biombo	69.7	23.3	4.7	2.3	20,459
Bolama/Bijagos	89.3	7.9	1.8	1.0	11,111
Bafatá	55.9	37.4	5.2	1.5	44,735
Gabú	59.6	34.9	3.4	2.1	40,743
Cacheu	37.1	54.8	6.3	1.7	36,893
Bissau	45.7	52.0	1.4	1.0	79,533
Whole country	49.3	45.5	3.7	1.4	326,615

Source: Unpublished materials of the National Election Commission.

Participation was relatively high among the registered voters on 3 July 1994. Altogether 400,417 voters had been registered, roughly equivalent to 81 per cent of the population of voting age.[46] Nearly 90 per cent of these actually voted, meaning that roughly 72 per cent of the total population of voting age took part.

The outcome as such, in terms of relative party strength, was not unexpected. The PAIGC victory shows that the old ruling party, in spite of rampant dissatisfaction with harsh conditions of life and high-level corruption, still remained a kind of self-evident representative of state power, particularly in the rural areas. But the result also demonstrates that the efforts of the opposition had not been in vain. Although the electoral system and divisions within the opposition favoured PAIGC, the opposition still took 38 seats out of 100 in the parliament. This alone is a great change in comparison with the previous single-party system.

The fact that the six-party coalition UM received no more than six seats may have surprised some observers. Basically it can be interpreted as an indication that the voters did not see it as a real alternative to PAIGC.

Participation was high on 7 August 1994 as well, although somewhat lower than in July. The number of registered voters was the same as before, but this time slightly over 81 per cent voted as compared to almost 90 per cent a month earlier, indicating some election fatigue among the citizens. Public interest was still strong, though, and was certainly heightened by the close struggle between the two final candidates. In spite of some uncertainty, the outcome was eventually accepted by all involved, including Koumba Yalá, who nevertheless let it be known that he considered the old regime to have been moving 'on the margins of the law' during the final days of the election campaigning (for earlier accounts, see Rudebeck 1977; 1986; 1988; 1991; 1992; 1996b; 1997a; and 1997b).[47]

The village level

The 1994 election and its aftermath can be examined in one single village, that of Kandjadja in northern Guinea-Bissau (for earlier accounts, see Rudebeck 1977; 1986; 1988; 1991; 1992; 1996b; 1997a; and 1997b). It has around 1,000 inhabitants and is the central village of a section

[45]The percentage figures for the two rivals are somewhat lower than those given earlier in the text. This is because the figures used in the public debate in Guinea-Bissau at the time (52 versus 48) did not include blank and invalid votes.

[46]Population of voting age (18 years of age and above, as before) is roughly estimated here as 45% of 1,100 000 = 495,500.

[47]The statement is found in the independent Bissau daily, *Banobero* 7 February 1995 (in chronicle of the year 1994). It is not uncommon that people express doubts in private about the outcome of the second round of the presidential elections, assuming then that the real winner might well have been Koumba Yalá rather than President 'Nino'. However, no firm evidence is available to support such allegations.

comprising 14 other smaller villages as well. Bissau, the capital city, is about 120 kilometers away, including 11 kilometers of track road through the forest, leading up to the main road. A large majority of the people are Mandinga, but people of Balanta and Fula ethnic groups also live in the section.

The livelihood of the people in Kandjadja is based on agriculture, as well as on earnings by migrants who have left for Bissau and abroad. In recent years, cashew nuts have taken the place of groundnuts as the major local source of cash income. Materially, the village subsists and survives. As yet, there have been only limited signs of economic improvement during the past 20 years.

The 1994 elections had taken place normally in Kandjadja, as well as elsewhere in Guinea-Bissau.[48] During April 1996, a poster stating in Creole that 'only you and God know how you vote' was still left on the wall of the local shop in the village of Kandjadja. Indications were that this rule had been well respected in the village.

The number of potential voters, that is citizens having reached the age of 18 at least 30 days before voting day, had been counted at 394 in Kandjadja. Of these, 371 had registered as voters. The actual turnout on 3 July was 82 per cent (304) of the 371, and on 7 August it was as high as 98 per cent (363).

As seen from Table 5.9 below, the position of PAIGC among the voters was stronger in the village than in the country as a whole. But the ruling party was not unchallenged, since the opposition was far from negligible. If the distribution of seats had been decided only on the basis of Kandjada's votes, the third mandate would have gone to PCD, a party that did not even manage to get any representation at all at national level. This shows that the democratic system functioned, in the sense that a specific opinion was able to manifest itself at the local level.

Table 5.9: Parliamentary election results in Kandjadja, July 7 1994

	Number of votes	Per cent
PAIGC	178	58.6
PCD	68	22.4
RGB/MB	28	9.2
PRS	15	4.9
PUSD	9	3.0
FD	4	1.3
FLING	2	0.7
UM	0	
Total	304	100

Sources: Notes taken on election day by the controller named by the PAIGC and approved by the National Electoral Commission for the local electoral district of Kandjadja.

The final result of the presidential election in Kandjadja differed even more strikingly from the national result. President 'Nino' won as many as 328 votes, which is 88 per cent of the total number of registered voters. Koumba Yalá got 35 votes (9 per cent), while the rate of abstention as already mentioned was very low (8 individuals). 'Nino's' position was thus seen to be very strong in Kandjadja, in fact much stronger than that of the party PAIGC.

To sum up, it seems clear that the local voters felt fairly free to express their opinions as voters and that many of them took the chance to manifest their criticism of 'the party', while not being prepared to see anybody else than 'Nino', the former hero of the national liberation struggle, as their president. In this, they were quite typical of rural people in many parts of Guinea-Bissau, excluding those parts where Koumba Yalá had his strongholds.

Electoral participation in a comparative perspective

It was noted above that electoral participation was relatively high in the first multi-party elections to be held in Guinea-Bissau. This is shown very clearly when compared with previous non- and

---

[48]As far as Kandjadja is concerned, I was able myself, in March and April 1996, to document the specific electoral process with the help of local interviews and documents.

single-party elections to have been held in the country. The following table is based on rough estimates of the percentages of eligible voters who actually voted in the various elections held in
Guinea-Bissau from 1972 until 1994.

It is striking that the multi-party election of 1994 mobilised many more voters than did the
preceding single-party elections, not to speak of the colonial non-party election of 1973. It does
not appear far-fetched to conclude from this that the 1994 election also had higher democratic
legitimacy than its predecessors did.

**Table 5.10: Approximate percentage of adult population voting in various
elections**

Election	Participation, per cent
1973 colonial non-party	2.9
1972 wartime PAIGC-controlled	31.7
1976 single-party	56.0
1984 single-party	48.4
1989 single-party	49.2
1994 multi-party parliamentary	71.8

Sources: See sources for Tables 5.1–5.6 and respective calculations of adult
population (population of voting age), notes 9, 11, 15, 21, 26, 28 and 46.

The representation of women

One important aspect of democratisation has to do with how it affects the position of women in
society. It is possible to consider various ways in which the opening up of the political system to
different opinions, an open debate of key contradictions in social and political life and a much
freer associational life than previously might affect the position of women favourably. The fact
that a woman was one of the candidates to be President of the Republic of Guinea-Bissau certainly
has symbolic significance too, in spite of the meagre percentage of votes she won in 1994.

It is nevertheless a fact that in sheer numerical terms, the representation of women at the
national level deteriorated as Guinea-Bissau moved from authoritarian single-party politics to
relatively liberal-democratic multi-partyism. In the National Assembly, indirectly elected under
the old regime in 1989, there were as mentioned 30 woman deputies out of 150. In the democratically and directly elected assembly of 1994, there were no more than 8 women among the 100
deputies. The percentage of women representatives had thus been reduced from 20 to 8.[49]

The only certain conclusion to be drawn from such a comparison between the two parliaments
elected in 1989 and 1994 is that electoral democratisation as such does not by itself guarantee
equalisation of the representation of women.[50]

All that can be said here about the village level is that three deputies were elected in 1994 to the
National Assembly from the sub-regional district to which Kandjadja belonged. All of them were
men.

Post-election developments

National level

Although interrupted by the war of June–July 1998, democratisation at the national level in
Guinea-Bissau had at least until then meant the institutionalisation of a new political system,

[49]Originally there were nine women elected, but one joined the government, leaving only eight in the National
Assembly.

[50]It is known, for instance, that when female suffrage was introduced in countries such as Germany and
Sweden soon after 1918, this was statistically correlated with electoral gains for those parties which had fought
against democratisation in that form. See Tingsten 1963 (1937), 36 ff. Tingsten's analysis of these seemingly
paradoxical correlations clearly shows that they cannot be used to substantiate simple conclusions about the
possible effects of democratisation.

under which the government was forced to accept scrutiny by the opposition and where civil and associational rights, without being perfectly guaranteed, were better ensured than before.

The daily life of the majority of the population, however, was far from the constitutional political system. Here, there were few indications of increasing popular sovereignty before June 1998. Generally, the overwhelming majority of the population found within the agricultural sector of the economy had not seen their relations with the state decisively altered through democratisation. Increasing differentiation favoured some farmers within the framework of the deregulated economy, but the new opportunities did not suffice for all, while old ones dried up and stagnated. Deterioration of educational and health facilities caused young people to move to the towns. But, in the urban sector, while unemployment increased despite lively commercial activity, the daily minimum money wage did not even cover the price of rice necessary for daily consumption.

Over the longer run it is difficult to reconcile such poverty with the democratic form of rule, although it is impossible to say in advance where the breaking-point will manifest itself. From a general point of view, we may assume that democracy, in the short and medium term, makes people more prepared to accept harsh conditions than do other forms of rule – but only as long as they, as citizens, perceive themselves to share responsibility for a better future. If this assumption holds, then the consolidation of democracy in Guinea-Bissau will hardly be possible without greater popular sovereignty in society as a whole than was found before June 1998. Post-war political and economic measures taken will thus be decisive.

The overriding threat to democratisation is poverty and those difficult conditions of life, which have not seemed to improve for the majority of the population. Discontent was manifested for example in a series of demonstrations and strikes by opposition parties and the national trade union organisation towards the end of 1995, under slogans such as 'against hunger, corruption, and a government moving backwards'.[51] Growing social differentiation and the intertwining of politics and economics under continued structural adjustment increased the vulnerability of ordinary people.

As in many countries, the official development ideology in Guinea-Bissau, both before and after the war of June-July 1998, is to leave a lot of space to the autonomous efforts of citizens within 'civil society'.[52] But such measures do not answer the question of how far the state can withdraw without leaving large groups of the population without access to common resources. In order to avoid this gap, the state may also choose to increase the space for citizen responsibility within state institutions, usually through democratisation by decentralisation. This possibility was on the agenda of the government of Guinea-Bissau during the mid-1990s. The strategic question is how these two approaches, state withdrawal versus the democratisation of the state, can be made to supplement and support each other. In order for the decentralised state organs to be credible in the eyes of the people, they must, for example, control financial resources for spending on public services.

Village level

The same basic national contradiction of development and democracy is also found in Kandjadja at the local level. The people have welcomed and positively viewed the new political system as contributing to personal freedom and the rule of law. This was welcomed and positively viewed. But the citizens feel betrayed, at the same time, as so many promises have been given without being kept. Two years after the elections, life was as harsh as ever. While the patience of the people is considerable, it is hardly unlimited. The question is complex, as reality is split. At a meeting held in Kandjadja to discuss democracy with some hundred villagers in March 1996, the following comment was made by a young man:

> Democracy has both positive and negative sides. Let us speak concretely. Thanks to democracy, an end has been put to some abuses in the prisons. Nor do we any longer have armed thieves in the forest stealing our timber. This is good. But where, in our part of the country, has the government helped us drill a well? Nowhere. If PAIGC does not do anything concrete for us, we will not vote for them. If no concrete improvements take place, we shall withdraw.

---

[51]*Nô Pintcha* 1 November 1995; *Voz de Bissau* 3 November 1995; *Banobero* 10 November 1995.
[52]Interview with Helder Proença, Minister in Charge of the Presidency and Parliamentary Affairs, 21 March 1996.

In Kandjadja, as in other parts of Guinea-Bissau, local government has not yet controlled any developmentally significant financial resources. Even if a local assembly were to be installed at village sector level within the coming years, it is uncertain whether it would carry enough weight to achieve credibility. Within civil society, on the other hand, a new phenomenon had appeared during the first half of the 1990s.

Before 1990, single-party rule had made it impossible in practice for non-governmental organisations to function in developmental work without being closely linked to state and party. Autonomous initiatives of more than local significance had been almost unthinkable. Kandjadja was only one of many villages where the economy stagnated and cultural and political life was turned inwards and often in ethnic directions.

But in 1990, political liberalisation and democratisation brought new opportunities. An African non-governmental organisation, *Résau Africain pour le Développement Intégré* (RADI) began to visit Kandjadja with new ideas, encouraging the people to develop local agriculture on the basis of their own organisational and cultural traditions.[53]

Popular response was strong. The innovative work of this NGO was carried on completely independently of local state and party structures. RADI provided seeds on credit as well as technical instruction. The participants divided work between themselves according to age groups and gender. Within each group, women took an active part. A large meeting hall and youth club was built with local means, as well as storage houses for seeds, tools and products. This was the first time, since the early years of independence, that something introduced from outside had evoked such broad trust in Kandjadja.

If a directly-elected local assembly is established in Kandjadja within the near future, then the question of how it relates to RADI will be crucial for its chances of functioning in the area. If, for instance, the closed state school could be re-opened thanks to state decentralisation, such an achievement would probably contribute greatly to increasing the local legitimacy of the state.

The example of Kandjadja demonstrates how the absence of the state in developmental work created a vacuum, as well as deep popular disenchantment. This in turn opened up chances for an organisation such as RADI to strike a chord of strong response within civil society. Thanks to democratisation this became legal. Still, it is difficult to see how continued development could take place without the presence of more dynamic state power than up to now. In spite of democratic elections, the gap between society and state was as deep as ever in 1996. The gap had possibly even deepened, since new hopes and expectations had been created and been quickly betrayed. The democratic decentralisation of the state under consideration in the National Assembly at the time was thus logical, although weakly rooted in local society.

War in 1998/99 and new elections

As already mentioned, the peaceful process of political transformation in Guinea-Bissau was abruptly interrupted by civil and regional war in mid-1998 (see for instance Rudebeck 1998b).[54]

In the early morning of Sunday, 7 June 1998, shooting was heard from the military installations in the north-eastern parts of Bissau, the capital city. Fighting spread quickly to the military base near the airport, in the north-western parts of the city. In a radio broadcast the same day, president João Bernardo 'Nino' Vieira held former commander-in-chief, Brigadier Ansumane Mané, responsible for an armed revolt against the legal government.

---

[53]RADI is an African NGO with national organisations in several other African countries (See its brochure *Le RADI. Ce qu'il est et ce qu'il veut* [*Résau Africain pour le Développement Intégré* no date]). The Guinea-Bissau branch of RADI was in 1996 directed from the Bissau office of the Swiss aid organisation, Swissaid. The office was headed by a Guinean who was at the same time the RADI coordinator in Guinea-Bissau and the local representative of Swissaid. RADI was able to function in Guinea-Bissau due partly to the material support offered by Swissaid. Thus, even RADI depended on foreign aid, despite the fact that all of its work was carried out by Guineans, that the administration was small-scale, and that it had strong local support.

[54]The following is based on own close research on developments in Guinea-Bissau during 1998–2000, including three periods of fieldwork in May and November–December 1999 and January 2000. An early account is given in Rudebeck 1998b. More detailed accounts and analyses will be provided in forthcoming publications by this author.

Two days later, on 9 June, spokesmen of Ansumane Mané announced that a military 'junta' had been formed. It demanded the resignation of the president in order to create proper conditions, according to the rebels, for democratic elections to be held within sixty days. As the holding of parliamentary elections before the end of 1998 and presidential elections in 1999, according to the constitution, had been the stated ambition also of the legal government, the real causes and motives behind the uprising did not stand out very clearly at this stage.

The initial impression conveyed by international media, based largely upon official as well as officious declarations from Bissau, was that this was a mutiny by a disgruntled group of military men that would in all probability be put down quite rapidly. Very soon, however, the situation appeared considerably more complex. As early as 9 June, the very day of the rebels' initial decla-ration, 1,300 soldiers from Guinea-Bissau's northern neighbour Senegal were already in place in Bissau on the president's demand to support the few loyalist troops. On the next day, the Senegalese were joined by 400 soldiers from Guinée-Conakry, the neighbour in the South, with even more Senegalese arriving in the following weeks. Thus the conflict was almost immediately regionalised.

The image of a simple mutiny against the legal, democratically-elected government was very far from the whole truth. Legality and political legitimacy seem in this case to have been far apart. After the first days of the war, the president appeared politically isolated and abandoned by most of his army, reduced to relying on the military force of the Senegalese army to remain in office, and thus totally dependent upon foreign troops.

The war was carried on primarily by destructive artillery fighting between the foreign forces supporting the government inside Bissau and the rebel forces surrounding the city. About five-sixths of the city's approximately 300,000 inhabitants fled into the countryside, while thousands of other citizens as well as almost all foreigners escaped abroad, mainly by sea.

The background was that Ansumane Mané, a veteran of Guinea-Bissau's anti-colonial liber-ation war where he served with president 'Nino', had been suspended from his post as commander-in-chief of the armed forces in January 1998. The alleged reason was negligence in regard to controlling the illegal sale of Guinean arms to the rebels struggling for the self-determi-nation of Casamance, the southern-most province of Senegal, across Guinea-Bissau's northern frontier. The Casamance rebellion had gone on with varying intensity since the first half of the 1980s. The Senegalese government had long been worried by the easy flow of persons and, as it seems, arms between Guinea-Bissau and Casamance. Furthermore, the majority people of Casamance, the Diolas, are culturally and historically close to important groups of people in northern Guinea-Bissau.

There were, however, no clear indications that the issue of arms trafficking as such could be traced specifically to the suspended commander-in-chief. A parliamentary commission with multi-party representation had investigated the charges under great secrecy. Its findings were to have been presented to the parliament and the public on 8 June. But on 5 June, Ansumane Mané was instead suddenly dismissed, followed two days later by the outbreak of fighting at his domicile. The public discussion of the investigation report was thus aborted.

Seven weeks of subsequent war hardly budged the initial front-lines. Finally, on 26 July, the military and diplomatic stalemate resulted in a provisional truce negotiated by the Portuguese-speaking countries' organisation *Comunidade de Países de Lingua Portuguesa* (CPLP). After initial rivalry, agreement was reached on cooperation between CPLP and the West-African states' regional organisation, Economic Community of West-African States (ECOWAS) on the matter, and the truce was transformed into a formal cease-fire on 26 August, 1998, in Praia, the capital city of Cape Verde. Heavy fighting resumed on two occasions in October 1998, on 9–10 and 18–21, resulting in decisive military gains for the rebel side and apparently causing president 'Nino' to give up his last hopes for a military victory. Having lost Bafatá and Gabu, the two major towns in central and eastern Guinea-Bissau, to the rebels and being completely encircled with his foreign protectors in central Bissau – almost empty after the population had fled again – the president saw no other choice than accepting to meet with Ansumane Mané, the leader of the self-proclaimed military 'junta'.

At a two-day meeting in Banjul, Gambia's capital city, the belligerents failed to agree on condi-tions for peace in spite of intensive negotiations. Instead they flew on together to Abuja, the capital city of Nigeria, where an assembled ECOWAS summit meeting finally pressured them, on 1 November, 1998, into signing a peace agreement.

According to the Abuja agreement, a transitional national unity government with military 'junta' representation was to be formed and remain in power, awaiting elections. The military forces of Senegal and Guinea-Conakry were to be withdrawn, and followed instead by ECOMOG (ECOWAS's 'peace-monitoring group') troops, expected to control Guinea-Bissau's border with Senegal and also, presumably, to act as a force of 'interposition' in Bissau. The airport which had remained under 'junta' control all through would be opened, as well as the harbour. The president would remain in office for the time being.

The Abuja agreement was a significant achievement in terms of African peace-making. In the end it was even implemented to a considerable extent, although only after many delays and two more outbreaks of military fighting. The final and decisive one of these occurred on 6–7 May, 1999. It resulted in the total defeat of President 'Nino's' forces, in the passive presence of 600 ECOMOG West African soldiers. The President himself was escorted by 'junta' commanders to the Portuguese embassy in Bissau where he found asylum, until allowed to leave the country for Portugal one month later.

The victorious 'junta' troops under Ansumane Mané promised withdrawal to their barracks, while the transitional government under Prime Minister Francisco Fadul continued in office, until parliamentary and presidential elections were finally held on 28 November, 1999. As none of the 12 presidential candidates reached over 50 per cent of the vote, a second and decisive round of the presidential election was held on 16 January, 2000.

The 1999/2000 elections would obviously have merited careful analysis in the present context. Due to the fact that they occurred too late for this to be possible in terms of publishing deadlines for our book, let it only be mentioned here that those elections were momentous in the political history of Guinea-Bissau for allowing the political opposition to gain a parliamentary majority and form a coalition government of its own as well as for allowing the leading candidate of the opposition to become the President of the Republic. The formerly dominant party PAIGC scored no more than 15 per cent of the vote which gave it 24 out of 102 seats in the National Assembly. The new President was Koumba Yalá, the same populist PRS politician who had been narrowly defeated by former President 'Nino' in the close second round of 1994. On 16 January 2000, Koumba Yalá scored an overwhelming victory over the PAIGC candidate Malam Bacai Sanhá, interim President since May 1999 and former Speaker of the National Assembly. The all-country outcome was 69 per cent of the votes for Koumba Yalá and 27 per cent for Malam Bacai Sanhá. reformist candidate of the old regime.

Not knowing the future, all that can be said with some certainty about the long-term significance of the violent events of 1998/1999 for democratization in Guinea-Bissau is that the setting and the givens of the political process in the country had been severely shaken. It remains to be seen how profound this was. It seems clear, though, that a minimum requirement for democratic legitimacy in Guinea-Bissau in coming years will be less governmental authoritarianism and less top-level corruption than before. Still, during the first six months after the country's return to democratic constitutionalism in January 2000, there were few signs of this materialising. On the contrary, the most promising indications in that direction were noted during the period of transition from May to November 1999, while after the elections there was instead more of a disturbing return to pre-war 'normalcy' and less of that real political and institutional change so intensely longed for by Guineans and also by concerned foreigners.

By way of conclusion

In the introduction to this chapter, the two concepts of constitutionalism and popular sovereignty/ autonomy were singled out as two crucial aspects to be distinguished in the historical processes leading up to the actually existing democracy of the 1990s. Democratic sustainability was said to depend largely on the simultaneous presence of both to some significant extent. The importance of the relative timing of their emergence in history was pointed out.

The historical example of Guinea-Bissau's experiences with national elections of three different types, in war and peace, and on six different occasions from 1972 to 1994, provided us with a significant case to evaluate these propositions.

The key question raised was about the conditions of the consolidation/sustainability of a newly introduced democratic system of rule. It was postulated that the democratic form of rule cannot survive into sustainability without being legitimate in the eyes of most citizens. At a very minimum, this particular form of rule must be accepted by a stable majority of the citizens. Anything else would be a contradiction in terms. Legitimacy is thus a necessary key condition of democratic sustainability.

In a general way, it could be said that democratic legitimacy has two types of foundations. One concerns what is deemed by people to be just and right, the other what they find useful and possible in their lives. This is the double foundation of democracy struggles across the world, both historically and in our own time (see introduction to Rudebeck ed. 1992, 8).

The meaning of this is that lofty ideals of justice and freedom and control over material conditions of life are simultaneously at stake. Whether or not democratic constitutionalism will survive in Guinea-Bissau depends therefore, in the first place, upon the actual relations of power in society at large, that is, the extent to which actually existing democratic constitutionalism is supplemented with popular sovereignty/autonomy.[55] This is a larger issue than this study of national elections taking place in Guinea-Bissau from 1972 to 1994. Hopefully, however, the study does illuminate some of the crucial and intricate interlinkages between competitive elections and democratisation.

---

[55]Referring to democratisation in Africa generally, the Guinean sociologist Carlos Lopes, resident representative of UNDP in Harare, observes that abrupt democratisation may well result in 'situations where the push for multiparty systems is the most appropriate way of maintaining a discredited elite in power' (Lopes 1997, 129, this author's translation). Even before the 1998 war, this observation was quite relevant to aspects of democratisation in Guinea-Bissau. Profiting from hindsight, the course of the war can be interpreted as demonstrating the actual extent to which legally democratic power in Guinea-Bissau was discredited by disregarding the need for citizen or popular sovereignty/autonomy.

6

The 1997 Elections in Kenya
The Politics of Communality & Locality

MICHAEL COWEN & KARUTI KANYINGA

Introduction[1]

On 29 December 1997, Kenya held its second post-colonial multi-party set of presidential, parliamentary and local government elections. As Tables 6.2 and 6.3 below show, the Kenya African National Union (Kanu), the party which has ruled Kenya since independence, won a majority of seats in parliament while Daniel arap Moi, the incumbent president since 1978, was returned to office. Despite some significance in the difference between the 1992 and 1997 results, as Tables 6.1 and 6.2 also indicate, the 1997 elections were not a momentous event in themselves. Indeed, it is likely that late-1997 in Kenya will be remembered more for the *El Niño* rains, which brought widespread death, disease and destruction in their wake, than the general elections of that year.

However, the 1997 elections were significant as part of a wider electoral process on two counts. Firstly, important political consequences during forthcoming years are likely to follow from the fact that the elections narrowed Kanu's majority over opposition parties in parliament. While we also point to the significance of some immediate post-election events towards the end of this chapter, it must be emphasised at the outset that the 1997 results produced a hung parliament. Kanu's thin majority meant that unless it were able to win electorally significant by-elections, the ruling party would be forced to negotiate with one or more opposition parties to stay in government and secure legislation. One such significant by-election during 1999 is also reported below.

Facts about voter registration and participation, electoral administration and campaigning may be important and of interest in themselves but, whether singly or taken overall, these factors do not appear to have affected the overall result of the elections to an extent which would have changed the configuration of political forces in Kenya.[2] Since it is the configuration of political forces which also best explains the facts of electoral administration, this paper concentrates on providing a political account of why Kanu and President Moi won the 1997 elections. As we will explain below, the 1997 election results are about the extent to which an anti-Kanu and Moi majority prevailed over the countervailing anti-Kikuyu majority. This paper focuses upon what accounts for change in the counterbalance between these two negative political forces.

Secondly, and following from the above, the 1997 elections encompassed an interlinked chain of constitutional, economic and violent events which came before and after the election campaign

---

[1]We are indebted to Michael Chege, Liisa Laakso, Suzanne Mueller and Scott MacWilliam for their exhaustive comments on earlier drafts of this chapter.
[2]For an account of the general administration of the 1997 elections, see Tostensen, Andreassen, and Tronvoll 1998. This report also includes that of the Donors' Democratic Development Group, the most substantial, and also controversial, of the apparatuses which were mounted to observe the elections. The most serious short-comings reported were the failure to register 1.5 to 2.5 million voters, aged 18–23, who had not been issued with identity cards before registration, and the possibility that parliamentary results were either rigged and/or flawed in ten constituencies.

and polling. Between April and September, pre-electoral events included a spate of mass meetings, demonstrations and rallies to advance the cause of constitutional and electoral reform; seemingly violent attempts to ethnically cleanse population in the Coast Province and elsewhere; and the suspension of loan finance by the IMF and World Bank in the name of conditionally asserting the need for 'good governance' in Kenya.[3]

Ramifications of the events were immediate and extended to widespread violence and the destabilisation of the economy. Violence involved the fatal shooting and maiming of protestors by police, in Nairobi and other urban centres, the lynching of plainclothes policemen, also at a demonstration in Nairobi, and the slaughter of at least 8 police officers and 110 civilians at Likoni and, later, elsewhere along the Coast. Destabilisation of the economy, following the suspension of an IMF loan facility to the government of Kenya, presaged a prospect of inflationary pressure since the effects of the immediate depreciation in the value of the Kenya shilling and rising import prices were amplified by indirect tax rate increases, necessary to fill part of the budget gap which was meant to be financed by the IMF loan. Furthermore, the violent events at Likoni, as earlier in Nairobi, threatened the tourist industry, a foremost foreign-exchange earning sector of the economy and, thereby, wage employment in the industry as well as the self-employment of small traders whose streetside premises were destroyed aplenty along the coast during the course of these events.

Events of this first period of the 1997 electoral prelude culminated in a parliamentary agreement of 11 September, between Kanu and opposition members of parliament, for a minimal programme of reform to change the constitution and electoral procedures as well as the general policing and administration of political practice. Detention without trial and torture were legally prohibited; the holding of meetings, rallies and demonstrations was to be freely allowed; all political parties which had applied for registration were to be registered; and public broadcast media were to be made non-partisan. Between September and November, the second period of the prelude, the agreement between the Moi government and a majority of opposition members of parliament was enacted in parliament. However, the agreement was contested by a political amalgam of some opposition parliamentarians, leaders of political parties, churches and other civil society organisations who did not view the parliamentary agreement as a sufficient means of securing 'free and fair' elections for 1997.[4] Earlier events continued to have an impact after the September agreement. Despite some equivocation over whether the reforms were to be enacted in full before the election, reform Bills passed into law in early November when parliament was dissolved and the immediate electoral period was set in train.

The electoral prelude was as significant as the electoral period in determining the outcome of the elections in both 1992 and 1997. It was during the electoral prelude that the potential outcome of the elections was contested within a non-parliamentary framework of action that was as much electoral in intent as the set of elections towards which they were directed. Bearing the electoral prelude in mind, the 1997 elections were also significant because they bring into question the pattern of multi-party politics in Kenya which seemed to be established by the holding of the first post-colonial multi-party elections in 1992.

In Kenya, as elsewhere in Africa, internal opposition parties and movements and international agencies have all held the belief that multi-party elections provide a potential for a progressive movement away from rule through authoritarian corruption and towards a more accountable system of government – the necessary condition for a general improvement in economic and social welfare. Since authoritarian rule and corruption in Africa has been long epitomised by the Moi regime of Kanu government, the belief in the progressive force of multi-party politics holds firm only so long as it can be anticipated that Moi and the Kanu government can be dislodged from power through elections.

Insofar as results of the 1997 elections have confirmed rather dislodged the ruling regime from power, one apparently paradoxical question arises. The question is whether the fact that President

---

[3]For both a survey of some aspects of electoral administration and an account of the electoral prelude events, see Cowen and Ngunyi 1997; also see Barkan and Ng'ethe 1998, 34–41.

[4]Churches, whether or not included in 'civil society', have played a substantial role in politics. For an overview, see Throup 1995.

Moi mobilised to counter the advent of multi-party politics in Kenya is the same one that the results of multi-party elections have only served to highlight by confirming his regime in power. This factor is that of an ethnic or tribal pattern of voting, which Moi claimed would tear the country apart, but that has ensured that his regime continues to command a plurality of votes in the face of opposition parties whose electoral basis has been primarily defined according to the ethno-regional attributes of tribe.

Our argument in this paper is that the well-addressed question of *tribe*, namely the territorial association between an ethnic people and a region, has been conflated with the *local* of political representation in Kenya.[5] It is as much the local as the tribal which has to be brought into play to explain national contours of political power and opposition in Kenya. Questions over the communal logic of political association arise out of the place that the local occupies in national politics. The expression of the contending logic of communal politics was repressed during the one-party period, which effectively lasted for virtually the first three decades of the post-colonial period when no multi-party *general* elections were held. One difference between the one- and multi-party periods is that the latent logic of political association can now be openly expressed, acted upon and conceptualised as a source of political action for multi-party politics. Given that the local has always played a major part in intra-party electoral contest, it is through the interaction between the national and the local of political action that we attempt to show why the paradox of multi-party democracy in Kenya has brought communal politics to the fore. Insofar as conflict within political parties has spilled over into the multi-party arena, it is the source of the conflict, as much economic as simply political, which has to be taken into account when unravelling the paradox of communality.

Ethnic identities of tribe, especially when invoked to have some communitarian value, have too long been presented as being an end of political action when they have been the political means to promote and secure indigenous African capitalist class formation in Kenya. Since the primary accumulation of capital, especially during the Moi period of government, has necessarily involved corruption, the local of political representation and the ethnic layering of capital have amplified communal patterns of voting. Corruption, as a conjunction between accumulation 'from above' and an authoritarian disposition towards the instruments of state power, has done much to explain the form of state rule in Kenya. This chapter attempts to show how different communal logics of political association bring the local into the interplay with the commanding heights of state power. Taken as a whole, the electoral process is one important way in which this interplay has occurred historically in Kenya.

Communal politics: 1963–1997

Communality has entered the organisation of politics in Kenya in two ways. The first is that of ethnic or 'tribal' identity, which arises out of territorial association between the space of an area of land and people of a given language grouping and/or culture. In Kenya, as in much of former British colonial Africa, the boundaries of administrative regions or provinces broadly corresponded to what was judged to separate different sources of 'tribal' identity.[6] Since the ecology of land varies between regions, and regions are identified with particular tribal groupings, the

---

[5]It should be noted here, and for what follows below, that there is little novelty in the conception that the 'tribal' and 'tribal identity' has often stood for other interests. Much of the social anthropological work, especially during the 1950s, of the Rhodes-Livingstone Institute in the former Northern Rhodesia, was centred on working through the social meaning of tribe in a 'modern' and/or urban setting. See Epstein 1958; Mitchell 1956; Watson 1958. We owe this point to Michael Chege.

[6]It is for this reason that Greet Kershaw (1997, 276–277), for example, has uncontroversially noted that the 'concept of a Kikuyu "tribe" is more colonial and post-colonial than pre-colonial' and that the 'belief that there had been a "tribe" became a self-fulfilling prophecy as boundaries hardened and [inter-ethnic] interaction was stifled'. Furthermore, 'this increased sense of ethnicity fostered the sense of being a closed entity, different and distinct from other entities'. These 'entities', as we mention further below, became 'tribal' because of the identity with a territory of land for economic subsistence and accumulation.

potential for different kinds of agriculture and other economic activities also came to be associated with tribal identity. However, for our purpose here, it is this political identity which, as Roddy Fox (1996, 603) has put it, is 'part and parcel of the continuing "game of tribal politics" in Kenya.' One significant institutional arrangement for elections is that the tribal and ethnic basis of the old administrative boundaries has been perpetuated for the purpose of mapping the distribution of parliamentary constituencies and which, as Fox has shown, thereby governs the basic rule of the political game.[7]

Secondly, communality enters political organisation as a result of a specific source of identity that cannot simply and unequivocally be reduced to the 'ethnic'. As usually understood, and however complex the relation between the ethnic and the 'tribal', ethnic identity arises in an arena where people of different language groups and/or cultures occupy the same area.[8] Notwithstanding, for example, the segmentation of urban space according to ethnic identities, as in the formation of residential ghettos, or the distribution of occupations or means of livelihood according to ethnic criteria, it is the heterogeneity of the city through which 'the ethnic' arises as a source of political mobilisation. However, communality has a different implication where and when a population is ethnically homogeneous in a territory of land. Ethnic identity arises from the 'tribal' conception of the territorial when and where the territory of land, or water in the case of fishing, provides the main source of economic subsistence, acquisition and accumulation. This second implication of communality, following from association of the ethnic with a region of land, and land with the means of production, makes 'the tribal' also more than simply a political game in cases such as Kenya.

From the foregoing, and for what follows below, it must be emphasised that the territorial space of tribe is not merely some historical or geographical given within which the political interplay of the local and the national takes place. While particular places have acquired an inherent economic and social meaning, territoriality has increasingly become a source of political power. Strategies, including violence, to politically control contested territorial space have been an integral part of sustained attempts to maintain political power and, thereby, give shape to the identities from which the political content of the local is largely derived.

Due to the extent of European landed settlement from the first years of colonial rule over the present territory of Kenya, the difference between the tribal and the ethnic has added meaning for the contemporary significance of communal politics. The scale of large-farm estate agriculture, predominantly in the Rift Valley, and along the lines of rail, first to Kisumu on Lake Victoria, and then through the present Western Province to the Uganda border at Malaba, created extensive areas of 'extra- or non-tribal' territory, the 'white highlands', which came to be politically contested, on economic grounds, during and after the 1960s transition to independence.[9] Secondly,

---

[7] Fox (1996, 597, 603) has shown how the Regional Boundaries Commission in 1962 'divided Kenya on the basis of either ethnic homogeneity, i.e. one tribe per district, or compatibility, i.e. more than one tribe per district where they were happy to coexist'. The 1987 delimitation of constituencies during the one-party period, within which the 1992 and 1997 multi-party elections were conducted, was based on the same principle. As will become clearer below, President Moi has been able to employ this principle to his and Kanu's advantage by creating new administrative districts and, thereby, effectively defining the boundaries of extra parliamentary constituencies.

[8] Kershaw's 'pre-tribal' entities, as mentioned in note 6 above, appear as ethnicities: 'Kinship created ethnicity; those within the boundaries of kinship – widely drawn – belonged to the same ethnic group. They were bound by the same moral order; they might speak the same language; their primary mode of subsistence was agriculture'. If ethnicity was created by kinship, kinship was created, according to Kershaw, 'through common land, through marriage and descent' (*op. cit.,* 276). For our purpose here, the key is this reference to the commonality of land, although not land held in common since Kershaw's main point in her historical account of the genesis of the Mau Mau revolt is that pre-colonial land right was not based upon communal as opposed to individual tenure. We take 'common land', in the sense of a territorial region rather than referring to some concept of ownership, to be the vital factor that makes 'the tribal' a significantly different political factor from that of the ethnic.

[9] As mentioned in the preceding paragraph, and as it will become clearer below, the tribal and/or ethnic identities which may have been contested during the colonial period do not simply run into the post-colonial period. Thus, 'extra- or non-tribal' refers to those territories and regions which were occupied and/or created by immigrants into the colony of Kenya and who, as in the case of the Rift Valley, displaced indigenous populations, especially Maasai and other pastorialists.

the twentieth-century development of Mombasa, as a port serving territories to the west of Kenya and, later, as the centre of the coastal tourist industry, and Nairobi, as a major commercial and industrial centre for East Africa as much as the political capital of Kenya, created two major urban arenas of ethnic populations. As indigenous African political organisations and voluntary associations first developed within the urban arena, especially in Nairobi, ethnic identities were brought back to mainly rural tribal territories from the first decades of the colonial period, thereby creating the basis for what has been called the 'ethno-regional' politics of Kenya.

Last, and not least, a singular fact of political geography has been the literal centrality of the Central Province for economic and political change in Kenya. As 'the Kikuyu' region of relatively high potential agricultural land, the Central Province bordered both the former 'white highlands' to its north and west and Nairobi to its immediate south. To the east of the Central Province, Embu and Meru peoples, of some significance for the case study which follows towards the end of this paper, came to be officially identified with, and incorporated into, 'the Kikuyu'. Two historical factors followed. Firstly, before the *Mau Mau* revolt of 1952–6, the agricultural wage-labour force in a large part of the white highlands and wageworkers in Nairobi were preponderantly of Kikuyu origin. After the revolt, and from the early 1960s, former wageworkers on sub-divided estates, following the de-racialisation of the highlands, laid claim to the non-tribal territory of the Rift Valley. Likewise, Kikuyu workers and migrants from the Central Province and Rift Valley countrysides re-occupied Nairobi. Secondly, small-scale commercial agriculture and trade was most developed in the Central Province and it was here that the first indigenous African layer of capital appeared as a singular economic and political force, dominating the first post-colonial regime of the Kenyatta period and ensuring, unlike virtually all the rest of former British colonial Africa, that there was no 1960s and 1970s experience of socialism in Kenya.

However, even without experiments in socialism, control over state power has been no less a vital part of the post-colonial economic and political experience in that it was by virtue of state action that the commitment to indigenous capitalist development was to be realised during both the Kenyatta and Moi periods of government. More generally, the command over state resources was to be regarded as the key for political action at the onset of the transition to self-government and political independence. The two historical factors mentioned above played a large part in determining the course of political conflict, including patterns of voting, during the post-colonial era. Thus, in the first of the two multi-party elections before independence, the 'Kenyatta' elections of 1961, for a representative parliament as part of constitutional self-government, and the 'Independence' elections of 1963, a communal pattern of voting, based on ethno-regional electoral blocs, was established. After the long one-party period, a very similar pattern of voting was apparent for the multi-party general elections of 1992 and 1997.

At the 1963 elections, for example, the Kenya African National Union (Kanu) won just half the number of parliamentary seats in the then House of Representatives and formed the Kenyatta government as the majority party. One major opposition party, the Kenya African Democratic Union (Kadu), won one-third of the 112 seats on offer. For the 1997 parliamentary elections, Kanu also won just half the number of 210 seats open to contest while the two major opposition parties, the Democratic Party (DP) and the National Development Party (NDP) also won one-third of the seats between them.

If we switch 'Kanu' and 'Kadu' around for 1997, the 35-year parallel becomes even more striking. Although Kanu, in 1963, then comprising a coalition of Kikuyu, Embu and Meru (the *Kem* of the Mau Mau revolt, now known as *Gema*) and Luo ethno-regional groupings, won seats in all the provinces, three-quarters came from Nyanza, Nairobi and the *Kem* districts of Central and Eastern provinces. These were the same provinces to which the main opposition parties were electorally confined in 1997: the DP to Nairobi, Central and the *Kem* area of Eastern, and the NDP, to Nyanza. Conversely, Kanu in 1997, as in 1992, polled predominantly in the three provinces – the Coast, Rift Valley and Western – where Kadu won seats at the 1963 elections. Kadu had been formed, for the 1961 elections, to represent the so-called 'minority tribes': mainly the Kalenjin, Maasai, Turkana and Samburu (*Kamatusa*) grouping, for the Rift Valley; the Luhya, for Western and smaller groups, such as the Mijikenda at the Coast; and the Somali in the North East Province. After the 1963 elections, and at the inception of the Republic of Kenya in 1964, Kadu dissolved itself to become part of the ruling party Kanu. From the early 1980s, if not before, and with political change associated with the trajectory of the Moi regime, 'Kanu' progressively became

'Kadu', thereby historically accounting for the logical inversion of the parties between 1963 and 1997. The minorities of 1963 formed the majority in 1992 and 1997 against what had always been feared – domination by 'larger tribes', and the Kikuyu in particular.

Moreover, the communal configuration of voting patterns has required that a winning party, itself a coalition of tribal groupings, has to win electoral support from what Throup and Hornsby (1998, 503–514), for the 1992 elections, called the 'swing communities'.[10] Thus, in 1963, although Kadu won the majority of seats in Western Province, the fissiparousness of the Luhya grouping meant that Kanu could count on one-third of the seats in this pivotal electoral area. In Nyanza Province, Kanu won all the seats in the populous Kisii district. Ukambani, in Eastern Province, voted in all eight seats for the exclusively Kamba African Peoples' Party (APP) which entered a compact with Kadu before the election but, after the election, was effectively aligned to the Kanu government before also dissolving itself. At the Coast, Taita-Taveta and Lamu returned Kanu candidates. Broadly, the same pattern of voting reappeared 30 years later, in the 1992 and 1997 elections, with the difference that these same or other groupings, some of which are mentioned below, swung to the 'Kadu' Kanu of the Moi period.

Historical parallels of the kind above seem to be so obvious that they lead to the strong version of a thesis that the obvious continuities in ethno-regional blocs of voting make communal politics *the* determinant of electoral outcomes in Kenya. A weaker, but different, version of the thesis, which forms the bulk of what follows, claims that insofar as communal politics do enter into the explanation of electoral outcomes, they do so as part of 'something else'. It is the something else which explains why the striking impression of a historical parallel is an impression of something that has the potential to make the meaning of communality very different from what its tribal and ethnic attributes presuppose it to be. The 'something else' refers to the national and the local, both of which have contained an interrelated economic interest and which, through the communal, comes to be represented by the political. If the impression of the communal appears to be so solidly striking, by way of a historical parallel, then it is not necessarily the communal which is so durable. *Far more durable is the organised intention to make economic interest find an adequate form of political representation.* And, as we suggested above of corruption, it is the political which affirms the 'something else' about trajectories of primary accumulation in Kenya.

Kanu was formed in 1960 as the successor to the Kenya African Union (KAU), banned as a nationalist African political organisation in 1953, at the onset of the *Mau Mau* revolt. In turn, KAU, formed in 1944, had enveloped the Kikuyu Central Association (KCA), the Kavirondo Taxpayers Association and other 'tribal' political associations of the inter-war period whose origin lay in the earlier East African Association, the extra-Kenyan association of the relatively privileged Africans mainly in colonial government employ as clerks, telephone operators, teachers and other occupations requiring educational certification. This oscillation in the form of political association, itself *partly* determined by colonial government regulation,[11] between the regional, whether extra- or intra-Kenyan, and local and the national, should not belie what was relatively constant about the leadership of the different associations which culminated in Kanu. Predominantly Kikuyu, the leadership was foremost of a salariat[12] whose nationalist aspiration was to find an economic place in the sun, the place which had hitherto been monopolised by those of Asian and European origin. In addition, to be nationalist meant the right to occupy a national arena for capital accumulation, including the 'non-tribal' territory of the Rift Valley and, indeed, the disputed Coastal strip, which was to become the location of the burgeoning tourist industry.

---

[10]See below for more on the swing communities. Throup and Hornsby are described by their publisher as having produced 'the most thorough analysis of any African election'. This is no mere blurb. Although our analysis of the trajectory of Kenyan politics might move in a different direction from that of the authors, and with different emphasis, we are hugely indebted to their detailed account of the 1992 election.

[11]Between 1953 and 1960, for example, the colonial government confined political organisations to the administrative boundaries of provinces thereby preventing the formation of countrywide parties. For the history of political parties, see Bennett 1963; Bennett and Rosberg 1961; Rosberg and Nottingham 1966; Ghai and McAuslan 1970; Harbeson 1973; Oyugi 1993; Kershaw 1997.

[12]For example, of the 53 candidates standing for Kanu in the 1963 elections, well more than one-half were teachers by way of occupation. Lawyers and civil servants accounted for another 10 per cent of the total (Bennett and Rosberg 1961, 142, Table 6.4). For the salariat, see Cowen and Kinyanjui 1977.

Within less than two years after Kadu was incorporated into Kanu, the original Kikuyu-Luo coalition of Kanu fragmented. In 1966, the then Vice President, Oginga Odinga, resigned his position and formed another party, the Kenya People's Union (KPU), which *ideologically* stood for socialism and in opposition to the capitalist orientation of policy which the Kenyatta leadership of Kanu had set in train. As the results of the 'Little General Elections' held in the same year showed, and as subsequent events revealed, the KPU proved to be a predominantly but not wholly Luo phenomenon. On ideological grounds, the KPU generated support within the Kikuyu heartland, especially in the Murang'a district of the Central Province. During 1969, the KPU was banned following violence, mainly in Nairobi and Nyanza, in the aftermath of the political assassination of Kenyatta's putative successor, the 'Luo' Tom Mboya, whose earlier trade union politics had developed in the non-tribal territory of Nairobi. Mboya had also commanded widespread political support in the Central Province during the Mau Mau emergency of the 1950s and had later, as in 1966, framed the strategic political conception of African Socialism against KPU doctrine.[13] Between 1969 and 1992, open political contest together with elections were conducted within the framework of a *de facto* and, after the 1982 turning point of the Moi regime, a *de jure* one-party state.

During the period of the Kenyatta regime, 1963–78, and especially after the KPU and other sources of opposition were fought off politically within the party, the original 'Kikuyu' intent of Kanu, incorporating the history of its predecessors, was broadly achieved. A layer of large-scale indigenous African capital was formed through the ownership and accumulation of enterprises across a range of economic sectors including agriculture, commerce, transport, finance, insurance, real estate and tourism. The significance and extent of African ownership and capital accumulation has been highly contested through what became known during the 1970s as the 'Kenya debate'.[14] Yet, despite continuing controversy, especially over an African presence in ownership and control of manufacturing industry, there is now little dispute that the first post-colonial government sought to promote African large-scale enterprise; that this presence was established through the command of the state apparatus as a whole; and that the extent of an African presence was enough to promote antagonism from those Africans within Kenya who had not shared in finding a place in this economic sun. In short, the phenomenon in question, that of indigenous capitalism and all it entailed was deemed to be by, of and for the Kikuyu. Kanu government was presumed to be a Kikuyu, and more specially, a southern Kikuyu regime centred upon Kenyatta's 'family' home of 'Gatundu' and his district of 'Kiambu'.

It is not difficult to identify the associations between 'the Kikuyu' and its more incisive connotations, indigenous capitalism and the way in which 'fields of accumulation' were commanded through the structure of the state.[15] Yet, despite these associations, a closer reading of the politics of the Kenyatta regime would show that there was considerable restraint on the part of the presidency in holding back the spread of Kikuyu-owned enterprise from regions where antipathy towards 'the Kikuyu' was marked. After 1969 especially, small-scale entrepreneurs of Kikuyu origin were repatriated from Nyanza Province; Kikuyu farmers, traders and artisans were largely absent from swathes of the Western and Eastern Provinces, especially Ukambani. While indigenous-owned corporate capital was largely free to roam nationally, its historical incubus of Kikuyu-owned small-scale enterprise was confined to the Kikuyu hinterland and the non-tribal territories mentioned above.

Kadu had been organised around the fear of both political and economic domination by fear of the Kikuyu-Luo Kanu coalition. In particular, the fear was that it would be Kikuyu farmers and traders who would swamp regions throughout Kenya, including the non-tribal territories and economic arena where claims to land and resources were contested on the ground that they could not be 'naturally' Kikuyu because they had historically been occupied by those of European, Asian or Arab origin. Despite, if not because of, Kadu's incorporation within the one-party state, and the destruction of open KPU opposition, the fear of Kikuyu domination was ameliorated by

---

[13]For the foregoing, see, for example, Rosberg and Nottingham 1966; Gertzel 1970; Mueller 1984; Barkan and Okumu 1979; Ogot and Ochieng' 1995; Goldsworthy 1982.
[14]For a survey of the debate and its significance, see Cowen and MacWilliam 1996.
[15]For what follows, see, for example, Leys 1975; Bates 1989; Berman 1992; Berman and Lonsdale 1992.

the policy of restraint. And, despite the extent to which state resources were unequally distributed, and that the non-tribal territories generally did become disproportionately Kikuyu, the policy of restraint, perpetually policed by the regional political bosses who the president acknowledged and rewarded, meant that the Kadu areas contained enough of indigenous-owned enterprise for its potential to be developed following a change in regime.

Moi's ascendancy to the presidency in 1978, and his tightening grip over state power during the 1980s, politically capitalised upon anti-Kikuyu majoritarian sentiment within the country as a whole. Kikuyu-owned corporate capital was conflated with small-scale enterprise to politically reverse the *direction* of a series of associations between state power, indigenous capital accumulation and regional privilege. President Moi, within the same party of Kanu, set about diminishing the place of 'the Kikuyu' within the state structure on the same grounds that the first historical layer of indigenous capital had been established, namely that tribal privilege in government captured the means to make a tribally-defined class rich in resources, wealth, assets and capital. The same series of associations, which had been used to de-construct a Kikuyu place in the state, were then used to build Kalenjin privilege into the structure of the state.

Tribal 'communities' of 'the Kikuyu' and 'the Kalenjin', as some historians and social anthropologists like to tell us, are politically imagined communities serving a particular purpose in a place in time.[16] 'Kalenjin' is a fairly recent historical innovation, formed as a tribal grouping between the late 1940s and early 1950s in the wake of the post-war surge of African nationalism. Elites from Kipsigis, Nandi, Tugen and other language- and culture-related groupings to the west of the Rift Valley started using *Kalenjin* ('I tell you') as a word-phrase which was common to the different groupings but which had the added meaning that there was now a basis of commonality between themselves.[17] The political purpose was to provide a larger grouping which had a sufficient weight of territory and population to stand alongside other tribal peoples during a period of rapid political change (see Kipkorir and Welbourn, 1973; Omusule, 1989; Kanyinga 1998a, 173–174). A decade later, Kalenjin had acquired a less-than-national purpose, now serving to denote a tribal grouping which, although larger than any of its constituent 'tribes', represented one of the smaller 'minority' tribes which made up Kadu's popular base. At the 1963 elections, Kadu and Kadu-affiliated candidates won all four seats in Kalenjin country, receiving between 80 and 90 per cent of the popular vote. One Kadu victor was Daniel arap Moi, in the smallest of the constituencies where less than 10 per cent of the population had registered to vote (Bennett and Rosberg 1961, appendix, 214–215). Yet, it was precisely because he was of the then politically insignificant Tugen, and not of the far more significant Nandi or Kipsigis, that Moi was able to become a commanding political figure for the Kalenjin.

Another major historical enlargement of 'the Kalenjin community' occurred after Moi became Vice-President and then succeeded to the presidency in 1978. To confront what had now become *Gema*, a larger politically-conscious confederation of peoples was created – that of the *Kamatusa* which, as mentioned above, incorporated the Maasai, Turkana and Samburu, who were not necessarily linguistically related to other Kalenjin groupings. Moreover, *Kamatusa* came to incorporate into 'the Kalenjin' those smaller groupings who were politically represented in Kadu – the Somali, Borana, Rendile, Gabra and others of the North-Eastern and Eastern provinces. Non-Nilotic populations, such as the Mijikenda, Taita, and Pokomo of the Coast Province have also entered into the *Kamatusa* pantheon. *Kamatusa*, therefore, is what makes Kanu a 'Kadu' government in state power. What Kenyatta was supposed to have done for 'the Kikuyu' and *Gema*, Moi and his government has striven for the *Kamatusa*, to enlarge the fields of accumulation for those who have politically represented the claims of hitherto 'minority tribes', thereby finding them an economic place in the sun. It is also for this reason that an alternative government to one ruled by Kanu is represented as nothing other than the original 'Kanu', the present opposition parties who are alleged to be under the political hegemony of 'the Kikuyu', and therefore, to be feared.

---

[16]See note 5; for Kenya, Berman and Lonsdale 1992, especially after Anderson 1983, and Hobsbawm and Ranger 1991.

[17]Students at either the Alliance High School in Kenya or at Makerere University College, Kampala, Uganda, then *the* University for East Africa, are believed to have been the first source for imagining 'a community of the Kalenjin'.

Yet, the Moi regime faced, from its inception, the historical given of two layers of indigenous capital, that of Kenya Asian and *Gema* enterprise which had developed during the colonial and post-colonial periods. In replicating the historical experience of the Kenyatta regime, therefore, the Moi presidency used the same method of commanding the state apparatus to favour Kalenjin and, then, *Kamatusa* interests. Through both appointments to the upper echelons of the administration, and in making the presidency the central and singular source of public policy, the Moi period of government looks as if it is similar to that of the earlier period.[18] However, on both economic and political grounds, President Moi has had to depend more upon the state as an arena for the primary accumulation of capital and, to retain political support, has centralised political patronage to a far greater extent than was apparent during the Kenyatta years.[19] Over and above these grounds, the Moi period has coincided with a different international economic and political environment than that of the earlier period, especially before 1979. This difference has accentuated the internal reasons for why the Moi government of Kanu has faced political opposition on a scale which not only brought multi-party politics to Kenya but also made it more necessary for the Kanu government to make communal politics more emphatic for the purpose of perpetuating its electoral hold over state power.

Primary accumulation within the arena of state institutions has meant corruption. The centralisation of political patronage has entailed authoritarian rule. Both corruption and authoritarianism have been the hallmarks of a regime that has faced open opposition, during the 1990s, from a wide range of economic interests. In the *Gema* territories, blame for declining proceeds from small-farm production, largely due to government mismanagement of parastatal institutions, has been attached to Kanu as a further source of grievance about Kikuyu marginalisation. As we further show below, despite attempts to incorporate Kikuyu big business into a Kanu firmament, the majoritarian élites and middle classes across a range of tribal groupings, from the Kikuyu and Luo to the Kamba, have made it their political business to contest the regime and its ruling party. Wageworkers, experiencing increasing rates of real wage-rate decline, have made common cause both with the above strata and the rapidly increasing ranks of the impoverished self-employed to express opposition to their economic predicaments. Nor has opposition been absent from the Kalenjin heartlands of the *Kamatusa* territories.[20]

In the same way that the 'Kamatusa' had been formed by extending the range of 'Kalenjin', and Kalenjin itself formed out of smaller tribal groupings, the enlarged compass of *Kamatusa* made the wider political grouping more economically heterogeneous. Thus, Kipsigis and Nandi territory consists of relatively high potential agricultural land, ecologically akin to that of *Gema* territory east of the Rift Valley and around Mount Kenya. Tea and dairy cattle farming, together with other relatively land and resource-rich agricultural activities, comprises the basis of small and medium-farm production in these regions. However, pastoralism, involving the rearing of cattle livestock, is the mainstay of economic activity for the majority of other, lesser-populated and land-poorer territories within the *Kamatusa* grouping. These ecological, and therefore, economic differences between the territories have also made the *Kamatusa* grouping less electorally homogeneous over time. While pastoralists' participation in elections has generally tended to increase over time, when comparing parliamentary election results for 1997 with 1992 and 1963, opposition party candidates have increased their shares of the popular vote in the Nandi and Kipsigis' districts such

---

[18]Four of the eight provincial commissioners, together with one-third of the district commissioners, in 1972 were of Kikuyu origin, as were the majority in the senior management positions in the extensive parastatal organisations. In 1990, for example, the above positions had now become occupied by those of Kalenjin origin in roughly the same proportions. Moreover, two-thirds of the permanent secretaries of government ministries were Kalenjin.

Africa Confidential 31(21), 26 October 1990; for resource distribution generally, see Rothchild 1973; Barkan and Chege 1989.

[19]Primary accumulation through manipulation and fraud of state institutions, including agricultural parastatals, together with misappropriations of publically owned land, especially in urban areas, has been legendary during the period of the Moi regime. For primary accumulation, see, for example, Cowen and MacWilliam 1996, 164–206; Kanyinga 1996; for the centralisation of public policy, see Widner 1992.

[20]For the reason for opposition in the 1980s, see, for example, Throup 1987; Anyang' 1989; Widner 1992.

as Kericho.[21] One marked fact of the political map in Kenya is the extent to which the Kanu heart-lands have increasingly become those of pastoral territories.[22]

It was in Nandi that opposition built up against the Moi presidency in the same way that Jean Marie Seroney, a former deputy speaker of parliament, had openly expressed opposition to the Kenyatta presidency, and Vice-President Moi, during the 1970s, on the grounds that the Kanu government had ignored the claims of the landless. Disaffection with Moi and others in the inner court of the *Kamatusa* confederacy began to show openly after the 1992 elections when it was argued that, as predominantly arable agriculturalists, the Nandi had suffered from bias towards pastoralist groupings within the confederacy (for more detail, see Kanyinga 1998a, 225–240). After 1992, a distinct Nandi faction emerged within Kanu, led by Uasin Gishu Kanu district chairman, Jackson Kibor, and the Cherangani MP, Kipruto Kirwa. By articulating Nandi griev-ances, this faction won several party elections in Uasin Gishu but then faced presidential retri-bution at the behest of Keiyo and Tugen petitioners who argued that the district was to be regarded as cosmopolitan rather than as an exclusive Nandi zone of interest (Kanyinga 1998b, 79–82).[23] As we shall show below, it was this Nandi opposition to the Kanu leadership that was to culminate in the formation of a new party, the United Democratic Movement, after the 1997 elections.

Kanu's advantage of incumbency, in making possible a disproportionate use of state resources and backing by the provincial administration, eased an expansion of the party's influence over several parts of the country, especially in the pastoral and 'undeveloped' regions occupied by the 'minority tribes' which Kadu had galvanised before the 1963 elections to confront the threat of Kikuyu and Luo domination through Kanu. It was through a widening, and then political fencing-in of the *Kamatusa* dominion, much of it accompanied by repeated assertions of *majimboism*, the demand for regional autonomous governments in Kenya, that Kanu's blocs of electoral votes were assembled for 1992 and kept relatively intact for 1997.

However, it was after the election, during April and May 1998, that both intra-Kalenjin and intra-*Kamatusa* conflicts were expressed over claims to land in Trans-Nzoia, of the former white highlands in the northern Rift Valley. Three Nandi MPs mounted a campaign to secure the

---

[21]Thus, for the single Kipsigis and Nandi constituencies in 1963, the Kadu and Kadu-affiliated candidates, Towett and Seroney, received over 90 and 80 per cent of the vote respectively against Kanu opposition. In 1992, the 'Kadu' Kanu candidates were elected unopposed in the then three Nandi districts constituencies of Mosop, Aldai and Tinderet. By 1997, there were signs of a shift against Kanu. Although NDP and Ford-K parties did not make much headway in Mosop and Tinderet against Kanu candidates, the Safina candidate in Aldai received 30 per cent of the vote as opposed to the 60 per cent for Simon Choge of Kanu. For the Kericho district, in 1992, elections were held in one of the four constituencies, namely Kipkelion where Tanui of Kanu won 75 per cent of the vote against his Ford-K opponent, Keino; two constituencies, now including Kipkelion, did not have elections in 1997. Furthermore in Eldoret North, Uasin Gishu District, Kipkorir Menjo of Ford-K polled nearly one-half of the 30,000 votes for Samoei of Kanu, albeit roughly the same that went to a Ford-A candidate against Kanu in 1992. Kanu's zoning of these districts on a tribal and ethnic basis in 1992 had virtually excluded the opposition. Despite the same attempts for 1997, and Luhya-driven opposition in areas such as Eldoret, the strength of intra-Kalenjin opposition was sufficient to make more elections possible and force Kanu to win votes at parliamentary elections. Bennett and Rosberg 1961, appendix, 214–215; Throup and Hornsby 1998, appendix 2, 623–625; *Daily Nation* Election' 97 website [http://www.kenyaelections.com/res3/riftvalley.htm].

[22]In summarising the 1992 elections, Fox (1996, 604) wrote: 'The Kanu support base, by and large, came from rural constituencies with relatively few voters, where the turnout was usually below average'. The same applied to 1997.

[23]Conflict between Moi, with the Tugen and the Keiyo axis, and the Nandi faction deepened during 1996 when the President objected to Kirwa as Kanu's nominee as the 1997 parliamentary candidate for the Cherengani constituency in the other contiguous 'cosmopolitan' district of Trans-Nzoia. Kirwa took on Moi directly by pointing out that the President had not been able to overcome his phobia of major 'tribal groupings', that any such grouping larger than his own minor Tugen 'community' should be cut down to size and that he has never forgotten the personal bitterness of his confrontation with the late Seroney (*Daily Nation* 29 March 1996; *The Weekly Review* 5 April 1996). In the event, Kirwa won both the Kanu nomination and the seat in a district where Kanu fared badly against Ford-K candidates owing to the voting strength of the Bukusu Luhya in Trans-Nzoia.

settlement of landless Nandi in territory that had recently experienced a new wave of cattle rustling and land occupation by Pokot pastoralists under the benevolent guidance of the Kanu political 'hawk' and Minister of Natural Resources, Francis Lotodo. 'The line between criminal activity perpetrated by the raiders and activism by the élite,' it was reported, 'has become thinner by the day':

> While it is difficult to say that the élite of the community is deliberately fanning the situation, it is clear that the activism is motivated by the opportunity for private gain which the raids on Pokot neighbours is opening to the élite of the community.[24]

In other words, the *Kamatusa* dominion has undergone the kind of primary accumulation which opens up rifts within the very entity that was politically constructed to obtain and maintain state power.

Much has been made in the literature on Kenya, and Africa more widely, of the extent to which the organisation of politics stems from struggle over access to, and control over, state power.[25] Political losers, who lose parliamentary seats, party positions and/or influence within the presidential cabals, have always faced the prospect of economic losses associated with exclusion from privileged access to state resources, especially within the politically demarcated fields of accumulation mentioned above. The fear of exclusion has acted as a powerful magnate in attracting loyalty to party, and especially to Kanu as the ruling party of government. Conversely, attachment to opposition parties is far more diffuse. Political loyalties shift far more easily insofar as a political voice expressed through opposition parties means an axiomatic exclusion from personal access to state resources. When political parties are mapped across regions on communal grounds, relative losses and gains are not merely personal but affect the constituencies of winning and losing politicians.[26]

Yet, as the state's capacity to deliver services withers away during a period of general economic impoverishment,[27] and decentralisation becomes the keynote of policy, the renewed emphasis on the local only reinforces the hold of the communal in politics. Decentralisation, in itself, is not necessarily an economic instrument for increasing the sum of resources available for public and communal good in any one locality. Rather, an effect, if not an intention, of decentralisation is to shift the burden of placating the disenchantment arising from the inability of central government to deliver services. Emphasis upon the local mobilisation of resources for decentralised development aggravates the pressure upon elected politicians to serve their constituencies by increasing local shares of a diminished central government resource base for state spending.

---

[24] 'Trans Nzoia erupts', *Weekly Review* 25 May 1998.

[25] See, for example, Gertzel 1970; Leys 1975; Berg-Schlosser 1992; Oyugi 1993; Widner 1992; Haugerud 1995.

[26] This phenomenon has been referred to as a process of 'unbounded politics'. See Steeves 1997. The empirical reference point is the extent of defections by Members of Parliament from opposition parties to Kanu after the 1992 elections and from one opposition party to another, as before the 1997 elections. For the extent of defections, see Steeves 1997, 38; and Tostensen, Andreassen and Tronvoll 1998, 18–22.

[27] Kenya's economy grew during the 1960s but the oil crisis of 1979 signalled balance of payments imbalances that had worsened during the 1970s. Structural adjustment, with IMF support, then began but without official commitment since political rule was to privilege the *Kamatusa* class of capital as mentioned above. The image of Kenya as an exceptional case for Africa began to fray from the early 1980s, when a far lower annual average economic rate set in, roughly at less than 2 per cent as compared to 6 per cent for the 1960s. A higher population growth rate meant a severe decline in national income per capita. Real wage-rate decline had set in from the early 1970s but accelerated during the 1980s. Agricultural production, with the exception of horticulture, has largely been stagnant. Finance, insurance, and real estate, together with general business services, and domestic services, have shown growth rates of between 6 and 9 per cent during the 1990s. Official aid commitments have also been scaled down after 1990. Several donors, citing corruption and political ineptitude and/or lack of commitment to privatisation, withdrew aid to the government. When aid flows did resume, as after the 1992 elections, the volume did not match government expectations. For overviews, from international agencies' points of view, see Hino 1995; and Azam and Daubrée 1997.

Accordingly, as we see below from the Meru case study, how much development a politician delivers to his or her constituency plays a very important role in election results, becoming even more emphatic than for the earlier one-party period.[28] Insofar as local pressure from below makes MPs and contending parliamentary candidates more dependent upon political patronage as a medium of accessing state resources, and as patronage is attached to political party, the communal dimension of politics in Kenya has also been made explicit for questions about party organisation and strategy.

Communal aspects of access to state resources have raised a question about extrinsic political strategy as much as the intrinsic question about communality as some essential political end in itself. Before and during the 1997 elections, two broad views of political association appeared in Kenya. By incorporating an understanding of the local factor into strategy, one logic was that political representation and action should first be based upon expressing an exclusive regional interest, encompassing all that is implied by tribal and ethnic affiliation, to instrumentally lever up access to state power and resources. The exercising of state power would then involve a negotiation of different communal-based interests, whether or not they belonged to the same ruling party or to different parties of and outside government. The alternative strategy was that while communality might be the source of any one political interest, of political party or faction, it was through coalescing communal interests, at both the local and national levels, that a party would maintain or obtain state power.

These two strategies of political association corresponded to the views of different opposition party leaderships. However, there is also political logic at play, involving different courses of action that appear behind the backs of the activists involved in formulating strategies. It is logic, as much as strategy, that accounts for the fission and fusion of political parties, including the emergence of the significant new parties which fought the 1997 elections. Different views of political logic, as much as personality, also accounted for a deepening factional rift within Kanu. Furthermore, factionalism, together with the *Kamatusa* differences and the local factor, meant that the 1997 elections produced a phenomenal turnover of MPs within parliament. A new cadre of Kanu parliamentarians in a hung parliament is likely to play no small role in making the post-1997 Kanu government different from its predecessors. Furthermore, as we show below, it has been the logic of association on communal grounds, as much as any voluntary strategy, which has driven hitherto astringent opponents of the Moi regime into cohabitation with Kanu after the 1997 election. This is why questions over the communal logic of political association could make 1997 a possible turning point in Kenyan politics.

Results of the 1992 and 1997 elections

Almost 70 per cent of the registered electorate, as Table 6.1 shows, voted at the 1997 parliamentary elections. The overall turnout was slightly higher than for the 1992 elections which, in turn, was less than that for the 1979 one-party elections, the first of the Moi period of Kanu government. However, multi-party election turnout has been far higher than the low points of electoral participation during the one-party elections of the 1980s. In short, while the two multi-party elections of the 1990s have fallen way below the 1961 or 1963 peak of voter participation, as indicated by the turnout rate rather than the proportion of the population eligible to vote through registration,[29] it

---

[28]Together with John Okumu, Joel Barkan conducted a survey of nearly 4,000 potential voters in 13 rural constituencies during 1974. When asked what was the 'most important activity' the MPs should perform, to 'tell government what people in the district want' and 'obtain projects and benefits for the district' were cited, respectively, by 29 and 25 per cent of the respondents, a far higher score than for any other activity. Moreover, Barkan (1976, 453–454) was able to show that this view corresponded with how respondents voted during the then one-party election. If this survey were to be replicated in 1997, we surmise that the scores for these two activities, and especially the second, would rank even higher. Barkan and Holmquist 1989 also provide an elaborate discussion on how élites appropriated *harambee* (pulling together for self-help development projects) as a base for political capital. See also Hornsby and Throup 1990, on the turnover of legislators during the single-party period.

[29]See note 2. Given that the last decennial population census was in 1989, it is far more difficult than it was in 1992 to give a firm 1997 estimate of the ratio of registered voters to the potential electorate. The best guestimate is that for a projected population of 30m for 1997, with 16m aged less than 18 years, the registered electorate of 8.6m was just over 60 per cent of an eligible electorate of 14m. Population Resource Bureau [http://gaia.info.usaid.gov/horn/kenya/prb/kenya/html].

would be mistaken to presume that voter apathy has been a general feature of multi-party politics in Kenya. It has been the regional variation in turnout, rather than its overall change, which was most significant for 1997.

Broadly, it was in the constituencies of the most politically contested regions, of the Rift Valley, Western and Eastern provinces, that turnout increased appreciably in 1997. In Nairobi and the Central Province, where that part of the electoral prelude reform movement – associated with the leadership of the leading 1992 opposition presidential candidate, Kenneth Matiba – had its greatest impact in persuading people not to vote in 1997, turnout generally slumped. Mwai Kibaki, and his Democratic Party, gained most from Matiba's abstentionism. Yet, abstention in the opposition heartlands, and especially Nairobi where constituencies are so grossly malapportioned,[30] did not affect the overall results to the extent that a higher rate of turnout would have prevented Moi from winning the presidential elections. It is also a moot point whether abstentions in constituencies where results were alleged to have been rigged, and/or elections were closely contested, would have prevented Kanu from winning the parliamentary elections.[31]

Table 6.1: Voter turnout of registered voters by province, selected general elections, 1961–1997

	1997	1992	1983	1979	1961[a]
	multi-party		one-party		multi-party
		percentage turnout			
Nairobi	52	60	30	59	92
Central	73	83	40	77	95
North-Eastern	60	50	38	56	–
Coast	51	48	40	77	77
Nyanza	68	65	43	59	83
Rift Valley	81	70	53	73	88
Western	68	63	48	70	85
Eastern	72	64	50	69	86
All Kenya	69	66	48	68	85

a: Only for 'open seats'.

Sources: Bennett and Rosberg 1961, appendix, 210–216; Ahluwalia 1996, 165, Table 4; Institute for Education in Democracy 1997, 189–195; Daily Nation [http://www.kenyaelections.com].

Furthermore, whatever the extent of electoral rigging and voting irregularities across different constituencies, including the extent to which these practices were less prevalent than in 1992, the administration of elections does not bear sufficient weight *in itself* for explaining the outcome of the 1997 elections. Nor does election campaigning, especially for the presidential election, seem to have had a measurable impact upon the results. Political opinion polling at the beginning of the election campaign produced a set of results which were remarkably similar to the actual election results in predicting both Moi's actual share of the vote and Kanu's share of parliamentary seats won. Table 6.2 below indicates that Kibaki gained most from the presidential election campaign insofar as he doubled his predicted share of the vote by both drawing potential votes away from Ngilu and, as mentioned above, by bringing in the absent votes for Matiba from those whom, we suspect, declared that they were 'undecided' to the pollsters.[32] Thus in Nairobi and the Central Province, the DP leader more than doubled his share of the vote (see Table 6.3). Likewise, Table 6.4 shows that the DP achieved a far better set of parliamentary results than was predicted by polling. This electoral shift owed much to the kind of political party factors which we examine below and it is by way of the change in political forces that the election results are to be explained.

---

[30]Broadly, one vote in the North Eastern Province was worth five in Nairobi. See Tostensen, Andreassen, Tronvoll 1998, 22–26. Also see Fox 1996.
[31]There was evidence of rigged results and other irregularities in Nairobi Westlands, Kitui West, Mombasa Changamwe, Kisauni and Mvita, Makueni Kilome, Kitui Bobasi, Imenti Central and Lamu East Donors' Democratic Development Group, *Kenya General Elections 1997 Final Report*, in Tostensen, Andreassen, Tronvoll 1998, 102–109.
[32]Institute for Education in Democracy, 'IED presidential poll results', Nairobi 1997.

Presidential results

As Table 6.2 shows, President Moi's 2.5 million votes in 1997 represented a 4 per cent gain over his 1992 result but the fact that an anti-Moi majority exists in Kenya as a whole is confirmed by his failure to win more than 40 per cent of the votes cast, let alone of a potential registered electorate. The incumbent president, as in 1992, won his plurality of votes through continuing to be able to associate a confederation of relatively small 'tribal' groups with larger groupings, such as the Luhya, together with smaller ones on the Coast and elsewhere. It is likely that Moi's gain over 1992 was accounted for by the fact, as indicated by Table 6.3, that he polled more votes in hitherto opposition strongholds than the extra votes which opposition candidates polled in the Kanu hinterlands.

All the five major parties that contested the presidential elections had solid tribal bases of support, drawing support from the ethnic regions of their respective candidates and/or areas which identified with their local political concerns. Significantly, as in 1992, each of the candidates performed badly in one another's territory. Only the Democratic Party's Mwai Kibaki managed to come anywhere close to satisfying the electoral rule that the successful presidential candidate must win at least 25 per cent of votes cast in at least five of the eight provinces. As Table 6.3 shows, he won the requisite threshold in Central, the Kikuyu province, and in Nairobi, and eastern provinces where Kikuyu, Embu and Meru voting strength was sufficient to make an electoral impact. Of the other candidates, Raila Odinga, of the National Development Party, Kijana Michael Wamalwa of Ford-Kenya, and Charity Ngilu of the Social Democratic Party polled beyond the threshold in their own but no other province. The popular opposition vote represented a majority of votes cast but it was segmented according to regional and ethnic affiliation in urban and 'settled' areas, especially in the Rift Valley and Coast Provinces. On the strength of the 1997 results, and as Table 6.4 indicates, the pattern of voting for candidates appeared to differ little from the 1992 presidential elections.

Much has been made of the failure of opposition parties to 'unite' by presenting a single candidate to face the incumbent president and thereby make the latent anti-Moi majority the active electoral source of removing the incumbent president from power (for example, Throup and Hornsby 1998, 453, 526; Fox 1996, 606–607). However, it should be understood why the political possibilities of party merger, coalition or understanding, including tactical voting are so implausible. What President Moi can do, and what no single opposition presidential candidate can manage, is to politically capitalise on the anti-Kikuyu majority which is also evident throughout Kenya as a whole. As we mentioned in our introduction, the 1997 election results were about the extent to which an anti-Moi majority prevailed over the countervailing anti-Kikuyu majority. Moi's plurality of votes indicates the extent to which two negative political forces counterbalanced each other. Yet, insofar as the counterbalancing forces were also segmented, the relative impact of each force also depends on the way that the two majorities were politically composed for the purpose of the general elections.

Table 6.2: Presidential elections, share of the national vote, 1992 and 1997

	1992	1997 actual	predicted[b]
		percentage share of vote	
Moi (Kanu)	36.3	40.4	40.8
Kibaki (DP)	19.5	30.9	13.7
Odinga[a] (Ford-K/NDP)	17.5	10.8	11.1
Matiba (Ford-A)	26.0	–	1.2
Wamalwa (Ford-K)	–	8.2	9.2
Ngilu (SDP)	–	7.9	12.2
Others (undecided)	0.7	1.8	(11.8)

a: Oginga Odinga (Ford-K) for 1992; Raila Odinga (NDP) for 1997.
b: Predicted results from Institute for Education in Democracy opinion poll conducted in 42 constituencies, 29–30 November 1997.

Sources: Throup and Hornsby 1998, 435 ; Institute for Education in Democracy, 'IED Presidential Poll Results', Nairobi, December 1997; *Daily Nation* [http://www.kenyaelections.com/res3/presidential results.htm].

Table 6.3: Presidential elections, share of the vote by provinces, 1992 and 1997

	Moi 1992	'97	Kibaki '92	'97	Odinga[a] '92	'97	Matiba '92	'97	Wamalwa '92	'97	Ngilu '92	'97	Others '92	'97
					percentage share of vote									
Nairobi	17	21	19	44	20	17	44	–	–	6	–	11	0.5	0.7
Central	2	6	35	90	1	0.7	62	–	–	0.3	–	3	0.7	0.7
Eastern	38	35	50	27	1.6	0.8	11	–	–	0.8	–	37	0.8	0.6
Rift Valley	68	72	8	20	6	1.6	19	–	–	6	–	0.7	0.2	0.3
Coast	64	63	11	14	17	8	8	–	–	3	–	11	0.8	0.5
Western	40	45	3	1.3	18	2	39	–	–	50	–	0.5	0.3	1.2
Nyanza	14	24	6	16	75	55	3.3	–	–	2	–	1.7	1.7	1.3
North-Eastern	78	73	4	19	7	0.3	10	–	–	7	–	0.6	1.0	0.2

a: Oginga Odinga (Ford-K) for 1992; Raila Odinga (NDP) for 1997

Sources: Fox 1996, 606, Table 2; Throup and Hornsby 1998, 435, Table 10.1. Donor Democratic Development Group Report in Tostensen, Andreassen, Tronvoll, 1998, 93.

Two of the major opposition parties, the Social Democratic Party (SDP) and Safina, were resuscitated or formed since 1992 with the deliberate intent of transcending tribal representation and ethnic affiliation as the motif of electoral politics in Kenya. Safina did not contest the 1997 presidential elections while the SDP result seemed to confirm the systemic force of ethno-regional voting patterns in Kenya. While we return to the question of the new parties below it should be emphasised here that there is evidence that the SDP did have electoral appeal for the growing ranks of intermediate strata, or so-called middle classes, who may well become a future strategic force in Kenya politics.

Parliamentary results

Table 6.4 shows the extent to which the 1997 election results produced a hung parliament insofar as Kanu's slight majority over all opposition parties in 1992 fell even further.[33] Furthermore, the 1992 election results showed that parliamentary and presidential and civic votes were broadly uniform in that the party affiliation of candidates made voting relatively consistent. This 'three-piece-suit' pattern of voting was not replicated for the 1997 election when results indicate, a far more 'mix-and-match' outcome. Thus, in virtually all constituencies, and particularly those outside the leading presidential candidate's home areas, the number of votes for a party's presidential candidates did not match those for a parliamentary candidate of the same party. The two main interrelated reasons for the change in the pattern of voting were party fission/fusion and the local factor in parliamentary representation.

Table 6.4: Parliamentary elections, number and share of seats won, 1992 and 1997

	1992 actual	%	1997 actual	%	predicted	%
Kanu	95	53	108	51	110	52
DP	23	12	39	19	28	13
NDP	–	–	21	10	20	10
Ford-K	31	17	17	8	17	8
Ford-A	31	17	1	0.5	n.a.	
SDP	–	–	15	7	13	6
Safina	–	–	4	2	11	5
Others	8	1	5	2.5	n.a.	
Total seats	188		210			

Sources: Throup and Hornsby, 1998, 443; Nation [http: //www.kenyaelections.com]; for predictions, Donor Democratic Development Group Report in Tostensen, Andreassen, Tronvoll, 1988, 99.

---

[33]Although the constitution allows for 12 nominated MPs, and who were overwhelmingly Kanu in past parliaments, this will continue to be a hung parliament due to the 11 September IPPG reform agreement. Kanu and the opposition parties agreed to share the nominations in proportion to their elected seats in parliament. Thus, Kanu nominated 6 while the opposition parties nominated 2 for the DP and 1 each for the NDP, Ford-K, Safina, and the SDP. All these parties, except for the NDP and Safina, reneged on one aspect of the agreement in nominating losing parliamentary candidates.

Party fission and fusion

The first reason for 'mix-and-match' was due to party decomposition and re-formation during the 1992–97 period, and as in 1992, especially during the electoral prelude. In 1997, 26 parties contested the parliamentary elections but as in the presidential elections, only five parties won a significant number of constituencies. Of these major parties, only Kanu and the DP remained *relatively* unscathed by party fission. The Forum for the Restoration of Democracy (Ford) and the DP were the major parties formed after multi-party politics was re-permitted in 1991. While DP retained its solidity as a political party, Ford had disintegrated into fragments by the time the 1997 election arrived.

Disintegration of Ford

Ford, originally the reform movement campaigning for multi-party politics, turned itself into a political party during 1991 in an attempt to recapture the original constituency of Kanu as it had been formed during the early 1960s as a compact of interests. This compact included the 'tribal' dimension of 'the Kikuyu' and 'the Luo', the 'major tribes of Kenya' who faced Kadu as the compact of 'minor tribe interests'. Kenneth Matiba, former senior civil servant, business tycoon, minister in Moi's cabinet, and then, more latterly, political detainee, locked horns with Oginga Odinga, former Vice-President and radical, over the leadership of Ford which split into Matiba's Ford-Asili (Ford-A) and Odinga's Ford-Kenya (Ford-K) to fight the 1992 election, alongside a third Ford fragment, the Kenya National Congress (KNC).[34] After 1992, the two Fords fissured further. By December 1997, the only politically significant Ford was confined to Wamalwa's Ford-K in particular Luhya areas of Western Province.

Ford-K's original influence had spread from the majority Luo areas of Nyanza Province, where Oginga Odinga was the 'religion' which shaped local politics, to parts of the Coast and Western provinces. At the Coast, the party had entered into an alliance with the Islamic Party of Kenya (IPK) which was founded to assert Muslim participation in government but which was not registered for the 1997 elections.[35] In the Western Province, Luhya support for Ford-K was variable, stemming in part from the role that veteran politicians such as Masinde Muliro and Martin Shikuku played in particular districts of the province.[36]

Raila Odinga and the NDP

Following Oginga Odinga's death in 1994, Ford-K's chairmanship was taken over by Wamalwa but he faced competition for leadership of the party from Oginga's son and presumed political heir, Raila Odinga. Wamalwa's faction claimed that there was no right to a dynastic leadership of the party and that Raila, a former political detainee, was too 'violent' and 'radical' to stand as leader for the Luhya-Luo compact in Ford-K. Thus, Wamalwa's argument ran, Raila would repel rather than attract ethnic groups from other regions on the 'grand march' to the State House, namely the gathering up other tribal groupings on the road to government.[37] Significantly, for what follows below, Raila's group rebutted the claim with the accusation that Wamalwa, standing in the middle of the road between the opposition and Kanu, had fundamentally compromised the party by doing business with Ketan Somaia, a leading Kenyan Asian business partner of President Moi.[38] It is

---

[34]For an extensive account of the pre-1992 opposition movements and parties, see Throup and Hornsby 1998, chs. 4–5.

[35]The alliance between Ford-K and the IPK proved to be unstable. While Ford-K and IPK supporters clashed violently with Kanu youth at the Coast before and after the 1992 elections, Ford-K and IPK youthful supporters were also locked in violent confrontation during this period. For example 'Violence in Changamwe', *Weekly Review* 2 June 1992.

[36]Originally of Kadu, Muliro and Shikuku had become long-estranged from Kanu and also been leading lights in the formation of Ford but then faced opposition from a newer generation of politicians, such as Wamalwa within the Luhya heartlands.

[37]From interviews conducted in Nairobi during 1996, with informants from both factions.

[38]Having accused Wamalwa of betraying his Oginga's 1992 presidential campaign promises, Raila's group became increasingly involved, through party elections and violent conflicts during 1995, in wresting the helm of the party from Wamalwa, citing among much else his 'corrupt tendencies'. 'Mob marches to instal Raila', 'Police disperse Odinga's meeting as rival Ford-K youths clash', 'Wamalwa must go -Raila', *Daily Nation* 17 and 18 April 1995.

instructive that business collusion and competition generally played no mean part in what has been construed simply as personality and tribal or ethnic conflict in accounts of intra-opposition disunity and party decomposition.

In any case, the younger Odinga effectively took the political heart out of Ford-K by asserting the central presence of the Luo dimension within the party. After failing in his strenuous efforts, since early 1995, to become the leader of Ford-K, Raila renovated a minor party, the National Development Party (NDP), as the vehicle for Luo political representation at the onset of the 1997 election. Formed and registered in 1994, the NDP had been led by largely political unknowns from Luo Nyanza, including its chair Omondi Oludhe, a businessman. Like other parties which emerged after 1992, the NDP 'leased a space' for Raila and his group who moved into the reno-vated party with Oludhe stepping down from the chair in Raila's favour in May 1997. Despite its own contrary claims, NDP's support then firmly rested upon the conviction that both the Kenyatta and the Moi governments had marginalised Luo Nyanza from the mainstream of politics and economic development in Kenya.[39] Only a cohesive Luo political force, it was argued, would be able to compensate for their past marginalisation through a 'redistribution in arrears'. As such, the NDP rapidly became a base for Luo politicians in Luo Nyanza and the Luo diaspora.

The NDP's 1997 electoral wave in Luo Nyanza washed away virtually all non-NDP affiliated candidates. Of the former Ford-K luminaries who did not switch to the NDP, only the radical James Orengo, still on a Ford-K ticket, retained his Ugenya seat in Siaya district where Wamalwa, the party's presidential candidate, polled a mere 180 votes compared to the 27,000 received by Raila. As the NDP presidential candidate, Raila received nearly 60 per cent of the popular vote in Nyanza, which includes the populous Kisii vote and the less populous Kuria. Luo Nyanza, therefore, voted overwhelmingly for the NDP. Of the 21 parliamentary seats in Luo Nyanza, 19 were won by the NDP.[40] Contrariwise, the party won only 2 seats outside Nyanza, the Kikuyu populated Limuru constituency of Kiambu district in the Central Province and the Lang'ata constituency of Nairobi which Raila retained fairly easily.

Lang'ata was of interest because it is perhaps the most multi-ethnic and -racial constituency in Kenya, embracing both the extensive Kibera slums and the wealth Karen area on the southern edge of Nairobi, now dubbed 'Karengata'. Raila Odinga won the constituency in 1992 on a Ford-K ticket against the incumbent Kanu candidate, Philip Leakey, who had sat as an Assistant Minister in parliament during the 1980s and was the brother of Richard who is discussed below. After he disembarked from Ford-K and renovated the NDP, Raila resigned his seat and won a by-election as the NDP candidate during early 1997 on a voter turnout of less than 10 per cent. For the general election of 1997, however, Lang'ata represented 'a new home', a political place in Nairobi symbolically occupied by the Luo 'like any other big ethnic group' in Kenya.

Raila drew on Luo votes from both the slums and suburbs of Lang'ata but for different reasons. Whereas slum dwellers in Kibera stressed that the Luo deserved a party of their own to enable bargaining and/or competition with other 'tribal' blocs, Luo élites in the constituency tended to say that Raila was a democrat and a principled politician whose defection from Ford-K was merited because the Wamalwa group was intent on seeking a compact with Kanu.[41] Ironically enough, as we see further below, it was Raila who took the NDP into 'constructive engagement' with Kanu and President Moi after the 1997 election. In the light of the views set out by Luo voters at these polls, it seemed that Raila's communal strategy was in tune with the opinion of the urban poor in Lang'ata. More generally, the communal logic of political association, which underlined the renovation of the NDP and its virtual electoral monopoly of Luo Nyanza, drove Raila and his party into cooperation with the ruling party.

The Ford-K rump

Wamalwa retained his Ford-K chairmanship and managed to keep the rump of Luhya Bukusu MPs in the party until the election. Broadly, Wamalwa and Moi shared the presidential vote in the

---

[39]'NDP not a tribal party, Raila tells Moi', *Daily Nation* 8 April 1997.

[40]The NDP candidate for Gem constituency failed to meet the nomination requirements. Voter apathy, therefore, resulted in a 46 per cent turnout that enabled another Ford-K candidate to win but with NDP support.

[41]From interviews conducted at polling stations in Lang'ata and Karen, 30 December 1997.

mainly Luhya-populated Western Province. While Bukusu voters mainly provided Wamalwa's 48 per cent share of the vote in the Western province, the Maragoli electorate voted overwhelmingly for Moi, whose 45 per cent share of the provincial vote played no small part in securing his overall target of achieving the 25 per cent threshold in this predominantly Luhya region. Ford-K's parliamentary presence also remained largely confined to one segment and area of the Luhya tribal grouping.

This split between the Bukusu and the Maragoli, in conjunction with that between a 'Luo' NDP and 'Luhya' Ford-K, points towards a more general logic of the association between party and tribal affiliation. Wamalwa's strategy of the 'grand march' was based upon a conviction, as mentioned above, that a political coalition can be built around a centre, in his case Ford-Kenya, by attracting 'tribal' groupings away from other regionally-based parties and towards a pole of opposition to the established party-state of Kanu and the Moi regime. An alternative strategy, as shown by Raila's re-formation of the NDP of Kenya, is that a party which secures total support in a particular region then has the political authority to negotiate with the ruling party for the advantage of a tribal group and development of the region in question. After the 1997 election, as we see further below, Raila indicated his intent to negotiate with the Moi presidency and Kanu for the purpose of Luo advantage and the development of Nyanza.

Likewise, the Maragoli vote for Moi and Kanu was predicated upon the belief that it was another politically favourite son, who would be confirmed as vice-president after the election, their Musalia Mudavadi – outgoing Minister of Finance and leading technocrat in Kanu – who did much to arrange the 11 September Inter Parties Parliamentary Group (IPPG) agreement. Under the Kenya constitution, the incumbent vice-president stands the best chance of succeeding to the presidency. After the 1997 elections, Moi kept the vice-presidency open and shifted Mudavadi sidewards, if not downward, to the Ministry of Agriculture. However, this event does not in itself invalidate the belief that it is direct influence upon state power, through bringing a firmly established regional political presence to the centre, which is what matters politically in contemporary Kenya.

As we shall see further below, the new parties which fought the 1997 election were also forced to think through the two communal logics of political association in contemporary Kenya. The disintegration of the 'other Ford', Ford-Asili, between 1992 and 1997, shows that the failure to act according to the logics of association, and to fall between them, leads the most powerful of opposition figures into a political wilderness.

Matiba in the political wilderness

Ford-A began to disintegrate immediately after the 1992 elections when it lost a majority of its Luhya MPs who had anticipated that a Matiba-led Kikuyu-Luhya alliance would be the way for their favourite non-Maragoli son, Martin Shikuku, to accede to the vice-presidency. Although Kanu played a part in engineering the 1993–5 defection of Luhya MPs, from Kakamega and Bungoma districts, it was the anti-Kikuyu push factor that reduced Ford-A's representation in parliament from 31 seats in 1992 to 22 in 1997.[42] Defecting MPs complained that Matiba had come to personally dominate the party in the name of the Kikuyu to the exclusion of other tribal groupings. Corresponding to the dispute between Wamalwa and Odinga within Ford-K, Shikuku stayed within Ford-A and wrested the chairmanship of the party away from Matiba. Yet, unlike the Ford-K tussles, there was no coherent political base for Matiba to retreat to and/or coherently re-form a party which would act according to the two logics of association.

Ironically enough, while Matiba made his way into big business during the 1960s from straddling propensities in state service, his political ambitions were highlighted by the central role he played in nationally organising football. If football was a distinctly non-Kikuyu pursuit, it was a markedly western Kenyan religion. If anyone was fitted to embark on the theory of the grand march it was Kenneth Matiba in the 1970s who then added political colour to his mast of leadership by assuming the mantle of principled opposition to the tyrannical excesses of the Moi regime during the 1990s. Welcomed back to Nairobi during May 1992, after exile in London, amidst scenes that were reminiscent of the return of Jomo Kenyatta to 1946 colonial Kenya,

---

[42]For defections, see *Weekly Review* 25 August 1994.

Matiba might well have been fitted to play the role of the second liberator of Kenya (see Throup and Hornsby 1998, 124–127).

In explaining why he failed to be reincarnated as a second Kenyatta, Matiba's post-1980s personality, seen to be 'arrogant', or 'ill' due to his earlier incarceration, is beside the point. No political figure who was so closely identified with 'the Kikuyu' could assemble the political coalition that would make the grand march through tribal groupings possible. Equally, no figure could assemble a coherent coalition of the urban poor in Nairobi, who were preponderantly Kikuyu, with particular business interests and the middle peasantry of a part of Murang'a district in the Central Province.[43] A Bonapartian analogy fits the explanation by default. Insofar as Louis Bonaparte successfully assembled such a coalition in mid nineteenth-century France, then he did so from an already-established position of state power. The second logic of association in late twentieth-century Kenya stems from a position of opposition. It presupposes a willingness and capacity of a communally coherent opposition party to negotiate its way into exerting influence over those, in Kanu, who hold the reigns of state power.

Matiba's political coalition that carried through to the 1997 election prelude acted on two fronts. The first was to renew the attack on Kenyan Asian capital which Matiba, one powerful personal representative of Kikuyu big business, had directed as one upshot of the 1990 *saba saba* protests, demonstrations and violence which turned against all Kenyans of Asian origin. Secondly, Matiba reasserted his earlier radicalism in refusing to countenance negotiation with Kanu and the Moi presidency over electoral and constitutional reform. The slogans of 'Moi-Must-Go', 'Moi-butu' (referring to the recent demise of Mobutu in the former Zaire) and 'No Reforms No Elections', which rang through Nairobi streets during the mid-1997 demonstrations for electoral and constitutional reform, were voiced by Matiba's followers, the predominantly younger of the urban poor who refused to either register for, and/or participate, in the December elections. Matiba, their 'man', did not stand in either the presidential or parliamentary elections. Rather, he claimed ownership of the original Ford and proceeded to form Saba Saba Asili, borrowing its name from the 7 July 1990 movement that ushered in demonstrations for multi-partyism.[44] This party has yet to be registered. The electoral upshot of Matiba's 1997 political role was that voter turnout in Nairobi averaged 53 per cent, below the 65 per cent estimated nationally. Likewise, his own constituency, Kiharu in Murang'a District, registered a 57 per cent turnout, also below the average for the Central Province.[45]

Solidity of the Democratic Party

The DP was founded at the end of 1991 by mainly experienced but disaffected and disengaged Kanu politicians, predominantly of Kikuyu origin from the northern areas of the Central Province, especially Nyeri district. If there was a distinct social basis of the DP, it was its embrace of the serried ranks of Kikuyu professionals and intermediate strata alongside farmers, artisans and business people whose scale of relatively prosperous enterprise ranged from the large to the small. Furthermore, DP influence extended into Ukambani and the Coast. There has been a conspicuous presence of some equally disaffected Kalenjin and Maasai élites who, even before 1992, became dissatisfied with the grip held by competing Kanu political hawks, and big business tycoons, for

---

[43]For more on Matiba and the urban poor, see Chege 1994.

[44]An old political hand, Kimani wa Nyoike, Ford-A's secretary-general, took those disaffected with Matiba's abstentionism out of the party to form another new party, Ford-People, which won only three seats, all in the Central Province. Two of Matiba's former closest associates, John Michuki and Francis Njakwe, won for Ford-People in Murang'a District, presumably because of a personal vote for their past association. Nyoike failed to win against a DP candidate in his own constituency.

[45]While the DP won a majority of seats in Central Province, the party had relatively less impact in Murang'a where it won three of the seven seats in the district. The other four were shared between Ford People (2), Safina (1) and SDP (1). The Safina candidate, a former chairman of the Nairobi Stock exchange, Ngenye Kariuki, won the Kiharu seat. Although the turnout in Kiharu, Matiba's former constituency, was one of the lowest in the district, other constituencies registered a relatively high voter turnout, at more than 60 per cent, despite Matiba's campaign against voter registration and voting. See Institute for Education in Democracy 1998.

the ear of President Moi.[46] Generally, membership of the party was confined to the educated, middle and high-income groups, and generally well-to-do households all of whom had a committed interest in private property rights. Its organisational acumen and conscious sense of élitism, which it portrayed at public functions and political rallies, served the party well during the 1992–7 period when Ford disintegrated and Matiba adopted an abstentionist stance for his political constituency. It is hardly surprising, therefore, that the DP made considerable gains in 1997. Significantly, however, 36 of the 39 parliamentary seats won were in the Central Province and areas of the Kikuyu diaspora. Although Kibaki shared the Kisii popular vote with Moi, the DP did not win any parliamentary seats in this district. And the party succumbed to the new parties, such as the SDP in Ukambani, in Eastern Province, where it had captured seats in 1992. Therefore, the DP remained solid as a preponderantly Kikuyu party.

Mwai Kibaki and the party's leaders managed to mesh the representation of predominantly Kikuyu business with that of 'the Kikuyu' in general. As we mentioned earlier, the trajectory of the Moi regime was to widen the basis of indigenous African capital in Kenya by doing for 'minority' tribes what the Kenyatta period had been understood to have done for the Kikuyu – promoting business through directing policy to this end at the uppermost reaches of state power. To succour and extend the basis of *Kamatusa* business, the Moi regime came to exclude, by both design and opportunity, a Kikuyu interest in big business from state power. The exclusion of what had gone by the name of the colonial-tainted Kem, and now known as Gema, the original 1970s political-cum-economic Gikuyu, Embu and Meru Association, came to be experienced as a general marginalisation of the Kikuyu from large areas of state service and public life. In short, the DP successfully represented this experience of tribal and ethnic resentment and, despite intense intra-party feuds involving the clash of generations and regions, the DP did not disintegrate after 1992.

Kibaki was often to meet criticism from DP activists who resented his policy stance towards Kanu attempts to incorporate representatives of Kikuyu big business within its ambit of securing a long-term place for *Kamatusa* business. Thus, talks between Kanu leaders and Kikuyu business tycoons were held following the spates of ethnic cleansing before and after the 1992 elections, which resulted in the displacement of 300,000 people, mainly smallholders of Kikuyu origin, from the Rift Valley. During 1993, and later in 1995 and 1996, the *Gema-Kamatusa* talks were about a 'constructive engagement' to protect the mutual interests of two layers of capital – the present fear of Kikuyu business that its 'fields of accumulation' would be circumscribed by politically influential *Kamatusa* tycoons in state power who, on the other hand, feared for their future business prospects under a possible non-Kanu government.[47]

Younger DP MPs, from 1993, had argued that the solution to ethnic clashes did not lie in talks between party élites but in comprehensive constitutional reforms to which Kanu was not committed. Their complaint was that DP participation in the *Gema-Kamatusa* talks, whether manifest or not, was tantamount to declaring that the party represented the interest of big business to the exclusion of the Kikuyu majority. Others, especially the non-Kikuyu MPs, such as Benjamin Ndubai (Tigania constituency and who appears in the case study below), Kennedy Kiliku (Changamwe, who lost his seat at the 1997 elections following the Coast ethnic cleansing campaign) and Charity Ngilu (Kitui Central, who later switched to become the SDP presidential candidate), objected to the talks for serving particular Kikuyu interests. Ndubai and Kiliku stood against Kibaki for the party's presidential candidate nomination but lost. Internal dissension saw the party lose several prominent founder members, such as Eliud Mwamunga and John Keen, to Kanu. In the event, it was Kanu's 1996 failure to win a by-election in Kipipiri, the *Gema* stronghold in the Rift Valley diaspora, which led to talks being called off by the *Kamatusa* influentials who argued that 'the Kikuyu' were not prepared to return to Kanu. Thus, the DP leadership was let off the hook by default.

---

[46]One exemplary activist was Tabitha Seii, the politically courageous DP candidate who stood against the ruthless leading *Kamatusa* tycoon and Kanu influential, Nicholas Biwott, in his Rift Valley bailiwick of the Kerio South constituency. Although winning only 80 votes against Biwott's 18,000 in 1992, Seii stood her ground as a local beacon of opposition to the archetypical figure of authoritarian corruption within Kanu.

[47]For more detail on the *Gema-Kamatusa* talks and what follows below, see Kanyinga 1994; Ngunyi 1995, 20; Steeves 1997, 42.

Another upshot of the Kanu ploy behind the *Gema-Kamatusa* talks positively benefited the DP. Matiba's radicalism, with his appeal to the urban poor in Nairobi, especially when coupled with his earlier powerful political base in Murang'a District, was offensive to some of the luminaries of Kikuyu capitalist enterprise. Also, the DP held little favour for the tycoons, given their antipathy to Kibaki's base in Nyeri District, itself a historical stronghold of intra-Kikuyu political antagonism towards the alleged domination of 'Kiambu', the Central Province district contiguous to Nairobi, during the Kenyatta period. In short, alongside those mentioned above, the DP represented the smaller groups of the bourgeoisie, and not necessarily only *petit bourgeoisie*, who felt they had been fettered by the concentration of economic and political power which had epitomised the Kenyatta regime. As such, the social feel of the party was not especially amicable towards a capitalist class that had outgrown its roots in the countryside of the Central Province. With an interest in business which was national and, beyond Kenya itself, in the wider East Africa region, it was hardly surprising that a coincidence of interest could seem to be found with those of the *Kamatusa* whose business propensities had been succoured through a regime committed to the widening of the basis of indigenous African capitalism in Kenya.

Nevertheless, if a common basis of, and for, capital accumulation suggested a transcending of the communal, of tribe and ethnicity, the incorporation of Kikuyu tycoons within Kanu was predicated upon a project to politically re-colonise their original hinterland. Going by the name of the Central Province Development Support Group (CPDSG), the leading lights of the *Gema* side of the aborted *Gema-Kamatusa* talks attempted to rebuild Kanu within the Kikuyu heartlands. Thwarted by the failure of the talks, and dependent upon the government for business contracts, the tycoons took another tack to protect their means of accumulating capital 'from above'. In consciously exercising a role of trusteeship[48] for the Central Province, and especially after the 1996 failure of the talks, the CPDSG set its sights on the 1997 elections. Despite their fabulous wealth, CPDSG candidates failed miserably at polling votes for Kanu against DP candidates within the Central Province. Whether it was the CPDSG or not which accounted for Moi's improved 1997 presidential performance within the Central Province, the disappointment with their 1997 electoral experience must be one explanation for the virtual disintegration of the Group after the elections.[49] The DP benefited from the CPDSG electoral venture in 1997 because it enabled the party to present itself more easily as the 'authentic', as opposed to 'alien', voice of an economically and politically marginalised Kikuyu population of Kenya.

---

[48]For earlier post-colonial ventures of trusteeship in Kenya, see Cowen and Shenton 1996, 316–330.
[49]Members of the CPDSG included Stanley Githunguri, former chairman of the National Bank of Kenya and owner of a plethora of enterprises; Samwel Gichuru, managing director of Kenya Power and Lighting; Walter Mukuria, managing director of the Housing Finance Company; Manga Mugwe, chairman of the Thika Cotton Mills.

Selected parliamentary election results, Central Province, 1997:

Constituency	winning candidate	party	votes	Kanu (CPDSG) candidate	votes
Nyeri Town	W. Kihoro	DP	30 763	P.G. Muriithi	3 567
Mathira	E.M. Wamae	DP	38 340	P. Kuguru	809
Gichugu	M. Karua	DP	30 736	H. Mugo	4 980
Mathioya	F.M. Njakwe	F-P	13 009	J.K. Kamotho	11 517
Gatundu South	M.N. Muihia	SDP	22 637	U. Kenyatta	10 632
Gatanga	D.W. Murathe	SDP	14 526	S.K. Macharia	8 123

Source: *Daily Nation*, http://www.kenyaelections.com/res3/central.htm

Of the above, J.K. Kamotho is notable as Kanu's secretary-general and political hawk, unelectable but nominated MP and cabinet minister who organised the links between the party and the CPDSG; S.K. Macharia stood alone in the CPDSG by April 1998 when virtually all the above-mentioned names had left the Group; Uhuru Kenyatta, son of the former president, has shared business interests with Gideon Moi, son of the present president. Moi polled 100,000 votes in the Central Province, more than his entire vote in his erstwhile North-Eastern Province stronghold. 'Exodus from the elite group', *Daily Nation* 10 April 1998.

New Parties

Roughly half of the 26 parties which contested the 1997 election were registered following the 11 September reform agreement. The majority of these new parties had little or no impact upon the election. One of the few parties to be refused registration was the Islamic Party of Kenya (IPK) whose first application had been submitted for the 1992 elections. Although no official explanation was given for the refusal to register the party, the IPK's non-secular base, its fundamentalist inclination and ability to erode Kanu's base at the Coast Province, and other Muslim areas, may be inferred as reasons why the party was not permitted to contest the 1997 elections. Two new parties, however, did have an impact upon the elections. Safina, as we see below, remained non-registered until the onset of the election period. The SDP was re-formed out of the shell of an already registered party (the SDP having been registered back in 1992 and headed by a Johnstone Makau from Ukambani, who later defected to Kanu leaving behind a party without a following). Both parties acquired high profiles during 1997 and much was expected, especially of the SDP, at the elections.

Both Safina and the SDP were about fusion, rather than fission, of political organisation on two grounds. The first was that they attracted middle classes, especially professionals and the salariat, who were acutely disaffected with the Moi regime's economic performance. They hoped for a change in regime and not merely a change of party of government. Secondly, and related to the above, the parties drew support from former members and activists of Ford-A, Ford-K and the DP who were either alienated from the communal feuding of existing opposition parties and/or their communal exclusiveness. Thus, these two parties were neither further fissures of Ford nor simply spin-offs from the DP.

Defeat had brought the opposition parties together in the immediate aftermath of the 1992 elections. However, it was the common cause of constitutional reform, the ostensible ground for opposition unity in the aftermath of defeat, which was also to cause intra-party rift and further inter-party conflict. Opposition parties, under the umbrella of the United National Democratic Alliance (UNA) between 1994 and 1995, differed on reform strategy to an extent that the Alliance withered away by the 1997 elections.[50] From early 1995, a new forum for reform started to emerge through pressure exerted by organisations, ranging from NGOs to churches, who found common cause in the name of 'the civil society'. Threatened by the shift of a strategic political project from the arena of political parties to that of civil society, opposition party leaderships reawakened their earlier campaign for reform.

However, by the end of 1995, differences between parties and factions of parties again reappeared. Two umbrella organisations now developed. The National Opposition Alliance (NOA) comprised the 'moderate' secondary factions of parties mentioned above, namely Wamalwa's faction in Ford-K and that of Shikuku Ford-A, together with Kibaki's leadership of the DP. Activists of the NOA tended to shun the ostensibly belligerent profile which had been adopted by 'the civil society' campaign for reform, especially through their insistence that the parliament was the appropriate forum for reform. The National Solidarity Alliance (NSA), on the other hand, comprised the aggressive activists drawn from the primary factions of the opposition parties, including Matiba's faction in Ford-A and Raila's radical wing of Ford-K. In taking on board like-minded politicians from the DP, and especially those who were opposed to Kibaki's 'middle of the road' and 'yellow belly' attitude towards the struggle for reform, the NSA rooted itself in 'the civil society'. Little over a year later, during early 1997, the NSA had become part of the National Convention Executive Council (NCEC), founded by non-party, civil society organisations. Events of the electoral prelude during mid-1997 brought the NOA and Kanu backbenchers together in IPPG to negotiate the reforms that culminated in the 11 September agreement.[51]

It was partly out of their experiences in the reform forums that former Ford and DP activists, especially from the NSA, were motivated to establish new parties. Instead of uneasily operating within the umbrella alliances and/or through NGOs, the activists sought to fuse the disparate

---

[50]Reports in the *Daily Nation* 3 July 1994, 31 December 1996, 13 April 1997, 20 April 1997; *Weekly Review* 15 March 1996.

[51]See Ng'ethe and Musambayi 1997, for an account of this period of the reform movements. For an account of events during the electoral prelude, see Cowen and Ngunyi 1997.

sources of political disillusion, on grounds of both reform and communality, within cohesive political parties. Above all, they sought to ensure that the new parties would not succumb to the process of fission that had governed the genesis of Ford.

Safina

Ford-K, after the 1992 elections, lost several of its younger generation of politicians, mainly professionals, who had uneasily worked with the elder generation as epitomised by Oginga Odinga. Interestingly enough, matters came to a head over the famed Goldenberg scam, the ostensible means by which Kanu had funded its 1992 election campaign, and one of the alleged culprits, Kamlesh Pattni. Oginga, who chaired the parliamentary Public Accounts Committee that investigated the scam, was alleged to have had an interest in Pattni's enterprises which included the Goldenberg Company (Throup and Hornsby 1998, 548). As we mentioned above, Oginga's son, Raila, had made exactly the same kind of accusation against Wamalwa and given this as the reason why he could not be trusted with the leadership to undertake the grand march of opposition forces against Kanu and the Moi regime.

Paul Muite, Kiraitu Murungi, Gitobu Imanyara and Farah Mohamed, all of Ford-K's activist younger generation, gave up their party positions but did not immediately defect to any other party. Both Murungi, who later defected to the DP, and Imanyara, who stayed in Ford-K, feature in the Meru case study which follows below. However, in 1994, all these Ford-K dissidents founded a NGO, Mwangaza Trust, whose purpose was to develop opposition constituencies that the Kanu government had vowed not to assist unless their MPs defected to the ruling party. Although Mwangaza proved to be popular, taking on board 'radical politicians', and other politicians who were disenchanted with opposition party factionalism and previously non-political luminaries such as Richard Leakey,[52] it did not last long. During 1995, the government de-registered the Trust on the grounds that it had 'subversive and political intentions'. Safina (the Kiswahili for the biblical Noah's ark) emerged out of the banned Mwangaza Trust as a fully-fledged opposition party which was committed to contesting the ethnic and tribal presuppositions of politics in Kenya.[53]

More than any other opposition party, Safina incurred President Moi's and Kanu's wrath. They attempted to do what they had done to all other concerted forms of opposition – play the ethnic and racial card to split the party. Moi began to 'undo' Safina in public meetings by referring to 'imperialist organisations led by non-patriotic Kenyans and former colonialists'.[54] Denied registration as an official party until the onset of the 1997 election period, and after the IPPG-based reforms, Safina abstained from the presidential election but performed creditably by putting up 45 candidates in the parliamentary elections in 6 provinces, winning 3 seats in the Central Province and 2 in the North-Eastern Province. What was significant, as indicated by the extent of its predicted vote in Table 6.4 above, is that Safina candidates came second in 11 other constituencies, thereby establishing a potential threat to Kanu where other opposition parties, especially the DP, did not have a political presence.

Notwithstanding its relative electoral success, Safina unravelled after the elections. Its two Somali MPs from the North-Eastern Province were reported to be Kanu 'moles' within the party, voting with the government on vital parliamentary motions. Having failed in attacking the DP's Kikuyu hegemony through the CPDSG, Moi turned to Safina as the next target. Richard Leakey, in making his peace with Moi, left politics and went back to the Kenya Wildlife Service and then,

---

[52]President Moi had sacked Richard Leakey, an internationally-renowned Kenyan European paleontologist and conservationist, from his directorship of the Kenya Wildlife Services (KWS). Leakey had refused to share donor funding of the KWS with *Kamatusa* business tycoons and Kanu influentials. His brother, Philip, had served the Moi regime amicably as an MP for Lang'ata and assistant minister before he was defeated by Raila Odinga in 1992.

[53]Reports in *Daily Nation* 21 June 1995; *Weekly Review* 23 June 1995.

[54]The following was Moi's rhetorical question, posed at weekly meetings across the country during 1996 and 1997: '*Tangu lini tutawalwee na mkoloni?*' (How can a colonialist govern us again?). Black propaganda, in diverse forms, was also spread through pamphlets, books and media reports, to undermine Leakey's personal integrity.

in mid-1999, into the highest echelons of government as Secretary to the cabinet and Head of the civil service. Last, but not least, the above-mentioned Pattni accused the party's parliamentary leader, Paul Muite, of having received Kshs20m ($3m) from himself during 1993. Thus, one of the main progenitors of Safina, who claimed he had walked out of Ford-K due to Odinga's association with Pattni, was alleged to have been another beneficiary of Goldenberg.[55] The circle had turned, again due to events involving business competition between a Kenyan Asian associate of Muite and Pattni. One question which therefore arises, is the extent to which Safina, whose candidates were two-thirds Kikuyu by origin, had merely taken up the political slack which the fission of Ford created and which the DP could not hold in 1997. The same question, in a different context, arises for the SDP.

The Social Democratic Party
The SDP, like Raila Odinga's NDP, was the shell of a dormant but officially registered political party. Given the reluctance of the Kanu regime to register new political parties which adopted a non-communal stance, it was apposite for the SDP to be re-formed in early 1996 by two 'academic politicians' – namely Peter Anyang' Nyong'o and Apollo Njonjo – to contest the 1997 elections on issue-based politics. As its name implies, the new SDP was committed to confronting the scourge of poverty which has swept across virtually all regions of the country, on an increasing scale since the early 1980s and to an extent which could not have been imagined during the 1960s and early 1970s. Household surveys, and poverty profiles complied from the surveys in 1994 and 1996, have indicated that Central Province, and Nyeri District in particular, have been least afflicted by the growing incidence of poverty. At the other extreme, it has been the Eastern Province, including the Machakos, Makueni and Kitui districts of Ukambani, where the number of absolutely poor households has grown most rapidly and the incidence of poverty is most marked.[56] By virtue of the 1997 election results, Eastern Province is also where the SDP has become most securely established as a new party.

Ukambani, at 1992, had been a Kanu stronghold, with the party holding 12 of the 15 parliamentary seats. Of the remaining three constituencies, Kangundo, Kibwezi and Kitui Central, which were won by the DP, two were represented by women MPs. One, Charity Ngilu, who had a very close 1992 run against a Kanu candidate in Kitui Central, defected from the DP to become the SDP presidential candidate for 1997. Ngilu had shown interest in the presidency while in the DP but the party's social mesh of the relatively prosperous Central Province could not contain an unequivocal commitment towards fighting against the kind of poverty which afflicted her Kitui constituency.

During the electoral prelude and the campaigning period, Ngilu was the presidential candidate whom Kanu seemed to fear most. Her obvious popularity in Ukambani threatened to deny Moi the 25 per cent threshold in the Eastern Province, thereby forcing him into a second round against a single opposition candidate who might well have been Ngilu herself. In the

---

[55] 'Succession: Moi can still make an honourable exit', *Daily Nation* 10 October 1998; 'Under Siege', 'Nothing for nothing' and 'A threat to Safina's future', *Weekly Review* 18 December 1998. Elias Barre Shill and Adam Keynan Wehliye, the respective MPs for Fafi and Wajir West, had defected to Safina after failing to secure Kanu nominations for the seats that they won, due to personal popularity in their constituencies.
[56] The *Economic Survey 1997* (Kenya 1997, 29–56) reported extensively on the compilation of poverty profiles for recent household survey data. Despite considerable inconsistencies in statistical frameworks for data collection, methodology and the compilation of poverty indices, household survey data from 1974/75, 1981/82 and 1992 suggest that the proportion of poor rural households in Kenya increased from between one-quarter and one-third for the earlier years to nearly one-half in 1992. Of seven provinces surveyed, Eastern Province ranked second in 1982 to Central Province, with regard to relative estimated 'rural food well-being'. A decade later, Eastern ranked lowest of all provinces. Apart from North-Eastern, the same change in ranking occurred for 'absolute poverty'. Roughly 60 per cent of rural households were calculated as being both food-poor and totally poor. The relative depth/gap of poverty, estimating the proportion of resources required to give expenditure needed for a recommended daily intake of calories for all persons, was also highest in Eastern Province for 1992. During 1996, a survey was conducted to provide subjective evaluations of poverty. Again, 87 per cent of Makueni respondents in Ukambani considered that they had become poorer during the past five years – the highest proportion for all surveyed districts.

event, since the SDP appeared to be too restricted to Ukambani within the Eastern Province, Ngilu came second to Moi who crossed the threshold with votes from other regions in the province. Elsewhere, as in Nairobi and the Coast, Ngilu's vote held up to roughly 10 per cent but the Rift Valley and Central Province proved to be elusive for the presidential candidate and her party.

While the SDP won three parliamentary seats in Thika District, largely by inheriting Matiba's legacy and engaging in closely fought campaigns against Kanu CPDSG candidates, the party's spread of votes for the presidential election remained very thin. Thus, in Thika, Ngilu polled only 8,000 against Kibaki's 94,000 votes for the presidency. There is no evidence one way or another that gender affected electoral performance. A striking instance of this point is that Beth Mugo easily won the Dagoretti constituency for the SDP in Nairobi, obtaining nearly 60 per cent of the vote against eight other male candidates. Yet, Ngilu received merely one-tenth of the presidential vote in Dagoretti which polled almost the same number of votes (21,773), as Mugo received (21,745), for the parliamentary election.[57] Apart from the aforementioned four constituencies, the SDP flushed Kanu out of Ukambani by winning nine parliamentary seats. If the SDP played a national electoral role in 1997, it was to deny Kanu a secure majority in parliament. Despite Kanu's improved performance in the Western Province, the SDP ensured that Kanu would be forced, after the election, to find a political understanding with one or more of the larger opposition parties. The fact that it was the erstwhile oppositionist to the Moi regime, Raila Odinga, who turned his NDP into the auxiliary party for Kanu after the election, tells us that whatever his radical bent and strategic inclination, it was the logic of communal politics that produced an outcome which the SDP might also not have intended before the election.

Factionalism within Kanu
Factionalism became very apparent during 1997. Ostensibly, the reason for the formation of two factions, Kanu A and Kanu B, was due to the changes in the constitution which accompanied the advent of multi-party politics for the 1992 election. A constitutional limit was placed upon the presidential tenure, confining a president to two terms of office. Unless he died in office, therefore, Moi's tenure would be forced to end by 2002, at the end of the parliament elected in 1997. But there was more to factionalism than the mere question of succession since it also involved the two communal logics of political association in Kenya.

Kanu A encompassed those who pushed ethno-regional political representation to the fore. Its key figures included, among others: Simon Nyachae who had long sought to make Kisii a durable Kanu district, and the faction's candidate to succeed Moi as president; William Ntimama, a Maasai business tycoon and openly anti-Kikuyu advocate of *majimboism* for Kenya; and Kipkalia Kones, a Kipsigis Kalenjin political hawk.[58] From political bases in their respective regions, this cabal sought to ensure that the central core of the Kanu leadership was composed of representatives who were regional and, thereby, tribal strongmen. They objected to the influence that was exerted upon the President by his inner-court, consisting of Kanu leaders who lacked the solidity

---

[57]Beth Mugo, after the 1997 election, maintained that the secret of winning lies in being with the people, knowing their problems and initiating development programmes. She claimed that this is what she did after losing the 1992 election. Martha Karua, for her rural Gichugu constituency in Central Province's Kirinyaga District, made the same point, leading to the following comment in Tostensen, Andreassen, Tronvoll (1998, 30): 'Women (and men for that matter) who have not played a role in the areas they claim to represent grossly underrate the maturity of the electorate if they expect to be re-elected'.

[58]During the Kenyatta period, Nyachae served a lengthy term as the Central Province provincial commissioner while playing a political role in encouraging Moi, then Vice-President, to build a northern-Kikuyu-Kalenjin alliance. Later, he served as head of the civil service. Ntimama played a major role in ethnic cleansing, especially after the 1992 election. Kones was a leading advocate of Kanu zones for the 1992 election, preventing opposition party campaigning in some Rift Valley and other districts, and the view that only Kanu-voting districts should receive famine relief and development generally. The extremity of his ultra-Kalenjin views was matched by his clumsy attempts at riding roughshod over intra-Kalenjin conflicts, including the economic, between the Nandi/Kipsigis, on the one hand, and the Keiyo/Tugen on the other. See Throup 1987; Throup and Hornsby 1998, 190, 539, 551.

of a regional political base. As such, the Kanu A perspective was akin to Raila Odinga's version of the communal strategy of political association, one that attempted to ensure that the presidency and the ruling party incorporated regional interests within its direction of state power.

Kanu B largely comprised President Moi's inner-court and cronies who included members of his family and State House officials, acting as gatekeepers to the president and doubling up as influential political operatives. Significantly, this cabal was also made up of leading Kanu figures who had lost their parliamentary seats in 1992 and/or did not possess a solid regional political base. Joseph Kamotho, whom we met earlier as the organiser of the CPDSG within Kanu and the party's secretary general, and George Saitoti, of mixed Maasai-Kikuyu parentage and Vice-President until the 1997 elections, best epitomised Kanu B as the cabal of electoral losers. However, the cabal also included the renowned Nicholas Biwott, no political loser in his own constituency but feared and disliked throughout Kenya as the ruthless business tycoon and alleged instigator of political violence who nevertheless appeared to have a longstanding hold over Moi. The Kanu A cabal deeply resented the political influence of these three, popularly referred to through the acronym of *Kabisa* ('completely' or 'conclusively'), for the reason that their advice to Moi over any major matter requiring a presidential decision was taken by him to be definitive.

In particular, Kanu B viewed Nyachae, from when he openly expressed political ambitions in 1988,[59] as *the* threat to their national economic and political ambitions, including installing Saitoti as the presidential successor to Moi. When Nyachae won in 1992, receiving a decisive majority of 64 per cent of the votes in his Nyaribari Masaba constituency, *Kabisa* of Kanu B did all in their power to thwart his and Kanu A's political project to reform Kanu from within. After 1992, Nyachae with his allies campaigned for Kanu elections 'to rid the party of those who lost in the 1992 elections and in particular those who did not provide a block of ethnic votes to KANU'.[60] Their targets were Kamotho, who lost his seat in Murang'a, and Saitoti, who only retained his Kajaido North constituency because of split opposition votes between DP and Ford-A candidates. Moi prevaricated over the Kanu A demand. When he reluctantly decreed party branch elections in a few selected districts, the election results only replicated feuding between the two factions at branch levels (*ibid.*). Therefore, while decreeing the postponement of national party elections until after the general 1997 election, the president also acted upon *Kabisa*'s advice in taking retribution against the Kanu A cabal by sacking Kones and demoting Nyachae and Ntimama to lesser ministries. Conversely, during this cabinet reshuffle in early 1997, Biwott returned to ministerial favour in the Office of the President. Furthermore, the cabal were denied permission, by the Provincial Administration who were now under Biwott's effective command, to hold campaigning meetings in their home districts. After the 1997 elections, roles were reversed. Nyachae was appointed to the Treasury while Biwott was demoted to a lesser ministry and Saitoti's tenure as Vice-President was not renewed.

Strategically, Kanu B had proved to be vital for party organisation, campaigning and funding *before* elections. Saitoti, as Minister of Finance, had played a key role in the Goldenberg scandal, authorising the export compensation for minerals, and which, along with fraudulent theft of National Social Security Funds, yielded the bulk of the Kanu 1992 election fund. Likewise, though in a more minor way, the State House operatives were involved in creating the 1997 Kanu election fund through a duty-free sugar import scam, thereby nearly destroying the Nyanza sugar industry, although there were also cleaner forms of fund raising. For example, on 6 December 1997, at the start of the election campaign, Kanu raised Ksh100m (US$17m) at a 'presidential luncheon attended by a cross-section of top local businessmen'.[61] Kenyan Asians were the preponderant contributors to the election fund which fell far short of Kanu's target of Ksh500m. Organisers of the function were the State House Comptroller, Abraham Kiptanui, and presidential aide, the famed State House operative, Joshua Kulei, who was also involved in the earlier sugar scam.

---

[59]Biwott acted upon the President to prevent Nyachae from contesting a Kisii seat for the last one-party 1988 elections.
[60]*Weekly Review* 17 February, 30 June, 18 August and 6 October 1995.
[61]'Sh100m raised at Kanu lunch', *Daily Nation* 7 December 1997.

Party funding enabled Kanu to distribute cash widely within targeted constituencies, especially in the swing constituencies of western and eastern Kenya.[62] Central control of the party, through State House, made it possible to distribute state spending to the Kanu hinterland, thereby keeping voters on side for 1997. Equally, it was State House-directed funding and spending which accounted foremost for the wrath of the IMF and the World Bank, thereby contributing to the suspension of loan finance in mid-1997. Kanu B represented the most corrupt impression of Kanu-ruled Kenya, both at home and abroad. However, more substantial than the corrupt episodes related to party fund-raising was the strategy that Kanu B brought to their understanding of a political trajectory for a Kanu government. *Kabisa* stood for a national arena through which capital was to be accumulated by way of private enterprise and political affiliations secured. This was the analogue of Wamalwa's 'grand march' of oppositional politics. It was to be through the central core of a political coalition that other particular interests, whether expressed on the grounds of the ethnic, racial or tribal, were to be incorporated.

Regionally constructed sources of state power, the presupposition of Kanu A's communal logic of politics, made little sense for a regime which had secured national fields of accumulation during the 1980s. Through partnerships with Kenyan Asian enterprises, Biwott, like the president, members of his family and close associates, had established a range of businesses which were spread throughout most economic sectors and operated within a national and/or extra-Kenyan market in East Africa. As we showed above, *Kabisa*'s political trajectory also involved bringing Kikuyu big business, from a historically earlier period of indigenous capital formation, into the Kanu coalition. It was through State House, and its òperatives, that deals could be struck giving political protection to particular interests while keeping open the national fields of accumulation upon which the formation of a *Kamatusa* layer of capital depended. If the Moi regime was deemed to be fundamentally corrupt, then it was in this second meaning of corruption that Kanu B's influence is to be sought. However, it could be that Kanu B's trajectory had served its purpose by the time of the 1997 election and the events of the electoral prelude which preceded it, thereby bringing into play another source of influence within the state as a whole.

While less conspicuous and coherent than either of the Kanu A and B cabals, and standing at a measured distance between both, an increasingly influential and confident body of political influence had emerged since the 1992 elections. Higher-ranking officials within the civil service and public services more generally, including the military and financial institutions, came to share a common body of opinion with some Kanu ministers and backbench MPs who had remained aloof from the two Kanu factions. It is possible, judging by the events of the 1997 electoral prelude, that it was this factionally 'neutral' body which drove the Kanu side through to the IPPG 11 September reform agreement. Kanu A's presumption of the regional offended the national perspective of what became known as the 'technocrats' of government; Kanu B's concerted intent and practices of concentrating state power within State House meant the effective exclusion of official government, which the technocrats purported to represent, from decision-making. Resentful of both cabals and their political feuding, it was the political influence of the technocrats that pushed forward the cause for reform.

Given that there are no sharp ideological or policy differences between the parties, the assertive role played by the Kanu technocrats in finding common cause for reform with the major oppo-

---

[62]It was reported that Kanu parliamentary candidates received up to one million shillings each to fund their campaigns, with most of it distributed in cash at campaign rallies. 'At one rally near Nairobi', it was reported, 'a Kanu candidate was almost lynched after his cash supply ran low.' When Moi arrived at Kisii in Nyanza Province, a key swing constituency, it was also reported that 'the big hotels were full of Kanu businessmen and stalwarts handing out money. Carloads of rowdy young men drive through town yelling "give us money".' After the election, at the Akiwumi Commission of Enquiry into the Coast violence during the electoral prelude, a nominated MP, Rashid Sajjad, admitted he had spent Kshs17m ($280,000) on election funding at the Coast. The money, Sajjad said, was to buy 'votes, feast people, pay school fees and give some to elders to take to their families'. Apart from his alleged role in the Coast violence, Sajjad had been implicated in the 1997 sugar import scam, widely believed to be a source of Kanu party funding and akin to the Goldenberg scam before the 1992 elections (see Cowen and Ngunyi 1997). 'Moi goes on cash spree in search of votes', *Times* (London) 26 December 1997; 'Kenya's Charity not for sale', *Guardian* (London) 22 December 1997; 'How we bought votes, by Sajjid', *Daily Nation* 23 October 1998.

sition parties is likely to have political reverberations beyond the 1997 election. For the 1992 election, Kanu – as for the previous one-party period elections – had depended upon state officials acting administratively as if they were party agents for the ruling party. In particular, the provincial administration was regarded not merely as an extension of the party apparatus but as the substitute for a functioning party organisation through organising, for example, primary elections for Kanu nominations of parliamentary candidates. More generally, as the Meru case study below amply indicates for the 1992–7 inter-electoral period, all ranks of the provincial administration acted as agents for an incumbent MP or an aspirant parliamentary candidate according to the state of play of the factional rift within Kanu.

One major aspect of the 11 September reform package was the agreement to take the state apparatus out of party politics. As a result of the agreement, the provincial administration was directed to play no part in party organisation. Although evidence is equivocal about the extent to which the provincial administration did play its normal Kanu role during the 1997 election, it is clear that party factionalism, coupled with the 11 September directive, disorganised the party to an extent that primary elections for Kanu nominations produced a new wave of parliamentary candidates. For seats which Kanu won, therefore, the 1997 election ushered in a new cadre of backbenchers who are likely to be more attuned to the technocratic view of the cause of reform at the national level. However, it was at the local level that an exceptionally high turnover rate of MPs, for all parties, was determined in 1997. It is to the politics of locality that we now turn.

Locality

As we mentioned above, local-level issues have increasingly come to inform the outcome of parliamentary elections. If there is little novel in this supposition then it is made to counter the presupposition that the 'tribal' explains all as some overarching contention about the abnormality of voting decisions in the Kenya case. In some constituencies, what were perceived to be the personal qualities demanded of a constituency parliamentary representative, including the proven capacity to 'deliver development', became one important basis upon which candidates were judged and votes delivered in return. Mix-and-match voting in the same constituency for presidential and parliamentary candidates with different party affiliations was a marked feature of the 1997 election.[63] For both Kanu marginal and relatively secure opposition party seats, voters might choose parliamentary candidates according to their 'development' record but would vote presidentially according to a band-wagon effect, as exemplified by anti-Moi voters who plumped for Kibaki as the candidate most likely to challenge the incumbent for the presidency.

Moreover, in a number of striking cases, candidates with a high political profile on the national and international scene fared spectacularly badly after changing their party affiliation and/or coming to participate in reform movements at the expense of cultivating their local political bases. Three examples suffice. First, Peter Anyang' Nyong'o, the incumbent candidate in the Kisumu rural constituency of Nyanza Province, was convincingly defeated on a SDP ticket in a NDP region. Anyang' paid electorally for rising above the Luo-Luhya tussles within the Ford-K, as mentioned above, and lost his local Luo political base. He was a leading public figure of both the NCEC and the IPPG, the two contending prongs of the 1997 electoral prelude reform movement. Second, Wangari Maathai is a household name in world environmental circles. She won precisely two votes in her Tetu constituency of Central Province's Nyeri district for the presidential election while receiving 900 against the winning DP candidate's 24,000 votes for the parliamentary election.[64] Third, Koigi wa Wamwere, another well known former MP with immense popular support, political detainee and exile, was defeated relatively easily on a Kenda party ticket by the DP candidate in the parliamentary election for the Subukia constituency in the Rift Valley. While Koigi received 10,000 votes for the parliamentary election, he polled only 475 against Kibaki's 31,000 votes for the presidential election. All these high-profile political figures may also have been punished for being regarded as spoilers in standing against the mainstream opposition to Kanu – the DP in Central Province and NDP in Nyanza.

---

[63]For example, Raila in Nairobi's Lang'ata constituency polled 22,000 votes for the parliamentary but only 15,000 for the presidential election.
[64]See note 45.

More generally, the 1997 parliamentary elections showed two counteracting tendencies. The first was that voting patterns showed no major shift in the regional distribution of seats between Kanu and the opposition parties. Throup and Hornsby (1998, 463), working on the 1992 elections, produced a classification of seats based upon 'five types of electoral region, characterised by the nature of the contest'. Table 6.5 sets out a comparison of the results, using the same classification for 1992 and 1997. While this aggregation may be questioned on a number of grounds, especially in that it was not clear whether 'the nature of the contest' was determined before or after the 1992 elections, the import of Table 6.4 above (for the presidential election) and Table 6.5 below is reasonably clear. The tables show that electoral support for both Kanu and the opposition parties became more concentrated in their tribal heartlands. If *Kamatusa* is taken to encompass both the Central Rift and those allied territories mentioned above, and noted below in the table, then Kanu's count of seats from these regions rose from 62 to 65 of all the seats which the party won. Likewise, the dependence of opposition parties upon their core regions of support increased from 56 to 62 per cent of all seats won. Apart from the intervention of the SDP in Ukambani which swung seats away from Kanu, as we saw above, there was relatively little shift in either the other major 'ethnic battlegrounds' or 'swing communities'. This first tendency, therefore, seems to confirm the general perception that it is communal politics that determines electoral outcomes in Kenya.

Table 6.5: Distribution of parliamentary seats won by Kanu and opposition parties according to type of electoral region, 1992 and 1997

| | Kanu | | | | Opposition parties | | | |
| | 1992 | | 1997 | | 1992 | | 1997 | |
	seats	(%)	seats	(%)	seats	(%)	seats	(%)
Ethnic homelands[a]	17	(17)	27	(26)	30	(34)	38	(37)
Allied territories[b]	45	(45)	41	(39)	19	(22)	26	(25)
Opposition conflicts[c]	1	(1)	1	(1)	17	(19)	17	(16)
Ethnic battlegrounds[d]	8	(8)	11	(10)	9	(10)	8	(8)
Swing communities[e]	29	(29)	26	(24)	13	(15)	15	(14)
All Kenya	100		106		88		104	

a: Central Rift; Luo Nyanza; Murang'a and Nyeri districts, Central Province.
b: Kilifi, Kwale, Taita-Taveta districts; Coast Province; Kajaido, Narok, Samburu, Turkana, West Pokot, Rift Valley; North-East Province; Isiolo and Marsabit, Embu, Meru, Nyambene, Tharaka-Niithi, Eastern Province; Kirinyaga and Laikipia districts; Bungoma district, Western Province.
c: Nairobi; Kiambu and Nyandarua districts, Central Province.
d: Nakuru, Mombasa, Trans-Nzoia and Uasin Gishu, Kajaido North and Narok North.
e: Ukambani, Kisii, Kakamega and Vihiga, Busia.

Sources: Throup and Hornsby, 1998, 514, Table 11.26; 476–513; http://www.kenyaelections.com.

However, the local factors, especially those that put pressure upon candidates for development, contributed towards much electoral instability in 1997. During the one-party period, one well-noted feature of elections in Kenya was the extent to which incumbent MPs lost their parliamentary seats. Thus, for the 1974, 1979 and 1983 elections, 56, 46 and 35 per cent of incumbent parliamentarians respectively lost their seats (Ahluwalia 1996, 164, Table 3). Almost 60 per cent of MPs who were elected in the 1992 multi-party elections lost their seats for one reason or another in 1997. Even in the Kanu *Kamatusa* heartlands of the Rift Valley, North-Eastern and Coast provinces, this turnover ratio was at least 40 per cent.[65] Party fission and fusion played its

[65] **Turnover rates, parliamentary elections: 1992 winning candidates who did not contest or lost seats in 1997 as a proportion of 1992 seats:**

Nairobi	Central	North-Eastern	Coast	Nyanza	Rift Valley	Western	Eastern	All
				percentage turn-over				
75	64	40	50	79	52	65	50	59

Sources: Throup and Hornsby 1998, Appendix 2, 611–630; http:/www.kenyaelections.com
Included in this ratio were 1992 winners who died or retired from politics between 1992 and 1997. 1992 winners who moved seats due to constituency delimitation and won in 1997 were excluded from those turned-over.

part in turning over parliamentary candidates but it has also been local electors who have registered the extent to which they are willing to protest electorally by disposing of politicians who are not trusted to meet what is taken to be local need. A case study of Meru, which follows, shows how the electoral dynamics of the local are more often than not governed as much by the substance of the economic as the politics of the communal.

The 1997 elections in Meru and Nyambene districts

Kanu, in 1997, won a mere three seats in the 'Gema' area, comprising the Central Province and the Meru and Embu areas of Eastern Province, one of the 'allied territories' mentioned above. Against the grain in the Meru area, where the DP reigned electorally supreme, and as Table 6.6 shows, Kanu candidates, namely Mathews Adam Karauri and Jackson Kalweo, won the Tigania East and Igembe constituencies in Nyambene district. In fact, Nyambene district generally proved to be a Kanu island in hostile political territory. Voters in this district's four constituencies – Tigania West and East, Ntonyiri and Igembe – polled 49,000 votes for Moi, less than the 54,000 which Kibaki received but almost the same as the President polled throughout the Central Province. Nyambene is significant because it was a newly created administrative district that was separated from Meru district in 1993, immediately after the 1992 elections.

Before the 1992 elections, the Moi regime had effectively started to split the district by taking previous administrative divisions out of Meru district according to ecological and sub-ethnic criteria. Thus, although all people of the former Meru district share a common Kimeru language, they occupy different land gradients, and ecological zones, of territory. Imenti, north and south of the relatively high potential land on the slopes of Mount Kenya could be easily distinguished from the lowlands of Tharaka, at the other extreme, where commercial agriculture and economic infrastructure have been far less developed. Yet, one administrative division of Tharaka-Niithi was first turned into a district although Niithi, occupied by the Mwimbi and Chuka peoples, is located towards the more southern slopes of Mount Kenya. Significantly, while campaigning in the area for the 1997 elections, President Moi decreed that Tharaka and Niithi be split into two further districts. His decision to further subdivide the district was announced as a reward to those who campaigned for Kanu and for the voters who loyally supported the governing party.

When Nyambene was turned into a district in 1993, the President was mindful that the Igembe constituency, like that of Tharaka and Imenti Central, had been won by Kanu candidates in the face of DP opposition. Prior to the 1992 election, Moi struck a bargain with Meru influentials who consisted of senior civil servants, heads of parastatals and politicians, including the octogenarian former minister, Jackson Angaine, Kabere M'Mbijiwe, Kirugi M'Mukindia and the above-mentioned Karauri and Kalweo who won for Kanu in 1997. Virtually all were from Tigania/Igembe and Imenti and had, or hoped to have, interests in private business and/or large-scale farming. As hitherto Kanu loyalists, they agreed that they would not shift their allegiances to the DP. In return, the President pledged that 'the Meru' would get favoured treatment to compensate for past (alleged) discrimination, by the Kenyatta regime who, despite the formal association in *Gema*, had treated the district 'as a political project to benefit from only to subsequently throw out the Meru when it was time for the Kikuyu to eat'.[66] This view was prevalent among Kanu candidates at both the 1992 and 1997 elections to protect the ruling party against the threat of a DP electoral onslaught in the district. Part of Moi's pledge was to create a new district, Nyambene, in which the Tigania/Igembe élite would have its own sphere of influence. In fulfilling his promise, the president hoped to further the Kanu objective of creating a fence around the DP in Meru and thereby further fragment *Gema* solidarity in the region.

The political ploy of creating a new district paid off since the former Tigania constituency, when part of Meru District, returned Benjamin Ndubai who easily beat his Kanu opponent, Karauri, in 1992. Following the split of the constituency for the 1997 elections, Karauri, who had come second to Ndubai in 1992, won the new constituency of Tigania East. Furthermore, Ndubai

---

[66]All the information, for the foregoing and what follows, was obtained from interviews with informants conducted in Meru District, and especially the constituencies reported on here, during December 1997.

was hard pushed to win in the new Tigania West constituency by his Kanu opponent, Stephen Mukangu. DP got the majority of votes in the Imenti constituencies while the two Nyambene constituencies were now won by Kanu.

Politics in Meru during the Kenyatta period was dominated by a single actor, Angaine, the self-styled 'King of Meru'. Since he had played a role in the aborted 1976 attempt to change the constitution, which was intended to prevent the then Vice-President Moi from succeeding to the presidency after Kenyatta, Angaine fell out of favour with the Moi regime. At the first one-party elections of the Moi period in 1979, Nteere Mbogori defeated Angaine in Imenti North. Karauri also proved to be a rising star in Tigania. The demise of Angaine also led to a change in issue-based politics throughout the entire district. Instead of the question 'who would help fight Angaine?', the issue became development of the district. Clan-based and 'sub-tribal' identities, upon which Angaine and his associates depended for political mobilisation, appeared to wither on the vine as a younger generation of Moi-supported politicians entered the scene.

Table 6.6: Parliamentary election results for Meru constituencies, 1992 and 1997

constituency	winning candidate	1997 party	percentage share of vote		1992 party	winning candidate
Nyambene district						
Igembe	J.I. Kalweo	Kanu	50	48	Kanu	J. Kalweo
Ntonyiri	R.M. Maoka	DP	60	63	DP	R.M. Maoka
Tigania West	B.R. Ndubai	DP	52	58	DP	B.R. Ndubai
Tigania East	M.A. Karauri	Kanu	53			
Meru District						
North Imenti	D. Mwiraria	DP	64	72	DP	D. Mwiraria
South Imenti	K. Murungi	DP	79	43	Ford-K	K. Murungi
Central Imenti	G. Imanyara	Ford-K	66	31	Kanu	K. M'Mukindia
Tharaka-Nishi District						
Niithi	B.N. Mutani	DP	36	74	DP	B.N. Mutani
Tharaka	C. Mwenda	DP	56	57	Kanu	K.F. Nyamu

Sources: Throup and Hornsby, 1998, Appendix 2, 615; *Daily Nation* website [http://www.kenyaelections.com/res3/eastern.htm].

Central Imenti

Electoral politics in Central Imenti had centred around the Angaine factor and the question of whether the Karuku or Abogeta clan would provide leadership in the area. Another youthful politician, Kirugi M'Mukindia, won the seat in 1988, when Gitobu Imanyara was allegedly eliminated at the public queuing, or *mlolongo*, stage of preliminary voting for candidates during this infamous and last one-party set of elections in Kenya. It was fitting, therefore, that Imanyara, a radical lawyer who had played a leading part in the reform movements of the late 1980s, should have trumped the Kanu sitting candidate in 1997. Nonetheless, M'Mukindia, who was elevated to the Cabinet before the elections in 1992, had changed the political configuration in the constituency by de-emphasising clan bases and the Angaine factor. M'Mukindia's assertion of the local politics of development made contending candidates realise that what mattered politically was what could be delivered for local development projects in the constituency.[67]

Significantly, M'Mukindia had won in 1992 against both Imanyara and the business tycoon, Henry Kinyua, who once headed the country's only umbrella coffee milling body, the Kenya Planters Cooperative Union (KPCU). Kinyua, like many other '*Gema*' senior civil servants and parastatal heads, had been dismissed from his position by President Moi during the late 1980s. And, like others who were so 'disengaged', Kinyua became a leading DP figure. However, wealth in itself was insufficient to win elections. For the 1997 contest, Kinyua polled less than one-tenth of the votes that were cast for the winning candidate.

[67]In an interview, 10 December 1997 in Meru town, a local political influential claimed that the local élite in Meru had supported M'Mukindia for opening a 'new chapter of politics' in the constituency.

If M'Mukindia was helped by being a government minister in the 1992 elections, his further elevation after the elections to the powerful portfolio of Minister for Commerce and Industry detracted from his 1997 campaign. Voters alleged that the Minister had abandoned the constituency after 1992. Since it was observed that he had attended more *harambee* project meetings in Moi's Baringo Central constituency than in Central Imenti, a commonly held belief was that M'Mukindia was more interested in playing national politics, by insinuating himself into the *Kamatusa* echelons of state power than cultivating his constituency on his own developmental terms. M'Mukindia's second marriage into a *Kamatusa* family also persuaded voters in the populous Kibirichia location that his neglect of local development was epitomised by the familial neglect of the first spouse who played a pivotal role in political mobilisation for the Kanu 1988 and 1992 campaigns. And, since M'Mukindia had not delivered since 1992, the popular inference was that his party, Kanu, had also not delivered development.[68]

Central Imenti exemplifies the 'mix-and-match' pattern of the 1997 elections. Kinyua's abysmal parliamentary poll for the DP was matched by a successful DP presidential result. While Moi received more presidential votes than his Kanu parliamentary candidate, Kibaki outpolled his corresponding counterpart tenfold. Wamalwa, on the other hand, underpolled the secretary-general of Ford-K, Imanyara, by roughly the same factor. Kinyua performed so badly in 1997 because trust could not be placed in either his relative wealth or old age. It is the *basis* upon which wealth is used that counts politically. Whether directly, to voters, or indirectly, as through development projects, handouts can only buy votes when there is no other source of local electoral commitment. However, in Central Imenti there was commitment to defeat the sitting MP. A majority of younger voters, who played a major role in mobilising for Imanyara in 1997, were intent on rooting out the first and second generation of leaders. Belonging to the Kenyatta and Moi periods respectively, Kinyua and M'Mukindia were regarded by the youth as being alike in that they belonged to the old era of politics. In order to avoid vote splitting and/or confuse the elderly and fence sitters, whom Kanu targeted during the campaign, opposition campaign organisers made a decision, which was communicated constituency-wide by mobile youth, to sideline Kinyua. Unlike 1992, when opposition votes were split between Ford-K and the DP, Kinyua was shunted aside by the Imanyara bandwagon.

Imanyara occupied the political space which M'Mukindia had effectively vacated since 1992. Like Matiba, as mentioned above, Imanyara possessed the credentials of a principled opponent to the 1980s reign of terror and a leading light of the early 1990s campaign for the second national liberation. As the publisher of the *Nairobi Law Monthly* journal that was critical of the regime, he had often been arrested on trumped-up charges. He stuck by Ford-K to symbolise the potential offered by a political coalition of tribal groupings. Yet, unlike other higher profile opponents of the regime, Imanyara carefully cultivated Central Imenti after his defeat in 1992. He continued to mobilise support in the constituency by both organising appeals for *harambee* projects and participating in civic education programmes that were intended to raise the consciousness of peoples' rights in relation to the state. Indeed, M'Mukindia blamed his defeat on the churches and NGOs who took part in the civic programmes. This complaint was an inversely logical implication of his own campaign that depended heavily on the apparatus of the provincial administration, including the very public use of government vehicles to move on rutted roads. Consciousness-raising had its effect: the Kanu candidate was accused of making political use of government resources instead of putting resources to work on improving the roads.

Thus, Imanyara won because he stood locally for material improvement and democracy, both of which Kanu had failed to deliver and for these, their candidate was punished. This was a case of acting according to the maxim which we meet below: 'Act locally, think nationally'. Central Imenti could also be construed, so it seemed in 1997, as one vindication of the grand march theory of political association in Kenya. Unlike the incumbent Kanu candidate who imposed his national ambition upon the constituency, Imanyara brought the idea of communal coalescence into local politics.

---

[68]Other interviewees argued that 'all the élites' who had supported M'Mukindia in 1988, withdrew their support for the 1992 and 1997 elections because 'politics in the area had taken a national dimension with the introduction of multi-party politics' and also because 'he had let people down by re-activating clan politics to strengthen the base of support from the uninformed peasants'.

Igembe

Jackson Kalweo's victory in Igembe at the 1992 elections was rewarded by his appointment to the cabinet position of Minister of State in the Office of the President. As a result of his elevation to this powerful position, Kalweo was pitted against M'Mukindia for control over the political leadership of Meru as a whole. The creation of Nyambene district did not diminish struggle among political influentials but, rather, accentuated it since control of the larger Meru area meant more influence at the national level through the presidency. From the other direction, struggle between Kanu A and Kanu B spilled over into Meru and the new district as two factions lined up between the two cabinet ministers to engage in political warfare.

Mathews Adams Karauri, eventually to be the Kanu victor in the new Tigania East constituency in 1997, lined up as the then acting Kanu branch chairman, behind M'Mukindia. Political warfare re-activated rivalry between the two dominant 'sub-tribal' groupings in the area: Igembe, including Ntonyiri and represented by Kalweo; and Tigania, represented by Karauri. Factional struggle not only eroded the social basis of party politics but also contradicted M'Mukindia's earlier programme to rid Meru of communal-related politics. As Table 6.7 shows, Kalweo's vote in the 1983 one-party elections slumped. His response to this electoral dumping was to turn to community politics. Likewise, the performance of Karauri, Kalweo's rival in the district, had also followed a declining trend since 1979, culminating in his 1992 defeat in the Tigania constituency. In facing the opposite trend, that of a markedly improving performance at the polls from his other longstanding opponent Benjamin Ndubai, a DP founding member, Karauri also asserted his communal identity, thereby setting communal politics in full train after his 1992 defeat. Communal politics, it should be noted here, arise as part of political decline, decay and decomposition on the part of politicians who also have abundant access to state power. Also, this was a case in which the reversal from an intended politics of development, to that of clan and other communal phenomena, occurred during the break between the one- and multi-party periods of government in Kenya.

However, Kalweo, after 1992, had an inbuilt advantage over his rival since his ministerial portfolio put him in charge of the provincial administration which he used to ample effect by creating new divisions in the district. After Nyambene was given district status, the number of administrative divisions increased from 3 to 13, with a similar proportionate increase in the number of intra-divisional locations and sublocations within the new district (Kenya 1997a; Kanyinga 1998a). Igembe, Kalweo's base, became especially well-endowed with new administrative units. New divisions meant extra district officers and administrative chiefs to build up patronage networks whose purpose was to block the re-emergence of Kalweo's electoral rivals, Karauri and Joseph Muturia, his old electoral opponent and the then Kanu branch secretary who had defeated him at the 1983 polls.[69] Furthermore, Kalweo used his ministerial position to press Kanu headquarters to arrange branch polls in the district during early 1995, to disestablish the then incumbent office holders. It was while Kanu attempted to arbitrate over the local party warfare, and perpetually postponed the calling of elections, that communal politics directly entered the fray.

Although the DP had more popular support than Kanu at the 1992 elections, the opposition party ran to ground after the elections. Its popularity subsided as the party organisation was dismembered and several DP local councillors decamped in Kanu. In 1997, the vote for Erastus Mbaabu, the DP candidate, slumped. Part of the reason for the DP's demise was that, without access to state power, the party could not offer the immediate promise of local material improvement that was demanded in Nyambene. Indeed, a majority of local activists argued along the lines that 'people wanted change or something different from Moi and Kanu but after Moi won, people drifted back to Kanu to avoid political backlash and opprobrium'.[70] Also, and what was specific to Nyambene, the creation of the new district symbolised the independence of Igembe and Tigania from Imenti, the

---

[69]Several interviewees in both Tigania and Igembe revealed that those who occupied the positions of chiefs and assistant chiefs in the new administrative units were Kalweo's close associates and/or those who supported him in the 1992 elections against Karauri and Muturia. A former clerk to the Nyambene County Council (interview 17 December 1997 in Maua, Igembe) observed that Kalweo instructed the Provincial Administration to employ only those he recommended to these positions, both for his Igembe constituency and Tigania and Ntonyiri more generally.

[70]Interview, former clerk to Nyambene County Council, 17 December 1997. Similar remarks were made by interviewees during interviews, 15 and 23 December 1997, in Maua and Muthara and Mikinduri locations, Tigania.

generally richer agricultural area and 'people' whom the majority in Nyambene thought had dominated them for far too long. It was this consciousness of being Tigania/Igembe, as opposed to Imenti, which countered one communal expression of politics against that which Kalweo and Karauri had reactivated after their electoral defeats of 1992 and 1983.

Kalweo's cabinet position helped him retain his seat in 1997. In addition to the factors mentioned earlier, the sitting MP claimed ownership of the activities of a NGO, Plan International, in the constituency while emphasising that, since the early 1980s, he had enabled the construction of schools and the provision of piped water. Civil servants, including chiefs, and teachers rallied around the Kalweo campaign, out of fear as much as gratitude, because his ministerial power and influence since 1992 also enabled him to cause the interdiction, retirement and sacking of public servants who represented the nationwide Kanu B faction in the district as a whole. Last, and like Central Imenti, there was a generational split for the 1997 election. Generally, the elderly seemed to back Kalweo while the relatively young campaigned for Raphael Muriungi, the NDP candidate who had been sacked from the international NGO working in the area. However, unlike Central Imenti, the youth vote was not plugged into an opposition campaign which had sufficient weight to confront the Kanu candidate whom, as Table 6.7 indicates, increased his 1992 share of the vote in 1997.

Table 6.7: Elections results in Nyambene, 1969–1997

constituency	electoral year	leading candidates[a]	percentage share of vote	constituency	electoral year	leading candidates[a]	percentage share of vote
'Kalweo'				*'Karauri'*			
Nyambene N.	1969	*J.K.Muturia*	47	Nyambene S.	1979	*M.A.Karauri*	62
		J. Kalweo	24				
				Nyambene S.	1983	*M.A.Karauri*	61
Nyambene N.	1974	*J.I.Kalweo*	31			B.R.Ndubai	1
		J.K.Muturia	30				
				Tigania	1988	*M.A.Karauri*	53
Nyambene N.	1979	*J.I.Kalweo*	33			B.R.Ndubai	47
		J.K.Muturia	32				
				Tigania	1992	*B.R.Ndubai*	58
Nyambene N.	1983	*J.K.Muturia*	55			M.A.Karauri	27
		J.I.Kalweo	15				
				Tigania East	1997	*M.A.Karauri*	53
Igembe	1992	*J.I.Kalweo*	48			N.Nkuraru	42
		E.K.Mbaabu	42				
				Tigania West	1997	*B.R.Ndubai*	52
Igembe	1997	*J.I.Kalweo*	50			S.Mukangu	47
		R.Muriungi	30				
		E.K.Mbaabu	16				

a: The winning candidate is listed first, in italics, for each election.

Sources: IED 1997, 44, 71, 102, 136–137, 160; Throup and Hornsby 1998, 615.

Tigania East

The Karauri-Kalweo political struggle within Kanu, including issues over local development in Tigania, resulted in a doubling of Karauri's share of the 1992 vote in the new split constituency. A majority of the constituents reported that, had they elected Karauri in 1992, he would also have become a powerful cabinet minister, serving Tigania in the same way that Kalweo had used state resources for Igembe. As such, 1997 offered a local opportunity that was not to be missed. A logical fallacy of composition loomed over this local view since, from a national perspective, there could only be one 'Karauri' or 'Kalweo' in a powerful cabinet position for Meru as a whole, a point proven by Kalweo's demotion to the Ministry of Health after the 1997 election, while Karauri was appointed as an Assistant Minister of Agriculture. Indeed, M'Mukindia's local difficulty in Imenti was that he understood that a national perspective was necessary to advance his political position and, for this reason as much as anything else, he had to counter Kalweo through Karauri. But, from the local perspective, the logic was reasonable in that Karauri and Kalweo were regarded as political equivalents and that the elected DP candidate, Benjamin Ndubai, 'took off from the constituency immediately after the elections in 1992 and failed to address problems such as those about poor infrastructure'.[71] Therefore, according to the predominant local view, the succeeding DP candidate, Ntaiwa Nkuraru, another effective activist during the struggle for democracy in the late 1980s and early 1990s, was not to be trusted as an MP.

A further dimension entered the Kalweo-Karauri equation. On communal grounds alone, Kalweo was disliked to the same degree that he had publicly expressed his vicious dislike for the Tigania in the district. Kalweo had seemingly assumed the role of an ex-officio MP for the constituency after 1992, and after Ndubai's effective departure, by playing the role which he performed in Igembe in sacking three chiefs for allying themselves with Karauri. It was not difficult, therefore, for some Tigania 'communalists' to mobilise support for Karauri on the grounds that he was the only force who could tame Kalweo's occupation of Tigania. Karauri's supporters composed campaign songs about the sins Kalweo had committed against the Tigania in Karauri's absence. One song, sung as a curtain raiser at all Kanu meetings in the constituency, included the words 'nontu buramwita Kalwo, Kalweo, giciu Kigera kirime nau' (you call him Kalweo, Kalweo, he is a blunt panga of no use for any farmer). As such, there was more to the communality of Tigania than that of clan, ethnic or 'tribal' identity.

Tigania borders on Isiolo district, the beginning of the extensive semi-desert ranges stretching northwards to Kenya's northern borders. In turn, the northern area of Tigania East, comprising the former Muthara and Karama administrative locations, is occupied by agro-pastoralists who graze cattle in the officially demarcated Meru Northern Grazing Zone. Small-farm tea and coffee production, together with that of food crops, maize, beans and bananas, is practised in the higher-potential agricultural land running down from the Nyambene Hills which span the district south-wards. Mikinduri and Thangatha locations, in the lower part of the constituency, are thus relatively rich in agriculture in the same way that Imenti, as a whole, is richer than Nyambene, also taken as a whole. These agro-ecological divisions correspond to differences in political attitudes, interests and electoral patterns.

Pastoralists in the northern locations of the constituency came to bear a fervent grudge against Kanu and Kalweo, in particular, after they lost thousands of head of cattle during 1996 to Samburu cattle rustlers. Cattle rustling has been one of the prime sources of primary accumulation by Kamatusa accumulators and of whom the Samburu are an integral part. Kalweo, whose ministerial portfolio included internal security, was approached by representatives of the Meru pastoralists to order the retrieval and security of their herds. Despite these appeals, Kalweo failed to respond, presumably because of his fear of the Kamatusa influentials in and around the presidency and the upper echelons of the state apparatus. In contrast, when Karauri had been an assistant minister for education between 1988 and 1992, he had implored the same Kanu government to provide 'home guards' who had earlier helped to relieve the Samburu rustling problem. Now, in 1996, when the problem had intensified, Kalweo had not responded.

In Muthara and Karama, the political inference to be drawn was that Kalweo had neither the desire and/or capacity to represent a Tigania economic interest. The only question was whether political representation was to be best secured, for an economic interest, by voting for Karauri – the benevolent political actor – or for an opposition candidate whose party might win the 1997 election and, thereby, form a new government which would act against Kamatusa accumulation through cattle rustling. In the event, the rustling question electorally split Muthara and Karama, with the Muthara electorate voting overwhelmingly for the DP candidate, Nkuraru. As Table 6.8 shows, of the four locations, it was only Muthara where Karauri failed to receive a majority of the votes cast.[72]

---

[71]Interview, Mikinduri, 23 December 1997. A leading businessman in Mikinduri mobilised support for Karauri around the argument that the last time Ndubai and DP activists visited the area was in 1992. He often cautioned that there was no guarantee that the DP candidate would not do the same after the 1997 election.

[72]Of the minor candidates at the 1997 election, Godreffrey Mwereria of the Green African Party was alleged to have the support of Kalweo while Kamenchu Ringera had crossed over to the NDP when he failed to secure a Kanu ticket for the election. It should also be noted that if the number of registered voters for each location had been proportioned equally according to the estimated population of the constituency, it is likely that the DP candidate would have won the election.

Table 6.8: Tigania East Constituency 1997 election results by locations

Location (agro-ecological zone)	Number of polling stations	Votes cast (per cent) for each candidate (party)				
		Karauri (Kanu)	Ntai wa Nkuraru (DP)	G. Mwereria (Green African Party)	Kamenchu Ringera (NDP)	Total
Muthara	22	752	4177	638	118	5685
(pastoralist zone)		(13.3)	(73.3)	(11.3)	(2.1)	
Karama	11	2914	1442	72	29	4457
(pastoralist zone)		(65.3)	(32.4)	(1.6)	(0.7)	
Mikinduri	17	6605	3087	57	697	10476
(tea zone)		(63.2)	(30.0)	(0.1)	(6.7)	
Thangatha	20	4370	2241	402	253	7266
(coffee zone)		(60.1)	(30.8)	(5.5)	(3.6)	
All	70	14641	10947	1169	1097	27854
		(52.6)	(39.3)	(4.2)	(3.9)	

Note: When official results were issued by the Electoral Commission, the total votes cast for Nkuraru (DP) were reported to be higher than as recorded at the constituency counts. This is why Nkuraru's share of the vote is lower here than in Table 6.7 above.

Source: Results recorded in counting halls of Tigania East constituency.

More generally as a set of agrarian issues, the economic interest at stake was revealed during campaigning for the presidential election. Karauri was regarded benevolently on the second ground that, before the Kanu MP was deposed in 1992, he had initiated more development projects than the incumbent DP MP had done after 1992. However, President Moi, it was often said by those participating in campaign meetings, had failed agricultural production abysmally. Kibaki, on the other hand, had been remembered as the Minister of Finance during the Kenyatta period of relative prosperity. Thus, one powerfully expressed view was that, as an economist, Kibaki was best suited to the presidency since he could be effective at cleaning up the economic mess that Moi had created. During several meetings, Karauri supporters warned their parliamentary Kanu candidate not to campaign for Moi. Karauri was urged to 'market himself', and himself alone, because 'even mentioning Moi would lead to a walk out or generate a resolute backlash on him – Karauri'.[73] So, despite the Karauri majority in Tigania East, Kibaki won a majority of presidential votes in the constituency, an exemplary case of the 'mix-and-match' pattern of the 1997 election results.

The electoral aftermath

In reflecting upon the 1997 elections during April 1998, Anyang' Nyong'o, the SDP national chairman, modified the slogan that has served as the aspiration for both international NGOs and international firms. 'Act locally, think nationally', Anyang' argued, should serve as the motif for the kind of 'political socialisation' which has served the SDP through 'ideological politics that post certain national issues and options as the substance of local politics'.[74] Meru, above, showed how and why 'certain national issues and options' have been brought to the substance of local politics. National-level economic and political issues have been both expressed by, and contested in, the name of the communal. We have seen how the communal, whether of 'the Meru' against

---

[73]Interviews with tea farmers, 27 December 1997 in Miciimikuru and Kigucwa, Mikinduri.

[74]'Minister will ease formation of coalition government – Nyong'o', *Daily Nation* 7 April 1998.

'the Kikuyu', 'the Nyambene' against 'the Imenti' or 'the Tigania' against 'the Igembe', has been as much abjured as asserted during the course of electoral politics in both the one- and multi-party periods. Yet, Anyang's immediate reflection about the local and the national was designed to contest the logic of political association which had been enunciated most forcibly by Raila Odinga, of the opposition NDP, and by the Kanu A cabal centred upon one leading putative successor to the presidency, Simon Nyachae.

Anyang's reflection was apposite because of two major issues that arose in the aftermath of the 1997 election. The first was that of party co-operation. After their electoral defeat, the main opposition party leaders re-affirmed the regional precept of communal politics. Thus, although Raila publicly appeared with Kibaki, on a shared platform when the final results of the presidential election were declared, to denounce the election as flawed and rigged and announce that they would contest the result through the courts to obtain a re-run, the NDP leader then acted according to the regional precept of his communal strategy of political association.[75] Raila forsook any opportunity for a united opposition front by striking a deal with Kanu influentials who were closely associated with the President through the State House operatives. Towards the end of April, the deal was approved by President Moi when he visited Luo Nyanza to 'restate', as it was reported, 'the benefits the pro-National Democratic Party region would receive following the high-profiled "co-operation" between the NDP and Kanu'.[76] Six months later, on 15 October 1998, the NDP amply reciprocated this gesture by voting with the government against a parliamentary vote of no-confidence proposed by Ford-K's James Orengo.[77] Then, six months later, NDP MPs, led by Raila, were reported to 'have told members of the Kikuyu community to stop using their numerical advantage in seeking the country's leadership' since 'they had their share of the leadership and should now forge for unity and leave the top seat to others'.[78] Such was the practice of the political strategy which Anyang denounced when he was reported as having 'described the post-election phenomenon of the so-called cooperation politics as justification for the "circulation of the élite" thesis'.[79]

Given the post-election fact of a hung parliament, namely that Kanu has a majority of two seats, and therefore one parliamentary vote, it was to be expected that the ruling party would require the tacit support of at least one of the larger opposition parties in parliament. The parliamentary arithmetic was especially compelling for Kanu since the Moi government decreed that the mandate of the Constitution Review Commission, providing for more fundamental reform than the 11 September IPPG interim agreement, would lie in parliament rather than an extra-parliamentary Constitutional Conference. Political logic, according to ideology and temper, might have presupposed Kanu cooperation with the DP leadership. However, as part of the communal logic of political association resting upon the precept of region, the most important immediate post-electoral event was set in train. Like the immediate aftermath of the 1992 election, implicit anti-Kikuyu campaign rhetoric found an explicit voice in extra-parliamentary violence.

---

[75]If the DP did not act so impulsively after the 1997 election, it was because its regional base had been affirmed earlier than that of the NDP and other parties.

[76]'Kenyans perplexed by Moi's criticism of inter-party forum', *Daily Nation* 29 April 1998.

[77]Despite much excitement before the vote of no-confidence, the opposition garnered only 67 votes against 137 for the government, with 6 abstentions by Ford-K MPs led by Wamalwa who argued that the DP effectively sponsored the motion. One Kanu MP, Kipruto Kirwa, voted with the opposition, but speculation that other Kanu 'dissidents' might do the same, or abstain, did not materialise. Two DP MPs, Njenga Karume and Kihika Kimani, old *Gema* stalwarts, did not participate in the vote. 'Political noose on Kanu government tightening', 'Government survives no confidence motion', 'Motion: NDP MPs explain' and 'Motion: Party to discuss MP', *Daily Nation* 15, 16, 19 and 20 October 1998.

[78]'Luo MPs caution the Kikuyu on quest for presidency', *Daily Nation* 15 March 1999.

Returning from having observed the Nigerian March 1999 presidential elections, Raila reported that the Hausa/Fulani 'tribes' had forsaken a presidential candidate 'to unite' other minority tribes and that Kenya should emulate this experience.

[79]*Daily Nation* 7 April 1998.

For the first time during the 1997 electoral process as a whole, rural Kikuyu populations were swept into the kind of ethnic cleansing campaigns which had been experienced during the electoral prelude at the Coast and elsewhere. Within a fortnight of the elections, a violent campaign was unleashed in the predominantly Kikuyu-populated Laikipia District where Kalenjin and Maasai raiding gangs killed, maimed and destroyed houses and property. Kikuyu smallholders and others defended themselves, to a far greater extent than before and after the 1992 elections, by counter-attacking in the same vein. Violence then spread to the Molo and Njoro divisions of the Nakuru districts, on the immediate west of the Rift Valley and heart of the former white highland non-tribal territories, which had borne the brunt of the worst violence during the 1992 electoral prelude. Over January and February, nearly 130 people died in Njoro and Laikipia alone, almost double the number of casualties of the 1997 Coast violence. At the end of April 1998, violence flared up again in Njoro.[80] In sum, 200 died violently, with countless others maimed, as a result of conflict over the 'tribal' association with territory.

Laikipia District, another former area of the white highlands, borders the Central Province. Political reaction to the 1998 campaign of violence on the part of the DP was immediate, buttressed by other opposition parties, especially the SDP, as well as the myriad of institutions, ranging from churches to NGOs, which self-consciously made up 'the civil society' of the 1997 electoral prelude reform movements. President Moi accentuated the tension by casting the political die through declaring that the DP was responsible for the violence, a resulting conjunction of post-electoral positioning at the national level, involving Kanu factional cabals, together with locally substantial issues of land ownership disputes and cattle rustling, an important feature of the Meru case mentioned above. It was against this background that Raila's NDP, like Wamalwa with his contrary 'grand march' thesis of communal strategy, opted for cooperation with Kanu thereby confirming, perhaps by default as much as by intent, the place of Luo Nyanza in the anti-Kikuyu political firmament.

When the NDP struck its accord of understanding with Kanu, it was clear that tacit cooperation would be immediately invalidated by state economic incapacities for delivering resources to Luo Nyanza, or any such province, upon the regional precept. While individuals of the NDP might benefit from business liaisons with Kanu influentials, the organising slogan of the party would be rendered immaterial for the party's political project. It was from this kind of reckoning that the DP, after the election, also set in train one other kind of event, that of the economic, whose immediate political consequence was also to be of some significance for the post-1997 political trajectory of Kenya.

Economic events of the electoral prelude, as we briefly mentioned in the introduction to this paper, wreaked havoc with the general government budget. Direct and indirect effects of IMF loan finance suspension at the end of July 1997 were aggravated by the first nation-wide teachers' strike for 30 years. Involving a quarter of a million teachers during October, the strike, unlike the less solid industrial action of nurses which followed, was settled at the politically pragmatic insistence of the President but at a financial cost which hung over the 1997 election and after. *El Niño* at the end of the year destroyed infrastructure on a scale in north-eastern and eastern Kenya which required repair at a cost also far exceeding the extent of the budgetary compensations, through borrowing and raising taxes, which had been made necessary by the IMF loan suspension. It was the implication of corruption that tied all these events together and it was a wide-ranging attack on corruption that the 1997 electoral process as a whole had brought into play.

After the incoming finance minister, Simon Nyachae of Kanu A, announced proposals for severe cuts in state expenditure, including the retrenchment of one-fifth of the civil service, Kibaki, the long serving finance minister of both the Kenyatta and Moi governments, called for a cross-party economic forum to resolve the crisis politically. The Mombasa forum, held at the end of April 1998, supported by the World Bank and other international agencies, and attended by both Kanu ministers and the bulk of backbenchers from all parties and addressed by Nyachae, was immediately denounced by the President. When Moi further repeated his accusations, at a Kanu Council, that the forum was subversive of his government, he was jeered and shouted down by

---

[80]*Daily Nation* 28 April 1998.

backbenchers from his own party.[81] For a large proportion of Kanu backbenchers to openly dissent from the President was a unique event in the annals of post-colonial Kenya. This event was to signal two other events of the electoral aftermath. The first was the formation of a new party, the United Democratic Movement (UDM) by Kanu dissidents; the second was the dismissal of Nyachae as Minister of Finance together with the later re-appointment of George Saitoti as Vice President – on 1 April 1999 – thereby bringing Kanu B, the *Kabisa* faction, back to the firmament of State House and its grip over state power.

Young Nandi MPs in Kanu, notably John Sambu of the Mosop constituency in the Nandi District and William Ruto of Eldoret North in Uasin Gishu, joined Kipruto Kirwa, the Kanu Cherangani MP, the leading Nandi dissident, to galvanise intra-Kanu opposition to the presidency after the 1997 elections. The 'Nandis' also took on board Cyrus Jirongo, the former chairman of *Youth for Kanu* (YK 92), who established a youth organ through which Kanu disbursed 1992 election campaign finance to the grass roots (Throup and Hornsby 1998, 353–356, 549–553). If Jirongo had thus been the political gleam in the President's eye during 1992, his accumulation of wealth during the elections irked Moi to the extent that he was shut out of favour soon afterwards. The new group of 'Young Turks', during 1998, also attracted some of their peers from Ford-K and the DP who were also disillusioned by their parties' leaderships. After announcing, during September 1998, that they were ready to form a new party because they 'had been let down', the group formed the UDM at the end of 1988 and faced interminable political wrangling in attempting, during early 1999, to gain registration for the new party. The formation of the new party both ignited a major debate within Kanu over whether UDM should be registered and re-ignited the factional cleavage between Kanu A and B, with Kanu A stalwarts, such as Ntimama, standing accused of implicit collaboration with the 'Young Turks'.[82]

As mentioned earlier in this chapter, the Nandi dissidents, especially Kipruto Kirwa, had consistently campaigned for agricultural interests, especially in dairy cattle, tea and cereal production. Appointed after the 1997 elections as an Assistant Minister in the Ministry of Agriculture, presumably as a presidential ploy to silence him, Kirwa was soon dismissed from his position by arguing that mismanagement of the Kenya Cooperative Creameries (KCC) and the National Cereals and Produce Board (NCPB), due to corruption, had let down farmers.[83] After Nyachae was dismissed as Minister of Finance during February 1999, he was reported as saying that 'life at the Treasury became nightmarish' after he had authorised the release of a 'list of the powerful people in the public and private sector who owe the National Bank of Kenya billions in unsecured and unserviced loans'.[84] Thus, the formation of the UDM together with the dismissal of Nyachae in the electoral aftermath only underlined the extent to which the implication of corruption had been brought to the heart of the ruling party. Given Kanu's wafer-thin majority in parliament, by-elections during the post-1997 parliament assumed more than their usual significance.

After the death of the incumbent MP for Tigania West – the veteran Benjamin Ndubai of the Meru case study – the Kanu candidate, Stephen Mukangu, won an April 1999 by-election, on a lower turnout, by increasing his share of the vote, up to 67 from 47 per cent in 1997. One reason for this Kanu victory was not merely that their candidate was able to take advantage of local ethnic antagonism but that a new administrative location was demarcated weeks before polling day. Furthermore, the Kanu government directed that resources should be deployed, for digging bore

---

[81]'Kenyans perplexed by Moi's criticism of inter-party forum' and 'Kanu MPs defy Moi to his face: MPs tell Moi he is wrong on talks', *Daily Nation* 27 and 29 April 1998; 'Kanu rebellion isolates Moi', *The Guardian* (London) 30 April 1998.

[82]'We have been let down', *Daily Nation* 14 September 1998; *The Standard* 16 January 1999; *Nation*, 31 January, 5 and 11 March 1999.

[83]One accusation was that the Kenya Cooperative Creameries (KCC) had accumulated debts when the President's son and other kin held senior positions within the corporation.

[84]'"Fighting graft cost me my job" – Nyachae', *Daily Nation* 19 February 1999.

holes for water, repairing roads and extending rural electrification, to the same locations where ethnic-based support for Kanu was expected to be forthcoming.[85]

There might be little unusual in the allegation that Kanu was able to defeat the DP candidate by throwing resources at the constituency, both by public spending and private largesse. Yet, one outcome of this and another simultaneous by-election in Kitui South, where the Kanu candidate kept his seat against SDP opposition in a campaign marked by extensive violence, was an intervention by the Chairman of the Electoral Commission, Samuel Kivuitu, who blatantly said that allegations of bribery 'must be true'. Politicians, Kivuitu continued, put their faith in the power of money: 'As a result, the voters have come to expect tips and largesse from politicians at this time. It seems that elections have been privatised so that voters are free to sell their rights.' Kivuito concluded by referring to the bribery of voters as 'peaceful violence' and thus incompatible with democracy.[86]

Whether or not it was what brought about the UDM or Nyachae's attempt to curtail privileged commercial bank lending or the official recognition of voter bribery, corruption openly appeared at the heart of the ruling party in the election aftermath because the private appropriation of public benefit could no longer be implied to be an assumption of what government effectively meant for the holding of state political and civil office. Opposition parties railed against corruption as the hallmark of the Kanu regime for the same reasons that the international financial institutions had aggravated the budgetary crisis during the 1997 election prelude.[87] In the election aftermath, however, corruption was explicated openly within Kanu because extended claims on state resources, as represented by the NDP's compact with the ruling party, went far beyond the *Kamatusa* heartlands and at the expense of particular interests within them. It seemed as if the presidency was no longer able to provide the means by which these claims, whether for private and/or political benefit, had been hitherto satisfied.

The continuing budgetary crisis, in conjunction with the post-electoral violence, confirmed the extent to which dissension within Kanu made the anti-Moi and anti-Kikuyu electoral forces so politically unstable. Following the austerity budget of June 1998, including the drawback of funding to implement the second phase of the October 1997 Teachers Pay Agreement, teachers

---

[85]Tigania West in 1999 showed how a communal logic of political association worked within any one particular constituency of a district, let alone at district, provincial or national levels:

Results of Tigania West by-election, by administrative location, 1999

Location	DP Mururu	KANU Mukangu	Total votes cast
Mbeu	336	2403	2751
Uringu	275	3659	3962
Mituntu	1136	1121	2269
Kianjai	3165	971	4181
Akithii	913	5348	3865
Kitheo	600	1102	1709
All	6425	14604	18737

Source: Results as recorded at polling stations.

Mukangu, on a Kanu ticket, received more votes than the DP candidate in Akithii location, Ndubai's home area, as well as in his own Uringu location, Kitheo and Mbeu. Mururu, the DP candidate, polled exceptionally heavily in his home location of Kianjai. When the administrative location of Akithii was created, the Akithii shifted their allegiance to the Uringu ethnic grouping. Uringu political influentials also argued that they had never been represented in parliament by one of their 'own' and that insofar as the Kianjai and Akithii had hitherto provided MPs it was now their turn, with the support of the Akithii, to claim their own member of parliament.

[86]'Electoral body, leaders condemn attack on Charity Ngilu', *Daily Nation* 27 April 1999.
Charity Ngilu, the SDP leader, was severely injured when she was stoned by Kanu youth during an altercation in Kitui involving voter bribery.

[87]Kibaki, for example, only repeated pre-election campaigning when he typically referred to 'corruption as the biggest evil facing the country' during February 1999 when accounting for why, as mentioned below, the ruling party seemed intent on frustrating the constitutional reform process.

went on a national strike for two weeks during the October 1998 school examinations period. Although backed by a polled 70 per cent of popular opinion, with substantial opposition party support, but in the face of the defeat of the 15 October parliamentary vote of no-confidence as well as state media manipulation and police brutality, the strike ended without the gains which teachers had won in their three week national strike during the electoral prelude.[88] However, the kind of 'crisis' which labour unrest had engendered, following a national strike of bank staff during August 1998, also played no small part in moving forward constitutional reform.

On Christmas Eve of 1998, almost exactly a year after the 1997 elections, President Moi signed the Constitution of Kenya Review Commission Act, passed by parliament on 8 December 1998, that provided the machinery to deliver constitutional and electoral reform by mid-2001. The next elections, due in 2002, are supposed to be fought according to new constitutional and electoral law as designed by a 25-member Commission in consultation with National Consultative and District Consultative Forums – the 'three tier system' of delivering reform. As stipulated by the Act, political parties will select 13 members to the Commission; 'civil society' would nominate 4 members, alongside 3 Protestant, Catholic and Muslim religious organisations. Women would be represented by 5 members, chosen from a list of 43 women organisations, in addition to a provision that at least one-third of the Commission would be female. Broadly, the terms of the Act fulfilled those set out by IPPG that, as a successor to the Inter-Parties Parliamentary Committee (IPPC) of the electoral prelude, played a major part in negotiating the reform machinery.

Between May and October, at 'Safari Park' forums, attended by all the above-mentioned 'stakeholders', dispute and walk-outs almost brought the reform process to a halt.[89] Likewise, during the first half of 1999, the reform process was stymied and suspended by the refusal of opposition parties, including the NDP on this issue, to refuse to accept a Kanu proposal that the ruling party should nominate the majority (7) of the 13 party seats on the Constitutional Commission.[90] Among accusations made by opposition party leaders was their belief that Moi, despite his own protestations to the contrary, was using the reform process to extend his presidential period of tenure beyond the constitutional limit of 2002.

It is in this perception of the President that we can view Raila's position as the leader of the NDP in cooperation with Kanu, and especially the role which he had carved out to express his position of 'leadership' in relation to 'the Kikuyu', as mentioned above. His stance appeared to be as one of many other Kanu leaders who had advanced claims to the vice-presidency and, thereby, to stand in a poll position as the putative successor to Moi's presidency. Thus, after a long hiatus, when Saitoti was re-appointed as Vice-President on 1 April 1999, it was reported that 'a horde of other aspirants' was likely to be politically 'crest-fallen'. Foremost of these aspirants were the regional party influentials, Musalia Mudavadi, Stephen Kalonzo Musyoka and Katana Ngala, from western Kenya, Ukambani and the Coast respectively.[91] All these Kanu leaders, like Raila, commanded influence due to their electoral support arising from regional constituencies. Cross-cutting these regional affiliations was the resurgence of Kanu factionalism, especially the resurgent *Kabisa*, made up of the 'hardliners' or 'hawks' who made the issue of constitutional reform so difficult to resolve. Insofar as Kanu B had trumped A during 1999, it might seem that

---

[88]'Shutdown' and 'High Stakes for the State', 'Back to Class', *Weekly Review* 9 and 23 October 1998; 'Teachers' strike brings out govt's comedy of errors', *Nation*, 15 October 1998. Comment from the *Daily Nation* was apposite: 'The growing democratisation of the country's institutions and in particular the increasing realisation and understanding of people's constitutional rights, has done great damage to the State's ability to wriggle out of issues through the use of misinformation and bully-boy antics.'

[89]Kanu's original proposal for a single Commission constituted by members chosen from the 65 administrative districts, thereby implicitly affirming the 'tribal' of locality as well as satisfying some strident calls for *majimboism,* carried little weight. At Safari Park III, Moi appeared to mollify the opposition, including Kanu dissidents, by 'talking about the need to curb the powers of the president and the necessity of writing a constitution that would ensure justice and equality for all'.

'New Forum' and 'Marching On', *Weekly Review* 10 April and 9 October 1998; 'Doubts over reform talks' and 'Constitution Review Act now law', *Daily Nation* 23 August and 26 December 1998.

[90]'Reform: parties trade accusations', 'MPs want constitutional review put off', '"Reject constitutional review lobby" hots up', *Daily Nation* 6, 16 and 22 February 1999.

[91]'Saitoti's return', *Daily Nation* 3 April 1999.

normal politics had returned to Kenya after the 1997 election. However, one upshot of the election, and its aftermath, was that the openness of Kanu dissention, as amplified above, had brought the issue of all that was entailed by corruption to the fore. It is this kind of political opening that makes it possible to surmise that any forthcoming government in 2002, if not before, is unlikely to resemble the shape or form of past, and any remaining future, years of the Moi regime in Kenya.

Conclusions

As a result of their exhaustive account of the 1992 elections, David Throup and Charles Hornsby (1998, 453, 526) forecast that Moi and Kanu would win the 1997 elections more easily than in 1992 and that Kenya 'would be on the verge of becoming a single-party state once more' (*ibid.,* 602). It should also be noted that Throup and Hornsby effectively revised their conclusion when they were apparently writing during the 1997 electoral prelude (*ibid.,* 576), thereby acknowledging that the elections would be more closely fought than in 1992. However, the question remains about the status of Kenya as a multi-party state when the ruling party continues to win general elections with a mere plurality of votes but without an effective threat from a parliamentary opposition.

Constitutional and electoral reform, as before 1992, was the case and during the 1997 electoral prelude and of the more substantial kind which is likely to follow by 2001, has progressively taken Kenya away from the authoritarian rule of the one-party period. But the institutional facts of reform, in and of themselves, do not necessarily mean a change in state regime that would prevent Kenya from continuing to be a single-party state. We have seen from the above that, as a single-party which has won multi-party elections during a continuing process of institutional reform, Kanu has become more rather than less the 'Kadu' party of old. It is also possible for the single party to transform itself into another political formation that meets the demands of a different historical period when the logic of the communal association itself undergoes a change. Kanu's post-electoral alliance with 'the Luo' NDP should be seen in this light.

The circulation of élites thesis, in its Kenya integument, as in Africa more widely, is often also called 'tribalism from above' or 'political tribalism' (see, for example, Berman and Lonsdale 1992), namely the political project of élites for maintaining political power as a means for both their private economic accumulation and reproduction of their general class positions. As we saw above, the shift between the Kenyatta and Moi regimes represented one form of élite circulation in that, whereas political power shifted from Kikuyu to Kalenjin élites, both were involved in the common endeavour to promote indigenous capitalist accumulation in Kenya and secure the basis of large-scale property on grounds of the political. Now, after the 1997 elections, the thesis meant that it was a Luo élite which was intent on bringing itself into the tribal circulation of power. It is against the background of the post-electoral violent, constitutional and economic events, as briefly mentioned above, that the thesis of élite circulation, or political cooperation, has to be assessed.

During the course of this chapter, we have seen at least two problems involved in positing the élite circulation thesis as a depiction of the conditions for political association and the assertion of class power in Kenya. The first is that the shift from Kikuyu and *Gema* to Kalenjin and *Kamatusa* domination of state power could not simply replicate the means by which the first African indigenous class of capital was formed. A different historical layering of capital, that of the *Kamatusa* phenomenon, happened not merely by straddling official positions within the state but through encompassing state institutions as *the* arena for private and primary accumulation. As well as the politically intended destabilisation of a swathe of state institutions, corruption – the phenomenal form of private accumulation during the period of the Moi regime – involved the unintended destruction of the capacity to deliver state-provided services. And corruption, with its substantive implications, has not only changed the basis according to which élites might be deemed to circulate but has short-circuited the very process upon which tribalism from above, or political tribalism, has been based.

One implication of corruption returns us to the second of the problems associated with the élite circulation thesis. Insofar as decentralisation, in the provision of public and communal goods and services, has been regarded as the only substitute for what denuded state responsibility and/or capacity cannot do, we have seen that local constituencies put aggravated pressure on their parliamentary candidates to place themselves proximately around state power to appropriate development resources.[92] 'Tribalism from below' thus gains an overt material content, expressed by a *desired* need to access state resources through 'one of our own' because this is the only way to 'eat'. Circulation does not then describe an exclusively élite phenomenon. The expression that it is 'our turn to eat because another group ate or has eaten' becomes the organising slogan around which the regional precept of the communal political logic is founded.

By way of local perception, the regional precept cannot simply be rejected because influence over state power, in and around State House, cannot realise resources, or that it is socially undesirable that a communal strategy should be employed as the means to deliver 'development'. Rather, the regional precept would be fallacious if it were presupposed that the national is composed of so many regions, so many localities from which political authority derives. Yet, as we attempted to explain above, the mix-and-match 1997 election results showed evidence of the local determining voting at the parliamentary election with the national playing a major part in accounting for presidential votes. According to this evidence, at least, and bearing in mind that the local aspiration is for state resources to be brought to localities, there is no simple fallacy about the perception that presidential authority, let alone parliament, derives from some formless mass of localities.

It is, therefore, the way in which the national is 'thought', when action is sought at the level of the local, which matters. For the Kanu B cabal, together with the CPDSG of Kikuyu business, locality had been transcended in the name of finding a national agreement to politically secure the gains of capital accumulation. That the Group was so generally defeated in its 1997 parliamentary excursion might have made the national level of reckoning only more emphatic for this political force. For the new parties, as Anyang's political motif suggests, it is the way of thinking about the national that gives material substance to local politics. One powerful way of thinking about the national is to implicate it in development, especially in the intent to develop 'the nation'.

One meaning of intentional development, that of the positive and constructivist, involves an industrial policy. Academic interpretation about the state in Africa as patrimonial or prebendary has been accompanied by its pervasive prescription in favour of a doctrine of agrarian development whose antipathy and forewarnings of industrial society are matched only by a long-held European belief that Africa is the world's natural industrial no-go zone. It is now clear that this belief, even for the Kanu governing regime, is no longer generally shared in Africa. Towards the end of the electoral prelude, the above-mentioned Minister of Local Government, Francis Lotodo, seemed to speak the acceptable development jargon of the age when he told a UN-sponsored conference on Urban Industrial Development for English-Speaking Cities in Africa that 'stakeholders' should favour 'a participatory approach between civic authorities, the central government and the private sector in urban development'. However, the minister was adamant that Kenya, like other African countries, was shifting its 'economic development approach from agriculture to industrialisation'.[93] Industrial policy and the political are implicated in each other.

Friedrich List is best known as the fountainhead of an industrial policy for 'national development'. For the Germany of the 1840s, List advocated a series of economic measures, including protection, which became the staple diet for making late industrialisation possible. Less known is List's advocacy of 'social' and 'moral conditions', entailing 'legal security' for 'persons and their properties' in addition to the free exercise of minds and 'high moral culture' which would be developed to make possible 'economical development'. Political freedoms, of the kind fought for

---

[92]One paradox which arises is that the earlier failure of the developmental state, made evident in Kenya from the mid-1970s, cannot be simply addressed by the prerequisites of 'good governance' which include the advocacy of decentralised government, including the local and communitarian provision of services. At the same time that multi-party elections are presumed to be the means to remove centralised, corrupt authoritarian regimes from power, electoral practices make the local more emphatic. And, as the local becomes more and not less emphatic, so does the regional precept of the tribe come into play, as 'tribalism', the other besetting sin which is meant to explain both the failure of the post-colonial developmental state and why failed regimes win elections to stay in power.

[93]'Lotodo's plea on progress', *Daily Nation* 15 October 1997.

during the 1990s in Kenya, were a fundamental attribute of, and condition for, industrial development. In contrast, political freedoms were reversed and restricted as part of the industrial policy which governed the latest experience of rapid late industrialisation – that of East Asia since the 1960s.[94] We can only point here to the conundrum that while the East Asian case seems to have served as the template for the recently-expressed official African intent to industrialise, it is the advocacy of political freedoms in Kenya, along Listian lines, which has stood as one vital condition for economic reform associated with both internal political movements and external pressures.[95]

Second, and in line with the basis of the agrarian doctrine of development, development doctrine has meant state action to compensate for the negative propensities of capitalist development (Cowen and Shenton 1998). It is significant that there was some attempt to transcend the direct issues of electoral reform when, during the prelude to the elections, a NCEC Nairobi *kumi kumi* rally was planned for Moi Day on 10 October 1997. Paul Muite of Safina explained on behalf of the NCEC, the alternative forum of reform to the exclusively parliamentary one, that the purpose of the rally was to draw attention 'to the poverty afflicting Kenyans, unemployment, the lack of drugs in hospitals, the collapse of the education system and infrastructure'.[96] While the police were beating up those addressing and attending the NCEC rally, held at the poorer east of the city centre, Moi spoke at its prosperous western edge about how the British New Labour government should be praised 'for emphasising poverty alleviation' and how he would further this cause of development in Kenya.[97]

Thus, it seemed that the Moi regime was moving towards its final era as it had begun in 1978, when the president came to office, suggesting that his regime was presenting itself as 'Kenyan populist nationalism' in reaction to the capitalism of the Kenyatta period (Godfrey 1982, 288). Moi, however, had no intention then, or now, of implementing a populist programme of state policy. The difference between then and now is that the period of corruption has probably run its historical course, in bringing the *Kamatusa* layer of indigenous capital into being, and that the two-fold meaning of development is necessarily part of the question as to what extent multi-party politics has forced the ruling party to address the problem of poverty at the same time as its leaders are mindful of their own imperative to secure conditions for the private accumulation of capital. While the 1997 elections seemed to have tied development more closely to that of the local, they could also have marked a further future opening of political space in which the wider meanings of development are not so tightly enclosed by what has gone by the name of the 'tribal' and all that it has politically represented in the past.

---

[94]For Listian themes, see Cowen and Shenton 1996, 158–169, 427–433.

[95]The *World Development Report 1997* has been written around the theme of authoritarian government and corruption as the cause of why development has 'faltered and poverty endured', predominantly in Africa, and why state institutional capability and effectiveness are the conditions for true development. The conundrum makes an immaculate appearance here. On the one hand, East Asia is referred to as a case in which state interventions 'for market enhancement' were used effectively. 'Countries that pursued an activist industrial policy successfully could not have done so without strong institutional capability'. Four pages later, this same World Bank report stresses the need for 'giving people a voice' through parliamentary voting, the representation of 'genuine intermediary organizations' in policy-making, decentralisation of government and participation in the provision of state services (World Bank 1997, 6,10).

[96]'Rally's venue surveyed', *Daily Nation* 9 October 1997.

[97]*Daily Nation* 11 October 1997.

7

Winning Elections, Losing Legitimacy
Multi-Partyism & the Neopatrimonial State in Malawi

HARRI ENGLUND

Introduction

In Malawi, where the 30 years of one-party rule were ended by orderly and peaceful multi-party elections in 1994, electoral campaigning has assumed some permanence through frequent parliamentary by-elections. More than 20 MPs died during the first three years of the post-transition parliament, each prompting the Electoral Commission to organise a by-election. Several by-elections are usually organised at the same time. Some constituencies appear to be the strongholds of particular political parties and attract little attention at the national level. Others are vehemently contested, either because they are seen to indicate the pulse of Malawian politics for historical and demographic reasons or because the balance of support between the main parties is precarious.

This chapter presents a case study of the 1997 parliamentary by-election in the Blantyre City Central Constituency, the heart of Malawi's biggest city. More than any other by-election, it was expected to enable Malawians to anticipate the 1999 general elections – both in its patterns of popular support and in the new rulers' commitment to liberal democracy.[1] Its conduct and outcome were disconcerting to all the parties and, not least, to the electorate. As such, this by-election provides an opportunity to explore questions of wider relevance during the apparent 'consolidation' juncture of multi-partyism. Relevant questions include those that interrogate, among others, the impact of multi-partyism and other liberal institutions on state formation, and the idioms and practices by which persons assess and contest 'high politics'.

This case study explores how present multi-party politics has failed to erase past practices and institutions, some of the latter promoting, some undermining, popular participation. On the one hand, liberal democracy, with its Lockean version of social contract theory, has not introduced the state-society divide and the discourse of human and citizen rights as the sole parameters of political idioms and practices. Tenets of liberal democracy co-exist with notions of moral partnership, of enduring relatedness, with ideas of accountability, personhood and of the 'self' which are distinct from what is implied by the ideas of metropolitan liberalism (cf. Lemarchand 1992; Werbner 1995). On the other hand, despite liberal reforms, personified notions of power continue to be integral to a particular state formation which, in Malawi, has long promoted neo-patrimonialism.[2]

I am grateful to D.B. Chinsinga and J.K. van Donge for assistance and discussion during research. I alone am responsible for my analysis and conclusion.

[1] Although this chapter was written well before the June 1999 parliamentary and presidential elections, the interpretation of this by-election helps to explain, as well as much else, why the Malawi Congress Party was able to make a very significant comeback at the later general elections.
[2] Clapham has defined 'neo-patrimonialism' as 'a form of organisation in which relationships of a broadly patrimonial type pervade a political and administrative system which is formally constructed on rational-legal lines' (Clapham 1985, 48). In Bratton and van de Walle's (1997, 62) more recent usage, the neo-patrimonialism of post-colonial regimes in Africa indicates the 'hybridity' of those regimes. Patrimonialism, they imply, is the

After the transition to political pluralism, clientelist networks in a 'rhizome state' (Bayart 1993) no longer find an apparently uncontested figure at their apex, but neo-patrimonialism itself has remained salient. One question is the extent to which new practices, such as multi-party electoral competition, lay bare the contradictions of neo-patrimonialism.

In other words, it is possible to analyse the interpenetration of quite disparate institutions in the current Malawian predicament. 'New' institutions do not simply displace 'old' ones; 'global' forms do not take over 'local' dispositions. Such analysis must, of course, go beyond the essentially *ahistorical* evocations of 'pre-colonial' political forms and the invented traditions of Africa's autocratic leaders (cf. Cowen and Laakso 1997b, 721, 735–736). Furthermore, by situating moral arguments within a particular state formation, this chapter counters the tendency to associate the problems of democracy in Africa with a 'political culture'. Such a tendency, as mentioned later, often proposes 'political learning' and 'civic education' as remedies to these problems.

Before presenting the Blantyre by-election in detail, I outline what neo-patrimonialism has meant for both Malawi's autocratic past and the current period of political pluralism. International and local efforts to introduce institutions of liberal democracy, whilst of some significance, have been more attuned to identifying democracy with certain 'paraphernalia' rather than with thorough reforms in the state formation. The Blantyre by-election provides a case study of the contradictions which are part of the present period of political pluralism. Towards the end of the chapter, I discuss how the notions of moral partnership underlie the apparently non-political associations of residents in Ndirande, a poor township in Blantyre. Burial societies are one example of associations that contribute to Ndirande residents' well-being, and a person's prominence in branch-level party politics often derives from work in them. The moral partnership established in such associations indicates political practice that is distinct from the 'high politics' of both neo-patrimonialism and liberalism.

Background to the by-election

The death in July 1996 of Witness Makata, the MP for the Blantyre City Central Constituency, triggered off events and arguments that were of immediate national interest. The core of the constituency is Ndirande, 'the Soweto of Malawi', a densely populated and predominantly poor township, where migrants from all the districts of Malawi began to outnumber local villagers from the 1940s onwards. As an historical site of Malawian politics, Ndirande provided a sharply symbolic and emotional edge to campaigning during the by-election. Ndirande had provided the setting for the emergence of the Nyasaland African Congress, Malawi's nationalist mass movement, during the 1940s. It was also prominent as a setting for the underground mobilisation of pro-democracy support during the 'second liberation' of the early 1990s.

Makata represented the United Democratic Front (UDF), the new party that won the 1994 multi-party elections. President Bakili Muluzi, who replaced Dr Hastings Kamuzu Banda as the head of state in 1994, attended Makata's funeral for two days and also visited Ndirande in order to campaign for the UDF before the by-election. The Malawi Congress Party (MCP), the ruling party during the period of the Banda regime and the main opposition party after the 1994 elections, was also supervised by the highest-level party authorities. Its campaign was led by John Tembo, the former Minister of State and Banda's close adviser, and the party's vice-president, Gwanda Chakuamba, appeared frequently at campaign meetings. Likewise, the Alliance for Democracy (Aford), the second most important opposition party, enlisted the assistance of its president, Chakufwa Chihana, during the course of its by-election campaign.

The by-election was originally scheduled to take place during November 1996. When the election finally took place five months later on 17 April 1997, the main opposition parties had effectively withdrawn from electoral competition, while the electorate appeared indifferent towards the contest. For this subdued anti-climax, only a little over 4,000 of the 37,000 registered

---

choice term for pre-colonial African societies. For Max Weber, who introduced the concept, however, patrimonial regimes were the literate pre-modern empires where the reach of political power had extended to formerly non-patrimonial areas. See Eisenberg 1998, 84.

voters cast their votes. Nearly all the votes went to the UDF candidate; the votes for small opposition parties amounted to about one hundred. What had begun as a serious contest with repercussions on national politics ended as a virtual mockery of multi-party electoral competition. As shown below, the delay in holding the by-election was caused by a court injunction, itself occasioned by allegations of violence during campaign meetings, of irregularities in voter registration and, above all, of abduction of opposition candidates by the ruling UDF.

The virtual exclusion of opposition, if disappointing to the majority of the electorate, did not lead to public protests in Ndirande. But nor was the general sentiment best described as apathy and disillusion with politics. Rather, the UDF government had, quite inadvertently, sowed the seeds of its own illegitimacy. If elections, as Tom Young has observed, 'make people aware of numbers, *their* numbers, in a way they often were not before' (Young 1993, 308), then this by-election made the electorate wonder just how many would have voted for MCP or Aford. Four thousand votes out of 37,000 potential votes seemed a very dubious election victory indeed. Many were sarcastic about the result, but they saw no other option than to accept the new MP as their representative. Others felt that the 1999 general elections were so close that the situation would soon be rectified. Far from legitimising the incumbent government, therefore, the by-election victory was bound to undermine it. For some Ndirande residents, hitherto oblivious to the new 'democratic' government's malpractice, the by-election was the first indication that the promise of multi-partyism could be betrayed.

Neo-patrimonialism and the paraphernalia of democracy

The common pattern by which newly-independent states in Africa came to be personified by their charismatic leaders (see Chazan *et al.* 1988, 157–160) assumed grossly autocratic proportions in Malawi. Promoted as the 'father and founder' of the nation, Kamuzu Banda embarked on an extreme centralisation of political and economic power even before the country was declared independent in 1964. All 'development' came to be identified with his personal efforts and wisdom, and all politicians and the populace at large were expected to display wholehearted loyalty. The extent to which such autocracy actually prevented dissent, overt or covert, varied within the country and during different periods of the Banda era (Englund 1996). It is clear, however, that the state percolated through virtually every sphere of Malawian society, sometimes bringing extensive patronage, at other times coercion and violence. The transnational sources of state formation during Banda's era not only included the support which this anti-socialist regime received in the Cold War configuration. Banda's regime especially during the 1970s also averted a serious economic crisis through controversial allegiances with the South African government and influential Portuguese businessmen (see Williams 1978; Mhone 1992).

Popular participation consisted in expressions of support and obedience for the head of state, known as the Life President since 1971. Different villages, government departments and other work-places competed amongst themselves to maximise the turnout of their members in political rallies where speakers competed over the extent to which their eulogies were obsequious to the Life President. After the 1961 multi-party elections, which gave a landslide victory to the MCP (Mair 1962), parliamentary elections, though held several times during the one-party era, were considerably less colourful events. All the candidates represented MCP and were accepted by the Life President, who also made several direct appointments of MPs. In the early 1990s, when both external and internal pressure towards multi-partyism intensified, many Malawians took pride in the fact that they had never voted in their lives. The 1993 referendum on the system of government was the first voting exercise for them and – closely supervised and monitored by international agencies – it was a success in terms of both voter turnout and logistics. Moreover, the 63 per cent vote for the multi-party system of government was immediately accepted by the Banda regime which proceeded to organise multi-party parliamentary and presidential elections in May 1994. UDF won the elections whilst failing to secure a two-thirds majority, and its leader Bakili Muluzi, as mentioned, replaced Banda as the head of state. Banda displayed statesman-like dignity by publicly conceding his defeat and congratulating Muluzi.[3]

---

[3]On the Malawian transition, see for example Kaspin 1995; van Donge 1995; Englund 1996; for a 'stock-taking' a few years later, see Phiri and Ross 1998.

An independent press had emerged before the formal transition to multi-partyism. From 1993 onwards, Malawi witnessed the launching of various governmental and non-governmental institutions designed to safeguard liberal democracy. Prominent among these institutions were judicial offices such as the Ombudsman, the Law Commission and the Human Rights Commission. Their duties vary from investigating allegations by the general public about malad-ministration and injustice to reviewing laws. The Anti-Corruption Bureau and the National Compensation Tribunal were introduced by the UDF government to compensate for corruption and atrocities committed by the previous MCP government and to prevent further abuses of power. In addition to the state institutions stands a motley collection of human and civil rights organisations and watch-dogs, many of them funded by foreign sources. New notions and agendas have thereby emerged in Malawian public discourses, with women and children rights, for example, opening up alternative avenues to political lobbying. On top of all this, a new consti-tution came into force in 1995 (see Mutharika 1996; Banda 1998; Kanyongolo 1998).

The repeated calls by virtually all the parties to amend the 1995 constitution is only one example of continuing arguments amidst reforms and new institutions. Two issues are particularly pertinent for understanding the limits of the democratic transition. On the one hand, the Malawian state formation has retained more than a measure of continuity through the strong executive powers of the state president. On the other, apart from a short period of coalition government between the UDF and Aford, the country has been mostly ruled by a *de facto* one-party government since the 1994 general elections. Despite the ostensibly unhindered conduct of oppo-sition parties, the impact of one-party government has certainly been felt by the Malawian populace. The Malawi Broadcasting Corporation, the most important mass medium in the country as a whole, has been under the tight grip of the UDF government which prevents the meetings and statements of the opposition parties from often receiving any coverage at all. Over 1996–97, the MCP and Aford also boycotted parliamentary sessions for several months in protest against what they viewed as President Muluzi's 'poaching' tactics among opposition MPs. After Aford had withdrawn from the coalition government, some of its ministers refused to resign accordingly. Muluzi compounded the tension by nominating more Aford MPs as cabinet ministers. Bundaunda Phiri, an MCP MP, in turn, was rewarded with a ministerial post after he had resigned from the MCP.

Although the MCP and Aford eventually returned to parliament, mismanagement and persistent scandals have continued to hamper the government of 'democratic' Malawi. Public resources have gone into attempts to marginalise, if not to eliminate, the MCP, albeit to little avail from the UDF government's point of view. The judicial probe into the 1983 murders of four politicians in Mwanza District began as a compelling case of national self-examination, with Kamuzu Banda and John Tembo among the principal accused. However, the lack of evidence and the sheer haphazard conduct of prosecution disclosed pitiable incompetence in the UDF camp (see van Donge 1998a). The accused were acquitted. MCP newspapers asked the uncomfortable question of why the UDF was not interested in exploring atrocities which were committed when Muluzi and certain other senior UDF figures were themselves high-ranking MCP officials. After court decisions went in different directions, the UDF government was eventually more successful in seizing the Press Trust, a commercial conglomerate largely owned by Banda, from MCP trustees. The aftermath of Banda's death in November 1997 has seen Muluzi's undiminished zeal in under-mining the MCP's economic base. The State President has thought it necessary to give his opinion that Banda's estate should be shared by the latter's relatives rather than the MCP or C. Tamanda Kadzamira, Banda's long-time companion and Tembo's niece.[4]

The blatant abuse of power by UDF politicians has occurred in the context of establishing a toothless Anti-Corruption Bureau which, by early 1998, has yet to complete its first case. Some abuses reveal clearly how the paraphernalia of liberal democracy often fails to curb neo-patrimo-nialism and greed under the Malawian state formation. In one appaling case, the press discovered that Brown Mpinganjira, one of the founders of UDF and Information Minister in the government,

---

[4]At the time of writing, recent news indicates that all government departments have been ordered not to advertise in the *Daily Times* and *Malawi News*, two newspapers closely associated with the MCP, thus depriving them of an important source of income.

had seized a 350-acre piece of land that had belonged to the Malawi Young Pioneers, the paramilitary wing of MCP banned during the democratic transition. The land was in Mpinganjira's constituency in Mulanje District, one of the most land-hungry areas in the country. It had been divided between four prominent persons: Mpinganjira, a deputy cabinet minister, a businessman and the General Manager of ADMARC, Malawi's foremost dealer in agricultural products and agricultural development.[5] In another example, the government was found to have diverted funds which were meant for Malawian migrants who had worked in South African mines. Although the practice appeared to have started during the MCP regime, several politicians and officials in the new government allegedly continued to misappropriate funds. The wife of Vice-President Justin Malewezi, for example, used migrants' funds to cover her South African medical bills.[6]

More examples could easily be furnished, both of the UDF leaders' greed and of their sensitivity to criticism which led, among other things, to the banning of public meetings held by the Malawi Congress of Trade Unions intended to address the Malawian economic crisis after the democratic transition. Due to the plummeting value of the Malawi kwacha and inflation, rising from 8 to 115.9 percent between 1991 and 1994, real wages and work conditions declined (Banda *et al.* 1998, 78–79). After a reduction in inflation after 1995, economic problems have reappeared more recently.

One reason for the government's failure to sustain the democratic momentum may be the background of some top UDF officials who were prominent in previous MCP governments. The democratic transition has introduced the marginalisation of the religious and intellectual contingent, who were at the forefront of opposition to the Banda regime, in favour of astute politicians with considerable involvement in commerce taking over the scene.[7] While good leadership would not go amiss, as mentioned earlier, deeper problems of state formation may be at issue. A complex set of historical and local reasons accounts for this state formation, in Malawi as elsewhere in Africa, including 'colonial autocracy, the nationalist political monopoly, and personalised patrimonial rule' (Young 1988, 58).

The political practice and discourse of moral partnership, reaching beyond liberalism and patrimonialism, disclose the entwining of the self and social relationships. In a Cameroonian case, one image for a model of a prominent person resembles a piggy bank (see Rowlands 1995, 33). A Malawian version would represent the piggy bank as a big man or woman who embodies the welfare of the dependants in his or her person and who, as such, is constituted in him- or herself by those relationships. The popular idea of political change is not to break the piggy bank and to dissipate its contents, but to ensure the growth of the piggy bank on a par with the prosperity of its subjects. The analytic quandary is to understand how such moral notions co-exist with a state formation which extends marginalisation and impoverishment while often being governed by leaders who evoke versions of the same moral notions as that of the piggy bank. It is important to appreciate, nevertheless, the subversive potential in the discourses of moral partnership, because they express 'the moral discredit incurred by the state' (Lemarchand 1992, 190). Another paradox arises towards liberalism. Even though its institutions, such as multi-party elections, may reveal the extent of moral discredit, the critical discourse itself may have little to do with the liberal notions of the self and the good.

Neo-patrimonialism and moral partnership in Ndirande

Witness Makata, the late UDF MP for the Blantyre City Central Constituency, was a striking embodiment of the image of a piggy bank. The man was not just big. He was huge. The son of a prominent Ndirande family that also produced leaders within the 'traditional' authority structure, Makata was the owner of a big garage in Ndirande and the husband of three women. He had not

---

[5]See for example 'Mpinganjira under Fire', *Daily Times* 30 December 1996; 'Man to Sue UDF Big 4', *The Nation* 30 December 1996; 'Ex-MYP Land for Landless', *The Nation* 3 January 1997. The article in *Daily Times* mentions 350 hectares rather than acres.
[6]See for example 'Migrant Labour Funds Diverted', *The Nation* 11 November 1996.
[7]For a partly personal account of the failure of the intellectuals, see Lwanda 1996.

been active in party politics before the transition to multi-partyism. Evance Makata, his younger brother, was an MCP MP before the transition and subsequently joined UDF. Evance Makata competed for the candidacy in the by-election, but lost to Peter Chupa, another businessman, in the UDF's internal ballot by receiving 909 votes as against 1484. Despite vague memories of his father's difficulties at the hands of the Banda regime, Chupa himself left much to desire in his credentials as an Ndirande person. He had lived in Sunny Side, Blantyre's posh low-density area, for a long time and had, unlike the Makatas, no visible business presence in Ndirande. He was an unknown figure among most residents in this impoverished urban constituency. Chupa's status was unlike not only the Makatas' but also Kapolomsungeni Manda's, MCP's first-choice candidate, who had a chain of stores in Ndirande and was known for his interest in its residents' well-being. A dynamic and youthful 34-year old, Manda was also determined to dispel the image of MCP as a moribund and conservative party. It was not surprising, therefore, that Manda's elimination from the by-election became a major concern for UDF.

The tension between moral partnership and neo-patrimonialism, as mentioned earlier and discussed below, became even more pronounced in the by-election, when a conflict emerged between Evance Makata and UDF campaign leaders. A brief historical comment may help to clarify the issue of commercial success and moral partnership. The Nyasaland African Congress (NAC), which later became the MCP, was established in Ndirande in 1944. Many of the NAC founders were self-employed businessmen, partly because of their earlier harassment by white employers and the lack of autonomy in the colonial civil service (Power 1995, 90–91). However, it is also clear that success in commerce brought resources to foster a moral partnership which, in turn, was integral to political prominence. Elderly Ndirande residents recall that James Sangala, one of the NAC founders, bought the first bus in Ndirande in 1947; his business therefore eased commuters' difficult journeys between town and Ndirande. The village headmanship, through which the different sections of Ndirande are still governed, was also subject to similar aspirations. During the mid-1950s, for example, Lawrence Makata, a prominent businessman, had an ambition to become a headman and founded a primary school. The authority of village headmen also competed with the prominence of many non-local wealthy tenants in the township.[8]

The current juncture of political liberalism has not erased the tension between piggy banks and neo-patrimonialism. In the run-up to the 1994 multi-party elections, it was widely observed that the new manifestos of all the parties differed very little from one another. Every party seemed to be committed to multi-party democracy and professed allegiance to the economic prices of Structural Adjustment. As a result, voters did not seem to make choices either on the basis of clear ideological differences between party programmes or as subjects disembedded from their immediate socio-cultural fabric. Rather, regionalism came to define Malawian politics, with each of the three main parties winning one of Malawi's three regions: UDF won the south, MCP the centre and Aford the north (see for example van Donge 1995). However, the case of Ndirande cautions against the conclusion that primordial identities, whether regional or 'tribal', have become the sole parameters of politics. A closer look at the conditions of popular support in an urban setting permits us to see what happens when no one ethnic group dominates the scene and where MCP can capitalise on discontent with UDF, and vice versa. A politician has to gain his or her credentials locally, through acts that disclose the politician as an embodiment of the constituents' welfare.

The different parties in Ndirande have tried to manage popular perceptions of their moral standing as political entities, irrespective of who represents them. Funerals, in particular, become important occasions for political parties during electoral campaigns. While funerals put pressure on poor families' material resources, their cosmological aspects compel large numbers of people to attend in order to honour the dead. For the political parties, the deceased's party allegiance, or whether there is any in the first place, is not an issue during campaigns. When the Blantyre by-election was still expected to take place in November 1996, for several weeks the funerals in Ndirande were often well-attended by politicians, who also provided material support. UDF often appeared quicker, and more generous, than the MCP; it even provided expensive coffins for well-known MCP members.

---

[8]Bettison and Apthorpe 1961, 18 and 36; for more discussion on Makata and other Ndirande 'big men' as nationalists, see McCracken 1998, 258–261.

Such interventions by UDF did not, however, erase the fact that it had, at first, a weaker candidate than the MCP. As mentioned above, MCP's Manda both lived and engaged in business in Ndirande. His late father's success as a labour migrant in South Africa explained Manda's own affluence at a relatively early age. Manda was known to receive troubled Ndirande residents and to look for ways to help them personally. Proudly regarding himself as an example of the 'new blood' that Kamuzu Banda had wanted to inject in MCP, he used several MCP rallies to criticise poverty in Ndirande, to much applause. It often seemed that MCP rallies were better attended by those who were actually entitled to vote than UDF rallies. The crowd in the latter was very young, attracted more by the performances of pop groups and general festivity than by the candidate or visiting cabinet ministers. It therefore came as a shock to MCP that Manda was disqualified by the Electoral Commission, only a few days before the expected by-election in November 1996, due to the fact that he was not registered as a voter. He had failed to register before the 1994 elections because of illness and, in 1996, was not in the age group of those who had become entitled to vote after 1994 and were therefore permitted to register. MCP hurriedly called on Edward Mlongoti to stand as the candidate since he had received 294 against Manda's 895 votes in MCP's internal ballot for nominating their candidate. Mlongoti, as shown below, soon created more problems for MCP, leading to the postponement of the by-election.

Top UDF politicians, as is shown below, allegedly played a role in MCP's difficulties. These leaders at the national level also produced divisions in the UDF camp itself. The divisions owed much to the contradictions between the candidates' local credentials and the party leaders' own interests – between locally-established moral partnership and top-down neo-patrimonialism. The suspicions of some local UDF activists in Ndirande began to emerge, when over 2,000 representatives were permitted to cast votes in the party's internal ballot for nominations. The 27 party areas in Ndirande had been invited to send 30 representatives each, thereby making a total of only 810 voters.[9] The extra voters were regarded as necessary to secure Chupa's nomination but after the results had been announced, Makata promised to support the nominated candidate. However, for Brown Mpinganjira, the UDF Campaign Director and the minister embroiled in the Mulanje land scandal mentioned above, Makata apparently remained too influential in Ndirande. Makata became a convenient scapegoat for the violence that disrupted some opposition meetings before the by-election, and in late November 1996, he was expelled from the party in a meeting attended by UDF leaders in Blantyre. The meeting followed rumours that all area committee members who supported Makata would be replaced. Makata's expulsion, in turn, was challenged by a group of 'indigenous' Ndirande families, who claimed that 'foreigners' lacked respect and were mismanaging the township. Their intent was to present a petition to Sam Mpasu, UDF's Secretary General. Rumours of a protest march to President Muluzi's residence had also circulated.[10]

The limits of popular participation had already been shown by the nomination of candidates for the by-election. Makata, apart from being the son of a prominent family and a former MP, also owned a large road-maintenance enterprise which, as a labour-intensive business, had given employment to innumerable young men in Ndirande. Yet, UDF leaders had opted for a candidate whom they could control more easily than an established Ndirande big man. In other words, Chupa owed his nomination more to party leaders' patronage than to any moral partnership he had generated in his constituency. By the time the by-election was held on 17 April 1997, few UDF supporters continued to feel strongly about the official candidate, while a family dispute seemed to leave Makata's political career in tatters. During March, he spent a weekend in Ndirande prison, because he had refused to surrender the keys of a lorry to his brother who had taken over the management of the late Witness Makata's garage but had run into debts and wanted to sell the lorry. Makata and his wife accused the brother of mismanagement and alcoholism but found themselves opposed by the mother and sisters. Evance Makata subsequently left Ndirande for an area

[9]Before the by-election, there were 88 UDF branches in Ndirande, the most localised level of party organisation.
[10]For more details on the Makata case, see 'UDF Split in Ndirande', *Daily Times* 27 November 1996; 'Makata Axed from the UDF', *The Nation* 2 December 1996; 'No to Strangers' and 'Mpinganjira Happier without Makata', *The Star* 9 December 1996. *The Nation*, a newspaper close to the UDF government, had an editorial which was surprisingly critical of top UDF leaders on the Makata case: 'Double Standards in the Ruling UDF', 4 December 1996.

some 30 kilometers outside Blantyre city. The brother, in turn, swore that he would stay clear of politics. After 16 years in Lilongwe, he was relatively unknown in Ndirande and, as such, unlikely to win popular support in the immediate future.

Promises, abductions and disputes

On the eve of the expected by-election in November 1996, the attention of the electorate was bound to shift from the candidates to the wider standing of the parties. All the three main candidates appeared somewhat implausible. Chupa was the puppet of the UDF leadership, Mlongoti had been the MCP's second choice, and Evance Kapesi, Aford's candidate and a stadium attendant living outside Ndirande, was unknown in the constituency. Alongside the attention which the local campaign was receiving at the national level, by-election campaign issues had also acquired a national dimension. The by-election had become a stock-taking event after the 1994 multi-party elections. UDF urged people to vote UDF, because it was in the government and had access to 'development'. It also reminded the electorate of its key role in the democratic transition. MCP and Aford, in turn, sought to discredit the UDF, freely elaborating on the impoverishment of the electorate, their lack of security and the corruption of the new government.

A water development project became one of the most contested issues. During September 1996, President Muluzi effectively launched the UDF campaign by nominally inaugurating the water project in the 'squatter'[11] areas of Ndirande. Muluzi's public meetings have always been UDF events whose party symbols and yellow colours are displayed in abundance. Donated by the German city of Hannover and supervised by UNICEF, the water project immediately raised the question about which political party should be associated with it. MCP complained that UDF was trying to own several development projects which, in fact, had been launched by the previous MCP government. Chihana, Aford's president, announced that he had personally negotiated funding for the Ndirande water project when he was in the coalition government of Aford and UDF. However, Muluzi's visit to Ndirande had left the other parties somewhat disadvantaged at the early stage of the by-election campaign. The State President had overwhelmed the crowd with promises, including the pledges to build a new primary school and extend two others; to establish two new markets; to provide a fully equipped hospital with a doctor; and to construct roads within the densely-built township to enable people to reach their homes by public transport. Some days after Muluzi's rally, several lorries came to take vendors from the Ndirande market to a special reception held at the State President's Sanjika Palace in Blantyre. Singing UDF praise-songs as they left the township on the lorries, the vendors were treated to free drinks and food in the State President's presence.

The politics of development becomes entangled with particular, personal relationships in the daily lives of Ndirande residents. The new water kiosks, for example, are managed by local committees which, in principle, are non-partisan, but often seen to be under UDF control. For some, whether for shifting personal reasons or more entrenched party affiliations, the water question was a means to assess the UDF government. Dramatic increases in the cost of water occurred during 1996, when the management was transferred from the Blantyre Water Board to local water committees. Although different committees had slightly different charges, a 14-litre bucket of water went from 7 tambala under the Water Board to 25 tambala and then to 40 or even 50 tambala when control passed to the committees. Some residents complained that known UDF supporters received preferential treatment in water queues, and often paid less than the average rate, and that the committee members had increased their own wealth at the expense of consumers. The latter claim, at least, was based on the misconception that UNICEF was still financing the running of the water kiosks. But the uneasy relation between wealth creation and poverty also informed most other political arguments. To take another example from 1996, the issue of credit for small-scale businesses was even more contested than water development. Upon coming to

---

[11]For the City Council and the central government, most Ndirande residents are 'squatters', because they live in the 'unplanned' areas of the township. From the residents' own point of view, they are not 'squatters' but persons who depend on local headmen and landlords for access to housing. As mentioned earlier, Ndirande has grown on a site of several villages which are still overseen by headmen.

power, UDF had declared its commitment to enhancing economic liberalisation by establishing several micro-credit funding arrangements. A central development strategy was meant to involve unemployed youths and women in commercial enterprises. However, while the credit fund for youths remained inoperative, most Ndirande residents, whilst scraping a living through petty business, also failed to obtain credit, despite being obliged to pay processing fees. It was becoming clear, even to UDF supporters, that credit institutions were searching for entrepreneurs whose existing affluence guaranteed the credit repayments. MCP supporters, in turn, spread the view that the decisions on credit were made on a political basis.

Under such circumstances, where 'development' and prosperity were as distant as ever, the political élite, including President Muluzi, seemed to think that popular support required acts of direct patronage. After Manda's disqualification, MCP was at a loss. Mlongoti had to stand as the MCP candidate, because he had become second in the party's internal ballot, as mentioned earlier, but he needed considerable support from the party machinery. He was a meter reader in the Electricity Supply Commission of Malawi (Escom), which he had joined as a temporary labourer in 1988. From his clothes to his house in Ndirande, he embodied poverty only slightly less searing than that of most Ndirande squatters. When he celebrated his nomination as MCP's candidate, he bought ten crates of Coca Cola for MCP supporters, a woefully inadequate gesture from a person aspiring to be a MP. There was no chance that he could assist fellow Ndirande residents in funerals or other hardships or that he could pay their children's school fees – all acts that would prove the person's capacities as a resourceful and moral being. In Mlongoti's case, MCP even revised his CV in order to make the candidate look more convincing. A sympathetic official at Escom grossly exaggerated Mlongoti's academic qualifications in his letter of recommendation to the Electoral Commission.[12]

It was a measure of UDF leaders' own uncertainty that Mlongoti became the target of some shadowy deception. First, immediately after Mlongoti's nomination, Escom issued a transfer order that was designed to move Mlongoti from Blantyre to Lilongwe. Escom was under the Minister of Energy and Mining, Dumbo Lemani, another active UDF campaigner in Ndirande, and few feigned surprise at the order. Mlongoti defied the order, only to receive more disturbing news from his company. An internal audit report disclosed 'discrepancies' in his meter readings. Although he was not a cashier, he was said to have pocketed some customers' electricity bills. The sums involved were very small in comparison with the scandals in which some prominent UDF politicians found themselves, but Mlongoti's case struck a popular anti-corruption chord. Simultaneously with the audit report, UDF leaders began to persuade him to leave politics. At first, Mlongoti was again defiant and publicly named Brown Mpinganjira, UDF Campaign Director and Minister of Information and Broadcasting, as his interlocutor. 'Mpinganjira', he informed a newspaper sympathetic to the UDF government, 'told me they will help me in my problems and that they will support me in any way.'[13]

The events took a serious twist, when Mlongoti disappeared only five days before the expected election day in November 1996. A taxi driver emerged to reveal that two men had hired him to drive them to pick up Mlongoti at his house, whence they had proceeded to Mpinganjira's residence in Sunny Side. Several MCP supporters gathered outside Mpinganjira's gate, but gunshots were fired to disperse them. A day after his disappearance, Mlongoti, unkempt and visibly shaken, appeared at an impromptu press conference in the waiting-room of the Acting Director General of the Malawi Broadcasting Corporation. Mlongoti announced his resignation from MCP, claimed that he would not join any other party, but refused to answer questions. On the same day, his wife also disappeared from their Ndirande home, and even close relatives professed ignorance about her and Mlongoti's whereabouts. The eventful November days also witnessed the disappearance of Evance Kapesi, Aford's candidate. He later reappeared and explained that he had been concerned about his personal safety. It was only after the by-election had been postponed that he also announced his resignation from politics.[14]

---

[12]See 'MCP Bosses Cook Up CV', *The Nation* 8 November 1996.
[13]See 'Don't Poach Our Man – MCP', *The Nation* 15 November 1996.
[14]On the Mlongoti case, see 'Mlongoti Joins UDF?', *The Star* 15 November 1996; 'MCP Candidate Mlongoti Misses', *Daily Times* 15 November 1996; 'MBC Boss Parades Mlongoti' and 'Foul Play', *The Star* 18 November 1996; 'No Elections in Ndirande', *Saturday Nation* 16–22 November 1996; 'Mlongoti Still in Hiding', *The Star* 4 December 1996.

More complaints by the opposition parties made the Electoral Commission postpone the by-election. All the parties accused each other of buying voter registration certificates. The buying and selling of certificates took place quite publicly in Ndirande market, with prices ranging from 75 Kwacha (US$ 5 at the time) to 500 Kwacha (US$ 33), but the motives of the buyers were kept secret.[15] Voter registration procedures were another contested issue, with all the parties again accusing one another of bringing supporters from other districts to register and to vote in the by-election. Refusals to register, or to re-register, voters were seen, especially by opposition supporters, as politically motivated. Violence, in addition to the abductions of its candidates, was more exclusively a problem for the opposition. At an early stage in campaigning during September 1996, the MCP and UDF tried to hold a rally simultaneously at the same venue. A clash between their supporters ensued, and several MCP women, dressed in their party uniforms carrying Kamuzu Banda's portrait, were humiliated and undressed by UDF youths. In October, Aford president Chihana arrived in Ndirande to introduce Kapesi in a mass rally. Before Chihana had taken the stage, however, the crowd had been dispersed by a mob of youths fighting with pangas and stones. They left the venue in a pick-up car which was later found at the UDF office in Ndirande.[16]

The Electoral Commission initially postponed the by-election to 23 December 1996. UDF protested and accused it of a bias towards the opposition, pointing out that the parliament was due to meet in December. MCP and Aford, which were then boycotting the parliament, would have been able to release more people and resources for campaigning. The two parties and nine individuals, including MCP's first-choice candidate, Manda, presented their complaints to the High Court and were granted an injunction on 9 December. The same High Court judge who had earlier granted the injunction withdrew it on 13 March, arguing that the Electoral Commission had established sufficient evidence to prove that the petitioners did not deserve the rights they sought to protect, particularly their demand for the re-opening of voter registration. The High Court ordered the Electoral Commission to proceed with the by-election, which was now slated for 17 April 1997. Meanwhile, MCP and Aford took their case to the Supreme Court of Appeal which announced its agreement with the High Court on the very same day that voting was taking place in the by-election. MCP and Aford announced earlier that they would boycott the polls. Many Ndirande residents thought it was curious that the Electoral Commission held the by-election when the opposition appeal was still under consideration.

On the by-election polling day, armed police were more visible than voters at the polling stations. Short queues had formed during the early hours of voting, only to leave the electoral officials, observers and police idle for the most part of the day. The observers consisted of representatives of UDF and the Public Affairs Committee (PAC), a watch-dog which had played a major role during the transition and which subsequently became closely associated with the religious community. The two contending lilliputian parties, the National Unity Party and the Social Democratic Party, had been unable to send their observers to every polling station. The name of Florence Limbe, Aford's new candidate after Kapesi's resignation, appeared among the candidates, although Aford had resolved to boycott the by-election and had no observers present at polling.

Nearly 3 million kwacha (US$ 200,000) were reportedly spent on this by-election.[17] Tight security amidst an indifferent electorate was symbolic of how the by-election had become a facade of orderly electoral procedures amidst interventions that undermined the precepts of liberal democracy. After the opposition appeal had been rejected, the PAC also found it difficult to criticise the by-election on any formal grounds.[18] Other by-elections in 1996–97 were hardly

---

[15] In late 1996 and early 1997, 1 US$ was about 15 Malawian Kwacha.

[16] This attack followed a recent incident during President Muluzi's visit to the northern district of Karonga. Kampunga Mwafulirwa, Aford MP for Karonga South, had used Muluzi's rally, broadcast live on the radio, to voice his criticism of the UDF government. When UDF officials tried to stop his speech, he asked them to be quiet, because the north was not their home. Playing on these regional tensions, the UDF youths in Ndirande had similarly shouted that Ndirande was not Chihana's home.

[17] 'K2.9 Million Spent on Ndirande "Apathy"', *Daily Times* 24 April 1997.

[18] PAC's silence was somewhat surprising, given its moral mandate to assess Malawi's democracy beyond formal judicial proceedings. In January 1997, for example, it had issued a short statement entitled 'Assessing Malawi's Democracy'. Although criticising the MCP and Aford for their parliamentary boycott, the statement also condemned Malawi's continuing dependence on 'hand-outs' from the state president and international donors.

more encouraging, and many witnessed almost as low a voter turnout as the Blantyre by-election, with less than a quarter of the electorate casting their votes. Accusations of bought, stolen or illegally printed voter certificates were routinely traded between the parties, leading one or the other of the parties to dispute some by-election results.[19] The most substantial evidence on intimidation and abuse usually came from opposition parties. In the southern district of Chiradzulu, for example, MCP's vehicle and public address system were set ablaze. In Machinga, another southern district and the home area of President Muluzi, the candidate of the People's Democratic Party (PDP) received similar attention to that of Mlongoti in Ndirande. One morning before the by-election in the district, the PDP candidate had been taken to see Muluzi. The same day's lunchtime radio bulletin broadcast the news that the candidate had resigned from the PDP and given up his candidacy. UDF's Publicity Secretary later admitted that Muluzi had supported the opposition candidate with 'cash and material assistance'. Muluzi, the UDF official explained, had felt that the opposition candidate was 'a boy from home who needed help'.[20]

Death and moral partnership

For those who do not find themselves in the category of Muluzi's 'boys from home', apathy may not be an unreasonable reaction to the procedures of Malawi's 'democratic' government. Behind their seeming abstention, however, the Ndirande electorate took a keen interest in the unfolding by-election events. Although anger rather than apathy was the prevailing mood, no violence or peaceful protest followed the by-election. MCP and Aford had advised their activists not to organise protests and to calmly await the 1999 general elections. For both non-activists and those holding branch-level posts, it was surprising that the main opposition parties should remain silent after their appeal had been rejected. Party followers complained that they had not even been told to boycott the polls. Some local MCP officials saw their own party leaders' conduct as cynical, because MCP Landrovers only began to appear in squatter settlements during the campaign. Afterwards, no signs of high-level interest were to be seen in Ndirande.

Among Ndirande residents, daily struggles to sustain their lives, in both material and moral senses, are also waged outside the realm of party politics. Several other forms of association are especially important outside electoral campaigns, and for many local party officials themselves, party positions are often outgrowths of prominence in other spheres. Kinship, business and ethnic associations, among others, deserve attention in this local account of Malawi's 'democratic' politics, because the associations throw the distinctiveness of a moral partnership into starker relief. The Blantyre by-election disclosed the cynical manipulation of opposition candidates' poverty by the UDF élite, manipulation that drew upon neo-patrimonialism in the attempt to consolidate political power. Greed and cynicism, therefore, would be seen as the *only* parameters of political practice, if the discourse of moral partnership were not also understood as a forceful way of representing relatedness between leaders and their subjects. There is a contentious discourse in moving from revealing the state's moral discredit to fostering personhood that hinges on social relationships rather than on individualism. This discourse is not a means to delimit a timeless 'community'. As mentioned earlier, however, moral partnership operates under the politico-economic conditions of a specific state formation. Hence, there is a need to discern contradictions between different moral notions and the challenges some notions can pose, in multi-party elections for example, for party political practice.

Funerals, as political parties in Malawi have also discovered, hold a cosmologically significant place in people's moral conduct. As such, it is not surprising that burial societies provide important avenues to prominence in other spheres of local politics. Mere instrumentality, as if persons were simply seeking private gain through the appropriate cultural practice of showing reverence for the dead, must not be the standpoint to interpret local political prominence. The gravest emotional passions are at issue, made all the more extreme by dire material conditions.

---

[19]See for example 'MCP and UDF Dispute Polls', *The Nation* 28 May 1997; 'UDF, MCP Protest', *Daily Times* 28 May 1997; 'MCP Protests Nsanje Results', *The Star* 28–29 May 1997.
[20]Quoted in 'Mpinganjira Named in Ndirande Elections Fraud', *Daily Times* 5 May 1997.

Ndirande township, in particular, is a setting for utmost anxiety in times of death, because the bereaved are both poor and often under the obligation to bury the deceased in his or her home village. A journey of hundreds of miles can await the bereaved, taking them through neglected rural roads to home villagers who, in turn, are likely to receive them as townspeople having an easy access to the benefits of town life. The predicament of death, always amounting to a crisis, puts the bereaved residents of Ndirande into a particularly harrowing position towards both the dead and the living. Improperly conducted funerals are feared as common sources for drawing out the fury of the dead, thereby culminating in possession by their vengeful spirits (*mizimu*). Among the living, death does not affect only those immediately bereaved but also anyone linked to them, whether or not that person actually knew the deceased. Funerals, more precisely, are occasions to make relationships visible and therefore reveal the moral standing of a person. Assistance in securing food, firewood and transport, and simply the person's presence during the wake, are acts that define moral being.

Burial societies have emerged to ease the crisis of death in the region's townships, both historically and currently (see for example Mayer and Mayer 1961, 81). In Ndirande during 1996–97, for example, one burial society managed by women had been built on their common Sena ethnicity, because the women who were involved had felt that Sena funerals were distinct from others in the township. At the core of their association was Nambewe (a pseudonym), whose leadership eventually led to her chairmanship of the local branch of MCP. Her corpulent stature was another striking embodiment of the piggy bank. Nambewe used resources from her trade in maize and other food to organise and maintain the burial society. Some 60 women belonged to the society, including the local MCP chairman's sister who became impressed with Nambewe's will to assist those in trouble and asked her to assume a position in the party. Dominated by Sena from the southern districts of Nsanje and Chikwawa, the branch cut across different neighbourhoods and professed special allegiance to MCP's vice-president Gwanda Chakuamba, himself from Nsanje. Nambewe's position in the party blurred the boundaries between the branch and the burial society. Both the party branch and the burial society were associations that maintained an important sense of 'home', conflated with a particular ethnicity, in town. Nambewe came to embody the imagined 'home', with all its remembered virtues of mutual assistance and security. Her person, in other words, was the locus of many relationships, of others' well-being and, ultimately, of party political prominence.

Nyasulu, Aford's local branch chairman, is a somewhat different example of participation in party politics and burial societies. Nyasulu, who hailed from the Northern Region, came to Blantyre in 1968 and has had his own stall in Ndirande market since the early 1970s. He was an MCP chairman until 1992 when he joined Aford and became its branch chairman. At the end of the 1990s, however, Nyasulu's main field of prominence owed more to his seniority in the market than to his activism in party politics. Nyasulu was the chairman of the Market Burial Fund, which had over 200 members across party, ethnic and regional divides. It contributed the substantial sum of 400 kwacha, when funerals took place in the families of its members. As the burial fund chairman, Nyasulu observed considerable discretion in establishing whether a particular family connection warranted support from the fund. Nyasulu's continuing chairmanship attested to his successful management of the fund and to his command of vital resources. The same popularity in the market made him the principal applicant in the bid for the micro-credit project which 27 Ndirande entrepreneurs jointly presented to a lending institution. Although, like most other entrepreneurs in Ndirande, this syndicate failed, Nyasulu's leadership among a group of entrepreneurs with different political affiliations was another example of how his prominence extended beyond the Aford chairmanship. His party political affiliation mattered less than his capacity to oversee the well-being and aspirations of a wide range of people.[21]

Nambewe and Nyasulu illustrate the imagery of prominent persons as piggy banks whose participation in party politics is merely an aspect of their authority. Through their moral partnership with their subjects, party politics is a consequence, rather than a source, of their authority. However, branch-level party positions also attract persons who have few prospects of embodying

---

[21]Given the distrust between MCP and UDF even at the local level, Nyasulu's identification with Aford probably contributed to his popularity in ostensibly non-party political contexts.

a wide range of relationships. Another example was Thoko, a young UDF branch chairman in Ndirande, who succeeded the previous branch chairman, a successful businessman, after he had returned to the MCP. Thoko's own poverty was unmistakable in that, despite living on their 'own' plot, his young family endured a perpetual shortage of food. Thoko supported them through casual labour (*ganyu*), occasionally undergoing periods of unemployment, since he was too poor to begin his own business. By the time of the by-election in April 1997, Thoko was working on a construction site in Blantyre's city centre. Trying to save something from his meagre salary, he walked every day to and from his work. Tired, hungry and with an aching body, he had little energy to expend on branch affairs. Worse still, the rains had destroyed his house so that his family had to rent a room in an appalling old building. First Lady Anne Muluzi, one of the president's two wives, had made a well-publicised visit to Ndirande to distribute blankets and other items among flood victims, but neither she nor her gifts ever reached Thoko's neighbourhood. Genuine interest in democracy may well have driven him to join UDF. It was clear that Thoko was desperately looking for a moral partnership in which his loyalty to the UDF would have brought material security. Thoko was no piggy bank, and when he failed to find one, he was left wondering whether the UDF government itself was established on the basis of a moral partnership.

Beyond neo-patrimonialism and liberalism

The immediate conclusion to this chapter is a sober one. Multi-party electoral competition belongs to the paraphernalia of liberal democracy that keeps international donors content. The appearance of orderly elections and the avoidance of large-scale political violence are essential for the international legitimacy of a post-transition government. By contrast, this case study, in exploring the conditions of political legitimacy among an impoverished urban electorate, has shown that by the time the Blantyre City Central Constituency by-election was held, the electorate had effectively been disenfranchised by the ruling élite's zeal to consolidate its own power. Neo-patrimonial idioms served to legitimise the undermining of opposition politics in the élite's own eyes while the electorate's appeals for a moral partnership fell on deaf ears. Other aspects of the post-transition paraphernalia provided little consolation. The Anti-Corruption Bureau, for example, had been launched in name only, and the new 'democratic' Constitution could be interpreted in many different ways. When asked about the defections of opposition candidates, Peter Fachi, UDF's legal adviser, gave a curt response: 'I don't see anything wrong with that, it's provided for in Section 40, Subsection 1 of the Constitution'.[22]

Domestic and international pressures combined in complex ways to trigger off the democratic transition in Malawi, like in many other African countries in the early 1990s (see for example Monga 1996; Bratton and van de Walle 1997). As the Blantyre by-election shows, the extent to which the transition has actually introduced greater popular participation is much less clear. By highlighting the township electorate's critical discourses of post-transition politics, this case study has sought to go beyond an unquestioned juxtaposition between neo-patrimonialism and liberalism as the opposing parameters of the Malawian polity. The two are more compatible than is generally assumed. This is true not only in the international context where, as mentioned, states must look 'democratic', whatever the moral discredit they accumulate locally. In a more profound sense, liberalism promotes the exclusiveness of power that has come to characterise the neo-patrimonial state in Malawi. The reason is the individualist presuppositions of liberalism:

---

[22]Quoted in 'UDF Attacks Commission', *The Nation* 4 December 1996. Section 40, Subsection 1 actually reads: 'Subject to this Constitution every person shall have the right:

a) to form, to join, to participate in the activities of, and to recruit members for, a political party
b) to campaign for a political party or cause
c) to participate in peaceful political activity intended to influence the composition and policies of the Government, and
d) freely to make political choices.'

For an insightful discussion on the limits of liberal constitutionalism in Malawi, see Kanyongolo 1998.

subjects are linked to the highest state officials as pawns rather than as the *constituents* of their power.[23]

Anthropological studies, informed by alternative notions of democracy, are indispensable for understanding how the precepts of liberal democracy lend themselves to greed and the consolidation of exclusive power (see for example van Binsbergen 1995; Karlström 1996). However, I have also argued for the need to understand the Malawian case within the political economy of a particular state formation. From its autocratic past to its pluralist present, the Malawian state has gravitated towards strong presidentialism, now supplemented with, but not effectively challenged by, networks of patronage other than those of the president. One recurrent observation emerging from this case study has stressed how the control of the modern state apparatus, from its resources for 'development' to its means of coercion, enables the political élite to disentangle itself from a moral partnership with the populace. Political prominence and material wealth derive from allegiance to the élite, whereas the élite owes its position to its subjects at best only intermittently. This is precisely the reason why neo-patrimonialism, and clientelism as its obverse, better describes the Malawian state formation than the subaltern discourses of democracy. Subaltern discourses, as I have indicated, do not simply entail clientelism. Far from relating to one another as 'patrons' and 'clients', political subjects in the subaltern discourses are mutually constituted in moral practice. The cosmological dimensions of that moral practice encompass, moreover, both the living and the dead.

Subaltern discourses, themselves constituted within the same post-colonial polity, have not been introduced here to suggest a coherent system of 'true' democracy. It is, nevertheless, important to highlight alternative notions in an age when liberalism is taken for granted in most political and scholarly endeavours. By the same token, it is also necessary to analyse the ways in which these alternatives are marginalised. In this regard, the problems of the state formation require a perspective that goes beyond 'political culture' and 'political learning' as key issues for the consolidation of democracy in Africa. Recent studies of regime transitions in Africa have drawn upon discussions of 'structure' and 'agency' in social theory in order to strike a balance between structural constraints and popular interventions (see Robinson 1994; Bratton and van de Walle 1997). According to these studies, the momentum that triggers off transition is not enough to secure consolidation because, it is argued, political learning is a slow process. However, what is not discussed is whether liberal democracy needs to be imported into Africa wholesale, without attempts to identify indigenous democratic resources. Liberal democracy, in effect, is a new gospel which is spread by even the most measured texts of political scientists. Significantly, Bratton and van de Walle's word for political learning is 'conversion' (1997, 235).

The concept of state formation is not intended to obscure the role of human agency, but to outline its conditions. In Malawi, the state represents, despite recent attempts at economic liberalisation, the gateway to affluence in a poor country. For example, between his release from detention and the transition, Brown Mpinganjira, a UDF cabinet minister and the campaign director mentioned above, is said to have been so poor that he could not afford to use public transport in Blantyre. After some years in power, Mpinganjira's personal businesses included a fleet of cars and trucks, allegedly both in Malawi and abroad. For many Malawians, Mpinganjira, a self-professed 'democrat', has come to symbolise the post-transition predicament. Nothing short of country-wide turmoil, such as occurred in 1992–93, will remove him from public office. The consolidation of power and wealth, and not democracy, appears to be Mpinganjira's agenda. One is reminded of the important punch-line in the Cameroonian proverb publicised by Bayart (1993, ix): the goat eats where it is tethered – but it should not eat *beyond* where it is tethered.

Rather than bemoaning the fate of liberal institutions, such as multi-party elections, after Africa's democratic transitions, analysis must proceed to identify indigenous resources for challenging and circumventing exclusive political power. The above discussion of burial societies was a brief account of indigenous resources. The general observation is that the scope of the 'political' must be enlarged to include practices and institutions that have no obvious place in liberal political science. Religious congregations, for example, must belong to the purview of almost any African political analysis (cf. Gifford 1995; Constantin and Coulon 1997; on Malawi, see Ross 1996). The

---

[23]For a succinct discussion of liberalism in African 'development', see Williams 1993.

corollary is that an analytic language itself must shift from liberal utilitarianism to a greater appreciation of local idioms and concerns. This was the reason for evoking cosmological dimensions in Ndirande squatters' associations. Finally, all this should not be reduced to one more obsession of liberalism – to the 'tension' between civil society and state. Ostensibly non-political practices may be geared to *accommodating* the state in everyday lives. People may prefer to live with the state despite its apparent illegitimacy rather than embark on uncertain projects of undermining it (cf. Bayart 1992). One question is whether Ndirande residents and so many other Malawians both in towns and the country – terrorised and intimidated, impoverished and marginalised – can hope for one more transition, this time 'democratic' on their own terms. Another question is whether the very idea of a transition has worn itself out.

8

Swapo Wins, Apathy Rules
The Namibian
1998 Local Authority Elections

IINA SOIRI

Introduction

The local authority elections were held in Namibia on 16 February 1998 in all 45 municipalities, towns and villages covering the proclaimed urban area in the country. Originally set for 2 December 1997, the elections were postponed to February 1998 only a month before the polling.[1] The most significant feature of these elections was the low voter turnout of only 34 per cent. It had dropped nearly 50 per cent from the previous Regional and Local Authority elections in 1992.[2] At the same time more parties and associations than previously contested the elections. Although the ruling party, South West African People's Organisation (Swapo), won the elections as widely predicted, the independent local associations managed surprisingly well by winning at least one seat in all municipalities they contested and even taking a majority of seats in 2 municipalities, Rehoboth and Otavi. Their success brought a new local dimension to Namibian political discussion which so far has been dominated by the liberation agenda.

This article studies the reasons why the Namibian electorate stayed away from the polls and tries to analyse the impact of these particular local elections on the future of democracy in Namibia. In order to discuss the different political agendas in Namibia, the article presents firstly the election process in detail in Katima Mulilo, where the ruling party took a majority in the local council from the former dominant party Democratic Turnhalle Alliance (DTA). Secondly, particular attention in this article is given to the local residents associations in those municipalities where they obtained power in their town council, namely in Otavi, Rehoboth and Gobabis.

Dominant party rule

Since independence in 1990, Namibia has been ruled by the Swapo party, the former liberation movement SWAPO.[3] Swapo has won all three sets of elections held in independent Namibia.

---

[1] See a detailed analysis of the postponement in Soiri 1998. The official reason for postponement was that the High Court found technical errors in the Election proclamation. Yet, the underlying cause was that Swapo failed to register its candidate list in a Northern town (Rundu) during the first registration period. As a consequence, it took the whole proclamation to the High Court, where the matter was dismissed because of an out-of-court settlement between Swapo and the Electoral Commission to postpone the elections.

[2] An impressive turnout of 97% of all registered voters occurred in the 1989 independence elections. Since then the turnout has decreased, being 83% in the 1992 regional and local authority elections and 76% in the 1994 presidential and parliamentary elections. The turnout of 1994 fell to 68% of the total population including those who did not register. Yet, all figures have been satisfactorily high even when compared to more established democratic systems.

[3] After independence the liberation movement SWAPO adopted 'Swapo party' as the official name of the party. In this article 'Swapo party' is used to refer to the party after independence, and SWAPO when referring to the liberation movement.

Swapo's president, Sam Nujoma, was elected President for the second time in 1994. As a result, Swapo has governed the country with a two-thirds majority in the National Assembly since 1994 and also held a clear majority in the National Council,[4] the upper chamber of parliament, and most of the Regional Councils.[5] Swapo has a majority in most town councils, the lowest administrative tier of government at the local authority level.[6] After independence, Swapo has also effectively employed its own members and supporters in the public service in order to replace, and supplement, the white-dominated administration inherited from the apartheid era. The former civil servants maintained their positions because of the national reconciliation policy which Swapo adopted as a leading guideline for building a post-war society. Swapo's leader, President Sam Nujoma, has adopted the image of 'a benign shepherd with a loyal flock' (du Pisani 1996, 1). The Namibian Constitution is often regarded as one of the most democratic in Africa. Over the years since independence, however, the powers of an executive president have been expanded significantly, both formally and informally.[7] In fact, as Namibian political scientist Keulder suggests, Namibia is moving in the direction of a typical African neo-patrimonial state (Keulder 1998, 36).

Consequently, the opposition parties, or any other social forces, do not pose a significant challenge to Swapo's leading position in Namibia's public life. At the time of the 1989 elections there were 56 registered parties in Namibia among a population of 1.4 million.[8] The parties formed 8 different alliances. A total of 4 unitary parties and 6 alliances put up candidates for the 1989 elections. Only 7 of them managed to gain enough votes to win a seat in parliament. By the time of the elections in 1992 and 1994, the number of functioning parties had decreased considerably[9] and only 5 of them presently occupy seats in parliament.[10] The opposition's support is altogether less than that of the ruling party, Swapo. Yet, there is a wide acknowledgment among Namibians of the importance of the elections as an exercise of the will of the people. Regularly held polls are highly valued by the whole population as one of the cornerstones of young Namibian democracy (National Democratic Institute for International Affairs 1996).

In a situation where the parliamentary opposition does not create enough of a challenge to the dominant party, other organisations become even more important to provide the necessary political checks and balances in society. If the opposition parties suffer from their history as collaborators in Namibia, the civil society movements, which were united behind the liberation alliance as partners, have also been at pains to reposition themselves in independent Namibia. The main actors – trade unions, churches, women and student organisations – were all effectively organised behind the fight against the colonial regime. They were important agents of the internal resistance providing a platform for protest and shelter for the victims of the regime. The white

---

[4]National Council members are elected by the 13 Regional Councils (2 from each) constituting a total of 26 members. It has the power to review legislation, but its refusal to accept a proposal can be overcome by a two-thirds majority vote in the National Assembly. Swapo has 19 councillors against DTA's, the main opposition party's, 7 seats.

[5]Swapo gained 67% of the popular vote in the 1992 Regional elections, winning outright control of 6 of the 13 regions and majorities in 3, while DTA – with a share of 27% – won in the Caprivi and two Eastern regions. In one region, Kunene, the United Democratic Front (UDF), holds the balance of power. Kössler, 1992; Pendleton *et al.* 1993.

[6]In the 1992 local authority elections Swapo got 57% of votes, DTA 33% and the remaining 10 per cent were shared by UDF and other small parties and associations. Out of 51 local authority councils, Swapo gained a majority in 32, DTA in 11, UDF in 2 while in 6 councils there was a balance of power. Kössler 1992; Pendleton *et al.* 1993.

[7]Formally, several new pieces of legislation such as the Namibia Intelligence Service Act granted the President substantial new powers *vis-à-vis* Parliament. Informally, the President's powers over Parliament are procured through his control over the Swapo party list. The President nominates the first 32 candidates in the Swapo list.

[8]A detailed analysis of the development of the Namibian party system can be found in Du Pisani 1986; and Pütz *et al.* 1990.

[9]The exact number is difficult to establish because some parties are still registered, but have in practice become defunct.

[10]These are: Swapo, 53 seats; Democratic Turnhalle Alliance (DTA), 15 seats; United Democratic Front (UDF), two seats; Democratic Coalition of Namibia (DCN), one seat; and Monitor Action Group (MAG), one seat in parliament.

population, which distanced itself from apartheid rule, established pressure groups to support the liberation alliance.

After Swapo became the ruling party, civil society movements took different forms of adapting themselves to the post-colonial period. Trade unions maintained their alliance although some member unions opted for independence. Many church leaders were co-opted by entering into important positions in the new administration. The student organisation, *Namibia National Student Organisation*, NANSO, split when it decided to break its alliance with Swapo. A minority fraction, which remained aligned, has later distanced itself from the ruling party. Recently, Swapo is said to have approached NANSO in order to build its power base among the youth. NANSO, however, publicly announced that it prefers to remain independent.

Civil society has begun to reorganise itself and has stepped up its watchdog role over government. NANGOF, a co-operation forum for most NGOs, has adopted the role of assessing and monitoring governmental performance and criticising its shortcomings. Legal and para-legal associations, such as Legal Assistance Centre (LAC) and National Society for Human Rights (NSHR),[11] have also increased their activities in policy advocating and formulation. The Namibia Institute for Democracy (NID) together with certain foreign foundations, is doing pioneering work in civic education. Some new political organisations, such as the Namibia Movement for Independent Candidates (NMIC), have been established to organise the younger generation's participation in political decision making. Furthermore, the Namibian media institutions have taken their mission of independent and quality journalism seriously, even though they are sporadically challenged by the regime. Any attempts to limit press freedom have been successfully defeated by the media and civil society. The uncompromising manner in which the leading daily, *The Namibian,* reports and comments on the government's performance has kept the public aware of political developments. The government publication, *New Era,* has also taken a more independent role. The Afrikaans and German press frequently present criticism toward the government but their criticism is likely to be undermined, because they are considered to be controlled by the opposition parties and to voice their grievances. The government-controlled Namibian Broadcasting Corporation (NBC) is trying to be independent of the ruling party, by giving voice to public opinion through its call-in programmes which are broadcast in several local languages. These extremely popular programmes have provided the public with a vehicle to comment on, and contribute to, public decision making.

Institutional arrangement for elections and the local authorities in Namibian administration

After the UN-sponsored elections in 1989 leading to independence in 1990, elections have been run by the Namibian government. The 1992 Electoral Act determines the legal framework for organising elections. Following the Act, an Electoral Commission, (EC), was established to initiate and supervise electoral processes. Chaired by a judge, the EC consists of five members selected by the government. The members appointed to the first Commission in 1992 held their positions until the 1998 local authority elections. The fact that the members are appointed by the President and answerable to him is continuously giving the opposition a reason to argue that the EC is not independent but represents the interests of the ruling party. This has contributed to a widely held belief that Swapo can mismanage the elections if it proves to be politically necessary.[12] But although given comprehensive and wide powers of control and supervision, the EC is a statutory body that can only exercise its powers subject to the provisions of the Electoral Act and the Constitution of Namibia (Tötemeyer *et al.* 1996, 15–16).

The Directorate of Elections administers elections. Its status as a department of the Office of the Prime Minister has given cause for concern to the opposition parties. However, although the Directorate of Elections is responsible to two bodies, the Electoral Commission and the Office of

---

[11]NSHR publishes an annual human rights report on Namibia, which is distributed widely.
[12]For example, in one case in the Katima Mulilo dispute, the opposition claimed that Swapo was manipulating the voters register. See below.

the Prime Minister, it does not receive any operational instructions from the Prime Minister. Nor has it ever been exposed to any intervention by the Prime Minister's office. The Directorate is headed by the Director of Elections, appointed by the President and approved by the National Assembly. The Directorate handles the whole election process including voters' registration, the registration of political parties, candidate lists and the conduct of the elections. Although not regulated by law, the Directorate of Elections has also assumed duties, with the assistance of some NGOs and donor agencies, for voters' education (*ibid.*, 57).

Elections to Regional and Local Authorities are regulated by the Regional Council Act and Local Authorities Act in addition to the Constitution and Electoral Act. The Local Authorities Act of 1992 (amended in 1997) describes the prerequisites, and the dates of election for members of local authorities, and meetings of local authority councils. The Local Authority Act also includes regulations concerning representation by gender. According to the Local Authorities Act, all parties must implement a gender quota in the candidate lists. All lists of 7 must contain at least 3 female candidates. The Directorate of Elections also encouraged, although based on voluntarism, the parties to arrange their lists on a 'zebra manner' meaning that women and men candidates were placed on the list one after another instead of putting the women at the end of the list as was also legally possible. This recommendation actually worked in achieving a gender balance among the local councillors. Out of 329 seats countrywide, 193 or 41 per cent were won by female candidates. The gender aspect will be addressed again later in this paper.

The regional and local authorities are new entities for the majority of the population. Prior to independence, most people were deprived of fully-fledged participation in local governance. After independence, the local authorities had to be reformed and restructured to gain acceptance and legitimacy among the population. After the first Delimitation Commission decided on 13 regions to replace the former ethnic homelands, new local authorities – municipalities, towns and villages – were also proclaimed. The local authorities cover only urban areas. In 1991, approximately 31 per cent of the Namibian population lived in the areas of local authorities including the village councils.[13]

The government had, prior to the 1998 elections, passed a law on the decentralisation of the allocation and organisation of certain public services to the regional and local authorities. There has been widespread consensus over the need for decentralisation of the state administration. Parties differ only as to the degree and pace of implementing decentralisation. The opposition parties have also raised concern over Swapo's real commitment to allow effective decision-making powers to be vested in the lower levels of administration. Swapo had earlier, quite reluctantly, even agreed to a limited decentralisation – not its tradition and policy. Its sudden change of mind has led some to argue that the government only wants to get rid of the functions and responsibilities it has not been able to fulfil in delegating problem areas to the authorities who have even less financial and human resources to solve them.[14] Following pressure upon the government to empower the local institutions with revenue-raising capacity to match the new demanding responsibilities, the Ministry of Regional and Local Government and Housing has formulated a comprehensive plan to implement decentralisation (Namibia 1996).

The first elections to the new regional and local councils were held simultaneously in 1992, when Namibians voted for regional councillors by the first-past-the-post system and representatives to 51 local authorities by the proportional party-list system.[15] Each local authority council consisted of 7 to 12 members depending on the size of the town or village. For the second local authority elections of 1998, the number of local authority areas had been restructured to 45 and the maximum size of the council increased to 15 members. Although the constitution stipulated that

---

[13]In 1991 the municipalities had in total 307,684 inhabitants and the towns 117,408 inhabitants. The average size of a municipality was 19,230 inhabitants and of a town 9,780 inhabitants. The villages may have some 1,000–4,000 inhabitants. For the 1992 elections a total number of 156,795 people registered as voters. Namibia's population is 1.6 million.

[14]The opposition has especially expressed concern that there is no capacity at the lower administrative level to handle new tasks. Interviews with DTA and UDF leaders.

[15]Walvis Bay local council elections were held in 1994 when the coastal town was incorporated into Namibia.

the second local authority elections should have been held according to the ward-based system, the old party-list system was still in use.[16]

Initially, the change of the electoral system was debated in parliament but in the end it did not get the support of the ruling party. The main reasons why Swapo did not accept the ward-based system had to do with the legacy of apartheid. Due to the previous settlement policy, the majority of the Namibian population still lives in housing areas determined by race and ethnic origin, especially in the bigger towns in central Namibia. To prevent these factors from having an impact on voting behaviour, the government found it more expedient to constitute a single constituency for each town.[17] Since, as mentioned above, two other electoral systems are already in use in Namibia[18] to introduce a completely new one was believed to cause voter confusion and thereby increase the number of spoilt ballot papers. According to the Director of Elections, the introduction of wards and voting pattern accordingly would have demanded a much longer period of voter education than was possible in the given period of time.[19]

The opposition parties opted for the ward-based system. Their leaders argued that it would increase the accountability of the elected councillors to the local residents. On the other hand, a simple arithmetical calculation showed that the opposition, especially DTA, would probably win more seats under the ward system. This is due to the fact that if a given town was divided into wards/constituencies, based on housing areas where each would select their own representative, the votes cast for Swapo in the densely-populated areas would not be counted together with other votes to help its candidates in other wards. Furthermore, it was believed that participating in the elections on a Swapo ticket gave an additional advantage to a candidate who might not be able to compete on the basis of his/her personal competence. Overall, the fact that the elections were to be held on a party-list system emphasises people's support for the given party instead of encouraging their attention towards local affairs.[20] These elections showed, however, that the proportional system favoured the small parties and associations, especially because the quota for a seat was small due to low voter turnout.

According to the Electoral Act, parties and associations which intend to participate in elections must be registered by the Directorate of Elections. Thereafter, the parties and associations have to present their candidate lists for local authority councils to the returning officers, appointed by the Directorate of Elections, in each municipality that they wish to contest. As stipulated by the presidential proclamation, the registration process was fixed for a given period of time, until 24 October in the case of the 1997 elections. After the ruling party failed to comply with the registration deadline, it appealed to the High Court to challenge the election proclamation. Finally, the party and the Electoral Commission reached an out-of-court settlement that the election process was called off and the elections were postponed until February 1998 (Soiri 1998).

The postponement of the elections affected the election process in a number of ways. First of all, the voter registration period was extended, which increased the number of voters registered by 2 per cent in the whole country. Yet, in some of the municipalities the number of registered voters increased more significantly. For example, in Katima Mulilo, a North-eastern town in Caprivi region, the number of voters increased by 25 per cent. In Ondangwa, a town in Northern Oshana region, it increased by nearly 50 per cent. In Gobabis, the number of voters grew by 20 per cent. Seemingly the increase in the voters' roll was a result of the registration appeal made by the Directorate of Elections in the mass media. It was also a product of the local mobilisation by contesting parties and associations, who actively urged their supporters to go and register.

---

[16]Accordingly, contesting parties present a list of candidates equivalent to the number of seats available in each respective local authority. The electorate has the choice of electing a party list instead of individual candidates.
[17]Interview with Swapo Secretary, General H. Pohamba, 26 November 1997.
[18]In general elections the candidates are selected on a proportional party-list system. In Regional Council elections candidates are elected by majority vote in each region divided in one man/woman constituencies.
[19]Interview with Gerhard Tötemeyer, 25 February 1998.
[20]This concern had already been spelt out during the first local authority elections. The argument was tested in the exit poll conducted during the last local authority elections. The result confirmed that the people relied on political parties for direction instead of voting for candidates on the basis of their individual competence. Pendleton 1992, 18–20.

Contesting parties and their election campaigns

Before the extension of the registration period, only 1 party, the main opposition party DTA, had registered a candidate list in all 45 municipalities, while the ruling party Swapo only managed to register a list in 44 municipalities. After the new registration period, Swapo finally managed to present its list in all municipalities. Three other parties attempted to contest in selected municipalities, increasing their participation during the new registration period; the United Democratic Front, (UDF), in 22 municipalities; the Democratic Coalition of Namibia, (DCN), in 3 municipalities; and the Workers Revolutionary Party, (WRP), in 1 municipality, namely Windhoek, the capital of Namibia. Furthermore, 5 local residents associations had initially decided to participate in elections in their respective local authority area.[21]

In addition to this, one party and three more local associations decided to participate in the elections using the opportunity provided by the new registration period. South West African Union, (SWANU),[22] reassessed its former position of not contesting these local elections and decided to contest in three municipalities. An existing local group in Windhoek, Local Residents' Association, which had already taken part in the 1992 local authority elections without winning a seat, was newly mobilised. It registered a list in the Windhoek municipality. Furthermore, a completely new group emerged in Otavi called Otavi Residents' Association, and another one in Okahandja, called the Okahandja Ratepayers' Association. That increased the number of parties taking part in the elections from five to six and independent local associations participating in elections to a total of eight.

Looked at by municipality, however, in 20 municipalities there were Swapo and DTA contesting the elections, whilst in the remaining 25 there was a choice of 3 or more parties. A record number of parties contesting for municipal seats was in Windhoek, where all 6 parties and a local association had put up a candidate list. Compared to the 1992 local authority elections the number of contesting parties had remained the same,[23] but the number of local associations had increased from 3 to 8.

The ruling party, Swapo

The ruling party, Swapo, appealed to its voters to give it a mandate to continue the nation-building and reconciliation process it has led since independence. It claimed that only the Swapo candidates had enough knowledge and expertise to run the local councils. Political rallies constituted the core of Swapo's election campaign. A lot of emphasis was put on rallies where President Nujoma was speaking. As expected, the presidential rallies attracted a large audience, yet not all of them were Swapo supporters and potential voters. Swapo also transported some of its supporters from the nearby towns to attend the rallies.

Although President Nujoma helped Swapo to draw attention to its political rallies, it is questionable whether his active role was an appropriate way to inform people about the elections. These were, after all, local authority elections, and not national or presidential elections. Many people were not well informed about the significance of the local authority councils and the separation of power between national and local representative structures. By the same token they were unaware of the purpose of their vote. The active participation of the national President in campaigning might have confused people even more about the tasks of the different levels of state institutions. The local candidates were left in the shadow of the popular President and did

---

[21]These were: Gobabis Residents' Association in Gobabis, in Omaheke region; Concerned People's Organisation in Keetmanshoop, a town in the Southern Karas region; Omaruru Residents' Association in the Western Erongo region; Rehoboth Ratepayers' Association in Rehoboth in the Southern Hardap region and Swakopmund Residents' Association in Swakopmund, in the coastal Erongo region.

[22]South West African National Union (SWANU), the first liberation movement in Namibia, established in 1958.

[23]In 1992, the parties participating in the elections were Swapo, DTA, UDF, WRP, SWANU and NPF. NPF was turned into DCN after its cooperation with SWANU in the 1994 elections did not materialise.

not have a chance to highlight the local issues or present their objectives for the coming five-year period.

Campaign rallies led by other Swapo leaders were not successful in attracting an audience. A rally in Windhoek presenting the Foreign Minister, Theo-Ben Gurirab, was attended by less than 100 people. Swapo also decided to hold rallies only in selected towns and left out towns in regions where it was confident of maintaining its leading role. Consequently, there was no major rally in any of the 5 towns in the former Ovamboland area, where the core of Swapo's supporters comes from. The absence of effective campaigning in former Ovambo might have been one reason why the voter turnout dropped drastically in the whole region. Instead, Swapo attacked the opposition parties in towns under their control or where residents associations were gaining ground. Swapo's biggest attention was given to Katima Mulilo, which until these elections was the only major town with a DTA majority on the municipal council.

The main opposition party, Democratic Turnhalle Alliance (DTA)

The opposition parties accused the ruling party of mismanaging the country's affairs and the local councils of inefficiency. They, like the ruling party itself, did not manage to draw attention to the local issues but kept the campaign on a national level. The main opposition party, the DTA,[24] built its campaign around criticism of Swapo's performance as the ruling party, but failed to bring any viable policy alternatives. Swapo's failure to speed up economic development, alleged misman-agement and corruption, as well as a lack of accountability played a main role in the DTA's campaign. It stressed the need for decentralisation, which the government had already decided to implement. DTA enjoys most support in the Southern regions of the country and in the northern Caprivi Region. Furthermore, many Herero-speaking Namibians and a large part of the white population vote for the DTA.

In practice, the DTA's chance of winning the elections, or even increasing its share of votes or seats, was minimal. Hence, the party concentrated on securing its seats in its stronghold areas. DTA's main problem is its historical legacy as a former collaborationist party of the apartheid regime. The party is mainly run by the same leaders, thereby undermining its legitimacy. Historical reasons prevent DTA from penetrating the populated Northern areas where it is asso-ciated with the former repressive and violent regime. The party does not appeal to the people because it has failed to restructure and reposition itself in relation to the ruling party and to come up with alternative programmes in the new situation after independence. This reason, among others, seems to contribute to the internal disunity from which the party suffers. A number of its activists have broken away from party ranks by assuming posts in the civil service at Swapo's invitation, joined the independent resident associations or left politics altogether.[25]

United Democratic Front (UDF)

The third-biggest party, the UDF, campaigned in its traditional stronghold areas, Erongo and Kunene region as well as in the South. Their followers are mostly from the Damara-speaking community, whose traditional leader, Justus Garoeb, is also the party leader.[26] UDF was formed in 1989 as a strategic alliance to contest the elections. Its leading group, an ethnic association, Damara Council, has a record of opposing all the internal regimes of South Africa. Yet, it utilised the second-tier administration in canvassing support in former Damaraland and to lobby for internationally supervised independence. The Damara Council participated initially in a Multi-Party Conference in 1983, one of the South African creations to establish an internal

---

[24]DTA holds 15 (of a total of 72) seats in the National Assembly and 7 councillors (out of 26) in the National Council. Furthermore it controls 3 out of 13 Regional Councils and 11 (out of 51) local authorities.
[25]See below. After the elections were postponed, one more veteran DTA politician decided to contest the elec-tions on the platform of a revived Local Community Association (LCA) in Windhoek. *The Namibian*, 17 December 1997.
[26]According to the Namibian Traditional Authorities Act, no person should hold an office both as a politician and as a traditional leader. Justus Garoeb was elected to parliament on a UDF ticket, but resigned when he was chosen to be a Damara King.

regime,[27] but broke away to support SWAPO. The Patriotic Unity Movement, (PUM), and the WRP, joined the UDF alliance for strategic reasons. They are both parties formed by anti-SWAPO activists, who had personal experience of the treatment of dissidents by SWAPO. The UDF alliance presents itself as a centrist alternative within the liberation tradition. UDF was re-formed as a unitary party in October 1993 and intended to work closely with other opposition parties (Pütz et al. 1990, 80). Its support is restricted to areas of former Damaraland – presently in Erongo and Kunene regions – as well as in the South of the country. However, the UDF has not been successful in disposing of its 'tribalist' image, although it gets modest support from the white community that supported the resistance movement before independence.

As a matter of fact, the two main opposition parties of DTA and UDF were negotiating to join forces and to establish an election pact to fight Swapo more efficiently. The pact would have included common candidate lists in all towns where both parties had decided to contest. That would have increased the resources and concentrated votes in helping to gain more seats under the proportional election system. The pact failed, however, because of personal disagreements. Both party leaders, Mr Muyongo (DTA) and Chief Garoeb (UDF) did not want the other party to appear in the candidate list of their own hometown, that is Katima Mulilo for DTA and Omaruru for UDF.[28] After the pact failed, both parties registered their own candidate lists and ran separate election campaigns. The failure of establishing cooperation even in a modest form such as an election pact is an indication of the deep historical and personal divisions which are still characteristic of the Namibian party system. Opposition parties have found it difficult to transcend the pre-independence political positions and readjust their policies and strategies to the present reality.

Other contesting parties

DCN contested the first elections in 1989 under the name of the National Patriotic Front (NPF), which was an alliance of factions of old existing parties (SWANU, CANU[29] and a Rehoboth group under the leadership of Kaptein Diergaardt).[30] They all participated in the 'Multi-Party Conference' in 1983. DCN was formed in 1994 by Moses Katjiuongua,[31] an MP, after his former

---

[27]South Africa organised internal elections in Namibia in 1978, managing to co-opt many ethnically oriented parties to participate. The elections failed to get international recognition, because all opposition parties, among others SWAPO, boycotted them. After the National Assembly, elected in 1978, lacked popular support, and was disbanded in 1982, South Africa invited all parties to a Multi-Party Conference, (MPC), in 1983, to look for independence based on group representation in order to avoid internationally supervised democratic elections. Although more parties, among others UDF, took part in MPC than in the 1978 elections, it did not succeed, because the main opposition parties opted for UN supervised elections on the basis of one man/woman one vote.
[28]Interview with Mishake Muyongo (DTA), 15 February 1998 and Allen Liebenberg (UDF), 27 February 1998. Mr Muyongo said that the planned pact failed, when Chief Garoeb did not allow DTA to appear on the list of Omaruru. The UDF's story was different, accusing Mr Muyongo of blocking UDF's participation in Katima and insisting that the Omaruru list should have been named as a DTA list, which was unacceptable to Chief Garoeb. In the end, DTA lost in Katima Mulilo, and UDF gained the most votes (UDF 326, Swapo 310 DTA 280) in Omaruru. A common list would not have changed the distribution of seats in Omaruru, however (UDF 2, DTA 2, SWAPO 2 and Omaruru Residents 'Association 1). It is impossible to assess whether the UDF list would have any support in Katima Mulilo. It is unlikely that it would have prevented Swapo's victory.
[29]Caprivi National Union, originally a resistance movement in Caprivi, which joined Swapo's liberation alliance. It had disintegrated several times and the group in NPF represented only one faction.
[30]Kaptein Diergaardt was the traditional leader of the Baster community, the descendants of the indigenous population and white settlers who mainly reside in the Rehoboth area. He was very vocal in advocating the return of autonomy to the Baster community.
[31]Moses Katjiuongua's involvement in politics originates from the tradition of resistance to the colonial rule by Herero people. His father was a personal advisor to Chief Kutako, one of the leading figures in the early resistance movement in Namibia, whose Herero Chief Council contributed to the establishment of SWANU, the first national resistance movement. Katjiuongua joined SWANU, went into exile and returned to Namibia bringing his faction of already then disunited SWANU to participate in the South African Multi-party Conference. He became the Minister of Manpower and Civic Affairs, and National Heath and Welfare in the transitional government 1985–89. Although his reputation was discredited by this co-option with the South African regime, Katjiuongua is regarded as a committed and talented MP across the party political spectrum. Efforts to unite SWANU have proved unsuccessful because of deep personal and political divisions.

alliance, the NPF, fell apart after disagreements over the manner of how the party list for the 1994 elections was drawn up. Katjiuongua formed the DCN, after SWANU of Namibia decided to contest the 1994 elections alone. Katjiuongua managed to secure a seat in parliament with just over 4 000 votes.[32] Initially DCN registered a candidate list only in the North-western town Opuwo but increased its participation to three other municipalities after the registration period was extended. A new interim leadership of SWANU of Namibia also decided to contest the municipal elections. DCN and SWANU both claim to represent the legacy of the liberation movement. SWANU failed again to contest the elections jointly and presented a separate candidate list in Opuwo, Windhoek and Okakarara, while in Outjo only DCN contested. SWANU had established a new office in Katutura and ran the election campaign by emphasising its historical legacy as a first liberation movement still committed to the well-being of the most disadvantaged groups. SWANU and DCN contested for the same votes coming mainly from the Herero-speaking community.

The small Trotskyist WRP, left UDF after the latter reconstituted itself as a unitary party. It is inspired by socialist ideology and criticises Swapo for not addressing the needs of the working class. It draws support especially from the coloured community south of Windhoek. WRP only intended to contest the Windhoek local authority. WRP's following is very modest, and it survives because of the personal commitment of its leaders, Hewat Beukes[33] and Erica Beukes. Yet, it managed to get only 63 votes.[34]

All smaller parties, in their campaigns, emphasised affordable and cost-efficient municipal services and pointed out the difficult financial situation many municipalities have faced since independence. They claimed that this was a result of the government's spending on housing and other living conditions without securing the necessary financial basis for the funding. Many local authorities have not been able to raise enough revenue to finance these projects. The smaller parties also criticised the lack of participation by the local residents in improving their towns. They stated that, because of the promises made by SWAPO during the liberation struggle, the people expect government to provide everything without their own participation. Furthermore, many of the houses and services which are provided are of such high quality and cost that the masses cannot afford them. UDF, especially, campaigned for low-cost municipal services towards which people would contribute directly, for example, in the form of labour.[35] Small parties mainly campaigned with the help of the free coverage given by the mass media and by organising political rallies in their stronghold areas. No posters or leaflets were distributed due to financial constraints.

The local residents' associations urged more local autonomy and expressed criticism against all parties being centralised and not giving the local inhabitants enough access to decision-making structures. The parties accused the local associations of being separatists, particularists and repre-senting only the interests of rather limited communities. In most cases it was true that the local asso-ciations were established by the minority groups of a particular town. In Omaruru, the members were mainly white commercial farmers, whereas in Swakopmund the core of the membership consisted of the German-speaking white business community. On the other hand, in some places like Rehoboth, the local association consisted of Basters, who form the majority of Rehoboth resi-dents. The local association in Otavi had attracted members from all population groups, who were disappointed with the parties' performance at the local level. All in all, the local associations kept their campaigns at a local level by holding meetings with their members, distributing leaflets and

---

[32]In the proportional system votes cast are divided by the number of seats available in order to establish a quota required for one seat. The quota seats are then allocated to the parties whose votes exceed the quota. After this, a few seats will usually remain free. These seats are taken up by those parties that have the most extra votes. DCN did not qualify for a quota seat but was the first to get a remaining seat.

[33]Hewat Beukes was a SWAPO member in exile, but resigned from the movement at the beginning of the 1980s when it was hit by the 'spy-drama' and some its members, among others many from the Coloured community, no longer felt it safe to continue working for the movement. Beukes returned to Namibia and established WRP with some former exiles with similar socialist views. See also Thiro-Beukes *et al.* 1986.

[34]In the 1992 elections WRP got 115 votes in Windhoek.

[35]Interview with Allen Liebenberg (UDF), 3 November 1997 and Eric Biwa (UDF), 7 November 1997, Windhoek.

canvassing votes in residential areas. Only a few of them used the opportunity to share NBC's free airtime on television, which was provided for all participating groups.

In general, the public discussion on elections was rather calm and quiet, although the mass media covered most of the major events of all parties in an equal manner and tried also to present local issues in their news coverage. No serious complaints were presented by any party or association about the media coverage being biased or impartial during the election campaign.

Financial situation of the political parties

Financial constraints also prevented parties from running big campaigns. Financially, the DTA and other opposition parties have been in dire straits. Since South Africa stopped its generous financial assistance to the parties, they have had empty coffers barely enough to run their day-to-day administrative routines, let alone any effective restructuring and wider community outreach. However, the financial situation of all parties in parliament has been improved since the last 1994 elections, because, after a long debate, finally in 1997, Parliament approved a bill for state funding for political parties. The necessity of such support to the impoverished political parties has been emphasised since the 1994 elections (Commonwealth 1995, 20). Parties receive a share from state resources according to the number of seats held in parliament.[36] Political parties which receive state funding have to submit their financial reports to the Auditor-General according to the guidelines, which have not yet been formulated in detail.

Thanks to the new funds, DTA especially was able to put more resources into political campaigning during the 1998 local elections. It printed and distributed a considerable number of election posters and placards around the townships. The visible posters, with campaign slogans, supplemented its political rallies held around the country. In fact, DTA presence was felt much more than that of Swapo during the election campaign.

Swapo's financial situation deserves a deeper analysis. Unfortunately, very little is released concerning the party's financial status. The liberation movement, SWAPO, enjoyed substantial foreign support during the liberation struggle. The funds and material donations were directed to maintain the exiled Namibians and improve their living conditions in the refugee camps, as well as their educational and social activities. Because the exact number of SWAPO refugees was difficult to establish, the material support sometimes exceeded the need. Some leftover donations were shipped to Namibia and sold to finance SWAPO's political activities during and after the independence elections.[37] The peace agreement in 1987 included an impartiality clause, on the basis of which many former donors, Finland among others, stopped direct assistance to SWAPO. However, with repatriation, SWAPO received massive donations from the Namibian business community in the form of offices, vehicles and other equipment. After independence SWAPO sold its headquarters to the Government, which built an office complex on the vacated plot in the Windhoek city centre. Another, more humble headquarters was built for Swapo in a cheaper area near Katutura, a former black township. It is believed that Swapo invested some of its funds in business companies, which run services in different sectors. For example, a popular bus company, Namibia Contract Haulage, started when buses donated for the SWAPO refugee camps were brought to Namibia, commercialised and supplemented by newly-acquired ones.

Despite its commercial activities, the party has been accused of financing its own political activities from state coffers. Most of the leaders of Swapo are also ministers or other top government officers, who enjoy a government salary. The recent decision to relieve Swapo's secretary general Hifikepunye Pohamba of his duties as the Minister for Fisheries and to appoint him as a Minister without portfolio caused a lot of criticism and claims that he now served the party full-time on the government's payroll. These arrangements, naturally, decreased the amount needed for salaries from the party's own budget. At the same time, the party has announced that it

---

[36]For example, Swapo receives 5.3 million Namibian dollars annually, approximately 1.1 US$ million. *The Namibian* 17 April 1998.
[37]There were so-called 'SWAPO' shops in Namibia, where one could find all kind of necessities, clothing and houseware at cheap prices. Some of the goods still carried a label of origin. The shops also sold goods, which were produced by exiles in the camps. Some donors and the press expressed criticism of the sale of the products arguing that the donations were not meant to finance the political work of Swapo.

has not been able to fulfil all positions established in the Party Congress because of the lack of funds. It seems, thus, that the party has become dependent upon the state for resources. There is no information as to how much the party receives in membership fees. The same applies to the share of funds that is allocated to its regional and local functions.

During the election campaign, Swapo was careful to ensure that it did not, at least in public, use government property for party campaigning. Yet, when President Nujoma held rallies, the arrangements were organised and funded by the President's Office. At the same time, there is no evidence that Swapo or any other party used its own or public funds for 'buying' votes. All political events were kept at a modest level and, for instance, participants in election *braais*[38] had to buy their own food and drinks. Another more complicated question is in what ways Swapo utilised its position of controlling state finances and development funds in order to link voting behaviour with the promise of economic development. I will return to this topic below with reference to the Katima Mulilo campaign.

Election process well organised, the outcome a surprise

After the elections it was widely established that the electoral process went well and without any significant problems. The postponement of the elections had provided more time for the Directorate of Elections to educate and inform the election officers and the public. The election material reached the polling stations in time. No irregularities were reported in the polling process. There were 186 polling stations countrywide where the electorate cast their votes, including 27 mobile stations. The low turnout of voters also eased the polling process. There were short or no queues at the polling stations, which hastened the voting procedure. In some areas in the Northern region, as well as in the capital, it was reported that the election officers were virtually unemployed.

Ignorance and unawareness produced most problems in regard to the election process. Many voters had come to vote with the wrong registration card. There was a nationwide confusion about different voters' cards for regional and local authority elections. Only those citizens who had lived for a minimum of 12 months in a given town or village were eligible to vote for the local authority council. Those voters who had registered in the last local and regional elections in 1992, were in possession of such registration cards. Some of them were, however, only eligible to vote for Regional Councils, because they live outside the proclaimed – municipal, town or village – area. Furthermore, those who had moved to the local authority area either from another town or from outside proclaimed areas from the countryside, had to re-register. The fact that people were not well-informed about the difference between the Local and Regional Councils, resulted in many trying to vote with a Regional voting card. Again, many people who had moved from one town to another failed to re-register before the elections, and thereafter were turned away from the polls because they had a registration card from a different town or village. This confusion of the two different voters' cards, as well as an unawareness of the need to re-register after migration seemed to have contributed to the low voter turnout to some extent.

In the final results, Swapo gained 60 per cent of the votes cast throughout the whole country. DTA came second with 24 per cent, UDF 7 per cent, DCN, SWANU of Namibia and WRP less than one per cent between them and the local associations together 8 per cent.[39] Swapo gained majority control in 25 towns, DTA in 9 and UDF in 2 towns. Otavi and Rehoboth have a majority from the local residents' associations and in the remaining 7 towns there is a balance of power between 3 or 4 parties or associations. Compared to the previous local elections in 1992, Swapo, which got 58 per cent in 1992 and UDF, having gained 6 per cent in 1992, increased their share of votes slightly, whereas the other parties lost in their share of votes.[40] The biggest winner was,

---

[38]An Afrikaans word for a barbecue. This outside festivity is a typical way of celebrating any event in Namibia. *Braais* are also organised to collect money in the case of funerals or other unexpected financial needs. A typical *braai* consists of a lot of meat and plenty of beer, which is sold at a price higher than in normal liquor outlets and shops in order to generate a surplus.

[39]Votes rejected amounted to 1%. DCN got 0.5% (332 votes), SWANU of Namibia 0.2% (142 votes) and WRP 0.1% of votes (63 votes) in the whole country.

[40]DTA was the biggest loser in the share of votes. It gained 33% in the 1992 elections, thus the loss was nearly 10%. SWANU of Namibia gained almost 2% of the votes in 1992.

however, the local residents' associations, whose total share of votes countrywide rose from 1 per cent in 1992 to 8 per cent. Most significant was that all 8 local associations managed to secure at least 1 seat in their respective municipality.

In a number of the municipalities contested, the ruling party did not perform as expected. Although Swapo maintained its domination in most municipalities, it suffered many defeats, losing in total six towns formerly under its control. It now controls 25 out of the 45 municipalities compared to 32 out of 51 previously.[41] Instead, Swapo took control of the Katima Mulilo town council from DTA in the North-eastern Caprivi Region.[42]

For the DTA, another major loss was the Rehoboth town council, where it had to give up its majority to a local residents' association. Compared to the 1992 results, the DTA lost 2 town councils, gaining a majority in 9 councils against the former 11. Yet, a significant success for the DTA was that it managed to maintain its seats in both the Ondangwa and Oshakati town councils in the Swapo-dominated Oshana region and even win a new seat in the Ongwediva town council in the same region. DTA, which has found it extremely difficult to build up a support base in the former Ovamboland area, benefited clearly from the fact that low voter turnout resulted in low quotas being required for a seat, which allowed DTA candidates to gain a seat even with a very small number of votes.

Among the winners of these elections were women. The gender quota in the candidate lists in a 'zebra manner' actually worked in achieving a gender balance among the councillors. An initial study of the results revealed that of the 329 seats contested countrywide, 193 or 41 per cent were won by women. Of the parties, Swapo was most gender-balanced having 47 per cent of its elected councillors women. 36 per cent of DTA's councillors and 32 per cent of UDF's councillors were women. The representation of women varied a great deal for the residents associations.[43] The large number of women councillors gave rise to positive comments and it was also seen as promising in the longer perspective as getting more women involved in the higher levels of state administration.[44] In Namibia, women's affairs are widely discussed overall and women's activism during the struggle for independence managed to maintain gender issues on the political agenda after

---

[41]In 1992 there were elections in 51 towns. After that eight villages and towns were integrated into another town, because of their small size, and two new ones were established. As a result, at the time of the 1998 elections, only 45 municipalities, towns or villages existed. Out of the integrated towns, Swapo had a majority in 5 towns while DTA had a majority in the 3 remaining ones. In these elections, Swapo lost Opuwo, the major town in north-western Kunene region, and Henties Bay, a coastal town in Erongo region to DTA. In addition to this, Swapo lost control of the Otavi town council in the Otjozondjuba region to a local residents' association. In Gobabis, in the Eastern Omaheke region, Swapo lost its former majority, when the new residents' associations gained 3 seats against Swapo's 3 and DTA's 1 seat. In Omaruru, in the Western Erongo region, Swapo lost its majority and there is now a balance of power held by the residents' association. The same happened in Kamanjab, in the north-eastern Kunene region, where Swapo lost 3 of its former 5 seats to UDF and DTA. The power balance was changed in favour of DTA also in Tses and Karasburg, which were previously run by Swapo-UDF coalitions. Swapo also lost seats in Maltahöhe, although maintaining their majority, in Stampriet, in Ongwediva (one seat to DTA) and in Okakarara.

[42]In addition, Swapo improved its majority position in Rundu, in Northern Kavango region, in Swakopmund, in the coastal Erongo region, in Leonardville, in the central Omaheke region, and in Tsumeb, in the northern Oshikoto region. Swapo also gained all 7 seats in the newly proclaimed northern towns of Eenhana, in the Ohangwena region, and Outapi, in the Omusati region.

[43]The only representative of the Local Community Association in Windhoek is a woman, whereas the Okahandja Ratepayers' Association, the Keetmanshop Concerned People's Organisation, the Omaruru Residents' Association and the Swakopmund Residents' Association had placed a male candidate at the top of the list, who was then elected as the only councillor. For the rest, the Gobabis Residents' Association, the Rehoboth Ratepayers' Association and the Otavi Residents' Association, the gender-balanced list made it possible to have both women and men elected.

[44]There are 14 women MPs out of 72 in the National Assembly and only 1 female member out of 26 in the National Council. Furthermore, there are 3 female ministers (out of 21) and 2 deputy ministers out of 21. Only 3 out of 95 regional councillors, selected without quota, are women. Women also occupy a few other high positions in the government such as the Director of the National Planning Commission, the Ombudsman and a few permanent secretaries. *Namibian Parliamentary Directory*, 1997.

independence (Becker 1993; Soiri, 1996). Although the attitudes towards gender equality are not always supportive, especially in the rural areas and among certain church communities, the ruling party has followed a rather liberal gender agenda. The gender quota in the local elections is a good example of this policy and has promoted women's further involvement in political decision-making.

After the elections, the Electoral Commission declared the elections free and fair. All contesting parties accepted the results in all municipalities except one. DTA, after having lost control of Katima Mulilo to Swapo, came up with accusations that the voters' register was rigged. As will be described below, the elections in Katima Mulilo reflect the different political agendas that exist in Namibia in regard to the questions of nation-building and ethnic identity.

The battle for Katima Mulilo[45]

For Swapo, gaining control of the North-eastern town of Katima Mulilo was one of the main objectives during these elections. It was not only a question of Katima Mulilo town as such, but an experiment in Swapo's national reconciliation policy. Katima Mulilo is situated at the end of a narrow corridor reaching to the Zambezi river to the east of heartland Namibia. It is the administrative and commercial centre of the Caprivi region, which has approximately 90,000 inhabitants. The region is rather isolated from the rest of the country. Cross-border activities to Zimbabwe, Botswana, Angola and Zambia are common. Only about 15 per cent of the population lives in the urban areas, the main centre being Katima Mulilo with an estimated population of about 15,000 inhabitants. Although the region has received some attention since independence, it is still in serious need of many services and a great deal of basic infrastructure, of which a rural water supply, an improved road network, telecommunications and electricity are the most serious (Tötemeyer 1997, 63–64). Another question which needs to be addressed is the modernisation and commercialisation of cattle farming, the main economic activity closely connected to control of land and the powers of traditional authorities in that respect.

After the 1992 Regional and Local elections, the Caprivi region was DTA's power base. In the regional council, DTA won four constituencies against Swapo's two.[46] In the Katima Mulilo town council, which is the only municipality in Caprivi with local authority structures, DTA had four representatives, while Swapo had three. Besides, DTA's president Mishake Muyongo comes from Katima Mulilo. He was a founding member of CANU, an anti-colonial Caprivi National Union, which formed an alliance with Swapo during the 1960s. Muyongo was elected Swapo's vice-president. At the beginning of the 1980s, Muyongo deserted Swapo, accusing it of ethnic favouritism and drew many CANU supporters with him. After returning to Namibia, he went back to Caprivi in 1985 and initiated merger talks with the Caprivi Alliance (CAP)[47] and the DTA, which resulted in the formation of the United Democratic Party (UDP) under a DTA umbrella.[48]

DTA supports greater regional autonomy and has emphasised the ethnic and geographic uniqueness of the Caprivi area.[49] According to Mr Muyongo, people in the region identify themselves

---

[45]In public discussions, the Katima Mulilo municipal elections were always referred to by this military term 'battle'.

[46]Yet, Swapo has recently slowly increased its support in the region by winning the by-election in the Katima Mulilo constituency in 1996.

[47]The Caprivi Alliance was founded in November 1977 by the members of the Basubia and Mafwe tribal authorities with the two chiefs as leaders. The party grew from a loosely-grouped alliance which was the name given to the Caprivi delegation at the Turnhalle Constitutional Conference (1975–77). It joined the DTA under the leadership of Mafwe Chief Richard Mamili in 1977. In 1980 ethnic elections, CAP got an unchallenged majority but the tribal differences paralysed the Caprivi Second Tier Representative Authority, the basic organ of the South African-created Bantustan system. CAP was officially disbanded in 1985 after the merger with CANU and the formation of UDP. Fosse 1992, 35; Pütz *et al.* 1990, 97.

[48]Both CANU and CAP dissidents have reconstituted their parties, split again and joined with alliances of other Namibian parties such as the Namibian Patriotic Front (NPF) and the UDF, and have – after independence – faded into oblivion. Fosse 1992, 35.

[49]Interviews with Mishake Muyongo, 5 November 1997 and 15 February 1998.

first and foremost as Caprivians and seek to maintain their separate identity from Namibians. Swapo, on the other hand, has since its establishment pursued a common national identity instead of separate ethnic or regional allegiances and adopted the policy of a unitary state.

Ethnic versus national political agenda

The question of ethnic identities versus a national identity is actually a phenomenon very typical of the Caprivi region and has its due political significance. It can be argued that people in Eastern Caprivi are more closely related in linguistic and cultural terms to neighbouring peoples in Botswana and Zambia than to other Namibian population groups (Nussey 1978, 289; Cluver 1991, 44). Traditional authorities in the area have also remained strong and enjoy a large degree of legitimacy. There are several closely related ethnic groups in the area, the biggest of them being the Basubia and Mafwe groups. The relationships between different groups and subgroups are characterised by the competing interpretation of history and of the settlement pattern of the Caprivi area, which culminated in the dispute over land.[50] Added to the South African deliberate 'divide and rule' policy, the ethnic identities were further divided and made distinct from each other as an essential element of gaining political power and influence within the colonial system. The political parties have also utilised the ethnicity aspect in gaining political influence. According to general belief, the Basubia traditional leaders have been more favourably inclined towards Swapo, whereas the DTA has gained a lot of support among the Mafwe traditional leaders, which has become a self-imposing prognosis in the pattern of political allegiance and voting. According to Fosse, the ethnic tensions in the area seem to be more closely related to (or at least aggravated by) external political developments and factors like the liberation struggle and South African administration in the area, than to the negligible differences between the two groups in terms of mode of production, occupational specialisation or class divisions, social organisation, religious practices or stereotyping based on such differences (Fosse 1992, 46).

The Caprivi area was, during the apartheid era, administrated directly from Pretoria and separate from rest of the Namibia until the end of 1970s, when the Caprivi Second Tier Representative Authority was established. Until then, South Africa totally controlled the Caprivi militarily and otherwise. Under the tribal administration, the traditional leaders enjoyed a certain degree of autonomy among their subjects, and their participation in administration and politics was encouraged by the South African regime, contrary to the situation, for example, in Ovamboland where the legitimacy of chiefs was undermined by the people. Thus they offered a natural source of identity and allegiance. Therefore, it was only in the 1970s that the Caprivians started to regard themselves as belonging to the rest of the country, probably beginning with the liberation struggle and the formation of CANU, the construction of the Trans-Caprivi Highway, the Turnhalle Conference in the mid-1970s and the more effective and administrative incorporation of the region into Namibia from the late 1970s (ibid., 36–37).

Consequently, in the case of Caprivi, it is difficult to establish whether politics have entered into ethnicity or whether ethnicity has entered into politics. By the same token, this vibrant and influential mixture of ethnicity and politics presents a significant challenge to Swapo's policy of nation-building. During the liberation struggle, the Caprivi Strip was an important base for Swapo guerrillas to get access to Namibia from the neighbouring countries. For that reason, the breakaway CANU faction under Muyongo's leadership was a significant loss to the liberation movement.

---

[50]Both Basubia and Mafwe ethnic groups claim to be the first inhabitants of the area. However, according to many sources, all of the groups in the area were subordinated to the Malozi as part of the Barotse Kingdom, which originates in what is present-day Zambia. This situation continued for centuries all the way up to the German occupation in 1890. It is thus possible to argue that all of the groups essentially are or have been Lozi. This is further strengthened by the fact that Silozi is the lingua franca in the area. If this is the case, what come across as more or less distinct 'tribes' and deeply-rooted ethnic differences today may have amounted to little more than mobile clans and dialect difference in the past. From this it can be argued that Mafwe and Basubia ethnic differences only crystallised or became significant in ethnic terms after their area was separated from the rest of the Barotse kingdom, and from which time they were treated as separate entities. Fosse 1992, 39.

Swapo campaigned for victory

Swapo decided to run a powerful campaign in Katima Mulilo. One obvious reason was its desire to beat the opposition leader on his home ground. Clearly, Muyongo's possible defeat would have political consequences concerning the whole party.[51] The importance of the region and the town of Katima Mulilo is also increasing because of the new transport link to neighbouring countries, the Trans-Caprivi Highway, which would give landlocked countries an access to Walvis Bay, Namibia's important port. Transport and crossborder trade has also been recently identified as one of the main potentials for Namibia to develop and diversify its economy (Namibia 1997, 4). Katima Mulilo was also the only major town in Namibia still controlled by the DTA. The decentralisation process recently embarked on would give more autonomy and power to the regions and municipalities to carry out governmental tasks. Taking into consideration the DTA's stand for deeper decentralisation and regional autonomy, Swapo might have found it ultimately important to control the local decision-making in Katima Mulilo.

Finally, Namibia and Botswana had been disputing over the ownership of a couple of small islands situated in the Chobe river between the two countries. The dispute originated from the disagreements over where the colonisers drew the border between Caprivi and British Bechuanaland in the 1890s. The dispute had led to tension in the area and increased military presence by the Botswana Defence Force (BDF). Although the islands are most of the year under water, and uninhabited, their soil is ideal for cultivation and the river rich in fish. The Caprivian people, who used to cultivate and fish in the islands, have suspended their activities for fear of the BDF. The Kasikili island question, which started the dispute a few years ago, has been referred to the International Court of Justice. The Namibian and Botswanan governments have set up a joint technical commission to define the border in the river. However, the dispute has recently been extended to other islands and is creating a lot of confusion among Caprivi residents. The local and essentially irrelevant border issue has now become a matter between two sovereign states and can no longer be handled by regional or local authorities, as has been the position of the DTA.

Swapo's campaign in Caprivi was under the supervision of a senior Swapo leader as was the practice in the whole country. The main event was organised around the President's visit to Katima during the weekend immediately prior to the elections. President Nujoma arrived in Katima on Friday afternoon, 13 February, and was met by the dancing and celebrating delegation from the Swapo Women's Council's local branch. After his arrival he met community representatives, traditional leaders and Swapo activists. An economic forum for the local business community was arranged for the evening, during which the president addressed the participants over the border dispute. Following the business forum, there was a *braai* hosted by the local Swapo district and those people who had donated funds or equipment for Swapo's campaign were invited. On the following day, the president held several consultations with the local community and traditional leaders mostly concerning the border dispute and the development needs of the region. Opposition leader Mishake Muyongo also paid a courtesy call on the president, interrupting DTA's campaign schedule.

The main rally was held at the Katima Mulilo sports stadium with just over a thousand participants. President Nujoma in his speech stated that Swapo was the only party capable of running the local authority. If Swapo were voted into power, the town would prosper and there would be much needed development. He said 'But for you to be able to participate in the administration of your town, you must vote for the right political party. On 16 February 1998, vote for Swapo-party' (Nujoma 1998). Another topic in Nujoma's speech concerned the border dispute and the lively cross-border activities in the region. The President warned that the government would not tolerate foreigners being invited into the country to become involved in issues of national interest. According to Nujoma, it is a serious offence if foreigners are invited to come and address political meetings in Namibia. Any such offence will be sternly dealt with by law

---

[51] As predicted, Muyongo's defeat started a leadership crisis in the DTA. It got deeper when Muyongo, together with some Caprivian traditional authorities demanded Caprivi's incorporation in South Africa. Following the denials of the DTA that they had promoted such secessionist plans, Muyongo was suspended from the party's leadership in August 1998.

enforcement agencies and the courts, once detected. The statement stems from the accusations both main parties had thrown at each other, that foreigners are being used to influence the politics of Namibia.

After Nujoma's speech, all seven local authority candidates were introduced to the audience. Thereafter, the programme was interrupted 'spontaneously' when about 50 people approached President Nujoma's VIP tent, and the speaker, a local Swapo activist, introduced them as former DTA members, who wanted to join Swapo. After this very symbolic act, the speaker announced that people in Katima Mulilo have been impoverished by the present DTA council, and that they need Swapo to bring development. Later on in the same evening, Swapo organised an election *braai* in the centre of Katima Mulilo. Its rival, DTA, organised a car convoy, which toured the town spreading DTA's message through loudspeakers. The atmosphere in Katima Mulilo was full of an enthusiasm over the elections not experienced in other areas in Namibia. It became clear that both main parties regarded 'the battle of Katima Mulilo' as an important issue in these elections carrying political weight beyond its actual magnitude.

In an interview on the following day, one day before polling day, Mr Muyongo dismissed the fifty ex-DTA members who joined Swapo, as insignificant, impoverished returnees, whom Swapo was only using as victims of its manipulation campaign. According to him, Swapo had deliberately refused to invest in the region and the town of Katima in order to discourage people from voting for the party of their choice.[52]

The dispute on voting rights

Already, during the registration period, there had been a dispute over the eligibility of some voters. DTA had accused the registration officers of discriminating against a group of little over 200 of its supporters who had not been allowed to register. Swapo had complained to the Directorate of Elections that non-residents were trying to register, and the complaint had been referred to the local magistrate. The magistrate had ruled on the basis of the residence of these people that only 38 of them were actually residents of Katima Mulilo and thus eligible to register and vote. DTA was not happy with the ruling, but there was nothing it could do about it. The old dispute started again in the early hours of polling day, when some members of the group tried to vote in the mobile polling stations by presenting a regional voters' card. After they were not allowed to vote, a DTA organiser had produced a handwritten document apparently signed by the Director of Elections, Mr Tötemeyer, claiming that these people were actually eligible to vote. In the middle of the heated dispute, Swapo organisers were called in to intervene. The polling process in the mobile unit was disrupted for a while. The Directorate of Elections was called by phone to clarify that no such letter of authorisation existed and that the decision of the magistrate remained valid. The disappointed DTA members threatened to bring the matter to the attention of the Electoral Commission.

Swapo won the election in Katima Mulilo by five seats against DTA's two. The votes cast in the town were altogether 2,215. The voter turnout was 44 per cent, well above the national average of 34 per cent. Swapo got 65 per cent of votes and DTA 35 per cent. This defeat on the home ground was difficult to swallow for DTA. Shortly after the results were declared, Mishake Muyongo announced that DTA did not accept the results. He claimed that the party had been betrayed and its supporters victimised and intimidated. DTA claimed that Swapo had managed to transport its own supporters from outside Katima to register by manipulating the voters' register. At the same time, eligible voters of DTA were denied their right to vote.[53] As a consequence, DTA rejected the results and the 2 councillors elected on a DTA ticket refused to take up their seats in the new city council when it convened at the end of the election week. However, despite Muyongo's claims, the party never made any official complaint concerning the election results to the Director of Elections or the High Court. Their complaint about the intimidation of DTA supporters was referred to the police, who investigated the matter. It seems that there was not evidence to prove their claims of rigging the voters' register. According to the Director of Elections, the voters'

---

[52]Interview with Mishake Muyongo, 15 February 1998.
[53]Interview with Mishake Muyongo, 17 February 1998.

registers were properly kept and inspected, and the magistrate's decision of not allowing the group of 190 DTA's supporters to vote remained legal.[54] In any case, had all those 190 voters been allowed to vote, and actually turned up to vote for DTA, it would only have changed the elections result in favour of DTA by increasing its seats from 2 to 3. Swapo would have still dominated the town council with a majority of 4 seats.

Swapo succeeded in its campaign to win a majority in the Katima Mulilo local authority with its effective message of development and economic prosperity. Its campaign was more organised and more attractive than DTA's. The role of the President was significant, because his rare visits to Katima Mulilo are always considered as important local events. Swapo also effectively employed the national agenda in the local elections. The inhabitants of Katima Mulilo were invited to share the national cake by voting for Swapo. On the other hand, the past five years of DTA's rule in the local council had not produced any visible development in the area. In the absence of real decision-making power at the local and regional level, DTA had in practice been powerless to invest in development. The only real improvements in the town have been a few new housing schemes, which have both been administered by national housing enterprises without the involvement of the local authorities.

In regard to ethnic voting in Katima Mulilo, it is impossible to verify any pattern in that respect. Katima Mulilo is an integrated town with people from all ethnic groups and subgroups. As a result, the voting pattern of a certain polling station does not indicate the political behaviour of any ethnic group. By analysing the results of the separate polling stations, it can only be concluded that Swapo's supporters dominated three out of five polling stations.[55]

Where have all the voters gone?[56]

In the whole country and contrary to the general belief immediately after the elections, Swapo did not succeed in the elections as well as was expected. Swapo's victory in Katima Mulilo and Windhoek was widely published and commented on in the media. But its loss in Opuwo, Henties Bay and four other towns was a surprise. The biggest defeat was probably the fact that in Ovamboland, people did not bother to go to the polls. Swapo could not realise its objective there of wiping out DTA from the town council of Oshakati and Ondangwa, but instead had to give one new seat to the DTA in Ongwediva.

Swapo's explanation for the low turnout was that people had been mixed up by the different voters' cards. It is, however, difficult to believe that if people were unsure of the documents, they would not have taken both of them with them, when they went to vote. Swapo also claimed that as polling day was not a public holiday, it prevented people from voting. A general observation, however, counteracts this statement, as people had time to go shopping and take care of their private affairs during working hours. The government had urged employers to exercise flexibility in allowing people to vote during office hours.[57]

A more reliable explanation for low turnout was the internal migration of people. It is estimated that the annual migration rate in Namibia is 20–30 per cent. Many people neglected their

---

[54]Interview with Director of Elections, Gerhard Tötemeyer, 25 February 1998.

[55]Even after the election, the political and ethnic rivalry in Caprivi was far from over. The tension in the region increased rapidly by the end of 1998. The former DTA leader Muyongo was accused of building up a secessionist military group to separate Caprivi from Namibia. He with some of his followers sought refuge from Botswana. Muyongo was later offered an asylum in a third country. After the incident the government of Namibia intensified its military presence in Caprivi which led to accusations of intimidation especially from the people belonging to the San ethnic group. The regional elections in Caprivi in December 1998 were largely boycotted by DTA followers. The exact details of the Caprivi incident have been difficult to trace and tension in the area continues.

[56]A headline in the *Namibia Plus* newspaper, 20 February 1998: 'Namibia in mourning – missing voters. Where have all the voters gone?'

[57]*New Era* 13–15 February 1998. The appeal was effective. The author witnessed an incident in Katima Mulilo, when Swapo organisers made a deal with an owner of a hotel to transport its workers to vote in shifts.

responsibility to re-register after changing their residential area. Yet, the most significant factor in the low turnout was a deliberate refusal to vote resulting from a number of reasons. To put it simply, for many, voting did not make sense anymore.

Before the elections, in urging people to go to the polls and cast their vote for Swapo, the party had acknowledged that its main rival was political apathy rather than the opposition parties. Slow economic growth and appalling social problems were believed to have frustrated even loyal supporters.[58] The pre-election period witnessed the most serious demonstrations by unemployed Swapo liberation army veterans, who had found it difficult to adapt to post-war society. The ex-combatants' frustration had been aggravated by a growing gap between the party's leadership and its rank and file membership. Another issue discrediting Swapo was its reluctance to deal with human rights violations during the war. In contrast to South Africa, where the government used the Truth and Reconciliation Commission to deal with and heal its past, Swapo has strictly refused to acknowledge its own past violations.[59] Thus those who were mistreated and killed remain as a sore wound in the nation's consciousness. The release of the book by a German pastor Siegfried Groth[60] has led to the creation of an organisation 'Breaking the Wall of Silence' (BWSM), which since its inception has been very vocal in keeping the issue in the public mind through publications and by organising seminars.[61]

The impact on the electoral system of the voting turnout and elections results was debated before and after the election in Namibia. The possibility of selecting between individual candidates, or a ward-based system was argued to have given the electorate a better opportunity to evaluate and assess their candidates' ability and performance.[62] On the other hand, the proportional system might have worked to the advantage of the minor parties and groups. Coupled with the low voter turnout, the smaller groups which managed to mobilise their voters to go to the polls gained seats when the large masses of Swapo's alleged supporters abstained from voting.

Low turnout in Swapo's stronghold areas

As already shown, the low turnout was most striking in the North, Swapo's stronghold area. Although there had been indicators that people were disappointed with the government and considering not voting, many thought that allegiance to the former liberation movement would overcome the present problems and that people would in the end go and vote for Swapo. That is why the absence of voters in some of the polling stations was a complete surprise to many, not least to the party leadership.[63] In the main centre of Oshana region, Oshakati, only 23 per cent of the people turned out to vote, scoring the lowest turnout in the whole country. The turnout was better, but not satisfactory, in the newly-proclaimed town Eenhana (54 per cent) and Outapi (42 per cent).

According to *The Namibian*, people in the North who were interviewed immediately after the elections said that they did not bother to vote because they felt the candidates were 'useless'. People claimed that the candidates lacked leadership qualities and the municipal offices provided poor services. They could not see what difference voting would make, because they still faced problems like poor education and unemployment. People commented that if they were not given a

---

[58]The burning issues in the Namibian economy can be listed as the following: high unemployment, unequal land distribution, high population growth, shortage of water and farming land as well as a narrow economic base (of largely mining and agriculture). See more in Namibian Economic Policy Research Unit (NEPRU) 1997.

[59]See, for a more detailed account of SWAPO's mistreatment of its dissidents, Leys and Saul 1994; Leys and Saul eds. 1995; Thiro-Beukes *et al.* 1986.

[60]Groth 1995. Rev. Groth worked among the Namibian refugees in Lusaka and witnessed incidents of mistreatment. In a direct NBC broadcast, President Nujoma declared that the book contained blatant lies and was written by somebody who did not have Namibia's interest at heart.

[61]The BWSM reprinted a report released by the then Political Consultative Committee (PCC) of ex-Swapo Detainees in 1989. It aimed at collecting sufficient evidence from the people involved before entering into a dialogue with Swapo.

[62]*The Namibian* 16 March 1998.

[63]The low turnout dominated public discussion in the press after the elections. *Allgemeine Zeitung* 19 and 23 February 1998; *Die Republikein* 19 February 1998; *The Namibian* 19 and 20 February 1998.

chance to cast a vote for a person instead of a party list, and if the municipal services were not improved, they would only vote in the presidential elections.[64] Despite people's dissatisfaction with the performance of the lower levels of the administration, the President still enjoyed a considerable amount of support.

On the other hand, some people also asked why they should vote again. They claimed that they had voted for Swapo already in three elections, and had not changed their mind. According to this logic, people thought that they would only need to go and vote if they changed their political allegiance. This shows that many, who had been denied the right to vote for almost all of their lives, had not yet understood the meaning of elections as a regular assessment of the performance of the elected representatives and consequently granting or denying their mandate to represent the electorate. The absence of effective education of voters has maintained the high level of ignorance.

Swapo's leadership held an internal meeting shortly after the elections and discussed the election results. After the meeting, Swapo local representatives were more willing to analyse the performance of their constituencies. Swapo's regional coordinator in the Oshana region repeated the official explanations of polling day not having been a public holiday. Furthermore, according to him, Namibia was following the worldwide pattern of voter apathy which is experienced in all societies after a few years of independence. 'When people finally have their freedom, what they strove for, the content of politics loses its meaning and people turn their attention to private affairs'.[65]

However, the Swapo representative also admitted that a great deal of apathy could be explained by the fact that people are not happy with the government's performance. According to him, a number of changes have not been made with the proper consultation of the people. The Swapo representative also argued that people are not well informed about the responsibilities of the local authorities and that they did not trust the local leaders. Based on this, he argued, they accused the local leaders of not solving the problems which they consider as within the local leaders' mandate, even though that is not the case according to the legislation.

The local reactions to election results also reflected the internal situation of Swapo and the party's relationship to the state institutions. Local Swapo leaders emphasised that as party representatives they see the problems arising rather from the government's performance and not from the party's policies. Before the elections, people's complaints were presented to the party leadership and to the government ministers, who instead of taking note were said to have ignored them. According to Du Pisani, Swapo, which is endlessly interested in the outward appearance of unity and solidarity, had in a recent Swapo Congress shown signs of internal disunity especially in regard to the elections of the Vice President. The influence of the party's democratic structures had receded *vis-à-vis* the growing autonomy of presidential power and the growing pre-eminence of the state bureaucracy. This has also limited internal party democracy, decreasing the powers of regional and local party structures in relationship to the all-powerful party executive (Du Pisani 1998). Yet, in the absence of well-established local and regional institutions and local apolitical civil servants to address people's needs and complaints, the party activists are the ones who have the closest interaction with the communities. For that reason they are approached by the people in need of services, the delivery of which actually belongs to the mandate of the local government. By the same token, the local Swapo activists also feel the burden of the criticism irrespective of whether it is targeted at the party or at the government. When the border between the party and the state becomes increasingly blurred, an ordinary citizen cannot tell the difference between the two organs, but directs criticism against the one that is closer to the community. Swapo party cadres, which are well connected with the community, then receive the sharpest brunt of complaints. The system of a party list in the election has exacerbated the unclear border between the government and the party, because some party cadres are imposed as candidates on the communities.

For the ruling party, the disillusion of its most reliable supporters in the North is a serious concern. With Regional Authority elections planned to be held at the end of 1998 and the presidential and parliamentary elections in 1999, Swapo cannot afford to lose its most loyal flock, especially if

---

[64]*The Namibian* 19 February 1998.
[65]Interview with Swapo Regional Councillor (Oshana region) Clemens Kashuupulwa, 4 March 1998.

arrangements are made to allow Nujoma to stand for a third term.[66] On the other hand, if the Swapo party's support is decreasing, it might be further encouraged to play a safe card, that is Nujoma, whose support is strong regardless of political affiliation. In other words, Swapo might be discouraged from contesting the presidential position in a situation where its supporters are deserting the party. Nujoma is considered to hold together different factions inside the party leadership, who are already struggling to safeguard their positions in the post-Nujoma era. The result of an internal contest is highly dependent on the behaviour of the Ovambo population.

Although Swapo has attempted to accommodate people from all ethnic groups on an equal basis, it cannot be denied that the core of its supporters are Ovambos.[67] Whilst people of Ovambo origin form the biggest ethnic group in Namibia, Swapo is highly dependent on this important voting bloc. The 1994 elections showed clearly that the four northern regions are unassailable SWAPO bastions (Diescho 1996, 13). In view of the fact that almost one-half of all registered voters live in those regions, even a majority in the rest of the country would not be enough to bring the opposition to power (Weiland 1996, 195). This demographic imbalance gives Swapo a built-in majority. Without Ovambo votes, no party can rule in Namibia. But on the other hand, this ethnic imbalance contributes to the fact that Swapo is sensitive about accommodating the needs of other ethnic groups for the purpose of avoiding the accusation of ethnic favoritism.

Swapo's position in the Northern regions has been so powerful that it has left little space for an opposition party to gain ground or independent political associations to emerge. As a general belief, politics in Ovamboland is still associated with the former liberation struggle. In that context, it is assumed that everyone is either with us (Swapo) or against us (DTA). Up until today, there has been no political issue or a group, which has been able to penetrate beyond that antagonism in the Swapo stronghold areas. It has been argued that, due to a historical legacy, the Swapo party seems to enjoy the highest political legitimacy among the Ovambo communities, which even exceeds the legitimacy of the Namibian Constitution. According to Director Gerhard Tötemeyer, the party is the highest political organ which other institutions – constitutional, legislative, other government institutions – fall upon.[68] To add to this, for many, the president of Swapo, Mr Nujoma, is the ultimate representative of this legitimacy. In this respect, the legitimacy of the political system is very personalised.

Local residents' associations

However, some other regions experienced the birth of the local groups, which participated in the elections. Initially, the legitimacy of those associations was denied because of their association

---

[66]According to the Namibian Constitution, the President can only serve for two five-year terms. Nujoma is presently on his second term. The Swapo Party announced after the extraordinary Congress in August 1998 that Nujoma's third term had already been decided, despite the opposition mainly by the press and academic community. Only a few days before the Congress, a veteran Swapo politician and Central Committee member, Ben Ulenga, resigned from his post as Namibia's High Commissioner to Britain in protest against the lack of discussion in the party over critical issues such as the third term, ex-combatants and Namibia's involvement in Congo unrest. His move signalled the first public criticism from a Swapo member, and was treated with silence by the party leadership. Although Ulenga seems to have made his resignation on a personal basis, he is supported by many Namibians critical of the Swapo executive's growing dominance and the party's administrative and procedural problems. *The Namibian* 27 August and 1 and 4 September 1998. President Nujoma himself has adopted publicly a rather passive role in regard to the third term. When asked about the possibility, he repeated his often indicated position that 'I will serve the people, if they so wish'. Interview with President Sam Nujoma, 14 February 1998.

[67]Discussion after the 1989 independence elections centred around 'tribalism' and ethnicity as explanations for voting behaviour, which, some argued, brought the victory to Swapo. Many analysts, however, had another opinion. The 1994 elections proved that Swapo drew support from all population groups, which does not, however, deny Ovambo's overwhelming association with Swapo. The reason why they vote Swapo cannot, though, simply be explained by their primordial sense of ethnicity, but also because of political socialisation through historical development. Many in Ovamboland consider themselves to be 'born-Swapo', which means that they have been involved in the struggle against colonialism. See Potgieter 1991; Lindeke *et al.* 1992; Soiri 1996.

[68]Interview with Director of Elections Gerhard Tötemeyer, 25 February 1998.

with certain minorities, especially the German- and Afrikaans-speaking white community in Swakopmund and Windhoek. Quite surprisingly, these elections showed that some of the associations attracted quite a substantial share of votes in their municipalities. Although the associations have many common characteristics, their diversity seems to be greater than the similarity in many respects.

The Electoral Act allows citizens' associations to register and take part in the elections in their respective municipalities. Eight different associations eventually emerged and nominated a full list of candidates in Gobabis (Omaheke region), Keetmanshoop (Karas region), Omaruru (Erongo region), Rehoboth (Hardap region), Swakopmund (Erongo region), Windhoek (Khomas region), Okahandja (Hardap region) and Otavi (Otjozondjupa region). Of these only the Swakopmund's Residents' Association and Windhoek local associations had participated in the 1992 elections. In Swakopmund, one of the candidates was voted onto the town council.[69] As a common approach, the local associations demanded more local autonomy and criticised the party-list system for centralising decision-making.[70] The associations levelled criticism against the incumbent town councillors for not looking after local interests and needs and for the existence of an ineffective administration.

Despite the popularity of their apolitical approach, the image of the independent associations suffered from the fact that they were tied to ethnic and racial particularities. Although the law forbids any association which is exclusively limited to a single race or ethnic group, the first associations consisted of mostly white residents who benefited from the all-white town administration and services under the apartheid era.[71] Furthermore, many of the residents' associations' core activists were not newcomers to the political arena. Many activists were previously members or supporters of the political parties, mainly of DTA, which have distanced themselves from the party for various reasons.[72] Although there is probably irreconcilable personal disagreement behind the phenomenon, a greater willingness to accommodate local initiatives and a change in the local structure of parties would have pre-empted residents' associations from emerging. On the other hand, people at the local level pointed out that the centralised manner of decision-making by the political parties had caused the establishment of the independent associations.

Before the elections, it was believed that the success of the residents' associations would depend on the way they can appeal to voters beyond party loyalty. Many considered their prospects rather bleak especially because of their stigma as whites-only interest groups. In the end, all of the associations managed to get a representative on their respective town council. Yet, a detailed analysis of their performance confirms the hypothesis of the limited support for some of these groups. The local residents' associations, whose core supporters were white minorities, did not manage to draw considerable support from outside their own communities. The eldest one, Swakopmund Residents' Association (SRA), managed to keep its one seat with a very small margin.[73] In Windhoek, the revised Local Community Association (LCA), under the leadership of the former DTA councillor, also barely managed to secure her seat.[74] In Omaruru, the association also won one seat, although it did not reach the quota.[75] The same applied to Keetmanshoop, where

---

[69]For the 1992 elections, three residents' associations put forward independent candidates to contest the municipal council in Swakopmund, Mariental and Windhoek.

[70]Interview with Margit d'Avignon (SRA), 8 November 1997.

[71]With the exception of the Rehoboth Ratepayers' Association which brought together coloured members of the community, or Basters. See below.

[72]For example, in Keetmanshoop the Concerned People's Association was initiated by a DTA councillor who had for a long time disagreed with his party leadership. The association was expected to draw votes from DTA rather than any other parties. This concerned the leadership of DTA. However, DTA leader Muyongo labelled them as outright racists and individualists who have failed to pursue their selfish interests through the party. Interview with Mishake Muyongo, 5 November 1997.

[73]The quota for a seat was 526 votes, while the SRA got 554 votes. The total number of votes in Swakopmund was 9,061 (51 rejected).

[74]Windhoek quota was 1,107, and the LCA got 1,210 votes. The total number of votes was 16,743 (127 rejected).

[75]The quota in Omaruru was 146, while the ORA got 106 votes. The total number of votes was 1,025 (3 rejected).

a former DTA councillor managed to secure his own seat with an independent Keetmanshoop Concerned People's Association (KCPA) ticket, by only 151 votes.[76] The Okahandja Ratepayers' Association, which was established after the postponement of the elections, gained one seat with a number of votes just exceeding the quota.[77] The votes seemed to have come from DTA, which accordingly lost one seat, while Swapo managed to maintain its four seats and a majority.

Common to all these associations is the fact that the leading figure is either an active member of the white minority community in the town and/or a former active member of DTA. This shows that in a polarised society like Namibia, any group, which is associated with a community integrated on the basis of colour, finds it very difficult to attract a following from the people of other colour. By the same token, these associations did not manage to attract a significant number of votes from Swapo or any other party. Their election success was a result of the low turnout, which produced low quotas.

Success in three towns

Three remaining local residents' associations differ considerably from the five previous ones. A unique case is the Rehoboth Ratepayers' Association (RRPA), whose history is closely connected with the history of a majority of the residents of Rehoboth, the Basters.[78] Before South Africa took control of Namibian territory, Rehoboth, which is only about 80 kilometers south of Windhoek, had a status of an autonomous 'republic', which had its own independent administrative structures.[79] Since autonomy was denied in 1923, the Baster community has struggled by all means to return self-government to Rehoboth. The Baster community is governed by a Kaptein, a traditional chief of Basters, who has been involved in the politics of the colony for decades. The late Kaptein Diergaardt was a founding member of several political parties among the Baster community. He originally resisted the South African regime, but finally chose the collaborative approach by leading his Rehoboth Liberal Party to the Multi-Party Conference in 1983. After independence, the Baster community sought to reinstall their autonomy. Their case was lost in the International Court of Justice, because the status of an autonomous town was in contradiction to the Namibian Constitution. The territory of Rehoboth was also reduced by the governmental delimitation commission, when the new regions and municipalities were proclaimed. This angered the Baster community, which had to (with resentment) receive new immigrants to the town after the apartheid settlement restrictions were stripped away.

The legal way to return autonomy of the town having been denied, the Baster community decided to try a political solution. They formed an election association to secure that local decision-making remained in the hands of the community. Although as stipulated in the Traditional Authorities Act of 1995, the traditional leaders are supposed to refrain from party politics, the late Kaptein Diergaardt was an active member of the newly formed RRPA. Swapo acknowledged the challenge of the new association and held one of the Presidential rallies in Rehoboth a week before the elections.

As expected, the RRPA won the majority of seats in Rehoboth, four altogether, DTA got two and Swapo only one.[80] Compared to the 1992 local authority elections, DTA was the biggest loser, having had four seats in the former council. Swapo lost two of its three seats. After having

---

[76]The total number of votes was 1,645 (16 rejected) in Keetmanshoop, giving a quota of 232 votes. The KCPO got 151 votes.

[77]The quota in Okahandja was 234 votes, while the ORPA got 279 votes. The total number of votes was 1,656 (19 rejected).

[78]The size of the Baster population was about 35,000 in the last census of 1985, when the population was still classified according to their ethnic origin. The Baster community is very homogenous and most of them live in Rehoboth. For the Basters themselves it is possible to distinguish another coloured person from a Baster on the basis of his/her birth and Afrikaans dialect.

[79]Rehoboth belongs to the Hardap Region, the council of which is dominated by DTA's four councillors against Swapo's two.

[80]In the 1998 local authority elections 9,166 voters were registered in Rehoboth, 3,343 of whom cast their votes. RRPA got the majority with 54 per cent, DTA came second with 24 per cent and Swapo got only 22 per cent of votes.

invested considerable resources in campaigning in Rehoboth, the result was a big defeat for Swapo. The separatism represented by RRPA irritates the Swapo government which advocates national unity. RRPA represents conservative and moralist values and at least in its rhetoric holds hostile sentiments against the other ethnic groups and their dominance of state affairs.[81] There exists a competition between different sources of identity in the Baster community, even though their sense of community and unity was formed to respond to the external threats from other communities during the colonial period.[82] The people of Rehoboth welcomed the good performance of the RRPA and hoped that their self-government would improve the well-being of all residents.[83] The RRPA was well aware of the fact that its victory in the elections might not automatically mean that more funds would be allocated to the development of the town. They were actually worried that the opposite would happen. Yet, the RRPA leaders were not prepared to change their policy for self-government in exchange for material benefits.

Another local association, which managed to get a majority in the town council, was Otavi Residents' Association (OTRA) in the central Otjozondjuba region. Since the 1992 regional and local authority elections, the Otjozondjuba region and the Otavi town council have been governed by Swapo.[84] In preparation for the 1997 local authority elections three parties, Swapo, DTA and UDF, initially registered a candidate list. The local Swapo supporters were not satisfied with the Swapo candidates, who were nominated without consulting the local Swapo members. As a consequence, the Swapo activists appealed to the party leadership to be allowed to select representatives of their own choice. They also argued that they were not satisfied with the performance of the incumbent councillors who had not kept in touch with the residents. After Swapo allegedly ignored the calls from the local activists, they used the postponement of the elections to register an independent association to take part in elections.

Their campaign, emphasising local needs regardless of the party political affiliation, proved to very successful among all communities and resulted in a majority of votes and four seats out of seven. Swapo collected the remaining seats, whereas the DTA and the UDF remained without seats. After the election, the association approached Swapo in order to work together for the improvement of the town and to set aside political differences.[85] Some of the leading figures of OTRA are still Swapo members and planned to vote for Swapo in the regional and national elections.[86] Their involvement in the local association was motivated by their commitment to improve their immediate environment according to the needs and ideas of the local residents, regardless of party political affiliation.

A similar development can be witnessed in Gobabis,[87] where Gobabis Residents' Association (GRA) also managed to gain 3 seats in the municipal council. The GRA was established approximately 2 years ago as a non-political platform to channel ideas and complaints to the town council. After it became clear that the incumbent town council did not react to these appeals, the association decided to participate in local authority elections. The membership of GRA is estimated to be around 500, and none of the activists have held a position in the municipal structures or any office in any political party. Yet, some have been connected with political parties but are now committed to the association.[88] The primary objectives of the Residents' Association were the promotion and protection of the general welfare of the residents of Gobabis, cooperation with all interest groups, organisations, local and regional authorities as well as with residents, and

---

[81]Interview with Kaptein Isaaks (RRPA), 28 February 1998.
[82]In the memorial service for the late Kaptein Diergaardt, Pastor de Klerk called on Rehoboth residents to distinguish when to be 'Basters first and Namibians later and vice versa'. *New Era* 16–19 February 1998.
[83]Interviews around Rehoboth, 8 and 28 February 1998.
[84]Swapo controls the Regional Council with four against DTA's two constituencies of the region, including the Otavi constituency. In the Otavi town council Swapo had five representatives and DTA two councillors.
[85]*New Era*, 23–26 February 1998.
[86]Interview with Marcus Damaseb (OTRA), 1 March 1998.
[87]Gobabis is the central town of the Eastern Omaheke region, which is one of the main areas of commercial and communal cattle farming activities. Gobabis also links Namibia to Botswana and serves as a supply centre for many western Botswanan farmers.
[88]Interview with GRA activists, Erwin H. Mukangi and Petrus Jacobus Derks van Zyl, 24 February 1998.

planning and maintenance of town structures and services in the most economic and effective way.[89]

Although Swapo managed to gain the majority of votes cast, the GRA gained the same number of seats, both winning three, in the town council. The remaining seat went to the DTA. UDF did not manage to gain any seats. Both Swapo and the DTA lost seats compared to the 1992 elections, because since then Swapo had held four seats against the DTA's three. The GRA activists themselves assumed that the bigger number of votes might have come from the white community although they managed to canvass support from all population groups in Gobabis.[90]

After the elections, the GRA invited all the other parties to a meeting to draw up a strategic development plan for the town. In the first council meeting, the GRA struck a deal with Swapo and shared the top positions in the council. That seemed to have been a surprise to many, because it was expected that the GRA would form an alliance with the DTA and gain control of all top positions. But in the spirit of the Election Manifesto, the GRA preferred broad cooperation in the town management involving all stakeholders in the community instead of trying to gather all power in its own hands.[91] Like the other residents' associations the GRA promotes rather conservative policies such as extending the moral and spiritual values of the inhabitants as well as combating 'social evils', including abortion, and also promotes Afrikaans as a means of communication in municipal affairs.

Introducing local agenda

Apart from the political victories, the main achievement of the local associations was the introduction of the local dimension to the Namibian political agenda. The country's political discussion is still dominated by the liberation struggle, which tends to determine political affiliation and voting behaviour. The local associations managed, for the first time, at least in some municipalities, to cross the traditional dividing line between Swapo and the opposition, and unite people under local interests. The associations were well aware of the stigma they were carrying as 'whites only' interest organisations, but decided to challenge the general distrust against whites in politics.[92] They demanded a new approach to politics, which would discard the antagonist politics and adopt a socio-economic programme for the well-being of all citizens regardless of their position in the past political conflict. The main parties, Swapo and DTA, lost their votes to the local associations, because they refused to include the local approach in their agenda. Frustration with the incompetence of the councillors selected on the basis of their party-political loyalty, and disagreements between the party leadership and local supporters over the suitable candidates, resulted in many activists and voters turning to the local associations.

Yet, the emergence of a local resident association was a rather limited phenomenon. It seems that the local associations have been a better breeding ground in the more established towns in the regions, which had already, under the apartheid regime, practised some form of municipal democracy, though segregated along colour lines. However, in the more remote regions, where the municipalities were only recently established, and where the residents lacked experience of local administration and decision-making, people voted for established political parties. In any case, the following five-year period will show how the local associations manage to fulfil their objectives and enhance local democratic culture. It will also be a challenge to the government structures to create communication channels and a working relationship with the associations, which are not under the political control of the ruling party.

---

[89]Election manifesto, Gobabis Residents Association.

[90]'We have 500 members from all communities. Accordingly we got 155 "extra" votes, which might have come mainly from the white section of the town'. Interview with Petrus Jacobus Derks van Zyl (GRA), 24 February 1998.

[91]In Keetmanshoop, for example, where the independent organisation holds a balance of power between Swapo and DTA, which both have three seats, the only councillor elected on the Concerned People's Organisations' ticket formed a majority alliance with DTA. He was elected Mayor of the town. He was, however, a former DTA councillor, who deserted the party because of dissatisfaction with his low position in DTA's candidate list.

[92]'Black people go to a white doctor, but why don't they trust a white politician?' Interview with Petrus Jacobus Derks van Zyl (GRA), 24 February 1998.

Conclusion: did the elections consolidate Namibian democracy?

The Namibian local authority elections were well managed and there were no irregularities. The election process was peaceful and the institutional arrangements for elections were professional. However, the ruling party Swapo used its administrative power to manage the elections to ensure its own success, firstly by maintaining the party list system and then by postponing the elections in order to avoid losing in Rundu. On the other hand, despite the criticism presented by the main opposition party DTA, the Electoral Commission remained impartial and objective.

Only nine years ago, Namibia experienced a transformation from authoritarian colonial rule into multi-party democracy. Thereafter the political system has been dominated by the ruling party Swapo. Namibian political culture is still polarised along pre-independence politics, which determines voting behaviour and political allegiances (Friedmann 1996).[93] Swapo has utilised its strong popular legitimacy in securing its position at all levels of administration and has not been able to transform itself from the movement of unity into a post-colonial political party, which could nourish diversity and open political culture in the new multi-party system.[94]

The Swapo leadership still practises the 'politics of command' from the top downwards. Apart from the party structures, the party tends to extend its command to other social spheres, such as the press and NGOs by directing them on what and how to carry out their tasks 'constructively'. A lot has been said and written about Swapo's internal disunity and prospects of a division among its ranks.[95] In fact, many analysts foresee that the only effective way of maintaining a functioning multi-party system with a strong opposition is through the splitting of Swapo as a unitary party.[96]

Weak and fragmented opposition

The attempted election pact between the DTA and the UDF failed because of personal disagreements. Serious merger talks have been blocked by the fact that both parties seem to regard mutual competition to be the biggest opposition party as more attainable than fighting against the gigantic ruling party. Yet, as admitted by one opposition politician, a realistic objective for a united opposition is to abolish Swapo's two-thirds majority in the legislature during the general election in 1999.[97] That would create a *de facto* multi-party democracy in Namibia by stripping Swapo of its power to change the Constitution if it so wishes.

On the other hand, it seems that at the local level opposition parties and even independent residents' associations have a real chance of gaining votes and getting elected to public office. If the opposition parties and residents' associations gain more legitimacy at the local level by performing their tasks satisfactorily, it might have a spill-over effect on the national level. Opposition parties would gain more legitimacy and the residents' associations would set an example that politics can also be a commitment to local affairs beyond party-political antagonism.

People's alienation from politics

These elections confirmed the observations that, despite a well-managed electoral institution, the most serious danger to the Namibian democratic political system and to Swapo's dominant

---

[93]A similar process seems to have taken place in South Africa after the democratic transition. Saul 1997.

[94]The national agenda has driven over ethnic minorities who have been alienated from the sources of power and whose demands for more regional and local autonomy have not been respected. For example, the government's plans to built a hydroelectric dam in the ancestral land of the so called Himbas in north-western Namibia met a lot of resistance among the local population. However, the government ignored their arguments and responded by banning their meetings and disrupting their assembly by force.

[95]See Dioooho 1996; Du Pisani 1996. The issue came up also in many interviews, which were conducted in Namibia in 1997 and 1998.

[96]Disunity in Swapo's ranks was more evident during the Swapo Congress in May 1997 when the vice-presidential contest divided congress delegates. Most serious challenge for SWAPO's unity originates from the process which was triggered by Ben Ulenga's resignation. After a lively political discussion, a new party, Congress of Democrats, was established in April 1999. Its leadership is multi-ethnic in composition and its members represent different walks of life. Large support is believed to come from the coloured community in Khomasdal, Windhoek, many of whom are former SWAPO supporters.

[97]Interview with Allen Liebenberg (UDF), 27 February 1998.

position is the emerging voters' apathy. Rare public comments from Swapo leaders acknowledge the problems witnessed in the Namibian political system. However, there is a tendency to explain the present situation by the antagonism still prevailing in the Namibian political culture. Racism and regional, ethnic and tribal schisms are phenomena still poisoning the democratic atmosphere. Accordingly, Swapo maintains that the concerted efforts at national reconciliation, which is the building block for the consolidation of social capital, are needed as well as confidence building (Angula 1998). Very little attention is paid to Swapo's own behaviour as an explanation of the absence of social capital.

Against this attitude, recent revelations of misconduct by some government ministers and top officials concerning the use of public funds have cast a further shadow on the party's image among the population. Enhancing the transparency of the public administration, increasing the accountability of the political office holders and stricter action against those who have committed criminal offences by exploiting their positions would prevent the total erosion of public morals related to political decision-making.[98] An alternative but undesirable vision is that Swapo, surviving from the syndrome of an all-powerful ruling party, will be tempted to maintain its dominant position by legislative, administrative and coercive power.

In search of a socio-economic political agenda

Instead of protecting its facade as a democratic and all-powerful party, Swapo should now seriously consider that the reasons for voters' apathy include its own shortcomings and adopt policies which would restore trust in the political system. As a basic guideline, it seems that people in Namibia do not respect democracy if their basic needs are not fulfilled. The election results in Katima Mulilo confirm the view that in Africa political behaviour is driven by an instrumental view of democracy. According to Ake, 'ordinary Africans do not separate political democracy from economic democracy or for that matter from economic well-being. They see their political empowerment, through democratisation, as an essential part of the process of getting the economic agenda right.' (Ake 1993, 239–244). Therefore, Swapo needs to embark on its socio-economic policies and improve its development efforts.

Another question is that, even if there were the political will to address socio-economic problems, would the Namibian government have realistic alternatives to address the deep-rooted structural problems – land allocation, market distortions, dependence on primary industry – within the framework of the neo-liberal policy it has adopted? A restructuring of the economic role of the state so that public decision-making makes sense for the welfare of the citizens should be necessary as much in Namibia as in other African countries which have lost their economic power as a result of economic globalisation and, by the same token, marginalisation of African economies (Laakso 1997a).

In any case, the present apathy witnessed in the elections is an indication of the fact that people's patience is running out. Swapo has succeeded in integrating the well-educated middle class into its clientelist network by allocating them the most wanted public sector jobs. However, in rural Ovamboland among the most disadvantaged communities, even the strong level of patronage Swapo commands among its 'loyal Ovambo flock' no longer drew people to the ballot boxes.

Civil society encourages participation

The most welcome phenomenon in these local authority elections was the emergence of the local residents' associations, which provided space for grass roots democratisation. They introduced the local dimension into Namibian politics, which seemed to have gained the people's support. The ability of grassroots activists and local political representatives to work for a common interest across party-political lines is presenting an alternative to what political decision-making is all about. The local residents' associations also represent a challenge to the former borderline between communities of a different colour. Yet, it should not be forgotten that a large number of

---

[98]NGOs have been active in raising issues related to misconduct and corruption in the public service. See for example Namibia Institute for Democracy and Konrad Adenauer Stiftung 1996a.

the people casting their votes for these associations acted only for the benefit of their minority right privileges, trying to secure their positions in their immediate environments.

Other civil society organisations have not been able to empower and mobilise Namibian people to take a more active part in public decision-making. The exception to the rule could yet come from the trade union movement, which has expressed a hardening criticism concerning the government's failure to address the socio-economic problems.[99] The trade unions, which are well established, organised and recognised by the government as a negotiation partner, could be significant in advocating better economic policies and keeping the progressive agenda alive. Yet, their leaders rely on a co-option strategy and the Central Union has maintained its affiliation with the ruling party. As a result, the trade union caucus has rather acted as a watchdog inside the party and managed to stop some of the most outrageous enrichment exercises the party leaders would have otherwise been guilty of. In regard to the post-Nujoma era of Swapo, the leftist faction of Swapo led by the trade union caucus is observed with concern by those who value the internal unity of the party above all other options. In any case, the trade union caucus will play a role in the competition for Nujoma's successor.

The role of traditional and ethnic identities

In regard to ethnic voting and the role of the traditional authorities who are the advocates of the ethnic identities in the electoral competition, it seems that the Traditional Authorities Act passed in 1995 has not cleared up the situation totally. Irrespective of the Act, some traditional leaders are still actively involved in politics. The ruling party itself does not have a clear record either, because the Nama leader, Hendrik Witbooi, was re-elected as Swapo's vice-president and holds the office of Deputy Prime Minister of Namibia. At the local level, the Rehoboth Ratepayers' Association is the most evident example of the involvement of the traditional leaders in politics. The Baster community is, however, a tiny and unique example and should be considered as such.

More relevant in the nation-wide perspective are the ethnic allegiances in the Caprivi region which have played a significant role in political affiliation. However, the economic agenda was dominant in Caprivi in these elections. The alleged political power of the Herero population is divided along party-political divisions and the three parties – the DTA, the DCN and SWANU – have competed for their loyalty. Yet, a big part of the Herero-speaking population votes for Swapo as well. In regard to the Ovambo-speaking population, their loyalty belongs to Swapo. Yet, as witnessed in these local elections, no loyalty is blind, if the party's performance is not satisfactory. To sum up; no clear ethnic voting pattern can be identified in Namibian voting behaviour during these 1998 elections.

The role and legitimacy of the traditional authorities have also proved to have been significant after independence, because the elected structures at the local and regional level have been too weak and uninstitutionalised although councillors were chosen for the first time in 1992 (Keulder 1997). In the light of the low voter turnout at these elections in 1998, some of the councils clearly lack popular support. As a consequence, it may mean that the major source of legitimacy is still vested in the traditional leaders. The traditional authorities, on the other hand, are also dependent on centrally allocated funds and all the recognised chiefs are on the government's payroll, because their right to raise funds among their subjects has been denied by new legislation. The Traditional Authorities Act limits the role of the traditional leaders to maintaining the cultural and traditional values of the community. There are plans, though, that they should play a role in land allocation as advisors to the local land boards, which consist of elected representatives.

Lack of participatory democratic culture

The future of the Namibian political system depends on popular demand for democracy. Democracy cannot be eaten, but do Namibians regard it as a precondition for getting the economic agenda right? Analysing electoral participation as an indication of the status of the democracy, Namibia's good record suffered a big loss in the 1998 local elections. A turnout of 34 per cent

---

[99] A few days after the elections the teachers voiced their demands for new staff norms and better working conditions and staged mass demonstrations in many Namibian towns.

dropped to less than half compared to the previous general election in 1994 (76 per cent) and to regional and local elections in 1992 (82 per cent). In other words, in the absence of a proper economic agenda, people did not regard the elections as a means of exercising their democratic will. None of the many parties, with the exception of some of the local residents' associations, seemed to have addressed effectively enough the basic interests of the electorate. At the same time, it has to be kept in mind that Swapo did gain 60 per cent of the votes cast, which shows its dominance in the Namibian political system.

Namibians still value the elections as an important institution and appreciate their long-awaited democracy and democratic institutions. A survey among university students indicates that the public institution enjoying most popular support and sympathy in Namibia is the president. In general, the students are in support of public institutions and democratic dispensation, but the parliament and the lower levels of administration including local councils do not seem to be regarded as being as important as the strong support for presidentialism (Keulder 1998, 61).

Another aspect of Namibian democracy is the absence of the idea of participation and self-government. In short, as the 'Report on Focus Group Research in Namibia: Popular Perceptions of Political Institutions' (National Democratic Institute for International Affairs 1996) indicates, people have little sense of personal empowerment or involvement in their government. There are several reasons for this, and many of them have to do with the apartheid regime, which violently discouraged people from participating in public affairs. Another significant reason is the culture of patronage of the ruling party, which allowed little space for individual and pluralistic initiatives to emerge. As the student survey also shows, although there is a strong commitment to a liberal political dispensation, Namibian society lacks a consistent set of liberal values. The students have a liberal political disposition but a conservative social one.[100] As a result there is an inconsistent mixture of liberal and conservative value systems ('modernity' against 'traditionalism') which is characteristic of a society in transition (Keulder 1998, 56).

In spite of the democratic and functioning legal institutions, people lack the capacity to exercise their democratic rights. Naturally, learning democratic practices is a long process in a society where they were denied for such a long time. Yet, it may happen that by the time people learn to appreciate democracy, there will be little of it remaining. Democracy is not equal to independence. Also, democratic government follows different rules of the game from the liberation movement. These rules include active citizens, who are able and willing to utilise their democratic rights and responsibilities.

---

[100]The students' attitudes and beliefs towards social issues commonly associated with a liberal social disposition such as legalised abortion, premarital sex, racially mixed marriages, pornography, legalised prostitution, gay and lesbian rights indicate rather conservative trends. The majority is in favour of strict discipline. Keulder 1998.

Appendix: Interviews conducted in Namibia

Mrs Margareth Abrahams,
Town Councillor (DTA) Keetmanshoop
Windhoek, 31 October 1997
Mr Kari Alanko, Counsellor
Embassy of Finland
Windhoek, 9 February 1998
Mrs Margit d'Avignon, Chairperson
Swakopmund Residents Association
Swakopmund, 8 November 1997
Mr Eric Biwa, Member of Parliament (UDF)
Windhoek, 7 November 1997
Mr Marcus Damaseb, Mr Gerson Gamibeb,
Mr Emmanuel Kauendje, Mr Gottfried
Ubugaeb
Otavi Residents Association
Otavi, 1 March 1998
Mr Clement Daniels, Lawyer
Legal Assistance Centre
Windhoek, 29 October 1997
Mr A.N. Elago, Deputy Director
Directorate of Elections
Windhoek, 13 October 1997
Mr J. Geingob, National Organiser
Namibia National Teachers' Union, NANTU
Windhoek, 5 November 1997
Mr Likando Gilt, student
University of Namibia
Katima Mulilo, 15 February 1998
Ms Lori-Ann Girvan, Programme Officer
USAID
Windhoek, 27 February 1998
Mr Hans-Dieter Göthje,
Regional Councillor (DTA), Erongo Region
Swakopmund, 8 November 1997
Mr Ranga Haikali, Secretary General (acting)
National Union of Namibian Workers
(NUNW)
Windhoek, 3 December 1997
Mr Peter Haitembu and Mr John Nghikongwa,
SWAPO officers
Eenhana, Ohangwena region
17 October 1997
Ms Josephine N. Hamutwe,
Member of National Council (SWAPO)
Ohangwena, 3 March 1998
Dr Lazarus Hangula, Deputy Director
Multidisciplinary Research Centre, UNAM
Windhoek, 27 October 1997
Mr Peter Ilonga, Secretary General,
Member of Parliament (SWAPO)
Namibia Public Workers Union (NAPWU)
Windhoek, 27 November 1997
Dr Nickey Iyambo, Minister of Regional
and Local Government and Housing

Windhoek, 28 November 1997
Mr Colin Kamehozu, Secretary General
Namibian National Student Union (NANSO)
Windhoek, 2 December 1997
Mr Daniël Hangula Kamho, Mayor (SWAPO)
Swakopmund, 9 November 1997
Mr David Jakobus Isaaks, Acting Kaptein
Rehoboth Rate Payers Association
Rehoboth, 27 February 1998
Mr Yrjö Karinen, Ambassador
Embassy of Finland
Windhoek, 13 October 1997
Mr Clemens Kashupulwa, Regional
Councillor (SWAPO)
Oshakati, Oshana region
16 October 1997 and 4 March 1998
Mr Moses Katjiuongua, Member of
Parliament (DCN)
Windhoek, 13 November 1997
Mr Joseph Kauandenge, President
and Mr Clemens Tuahuku, National
Organiser
Namibia Movement for Independent
Candidates
Windhoek, 12 November 1997
Mr Christiaan Keulder, Researcher, UNAM
Windhoek, 7 November 1997
Mr Theunis Keulder, Executive Director
Namibia Institute for Democracy
Windhoek, 29 October 1997 and 26
February 1998
Mr Richard Klein, Programme Officer
National Democratic Institute for
International Affairs
Windhoek, 5 March 1998
Mr Allen Liebenberg, UDF Secretary General
Windhoek, 3 November 1997 and 27
February 1998
Mrs Gwen Lister, Editor in Chief
Namibian
Windhoek, 25 November 1997
Mr David Lush, journalist
Windhoek, 23 February 1998
Mr Louis Mazel, First Secretary of Embassy
American Embassy
Windhoek, 11 February 1998
Mr Libertus U. Mbaumba,
Executive Secretary (SWANU of Namibia)
Windhoek, 10 February 1998
Mr Erwin H. Mukangi and Petrus Jacobus
Derks van Zyl,
Gobabis Residents' Association
Gobabis, 24 February 1998
Mr Michael Mukwame, Chief Reporter: TV
news, Election Desk

Namibian Broadcasting Corporation (NBC)
Windhoek, 27 October 1997
Mr Rajah Munamava, Editor
New Era
Windhoek, 12 November 1997
Mr Mishake Muyongo, DTA President,
Member of Parliament
Windhoek, 5 November 1997
Katima Mulilo, 15 and 17 February 1998
Mr Phil Ya Nangolo, Executive Director
National Society for Human Rights
Windhoek, 28 October 1997
Mr Samson Ndeikwila, Chairperson
Breaking the Wall of Silence Movement
Windhoek,10 November 1997
Mr Immanuel Ndilimondi, Town Councillor
(DTA)
Oshakati, 22 October 1997
Mr J K Nghihepa, Town Clerk
Oshakati, 21 October 1997
His Excellency President Sam Nujoma,
Republic of Namibia (SWAPO)
Katima Mulilo, 14 February 1998
Ms Dawn Oxenham, Manager
Ichingo Chobe River Lodge
Katima Mulilo, 13 March 1998

Mr Hifikepunye Pohamba,
SWAPO Secretary General, Minister of
Fisheries
Windhoek, 26 November 1997
Dr Hetty Rose-Junius, Chairlady
Local Community Association Windhoek
Windhoek, 12 February 1998
Mrs Elizabeth Shiyagaya,
Deputy Mayor (SWAPO), Lüderitz
Windhoek, 31 October 1997
Mr Max Silas, teacher
Namibia Institute for Democracy
Oshakati, 22 October 1997
Mr Nico Smith, Administrative Secretary
(DTA)
Windhoek, 29 October 1997
Ms Ulla Ström, Ambassador
Embassy of Sweden
Windhoek, 24 February 1998
Dr Gerhard Tötemeyer, Director of Elections
Windhoek, 27 October 1997 and
25 February 1998
Mr Bisey Uirab, Manager Personnel/
Administration
Legal Assistance Centre
Windhoek, 28 October 1997

9

A Transition to Nowhere
Electoral Politics in Nigeria during the Abacha Years 1993–8

ADEBAYO O. OLUKOSHI

Introduction

The period since the late 1980s has witnessed a significant growth in academic and policy interest in electoral politics in Africa. This development has gone on side-by-side with the formal demise of many one-party and military regimes on the continent and their replacement by multi-party systems that are supposed to give content and meaning to the new era of electoral pluralism. The new industry that is developing around electoral politics has grown in various inter-related directions. At one level, scholarly publication on the subject of elections in Africa has been undergoing a boom since the early 1990s (see the extensive review in Cowen and Laakso 1997a or 1997b). Academic interest in this regard has been focused, among other things, on the politics of the decline of one-party/military rule; the domestic and international factors accounting for or facilitating the return to multi-partyism; the dynamics of party formation; the mode, pace, and content of constitutional reform, including especially the host of (sovereign) national conferences held across Francophone and Lusophone Africa; the institutions that have been established to manage the transition from one-party/military rule to multi-party politics; the practice of electioneering, including the issue of the extent to which a level playing-field has been established for all contestants; the role of the mass media and civil society groups in the reform process; the issues and personalities at the heart of the political process; the socio-economic conditions within which electoral/political reforms have occurred and the extent to which they hinder or enable the reform process; the role of donor political conditionality in encouraging/hampering political change; and what the changes that occur between first and subsequent multi-party elections portend for democratic consolidation.

At another level, the business of international election monitoring has also emerged as a distinct area of policy and activist interest involving international and local NGOs, inter-state regional organisations such as the Organisation of African Unity (OAU), and international agencies like the United Nations (UN), the Commonwealth, and the recently-established International Institute for Democracy and Electoral Assistance (International IDEA). Furthermore, the training of African electoral officials/civil society activists in the 'art' of managing/observing elections has become integrated into the agenda of many international non-governmental groups and the development co-operation programmes of some of the leading donors. Exercises are also being promoted whereby the nature of the electoral system in various African countries, including especially those that have recently emerged from situations of conflict, is assessed for its suitability to the task of national reconstruction and power-sharing. In this regard, policy debates have been raging on the merits and demerits of the British first-past-the-post electoral system as compared, for example, to the proportional representation system. Donors have also immersed themselves in discussions on the merits and demerits of parliamentary as opposed to presidential systems of government, and federalist as opposed to centralist modes of administration.

Basic Pitfalls of Prevalent Efforts at Understanding Elections in Africa

Without doubt, the increased focus on elections as an exercise that is central to the effort at promoting democracy in Africa has served the useful purpose of illuminating some of the progress that has been made, and the difficulties that continue to dog the process of political reform on the continent. However, there are also several other important ways in which our understanding is beclouded by the dominant approaches to interpreting the role and place of elections in the struggle for meaningful or lasting political change in Africa. Some scholars, for example, have expressed justifiable concern that there is an uncritical tendency first, to isolate and then, simplistically to equate the fact of 'free' and 'fair' elections with the dawn of a new democratic era. Because of this, the advantages that could have been gained from a more sober, less hasty understanding of democracy as a *process* rather than as an *episode* is lost. Thus, many African countries where authoritarian political practices are still widespread are declared 'democratic' on the basis of the fact that they have held multi-party elections. The notions of '*democratie tropicalisée*' or 'pro forma' democracy that flow from this approach have been rejected by a host of African scholars who, instead, make the case for an understanding of democracy as a process that entails much more than intermittent electoral episodes. They also insist on the need for a careful study of the African state form and the extent to which it has been reformed to make it both representative and accountable in a framework in which basic rights are respected and political pluralism is upheld. Within this context, electoral pluralism becomes only one of the important elements necessary for ensuring the establishment of a state that is both representative of and accountable to the citizenry (Olukoshi ed. 1998).

For other critics of the one-sided electoralism that is rife in policy and academic circles, what is worrisome, especially with regard to the integrity and sustainability of on-going efforts at political reform, is the fact that, in many countries, elections not only depend on foreign/external certification for their international recognition but can only take place with donor financial support. In some cases, even the political parties whose activities are indispensable to a sustainable democratic outcome are unwholesomely dependent on external sources of finance in order to be able to operate. Attention has been drawn to several dimensions of the distorting consequences of this *donorisation* of a central element of the African political system for the transition to democracy on the continent, not least in terms of the potential conflicts that could arise between a prevailing system of international legitimation and the demands of internal legitimation that are closely tied to local history and grow out of deep-rooted domestic considerations/aspirations. Here again, the case has been made for the political reform process to be more fully anchored in domestic political processes, structures and actors/actresses as the only sure way to ensure its long-term sustainability. Such questions as the funding of elections, electoral bodies and political parties are too central to be left to external actors alone to determine (Mkandawire 1996).

Objectives and Underlying Assumptions of the Nigerian Study

At a general level, our interest in this chapter, based on the Nigerian experience, goes well beyond the limiting consequences of the local and international cults of electoralism, as well as the well-founded concerns that have been expressed about excessive donorisation, to include the related problem of the enthronement of technical perspectives at the expense of political ones and the failure to grasp the role of elections both as an instrument of regime and state legitimation and de-legitimation. More specifically, we are keen to understand the ways in which elections serve as an instrument for the confirmation or alteration of all or specific aspects of existing power relations in the Nigerian political system, whether these relations be actively contested or not and the alteration be radical or mild. The elements that make up the power relations in any given polity are central to the way in which political questions are tabled and sorted out. These different elements will undergo shifts from time to time in terms of their saliency to the political struggles at hand. It is our argument here that a clear understanding of the various constituent elements of the power relations in a given polity is indispensable to an understanding of the politics of its electoral process.

There are various dimensions to power relations in contemporary Nigeria. These dimensions often express themselves in terms of the overlapping, cross-cutting contradictions that have been built into the national political process and which pitch one group against the other with varying degrees of intensity. They include the struggle between the rich and the ever-growing army of the working and unemployed poor; the conflict between the bearers of a vision of autonomous national development and the forces of local and international capitalism; the political competition among the different geo-political zones in the country (broadly, north versus south and within this east versus west, west versus north, and east versus north); intra-regional contradictions (such as those between the middle belt and the emirate north, the minorities of the oil delta and the Igbos of the south east, and among the minorities themselves); the closely related tensions within and among the diverse ethnic groups that make up the country; the tensions between ethnic minorities and majorities; the contradictions between rural and urban Nigerians; the widening gulf between chiefs/emirs and their 'subjects'; the contradictions between Christians and Moslems; gender- and generationally-based disparities that display varying degrees of rigidity in different parts of the country; and the contradictions within and between military society and civil society. The way in which these contradictions alone and in combination play themselves out is central to an understanding of the nuances of politics in contemporary Nigeria (Mustapha 1986).

The underlying thesis that informs our argument here is that where elections confirm the existing balance of power relations and where those relations are relatively or temporarily *settled* in the sense of not themselves being the subject of active, radical or popular contestation, the results tend, on the whole, to confer legitimacy on the state form and the authority structure on which it rests. This is not to say that the results themselves may not be disputed in their details or that the incumbent government will not face serious challenges from its electoral opponents. The important thing is that such contestations do not (ultimately) so question the legitimacy of the state itself as to completely undermine the political system. But where the underlying power relations are not settled in the sense that they are actively contested and elections either fail to deliver the change that some groups are fighting for or result in the radical alteration of existing power relations along lines that some groups do not want to see, it can be expected that the outcome will be hotly disputed and, depending on the responsiveness of the political system, might result in the legitimacy of not just the governmental system but also the state being called into question. Central to this formulation is the extent to which the various structural and non-structural contradictions that are built into a polity overlap and get played out; it is also tied to the perceptions of various groups as to the capacity of the existing political system to accommodate their concerns.

In much of Africa, the bitterness that tends to accompany elections has to do with the fact that various aspects/dimensions of power relations are mostly not yet 'settled' and electoral exercises could carry zero-sum consequences where they result in shifts in all or some of the overlapping power equations that were built into the fabric of politics from the late colonial period. This should not be surprising: although considerable energy has been invested in the task of nation-building, a stable national political equilibrium that could underpin the quest for unity and development in multi-ethnic nation-states has not yet been achieved in most countries. Indeed, this task has been compounded by the deepening social polarisation in many countries as manifested, for example, in the ever-growing gap between a rich and powerful minority, on the one hand, and the growing army of poor and marginalised people, on the other. When this is taken together with the precarious economic foundations on which the political system in most countries rests and the fact that the state and access to it are central to the definition of individual and group opportunity, then we will begin to understand why elections could mean so much to contestants and their constituencies (Ake 1996).

We argue that recent electoral experience in Nigeria has been aimed at altering central aspects of the power relations in the polity, with the most important element in this process being the balance between the military, on the one hand, and the politicians and civil society, on the other. In this endeavour, an attempt was made during the 1980s and 1990s by incumbent military regimes to employ elections as the principal instrument for effecting a decisive shift in the balance of power between civilians and the military. Significantly, this effort was undertaken at a time when the other contradictions in the polity were at a new height, fired by the prolonged economic crisis which the country has been faced with since the early 1980s and which created an environment of intensified competition for resources and power (Adekanye 1995; Osaghae 1996; 1998; Egwu

1998). Of particular importance to the military-supervised electoral politics of the 1990s are those contradictions that expressed themselves, in an overlapping manner, in ethnic, north-south regional, minority-majority and rich-poor terms. As we will attempt to show in this chapter, the push by the military to use the electoral system to cling on to power both profited from these contradictions but also ultimately foundered on their account.

The effort at using elections to alter important pillars of politics in Nigeria represented a new dimension to electoral politics in a country where the act of voting has always been dogged with deep-seated controversies that have served, ultimately, to undermine the episodes of civilian, elected governance that the country has experienced. It is, therefore, a central premise of this chapter that although regular elections may constitute an essential defining feature of any political system that claims or aspires to be democratic, those exercises could also become important building blocks in the consolidation of political exclusion and authoritarianism. This premise immediately broaches the question of regime type, the form of the state, and the nature of state–society relations in any effort to understand the significance of elections in the political development of African countries. In the Nigerian case, it leads us to a discussion of the ways in which a programme of transition to 'democracy' on the basis of scheduled elections is integral to the development of a strategy for the re-composition of a key pillar of the basis of power in the country in a direction that was, in design and content, authoritarian and repressive whilst appearing, on the surface, to respond to the international movement towards political reform.

Scope of the study

This case-study of electoral politics in contemporary Nigeria covers the experience from November 1993 to June 1998 when the military government headed by the late General Sani Abacha was in power. Following its rise to power on 17 November 1993 through a military *coup d'état*, the Abacha junta, under intense international and local pressures, held five elections as part of a three-year 'transition' programme to 'democracy'. This was in spite of the fact that the regime had spent its first year in office refusing to discuss its plan for returning Nigeria to elected governance beyond vague promises which critics felt were meant to buy the junta time to consolidate itself in power and, thus, be better able to determine the pace and content of whatever transition programme it decided to unfold (Osaghae 1998). The elections that were held included those for a constitutional conference that was charged with drawing up a new constitution, the country's local government councils (first on a non-party and then on a party basis), the 36 state houses of assembly, and the National Assembly. Only the elections into the offices of governors and the President were still outstanding when news came of General Sani Abacha's sudden death on 8 June 1998. With the death of the general also came the death of the entire transition programme over which he had presided; so discredited was the programme and the elections that were held under it that General Abacha's successor, General Abdulsalam Abubakar, had no option than to bow to local and international pressures to cancel them and start the quest for political reforms afresh.[1] Both in a literal and metaphoric sense, the Abacha transition programme had been a transition to nowhere.

Understanding the Abacha Transition Programme: The immediate political context

The gathering storm of internal opposition and international condemnation

The decision of the Abacha regime to convene its first elections in May 1994 was not one which it took voluntarily. Instead, the decision was forced upon it by steadily building local pressures for the government to unfold its political agenda in a more concrete manner nearly six months after it

---

[1] *Post Express* 22 July 1998.

came to power. The most decisive factor in the domestic pressures that were piled on the regime came from the activities of the civil and political society groups at the centre of a renewed effort to push for the recognition of the results of the 12 June 1993 presidential elections that had been annulled by the Babangida military administration, a government in which General Abacha was a key player. M.K.O. Abiola, who was the winner of the annulled presidential elections, emboldened by the growing popular agitation for the re-validation of his mandate, undertook consultations with a range of politicians and activists across the country as part of the spirited campaign which he decided to embark upon against the Abacha regime.[2] At the same time, some of General Abacha's erstwhile military colleagues, most notably the freshly-retired Brigadier David Mark, who played a major role in the overthrow of the interim government of Ernest Shonekan, alerted the nation to Abacha's determination to cling on to power at any cost and against the agreed plan on the basis of which other officers supported his seizure of power.[3] The regime, therefore, hastily called its first elections primarily to scuttle the momentum that was gathering in support of Abiola's claim that he was the legitimately-elected President of Nigeria and to appear to discredit Brigadier Mark's accusation that a hidden political agenda was in the making to perpetuate Abacha in office until 1999 at a minimum. Those elections were for participation in a constitutional conference whose creation was initially promised on 17 November 1993 in Abacha's maiden speech after he seized power but which was not inaugurated until 27 June 1994.[4]

It was, however, only after the hanging of Ken Saro-Wiwa and eight other Ogoni/minority rights activists on 10 November, 1995 that the Abacha junta, now under considerable international pressure, including the suspension of the country from the Commonwealth, unfolded a programme of 'transition' to civil rule that was expected to end with the inauguration of an elected president in October 1998 (see Figure 9.1 for the transition programme as it was first spelt out and the subsequent amendments it underwent). Interestingly, by the time of the execution of Saro-Wiwa and his colleagues, the alliance which Abacha struck with sections of the populist political elite had clearly failed to deliver regime stability and legitimacy to the junta. Upon seizing power from Ernest Shonekan, Abacha had constituted a cabinet which had a number of prominent politicians and activists closely associated with the 'progressive' current in Nigerian politics. In doing this, his hope was that their relative political credibility would be translated into credibility for his regime and that this would be sufficient to take the heat out of the clamour for the restoration of the results of the 12 June 1993 presidential elections. It was a strategy that worked for a short period but which also very quickly ran its course as evidenced by the fact that the government was to find itself confronted by opposition on several fronts over the period between May and December 1994.[5]

At one level, and as noted earlier, there were the spirited challenges from the Abiola-led section of the civilian political elite, including leading figures from the Third Republic National Assembly which Abacha had dissolved in November 1993. This group was intent on undoing the dissolution of the Third Republic and pushing for the confirmation of the 12 June 1993 presidential elections which Abiola had been poised to win. Apart from Abiola himself, it had in its ranks several prominent legislators from the dissolved national assembly as well as a number of the elected civilian governors who had been sacked following the *coup d'état* which Abacha led. Indeed, Ameh Ebute, the president of the dissolved senate, went so far as to contest the right of General Abacha to disband the National Assembly; following a meeting with a group of senators in Lagos, he issued a statement in June 1994 declaring the Abacha junta illegal and notifying his colleagues that the Senate stood reconvened. At the same time, amidst the intensification of his campaign to have his electoral victory recognised, M.K.O. Abiola proceeded with arrangements to have himself inaugurated as President. He did this symbolically on 11 June 1994 at a secret assembly in Epetedo, Lagos and his speech also contained a proclamation reconvening the dissolved National Assembly and restoring all elected officials to the positions they occupied before General Abacha's takeover.[6]

---

[2]*Newswatch* 10 July 1995.
[3]*Newswatch* 20 April 1994 and 4 May 1998; *Economist Intelligence Unit* 3rd quarter 1994.
[4]Human Rights Watch 1996a; Economist Intelligence Unit 1996; Osaghae 1998 *Economist Intelligence Unit* 3rd Quarter 1994.
[5]Agbu 1998; Human Rights Watch 1996; *Daily Times* 1 October 1995.
[6]*Newswatch* 10 July 1995 and 4 September 1995; Agbu 1998.

Figure 9.1: The transition time-table of the Abacha regime in its original and amended versions

Original Version (Released on 1 October 1995)	Amended Version (Released on 2 July 1997)
Date	Date
4th Quarter 1995 Approval of Draft Constitution (NB: This was not implemented until Abacha's death)	
2nd Quarter 1996 Creation of new states and local governments (NB: This was delayed by about four months)	
4th Quarter 1996 Elections into local government councils (NB: This only took place in March 1997)	
3rd Quarter 1997 State Assembly Elections	3rd Quarter 1997 Local Government By-elections arising from ward adjustments and of litigation to be held in July 1998
4th Quarter 1997 Governorship Elections (NB: This was postponed to 1998)	4th Quarter 1997 State Assembly Elections on 6 December 1997
2nd Quarter 1998 National Assembly Elections (This was postponed to the Fourth Quarter of 1998)	2nd Quarter 1998 National Assembly Elections on 25 April 1998
3rd Quarter 1998 Presidential Elections	3rd Quarter 1998 Governorship and Presidential Elections on 1 August 1998
4th Quarter 1998 Swearing in of President and National Assembly	4th Quarter 1998 Swearing in of President and National Assembly on 1 October 1998

Source: *The Guardian* (Lagos) Thursday 3 July 1997; *Thisday* Thursday 3 July 1997.

At another level, an assortment of pro-democracy civil-society activists, including trade unionists in the strategic oil sector, who were unhappy with the brazen disregard by the military for the democratic aspirations of Nigerians, decided that, nearly one year after it seized power, the time had come to confront the Abacha junta head-on in order to dislodge it through popular mass action. The Campaign for Democracy (CD), an umbrella grouping of pro-democracy groups in the country which played a key role in General Babangida's downfall after he announced the annulment of the June 1993 presidential elections, once again took on a front line role in organising Nigerians, particularly in the Lagos area, for civil disobedience and demonstrations against the Abacha regime. As in the period from June to November 1993 when it coordinated opposition first to General Babangida and then to the puppet interim government to which he handed over power, the CD was joined in its campaign by some of the most powerful trade unions in the country, especially the National Union of Petroleum and Engineering Workers (NUPENG) and Petroleum and Engineering Senior Staff Association of Nigeria (PENGASSAN). Their joint action brought the country into a state of paralysis between June and September 1994.[7]

Furthermore, the minority oil-producing areas of the country were becoming ever more restive, nowhere more so than in Ogoniland where Ken Saro-Wiwa and his colleagues in the Movement for the Survival of the Ogoni People (MOSOP) had succeeded in mobilising popular opinion against the military government as an unrepresentative and remote organ working in league with Shell and other oil companies to undermine the livelihood of the oil minorities of the country. The campaigns of MOSOP captured the popular imagination of the oil-producing areas of the country even as it was becoming increasingly well-known internationally. MOSOP had, through its direct actions of daily demonstrations and occupation of oil production sites, succeeded in chasing Shell

---

[7]*Newswatch* 10 July 1995 and 4 September 1995; Agbu 1998.

out of Ogoniland; its charter of demands which called for massive compensation to the Ogoni by Shell and the Nigerian government for the despoliation of their environment and the destruction of their livelihood struck a chord with many in the other oil-producing parts of the country. In time, the entire Nigerian oil delta was gradually transformed into a delta of discontent. This discontent fed into wider challenges against the Abacha regime across the country and resulted in the formation of an assortment of political movements (see Figure 9.2) with varying agenda for the reform of the entire basis of Nigerian federalism in order to satisfy their competing visions for the creation of a more representative national political system.

Figure 9.2: Some of the main opposition associations formed to resist the Abacha junta

Name	Geo-Political Base
Afenifere	South-Western Nigeria;
National Democratic Coalition (NADECO)	National
National Liberation Council of Nigeria (NALICON)	Abroad
Mpoko Igbo	South-Eastern Nigeria
Movement for the Survival of the Ogoni People (MOSOP)	The Oil Delta; Abroad
Eastern Mandate Union (EMU)	South-Eastern Nigeria
Campaign for Democracy (CD)	National (established as an umbrella association for many civil liberties and human rights groups)
Democratic Alternative (DA)	National (formed out of CD)
United Action for Democracy	National (combining CD and DA)
National Conscience Party (NCP)	Lagos (led by Gani Fawehinmi)
Joint Action Committee (JACON)	Lagos (led by Gani Fawehinmi)
United Democratic Front of Nigeria (UDFN)	United front of various groups formed by exiled activists
Oganiru	South-Eastern Nigeria
Middle Belt Forum (MBF)	The Nigerian Middle Belt
Northern Christian Elders Forum (NCEF)	Northern Nigeria
Association of Patriotic Professionals (APP)	South-Western Nigeria

Source: Author's Field Survey 1996, 1997, 1998.

From benign dictatorship to neo-fascism

In responding to the challenges to the authority of his regime and opposition to his continued stay in office, General Abacha was to quickly shed all pretences to moderation and decency. The regime transformed itself into a neo-fascist dictatorship, unleashing an unprecedented reign of terror, sadism and thievery on the Nigerian populace.[8] Moderate civilian elements in the cabinet were purged as were moderate military members of the Provisional Ruling Council (PRC), including Major-General Mohammed Chris Ali, the Chief of Army Staff, and Rear Admiral Alison Madueke, the Chief of Naval Staff. Three independent newspapers – the *Guardian*, *Punch* and Abiola's *Concord* group – were proscribed and placed under prolonged armed occupation (Article 19 1997). Weekly news magazines such as *Tempo*, *The News*, and *Tell* had their operations routinely disrupted; at one point, even a newspaper (*Sketch*) and a local radio station (Ogun State Broadcasting Corporation), both owned by state governments, were shut down by the security agents of the federal government. Furthermore, several journalists were arraigned before military tribunals and sentenced to long terms of imprisonment for challenging the authenticity of the claims which the regime made of plots to topple it (Amnesty International 1996; Human Rights Watch 1996; Article 19 1997).

The security apparatuses of the government were revamped and were given a wide, unprecedented latitude to 'contain' and eliminate opposition to the regime by all means necessary. Abiola and his leading political, trade-union and civil society allies were arrested. Other opponents of the regime were either forced into exile, murdered, or placed under permanent harassment and intimidation. Trade unions were proscribed, civil and human rights NGOs placed under siege, with their

[8]Human Rights Watch 1996; *Post Express,* 10 November 1998; *The Punch,* 10 and 11 November 1998; *The Diet,* 11 November 1998.

leaders and members subject to arbitrary arrest, imprisonment and torture, often without trial; the travel documents of known and suspected critics of the regime were routinely impounded to prevent them from travelling out of the country; Ken Saro-Wiwa and his colleagues were hanged in November 1995 as part of a wider policy of 'pacifying' the oil Delta by naked, brutal military force and a scorched-earth strategy; distinctively pro-military politicians drawn from the conservative tradition in Nigerian politics were brought into the federal cabinet and various other institutions of government; the PRC was transformed into a fully-fledged military organ through the removal of all its civilian members and their replacement by military officers; and the regime openly and opportunistically declared itself as a 'northern' government as part of its effort to prevent the emergence of cross-national opposition to General Abacha's rule. In sum, Nigeria was transformed by the Abacha junta into a security state that increasingly seemed to be at war with a significant section of the citizenry.[9]

It was against this background that the electoral programme of the Abacha junta was unfolded. In spelling out the programme, General Abacha stated that it would last for three years from October 1995 to October 1998. On the face of things, the programme *appeared* to respond to local and, especially, international concerns for the country's return to elected civilian governance in the shortest time possible. It was also scheduled to follow on from the presentation of a new constitution by the constitutional conference. Indeed, immediately after the announcement of the programme, the initial concerns that were expressed internationally had less to do with its content and more with the three-year time period over which the junta claimed to intend to implement it; the Commonwealth, in suspending Nigeria from its ranks after the execution of Ken Saro-Wiwa and eight of his colleagues, had insisted on a return to full civilian rule within a maximum period of two years. Within Nigeria itself, some of the politicians who participated in the Constitutional Conference had hoped that the transition programme would offer them an opportunity to freely seek office, including the presidency, under rules spelt out and supervised by the military government. Effectively, however, as the mechanics of the programme were unfolded, it became clear that it was designed with one goal in mind: to consolidate military rule in Nigeria under the person of General Abacha.

Preparing the grounds for using the facade of elections to consolidate military rule

Three approaches were central to the strategy of the Abacha government for the realisation of its project entrenching military rule in Nigeria. The first had to do with the elevation of 'security', meaning regime security in the pursuit of the objective of prolonged military rule under General Abacha, to the status of the primary, almost sole objective and directive principle of state policy. In pursuit of this goal, not only were the security services given a wide latitude to act in the interest of the regime but also to pro-actively destabilise opposition to the political agenda of the junta and, if need be, retroactively enforce the wishes of General Abacha as his version of personal rule took hold. Within this framework, opposition to the regime, peaceful or not, was defined as constituting a threat to national security and unity. In addition to the State Security Services (SSS), the Nigerian Army Intelligence Corps (NAIC), the Directorate of Military Intelligence (DMI), the police, and the National Intelligence Agency (NIA) which were at the core of the security structure that the regime inherited and reorganised for its own purposes, new, clandestine and shadowy security units were established. These included the Body Guards (BGs), the Intelligence Group, the Israeli and North Korean-trained Strike Force, and the so-called K-Squad, all of which mostly reported directly to Major Hamza Al-Mustapha, General Abacha's Chief Security Officer. These organisations were central to the extra-judicial punishment of the opponents of the regime and the generalised campaign of terror which the ruling junta unleashed against the populace. The services of the Presidential Task Force on Terrorism and the General Musa Bamaiyi-headed National Drug Law Enforcement Agency were also enlisted in the pursuit of the opponents of the regime, real and imagined.[10]

---

[9]Human Rights Watch 1996; Amnesty International 1996; Agbu 1998; *Daily Times* 1 October 1995; *Newswatch* 4 May 1998; *The News* 2 November 1998.
[10]Human Rights Watch 1996; Amnesty International 1996; Agbu 1998; *The News* 2 November 1998.

In order to convince Nigerians that there was a credible, if hidden, threat to the security and unity of the country, the agents of the regime proceeded to organise a spate of bombing activities primarily in Lagos, the bastion of opposition to the government. These orchestrated bombing campaigns were mostly targeted at military convoys and served as justification for clamping down on the opposition as well as convincing sceptics within the military that civilian opposition to Abacha's junta was tantamount to opposition to the collective interests of the military as an institution and a political force.[11] Show trials were also organised against civilians as well as retired and serving military officers whom the regime saw as threats to its plan of holding on to power. The most notable of these trials was the one held in 1995 in which former head of state, retired General Olusegun Obasanjo and his deputy, General Musa Yar' adua were arrested together with Beko Ransome-Kuti, the leader of CD, and several serving military officers on charges of plotting to overthrow the regime. Their conviction, along with 32 others, was already a foregone conclusion and helped the regime to eliminate some of the most formidable opponents of the regime from the political scene.[12] Huge, mind-boggling sums of money were also withdrawn from the Central Bank of Nigeria purportedly to beef up the 'national security' and weaken the opposition; revelations published after the death of General Abacha suggest that close to US$2 billion was withdrawn outside of the budgetary framework allegedly for this purpose.[13] Clearly, security was a central alibi for the perpetration of wholesale theft of national resources by Abacha and his inner circle which included members of his family (nuclear and extended), his security advisers, and favoured *agents provocateurs*.

The second approach that was integrated from the outset into the strategy for the prolongation of military rule was the designation of principal transitional organs which enjoyed wide discretionary powers and whose actions were beyond judicial scrutiny through the inclusion of ouster clauses in the legal instruments establishing them. The most important of these organs were the National Electoral Commission of Nigeria (NECON) headed by Summer Dagogo-Jack and the Transition Implementation Committee (TIC), headed by Mamman Nasir. The latter had responsibility for the design and implementation of much of the transition programme; the former set the electoral rules, screened candidates for elections and announced the results of elections. Both of these agencies were, with the security services, central to the manipulation of the rules of the 'transition' process and the political game in order to ensure that General Abacha remained in power. Because the political equation in the transition process always changed as rapidly as politicians attempted to surmount obstacles put in their way, the rules governing the programme were also frequently altered in order both to wrong-foot the politicians and to ensure that the political advantage was always on General Abacha's side. It is perhaps instructive to note that the head of the TIC was one of the first people to suggest to Nigerians that General Abacha might be the best candidate for the office of president, pointing to the need to keep Nigeria united in the face of domestic and international opposition.[14]

The third approach consisted of the institution of a programme of political engineering that covered the entire spectrum of 'transitional activities' from the election of delegates to the constitutional conference and the writing of a new constitution to the formation of political parties and the nomination of candidates for elected office. The security services NECON and the TIC were all active in weeding out 'trouble makers' from the list of people eligible to participate in different aspects of the transition. Where security clearance had been inadvertently issued to potential or little known opponents, such candidates were often disqualified even after they had won the elections for which they competed. The government also passed a decree granting itself the right to remove any elected official from office and replace him/her with an appointed administrator as it may deem necessary. With specific regard to the 1994 Constitutional Conference, the regime only permitted the election of 272 out of the 398 delegates; the remaining 96 were nominated by the

[11]*Nigeria Now* January–April 1997.

[12]Human Rights Watch 1996; Amnesty International 1996; *Nigeria Now* January–April 1997.

[13]*The News* 2 November 1998 and 9 November 1998; *The Punch* 11 November 1998; *The Diet* 11 November 1998.

[14]*Newswatch* 8 July 1998 and 27 April 1998; *Thisday* 3 July 1997; *The Guardian* (Lagos) 3 and 7 July 1997; *Nigeria Now* January–April 1997; Human Rights Watch 1996.

presidency which was also responsible for naming the conference's chair and deputy chair. Furthermore, the decree setting up the conference fixed the quorum for meetings at 123 delegates; such quorums would only be valid if the conference chair and his deputy were present. Clearly, the aim of the regime's political engineering was to fill the various layers of state and party elective offices with individuals who were known to be loyal or pliable to the increasingly thinly-disguised project of keeping General Abacha and the military in power beyond October 1998.[15]

Understanding elections under the Abacha Junta: The historical and national contexts

Elections, electoral violence and military rule

It is not possible to understand the 'transition' programme of the Abacha junta without situating it in the wider context of the history of elections and politics in Nigeria. With regard to the former, the first point to bear in mind is that, together with the politics of revenue allocation and population census, elections have always constituted a bitterly contested issue in Nigeria. The intensity of this contestation is linked to phenomenon of competing ethnicities and regionalisms that is integral to the multi-ethnic character of the country, the uneven development of the country's main geo-political regions that tends to feed into and fuel inter-ethnic and inter-regional rivalries, and the increasing importance of access to the federal centre in the political economy (Dudley 1972; 1982; Nnoli 1980; Otite 1990; Oyediran 1996; Osaghae 1998). No election in Nigeria's late colonial and post-independence history has, therefore, ever gone uncontested because of the direct connection which most actors make between it and access to/control of local and national resources. So intense was the contestation of the first post-independence elections that it not only resulted in the collapse of the First Republic (1960–66) and the onset of military rule but also paved the way for the onset of the country's civil war. It was also the violent contestation of the results of the 1983 elections, together, this time, with the gathering crisis in the national economy, that provided justification for overthrow of the Second Republic (1979–83) by the military.

Arising from the foregoing is the second point worth noting, namely that the bitterness of electoral disputes has often been associated with incidents of massive rigging, thuggery and violence on the part of the key players in the political process. *Under these conditions, electoral outcomes have, for a long time, been integrated into informal pacts that allow for results to be upheld and, thus, provide the country with short periods of relative stability under elected civilian administrations.* Perhaps the most important element in these pacts is the basic respect by the different political players of the core 'spheres' of influence of their leading rivals, spheres of influence that are integral to the original, regionally-based structure of Nigerian federalism and the geographical distribution of the three major ethnic groups. In practical terms, this has translated into a tendency for the emergence of political organisations closely associated with specific geo-ethnic groupings. These groupings establish their credibility essentially by using all means necessary to build their political and electoral dominance in their regions of origin. The extent to which their rivals recognise their position is central to the maintenance of political order and stability. Indeed, it was precisely the attempt to breach this pact through manoeuvres aimed at weakening and dislodging the dominant political party in the old Western Region both during the First and Second Republics that resulted in the violent breakdown of political order and the takeover of power by the military.

Deriving from the strong regional roots of the leading political organisations is the fact that none of them is ever powerful enough to be able to gain a commanding national presence and dominance. The exercise of power in the federal centre has, therefore, always had to be built on an alliance between parties from at least two of the geo-ethnic groupings; similarly, the effectiveness of the federal opposition has also often been enhanced by alliances among the groupings that are outside of the ruling coalition (Dudley 1966; 1972; 1973; Oyediran 1996). By their nature, both the ruling and opposition alliances are unstable and, therefore, the history of alliance politics in the country has fed into a widespread notion that not only is civilian rule prone to violence but it also

---

[15]Human Rights Watch 1996; *Nigeria Now* January–April 1997; *Newswatch* 4 May 1998.

exposes the country to chronic instability. Not surprisingly, the elimination of political violence and the assurance of stability, together with the control of corruption among public officials, have always been the main bases on which the Nigerian military have sought to justify their intervention in the political process.

Regarding the framework of national politics within which we attempt to situate the transition programme of the Abacha regime, and related to the inability of civilian politicians to respect the underlying pacts that could make for post-election political stability beyond the short term, military intervention has been a prolonged feature of Nigerian life. In the period since 1960, when the country attained independence, it has had 8 military heads of state leading 7 military administrations. Out of the 40 years of independent nationhood, the military have ruled the country for about 28 years. Military *coups d'état* have, clearly, been far more important than elections in the organisation of the politics of succession, with the implication that the sources of pressure for change in Nigeria have lain less in political society as such and more in the confrontation between strong, national-territorial interest groups and an assortment of regionally-based power blocs, on the one hand, and military society, on the other hand. In this contestation, political society – the arena of civilian politics – appeals, mostly opportunistically, to the military for the resolution of differences among the politicians; civil society is considered to be important only to the extent that it can be mobilised to create a *prima facie* case for military intervention in the political process. It was only after the seizure of power by General Abacha that concerted efforts began to be made, for the first time in Nigeria's history, to organise civil society forces to resist military rule and insist on the supremacy of elected civilian governments over the military.

Prolonged military rule without military hegemony

Yet, in spite of the fact that the military have dominated national politics in Nigeria for most of the post-independence years, it is one of the big ironies of Nigerian politics that military rule as such has never been accepted, even within the military, as a wholly legitimate form of long-term governance. The point needs to be emphasised that within both military and civil society, the ideological position that military rule in Nigeria is an illegitimate aberration and, therefore, only transitory has deep roots. For civil society groups, it provided a basis for struggling for the retention of the local democratic space in spite of the fact of military rule. For the politicians, the very fact that military rule was seen as temporary meant that they could live to fight another day. For the military, the ideology provided an immediate instrument for regime stabilisation in the immediate aftermath of a *coup d'état*. It also provided a basis for the maintenance of a degree of internal coherence and professional discipline. All key players in the political system, therefore, had objective and subjective interests in the propagation of the ideology. It is an ideology that has ensured that in spite of the fact of prolonged military rule and the increasing militarisation of society, the hegemony of the military remains highly contested. This is also why, interestingly, every military government regime has either had to declare itself as a 'transitional' government committed to restoring elected government at the earliest opportunity or face the danger of being dislodged by other sections of the armed forces as was experienced by the Gowon (1966–75) and Buhari (1983–85) regimes.

The preservation of the notion that military rule, being illegitimate, had to be temporary meant that most programmes of transition to elected government were conducted in a framework in which the military were, formally at least, above the fray, presenting themselves as a neutral umpire in the electoral process (Adekanye 1981). It was also reflective of a balance of relations within the military between the 'professionals' and 'the political soldiers' as well as between the military and political society, on the one hand, and the military and civil society, on the other. It was, in a sense, one of the relatively settled aspects of power relations in post-independence Nigeria and it operated on the following implicit assumption: the military could intervene in the process of governance if the circumstances necessitated such an intervention but their rule would always have to be temporary, tied to the restoration of stability in periods of civilian political infighting that actually or potentially threaten the unity of the federation. That is why, in spite of the fact that Nigeria has experienced long periods of unbroken military rule, as for example between 1966 and 1979 or 1983 and 1999, those periods are spoken of in terms of an interregnum, not an accepted governmental norm. It also explains why the military retain the constitution operated by the civilians whom they overthrow, only suspending those aspects that provide for political parties, the legislative arm of government and the functions of various elected officials.

Closely related to the notion that military rule is a temporary aberration is the fact, now considered as one of Nigeria's political myths, that the sheer complexity and size of the country, including the existence of multiple centres of power and influence, are such that no military ruler can successfully succeed himself either by remaining in office to preside over an elected civilian administration or by transmuting from a soldier to an elected civilian head of state/government. This is a practice that has been widespread in the rest of West Africa: military rulers who come to power through a *coup d'état* have always quickly organised to transform themselves into civilian rulers without first leaving office.[16] Various attempts at promoting the notion of a diarchy in Nigeria whereby a serving military head of state/government presides over layers of elected officials have invariably failed to materialise. General Yakubu Gowon's government (1966–75) was toppled partly because of the widespread conviction, which his repeated postponement of the terminal date of his administration created, that he intended to foist a self-serving diarchical arrangement on the country. Similarly, the spirited attempt which General Babangida made to succeed himself was completely undermined following the annulment of the June 1993 presidential elections. As we shall see later in this chapter, General Abacha too made an even more brazen effort than his predecessors to succeed himself but that also came to nothing. Suspicion of an agenda of self-succession by serving military rulers has not only always unsettled the armed forces but also served to rally national civilian opposition which the incumbent military regimes find hard to ignore.

The process by which the ideology of the essential illegitimacy of military rule began actively, self-consciously, and systematically to be jettisoned could be traced to the Babangida years (1985–93); the Abacha junta, in a sense, therefore, only sought to carry the process to a logical conclusion. The contestation of this project by sections of military, political and civil society constituted the essence of opposition to the electoralism of the Abacha junta. This contestation was certainly marked by a host of internal weaknesses but its effectiveness was also severely undermined by the extremely harsh repressiveness of the junta and the susceptibility of many political players to the regional, ethnic and religious sentiments so brazenly and artfully manipulated by the regime to atomise opposition and prevent the coalescence of a national–territorial movement against it. Without doubt, the Abacha regime has been the crudest, most narrowly-based, and violently repressive in the county's history. The extent which the junta proved ready to go in order to weaken the opposition was, in itself, a source of shock to its opponents; the deliberate targeting of its repressive actions to create the impression of an ethnically-based campaign challenged the political capacities of the mainstream and radical opposition, which was most active in the Lagos area.

Yet, it was also General Abacha's tragedy that the scheme which he and his faction of the military tried to implement was unfolded at a juncture in Nigerian politics when resentment in various parts of the country, but especially in the geographical South, had built up against perceived exclusion from the national political process, a process which years of military rule had also transformed into a *de facto* centralised system of control. The view was strongly canvassed that the time had come for power to be rotated from the northern political elite, civilian and military, who had dominated it since independence to the southern political elite. Increasingly, military rule came to be equated with rule by northern military officers and, therefore, with the continued 'monopolisation' of the presidency by the northern political elite (Agbu 1998). As can be expected, this interpretation was contested by politicians in the north of the country who also outlined their own grievances against the country's political and economic arrangements. Without doubt, the deepening crisis of the national economy and the heavy toll which this took on the standard of living of the overwhelming majority of the populace reinforced the resentment that was building up in the system. Similarly, the gross mismanagement of basic public services added to the air of disaffection that was spreading across the country. Manipulating ethnic and regional sentiments as the Abacha regime did had the double-sided effect of both generating support and opposition to the government at one and the same time.

---

[16]*Newswatch*, 4 May, 1998.

Altering the civilian-military balance during the Babangida years

Systematic demobilisation of civil society

In attempting to lay the basis for the reversal of the ideology that military rule is essentially a temporary aberration, one of the first steps which General Babangida and his colleagues embarked upon was the systematic weakening and dismantling of the key structures of non-party popular political mobilisation in the country. The regime was aided in this regard by the deep-rooted crisis in the Nigerian economy which the IMF/World Bank structural adjustment programme that the government embraced in 1986/87 exacerbated and which resulted in a sharp, unprecedented decline in the incomes and living standards of most Nigerians. The context of a declining national economy and collapsing livelihood laid civil society forces – trade unions, professional associations, the independent media, student and youth groups, etc. – open to a systematically articulated programme aimed, at one level, at co-opting and corrupting them and, at another level, at repressing them with a view to precipitating their decay from both within and without. One after the other, the main associations were emptied of their vitality as a combination of the carrot and the stick was applied by the government to weaken their political instincts, create divisions within their leadership structures, and establish a wide gulf between the leaders and their members. Thus it was that the Nigeria Labour Congress (NLC) and some of its affiliate unions, the Nigerian Union of Journalists (NUJ), the Nigerian Bar Association (NBA), the Nigerian Medical Association (NMA), and the National Association of Resident Doctors (NARD), among others, were targeted by the regime for disorganisation and demobilisation. Failing to corrupt some of the groups, the military government adopted strategies for repressing them or dividing their ranks, including the proscription, by decree, of the NMA, NARD, the National Association of Nigerian Students (NANS), and the Academic Staff Union of Universities (ASUU). Several independent newspapers were also shut down by the government as part of its attempt to contain the opposition to General Babangida (Olukoshi 1997).

At the same time, the Babangida regime took the unprecedented step of inventing its own civil society that would not only propagate the idea that the military under Babangida should continue in power but also serve as a counter-weight to the growing number of civil liberties, human rights and pro-democracy groups that were created during the course of the 1980s and which were actively scrutinising the actions of the government and mobilising against General Babangida's continued stay in office. Among the most prominent of these civil liberties/human rights/ pro-democracy groups are the Civil Liberties Organisation (CLO), the Constitutional Rights Project (CRP), the Committee for the Defence of Human Rights (CDHR), and the National Association of Democratic Lawyers (NADL). Most of these groups were to work together under the umbrella of the Campaign for Democracy (CD) (Olukoshi 1997). It was in a bid to check the growing influence of these groups that the Babangida regime took to creating its own civil society. Some of the groups created by the regime remained faceless, operating under such names as Third Eye and, with the backing of the security services, engaging in newspaper and poster campaigns for General Babangida's self-succession. Others like the Association for a Better Nigeria (ABN), led by the infamous Francis Arthur Nzeribe, were heavily funded by the state to campaign across the country for military rule to continue and to agitate political society in order to create an objective basis for the prolongation of military rule. It is worth noting that the ABN was instrumental in the manufacture of the series of events that paved the way for the annulment of the 12 June 1993 presidential elections (Olukoshi and Agbu 1996; Diamond *et al.* eds. 1997).

Deliberately wrong-footing the politicians

Economic decline also enabled the Babangida junta to exploit the opportunism of Nigerian politicians to the fullest, playing different factions against one another. Apart from playing on the traditional regionalist concerns of the politicians, the regime also attempted to pitch 'old breed' politicians, defined to include almost all of the leading actors in the politics of the First and Second Republics, against the 'new breed', defined to include a new, younger generation of aspiring politicians. In support of this strategy of dividing the politicians from within, the government adopted a policy of banning and un-banning various individuals from participation in the transition process as it was unfolded. This policy not only created an air of permanent uncertainty among the politicians, it also fed into the regime's deliberate strategy of wrong-footing them at every stage of the transition process. This strategy was extended to the party formation and registration process that was announced in 1989. The basic rules that were defined for the formation of political parties were so stiff – and unreasonable – that no grouping could, in all honesty, meet them within the time frame of three weeks allotted by the electoral commission. Not only were the parties required to have a presence in at least two-thirds of the local government areas of all of the states in the country, they were also expected to submit physical evidence of their membership, including the names, ages, addresses and even photos of card-carrying members down to the ward and local government levels. The parties were also required to have a minimum of 480,000 members in each state and were to submit 25 certified copies of their serially-numbered membership lists. Furthermore, their principal officials had to undergo a hazily-defined security clearance and their manifestos were expected to contain specific policy proposals on how they intended to tackle Nigeria's political, social and economic problems, including a clear declaration of their attitude to structural adjustment which the regime knew was deeply unpopular in the country.[17]

Nigerians were treated to a spectacle of politicians scrambling to meet the deadline for registration set by the electoral commission and arriving at its headquarters with lorry loads of documentation that included evidence of their membership as well as printed copies of their constitutions and manifestoes. Nobody was surprised when the regime announced that none of the 13 political associations that applied for registration was able to meet the requirements set by the electoral commission. A meeting of the Armed Forces Ruling Council (AFRC) called to consider the report of the National Electoral Commission (NEC) on the performance of the associations accused them of factionalism, rigging and falsification of claims, links to the banned political parties that dominated the First and Second Republics, and general disregard for the party registration guidelines announced by the government. The government, therefore, announced that since none of the associations met its requirements, they all stood dissolved. That announcement was swiftly followed by the unfolding of the regime's pre-arranged plan to impose 2 political parties of its own creation on Nigerians. At a dramatic press conference in Lagos, General Babangida informed Nigerians in 1989 that, on account of the failings of the parties that sought registration, his government had, after a careful study of the political history of the country, decided that it was best to have two parties competing for power. This was to ensure that the unity of the country was not unduly threatened by political competition; it was also to insulate the political transition from the negative influences of 'money bags' and the old breed politicians. With the government as the founder and financier of the two parties, politicians were invited to join either of them as individuals and ordinary members with equal rights.[18] Critics of the transition programme were to instantly describe the parties as little more than parastatal agencies of the Babangida regime.

The two parties were named the National Republican Convention (NRC) (which was, according to Babangida, to be a 'little to the right') and the Social Democratic Party (SDP) (to be a 'little to the left') (Olagunju et al. 1993; Diamond et al. eds. 1997). It marked the first time in the history of Nigeria that a two-party system was foisted on the country by the military; it was also the first time that the military would involve themselves openly in the creation of political parties which the politicians were then invited to join as individuals acting in their private capacity. General Babangida and his colleagues had pursued this programme of political engineering in a self-conscious manner, insisting that failure to carefully guide previous transition programmes was responsible for the short life span of elected civilian administrations. The notion of a 'gradual transition' and 'staggered' elections based, at one time, on the so-called 'open' ballot system, whereby voters queued behind the symbol of the candidate or party of their choice, and, later, on the 'modified open ballot' or option A4 system, was pursued such that elected civilian officials at the local and state levels co-existed with the military officials who controlled the federal administration (Olagunju et al. 1993; Diamond, Kirk-Greene and Oyeleye eds. 1997; Osaghae 1998). The National Assembly, though elected in 1991, was not inaugurated initially; when it was eventually allowed to sit, its remit was strictly limited to ecological issues, including desertification and

---

[17]Olagunju et al. 1993; Newswatch 8 July 1996; Diamond et al. eds. 1997.
[18]Olagunju et al. 1993; Newswatch 8 July 1996; Diamond et al. eds. 1997; Osaghae 1998.

erosion. It was only in the thick of the crisis that followed the annulment of the 12 June 1993 elections that General Babangida was driven, in desperation, to confer full powers on the National Assembly. That gesture was not enough, however, to save his presidency (Olukoshi and Agbu 1996; Osaghae 1998).

In deciding to closely engineer and guide the transition process over which he was presiding, General Babangida abandoned the semblance of neutrality which his military predecessors always adopted in relating with politicians during the implementation of programmes of return to elected civilian rule. Indeed, he was to declare during the early stages of the transition that 'we don't know who will succeed us but we know those who will not succeed us'. The regime was also not content with just creating and naming the only two political parties that were to be allowed to participate in the transition; it proceeded to write their constitutions and manifestoes, fund their activities, build their offices across the country, design their logo, and appoint interim officers for them. All of these actions were part of a prolonged game of hide-and-seek between Babangida and the politicians, a game which in its early stages earned him the nickname of Maradona but which, as it became long-drawn-out and resulted in the repeated postponement of the terminal date for military rule, began to discredit the entire transition programme itself. Thus, by the time the two government-created parties were launched, the notion that General Babangida's game with the politicians was part of a hidden agenda to perpetuate military rule in one form or another had gained ground; the very Maradona antics that had apparently served him well in the early years of his regime ultimately became the main source of disquiet as the country increasingly worried that General Babangida was taking the citizenry on a long, endless ride.

Remoulding the military for the prolongation of General Babangida's rule

The attempt to alter the balance of power between the military and civilians also had implications for the armed forces. As has been observed by various commentators, the military was increasingly characterised by a breakdown of internal discipline associated with General Babangida's strategy of containing it as a source of check on his power. As part of this process, military officers were brought into public life in unprecedented numbers: apart from the key political posts in the federal and state governments, officers were offered positions in leading parastatals, special task forces were created for them with rent-generating capacities, and an unusual rapidity of turnover of appointees was introduced to create the impression that all 'deserving' and 'loyal' officers would have their turn on the gravy train of the Babangida express (Adekanye 1993). It is generally reckoned that during the eight years of General Babangida's rule, the total number of officers who were offered public office of one type or the other almost equalled the combined total number of military men offered political appointments by the Gowon (1966–75), Murtala-Obasanjo (1975–79), and Buhari (1988–85) administrations put together. This use of the carrot of political office/appointment to buy support from the military was supplemented with the distribution of presidential gifts to younger officers as happened when new cars were acquired and distributed to majors and captains in the armed forces. Special dispensations were also awarded to more junior officers to enable them 'cope' with the pains of structural adjustment.

The wholesale attempt by General Babangida to completely politicise and corrupt the officer corps of the armed forces inevitably took its toll on their professionalism; indeed, General Salihu Ibrahim, the second Chief of Army Staff in the Babangida regime, was to declare, on being retired, that the army he was leaving had become an army of anything goes, lacking in discipline, *espirit de corps*, and a sense of public service. Politicisation also resulted in an acceleration of the pace of retirements from the armed forces, a process which, in a sense, was a logical outcome of the gravy train culture that General Babangida so artfully forged and which meant that those who had had their turn necessarily had to move on to create room for others. Perhaps not surprisingly, this process of politicisation created severe internal instability as disaffected officers who felt left out in one way or the other posed open challenges to the regime. The most dramatic and bloody of these challenges came on 22 April 1990 when a group of middle-level officers attempted to violently overthrow General Babangida (Diamond *et al.* eds. 1997; Osaghae 1998). Less dramatic but no less significant was the tension that developed between the 'political officers', i.e. those who craved political office and worked for prolonged military rule and the 'professionals', those who emphasised the temporariness of military rule and stuck to command appointments within the army.

The collapse of General Babangida's strategy for prolonged military rule

In laying the basis for the possibility of the reversal of the ideology of the illegitimacy of military rule, the Babangida regime did not refuse to commit itself to restore elected government to the country. Indeed, one of the key justifications for General Babangida's coup of 27 August 1985 was precisely that his predecessor, General Buhari, had refused to commit himself to a specific date for returning the country to elected government, opting instead to prohibit all debates about the country's political future. It was this that General Babangida and his supporters seized upon to take power. Unable to avoid committing itself to a date for returning the country to elected civilian rule, the regime sought, instead, to manipulate the entire transition programme in order to make the process unending, and thus prolong military rule (Diamond *et al.* eds. 1997). In pursuit of this objective, the terminal date for military rule was postponed four times and this was only one of the several policy and political somersaults which the regime undertook. But the strategy was to become a victim of its own success, leading to a spirited domestic campaign against Babangida's 'hidden agenda' to stay in power as President. This campaign was spearheaded by the CD and its affiliates but it was also increasingly taken up by politicians who were disillusioned by the repeated postponement of the terminal date for military rule (Olukoshi and Agbu 1996).

Central to the growing concern that General Babangida and his colleagues were intent on prolonging military rule was the deliberate effort made by functionaries and supporters of the regime to create as much confusion as possible around the last stage of the transition programme involving the selection of presidential candidates by the two parties. Having conducted elections to the local government councils, state houses of assembly, state governorships, and the national assembly within the framework of the two political parties which it had created, the government repeatedly stalled the process of the selection of presidential candidates at the same time as the Third Eye and the ABN, two of the front organisations which it set up, were given a new prominence in their campaign for General Babangida to remain in office and preside over the already elected structures of government. The ABN, in particular, was funded to set up a national campaigning structure to discredit the idea of an elected civilian president and infiltrate the two political parties in order to create confusion within them. The worst fears of many Nigerians were fulfilled when the presidential primaries conducted by the two parties in 1992 were cancelled by the regime and the contestants banned from further participation in the transition process. The executives of the two parties were dissolved for being partisan in support of some of the contestants; their reconstitution and the selection of their new presidential candidates provided yet another justification for the prolongation of the terminal date for military rule to 27 August 1993. New presidential elections were scheduled for 12 June 1993 (Olukoshi and Agbu 1996; Diamond *et al.* eds. 1997).

Precisely because of the widespread recognition that the Babangida transition programme was being deliberately manipulated to prolong military rule, various sections of political society made a determined effort, against all the odds, to ensure that the 12 June 1993 presidential elections which the regime called ended conclusively with an outright winner. As decreed by the government, the two parties held their primaries and national conventions to choose their presidential candidates. The NRC, meeting in Port Harcourt, selected Bashir Tofa as its candidate while the SDP, meeting in Jos, selected M.K.O. Abiola as its flag bearer. Both candidates were millionaires who were extremely close to Babangida, Abiola as a friend and one-time benefactor, Bashir Tofa as a client who once confessed that he owed his wealth to Babangida's generosity. However, of the two candidates, Abiola, who also had a long-standing national reputation for philanthropy, was generally seen as being more 'relatively autonomous' of Babangida than Bashir O. Tofa. Whereas Tofa got the NRC ticket without any serious internal opposition within the NRC – indeed, before the party's convention, it was already established in the media that he was the favourite candidate of the Babangida regime – Abiola had to fight off an intense challenge from Babagana Kingibe who was later to be his running mate. Inevitably, in order to carry his party behind him and also gather a broad coalition behind his ticket, Abiola had to enter into negotiations with a broad cross-section of opinion within the SDP and across the country.

In the calculations of the Babangida regime, the likely outcome of the presidential elections would be a victory for Tofa and the NRC. Not only was the NRC seen as the reincarnation of the principal parties of power in the First and Second Republics, Tofa had the added advantage of being from the Moslem North of Nigeria with a Christian Igbo from the East as his running mate. In the view of the party's strategists, that combination gave a reasonable assurance that the NRC would be dominant in the North and the East. Moreover, it was such a combination that delivered victory in the 1979 presidential elections to Alhaji Shehu Shagari; it was reckoned that nothing appeared to have changed much in the country to prevent a repeat performance. Abiola, on the other hand, not minding his own background as a moslem, selected Kingibe, another Moslem, as his running mate, a choice which drew the ire of the Christian Association of Nigeria (CAN) and forced him into negotiations with the organisation after it threatened to ask Christians not to support his ticket for its insensitivity. Moreover, unlike the NRC, the SDP on whose platform he was to compete was a more internally diverse and divided party and bitterness over the outcome of the Jos convention where he emerged victorious continued to linger in spite of the attempts to mend fences and present a united front. On the face of things, therefore, the NRC and Tofa appeared headed for victory.

In anticipation of a possible Tofa victory at the polls, agents of the military government began a campaign against him, claiming that he was not fit for the office of president on account of previous involvement in alleged fraudulent activities. In support of this campaign, Abidina Coomasie, a shadowy businessman with close links to the government, filed an affidavit challenging Tofa's qualification for the office of president. All of this was taking place at the same time as the ABN was intensifying its campaign against the prospects of a presidential election. But the fact that Tofa was particularly targeted for attack was seen as indicative of the preparation of a judicial basis for discrediting him and, once again, cancelling whatever the outcome of the presidential elections might be. Barely a few days before the elections, the ABN itself went to court to seek an injunction preventing the electoral commission from going ahead with them. That suit was filed in spite of the fact that a decree existed which ousted the jurisdiction of the courts over the activities of the commission. On the very eve of voting, confusion was let loose on the country when an Abuja High Court judge, sitting well after hours, issued a ruling granting the ABN's prayers that the electoral commission should not go ahead with the elections but also stating that, in view of the enabling decree setting it up, the commission was not obliged to obey its ruling. Amidst the confusion, Nigerians were not sure if polling would go ahead on 12 June as planned, especially as the preparation of polling stations was more lukewarm than had been the case in previous elections. It was only late in the evening of 11 June 1993 that the electoral commission announced on radio and television that the elections would be going ahead.

On the polling day itself, it rapidly emerged that Tofa was not even a registered voter and questions quickly arose as to whether, if he emerged victorious, he would, under these circumstances, be able to claim his mandate. In the event, these concerns were not necessary as Abiola and the SDP, against all the odds and forecast, headed for an emphatic victory that stunned the NRC as much as it stunned the military government. Not only did Abiola beat Tofa in his constituency, he also got more votes in the North and West than his rival, while giving a very good account of himself in the East. In sum, the outcome of the election was clear and indisputable: Abiola and the SDP were headed for an emphatic victory. The conclusiveness of the elections represented a significant setback for General Babangida and his closest military colleagues (see Table 9.1). They responded to Abiola's impending victory by first stopping the electoral commission from continuing with the announcement of the results. They then proceeded to annul the results without being able, to this day, to give clear reasons for their action. That annulment precipitated a major political crisis from which the country is yet to recover; it also provided the immediate background for General Abacha's *coup d'état* and the unfolding of his own version of a supposed transition to civilian rule (Osaghae 1998).

The annulment of the presidential elections elicited widespread strikes and protests across the country. It also severely weakened General Babangida's authority, putting paid to any hope he might have had of remaining in office. Pressures also mounted on him from within the military where opponents and supporters of the annulment were locked in a tense struggle. Amidst the confusion, Babangida bowed to pressures to step down and an Interim National Government

Table 9.1: Results of the 12 June 1993 elections that were annulled by the Babangida junta

State	SDP votes	%	NRC votes	%
Abia	105,273	41.0	151,227	59.0
Adamawa				
Akwa Ibom	214,782	51.9	199,342	48.1
Anambra	212,024	57.1	159,258	42.9
Bauchi				
Benue				
Borno	153,496	54.4	128,684	45.6
Cross River				
Delta				
Edo	205,407	66.5	103,572	33.5
Enugu				
Imo				
Jigawa				
Kaduna	389,713	53.5	336,860	46.4
Kano	169,619	52.3	154,809	47.7
Katsina				
Kebbi				
Kogi	222,760	45.6	265,732	54.4
Kwara	272,270	77.2	80,209	21.8
Lagos	883,965	85.5	149,432	14.5
Niger	136,350	38.1	221,437	61.9
Ogun	425,725	87.8	59,246	12.2
Ondo				
Osun				
Oyo	536,011	83.5	105,788	16.5
Plateau	417,565	61.7	259,394	38.3
Rivers				
Sokoto				
Taraba				
Yobe				
FCT Abuja	19,968	52.2	18,313	47.8

Source: *National Concord* 15 June 1993, 1–2.

(ING), headed by Ernest Shonekan, was set up on 27 August 1993 to organise fresh presidential elections. But the ING was a lame duck headed by an equally lacklustre figure who was seen as a puppet of the military. From the time it was inaugurated to the time it was toppled, the interim government was buffeted on all sides by opposition protests and nowhere was this more intense than in the south west of Nigeria, Abiola's home region from where Shonekan also came. Shonekan was dealt a further blow when on 10 November 1993, a Lagos High Court judge, ruling on a petition filed by Abiola, declared that the ING was illegal and restrained Shonekan from parading himself as head of state. It did not, therefore, come as too much of a surprise when on 17 November 1993, General Abacha, easily the strongest figure in the interim government, announced that he had taken over power (Human Rights Watch 1996; Osaghae 1998).

The Abacha Transition Programme:
attempting to re-engineer the prolongation of military rule

The Abacha regime was inaugurated at a time when all of the various divisions in the Nigerian polity had been brought to a head by the annulment of the 12 June 1993 presidential elections. Compounding the divisions was the deteriorating state of the national economy and the decaying condition of much of the physical and social infrastructure in the country. Nigerians were as worried about the deteriorating political situation in the country as about the continuing decline in their living standards. But any expectation that the Abacha regime would act quickly to stabilise the political and economic situation, either by holding fresh elections into the presidency or restoring the mandate of Abiola, was soon dashed by the government's decision to proscribe the NRC and SDP and dissolve all the elected structures of government that it inherited. Thus, not only were the national and state assemblies sacked, military administrators were appointed to take charge of the states; civilian sole administrators were also put in charge of the local governments. At the federal level, the PRC was vested with the powers of running the country with a membership that initially included some civilians but which was later to be transformed into a fully military organ.

Continuing Babangida's unfinished agenda

In many respects, based on its contents and the way in which it was unfolded, the transition programme of the Abacha regime was little more than a continuation of the Babangida administration's project for the entrenchment of military rule but, this time, with an apparent determination not to repeat the 'errors' that resulted in the collapse of the self-succession strategy of General Babangida. Thus, like the Babangida regime, the Abacha junta was, from the outset, very heavily involved in the manipulation of the transition process, although without the pretensions to finesse or sophistication that characterised most of the Babangida years. In place of the carrot and stick approach of Babangida, Abacha mostly opted for draconian, sledge-hammer measures aimed at silencing, even eradicating all opposition. The junta's philosophy seemed to be that nothing would be left to chance this time round and, in this task, all pretences to intellectualism and public discussion of the government's political options were dropped. Secrecy and conspiracy were, therefore, the flip side of the Abacha regime's sledge-hammer approach to the opposition.[19] Like the Babangida regime, the Abacha junta financed the creation of a host of organisations whose mandate was to campaign for the continued stay of the military under General Abacha in power (see Figure 9.3 for the list of associations that were involved in the campaign for Abacha to stay in power). The most prominent of these organisations is the group known as Youths Earnestly Ask for Abacha (YEAA), which was led by one Daniel Kanu. Alone and with other groups, it printed posters and badges for circulation in support of the entrenchment of military rule. It also organised rallies and seminars with open support from various state agencies, including the security services and military administrators. Musicians were mobilised with huge fees to perform in public in Abuja as part of the campaign for Abacha to stay in power.[20] Both the government and these organisations were involved in the circulation of Abacha-label consumer goods – rice, milk, television sets, mobile phones, tee-shirts, etc. – across the country. The central message which they tried to push through was that an independent, self-propelling, popular bandwagon had developed for a 'reluctant' Abacha to stay in power and that this self-succession bid had grassroots support across the length and breadth of the country. Yet, participants at pro-Abacha rallies and seminars were often paid attendance fees both in cash and in kind; suggestions were made by the leaders of YEAA that both Nigerian youths and the rural populace were solidly behind the campaign to persuade General Abacha to stay in power.

Again like Babangida, the Abacha regime took an active part in engineering the formation of political parties and in monitoring the results of elections in order to weed out opponents. It differed from its predecessor, however, in its determination to ensure that the only players allowed in the political game were civilians who were either not seen as a source of threat or who had been certified to be willing, at a minimum, to accept the regime's plan for entrenching military rule under General Abacha. This much was made obvious when the government, under intense local and international pressure, scheduled the election of delegates into the constitutional conference as the first stage of its transition programme. As we noted earlier, only some of the delegates were to be elected while the remainder were to be nominated by the government which also reserved the right to name the conference's chair and vice chair. The elections were conducted on a non-party basis and primarily targeted for exclusion from the process were pro-12 June 1993, as well as radical civil society, activists. Their exclusion was ensured through the mandatory security clearance which candidates were expected to undergo; this instrument was also used to weed out all those who were expected to use the floor of the conference to seriously call for the re-visiting

---

[19] *The Guardian* (Lagos) 10 August 1997; *Thisday* 19 April 1998.
[20] *Newswatch* 27 April 1998.

Figure 9.3: Associations set up to campaign for General Sani Abacha's self-succession in office

Name	Leader/Spokesperson
Youths Earnestly Ask for Abacha (YEAA)	Daniel Kanu
National Tranquillity Movement (NTM)	Ahmed Gashash
General Sani Abacha Movement for Peaceful and Successful Transition (GESAM)	Yomi Tokoya
National Youth Consultative Forum (NYCF)	
Vision '98 National Mobilisation for Abacha	Azeez Arisekola Alao
The 21st Century Generation	Babalade Oriwu
National Council of Youths Association of Nigeria (NACYAN)	Ilya Ibrahim, Emmanuel Okereke, Bature Ahmed, Basirat Ajiborisha
Sani Abacha Initiative for National Transformation (SAINT)	Emeka Kalu/Sam Ezenwanne
National Mobilisation and Persuasion Committee (NMPC)	Godwin Daboh
New Generation Youth Movement for Sani Abacha (NGYMA)	Edozie Madu
National Mass Movement of Nigeria	Zanna Bukar Mandara
Movement for Indigenous Democracy in Africa (MIDIA)	
Northern Elders Forum	Abdulrahman Okene

Source: Author's Field Survey 1997.

of the 12 June 1993 elections. In the event, the election was greeted with widespread voter apathy across the country, with a turnout put at 300,000 voters compared to the nearly 12–14 million who voted in the 12 June 1993 elections (Human Rights Watch 1996). That did not stop the government and some of the newly appointed and 'elected' conference delegates from claiming that the electorate had given them a new mandate which now superseded the mandate won by Abiola and for which his supporters were still vigorously campaigning.

The constitutional conference itself was initially given six months to carry out its task of writing a new constitution for the country. That deadline was to be extended in part because of the many unresolved issues that divided the delegates but also because the extension suited the regime well since it hinged both the content and time frame for its expected transition programme on the successful completion by the conference delegates of their work. Through its three special duties ministers and the security agencies, the regime closely monitored the formal debates of the delegates and their informal caucusing preparatory to the lifting of the ban on party politics. Some of the politicians who were delegates to the conference, eager for the work of the conference to be completed and for party politics to be resumed, mustered support for a resolution that was passed on 6 December 1994 asking the government to introduce a transition programme whose terminal date would be 1 January 1996. The two main actors behind this resolution were retired General Shehu Musa Yar'adua, once the deputy to General Obasanjo, and Alex Ekwueme, vice-president to Shehu Shagari during the Second Republic. That resolution stung the Abacha regime; the security agencies responded initially by puncturing the tyres of the cars of the conference delegates and then making a series of threats against them. Soon after the resolution was passed, the government announced (on 25 March 1995) that it had uncovered a plot to violently overthrow it and that, in addition to serving officers, the plotters included none other than Yar'adua, its most formidable opponent within the conference; Obasanjo, its biggest critic outside the conference; and Beko Ransome-Kuti, the leader of the CD. Few Nigerians believed that there was a plot but the government quickly proceeded with a secret trial that resulted in the jailing of several of its most fearless critics, including journalists who published comments on the travesty of justice that was enacted by the military tribunal that carried out the trials. With Yar'adua out of the way and the rest of the conference intimidated back into conformity, the government succeeded in getting the delegates to reverse their earlier resolution asking it to hand over power to elected politicians in January 1996; the new resolution which they adopted on 25 April 1995 asked the government to design, at its own pace, a transition programme that took account of the challenges of stabilising the national economy and the domestic political situation. It appeared to be a triumph for the first phase of the self-succession game plan of the regime.[21]

Creating political parties in the service of prolonged military rule

Following the conclusion of the work of the constitutional conference and the submission, on 27 June 1995, of the draft Constitution which it produced to the government, the next significant stage in the Abacha regime's transition programme was the formal lifting of the ban on politics. This was announced in June 1996, allowing several of the political caucuses/associations that had been established during the Constitutional Conference to come out into the open, hoping to be registered as parties. The National Electoral Commission of Nigeria (NECON) spelt out the rules that would govern the registration of parties on 17 June 1996 and, as usual, they included stipulations that the parties must be national in outlook and presence. Each of the prospective parties was required to satisfy NECON that it had at least 40,000 members in each of the states of the federation and 15,000 members in the Federal Capital Territory, Abuja. They were also required to submit a certified copy of the list of their members, complete with verifiable documentation such as names, addresses, age, and passport photos. Officials of the associations from the ward through to the local government, state and national levels were required to submit court-registered documentation declaring their assets. Furthermore, the associations were to make ten copies of their constitutions and manifestoes available to NECON and they had four weeks from 19 June 1996 to comply with all of the requirements contained in the Commission's guidelines.[22] Though not formally stated, it was clear that those politicians who were adamant in their defence of the mandate of Abiola would not be welcomed to participate in the party formation process; the ubiquitous requirement that all politicians must go through security clearance was also harped upon by NECON's chairman.

In the event, over 60 associations were formed, of which 23 paid the N500,000 registration fee required by NECON to obtain the necessary application forms to enable them to compete for recognition as one of the 5 parties that were to be selected to participate in the electoral and political process (see Figure 9.4).[23] After the first round of screening, NECON sent shock waves through the political establishment when it announced that none of the parties had met its requirements, not even the essentially establishment All Nigeria Congress (ANC) that was founded by leading figures from the Northern Peoples' Congress and the National Party of Nigeria that were the dominant parties in the First and Second Republics respectively. NECON, thereafter, proceeded to encourage the associations to explore the possibility of merging; politicians were to accuse it of engineering the merger of the 5 parties that it eventually registered. These parties were the United Nigeria Congress Party (UNCP), Congress for National Consensus (CNC), National Centre Party of Nigeria (NCPN), Grassroots Democratic Movement (GDM), and Democratic Party of Nigeria (DPN).

What was most remarkable about the five registered parties is that they did not initially include any of the big names in Nigerian politics; their members and leaders were mostly people who were not known on a national scale.[24] Moreover, the registered parties did not represent any of the established traditions in Nigerian politics; indeed, their manifestoes were astonishingly similar in terms of what they claimed to represent and the policy options they espoused. Infuriated by what they saw as the extreme partisanship of NECON and convinced that there was a deliberate attempt to sideline them, the most prominent of the establishment politicians who had also been active in the ANC called press conferences to protest the actions of the government and to declare that they were formally withdrawing from further participation in the Abacha transition programme for as long as it lasted. Their action was significant to the extent that it represented the first serious blow against the transition from among establishment politicians, predominantly drawn from the geographical north, who earlier on believed that participation in the transition would enable them to gain access to political power in the elections that were to be held. They

---

[21]Human Rights Watch 1996; *Newswatch* 4 May 1998.
[22]*The Guardian* (Lagos) 27 June 1996; *Newswatch* 8 July 1996.
[23]*The Guardian* (Lagos) 27 June 1996; *Newswatch* 8 July 1996; *Thisday* 19 April 1998.
[24]*Thisday* 19 April 1998.

Figure 9.4: List of political associations that sought registration as political parties under the Abacha transition programme by purchasing party registration forms

All Nigeria Congress (ANC)	National Democratic Congress (NDC)
All People's Alliance (APA)	National Solidarity Peoples Alliance (NSPA)
Committee for National Consensus (CNC)	Nigeria Centre Party (NCP)
Democratic Congress of Nigeria	People's Consensus Party (PCP)
Democratic Party of Nigeria (DPN)	People's Democratic Congress (PDC)
Grassroots Democratic Movement (GDM)	People's Progressive Party (PPP)
Labour Democratic Party (LDP)	People's Redemption Party (PRP)
National Congress for Unity and Democracy (NCUD)	Progressive Party of Nigeria (PPN)
	Social Progressive Party (SPP)
National Congress of Nigeria (NCN)	Solidarity Group of Nigeria (SGN)
National Congress Party (NCP)	United Nigeria Congress (UNC)
National Democratic Alliance (NDA)	United Nigeria Party (UNP)

Source: *Newswatch* 8 July 1996, 8.

NB: It was after the declaration that the parties did not meet NECON's registration requirements that 'merger' talks among some of the associations were officially organised and the five parties, namely, the CNC, DPN, GDM, NCPN, and UNCP, that were to take part in the transition process were created and then formally recognised by the electoral commission as having met its requirements. All the other formations that were not included in the merged organisations were thereafter dissolved and told to stop operating.

were also joined in their condemnation of the party registration exercise by those politicians from the 'progressive' current in Nigerian politics who were not part of the pro-12 June 1993 National Democratic Coalition (NADECO). Particularly notable in this regard were the Social Progressive Party (SPP), the People's Redemption Party (PRP), and the People's Democratic Movement (PDM).[25] As to NADECO, its political front for participating in the transition process, namely, the People's Progressive Party (PPP), probably stood the least chance of gaining any form of acceptance from the regime. Having been left in no doubt that there was no room for its members in the Abacha transition process – indeed, its key leaders/members were to be driven into exile, arrested and detained under various trumped up charges, or targeted for assassination – NADECO's response to the outcome of the registration exercise was to proclaim that the five parties that had been approved were the five fingers of the same leprous hand. It pointed out that the five parties were created with only one mandate: to ensure the self-succession of General Abacha.

Thus it was that at the end of the party registration exercise, opposition to the government and its transition programme not only came from radical quarters like NADECO, the CD, and the newly-formed Democratic Alternative (DA) (a splinter umbrella organisation of civil liberties/human rights groups that were once part of the CD), but also from non-12 June 1993 'progressive' politicians and influential sections of politicians drawn from the conservative/establishment current in Nigerian politics. Opposition also continued against the regime among the various ethnic minority rights organisations, especially MOSOP, that had been set up by the peoples of the oil-producing Niger Delta. The pressure on the regime emanating from these various sources, especially with regard to Abacha's self-succession plan as it unfolded, was complemented by international pressure and the vociferous agitation of a growing army of Nigerians driven into exile by the increasing brutality and bestiality of the regime. Indeed, a host of exile associations was formed which canvassed public and governmental opinion against the Abacha regime in Africa, Europe and North America. As it became increasingly evident that General Abacha was intent on staying in power, the domestic civil society-based opposition to the regime was later to crystallise into the formation of the United Action for Democracy (UAD) set up by organisations affiliated to the CD and the DA.

---

[25]*The Guardian* (Lagos) 27 June 1996; *Newswatch* 8 July 1996.

Elections as the selection of delegates to endorse prolonged military rule

Elections were held over the period between 1996 and 1998 to the local government councils, the state houses of assembly, the mayoralty of Abuja, and the National Assembly as part of the transition process. A distinguishing feature of these elections was the use of the security card by the government to eliminate candidates whom local-level and national officials did not like. Ministers, military administrators and even pro-regime local power brokers used 'national security' as their justification for interfering in the electoral process to remove candidates whom they perceived as potential rivals or people sympathetic to the opposition, especially NADECO. Newspaper reports suggested that, in a significant number of constituencies, results were pre-determined even before polling; in other cases where candidates who were not favoured managed to win their seats, the results were annulled by military administrators and ministers and the preferred candidates sworn in as the winners. The most dramatic, but by no means an isolated case of this brazen interference in the electoral process, concerned the mayoralty of Abuja where the Minister of the Federal Capital Territory and close confidant of Abacha, General Jeremiah Useni, openly defied the courts to swear in the candidate of his choice for that office. His example was replicated by several state military administrators. The election tribunals set up by the regime to hear petitions were mostly reduced to instruments for reversing outcomes that the regime or local power brokers allied to it did not like.[26]

Another distinguishing feature of the elections was the massive deployment of governmental resources in favour of the UNCP.[27] Thus, although the five registered parties were the creations of the government and owed their continued existence to the regime, the UNCP was singled out for special support by various government functionaries for the simple reason that it was seen as the most likely platform on which Abacha would run should the circumstances be such that he would have no option than to contest the presidency with other candidates.[28] It is solely on account of this that the UNCP easily became the most successful of the five parties as military administrators and ministers struggled to ensure that it was awarded more seats in their state as a sign of their loyalty to the regime and the ambitions of General Abacha (see Tables 9.2 and 9.3; and Figure 9.5 for the results of the elections). As can be expected, this fact created rancour and bitterness among the five parties. The four other parties openly accused ministers in the Abacha government as well as state military administrators of campaigning for the UNCP on account of the increasing signals that emanated from Abuja that General Abacha might decide to run on the party's platform for the presidency. Independent evidence exists to suggest that government functionaries actively interfered in the elections to produce outcomes that were in favour of the UNCP. At the same time, there was no missing the fact that for each of the elections, the turnout of voters was very low, none more so than the elections for members of the National Assembly which, even by the government's own admission, witnessed less than a 10 per cent turnout. Most Nigerians who had registered to vote increasingly realised that, apart from the problem that the five officially recognised parties did not really offer them a choice, their vote counted for little as results seemed to be fixed well in advance and the entire transition programme was simply being tailored to ensure Abacha's continued stay in office. The consistently low voter turnout that characterised the elections was seen a source of constant encouragement by NADECO, the UAD, and other opposition groupings which actively campaigned for a popular boycott of the entire transition as a way of discrediting it.[29]

Packaging Abacha for office as 'elected' president

Soon after the conclusion of the work of the Constitutional Conference in 1995, open suggestions began to made from within and outside the government that General Abacha might be the best candidate for the office of president. One of the first hints in this regard was dropped by none other than his wife who told a televised audience in 1996 that, as a Nigerian, her husband was

---

[26]*The Guardian* (Lagos) 23 March, 8 July, 11 August and 17 August 1997; *Daily Times* 25 March, 13 December, 16 December and 18 December 1997; *The Punch* 9 December 1997.

[27]*Daily Times* 25 March, 12 December, 13 December, 15 December, 16 December and 18 December 1997; *The Punch* 9 December 1997.

[28]*Thisday* 20 August 1997.

[29]*The Guardian* (Lagos) 8 July, 11 August, 18 August and 20 August 1997 and 26 April 1998; *The Punch* 9 December 1997; *Newswatch* 11 May 1998.

Table 9.2: Results of the 15 March 1997 party-based local government elections

State	UNCP	DPN	CNC	NCPN	GDM	Remarks
Abia	5	5	–	4	–	
Abuja FCT	5	–	–	1	–	3 run off
Adamawa	86	5	2	3	–	5 awaited
Akwa Ibom	21	4	1	3	–	1 cancelled
Anambra	2	2	6	–	1	10 awaited
Bauchi	10	6	–	–	1	
Bayelsa						
Benue	8	–	6	1	–	
Borno	17	1	–	–	9	
Cross River	4	3	–	1	–	3 run off, 7 awaited
Delta	7	5	1	–	3	2 awaited
Ebonyi	4					
Edo	12	–	–	4	–	2 run off
Ekiti	7	–	3	–	–	5 run off
Enugu	10	4	–	1	–	2 run off
Gombe	5	5	–	–	1	
Imo	9	11	–	–	–	11 run off
Jigawa	8	4	1	8	4	2 run off
Kaduna	13	9	–	–	1	
Kano	5	13	2	5	6	12 run off
Katsina	20	14	–	–	–	
Kebbi	9	7	2	3	–	
Kogi	5	3	7	3	–	3 run off
Kwara	3	–	11	–	2	
Lagos	8	3	1	–	2	7 run off
Nassarawa	9	1	–	–	2	
Niger	10	3	3	5	–	
Ogun	12	1	–	4	–	1 run off
Ondo	7	2	–	–	–	8 run off
Osun	9	10	4	–	–	
Oyo	7	16	4	1	1	4 run off
Plateau	9	1	5	–	1	1 cancelled
Rivers	8	3	–	1	3	
Sokoto	10	12	–	–	–	
Yobe	8	6	–	–	3	
Zamfara	3	6	–	–	2	

Source: *Nigeria Now* January–April 1997, 27.

NB: The results are not complete because in a number of constituencies, NECON cancelled the results and ordered a re-run. In some cases, the results were cancelled by election tribunals set up by the government. Until the collapse of the transition programme, the runoff elections had not been held.

fully qualified to run for office should he so decide. These hints were to grow in intensity after the registration of the five political parties; the chair of the TIC, retired Justice Mamman Nasir, and his deputy, the late S.G. Ikoku, as well as Justice Mohammed Bello, freshly retired as the Chief Justice of the federation, were to take turns in suggesting that in law and constitutionally, nothing stood in the way of General Abacha and the presidency should he choose to run. Abdulrahman Okene, chair of the so-called Northern Elders' Forum, also joined in the growing chorus, arguing that the domestic political situation called for the adoption of General Abacha as a consensus presidential candidate. All of these orchestrated pleas were significantly carried forward when, on 3 February 1998, Justice Nasir directly suggested to the political parties at an official meeting they had with the TIC that they ought to consider encouraging General Abacha to seek the presidency in the national interest. He was joined by some of the ministers in the federal cabinet, including Wada Nas, one of the three members of the Federal Executive Council responsible for 'special duties', generally interpreted to mean the engineering of Abacha's self-succession plan.[30]

---

[30]*Thisday* 19 April 1998; *Newswatch* 27 April and 4 May 1998.

Table 9.3: Results of the 6 December 1997 state houses of assembly elections

State	UNCP	DPN	CNC	GDM	NCPN
Abia	16	5	–	–	3
Adamawa	8	5	3	–	3
Akwa Ibom	16	1	–	9	–
Anambra					
Bauchi	22	9	–	–	–
Bayelsa	15	1	–	3	1
Benue	17	1	7	–	–
Borno	22	–	1	5	–
Cross River	9	9	–	5	1
Delta	10	2	–	4	–
Ebonyi	13	3	–	2	1
Edo	20	4	–	–	–
Ekiti					
Enugu	19	4	–	1	–
Gombe					
Imo	24	2	1	–	–
Jigawa	20	3	1	1	–
Kaduna	21	13	–	–	–
Kano	11	16	1	6	5
Katsina	27	6	–	–	–
Kebbi	15	9	–	–	–
Kogi	16	4	5	–	–
Kwara	9	–	15	–	–
Lagos	31	5	1	3	–
Nassarawa	19	2	1	–	–
Niger	9	13	2	–	2
Ogun	17	7	–	–	–
Ondo	22	3	1	–	–
Osun	9	13	–	1	–
Oyo	13	16	3	–	–
Plateau	23	1	–	–	–
Rivers	27	1	1	–	–
Sokoto	22	8	–	–	–
Taraba					
Yobe	15	6	–	3	–
Zamfara					

Source: *The Punch* 9 December 1997, 2.

NB: The results are not complete for the reasons given in Table 9.2.

An early test of the extent to which General Abacha and his closest advisers were prepared to go in paving the way for his transmutation from military head of state to elected president came when one of his former ministers, Don Etiebet, who held the petroleum portfolio in the first cabinet, formally declared his intention in March 1997 to run for the highest office. He made public his intention to contest the presidency on the platform of the NCPN; it was a party in which he held a key leadership position and was a major financier. Within days of declaring his intention to run for office, Etiebet was arrested, accused of obstructing the voting process for the March 1997 election of local government councillors in his native Akwa Ibom state, and sent to Abuja for further questioning. In Abuja, Etiebet was formally confronted by the most senior security advisers to Abacha; after 'discussions' with them, he summoned a press conference in which he announced that he had decided to first drop his presidential ambition and then to quit the NCPN and join the UNCP, all in the 'highest national interest'. It was the strongest signal from the regime at that early point in the transition process that the presidency was not vacant. Following the treatment meted out to Etiebet, several other politicians such as Olusola Saraki, Lema Jubrilu, Abel Ubeku, Odumegwu Ojukwu, and Emmanuel Iwuanyawu, who were known to be nursing presidential ambitions of their own within the Abacha transition programme, quickly lowered their profiles, revised their strategies, and set their sights on other things.[31] Nigerians were subsequently to witness for the first

---

[31] *Post Express* 8 May 1997 and 10 June 1998; *The Guardian* (Lagos) 11 August 1997.

Figure 9.5: Results of the 6 December 1998 State Houses of Assembly election classified according to the dominant party in each State House of Assembly and in the six geo-political zones delineated by the 1994/95 Constitutional Conference

North-East Zone	North-Central Zone	North-West Zone
Yobe – UNCP	Niger – DPN	Kano – DPN
Borno – UNCP	Plateau – UNCP	Jigawa – UNCP
Bauchi – UNCP	Nassarawa – UNCP	Katsina – UNCP
Adamawa – UNCP	Benue – UNCP	Sokoto – UNCP
Taraba – UNCP	Kogi – UNCP	Zamfara – UNCP
Gombe – UNCP	Kwara – CNC	Kaduna – UNCP
		Kebbi – UNCP

South-South Zone	South-East Zone	South-West Zone
Edo – UNCP	Enugu – UNCP	Oyo – DPN
Delta – UNCP	Ebonyi – UNCP	Ondo – UNCP
Cross-River – UNCP	Anambra – CNC	Osun – DPN
Rivers – UNCP	Abia – UNCP	Lagos – UNCP
Bayelsa – UNCP	Imo – UNCP	Ekiti – UNCP
Akwa Ibom – UNCP		Ogun – UNCP

Source: *The Independent* 9 December 1997, 1.

time in the history of their country, a situation in which politicians, big and small, competed furiously for various elective offices except the presidency for which none dared declare an open interest. It eventually took two outsiders, Tunji Braithwaite and M.D. Yusuf, to change this situation by joining the GDM and seeking the party's nomination for the presidency; we shall return to this point later.

Once elections began to be held, especially after the polling for the state houses of assembly on 6 December 1997 and the National Assembly on 25 April 1998, the orchestrated calls on Abacha to stay in office and for Nigerians to rally in support of this choice became a din. Traditional rulers were summoned by Abacha's political advisers and security chiefs and pressurised, allegedly in return for gifts, to issue a communiqué to the effect that General Abacha was the Nigerian best suited for the office of the president. Their communiqué was read by none other than the Sultan of Sokoto; other prominent traditional rulers, including the Ooni of Ife, Shehu of Borno, Obi of Onitsha, and Oba of Benin flanked him and nodded their approval. Elected local government chairmen were also enlisted into the Abacha-for-president drive as were an assortment of groups claiming to represent Nigerian youths, women and even rural residents. As the self-succession campaign intensified, Abacha, the Minister of the Federal Capital Territory, General Useni, and several state military administrators spent some of their time playing host to sponsored delegations from various parts of the country appealing to the military ruler to run for the presidency. Prominent musicians were also invited to Abuja to perform at a so-called 'two million man march' of Nigerians intent on 'pressurising' Abacha to stay in office. Organised by YEAA with funding to the tune of N500 million (US$6.2 million) from the government, the march was attended by rented crowds and civil servants who were threatened with the sack by state military administrators if they did not go to represent their states and local governments. Free transportation was provided in all major cities of the country, as was free food and music. In the event, the rally attracted only 200,000 people.[32]

Furthermore, the press secretary to General Abacha was to plead with Nigerians to pressurise Abacha not to leave office. Taking their cue from this, state-owned print and electronic media devoted much of their time to distributing daily reports about the demands of an endless stream of groups from different sections of the country demanding that Abacha should 'save' Nigeria by

---

[32]*Post Express* 13 and 14 June 1998 and 11 August 1997; *Thisday* 17 and 19 April 1998; *Newswatch* 27 April and 4 May 1998; *Sunday Times* 19 April 1998; *The Guardian* (Lagos) 20 April 1998.

staying in/running for office. The reports distributed by the official media were meant to reinforce the government's own propaganda that there was a genuine groundswell of popular opinion in the country that Abacha was the best possible material for the presidency, and that opposition, to the extent that it was there, was confined to NADECO, 'unpatriotic' activists who were in exile and their 'masters' in the United States and Europe. It is needless to add that the official media hardly reported stories of opposition to the self-succession plan of General Abacha; even the decision of some students to launch a Youths Earnestly Against Abacha movement went unnoticed. What is more, those independent journalists who gave prominence to opposition activities or took a position against the prolongation of Abacha's period in office were relentlessly pursued by the security agencies. Not a few of the media organisations were routinely shut down by the government; copies of their publications were frequently seized and vendors selling them arrested. On a number of occasions, the government produced fake versions of the independent publications at the same time as funding several individuals to also start 'independent' news organisations that would be friendly to the regime and its policies.[33]

Imposing Abacha as consensus presidential candidate

By the beginning of 1998, few in Nigeria and beyond doubted that General Abacha was intent on succeeding himself as Nigeria's ruler. But it is noteworthy that in all of the officially sponsored or sanctioned campaigning that was going on around him, Abacha himself did not openly declare his interest, leaving it to his close aides, officials, family members, friends, and paid agents to act as his spokespersons. Clearly with an eye on the military, General Abacha did not want to openly and personally play his hand without being absolutely sure that the army was fully under control. Indeed, he was to tell a group of foreign journalists who asked him in mid-January 1997 if he had ambitions to be president that his final decision depended primarily on what his 'constituency', the military, thought. This did not, of course, mean that he was about to leave the military to make a decision all by itself; like Babangida, he engaged in a series of manoeuvrings as part of his bid to master the armed forces. These manoeuvrings included frequent retirements targeted at officers across the ranks whose 'loyalty was in doubt, the arrest and detention of officers and civilians for 'coup plotting', and the frequent reshuffling of key military commanders. One of the more dramatic acts of manoeuvring within the military came on 21 December 1998, when Abacha ordered the arrest of his deputy, General Oladipo Diya, his entire military staff, some of his civilian friends and advisers, and several other senior officers on the grounds that they were involved in planning a coup to violently overthrow the government. Most of the arrested persons were put on trial in the course of the first four months of 1998; several of them, including Diya, were sentenced to death on 28 April 1998 by the tribunal which was set up to try them.[34] That sentence was yet to be ratified and carried out when General Abacha died.

Whilst working on the military in order to pave the way for the imposition of his desire to stay in office, General Abacha and his advisers intensified their manipulation of the political parties and the polity for his presidential ambitions. Direct pressure was brought to bear on the parties to sort out whatever differences they had and work towards the common goal of presenting Abacha as a candidate for the presidency. Politicians, including those who were already elected into various positions and those who had their eyes on one office or the other, were also urged by senior state security personnel to join in the campaign within their parties for Abacha to be adopted as their presidential candidate. Partly in response to these orchestrated pressures, the parties decided in February 1998, under the direct supervision of the TIC, that they would jointly present Abacha as their presidential candidate. Their resolution to this effect was immediately forwarded to General Abacha, but with a separate plea from four of the parties that the results of the 6 December 1997 state assembly elections be voided because of the many irregularities that occurred for the sole benefit of the UNCP. In the face of this plea, the agreement which the TIC got the parties to sign began to unravel as the UNCP, by then widely regarded as the most favoured of the five government parties, repudiated it because it did not want the 'gains' it had made in the local government and state assembly elections to be jeopardised at a time when the four other parties

---

[33]*Newswatch* 27 April 1998.
[34]*The Guardian* (Lagos) 22 and 23 December 1998; *Daily Times* 21 April 1998.

were calling for a re-run of the state assembly elections. The leaders of the UNCP instead decided to concentrate on getting Abacha to be their presidential candidate. Another party, the GDM, always the least connected to senior and well-placed government officials, dissociated itself from the agreement because it said its constitution did not provide for a consensus candidate.[35]

The UNCP's desire to 'monopolise' the candidature of General Abacha for the presidency was, however, not favoured by the General's advisers as it implied that other parties would be free to present their own candidates. The risk of having Abacha compete with four other candidates was one which they were not prepared to take, especially as they could not be sure that, in spite of the machinery of state at their disposal, he would still win. Furthermore, although Abacha had built a reputation among Nigerians for his untrammelled brutality, he was not known to be an engaging public speaker and the thought of him addressing campaign rallies was one which his political and security advisers ruled out. Moreover, politicians marginalised from the Abacha transition were actively regrouping, determined to make the self-succession programme as difficult and bumpy as possible.[36] Indeed, as we noted earlier in a different context, two candidates, Tunji Braithwaite, a Lagos lawyer, and M.D. Yusuf, a former Inspector General of Police during the Murtala-Obasanjo days, had emerged to openly defy Abacha and his advisers by declaring their determination to run for the presidency of Nigeria on the platform of the GDM. Both of them not only addressed press meetings condemning the self-succession scheme, they also began to travel around the country to promote their candidature, promising Abacha a run for his money.

It was against this background that in April 1998, as manoeuvrings intensified to, once again, get the five registered political parties to settle their differences and jointly endorse General Abacha as their consensus presidential candidate, NECON issued a sudden directive asking them to convene their national conventions on the 16th of that month to select their presidential candidate. The UNCP was first off the block, holding its convention in Kaduna where it duly selected Abacha as its candidate. The CNC, NCPN, and DPN followed on 18 April with conventions of their own held, respectively, in Makurdi, Owerri, and Port Harcourt, where they too duly endorsed motions adopting Abacha as their presidential candidate. The only party that was left was the GDM whose leadership was faced with the dilemma of how to handle the candidatures of Yusuf and Braithwaite, who had declared their interest in the presidential ticket. After protesting NECON's directive to the parties on their conventions and having failed to secure the postponement of the National Assembly elections scheduled for 25 April, a postponement which it had requested in order to be able to accommodate the convention, the GDM finally decided to meet in Maiduguri on 19 April 1998.[37]

The choice of Maiduguri as the venue for the GDM's convention was immediately contested by critics of the regime who insisted that it was a calculated move to guarantee Abacha victory given that Maiduguri was the place from which his parents originated before settling in Kano; some of Abacha's strategists gave credence to this concern when they stated that they were sure that the ethnic Kanuri of Borno State would 'flood' the GDM convention in order to deliver a 'landslide' victory to the military ruler. Added to this was the thinly-veiled threat of violence and mayhem that was issued if, somehow, Abacha was not declared winner. It was against this background that, as the debate raged on the proposal tabled by pro-Abacha elements at the convention for the party's constitution to be amended to allow the nomination of a non-party member for the presidency, Braithwaite withdrew his candidature, insisting that pro-Abacha elements, including the party leadership, had determined to prevent a free and fair contest. Braithwaite argued that his continued participation would only serve to give a gloss of legitimacy to an outcome that had already been pre-determined in Abacha's favour. Yusuf, however, decided to stay in the race, with Abacha nominated on the floor of the convention as a second candidate. As the party debated the merits of the two candidates, proceedings were disrupted by a combination of state security agents and hired hooligans who created an atmosphere of generalised confusion, beat up some delegates and shouted calls for the quick endorsement of Abacha. The convention was temporarily

[35]*Newswatch* 27 April and 4 May 1998; *Thisday* 19 April 1998.
[36]*Thisday* 19 April 1998; *Newswatch* 27 April 1998.
[37]*Newswatch* 27 April and 4 May 1998; *Thisday* 17 and 19 April 1998; *Daily Times* 17, 18, 19 and 21 April 1998; *The Guardian* (Lagos) 17, 18, 19 and 20 April 1998.

suspended, to be reconvened in the dead of the night with the hall consciously packed full of pro-Abacha participants, some of whom were, allegedly, not even registered convention delegates. As was expected, Abacha 'won' the 'election', scoring 1,356 votes against Yusuf's 408. Thus it was that Abacha became the GDM's candidate for the presidency. Yusuf and Braithwaite immediately headed for the courts to challenge the 'victory'; they were joined by veteran anti-military campaigner and human rights activist, Gani Fawehinmi. These challenges were, however, swiftly dismissed by the judges who heard the cases.[38]

Thus it was that the stage appeared fully set for Abacha to be transformed from a military ruler to 'elected' president. Two questions, however, remained outstanding. First, were Nigerians still going to have to vote for a president if the five parties had all endorsed Abacha as their candidate? Second, would Abacha run as a retired or serving general? (The legal situation as of the time of Abacha's endorsement by the five parties was that all public officials seeking elective office must first resign from their posts before contesting elections). Regarding the first question, Abacha's political advisers announced to Nigerians that rather than a vote on 1 August for a president, the relevant decrees guiding the transition would be amended to allow for a referendum in which Nigerians would be asked to endorse Abacha as president. As to the second question, Wada Nas, one of the Special Duties Ministers, let it be known that Abacha had no intention whatsoever of quitting the army and that if he was endorsed by Nigerians as President, it would have to be in his capacity as a full general. Clearly, there was still concern within the government as to what the response of the armed forces would be, in spite of the fact that General Oladipo Diya, and several other senior and middle-ranking officers, had already been decisively eliminated from the power equation within the military.[39]

Re-grouping for opposition to Abacha's self-succession

In the meantime, following his endorsement by the five parties, many of the old politicians from across the country who had either been deliberately marginalised from the transition process or who felt themselves unable to accept being puppets for Abacha's political ambitions came together with some of the disaffected members of the registered parties to oppose Abacha's plan to transform himself into a civilian President. First, a group of so-called Northern Elders, organised into the G-18, and drawn from both the conservative and progressive currents of northern Nigerian politics came together and signed a letter to Abacha, warning him not to accept the offer to run for office both for his own good and that of the country. This call came hot on the heels of a statement issued by a group of northern Nigerian academics and civil society activists who condemned the naked manoeuvrings for Abacha's self-succession as both self-serving and not in the national or northern interest. The G-18 was joined by other politicians from other parts of the country and they constituted the so-called G-34 of politicians who also repeated calls for Abacha not to accept to run for office if the already severely discredited transition was not to be further damaged and Nigeria put on the path of prolonged instability that could threaten its existence as one country.

General Abacha mostly responded to the open and angry pleas that were made against his self-succession plan by arresting some of the people who signed the letters. Most prominent among those who were held were Bola Ige of NADECO, Abubakar Rimi and his close associate Sule Lamido, Arthur Nwankwo of the Eastern Mandate Union (EMU), Olisa Agbakoba of the UAD, and Ola Oni, the veteran socialist activist. At the same time, the regime stepped up its attempts to hold Abacha-for-president rallies in Ibadan and Lagos in order to demonstrate that it enjoyed support even in the bastions of the opposition. However, the Ibadan rally that was held on 15 April 1998 and which was addressed by the Oyo state Military Administrator, ended in severe violence, with several fatal shootings and widespread arson; the opposition, working under the auspices of NADECO and the UAD, was able to successfully mobilise the populace to disrupt the pro-Abacha rally and underline popular anger at what was going on in the country. The Lagos rally never took off as the UAD and NADECO promised a repeat of the popular resistance that was witnessed in Ibadan if its organisers tried to hold pro-Abacha public meetings in the city. The UAD also

---

[38]*The Guardian* (Lagos) 20 and 21 April 1998; *Daily Times* 20 and 21 April 1998; *Thisday* 20 and 21 April 1998.
[39]*The Guardian* (Lagos) 20 April 1998; *Daily Times* 18 April 1998.

organised meetings of its own to underline the fact that it found the prospect of the prolongation of military rule in whatever guise totally unacceptable.[40]

Students across the country also regrouped, issuing statements of their own, denouncing General Abacha's agenda for prolonging military rule and promising mass action in all campuses to resist the regime. What was significant in all of this was that, for the first time since General Abacha seized power, a pan-Nigerian opposition movement had begun to develop in contrast to the atomised, regionally and even ethnically based specific kinds of resistance that had been dominant until that point in time. This internal opposition was reinforced by international condemnation, with several Western countries underlining the position that they were not prepared to countenance Abacha's continued stay in office under whatever guise. Civil society groups in Europe and North America and in a number of African countries, including South Africa, also drew up action plans for intensifying their campaigns for tougher action by their governments against General Abacha, the Nigerian military and its civilian collaborators. The Nigerian diaspora across the world, including the large army of people driven into exile by the junta, joined in the renewed campaign of opposition to General Abacha's self-succession plan. A key instrument in this campaign was Radio Kudirat, the voice of the pro-democracy movement which was named in honour of the memory of Abiola's wife after her assasination in June 1996. The radio broadcast its messages to the country from abroad.

This was the state of play when, on 8 June 1998, Nigerians were informed that General Abacha had died suddenly in Abuja of heart failure. Speculation has been rife in Nigeria and abroad as to whether Abacha's death was natural or a calculated act of murder by elements within the regime who were concerned that his determination to cling on to power was both damaging the military irreparably and leading Nigeria towards civil war. Whatever the source of his death may have been, it immediately laid bare his entire transition programme. It was by far the most personalised programme of self-succession ever attempted in Nigeria's history, with a spirited attempt made to mobilise all of the machinery of government and the state in support of General Abacha's ambition. Sections of civil and political society were also recruited into this scheme. While opposition from pro-democracy civil society activists and politicians was not in doubt, it was never entirely clear if Abacha was able to convince the military that the prolongation of his stay in power would also be in their collective institutional interest. Whatever the case, succeed or fail, the way the transition programme had been crafted was such that it would have amounted to a transition to nowhere: If it had succeeded in delivering the presidency to Abacha, Nigerians would have been stuck, for a while at least, with the brutal, anti-democratic mode of administration that had become the trademark of his regime; if it failed, Nigerians would have had, yet again, to go back to the drawing board in their long search for democracy. The latter situation was precisely what was brought about by the death of General Abacha in June 1998.

Post-Abacha quest for political reforms

Perhaps not surprisingly, given the strong opposition that had built up against it, the death of General Abacha led inevitably to the death of his transition programme. His successor, General Abdulsalam Abubakar, who was the Chief of Defence Staff during the Abacha years, came under intense pressure at home and abroad to dissolve the five parties, cancel all the elections that Abacha had held, and free all political prisoners. After what seemed like some initial procrastination that may not have been unconnected with considerations of regime security, Abubakar and his colleagues began to bow to the pressures piled on them by freeing scores of political prisoners, meeting with the opposition NADECO on ways of resolving the political stalemate in the country, and dissolving the so-called National Reconciliation Commission (NARECOM) and the National Committee on the Devolution of Powers that were both set up by Abacha, basically to appear to be responding to demands for internal political dialogue and administrative decentralisation. It was also announced that meetings had been held between the most senior functionaries of the government and M.K.O. Abiola, although the outcome of the discussions that were held remained

---

[40]*Tribune* 16 and 17 April 1998; *Daily Times* 16 and 17 April 1998; *Newswatch* 27 April 1998.

inconclusive as Abiola made it clear that he was not about to surrender his mandate of 12 June 1993 as demanded by the new military rulers. This was a position he held on to in the face of pressures that were brought to bear on him by the United Nations and Commonwealth secretaries general who, in paying swift visits to Abuja, were among the first set of international and foreign dignitaries to respond to the charm offensive launched by General Abubakar in order to break Nigeria's international isolation.[41]

By the beginning of July 1998, it was clear that the new military leadership was going to jettison the entire transition programme of the Abacha regime; the only question that remained was how long a new programme would take to organise and how Abiola would fit into it. A substantial political dilemma was partially solved, at least temporarily, for the government when, on 7 July 1998, Abiola died suddenly while he was still in the custody of the military as a political prisoner. He allegedly died of a heart attack that developed while he was meeting with a visiting delegation of senior American government officials;[42] many raised questions about the circumstances of that death but few doubted that it was one death that was very convenient both for the regime and the leading Western countries interested in Nigeria's domestic political situation. In the aftermath of Abiola's death, General Abubakar and his colleagues moved swiftly to dissolve the five political parties, cancel all the elections that were conducted during the Abacha years, and announce a new transition programme that would begin with local government elections on 5 December 1998 and terminate on 29 May 1999 with the swearing in of an elected president. An Independent National Electoral Commission (INEC) was also set up to replace NECON while the TIC was dissolved. Without doubt, the government's attempt to promote a new transition programme was made relatively easier by Abiola's death even if little comfort could be derived from the knowledge that he died as a prisoner of the military whilst holding on tightly to his claim of being the legitimate, popular elected leader of Nigeria.[43]

Within a few days of its establishment, INEC held consultations with various political associations with the primary aim of seeking their views on the rules that would govern party formation and the electoral process. Following the consultations, it announced that Nigerians were free, at the initial stage, to form parties which would then be evaluated for their national-geographical spread and granted temporary registration until after the December 1998 local government elections. In October 1998, INEC announced the interim registration of 9 political parties out of the 29 that applied for recognition. The provisionally registered parties were the All Peoples' Party (APP), Alliance for Democracy (AD), Democratic Advance Movement (DAM), Movement for Democracy and Justice (MDJ), National Solidarity Movement (NSM), People's Democratic Party (PDP), People's Redemption Party (PRP), United Democratic Party (UDP), and United People's Party (UPP). The leadership and membership of these parties included people who were once detained or exiled by the Abacha regime side-by-side with people who were marginalised or chose to keep their distance from the Abacha transition programme and people who actively participated in the 5 parties that were dissolved, including some of the prominent individuals who campaigned for Abacha's self-succession. To confirm their registration, the parties were required by INEC to win at least 10 per cent of the total votes cast in two-thirds of the 36 states of the federation in the December 1998 local government elections. Those parties that failed to achieve this target automatically lost their registration after the local government elections.

In the local government elections that were held on 5 December, 1998 (see Table 9.4), three parties, namely the PDP, the APP and the AD, emerged as the biggest players in the new transition programme. They were subsequently granted certificates of full registration by INEC to continue to function as political parties and participate in the remaining elections that were to be organised. The remaining six parties that were not granted full registration were ordered to dissolve themselves even though several of them had elected local government chairmen and councillors. The elections into the state houses of assembly, the state governorships, the National Assembly (consisting of the Senate and the House of Representatives), and the presidency (see Tables 9.5, 9.6, 9.7 and 9.8) followed the broad patterns that had been set in the earlier local

[41]*Post Express* 20 June 1998; *The Guardian* (Lagos) 22 June 1998.
[42]*The Guardian* (Lagos) 8 July 1998.
[43]*Post Express* 22 July 1998; *The Guardian* (Lagos) 22 July 1998; *Thisday* 22 July 1998.

Table 9.4: Nigerian local government elections, 5 December 1998

| | Parties | | | | | | | | |
	AD	APP	PDP	UPP	PRP	MDJ	DAM	NSM	UDP
No. of states with 5% of votes	13	35	36	1	0	2	0	1	0
Elected Chairmen	102	192	464	1	2	3	0	2	0
Elected Councillors	1101	2599	4840	35	21	71	4	17	11

No data for 8 Chairmanship and 112 Councillorship positions.

Source: SPMGN Report.

Table 9.5: Nigerian local government elections, 5 December 1998: Party support by zone

		Parties							
		AD	APP	PDP		AD	APP	PDP
			Chairmen				Councillors	
Zones	Total				Total			
SW	137	95	19	21	1542	931	205	384
SE	95	2	23	67	1249	41	361	768
SS	123	3	35	79	1406	67	436	807
NW	186	0	46	137	2005	6	635	1325
NC	115	2	31	81	1337	45	444	821
NE	112	0	37	74	1210	11	502	694
FCT	6	0	1	5	62	0	16	41

No data for 8 Chairmanship and 112 Councillorship positions.

Source: SPMGN Report; *Guardian* (Lagos) 10 December 1999.

Table 9.6: Nigerian gubernatorial elections, 9 January 1999

| Party | Zone | | | | | | Total | Total |
	SW	SE	SS	NW	NC	NE	(States)	(Votes)
AD	6	0	0	0	0	0	6	3,163,587 (11.52%)
APP	0	0	0	4	2	3	9	9,854,222 (35.89%)
PDP	0	5	6	3	4	3	21	14,434,037 (52.58%)
Total (States)	6	5	6	7	6	6	36	27,451,846

Source: SPMGN Report; *Vanguard* 14 January 1999.

Table 9.7: Nigerian national assembly elections, 20 February 1999

| | Party | | | | |
Chamber	AD	APP	PDP	To be declared	Total
Senate	20	24	59	6	109
House	68	74	206	12	360

Source: SPMGN Report; *Guardian* (Lagos) 23 February 1999.

Table 9.8: Nigerian presidential elections, 27 February 1999

	Olusegun Obasanjo	Olue Falae
Total Votes	18,738,154	11,110,287
No. of States won	27	9
No. of States with >25% of votes.	32	23

Source: SPMGN Report; *Vanguard* 2 March 1999; *Guardian* (Lagos) 2 March 1999.

government elections, with the PDP emerging as the biggest party, the APP following as the second party, and the AD as the third. Broad ethno-regional trends were in evidence in the support base of the three parties, with the PDP drawing considerable support from the north-central and the south-east and splitting the north-west and the south-south with the APP, the APP being firmly rooted in the north-east, and the AD being the dominant player in the south-west of the country. There was, however, little or no ideological difference among the parties although the PDP had a preponderance of establishment politicians and retired military officers, the APP had a disproportionate number of politicians who associated themselves with Abacha's regime (hence it was derided from birth as the Abacha People's Party), while the AD was home to many of those who were associated with NADECO and the pan-Yoruba *Afenifere* political grouping (Mustapha 1999).

The process of the nomination of candidates for elective office was marred by considerable controversy and manipulation, including vote-buying and outright rigging. Indeed, after the local government elections, all the three parties suffered different degrees of internal crisis over the nomination of candidates for various offices. The selection of presidential candidates within the parties was particularly marked by acrimony and the exchange of huge sums of money. Indeed, the APP was to split into different factions following the internal disagreement that greeted the effort by a section of its leadership to zone its presidential ticket to the geographical South within the framework of a contested alliance with the AD. The general membership of the AD itself was stunned by the decision of party leadership to choose Olue Falae over the highly-favoured Bola Ige to be the party's candidate in the alliance that was struck with the APP for the presidential election. The PDP which also had a highly-charged convention selected retired General Obasanjo as its presidential candidate and moved quickly to try to patch up the divisions which the mud-slinging and vote-buying associated with the selection process caused. The presidential contest that was held on 27 February 1999, therefore, pitched Olu Falae, representing a highly shaky alliance between the APP and the AD, against Olusegun Obasanjo, heading a PDP which was by and large more united and confident.

The presidential elections were, like the earlier elections, marked by different kinds of irregularities, only this time they seemed to be on a much bigger scale. Obasanjo was declared winner by INEC with a vote of 18,738,154 to Olu Falae's 11,110,287. While most independent observers believed that, on the strength of earlier patterns, it was highly probable, even certain, that Obasanjo and the PDP won the presidential election, they strongly doubted that the margin of the victory was as wide as the result that was proclaimed. Falae himself was to emphatically reject the result, alleging massive fraud by the PDP and some electoral officials and taking his case to the presidential election tribunal. His petition was, however, dismissed by the tribunal and amidst pleas that he should not do anything that might encourage hawks within the military to scuttle the transition to civil rule, he decided not to make an appeal to the Supreme Court. Thus it was that the way was cleared for Obasanjo and the elected state governors to be sworn in on 29 May 1999, marking the end of nearly 16 years of unbroken military rule. It was now the task of the elected officials to grapple with the legacy of institutionalised corruption, an eroded national moral fibre, a brutalised national psyche, deepening ethno-regional suspicion and religious intolerance, and a collapsed national physical and social infrastructure which the military bequeathed the country. The politicians were to tackle these problems within the framework of a flawed electoral mandate, a dubious, even illegitimate constitutional framework, increasing campaigns for a far-reaching restructuring of the system of national-territorial administration, and growing poverty in the country. Few doubt that the tasks will test all the managerial and political skills of the country's new rulers; their success or failure might well play a central role in determining if elected governance and the Nigerian state will endure.

Concluding remarks

With the armed forces having been severely discredited and internally demoralised by the record of the Abacha years, and conscious of the deep unpopularity of the military among the majority of the citizenry, it is not surprising that the Abubakar junta did not seek to play the kinds of self-succession games that its immediate predecessor and, before that, the Babangida regime, tried to foist on Nigerians. Indeed, there seemed to be a conscious attempt to avoid the kinds of open, manipulative political engineering that were a hallmark of the Babangida and Abacha transitions. For the first time in Nigeria's post-colonial history, a military government came to power which committed itself to handing over power to elected politicians within a space of less than one year; although the internal political balance would, in all probability, have made a much longer transition difficult to sustain, it is still significant that the new military regime itself felt the need to retreat from the political scene as quickly as possible. Whether the much-delayed Fourth Republic will be sufficiently democratic in content and capable of resolving the myriad of problems that are the legacy of military rule remains to be seen.

What is, however, clear from the experience of electoral politics during the Abacha years is that the transition programme, born, as it was, out of a highly authoritarian, neo-fascist environment, amounted to little more than an attempt to prolong military rule using the facade of elections that neither offered choice to the citizenry nor the prospects for an opening up of the political space for oppositional activity. If anything, the political space available for autonomous citizen action was increasingly narrowed as the implementation of the transition programme progressed. It is little wonder then that voter turnout was consistently dismal throughout the transition programme; most Nigerians were not persuaded that the prolongation of military rule under General Abacha, together with the loss of their most basic political freedoms, was a price well worth paying for whatever promise of national stability and unity the regime tried to market as its main objective. Indeed, the methods by which it attempted to organise its continued stay in office increasingly came to be seen as the single biggest threat to national unity and stability; as the self-succession programme developed, it, therefore, only served to focus opposition to continued military rule. The goal of permanently keeping the military out of national governance and avoiding a repeat of the experience of the Babangida and Abacha regimes has already emerged as one of the key political challenges facing the politicians who came to power on 20 May 1999 following the handing over of the reins of power from the military government of General Abdulsalam Abubakar to civilians.

10

Multi-Party Elections & the
Predicament of Northern Hegemony
in Sudan

ATTA EL-BATTAHANI

Introduction

The Sudan has had a rich experience of elections to the extent that even one-party, totalitarian regimes have found it difficult not to concede to the principle of allowing publicly contested elections, however inadequately these elections may have been organised. Many scholars have sought, with varying degrees of success, to account for elections and their political significance (Bechtold 1976, Karar 1986, Mahmoud 1986, Niblock 1987, Hamid 1990, Kursani 1997). Though these studies have yielded some useful material and made some perceptive observations about the issues over which elections were fought, the analysis of elections in the Sudan has generally been deficient. The main deficiencies include an inadequate treatment of the underlying pattern of conflict over state power, a lack of in-depth sociological and economic analyses of elections and of political mobilisation, especially regarding the use of ethnic and religious ideology and symbols during elections. Gender has been neglected.

A political economy perspective is adopted in this chapter to provide a different approach to elections in the Sudan. Representative democracy, in conventional perspectives, usually means practices of multi-party politics, electoral competition and an independent judiciary and/or electoral competition, while an absence of these practices is often taken to taken to mean dictatorship and authoritarianism (see Chapter 1). However, this equation between multi-party elections and democracy does not always hold true. From a non-conventional perspective, the general historical overview that is provided in the first part of this chapter tells a different story about Sudanese elections. While multi-party elections are not necessarily democratic, elections under a one-party regime should not be dismissed out of hand as undemocratic and irrelevant. One important point that emerges from a general view of elections is that the representation of minorities, including the South, has often been greater during one- than multi-party parliaments. Another point, as shown by the more detailed study of the 1996 elections in the latter part of this chapter, is that a totalitarian regime is capable of adopting practices of participatory democracy to serve as the institutional means for conducting elections.

Nevertheless, the main purpose of studying elections in the Sudan is to show how a predominantly northern power-bloc has managed to maintain its hegemony during periods of civilian, military, one- and multi-party rule. In maintaining their political hegemony, ruling classes have successfully manipulated both capital and the state by keeping various sources of opposition in their place. The main questions, therefore, are about how 'democratic' democratic, multi-party elections really are and in what way elections under one-party, totalitarian regimes can be said to be undemocratic. My intention is to answer these questions by assessing the impact of elections and electoral processes on the capacities of working masses, ethnic-national groupings in peripheral regions (especially the South), and women to organise autonomously of the manipulations of both capital and the state.

In view of the fact that seven general elections have taken place in the Sudan between 1953 and 1996, a body of material is available to justify a historical, diachronic analysis with the main objective of bringing out the political significance of elections.[1] It is evident that Sudanese elections and parliament have not been an imitation of the Westminster model of parliamentary democracy despite the former British colonial influence. More generally, it is through the Sudanese electoral system that it has been possible and credible for political parties that are ethnically-based and non-democratic in structure to act democratically and abide by the rules of democratic politics. Both traditional-sectarian parties, such as the Umma and the Democratic Unionist Party (DUP), and those non-democratic in discourse and orientation, such as the National Islamic Front (NIF), have competed in multi-party elections. In particular, this chapter, in paying particular attention to the factors that contributed to the electoral gains achieved by the Islamic-dominated party between 1986 and 1996, brings out the systematic tension between a genuine representation of voter choice and the formal procedures of democracy. Underlying this systematic tension is a gradual, uneven process of an emerging citizenry, determined to fully acquire and enjoy political and economic rights *vis-à-vis* a conservative, northern-based hegemonic power bloc of ruling classes and groups.

Elections before 1989

When the British took over the administration of the country at the turn of the twentieth century they found a relatively developed local trade network in the riverine areas where a number of associational groups were active. Artisans, carpenters, dealers, and merchants, together with other religious, sectarian and tribal orders, associations, organisations, all formed part of the Sudanese political community. The British administration adopted a two-pronged strategy. Firstly, to counter the potential threat of the religious Mahdist force, quasi-liberal colonial policies encouraged the growth of a market economy and 'modern' social strata such as merchants, technicians, administrators and intellectuals. Secondly, however, the interest of the British administration in political stability dictated that it could not develop a fully-fledged market economy, together with modern secularism, for fear of provoking the spread of nationalism. Therefore the associations of modern strata, corresponding roughly to what I refer to as civil society, have developed in a process of gradual evolution (for more general histories of what follows, see Holt 1961; Beshir 1974; Niblock 1987).

Of special significance here is the conflict of interest between three broad coalition forces: urban merchants and educated groups, an alliance of traditional, sectarian groups, mainly the Ansar and Khatmiyya, and the colonial state. The South, on the other hand, was administered separately after the 'pacification' of resistance to colonial rule and the imposition of the Closed District Act of 1922. The gradual spread of nationalism from Egypt into the Sudan, and the events of 1924, when Sudanese and Egyptian armed forces orchestrated an armed mutiny, had altered the balance of power between these three groups in many fundamental ways. In the years that followed, the closer collaboration between British colonialism and religious sectarianism had alienated the educated and merchants from colonial rule and sown the seeds of conflict between these groups and the state.

During the first years of the British colonial administration, the intention of administrators was to renovate those northern Sudanese societies that were thought to have been destroyed by the Mahdiya. However, in adopting a rather peculiar liberal social philosophy, the British administration left indigenous cultural and social structures untouched except when these interfered with their overriding concern of maintaining law and order. Both political and economic arrangements reflected this principle of political stability. State-run schemes, sharecropping formulae and control of movement of local merchants were all elements of guided or controlled change. Among the factors that contributed towards the prevalence of political space during the colonial period were the 'fair' dispensation of economic schemes; the nurturing of local collaborators among religious and sectarian groups; a

---

[1] A number of data sources were used for this research: interviews with state and non-state officials and political parties across different regions; archival records and reports at the National Record Office, the National Electoral Commission in Khartoum and at the University of Khartoum Library; and, not least, newspaper archives.

concern not to deepen social differentiation; the incorporation of native administration within the system of government and a tolerant attitude towards the newly emerging educated élites. The roots of present-day civil society, encompassing political parties, trade unions, pressure groups, the press, regional and tribal associations were laid down during the colonial period.

Since their interests were frustrated, both the *jallaba* merchants and educated *effendiyya,* the cornerstones of civil society, had an antagonistic attitude towards the state of both the colonial and post-colonial periods. Lack of trust and suspicion shaped the relationship between the colonial administration and the *jallaba* and *effendiyya* who regarded the state as a source of colonial power, repression and, later, as a tool in the hands of traditional groups. While the *jallaba* and *effendiyya* increasingly overlapped as class groupings, during the 1950s and after independence, they competed for state power. Although commercial interests came to find a voice in state institutions, professionals, in particular, continued to view the state with suspicion after independence. On the other hand, both the colonial and post-colonial state administrations had a deep suspicion of these 'new' or 'modern' classes which were seen as determined to undermine the power and privileges of traditional authorities (Al-Hardallo 1998).

The Sudanese nationalist movement's gradual and steady emergence during the 1930s and 1940s was partly based on a fit, or correspondence, between an emerging civil society and a growing market economy. Social and tribal associations from the 1920s, and especially the Graduate Congress of the 1930s, spearheaded the nationalist call for self-rule and political independence from Anglo–Egyptian colonial rule. To placate the nationalist forces, the British administration instituted the Advisory Council in 1944 and the Legislative Assembly in 1948. Both, however, were boycotted by the mainstream nationalist movement, though the colonial rulers did not fail to find allies and collaborators among the tribal aristocracy and religious sectarian leaders. By taking part in these 'legislative' bodies, rural and religious groups, with their interests in agricultural schemes, trading companies and external trade, were co-opted into government.

Furthermore, the colonial administration used the coalition with the 'traditionals', of the native/tribal administration and religious aristocracy, to control the rural masses and check the growth of the nationalist movement in urban areas. For its part, the nationalist movement organised and galvanised the gradually emerging new social groups and classes of teachers, lawyers, technicians, workers, artisans and students. But controversies over what tactics to adopt in the struggle for independence, among other issues, led to a split among the nationalist élites. Calling for 'Sudan for the Sudanese', and preferring co-operation with the British, the Ansar formed a political group whose objective was an independent Sudan. Pro-Egyptian forces called for 'Unity of the Nile Valley'. Both parties, however, were organised under the leadership of an educated, secular and modern élite of the Graduate Congress.

Subsequent failures to reach out to the masses forced urban élites to seek rapport with religious leaders and tribal aristocracy. One result of this turn of events was the formation of political parties. A section of élites and the Ansar sect formed the Umma party in 1945; later during 1954–5, another group joined the Khatmiyya sect with the blessing of its patron, Sayyed Ali Al-Marghni, and formed the People's Democratic Party (PDP), led by Sheikh Ali Abdelrahman and others who professed pro-Arab sympathies with Nasserite Egypt. For a period, non-sectarian élites led the National Unionist Party (NUP) that was politically influential during the 1950s. However, collaboration between the PDP leadership and the military regime of General Abboud, during 1958–1964, alienated party supporters and weakened its support in the aftermath of the downfall of the Abboud military regime in 1964. Sensing its probable electoral failure, the PDP boycotted the 1965 general elections and negotiations with the NUP, in 1967, led to the formation of the Democratic Unionist Party (DUP) which was able to effectively compete and win more seats than its arch rival, the Umma party, at the 1968 elections.

A more radical élite group allied itself with workers, peasants, professional strata and students in what came to be the Communist Party, while another group formed the Islamist movement by way of reaction and challenge to the Communists. Regional political parties and movements emerged to express the discontent of the marginalised population in less-developed regions of the South, West and East. Although Northern political forces were not united, as I have indicated above, nonetheless the discontent and frustration of regional and ethnic political movements were directed at these predominantly northern ruling forces. In fact, the above-mentioned groups and parties generally dominated the political scene in post-independence Sudan.

The northern political culture in the Sudan has been based on openness to outside cultural influences from the Middle East and Europe. However, this openness has not extended towards an African and Christian South. As a result, there been a historic tendency for a missionary attitude towards assimilating non-Arab and non-Muslim Africans within the country, an attitude based on the eventual southward spread of the twin processes of Islamisation and Arabisation (El-Bashir 1987, 161). In its extreme form, northern political culture takes the shape of the Islamic Fundamentalism of NIF. Its moderate form has been expressed by the more tolerant stance of the popular sectarian traditional parties of Umma and the DUP. Due to the racial and religious discrimination practised by post-colonial governments after independence, and experienced most by the educated élite of the South who have resisted Islamisation and Arabisation, southern Sudan has been rent by war for most of the post-colonial period.

After the Second World War, and following the success of the Gezira Scheme and other economic ventures, the state emerged as an important economic proposition for indigenous merchants and traders whose nationalistic sentiments were directed towards displacing foreign merchants and companies in gaining access to state resources. This tendency among indigenous merchants began to sow the seeds of friction between the two cornerstones of civil society, represented by the *jallaba* bourgeoisie, on the one hand, and the *effendiyya*, who now embraced peasants, workers and professionals, on the other. In particular, this was the case during the 1950s and 1960s when the nationalist leaders presiding over NUP, Umma and the PDP sought the support of both merchants and the rural aristocracy, making state support and resources available for enriching these groups but incurring the wrath of workers, peasants and professional groups within civil society.

The 1953 self-rule elections

The Sudanese politicians adopted a Westminster model, with some significant modifications, during the early 1950s. One modification was to establish graduate constituencies to give weight to educated Sudanese and reflect the role they played in politics. Boundaries of constituencies were defined on a special basis while there was no female participation in elections at least until 1965. Yet, it was generally agreed that the first general multi-party elections, following the Self-Rule Agreement of 1953, were free and fair, even though the Umma party and some British press reports alleged Egyptian interference in the electoral process.

The 1953 elections were held during a political conjuncture largely shaped by the ascendancy of NUP activists who had formed the Graduate Congress in the 1930s and played a leading role in the formation of political parties and trade unions during the 1940s. After the Juba Conference of 1947, southerners joined the national political process. Only after receiving pledges that their calls for federalism would be treated favorably by the northerners did they support the declaration of Independence of Sudan from both Britain and Egypt in 1955.

Table 10.1: The distribution of seats after the 1953 general elections

Party	Parliament	Senate-elected	Senate-nominated	Senate-total
NUP	50	21	10	31
Umma	23	4	4	8
SRP	3	1	0	1
Southern Party	9	3	3	6
Independents & South	12	1	3	4
Total	97	30	20	50

Source: Bechtold 1976, 180.

A number of national and regional factors had contributed to the electoral success of NUP at the 1953 elections. NUP drew support from both secularised urbanites and followers of the Khatmiyya sect, the traditional opponent of the Ansars. Secularism in Sudan does not involve a rejection of the Koran and of Islamic principles; nor does secular behaviour manifest itself in a refusal to perform the normal obligations of a Muslim. It was the Muslim Brotherhood, an offshoot of the Egyptian Muslim Brotherhood, who distinguished themselves by adhering, or claiming to adhere, to strict codes of Islamic behaviour. Followers of the two religious sects, the Ansar and Khatmiyya, were distinguished by an unquestionable, personal allegiance to their sectarian leaders. The Khatmiyya supported the NUP because it was anti-Ansar. The Khatmiyya within the NUP were at the forefront of abandoning their cause of union with Egypt after the NUP defeated the Umma at the 1953 elections.

Thus, the NUP brought together two distinct groups who had very little in common on social, religious or economic grounds (Bechtold 1976, 186). The El-Azhari leadership of the NUP was an asset to the party, together with a dynamic hierarchy at the top and an efficient organisation at local levels. The NUP landslide victory was attributed, among other factors, to its success in presenting a platform attractive to the Sudanese at this particular juncture in time, superior organisational talent and an effective use of resources made possible by solid financial backing, especially from Egypt (*ibid.*, 184–186).

One reason for Umma's electoral defeat was attributed to its visibly pro-British stance, whereas the original 'struggle for self-determination' was dominated and led by Ismail el-Azhari of the NUP.[2] Also, the militant fanaticism of the Ansar sect had alienated a large proportion of the electorate. Another important reason was possibly that the 1948–52 period of the Legislative Assembly, when the Umma Party shared the burden of government with the British, was one of labour unrest, demonstrations and economic hardships. Hence the Umma party was much more exposed to criticism than the rival parties that had boycotted the Legislative Assembly.

The Southern Party that fought the 1953 elections was formed by some southern politicians, including 'leaders of those southern tribes who could not be bought by northern parties' and who had the support of southern intelligentsia and the 'great bulk of southerners' (*ibid.,* 178). It is instructive to note, for what happened during the following decades, that the party aimed to secure the interests of southern Sudanese by working and cooperating with coalition governments in the North to achieve regional autonomy for the South.

The 1958 elections

The NUP elected government of 1953 was generally of a centrist nature, winning a broad-based support of urban middle classes, but attracting the wrath of both the conservative, sectarian parties of Umma and PDP as well as radicals and Communists on the left. Power struggles and intrigues led to pro-Khatmiyya leaders breaking away from the NUP and, as mentioned above, forming the PDP. Following the PDP succession from NUP, El-Azhari, Prime Minister and leader of NUP, lost a vote of confidence and was replaced by a coalition government formed by Umma and PDP in 1956. The sectarian coalition extended the life of the Constituent Assembly which adopted a new Parliamentary Election Act that enabled general elections. The 1958 elections were contested by the NUP, Umma, the PDP, the Southern Liberal Party and the Anti-Colonialist Front (Communists).

What characterised the 1958 elections was growing friction among northern political parties. The emergence of a new alignment between Umma and PDP parties seemed poised to challenge 'the new secularism of the Unionists', a development that prompted the Unionists to muster the forces of educated urbanites against traditional sectarianism (Bechtold 1976, 189). On the basis of an effective electoral pact, the Umma and PDP avoided confronting each other in constituency elections and pooled their resources to defeat the NUP, which won support from communists and radicals. The NUP won the largest number of votes but only one-half the seats won by the coalition parties, thereby suffering from the malapportionment of constituencies for 1958. Other factors cited by Bechtold (*ibid.*, 193–196) to explain the NUP failure included a loss of the outside financial support which the party mobilised in 1953, together with complacency on the part of the leadership.

---

[2]Likewise, the NUP and Umma labelled the Socialist Republican Party (SRP) as British stooges who wanted to maintain British rule and influence in the Sudan. The SRP was made up of conservative tribal leaders who advocated independence for the Sudan but were opposed to Mahdi domination. According to Bechtold, almost immediately after the 1953 elections the party collapsed and has not been revived since (Bechtold 1976, 177–178).

Umma gains were attributed, firstly, to a revision in eligibility requirements, enabling all male Sudanese over 30 years of age to vote. According to Bechtold (*ibid.*, 191), this revision helped to overcome 'the built-in advantage that the NUP had formally enjoyed when Senate electors had educational prerequisites'. Secondly, the Umma managed to hold to its traditional regional, rural power bases in west-central Sudan and to maintain its historical support base in both east and north Sudan, the original area of the historical leaders of the Mahdist Revolution, Osman Digna and Mohammed Ahmed Al-Mahdi. Thirdly, the territorial delimitation of 9 constituencies was gerrymandered in order to improve the prospects of Umma or PDP candidates who won in 8 of these 9 constituencies (Niblock 1987, 212). Whereas the delimitation of constituencies in 1953 was determined by an international commission and, later in 1965, by a non-partisan electoral committee, the government controlled the electoral process for the 1958 elections.[3]

Deep-seated tribal cleavages racked southerners who, however, found a semblance of unity in supporting the Southern Liberal Party's call for 'federalism for the South', the electoral slogan of the party at the elections. As shown in Table 10.2, the Southern Liberal Party (SLP), successor to the Southern Party, emerged as the third largest party in parliament in 1958. Although the SLP's gains seemed to show that the electorate in the South had voted to pursue its own political trajectory, many winning candidates in the South were either independents, devoid of any political party affiliation, or in effective alliance with Northern parties.

Table 10.2: The distribution of seats after the 1958 general elections

Party	House of Representatives	Senate
Umma	63	14
NUP	44	5
PDP	26	4
Southern Liberal Bloc	40	7
Total	173	30

Source: Bechtold 1976, 190.

Party political ferment after the 1958 election was compounded by economic hardships as 'foreign exchange reserves had dwindled from £62 million to £8 million and the balance of trade continued in a negative spiral with no relief in sight' (Bechtold 1976, 197). The electoral pact between Umma and the PDP fractured amidst a gathering momentum of popular opposition and increasing Egyptian pressures on the government to amend the Nile Waters Agreement. To avert the threat of parliamentary defeat by the opposition, the government parties agreed to adjourn Parliament until their differences were ironed out (Ali 1989, 144).

For our purpose here, it is necessary to stress that the opposition against the government, including its intentions to accept American aid, was led by the Sudan Workers Trade Union Federation (SWTUF) which had been able 'to play a more active role in, and leave a greater mark on, public affairs…than most of its counterparts in Africa and the Middle East' (Bechtold 1976, 113). When the government withdrew its recognition of the Federation, the SWTUF organised a successful nationwide strike, supported by the tenant farmers' union, student organisations and the communists. With the alleged connivance of the Umma party, senior army officers intervened in politics to topple the elected government during November 1958. Basically, the 1958 coup happened because political and economic instability ran together with the failure of any fraction of the predominantly Arab Muslim bourgeoisie to impose a stable form of political domination. Military rule was meant to have provided a period of reprieve during which the power bloc would be reorganised and its control over the dominated classes reasserted and secured (Ali 1989, 146). Yet, if anything, it was the military regime's mishandling of the Southern question, together with the economic development projects

---

[3]Other measures taken by the Umma-PDP coalition government to manipulate the electoral process included dropping the educational requirement for electors in the Senate constituencies, loosening the nationality provisions to make it easier for Fellata and other West African immigrants, known as supporters of the Umma Party, to vote, and introducing mobile polling units in nomadic areas to increase electoral participation by other well-known supporters of the ruling coalition (Niblock 1987, 211).

established in the North, within the context of the Ten Year Socio-Economic Development Plan (1960/61–1970/71), which were to sow the seeds of its eventual overthrow.

The 1965 elections

After six years of military rule, the forced Arabisation and Islamisation of the South had proceeded apace, tacitly supported by northern 'conservatives'. The response in the South was an escalation of war as thousands of southerners fled to the bush to fight the military regime by joining the Anya Nya movement. Also the outcomes of the Ten Year Socio-Economic Development Plan had contributed to an unprecedented expansion in irrigated agriculture, rain-fed mechanised farming, infrastructural and communication networks, urban areas and industrial production. In the face of the growing economic and social power of the middle classes, professionals and a state salariat which the Development Plan had brought about, the traditional ruling classes concluded that the military regime had outlived its purpose. Furthermore, the increased power of these social strata fed into popular resistance against the military regime.

During 1964, popular opposition to military rule reached its peak when politicians in the North made the direct link between the attempt to enforce a military solution upon the South and the lack of democracy in the North. Protests by university students and clashes with the police were followed by street demonstrations that culminated in a successful general strike. By October 1964, the fate of the military junta was sealed.

A new transitional government was formed in October 1964, comprising the Communist Party (CPS) and representatives of professional associations, the tenants' and farmers' unions and workers' unions as well as those from the older political parties. The CPS was legally recognised for the first time, women obtained full political rights, and the SWTUF regained official recognition that was extended to workers in the private sector. This extension of trade union rights, alongside that of other associations in government, disturbed employers to an extent that the Umma Party incited its fanatical followers, of the Ansar sect, to demonstrate against the transitional government (Niblock 1987, 228).[4] Following further unrest, the northern conservative parties, including the PDP and NUP, succeeded in forcing the resignation of the Prime Minister, Sir al-Khatim al-Khalifaa, and his provisional government and secured a return to coalition government including Umma, the NUP, the Islamic Charter and the Southern Front. The scene was now set for a return to electoral politics on terms that favoured the northern conservative parties and their allies.

Table 10.3: The distribution of seats after the 1965 general elections

Party	Territorial Constituencies	Graduate Constituencies	Total
Umma	76	–	76
NUP	52	2	54
ICF	3	2	5
PDP	3	–	3
Communist	–	11	11
Independents & Beja[5]	24 (10 Beja)	–	24
Total	158	15	173

Source: Sudan 1967.

---

[4]Also interview with Ahmed Al-Sayid Hamad, Cairo, 23 February 1999.
It was the intention of the Professional Front, the alliance that led the uprising against military rule, to allocate one-half of all seats in a new Constituent Assembly to representatives of workers' and peasants' associations.
[5]Beja are an ethnic grouping in Eastern Sudan who are traditionally followers of the Khatmiyya sect and loyal to its patron, Sayyed Ali Al-Marghani. In an attempt to struggle against marginalisation and deprivation, the Beja Congress was organised after the overthrow of the Abboud military regime in 1964. After 1964, a number of regional political movements emerged, such as the Darfur Front, also suspected to harbour anti-Umma sentiment, and the Nuba Mountains General Union, formed to work for regional autonomy and balanced development in the whole country. These regional political movements had tacit radical support, including the Communists and the Southern politicians who saw them as potential allies against the Umma-led coalition.

Two new parties, the Islamic Charter Front (ICF) and the CPS, fought the 1965 election. As Table 10.3 shows, the CPS won 11 out of a total of 15 of the graduate constituencies, thereby indicating the extent to which it represented the educated élite. However, the communists also included workers and students in their ranks, as well as a disproportionate number of women. 'Ethnic minorities' searching for an alliance with politicians in the South were also involved in the CPS. By calling for the nationalisation of the means of production, the CPS provoked the Umma, PDP, NUP and ICF to form an alliance in 1966 for the purpose of banning the party and excluding its MPs from parliament. For this purpose, the Constitution was amended by a minority vote. Social change and ferment during the 1960s had led to political change within the established parties. During the 1950s, for example, the NUP opposed the traditional sectarian parties, then the bedrock power of northern establishment. However, by 1966, all NUP MPs supported the exclusion of the CPS from parliament. According to Mahmoud (1984, 139) this change reflected a shift in the NUP party leadership towards favouring capitalist interests.

More generally, the established political parties underwent change during this period. Fearful of the outcome of Umma's success at the 1965 elections, and largely due to the efforts of its leader, Ismail Azhari, the NUP merged with the PDP to become the Democratic Unionist Party (DUP), although attempts to unite El-Hadi's and El-Sadig's factions within Umma failed. Despite their political rivalry, and endemic factionalism within Umma, the leaderships of these parties represented different fractions of the same social class, that of the Arab-Muslim bourgeoisie (Mahmoud, 1984). Both parties during the post-1964 period developed electoral programmes appealing to the Arab-Muslim constituency in the North and, in varying degrees, calling for the institution of an Islamic Republic. The NUP, in particular, had transformed itself, within the coalition with the DUP, from a secular party to one searching for support on an increasingly religious basis.

The 1968 elections

Table 10.4: The distribution of seats after the 1968 general elections

Party	Number of Seats
DUP	101
Umma	72
Islamic Charter Front	3
SANU	15
Southern Front	10
Beja & Nuba Mountains	5 (3+2)
Independents	10
Communists	2
Total	218

Source: Bechtold 1976, 249.

As Table 10.4 shows, both the CPS and the Islamic Charter Front failed to broaden their appeal at the 1968 elections. In the South, the northern political parties had continued to pursue co-option and divide and rule tactics towards the southern political parties. Recommendations by the 1965 Round Table Conference were quashed since the dominant attitude among northern politicians towards the Southern Question was one of indifference and marginalisation. The performance of southern political parties, the Southern Front and SANU, did not meet expectations. In fact, the northern major parties, the DUP and Umma, won nearly 60 per cent of the southern vote (Bechtold 1976, 250). The reason for this phenomenon was that the war prevented voter registration of the southern Sudanese, especially in Equatoria which recorded the lowest number of registered voters throughout the whole country. It could be said, therefore, that the southern Sudanese were deprived of participating in the 1968 election. (ibid., 246–57).

From 1963 onwards, economic conditions had worsened in the Sudan, resulting in a severe deterioration of living standards among the poor. Large numbers of people, particularly in urban centres, were becoming more radical despite the failure of the CPS at the 1968 elections to electorally capitalise on what had seemed to be gains in popular support. Internal stability was increasingly undermined by the war in the South and increasing repression, while the external situation was worsened by the impact of the 1967 Arab-Israeli war. The drain on resources represented by the civil war in the South, which consumed up to one-third of the government budget, together with decline in foreign aid after the Arab-Israeli war led to a substantial increase in deficit financing. During the period 1964–69, foreign debt doubled to US$260m. Economic pressure hit the poor hardest since indirect taxation on basic commodities brought in over US$153 million in revenue for 1968/69, in contrast to only US$22m in income tax. The scene was set for the military coup of May 1969.

The May 1969 military regime: the 1974 and 1978 one-party elections

General Numeiri came to power in the face of worsening economic conditions and won support from the CPS. However, in wavering between pursuing a 'socialist' path or retreating to a capitalist policy, the Numeiri regime bowed to the pressure of the capitalist class and its links with international capital (Mahmoud 1984, 141). Growing conflicts with the CPS led to the regime's failure to maintain a 'progressive alliance' against 'the conservatives'. CPS ministers were dismissed from government in 1970 and open conflict ended in an aborted coup by Communist army officers during 1971 (Niblock 1987, 249).

Immediately after the Communist-inspired abortive coup of July 1971, the political leadership of the May regime went ahead with laying down new political and constitutional structures of the new regime. Presidential elections were held on 15 September 1971, with the chairman of the Revolutionary Command Council, Numeiri, elected president as the sole candidate, polling 99 per cent of votes cast on a turnout of 26 per cent of registered voters.

A new constitution, of 1973, turned the Sudan into a one-party state, with a secular presidential form of government, after the May regime outlawed all political parties, confiscated their properties and arrested almost all conservative political leaders. The Sudanese Socialist Union (SSU) became the sole official political organisation. SSU members, some of whom were elected according to a limited franchise, constituted a People's Assembly which shared legislative powers with the President who took absolute power over the executive and judicial organs of the state.

Half the 250 seats in the People's Assembly were deemed to be elective. The remaining 125 seats were nominated by 'People's Organisations', consisting of 30 members from women, youth and village organisations; 40 were nominated by 'Allies of the People's Forces', interpreted to mean peasants, workers, and army personnel; 30 by administrative workers, and 25 by President Numeiri himself. In the North, each elective seat was contested by at least 2 candidates, while in the South, and as a result of the 1972 Addis Ababa Accord which secured peace, elections were more competitive and, on average, between 6 and 12 candidates were nominated to contest each seat. The South was represented by at least 45 members, of whom 25 were elected.

At the 1974 general elections, some Umma and DUP members, who had past grudges against the leaderships of their parties, were able to participate for the elective seats under SSU tutelage. Nevertheless, as might be surmised, there was no *real* contest of the kind shown in earlier elections. Despite the government orchestration of the presidential elections, no genuine enthusiasm was generated except in some rural areas where opponents of Khatmiyya and Ansar exploited the chance to build links with the new regime and received their due benefit (Karar 1989, 94).

The 1978 elections to the People's Assembly took place after the *National Reconciliation* between the one-party regime and the opposition coalition of Umma, DUP and the Muslim Brothers. While the Numeiri regime entered into reconciliation to widen its base of support, the coalition of traditional political parties attempted to undermine the regime from within by playing the rules of the game set by the regime. Representatives of political parties were permitted to stand for elective seats as members of the ruling party. In some areas, especially Khartoum where both the regime and the opposition claimed to wield solid support, the 1978 elections were expected to appear as multi-party elections under the disguise of a one-party cloak. However, voter turnout in Greater Khartoum as a whole barely reached 50 per cent. Although the lowest turnout in Khartoum was 31 per cent, it was only for two constituencies in the Eastern Area (57 per cent) and Bahri East (78 per cent), both in Khartoum North, that turnout ratios exceeded 50 per cent (Sudan 1978). Thus, despite the participation of opposition candidates, the main urban electorate had largely shunned elections under Numeiri's totalitarian, one-party regime. If electoral participation was considerably higher in parts of Khartoum North, it was because these areas, such as Bahri, were more rural and less urban than Khartoum Central, Khartoum South and Omdurman. As will be shown further below, tribal and religious families in the countryside have shown a consistent tendency to participate in elections, irrespective both of the nature of the political regime in power and whether the regime conducts multi- or one-party elections.

The main rationale which had been put forward after 1971 to justify the regime was that it constituted an effective instrument to achieve economic development and national unity. However, the regime was undermined by the evident failure of its development strategy and by the re-emergence of civil conflict in the South. The Numeiri regime gradually began to change its objectives and orientation. Prompted by the same kind of political expediency which first turned him towards the CPS, President Numeiri moved towards creating a basis of Islamic legitimacy for his regime, ultimately attempting to fundamentally change the new constitution which he himself introduced in 1973 (Niblock 1987, 289).

An expanding parastatal sector of the economy that emerged after the nationalisations of 1970, as part of Numeiri's 'CPS period', became the seed-bed for a state bureaucracy and state capitalist interests that, among other factors, had driven the regime to reach a national reconciliation with the Umma and DUP parties as well as, most significantly, the Islamic Brothers (*Ikhwan el-Muslimien*) during 1977. While the Umma and DUP gave lukewarm support to the regime and later pulled out to join the opposition, the Islamic Brothers took full advantage of sharing power, especially after Numeiri declared his intention to adopt *sharia* law. For a fringe political force such as the *Ikhwan*, desperate to build a secure constituency, the use of religion to create a political base of support was an obvious strategy. A number of local, regional and international factors enabled the *Ikhwan* to emerge as what can variously be called a 'parasitic comprador capitalist class', 'the new aristocracy' or 'new finance capital' (El-Battahani 1996, 15–16). Whatever label is used, a fraction of the predominantly Northern Arab-Muslim capitalist class had taken advantage of an ensemble of factors to enrich itself while at the same time deepening the crisis of the Sudanese economy. An important result was the economic and political ascendance of Ikhwan as an Arab-Muslim fraction of capital competing with Umma and the DUP for the political leadership of the Arab-Muslim bourgeoisie in the country. The adoption of *sharia* by Numeiri in 1983 and other Islamisation measures reinforced the political position of the *Ikhwan* in both government and the economy.

During the period of the Numeiri regime, the relationship between the market economy and civil society passed through one of its evolutionary phases. While Numeiri's authoritarian form of rule brought civil society and the market economy under the control of the state, both enjoyed a degree of freedom. Civil society and the market economy were left with a limited space mainly because the regime did not attempt to thoroughly restructure Sudanese society in a totalitarian way. In fact, there was a dual political system, represented by the authoritarian structures of government in the North and a 'democratic' form of government in the South following the 1972 Addis Ababa Peace Accord. However, political tension and economic crisis, particularly after adopting IMF policies, led the regime to be more authoritarian during the early 1980s, culminating in the abrogation of the Addis Ababa Agreement and implementation of the September or *Sharia* Laws of 1983.

Once again, a broad coalition of forces including the traditional and bourgeoisie classes, together with trade unions and professional associations, was put together in opposition against Numeiri's rule in the North. In the South, renewed fighting led to the formation of the Sudan People Liberation Army/Movement (SPLA/M) which was also formed in 1983. Widespread corruption, deepening economic hardships and the repressive policies of Numeiri following the *sharia* enforcement led to growing popular opposition to the government. The formation of the SPLA/M and its armed opposition strengthened the secular, national character of the opposition to the Numeiri regime and eventually contributed to its collapse in 1985.

Prelude to the 1986 elections

The modalities of changing the state regime in 1985 meant that the change was not fundamental in the manner sought by anti-Numeiri *intifada* (popular uprising) forces. The National Alliance of trade unions, professional associations and political parties, with the exception of the *Ikhwan*, led the uprising. However, the initial failure to make the repeal of the *sharia* laws a central plank in the National Alliance agenda, miscalculation on the part of Northern political parties and the refusal of SPLA/M to take part in the democratic process had all contributed to the weakening of the

National Alliance, which gave one concession after another to the sectarian political parties and the army (El-Bashir 1987, 160–161).

More fundamentally, the new liberal democratic regime could not create a conducive fit between the market economy and civil society. It does seem that the traditional northern ruling coalition of Umma and the DUP tried to revert to the strategic outlook of the 1960s in a different conjuncture between economic and political power. The post-Numeiri government failed to stop the continuing civil war in the South, stem the tide of widespread corruption and curb the mounting activities of ultra-right wing movements represented by the National Islamic Front (NIF). In acting against the CPS and the emancipation of women, together with its militant stance on the Southern question, the NIF's well-known anti-democratic credentials stretched back to the 1960s. Now, in May 1985, the *Ikhwan* moved into the political vacuum, which the new government had opened by wavering over *sharia* and the other factors mentioned above, by holding a constitutional conference. It was from this conference that a broad front of like-minded fundamentalist groups was formed, comprising retired army generals and influentials of the defunct Numeiri regime and the NIF, with its leader, Hassan el-Turabi, selected as the Secretary General of the front.

Utilising its newly acquired wealth, and the most modern techniques of public mobilisation, the NIF moved very quickly to dominate the political scene and present itself as an alternative leadership of the Northern Arab-Muslim political constituency. Instead of taking the defensive, NIF took the offensive, 'daring any group to abrogate the Islamic *Sharia* Law and threatening to resort to *jihad* if need be' (*ibid.*, 159). To many, *sharia* was elevated to the status of a taboo, while the imminent danger threatening the identity of the Arab-Muslims in Sudan was perceived as coming from the South, especially the SPLA/M and its leftists allies in the North. Between 1985 and 1989 the Islamists, led by NIF, fought an intensive and combined political battle against both the National Alliance and the traditional parties. To achieve its political goals, NIF occupied the space of democratic politics while at the same time doing everything to undermine democratic rule (El-Battahani 1996a and 1996b).

The 1986 elections and after

Table 10.5: The distribution of seats and votes at the 1986 general elections

Party	Sudan		Khartoum		Gezira	
	seats	votes %	seats	votes %	seats	votes %
Umma Party	99	38	6	21	29	47
DUP	63	24	29	21	15	31
NIF	51	20	13	21	4	13
Communist Party	3	1	2	6		1
Others	39	17				

Source: Compiled from Sudan 1986; Tahir 1986; Karar 1989.

As Table 10.5 shows, the two major traditional religious-sectarian parties, the Umma and DUP, managed to hold their rural strongholds with the Umma drawing exceptional support from Gezira as well as Darfur and Kordofan regions. However, it was in Khartoum where the NIF made its advance relative to the other parties, especially at the expense of the DUP. During the 1969–85 Numeiri regime, socio-economic changes undermined the social bases of the Unionists, particularly in areas where they had strongholds, mainly in Greater Khartoum and the very north. Prospects for the expansion of the urban commercial and business class, the public-sector salariat and the *petit bourgeoisie* more generally had been undermined. It was during this period that particular conditions of existence for petty traders and business had been eliminated, thereby differentiating between those who prospered and became part of 'the bourgeoisie proper' and those who sank into a semi-proletariat of the impoverished.

Secondly, DUP support for the *sharia* laws had dented its image, alienating the party's leadership from the mass membership who, finding no difference between it and the NIF, switched to the 'real' Islamic party. Being much more organised than the DUP, the NIF took on board the party's traditional constituencies. Some observers went as far as implicating the Khatmiyya leadership in conniving with the NIF to facilitate its electoral success. For example, the Khatmiyya nominated more than one candidate in one constituency and directed voters, in some cases, to vote for the Islamic Front, 'either by order or by image specially in rural Sudan' (Mahmoud 1986, 12). Fearful of Umma winning a electoral landslide victory, and driven by enmity towards their traditional opponents, the Unionists did not appear to take a public stance against the NIF even if they did not openly co-operate with it.

Umma succeeded at the 1986 polls because the socio-economic changes of 1969–85 had not gone deep enough to change the political landscape of the country as a whole. In particular, economic changes, drought and famine in Western Sudan had induced population movements and partially eased geographical and social mobility but these changes, nonetheless, did not undermine the party's strongholds. Secondly, Sadiq Al-Mahdi's continued criticism, and effective withdrawal from the 1977 process of national reconciliation, gained Umma's leader the support of the anti-Numeiri coalition and placed him as a leader of the 1985 popular uprising that toppled the regime. In Darfur and Kordofan, the Ansar still believed that Sadiq Al-Mahdi inherited the spirit of Al-Mahdi, the legendary Grandfather, nineteenth-century revolutionary and scourge of the British, and therefore represented the leadership of the Sudanese community. Third, Muslims who were reluctant to vote for the NIF because of its association with the Numeiri regime voted enthusiastically for Sadiq's 'Islamic Awakening', a liberal, tolerant and more accommodative version of Islamisation. One merit of Sadiq's liberal introduction of Islam was his recognition of the status of women in society and politics by proposing women constituencies as part of 'the modern forces' of politics. Sadiq also promoted the role of his wife Sarra Al-Mahdi in politics, thereby emulating the South-east Asian phenomenon of female political leaders.

The NIF made an electoral breakthrough because, after the 1977 signing of national reconciliation, the various elements of the party were either in total or semi-total control of political activities throughout the country. As a result, firstly the NIF was far ahead of other political parties in terms of financial, organisational and propaganda facilities. Secondly, the NIF was successful in establishing a solid economic base, mainly in the banking sector, through its control of the Islamic Banks, and winning the political support of a new class of business entrepreneurs. Mainly involved in trading, this new class moved to the NIF when they realised that Umma and DUP politicians were bent on using state economic policies to enrich their own supporters at the expense of their competitors.

Thirdly, its close collaboration with the Transitional Military Council in 1985 gave the NIF a say in the drafting of electoral laws and the drawing of constituency boundaries. In designing the graduate constituencies, which worked electorally in favour of the NIF, the Transitional Government hoped to temper the threat of *intifada* popular forces. The Communist Party suffered most from this electoral ploy. As is shown further below, the CPS won 11 out of the 15 graduate seats in 1965 while the Muslim Brothers and the National Unionists gained 2 each; in 1986, the NIF won 22 out of the 25 seats on offer.

NIF's gains at the 1986 elections alerted both the National Alliance and the traditional parties. Yet, without reorganising an effective anti-NIF coalition, the traditional party leaders found that they had little with which to challenge the NIF and maintain their precarious political influence. Therefore, it was along these lines that the DUP cautiously moved to reconcile its differences, with both the National Alliance and the SPLA/M, to eventually reach the 1988 Sudan Peace Initiative Agreement. Part of this agreement with the SPLA/M stipulated the convening of a National Constitutional Conference to resolve the political crisis in the country. To forestall the peace initiative and prevent the constitutional convention, the NIF took state power through a *coup d'état* in 1989. The coup met with little popular resistance and commanded an undeniable degree of popular support. This was because there was some belief in the declared policies of the military regime to fight corruption, stimulate the economy and maintain the territorial integrity of the nation against the threat that an agreement with the SPLA/M might pose. It was the NIF that was able to politically capitalise upon popular support for the coup and it soon became the ideological wing of a regime whose effective intention was to put the house of the predominantly Northern Arab-Muslim bourgeoisie in order under its hegemony. During the 1990s, the NIF's declared policies proved to be as difficult to realise as had been the case for previous regimes and popular disillusion mounted.

General reflections on elections before 1989

Locality, social forces and the Graduate Constituencies

One key factor of elections in the Sudan has been that of locality, especially in rural areas of the country. Religious sects and tribal aristocracies mainly dominated elections at the local level. Modern urban political parties, such as the CPS and the Muslim Brotherhood, have had no bases of popular support in rural constituencies. In an attempt to undermine rural support given to sectarianism and tribalism and encourage modern agricultural production, the Numeiri regime abolished the 'native' administration in 1970, replacing it by 'people's councils'. However, for the Umma and the DUP, administrative changes have not fundamentally affected their domination over rural power structures.

During periods of rule by one-party regimes, electoral systems were also generally designed to give 'modern' urban social forces a fixed share of representation in parliament to counter the influence of 'traditional' forces. For example, during the Numeiri regime, more than 40 per cent of the seats of the People's National Assembly were reserved for women (discussed further below), students, youth, intellectuals, professionals, business-men and -women and the armed forces. By contrast, these social forces were poorly represented in multi-party parliaments. During the 1953, 1958 and 1986 elections, only 3.5, 9.5 and 8.6 per cent of respective MPs were 'fixed share' representatives of modern social forces (General Secretariat for National Congress 1996).

As mentioned above, in marking a departure from the Westminster model, Graduate Constituencies had been an important feature of Sudanese elections since 1953. The idea for these constituencies was first debated in the Legislative Assembly during early 1950 and was incorporated into the draft of the Sudan Constitution through the 1952 and 1953 Self-Government Act. Though the remit of the Electoral Commission in 1953 was supposed to be purely of a technical nature, it was nevertheless vested with a wide range of powers in making a distinction between geographical and functional constituencies. Ostensibly, the justification for a graduate franchise was to give disproportionate political weight to 'the educated' from whom potential cabinet members could be drawn. However the implicit reason, as mentioned above, was to counterbalance the anticipated political influence of 'traditional' party representatives drawn from rural territorial constituencies. In particular, given the history of Egyptian influence in the Sudan, the idea of the Graduate Constituencies was especially intended to weaken the Umma.

The 1953 Self-Government Act provided that 3 to 5 seats in the House of Representatives should be filled by candidates in Graduate Constituencies. Voters in these constituencies were to be graduates whose qualifications were essentially the same as those of ordinary voters, except that they did not have to fulfil the residential or gender requirement and had to have completed at least the secondary school or its equivalent (Bechtold 1976,169). While it was decided to reserve 5 constituencies for graduates for the 1953 election, these constituencies were abolished in 1958 by the ruling coalition of Umma and the DUP simply because the idea was not in their interests. Moreover, it was argued that the idea of exclusive seats was fundamentally irreconcilable with democracy. After the leading role played by students, professionals and women's groups in the successful 1964 and 1985 opposition movements against the military regimes of Abboud and Numeiri, Graduate Constituencies were once again introduced, this time raised to 15 constituencies for the 1965 elections and 28 for 1986.

Except for the 1986 elections, the results of Graduate Constituencies had consistently favoured relatively radical, secular parties. In the 1953 elections, 83 per cent of 2,250 registered voters turned out to vote in the Graduate Constituencies (Bechtold 1976, 180). The NUP won 3 seats with the other 2 going to Umma and the Communist-controlled Anti-Colonialist Front. By 1965, the electorate for the Graduate Constituencies had increased 100-fold. As Table 10.6 shows, the CPS won 11 of the 15 constituencies but the Islamic Charter, led by Hassan El-Turabi (who won the highest number of personal votes at these elections), could have considered that the first-past-the post voting system unjustifiably prevented the party from converting votes into seats. Be that as it may, the 1965 Graduate Constituency results played no small part in leading to the backlash against the CPS, including the exclusion of its MPs from parliament and its banishment.

Table 10.6: Graduate Constituencies results at the 1965 elections

Party	No. of votes	Percentage of votes	No. of seats
CPS	63,662	34.7	11
Islamic Charter	49,790	27.1	2
NUP	45,854	25.0	2
Others	24.092	13.2	0

Source: Karar 1986; Mazoub Abdoun 1988.

At the 1986 elections, it was the NIF that proved to be the beneficiary of the voting system. As Table 10.7 shows, it was now the Communists who suffered, winning only one seat for nearly 20 per cent of the graduate vote. Although expressing some scepticism towards the Graduate Constituencies, the Islamists had recruited a relatively large number of urban entrepreneurs and professionals during the 1980s. Benefiting from superior organisational and financial resources, and drawing on its electoral experience during the period of the Numeiri regime, the NIF was also tactically well positioned to win the majority of the graduate seats at the 1986 elections.

Table 10.7: Graduate Constituencies results at the 1986 elections

Party	No. of votes	Percentage of votes	No. of seats
NIF	79,336	38.2	23
CPS	39,799	19.2	1
Umma	32,967	15.9	0
DUP	19,997	9.6	0
Independents(a)	14.561	7.0	4

a. Almost all from the South, including the Sudanese African Congress (SAC) and the Southern Sudan Political Association.

Source: Sudan 1986.

Gender

Table 10.8 below shows that women only entered parliament in any numbers during the early years of the one-party period of the Numeiri regime. It was also during this period that women secured many civil, economic and political rights that had been fought for but not extensively achieved during the earlier multi-party periods when the traditional parties held sway. Of particular interest here is the contradictory stance that the Islamists took towards women during the 1980s because this stance played a part in explaining participation in the 1986 elections. Further, as is shown below, the official Islamic stance towards women was important for the 1996 elections.

On the one hand, the NIF understood that women would not easily forgo the rights that had been won during the 1970s. The Islamic party therefore acted politically to do all possible to win women over to their side in 1986. Education, urbanisation and economic crisis have all contributed to make women visible, by being out in the open as food vendors, in workplaces, factories, the civil service and the universities. In facing the visible presence of women, the Islamist movement developed a pragmatic and flexible discourse on gender questions, believing that it was possible to support and extend women's rights within society at large. However, what was politically opportune did not fit the dictates of religious orthodoxy, and especially that associated with the ascendancy of a strict, fundamentalist version of Islam as the cornerstone of state policy. In this version of Islam, the assertion of women's rights was interpreted as a source of moral disorder, thereby favouring legal and institutional arrangements to control and keep women in a subordinate position. This contradiction between what was politically opportune and doctrinally necessary for a theocratic state continued to be played out during the 1990s.

Table 10.8: Women's representation in parliament, 1954–1996

	All seats	Women Seats	Elected	Appointed	Women seats %	Type of regime
1954	95					
1958	95					multi-party
1960–64	–					military
1965	233	1	1		0.4	multi-party
1968	233					multi-party
1972–73	255	14	10	4	5.5	one-party
1974–77	250	12			4.8	one-party
1978–80	304	18			5.9	one-party
1980–81	368	18			4.9	one-party
1982–83	153	14			9.2	one-party
1986	272	2	2		0.7	multi-party
1992–96	301	24		24	7.9	one-party
1996	400	21	1	20	5.7	one-party

Source: Compiled from Bechtold 1976; Tahir 1986, 192; Karar 1989, 154–56; Sudan 1996.

Political dynasties and party spending

Generally in rural Sudan, as well as in urban centres, some individuals and families have controlled electoral votes through different political regimes since independence. For example, in the East Nile area of North Khartoum, Sheikh Mohamed Sidiq Talha, the Nazir of Elbattahin, has won almost all elections since independence without effective contest. Other names include Nazir Hussein zaki-eldin of Bedeiryia of North Kordofan, the family of Yousif al-Agab of Rufa's al-Hoy in Blue Nile, the Habanbi family of Hasaniya in White Nile, and the Madipo family of Riziegat in Darfur (Karar 1989).[6] Partly as a result of capitalising on these dynasties, the traditional political parties are able to spend money lavishly during election campaigns. Lavish spending wins votes and elections. At the 1986 general elections, the NIF was also able to spend abundantly. For example, whereas the CPS did not possess enough transportation to exhaust its quota of oil and petrol allocated to the party by the National Election Committee, the NIF used its allocation fully. Another facet of the phenomenon of political dynasties is that electorates complain that they often only see their MPs and parliamentary candidates during election campaigning.

There has usually also been an element of external intervention in multi-party elections in the Sudan, particularly from Britain, the former colonial power, during the 1950s. Egypt, with its strategic need to protect the Nile waters, has always intervened overtly and covertly during elections in providing support for the DUP. At the 1986 elections, Libya, Saudi Arabia, Iraq and Iran, as then oil-rich countries, were foreign patrons for the Revolutionary Committees, Ansar el-Sunna, the Ba'thists and Islamists respectively. There has also been a marked United States and Western European interest in the Umma party; before 1989, there was a former Soviet and East European interest in the CPS.

The South and Northern Hegemony

Contrary to its more usual justification, the application of the Westminster model in the Sudan for multi-party elections has generally prevented one party from clearly winning elections. As Woodward (1994, 248) argues, and Table 10.9 confirms, multi-party elections have resulted in coalition governments that proved to be weak and unstable. At the same time, the capacity for extending political participation through parties with a share in the system has been limited to

---

[6]Other families include those of Bahr el-din and Taj el-Din of Masalit in Darfur, Ali Dinar Darfur, Fadl alla, al-Ie'sir and Ali al-Tom of Kababish in Kordofan, Zubeir Hamad al-Maek in the Dongula area of North Sudan, Bakr Mustafa in Gedarif, Abu-Sin in Butana, Sherif el-Hindi in Gezira, Ahmed Yousif Algam in North Gezira, Sarour Ramly in the North Khartoum Area, Abdel Rahman Nagdalla in the South Gezira area, Babu Nimr of Messeriyya of Kordofan, Al-Amin Tirik of Hadandawa of Eastern Sudan, Mikashfie in Gezira.

Table 10.9: The performance of parties in general elections, percentage of the vote, 1953–86

	1953	1958	1965	1968	1986
Umma	23	40	45	39	38
NUP	52	25	35		
PDP		15	1.5		
DUP				46	23
(NUP+PDP)					
NIF			5		21
CPS			1.5		1.6
Southern		20			
Others	25		12	15	16

Sources: Compiled from Bechtold 1976; Tahir 1986, 192; Karar 1989, 154–6.

northern Sudan. The result is that the South, in particular, and other peripheral regions in the West and East, have been alienated, if not deliberately excluded, from the political process.

When the British colonial administration held the Juba Conference in 1947 to consider the future of southern Sudan, and despite reservations by some southerners, debate was confined to the question of what form of regional autonomy within a unified Sudan would be appropriate for the South. However, in August 1955, and following ethnic and 'racial' practices by the new Sudanese administration in the South, the Equatoria Corps mutinied, forcing Northern political parties to pay attention to the South by agreeing 'a federal option for the future government of Sudan'. On the basis of this pledge, southern representatives in the Constituent Assembly agreed to support the Declaration of Independence in 1956. However, the northern pledge was never translated into a meaningful change in policy towards the South. Instead, the Sudan government ruled through excluding southerners from the power structures of the state. For example, south-erners comprised a mere 3 of the 43 members of the Special Commission that was appointed to prepare a draft federal constitution. With typical northern insensitivity towards the pledge made to the South, the Commission voted against the federal option. Although northern parties had won 46 per cent of seats on offer in the South for the 1953 elections, results of the 1958 elections showed the extent to which southerners, in turn, rejected the Commission's decision by voting over-whelmingly for the Southern Federal Party (SFP). Although the SFP won 40 of the 46 seats in the South at the 1958 parliamentary elections, northern political leaders shrugged off this electoral verdict by dismissing the main southern party as an insignificant political force (Hamid 1988, 15–16). In further opposing the new draft constitution, SFP party representatives voted with their feet by walking out of the Constituent Assembly after the elections.

As might be expected, there has only been effective southern representation in the Sudanese parliament during times of peace. Thus, after the escalation of armed conflict from the early 1960s, and during periods of war, political parties and movements have not been able to contest elections in all constituencies of the South. Due to 'the security situation', the general elections of 1965 were deferred in the South and held during 1967. Except for two months during this year, there was no southern representation in the Sudanese parliament until the 1972 peace accord. The deferral of elections, or confining them to parts of the South, amounted to partial representation if not virtual exclusion from the national political process. In 1968, the southern electorate was able to vote in only one-fifth of the constituencies; at the 1986 elections, when northern political parties won just over 4 per cent of votes in the South, the electorate was able to vote at less than one-half of the constituencies in which contests were due to be held. For the 1986 elections, turnout rates in southern constituencies ranged between 12 and 53 per cent, with the average at little more than 35 per cent (Sudan 1986, 223–224). Paradoxically enough, it was only during the one-party period of the Numeiri regime, 1969–85, when there was peace in the South for much of the time and the southern electorate enjoyed a far more marked degree of electoral participation and competition.

Apart from 1986, during periods of multi-party government, the Umma and DUP seemed to have some success in wooing southern MPs and encouraging them to defect to their ranks, thereby reflecting the deep paternalistic attitude of the North towards 'ethnic' parties: non-northerners were to be politically contained or manipulated. The same attitude applied to other ethnic or 'regional' political parties from Darfur, the Nuba Mountains or Beja in eastern Sudan. Irrespective of political party competition, northern political parties, especially Umma, the DUP and the NIF, have shown, through their election programmes, strategies and policies adopted when in government, that they were gradually converging towards a historically emerging power-structure which has been dominated by a northern hegemony over the South. This northern hegemony arises out of a common presumption that only a strong centre of authority can hold together a multiplicity of ethnic, racial, tribal and religious entities associated with particular regions. Any threat to the centre is ultimately seen as a threat to the unity and integrity of the nation upon which the predominantly northern Arab-Muslim hegemony has been based and underpinned by both one- and multi-party elections.

Politics and elections during the 1990s

Immediately after its seizure of power in June 1989, the junta suspended the 1985 Constitution, which guaranteed civil and political rights, dissolved the elected government and banned trade unions and the free press. All political parties including the NIF were banned on 30 June 1989. To provide a legal framework for their rule, the junta issued a number of constitutional decrees which were designed to transfer power from elected bodies to the Revolutionary Command Council (RCC). Within this framework, new structures were created, including a Transitional National Council (Parliament), Popular Committees and a new political organisation, the People's Congresses.

One of the justifications for overthrowing and dismantling the structures of the former liberal parliamentary regime was the NIF's idea that the leaderships of traditional parties manipulated representative democracy for their own narrow and sectarian interests. Therefore, so the argument ran, 'the people' were never given the chance to 'genuinely' elect their representatives and a government that was accountable to them. The new regime promised to break the monopoly of power which had been exercised by the traditional parties and hand power back to the people, with the claim that the NIF would arrest political decay and lead the process of regenerating and renewing Sudanese society (El-Affendi 1995; Woodward 1994).

Hassan El-Turabi, the longstanding practising theoretician of the NIF and its predecessors, drew upon an Islamic concept of democracy, *Shura,* which he proposed as a positive alternative to 'western' liberal democracy in shaping the relationship between the rulers and the ruled. *Shura,* hitherto understood as the process of consulting 'learned male' people, was now conceived as a way for empowering the Sudanese people, in making it possible for ordinary citizens to influence governmental decisions. Turabi and other regime-intellectuals suggested that any political system should rest upon an indigenous psychological and social background. Thus, it was claimed that 'Western values of individualism and personal self-interest cut a sharp contrast with those shaping the Sudanese psycho-social build-up of conformity, consensus and communality.'[7]

Further, this Islamist theory of governance put forward its own concept of 'civil society' in requiring that associations of people, especially non-governmental organisations, should participate fully in designing and implementing policies for liberating 'the people' from state control. *Shura,* when buttressed by a set of civic associations, would thereby play a role in creating the environment in which people could attend to their own political and social welfare. Economic growth was to be combined with greater self-reliance and food security. Poverty was to be combated by reducing distributional and social inequality and the improvement in basic social services. Overall, so it was believed, the human quest for dignity and freedom could be balanced with the need to improve the conditions of economic, social and cultural life. It was through the above administrative structures, and declarations contained in statements such as the Three Year Salvation Programme (1989–92) and the Comprehensive National Strategy (1992–2002), that *Shura* was to be institutionalised in the Sudan (El-Battahani 1996c).

Unsurprisingly, realities of political and economic developments in the Sudan during the 1990s proved to be contrary to what the theory prescribed. Representative or legislative bodies, from the Transitional National Council (TNC) to the 'elected' National Council have played no role in

---

[7]*Sudan Focus* 15 May 1996; Sudan Television, interview with Hassan El-Turabi, 1 September 1996.

government. Major policy issues are not debated. The National Council has been reduced to a rubber stamp, discussing issues such as 'the integrity of the nation' and 'the civilised orientation'. Bread and butter issues, including labour conditions, are reserved as concerns for the state National Councils and local authorities. When the National Council attempted to play its role as a supervisory body over the executive organs of government, the regime responded by further marginalising its functions. Similarly, when the Hisba Committee comprehensively reported on documented cases of widespread corruption, the regime's response was to dissolve and dismiss the Committee during 1995.

Furthermore, the NIF regime attempted to turn Sudan into a federal, decentralised state, dividing the country into 26 states, each with its own parliament, cabinet and governor. In reality, however, the Islamists have possessed firm control over the hidden network of resources and personnel, consisting of highly authoritarian officials, needed for the normal functioning of government. In effect, the Islamic system of government has become highly centralised (El-Affendi 1995). Opponents of the regime refer to a 40-strong council which rules the country from behind the scenes, while the regime's own supporters have also pointed to a 'super organisation' which has outlived the formal dissolution of the NIF and now effectively monopolises state power (*ibid.*).

Two important implications have followed from the centralisation of state power. Firstly, since politics has become a function of the security imperative, political activities are the exclusive domain of regime loyalists. This point is succinctly captured by the title of a chapter, Politics via Security Organs, in El-Affendi's book, *Revolution and Political Reform in Sudan* (*ibid.*). A one-party system has been established under the name of the People's Congresses that were supposed to provide a platform for all citizens to engage in politics through organising meetings, taking political initiatives and contesting elections. Since popular support for the regime has narrowed and cannot be assured, a number of security and/or paramilitary organisations have been created, or legitimised, by the government. These organisations include several security services, armed neighbourhood committees and the Popular Defence Forces, together with the Truth and Authentication Department as the regime watchdog against any challenge to political, social or religious orthodoxy (Fraser 1996, 20–25). Older established civil society institutions no longer function, either having been destroyed or disintegrated. The judiciary and universities have been purged and, as mentioned earlier, trade unions and professional groups have been dissolved and newspapers banned. As Fraser (*ibid.*) comments, the 'ethos of militant Islam that informs the rulers is deeply hostile to any form of dissent', even if couched mildly and motivated by an intent to serve the Islamic state.

Secondly, the economic policies pursued by the regime have undermined the livelihoods of what, until recently, were relatively well-established middle and professional classes in the Sudan. Middle classes, especially professionals in the public service, have been impoverished to an extent that they have been forced into exile. Economic policies, whether intended or not, have been linked to the regime's relentless efforts to impose its own mixture of theocratic and modern social structures to counter the previous, traditional, pre-Islamic or secular forms through which the old middle classes became established. In effect, urban middle classes have become so disenfranchised through fear of the regime that they might endorse secular, more liberal politics. One result of the process of replacing an old with newer middle classes has been the social splintering of the Sudan and the fragmentation of 'the body politic' (*ibid.*).

Economic developments

According to the Islamic economic doctrine that has been associated with *Shura* in the Sudan, state-directed economic management and public-sector ownership were the main causes lying behind economic stagnation and crisis. The state, it has been argued, should not participate directly in the market through direct control over production, accumulation or exchange. Rather, the state's role in the economy should be restricted to regulation and policy making with a view to creating a conducive market-oriented environment for private investment. Thus, as a panacea for Sudanese economic malaise, the new NIF-dominated regime carried out liberalisation and privatisation policies through issuing a number of decrees and setting up a number of committees.

Serious doubts have hung over the proceedings of these committees. Given the influence of NIF, and the general atmosphere in which these committees conducted their work, the regime acted to privatise rather than liberalise. Since these 'privatisation' committees conducted their work without abiding by neutral, objective or open measures of deregulation, they were able to transfer the ownership of state-owned corporations to regional state governments, Islamic organisations and individuals or business groups. What has been written about the market elsewhere applies here insofar as it is not to be regarded as a means for achieving 'allocative efficiency, but as the mechanism for extraction of surplus by one class from another'. Thus, 'the function of exchange is not to "clear" the market in some cases, but simply to gain advantage to one party at the cost of another' (White 1993, 3–6; also see Umbadda 1990).

Since economic access was facilitated by political office, disposing of commercial enterprises under state ownership gave undue advantage not to 'the old-boy network of the capital-rich, better-positioned and well-established Northern merchants and business groups' but to relatively new groups of urban entrepreneurs and financial networks (Umbadda 1989). The political affiliation of these new groups, and the gains they made out of the privatisation of the economy largely explain the intense conflict between old-boy and new-boy networks in the business arena. While the ascendancy of the new entrepreneurs is also to be explained by the overall orientation of the Sudanese economy since the mid-1970s towards non-productive, speculative activities that gave impetus to the newer business groups, they have been increasingly assisted by the economic policies of the 1990s.

A 1996 report partly attributed the rising inflation rates, and a deteriorating exchange rate, to rising government expenditure. However, the main factor explaining inflation was attributed to the volume of money circulating outside the banking system, estimated to be nearly 80 per cent of the total money supply.[8] The power that speculators have wielded over all sectors of the Sudanese economy can be traced back to the late 1970s and early 1980s when the Islamic Banks, under the management of NIF members, moved into the rural economy. During the 1990s these same banks have also won control over the urban economy.

The other aspect of non-productive activity has been the extent to which the government has engaged in military spending. Military expenditure as a percentage of GDP declined from an annual average of 3.8 per cent over 1970–75, to 2.9 per cent during the period 1980–85 and then jumped to 4.1 per cent for 1985–90 and 13.1 per cent during 1990–95 (United States of America 1996; Camps *et al.* 1997). Although precise numbers have not been officially released, it has been estimated that, during the early 1990s, the government spent 40 per cent of its budget allocation on the security forces (Khalid 1993, 329). Apart from expenditure on security and defence, it is instructive to note that for the 1993/94 budget, whereas the Television and Broadcasting Corporations were allocated Ls 294 billion, the budget for the whole health sector was less at Ls 290 billion (El-Battahani 1996b). Furthermore, it has been estimated that between 1989 and 1994, Ls 114 billion of public funds were embezzled, with over 80 per cent of the cases, as reported by the General Auditor, arising at the federal level of government (Al-Mahdi 1996). Government performance in the economy generally and for agriculture and education, as well as health, has been dismal. Cabinet ministers allegedly implicated in cases of corruption, and known for their dismal performance, either remain in office or are rotated to new portfolios.

The misallocation of resources, together with other factors, has contributed to widespread poverty and impoverishment. It has been estimated that the income share of the richest tenth of the population soared from 40 to 60 per cent between 1978 and 1990 while that of the poorest 40 per cent fell from 12 to 8 per cent over the same period (El-Battahani 1996b). While official estimates from the early 1990s suggested that 65 per cent of the population were living below the poverty line, other data put the proportion at between 80 and 90 per cent (Ali 1992). During the 1990s, this gross incidence of poverty worsened for both rural and urban populations. For example, in 1998, the government-funded Centre for Strategic Studies reported that 94 per cent of the Sudanese population were below the poverty line (Centre for Strategic Studies 1998). The minimum cost of living for food alone rose nearly 350-fold between 1992 and 1996 (Nour 1995). The middle classes have shared in economic impoverishment within the general Sudanese setting of repeated famines, civil wars, political decay, social unrest, and centralised state repression (Harir and Tvedt 1995).

---

[8]*Al-Rai Al-Nam* 40, 26 October 1996.

The 1996 elections

From the perspective of the regime, the 1996 elections were considered to be an important phase in the process for completing the reforms of its constitutional and political institutions. As mentioned above, the new political system of Popular Congresses had been laid down in 1990 and the 1996 elections were based on the new political system that comprised popular and sectoral congresses. Instead of the pre-1989 parliamentary system, a presidential system was adopted to give supreme power to an elected president as head of a federal structure of government. Most importantly of all, although political participation was formally based upon citizenship, religion was deemed to be the authoritative source of public life.

Participation

An Electoral Law of 1994 entrusted the Electoral Commission, funded from an independent government budget, with the task of preparing and maintaining a permanent, central voter register. For the geographical constituencies, the Electoral Commission, known as the National Electoral Committee (NEC), was also given the task of supervising electoral campaigning by ensuring that all candidates would be given equal access to public platforms, the mass media and political rallies. Candidates were not to be permitted to mobilise support on the basis of tribal, racial or regional partisanship. However, candidates were required to abide by the National Political Charter in presenting their views on the role of religion in public life and how it should relate to general government programmes. In coordination with other concerned bodies, the NEC was also responsible for appointing observers to oversee the counting of votes at polling stations. Therefore, the 1996 elections were governed by a rigorous procedure of conducting elections, including specifying how candidates were to conduct themselves during campaigning.

Another feature of the 1996 elections was the machinery set in motion to vet candidates. The 1994 Electoral Law also established Nomination Councils to screen parliamentary candidates with a view to ensuring that a nominee could not be disqualified on grounds of political, tribal, ethnic or religious affiliation. Nomination Councils were also empowered to consider appeals from those who failed to be nominated as candidates. Following another 1995 Electoral Law, Consensus Councils (*Majalis el-wifaq*) were also established at the constituency level according to the principle of *al'afu wa alrida* (forgiveness and consent). In an effort to distinguish their electoral system from previous ones, the Islamic government sought to limit the number of candidates for each constituency, on the ground that political competition damages the cohesion of 'community'. Electoral laws of 1994 and 1995 thus prohibited candidates, including those for the presidential election, from nominating themselves (Sudan 1995). However, what might look like a virtue of political modesty was little other than a device for excluding putative 'anti-government' candidates from the elections.

Consensus Councils (CCs) were authorised to make contacts with, and consult, potential candidates with the purpose of persuading one or more to withdraw their candidature for the sake of the one candidate who was considered to be more 'competent', of 'strong moral character' and more 'committed' to the National Charter and policies of the People's Congresses. This consultation exercise was especially harmful to the possible candidatures of government officials who might have stood against the government and yet were not bound by the National Charter of the regime. Thus, a hierarchy of candidates was effectively established with candidates campaigning for and working within the context of the National Charter cast as 'first-class' candidates, while those who disagreed with the National Charter, and were opposed to government policies, emerged as second-class candidates. In practice, some candidates were considered to have no chance of winning. Since the government undertook to finance election campaigning, it was also believed that a reduction in the number of candidates would save public finance.

It should be emphasised that the power of these CCs was deemed to be morally rather than legally grounded. A Consensus Council would have no right to decide over the eligibility of candidates or annul the candidature of those who were not members of the ruling political party. The idea of the CCs was based upon the tradition of *agawied*, an indigenous institution for conflict resolution, usually composed of elderly people, that works to contain and resolve conflict in 'a community'. However, the CCs were constituted differently when reinvented as *agawied* for the

1996 elections. Each CC consisted of nine members, drawn equally from the State Council, the Province Council and the Secretariat of the People's Congresses, and therefore composed of officials of the ruling party and government bureaucracy rather than from the elderly of the local community.

Despite official logistical support and propaganda, the 1996 parliamentary and presidential elections failed to entice the active engagement of the electorate. Given the rich electoral experience of the Sudan, a lively interest in an uncertain contest might have been expected. Paradoxically, it could be argued that the elaborate electoral rules might have contributed to the low turnout at the polls. Since the NEC exercised such a high degree of control over the electoral process, there was minimal interest by an electorate that was accustomed to hotly contested multiparty elections. Of an estimated 12.8 million eligible to vote, 8.2 million were actually registered and 3.7 million people, or 45 per cent of registered voters, actually turned out to vote at the 1996 elections (Sudan 1996). These ratios were far lower than for 1986 when voter turnout was 80 per cent and the proportion of registered voters higher than for 1996. Registration for the 1996 elections was based on the sugar quota register, thereby excluding many urban residents as well as a large proportion of Sudanese expatriates working abroad.[9] Turnout rates varied widely between different states and constituencies for the 1996 elections. Although turnout was lowest in the South because of the war, as Table 10.10 indicates, voters also stayed away from the polls in Khartoum and other major towns.

Table 10.10: Voter turnout in selected constituencies, Khartoum, 1996

Constituency Number	Potential voters (a)	Registered voters (b)	Actual voters (c)	b/a %	c/b %	c/a %
1	51041	29212	14353	57.2	49.1	28.1
2	51815	27950	14357	54.0	51.4	27.7
3	52793	23064	14464	43.7	62.7	27.4
13	53843	20741	11332	38.5	54.6	21.0
14	51513	16742	7645	32.5	45.6	14.8
37	59845	32554	13144	54.4	40.4	22.0
38	63056	34262	13336	54.3	38.9	21.1

Source: Sudan 1997, 79.

Furthermore, the 1996 parliamentary elections were marked by the extent to which contests were avoided. Of the 400 incumbent members of the National Council, nearly one-third were elected through the electoral colleges of the National Congress. Another 12 per cent (15 per cent in the South) were selected through a 'silent consensus', or *el-igmaa el-sikouti* (literally meaning collective silence), and did not need to contest their seats. There were only 3 such non-contested constituencies, with only 1 candidate selected in each, for the 1986 parliamentary elections. Yet, non-contested constituencies in 1996 amounted to 64, since vetting procedures and rules meant that only 53 per cent of the existing National Council were required to contest an election.[10] It does seem that the Consensus Councils succeeded in reducing the number of candidates in many constituencies. Thus, in the Red Sea State, the total number of candidates was reduced from 51 to 20; in White Nile State, from 114 to 62; in West Kordofan State, from 106 to 59. In other constituencies, as mentioned above, it was the work of the CC that prevented contests by arriving at a single candidate for each constituency. Thus, given the overwhelming influence of the National Congress, the electorate were effectively prevented from exercising their franchise at the 1996 elections.

Actual voting in the South took place in roughly one-half the number of constituencies delimited by the National Electoral Committee, thereby confirming the comment that 'war prevents the South from participating in general elections'.[11] From official data it can be calculated

---

[9]*Akhbar Al-Youm* 9 March 1996.

[10]Apart from six states, all experienced *igmaa sikouti* at the 1996 General Elections. Constituencies of *el-igmaa el-sikouti* were distributed by region as follows: Khartoum 2, Central 11, Eastern 8, Northern 5, Kordofan 2, Darfur 20, Equatoria 5, Bahr el-Gazal 6, and Upper Nile 5.

[11]*Al Asharq Aswat* 21 March 1996.

that since only 170,000 voted in the South, the actual southern electorate accounted for a mere 4.5 per cent of those who voted nationwide (Sudan 1996). Due to a worsening security situation in early 1996, the NEC *initially* excluded the 5 states of Jongeli, East Equatoria, North Bahr El-Gazal, Warab and Wahda from the general election. Elections were permitted for 4 states, Bahr el-Jabel, Upper Nile, Lakes and West Bahr el-Gazal, where movement by truck transport was possible. For the West Equatoria State, it was decided that elections could take place in only 1 constituency. However, later in the electoral process, decisions were reversed to permit elections to go ahead in the South as a whole. Since it was the military authorities who effectively decided whether elections could take place, and when the CCs were also brought into place in the South, it seemed that the 'security situation' had improved.[12] Election contests were held in 22 of the 45 constituencies delimited in the South. Elections did not take pace in 8 constituencies, while *el-igmaa el-sikouti*, the silent consensus, was deployed in the other 15 constituencies where patron-client networks assured the selection of a single candidate whose allegiance was to the Khartoum regime.

Thus, to take one example of a contest in West Bahr el-Gazal, Ali T. Farak, a Muslim Southerner and NIF leader, had the full backing of the regime, army and other security forces. Although he lost by a slim margin to Charles Majak, Ali's strong showing at the polls was only possible because of the support that he received from Khartoum. This contest was also of exemplary interest because the winning candidate also received indirect support from Khartoum, largely through the protection and other assistance provided by Riek Machar and Carbino Kwanine, former SPLA dissidents and warlords whose armies were engaged in warfare against the main southern threat to the regime.

The number of women candidates standing in the 1996 parliamentary elections rose considerably from a very low base in 1986, as shown in Table 10.8 above, and unlike a decade earlier, a woman candidate won in a geographical constituency, Khartoum East, with nearly 60 per cent of the popular vote. However, the participation of women in voting was relatively low, at just less than 30 per cent of the total electorate (Sudan 1997). Among other reasons for the low participation of women in 1996, the ruling party's General Secretariat suggested the following: traditions and convention inhibit women from participating in public affairs; the National Congress failed to establish constituent women's units at local and regional levels; and the General Elections Secretariat failed to provide voters with transport facilities, particularly in some rural areas (*ibid.*). However, one of the important reasons explaining the gender gap in participation was the perceived anti-women discourse of the NIF, a factor that had especially prevented urban women from taking part in elections. This anti-women aspect of the official Islamist discourse in the Sudan was indicated by the practices involved in the nomination of women candidates in electoral colleges confined to women. Within these electoral colleges, women who were well-known for their vocal and assertive political personalities, such as Lubaba El-Fadl, were excluded despite protest from other college members, while those of a milder and more deferential disposition were nominated.[13]

My own surveys for the 1996 elections showed that where women voted in larger numbers, they were often induced to do so by members of Popular Committees who spread rumours warning that those who boycotted elections would be deprived of their weekly subsidised sugar ration.[14] Reprisals of this kind, whether threatened or actual, were used as a stick by state officials to coerce people to turn out to vote. Given their need for public-sector employment or the weekly sugar

---

[12]Seven of the eight states nationwide with the lowest turnout were in the South: Upper Nile (30 per cent), Bahr el-Jebel (30), West Bahr el-Gazal (25), Wahda (24), Jongeli (11), Noth Bahr el-Gazal (1). Elections were not held in Warab. The displacement of populations, induced by war, was the main reason for these low turnout rates. From 1992 until early 1996, it was estimated that at least 1.3m died due to war and famine, with 3.5m displaced, seeking refuge in the North, major towns such as Juba, Malakal and Wau in the South or in neighbouring countries (*Asharq Al-Awsat* 21 March 1996). No other area of the world, since the end of the Second World War, has experienced war as long as that of southern Sudan. It is also here that more people have died than in any other war-torn area of the post-1945 world.

[13]Personal communication, 1996.

[14]Details of surveys.

ration, women were particularly vulnerable to coercion. Without coercion, it is likely that participation in the 1996 elections would have been even lower than that indicated by the actual turnout.

State resources were deployed to favour selected candidates, especially for the presidential elections. When the 1996 elections were announced, the NEC announced that it would allocate Ls 3 billion (US$15 million) to presidential candidates on condition that they would abide 'by the law' during their campaigns (Sudan 1996). However, after the final list of candidates was officially announced, and just before the start of election campaigning, candidates were informed that it was their own responsibility to finance campaigning, including travel expenses, political rallies and advertisements.[15] As a result, the incumbent presidential candidate, President Omer al-Bashir, had a built-in advantage over all other candidates. The government monopoly of mass media ensured him unlimited and biased coverage and, importantly for a country at war, privileged access to the Armed Forces. While al-Bashir was able to address the Armed Forces in his capacity as Army Chief Commander, other candidates were not even permitted to enter military barracks. Furthermore, presidential candidates were only allowed to campaign in Khartoum State, one of 26 states in federal Sudan, and were not allowed to travel outside Khartoum without official permission.[16]

Outcomes of the 1996 elections

The Islamic government's intention in 1996 was to politically undermine the bases of its opponents' support in both rural and urban areas. To undermine the patronage networks of the traditional parties, Umma and the DUP, the regime sought to nurture and support its own clients among some small tribes and religious sects whose 'representatives' had expressed grievances against larger tribes and the main religious sects. Table 10.11 shows the extent to which traditional leaders and farmers had been eclipsed in parliament by 1996. Although, as shown above, this tendency had stretched back over past decades, the 1996 elections made it far more emphatic.

Table 10.11: Occupations of elected Members of Parliament, 1958 and 1996

	1958	1996
	percentage	
Traditional leaders	20	
Farmers	24	5
Merchants	10	22
Politicians	13	5
Public employees, teachers and professionals	33	68

Source: Karar 1989; Interview with Hassan El-Turabi, Sudan Television, 15 September 1996.

Examples can be given of candidates who won as a result of the support they received from their local, tribal communities. Adam Salih Sabiel, elected for constituency 146, Gadaref State in eastern Sudan commented: 'I was in Saudi Arabia when I was nominated by my people here and all tribes in the area supported my nomination'.[17] Abdel-Rahman Abdalla Amir, for constituency 132, White Nile State recounted a similar story. Hasanat, Dowieh, Hasaniyya, with parts of Shanabla and Awamra, covered the cost of election campaigns on behalf of their candidate whose own contribution to the total cost of his election campaign did not exceed Ls41,000 (US$20).[18]

---

[15]*Al-Hayat* 27 February 1996.

[16]Some potential candidates who objected to the candidature of al-Bashir, the incumbent President, took their case to the court and demanded his resignation. Their complaint was about the lack of impartiality of mass media and that the National Electoral Commission was duty bound to follow complicated judicial procedures in such cases. *Al-Hayat* 5 March 1996; *Asharq Al-Awsat* 7 March 1996. The complainants, who also demanded the postponement of the elections until such time as they could be deemed to be *fair and free,* lost their case on 11 March 1996.

[17]Interview, quoted in Al-Karsani 1997.

[18]Interview, *ibid.*

Ahmed Sharif Musa, elected for constituency 104, West Darfur State, did not have any previous link with the Peoples Congresses but he was known to be a keen competitor of the tribal chief in the area and played a key role in the local cooperative society.[19] Thus, locality was a key issue for the 1996 elections since to have had a history in serving 'the community' and be seen as having been devoted to a community was of paramount importance for electoral success. As mentioned above, it was the emphatic intention of the regime to stamp out 'tribalism' throughout the country. The emphasis upon locality should be understood in this light.

Largely integrated into patron-client networks, the rural population in Sudan has always provided the traditional religious-sectarian based parties with solid political support. However, the steady expansion of the market economy, together with the encroachment of agricultural capitalist enterprise on the resources and means of livelihood of pastoralists and peasants in rural areas during the 1980s and 1990s, has gradually undermined farmers' support for Umma and the DUP. In benefiting from the exposure of rural masses to political radicalisation, it was a new alliance of religious élites (*ulamma*) and rural business groups that coalesced under the NIF to challenge the sectarian parties and undermined their constituency support.

However, political party competition and struggle, as mentioned above, was conducted within the parameters of the power-bloc of northern hegemony. During the 1990s, especially, the northern hegemony faced a serious crisis as a result of, among other factors, a growing resistance from ethnic, racial and other groups of non-Arab-Muslim origin. Hence, to re-organise the fragile northern power-bloc, mobilise the northern rural and urban masses and maintain the status quo, the Islamist élites resorted to religion. Islam, or more precisely a particular version of Islam, came to be deployed as a new ideology for the purpose of political mobilisation. A number of questions can be raised about how a fundamentalist Islam could be deployed in a country for which the faith of the majority of the population was Sufi Islam. Bearing in mind how *Shura* has been developed by the NIF along lines that formally parallel injunctions for 'civil society' and 'community' as sources of good governance throughout Africa, some interpretations of the current orthodoxy in the Sudan have cast the NIF version of Islam as modern and tolerant with 'secular' overtures. Others, however, have not failed to notice that there is little that is either civil or communitarian about the 'racist element in Islamic absolutism in the Sudan' (de Waal 1993). That said, there is one aspect of religious ideology that had an immediate bearing upon the 1996 election.

One of the more perplexing phenomena during the 1996 elections was the concerted campaigns that were organised by the ruling regime to make people take an oath of allegiance, *baya*. During the course of these campaigns, electorates at local and regional levels were implored to show their loyalty to the regime by taking a public oath to show their support and defend it against 'traitors' and other sources of external aggression. It is difficult to evaluate the impact of these *baya* campaigns upon popular opinion. However, the fact that the campaigns were organised as part of an electoral process carries the implication that the 1996 elections were designed to ward off the threat to the northern power-bloc that was posed by continuing and escalating war in the South, as well as the East where some cadres of the 1980s National Alliance now took to organising armed warfare against the Islamist regime.

Against this background, Islamic absolutism through concepts of the Islamic state and Jihad furnished the basis and justification for a thorough militarisation of society. As a result, there has been proliferation of security and paramilitary organisations created or legitimised by the government, including several security services, armed neighbourhood committees and Popular Defence Forces. Further, the presence of Islamist militia from the Arab and Islamic countries to support the Sudanese Islamic State has aggravated an atmosphere of institutionalised repression and fear. Although one result of this repressive atmosphere in the Sudan has been popular submission, as elsewhere, another result has been to escalate class, ethnic and religious conflict, including the pitting of Muslim against Muslim throughout the country, as well as the waging of total war in the South.

Given that the allocation of economic resources is a monopoly of the centre and that the political system is fundamentally authoritarian, there was no way for an independent candidate to stand in the 1996 elections on his or her own platform against the regime's nominees or favourites.

---

[19]Interview, *ibid.*

More significant than the absence of political contest in 1996 was the fact that it was the electoral machinations of the centre that thwarted the peace process in the South. In order to win the support of their local constituencies, as emphasised above, rival candidates resorted to their former tactics of political mobilisation according to tribal and ethnic sources of association. However, candidates favoured by the centre and believed to be anti-SPLA/M had a much more favourable chance of winning their contests because they expected that an anti-SPLA/M stance would secure unlimited support from the Khartoum government. Seeing their candidates losing mainly because of intervention from the centre, the Southern warlords, who had earlier joined the peace process, were forced to reappraise the links they had established with their Northern patrons.[20]

Conclusions

The history of elections in the Sudan has been one of the failure of dominant classes to build an effective power-bloc that has been able to rule and exercise hegemony, whether according to the precepts of liberal democracy or any other system of government. Between 1956 and 1958, the nationalist élites and representatives of the incipient bourgeoisie, the NUP, joined the political radicals when they were excluded from power by the religious-sectarian Umma and PDP parties who held state power. Joined by the southern rebel movement, the radicals, comprising the CPS and their supporters among workers, peasants, students, as well as some other ethnic nationalists, were able to withstand the repression of the military regime of Abboud from 1958 to 1964. For a short period, the fall of the military regime boosted the morale, strength and image of the radical left in challenging the hegemony of the dominant classes.

However, alongside this radical mobilisation, another political realignment of hitherto opposed social forces, that of the traditional, rural aristocracy and the urban bourgeoisie and entrepreneurs, was taking place. Development planning, as exercised by the Abboud regime, had led to a considerable expansion of agriculture and industry, accelerating the creation of a wage labour force, thereby reinforcing the potential threat posed by the boost of the radical movement during the mid 1960s. Political conflict between the radical movement and the newly aligned coalition of dominant, propertied classes had become class-based. Insofar as the coalition had been formed as a result of a class threat, it appeared to be politically solid. For example, as political conflict escalated during the late 1960s under multi-party politics and elections, while the former secularists of NUP joined the coalition of the propertied classes, by forsaking their former secularism in favour of advocating an Islamic constitution, the radical movement stood steadfast in supporting a secular constitution. Multi-party elections in 1965 and 1968 had brought the Communist Party into parliament. However, the manipulation of wealth, religious influence, tradition and the political power that the older parties were able to exercise during elections contained the threat posed by the radical movement in a competitive process for gaining power over state institutions.

It was the exclusion of the Communist Party from parliament after the 1968 elections, as recounted earlier in this chapter, which led to a series of events that culminated in the Numeiri period of one-party rule, lasting until the mid-1980s. Given that the patron-clientelist form of rule of Umma, the PDP and the DUP attempted to make access to state benefits conditional upon the political subordination of rural peoples, Numeiri's ostensibly populist takeover in 1969 was meant to free rural 'clients' from the shackles of their 'patrons' and institutionalise their access to state power on a new basis. Elections during the Numeiri period were designed to undermine the traditional, sectarian and bourgeois sources of authority and substitute it by that of 'the people'. Yet, the outcome of Numeiri's reforms was only to assert the authoritarian rule of a state administration some of whose personnel in the army and civil service were eventually to turn against their benefactor in making common cause with the National Alliance, inheritors of the 1960s radical movement, in successfully bringing down the regime. Unlike the 1960s, however, the renewed

---

[20]Thus, Kerubino Kwanyen was dissatisfied because he did not receive the personal appointment he considered he deserved as a reward for supporting the Northern regime; Riek Machar and Paulino Mathip have engaged in electoral and military warfare against each other with the support of different factions of the regime.

advent of multi-party politics after the demise of the Numeiri regime appeared during a period when the radical movement in the Sudan was far weaker. Correspondingly, since it did not face a radical threat of the kind experienced during the 1960s, the political coalition of propertied classes could also not be coherently reassembled without the intervention of a radical Islamic party, the NIF, that ushered in another period of one-party rule for the 1990s.

Against this historical background of a repeated cycle of critical political events, it can also be suggested that the relatively peaceful coexistence, in the North, between social forces, such as the traditional aristocracy, the merchant business class, unions of workers and professionals and state officials, was facilitated by a 'fit' between a fragile market economy and an emerging, burgeoning civil society. Democratic freedoms and space enjoyed by the various political groupings of these social forces positively correlate with the degree to which the economy had developed in a relatively balanced way. During the 1960s, for this complex of reasons, even when there were legal and other formal restrictions on political activity, northerners enjoyed a range of democratic rights. By contrast, for the 1990s, when formal democratic rights have been set out on paper according to an Islamic constitution of government, northerners have far less freedom to engage in political activity even within a relatively minimal area of democratic space.

The fit, or symbiotic relationship, between the market and political democracy was shattered when, as in 1958 and 1969, military intervention consolidated the power of state bureaucracy. Dominant classes of the North were generally reluctant to confront forms of authoritarian rule that undermined civil society and manipulated the Southern question, in making war in the South while attempting to incorporate southerners into the power bloc of the North. In preserving the fragile market economy, despite often taking measures to the contrary, periods of military rule did not fundamentally threaten the interests of the traditional aristocracy and merchants. As long as the northern radical movement, as represented by trade unions and professional groups, was put under control, and the South was thought to be pacified, Northern political parties might prefer to engage in multi-party politics but were resigned to one-party rule when it happened.

Periods of one-party rule in the Sudan have been punctuated by elections. Electoral 'innovations' have appeared in the Sudan as a singular feature of the process to both justify the failure of multi-party democracy and make one-party rule legitimate. There is a genuine case to be made for adapting the Westminster model of representative democracy to fit the experiences of African electorates. Graduate Constituencies, during the early years of independence, may have been one such meaningful example in the Sudanese case. However, what is practised in the name of 'originality' or 'innovation', or even 'Islamisation', during one-party periods has failed to transcend the dichotomy between elections as means to confer legitimation upon the state by the electorate and to provide voters with real choice. Indeed, the Sudan experience has only aggravated inherent tensions between the two reasons for why elections are held.

For public-orientated representatives of an enlightened citizenry, a major concern is to cede access to state power, and the resources that power brings, to less powerful and less privileged social forces in both the Sudan's North and South. Relative success in elections, or electoral success for the people's representatives, occurs if state institutions are brought under the scrutiny of, and made accountable to, those whom the public elects. People's representatives often attempt to occupy whatever democratic spaces can be opened, demanding a broader access to the state while trying to defend their capacity to articulate their own interests autonomously and to defend whatever gains they have made in the past.

I have provided a historical account of elections in the Sudan, as summarised above, to show how efforts at translating electoral gains into what can be called political capital formation usually provoke a backlash that brings authoritarian regimes to power. These regimes, as history has shown, turn the cycle by which the state structure was opened up from below, and in acting from above to close off democratic space have undermined the infrastructure for independent action from below. While there is no guarantee that cycles move through a unilinear path over time, these recursive cycles of opening and closing space for independent action *may* gradually foster a democratic culture, build independent mass-movements and enlarge the official tolerance for autonomous social organisations. According to the concept of political capital formation, the key issue is how much political capital is left after the cycle turns towards a democratic phase of multi-party elections and how democratic space can be maintained when the cycle turns towards an authoritarian phase. In the Sudan, this cyclical process has been slow, gradual and uneven.

The iterative process is highly uneven, helping to explain why such different patterns of state-society relations can coexist simultaneously within the same polity at one point in time. Thus, during the 1990s, and as the 1996 elections indicated, persistent authoritarian clientelism can coexist with new enclaves of pluralist 'tolerance'. These two authoritarian and pluralistic forms of polity fix the poles of a continuum extending from clientelism (obedience) to citizenship (civil-political rights). Between the two poles, there are multiple forms of political relationships for a political system in transition within which regimes get stuck short of a democratic threshold. This framework suggests that the concept of 'semi-clientelism' might be useful to frame those state–society relations that fall between authoritarian clientelism and pluralist citizenship rights. Semi-clientelist authorities attempt to condition access to state benefits upon the basis of political subordination. In contrast to conventional models of authoritarian clientelism, however, the leverage of incumbent ruling regimes is the threat to withdraw carrots, without the need to deploy the threat of sticks.

Within this framework, elections can be seen as relatively peaceful means for different social forces to gain legitimate access to institutionalised state power. However, as long as social differentiation, inequality and ethnic repression are accentuated by state policy, competition for the control of institutionalised state power may reveal the repressive, violent nature of political conflict. Whether intended or not, different state regimes have created more dimensions of social inequality, by adding those of race, ethnicity and religion to that of class. The accompanying tendency has been for a regime to resort to coercive power, thus making it more likely that conflicts are to be resolved through violent rather than peaceful, and electoral, means of political action.

11

Elections at the Borderland
Voter Opinion in Arusha & Kilimanjaro Tanzania

TUULIKKI PIETILÄ, SANNA OJALAMMI-WAMAI
& LIISA LAAKSO[1]

Elections and voter opinion are usually analysed in the framework of nation states and national politics. Yet it is a well known fact that state boundaries only seldom coincide with people's political identities or their socio-economic activities. Therefore perceptions of national politics in the borderlands of multi-ethnic states are particularly interesting. The position of people living on both sides of a state border, or crossing it frequently, might be particularly complex *vis-à-vis* national politics and not only due to the not-so-rare government suspicion concerning their loyalties. Their position can explain the low level of their political participation, but it can also contribute to the durability of their traditional political organisations. The state border can also be an asset not least due to the opportunities it provides for petty traders. In addition, the very fact that people in the borderland often follow and are affected by political development on the other side of the border can provide them with a wider perspective to reflect upon domestic politics and its prospects.

Tanzania is an example of a country where the borderlands have remarkable dynamics of their own. First of all ethnicity and regionalism in general are anything but politically irrelevant notions there. However, the peaceful coexistence of about 120 different ethnic groups in the country has to be considered as a major achievement of the policy of national unity. Based on a survey study of voter opinion in Tanzania in 1970 by Jon Moris, Joel Barkan has argued that when power and political recruitment were monopolised by a well-organised ruling party, ethnic or regional background as such was rarely a deciding factor in the way individuals voted (Barkan 1979, 84, 89). Yet the rural dwellers were not passive political actors ignorant of the national political community in which they lived. Nor did they base their political behaviour mainly on ascriptive or 'identity' considerations. Instead, most voters had a clear set of role expectations as to what constitutes the proper duties of a member of the National Assembly. They defined the role of the legislator primarily in terms of the representation of constituency interests at the centre. Most voters knew their MP and what he had and had not done to further the interests of the local community (Barkan 1979, 83).

Thus the elections during the one-party era were basically a series of local contests where a voter tried to select a representative of the periphery to lobby at the centre. By the same token, the election campaigns were dominated by discussions about local rather than national or ideological issues. Additionally the voters preferred to vote for the educated candidates or well-known

[1]T. Pietilä is responsible for the Kilimanjaro part. She conducted fieldwork in an ex-chiefdom called Mayanka (pseudonym) in the contemporary Moshi rural district in Kilimanjaro during 1994 and the beginning of 1997. S. Ojalammi-Wamai is responsible for the Arusha part. She conducted fieldwork in the Loliondo Division in the Ngorongoro Constituency from May 1994 to June 1995 and in May 1997. She would like to thank Metui Ole Tipap from Loliondo Division for the work done together. L. Laakso is responsible for the general part.

persons, who had been successful in life (see Barkan 1979, 82; Bavu 1989, 24; Mukandala 1994, 63). Mobilisation for registration and voting relied more on 'statecraft', including force, but also on the general acceptability of the party or the candidates. Voting was regarded as an important manifestation of people's participation in general (see Samoff 1987, 169). The number of voters registering to vote and the actual turnout varied from year to year at both national and local level. With low participation the voters could show, even during the one-party system, some of their disapproval of the political system, as happened in 1985 (see Othman *et al.* 1990).

When reintroducing multi-party competition in 1992, the government explicitly prohibited regional and religious political parties. In a way this represents an important continuity in the policy of national unity. Yet the results of the first post-reform general elections in 1995 show that regionalism and ethnicity played a role. In addition to the cases of Zanzibar and Dar es Salaam – where the official election results most likely did not reflect the will of the voters (Vesa *et al.* 1997, 10) – the Kilimanjaro area, on the Kenyan border, stood out as a stronghold of the opposition. The most important and colourful opposition leader, former minister Augustine Mrema of the NCCR-Mageuzi, came from the Chagga ethnic group living in the Kilimanjaro area. It was the only region on the mainland where the opposition gained more votes than the ruling party. Another striking peculiarity was the low participation of the Maasai pastoralists on the Kenyan border.

This article studies and attempts to explain the voting behaviour of these two borderland groups. While sharing the geographical and political borderland status, the Maasai and the Chagga differ remarkably in their socio-economic status and position in the state. Whereas the Chagga form one of the most modernised and 'advanced' ethnic groups in Tanzania – mainly because of their entrepreneurial and trading activities and good representation in civil service positions – the Maasai as a pastoralist group are much more marginal and weakly integrated into the state. The two areas studied in this article are the Vunjo constituency in Kilimanjaro and the Ngorongoro constituency in Arusha. Before looking in detail at the electoral history and the recent elections in the two areas, a summary of the transition period and the general conduct of the elections in the whole country is given.

Transition to a multi-party system

Tanzania arranged elections regularly under the one-party system. There had been parliamentary and presidential elections in 1965, 1970, 1975, 1980, 1985 and 1990, which were all carried out peacefully. Despite the party executive's influence in the nomination of candidates, the elections were competitive as each constituency was contested by 2 candidates. Thus the elections often contributed to significant changes in the composition of the political elite. In the 1990 parliamentary elections, for instance, as many as 203 (or 58 per cent) of all the candidates were new faces (Luanda 1994, 257). In the presidential elections, there was only one candidate and the electorate was asked to vote 'yes' or 'no'. What was remarkable in Tanzania when compared to the other African one-party states, however, was that the incumbent President Nyerere decided to step down in 1985 and the ruling party nominated a new candidate Ali Hassan Mwinyi, who was then elected.

It took less than two years to abolish the one-party state in Tanzania after *Mwalimu,* Tanzanian president and a theorist of one-party democracy in Africa, Julius Nyerere, initiated a debate on it in 1991.[2] The salient point of this process was that right from the beginning all aspects of it were controlled by the ruling party *Chama Cha Mapinduzi* (CCM), which has its history in the anti-colonial struggle and liberation movement and still enjoyed legitimacy in the eyes of the majority of Tanzanians.[3] To a large extent the power and legitimacy of the ruling party was based on an

---

[2]In February 1991, Nyerere said at a press conference at his Dar es Salaam residence that 'the time had arrived when Tanzanians should begin to question the wisdom of retaining the single party system or disregard it altogether' (Sundet 1995, 19, 20).

[3]After independence, Tanganyika was ruled by the Tanganyika African National Union (TANU) which in 1977 united with the ruling party of Zanzibar, the Afro Shiraz Party (ASP) and formed the CCM. Although Tanzania was in practice ruled by those two parties before 1977, it had formally already introduced a one-party state in 1965.

administrative structure that was made up of vertical linkages right through the state hierarchy, from village, ward, district and region up to the national level (see Sundet ed. 1996, 26). Contrary to what happened in neighbouring Zambia and Malawi, where the ruling party had to 'surrender', due to growing opposition not only among educated urban people and workers but also among the rural majority, in Tanzania there was relatively little internal pressure towards transition. A case in point is that the first mass demonstration of the opposition took place only after the opposition parties were legalised in December 1992.

Thus Nyerere's initiative, rather than being an attempt to open space for opposition and alternative political coalitions to compete for state power, was perhaps merely an initiative to safeguard CCM control in a development which was almost certainly spilling over to Tanzania. By mid-1990 Nyerere had already predicted that '[A] multi-party system is inevitable'. Therefore, 'CCM must be at the forefront of bringing about those changes, including CCM overseeing change to multi-party politics'.[4] Nyerere's own rhetoric on the need for political reform was restricted to the problems inside the party and not so much to reorganisation of the party's position vis-à-vis the state (Erdmann 1995, 3).

The transition was based on comprehensive preparatory work (Vesa et al. 1997, 5, 6). In 1991, President Ali Hassan Mwinyi established a twenty-member Commission under the chairmanship of Chief Justice Nyalali to investigate public opinion on one-partyism. In the course of its work, the Commission toured the entire country and gathered information and views from over 36,000 people (Sundet ed. 1996, 20). It found that a majority of Tanzanians favoured the retention of the one-party state. Some observers claimed that, as a governmental body, it was not able to get honest opinions from the people. However, independent surveys seem to confirm its findings. According to one survey conducted in 1994, about 60 per cent of Tanzanians regarded the multi-party system as a threat to national unity and not beneficial to the country (Erdmann 1995, 8–10). Yet the Nyalali Commission decided to recommend the introduction of a multi-party system saying that 'although the majority of Tanzanians wanted the one-party system to continue, they proposed very many modifications, some of which, in the Commission's view, could only be effectively introduced under a multi-party political system' (Ngasongwa 1992).

In 1992, the Constitution was amended by removing the one-party rule and legalising the founding of new parties. The first elections arranged under the new legislation were for the district councillors in 1994 (Reeves and Klein eds. 1995,12). The multi-party political mobilisation still remained minimal and it was not until the parliamentary and presidential elections in October 1995 that the opposition parties gathered pace. However, some of these parties were crisis-ridden from the beginning, and the opposition as a whole was very divided.

The 1995 elections witnessed the participation of 13 registered political parties in the parliamentary elections and 4 political parties in the presidential elections. These 4 parties were among the 5 biggest parties considering the number of running candidates in the parliamentary elections. These were the ruling party, CCM, with Minister Benjamin Mkapa as presidential candidate and 232 parliamentary candidates covering the whole country; National Convention for Construction and Reform (NCCR-Mageuzi) with Mrema as presidential candidate and 196 parliamentary candidates; Civic United Front (CUF) with Professor Ibrahim Lipumba as presidential candidate and 177 parliamentary candidates; Chama Cha Demokrasia na Maendeleo (Chadema) with no presidential candidate and 157 parliamentary candidates; and the United Democratic Party (UDP) with businessman John Cheyo as presidential candidate and 125 parliamentary candidates. In August 1995, it seemed that NCCR-Mageuzi, CUF, and Chadema might join their forces as they had signed an electoral pact. By the end of the month, however, the opposition had failed to keep to the pact and the coalition fell apart.[5]

While CCM's manifesto was still advocating socialism and self-reliance, the opposition parties were highly populist, mainly concentrating on blaming the ruling party. According to a survey made before Mrema left CCM and joined NCCR-Mageuzi, Chadema was the best-known opposition party and its leader, Edwin Mtei, former Minister of Finance, also from Kilimanjaro, was the best-known opposition leader (Erdmann 1995, 17). But Mrema, who was a vocal critic of

[4]Daily News, 27 June 1990.
[5]Economist Intelligence Unit 4th quarter 1995, 8.

corruption gave NCCR-Mageuzi a popularity boost. He was able to draw crowds at Dar es Salaam's Mnazi Moja grounds which observers described as the biggest ever seen. The party's membership rocketed in the city, as well as parts of the Kilimanjaro and Arusha regions.[6] However, Mrema's popularity was very much restricted to urban areas and Kilimanjaro and to the Chagga ethnic group. The CUF and Lipumba, known as a pious Muslim, had their base in Zanzibar and Zanzibari nationalism. While all the opposition parties saw restructuring of the relationship of Tanganyika and Zanzibar as necessary, the CUF's political programme was the most 'radical' in the sense that it was promoting individual National Assemblies to both parts of the country.

Currently Zanzibar is represented in and ruled by the national bodies, but it has its own House of Representatives and its own President, too. The President and House of Representatives of Zanzibar were elected a week before the national elections.The official results gave CCM's Salmin Amour a marginal 0.4 per cent victory over the CUF's Seif Hamad in the elections for the President of Zanzibar. In the House of Representatives of Zanzibar, CCM won 26 seats and CUF the remaining 24 seats.[7] However, as was widely published in the international media, the official figures differed critically from those registered by observers and agreed among the polling officials.[8] All the donor countries, financing up to half of the election budget, expressed their concern and demanded a recount, which was not carried out.[9]

Many problems characterised the conduct of the elections on the mainland, too. The situation in Dar es Salaam, which was also one of the strongholds of the opposition parties, was the worst. Due to the chaos there, the vote had to be annulled. This then opened up all sorts of speculations and theories, including charges of planned recklessness that benefited the ruling party. Naturally completing elections in the rest of the country affected the rescheduled Dar es Salaam elections, which followed almost a month later. The opposition parties said they would boycott the whole rerun in the capital, but from the beginning there were disagreements inside the parties. Most candidates in the parliamentary elections encouraged their supporters to cast their ballots. However, all three opposition candidates in the presidential elections decided to withdraw from the competition. This withdrawal was not legal according to the authorities, but it apparently affected the voters' behaviour as the turnout was very low, estimated to be between 30 and 40 per cent of the registered voters.

The final results in the whole country showed turnout at about 77 per cent of the registered voters. The ruling party, CCM, won both the presidential elections and the parliamentary elections. In the presidential elections, CCM's Benjamin Mkapa won with 62 per cent of the votes, while Augustine Mrema of NCCR-Mageuzi received 28 per cent, CUF's Ibrahim Lipumba 6 per cent and UDP's John Cheyo 4 per cent. In the parliamentary elections, CCM got 186 seats, CUF 24, NCCR-Mageuzi 16, Chadema 3 and UDP 3. As stated in the constitution, 36 seats were reserved for women representatives, who were appointed according to the number of seats won by the contesting parties. Thus, CCM gained 219 out of the total 274 seats or an 80 per cent share, although the opposition parties collected nearly 40 per cent of the votes.

---

[6]*Economist Intelligence Unit* 2nd quarter 1995, 7.

[7]As expected, Unguja island gave a majority to the CCM but Pemba voted for the CUF. This political division stems from the peripheral position of Pemba *vis-à-vis* Unguja, which has been the administrative centre since colonialism.

[8]At the request of the Tanzanian government, the United Nations coordinated the International Observation of the Zanzibar elections as well as the elections in the whole of Tanzania. In Zanzibar, the International Observation team observed, for instance, the counting process in Mlandenge constituency. According to the team figures and those of the Assistant Returning Officer, the results of the presidential elections announced by the Zanzibar Electoral Commission (ZEC) gave 473 additional votes to the CCM and 473 fewer votes to the CUF. Because the margin of victory for the CCM candidate was only 1,556 votes in the whole of Zanzibar, the observation team asked for a reconciliation of the counts at the ZEC, but without success (Karanko 1995).

[9]According to the Coordinator of the International Observers, Kari Karanko, this was also due to the coordination of the UN in Dar es Salaam, which actually delayed the activation of the donors' political pressure. There was no immediate diplomatic action to ensure that the ZEC postponed its declaration of the final results, even though the observers had already informed the UN of the serious shortcomings in the final counting. The pressure started only after the declaration, which was apparently too late for the Zanzibar Government to countenance any further scrutiny (*ibid.*).

Most importantly, after the elections the opposition was no more united in its relation to the ruling party (to which many opposition MPs once belonged) than it had been before the elections (Vesa *et al.* 1997, 7). In 1998, the opposition leaders were alleged to lack the unity and will to cooperate, with NCCR-Mageuzi being torn into two factions.[10]

Maasai in Loliondo Division, Arusha

The first region studied for this article is the Loliondo Division in Arusha. It is part of the Ngorongoro constituency and lies about 370 km from Arusha town on the Kenyan border. Economically, the Loliondo Division can be qualified as a marginalised area in Tanzania. The major pastoral group of Tanzania, the Maasai, constitute a majority, 90 per cent, of the population. Other groups are the Batemi/Sonjo, or 'newcomers', people who have moved to the area from other parts of Tanzania. They include the Chagga, the Irawq and even Kenyan Kalenjins and Kikuyus. According to the 1988 census, the population in the Loliondo Division was about 12,000 and in the Ngorongoro constituency about 50,000 (Tanzania 1988). The Ngorongoro constituency is wealthy and poor, marginalised and centred at the same time. Famous natural parks, wildlife and increased tourism in the Ngorongoro Conservation Area and in the Serengeti National Park have an effect on the local people and politics. The Loliondo Division borders on the Serengeti National Park and the Ngorongoro Conservation Area and the people living there distinctively classify themselves as 'indigenous people' in Tanzania.

In a way, similarities can be found between the Loliondo Division and the Mtwara Region, which Mmuya (1994, 252) has described as a marginalised area. According to him, marginalisation restrains democratic development and does not provide the context for active and unrestrained political participation. Politics becomes diffuse and backward. Within the context of elections, this means little or no effective participation. The election process itself is usually formalistic and ritualistic. According to Sjørslev (1998, 307, 308), for indigenous people like the Maasai their social inequality leads to political exclusion and the other way around. While being socially and economically marginalised, the Maasai are disqualified from national-level politics. At the same time, the Maasai feel that national politics since colonialism has too often overlooked their interests and specific cultural characteristics and thus undermined their position in society.

Among the Maasai, the level of education is low and generally men are more educated than women. Illiteracy is a general phenomenon and most Maasai women use their own Maasai language and speak Kiswahili very little, if at all. As is the case in many pastoral societies, Maasai society is patriarchal and women's role is more passive than that of men. Traditionally, the woman's domain consists of child care and household activities, while livestock rearing, public participation and representation belong to the men. However, a few Maasai men have played an important role in the administration, the police force and, during independence, also in politics through the ruling party in local government as councillors or village chairmen.

Newspapers do not, daily, reach the peripheral Loliondo Division behind the Serengeti National Park and both radio and television are rare commodities in Maasai families. The few influential educated Maasai – politicians, businessmen or government officials – who do travel frequently from Loliondo to Arusha town, bring the news and connections to the 'outer' world with them. The most educated people also tend to read newspapers, which come to the local shops and to the District headquarters weekly. Few of them have a television or video set. While the commonly read newspapers are Tanzanian, when radios are available, many people tend to listen to Kenya Broadcasting Company (KBC).

The Maasai often cross the national border to meet their relatives or to attend Maasai meetings or celebrations on the Kenyan side, and the Maasai from the Kenyan side are regular visitors for the same reasons to the Loliondo Division. Usually the journeys are made on foot. In some situations like during a severe drought or a possible famine in their home area the Maasai families can even move to settle down and use common natural resources with their fellow Maasai on the other side of the border. In marriage transactions, the bride might come from the Kenyan side. There is

---

[10]*Sunday News,* 1 March 1998; *East African* 2–8 June 1997.

also a tendency for the wealthiest Maasai families to educate their children in Kenyan secondary schools (Narok or Kajiado District). For the young Maasai men (warriors) very important cattle-sale journeys are made across the border on foot to livestock markets in Kenya. Usually the trip takes seven days one way and goes as far as the Ngong Hills near Nairobi in Kenya. A special feature of the Maasai is also how they cooperate for development issues across the borders. The Kenyan *harambee* (fundraising) is frequently organised in the Loliondo Division. When the local Maasai invite their prominent Maasai friends (i.e. politicians) from Kenya, they can end up raising large amounts of money for their own development projects in the area, such as school buildings or various women's projects.

During recent years the border has also brought some unpleasant features to the area; cattle raiding and poaching have increased. The Tanzanian newspapers report that Kenyan Somalis come across the border as bandits and violate and kill the locals.[11]

Chagga in Vunjo, Kilimanjaro

The other region studied is situated on the Eastern slopes of Mount Kilimanjaro. The material was gathered in Mayanka (pseudonym), an ex-chiefdom that today administratively belongs to the Moshi rural district. The larger area to which Mayanka belongs is customarily called Vunjo, which formed a constituency of its own in the 1960s and 1970s elections, and again in the 1995 elections. In the intermediate elections of 1985 and 1990 Vunjo was attached to the Moshi rural constituency. Moshi rural district is one of the four Chagga-predominated districts of the Kilimanjaro region, while two districts are mainly populated by the Pare ethnic group. The population of the whole Kilimanjaro region was estimated to be at 1.1 million in 1998, of which the Chagga predominated districts amounted to 840,000 (forming 3.7 per cent of the national population), and the Moshi rural district about 343,000 (Tanzania 1988, 45, 50).

Kilimanjaro has long been one of the strongest regions in the country both economically and politically. The early adoption of education and coffee cultivation during the first decades of this century had, by independence, raised the region's standard of living higher than that in most of the other regions. The coffee cooperative, KNCU, and the chieftaincy institution were important regional power bases. During the colonial time, the main political struggles centred on the local and regional issues of chiefs and chieftaincies, and the national independence movement gained little attention. Kilimanjaro was the last area in Tanganyika to be penetrated by the national movement TANU, which occurred only at the end of the 1950s.

In the independent state, the position of Kilimanjaro and the Chagga has been somewhat ambivalent. As coffee producers they have been important for the nation's foreign-exchange earnings, but simultaneously, as they have potential as a regional power base for a possible opposition, the government has taken certain measures to even out and suppress that power. These include restricting secondary school places open to Chagga candidates immediately after independence, the abolition of the chieftainship institution, and during the 1970s, as part of the national restructuring programme, the abolition of such important local institutions and power bases as the coffee co-operatives and the District Councils. According to Hopkins (1971, cited by Hartman 1990, 22), Chagga, together with Haya, Hehe, Sukuma and the Coastal people were under-represented in the high politics of Nyerere.[12] Yet, due to their education, the Chagga have been well represented in the salaried public sector.

Rather than as high politicians, the Chagga are known for their entrepreneurship. For business, studying and employment reasons – and often all three – Chagga can be found in all the major towns in Tanzania, in Nairobi and Mombasa in Kenya, and in other African countries as well as in Europe, Asia and the USA. However, even the most cosmopolitan and mobile Chagga usually wish to maintain their links to their rural homes in Kilimanjaro. Thus, through their travelling relatives and neighbours, even those who remain on the mountain are relatively well connected with the larger world. Local mobility is also important. Nowadays, numerous people commute daily

---

[11]*Daily News* 23 August and 8–9 November 1998.
[12]The publishing year of the book should be noted, however. It does not cover the 1970s and 1980s.

between the mountain villages and Moshi town and bring in their news, spoken and written. Additionally, the old nexus of market places on the mountain form a network where both information and commodities circle, also across the Kenyan border. Even after the economic liberalisation, much of the cross-border trade continues illegally, although decreasing profits and persistent risks have made it less common. Cross-border trade also touches those not directly involved in it. The local population constitute consumers of the minor industrially-produced articles that are imported from Kenya and producers or intermediaries of food commodities, especially rice, maize, and beans, that are exported to the Kenyan side.

People living on the mountain eagerly follow and comment on national and international news. Tanzanian newspapers circulate from hand to hand. In Mayanka there are two daily newspapers available, and many more can be bought in town. Nowadays practically every household has a radio and men especially listen to it keenly. Kenyan radio is often more accessible than Tanzanian, but people are most interested in and strive to listen to the Tanzanian news broadcast from Dar es Salaam.

Voting history in Arusha and Kilimanjaro

Ismael Mbise and Jon Moris have described elections in Arusha in the first years of independence. Referring to the 1962 elections in Arusha they wrote: 'The national election came almost as a surprise. A general election was then a new phenomenon: for most people it was complicated to understand the meaning of electoral procedures.' More than anything else these elections meant the same as the defeat of colonialism. The Maasai still describe them as an exciting experience. They eagerly gave their vote to Nyerere because they saw him as the founder of the independent state of Tanzania and saw no need to vote for anyone else.

During the second elections in 1965, Arusha District was divided into three electoral constituencies: Arusha urban, Arusha rural and Masai constituency. In the latter, Nyerere received 7,700 'Yes' votes while only 100 voted 'No'. In the parliamentary elections, there were two Maasai candidates: the sitting MP, E.C. Mbarnoti, and his challenger, Edward Moringe Sokoine. They can be regarded as the best known Maasais in Tanzania during the 1960s. Mbarnoti was appointed a paramount spokesman in 1959 and since then had become an executive officer of the district council. Sokoine was a young educated Maasai and had been elected as an executive officer of the district council in previous years. In 1965, he won the elections with eight times more votes than Mbarnoti. He was the only young Maasai who had the confidence of both older traditionalists and his own generation (see Cliffe ed. 1967, Appendix, 361, 362). In the 1970s, Sokoine became Minister of Defence, and in the 1980s he was elected Prime Minister of Tanzania.

For the 1965 elections, the Kilimanjaro District was divided into four constituencies, one of them being the Vunjo constituency. The TANU National Executive retained all the choices of the candidates of the District Conference. A large number of the selected candidates were drawn from the teaching profession, business, and cooperatives. Most of them stood either in their residential or home constituencies and were important figures in local politics – and many of them also in national politics. In some parts of the mountain, especially Vunjo and Rombo, an unprecedented proportion of women registered, mainly due to the influence of local women's organisations. In the Vunjo constituency, Mrs K.T. Mtenga, a vice-president of the national women's organisation, was clearly defeated by Naftal Kida, a veteran trade unionist. Mtenga received about 3,000 votes and Kida more than 21,000, reflecting a relatively high participation of the 29,000 registered voters (see Cliffe ed. 1967, Appendix, 375).

Mtenga and Kida were born in the same ex-chiefdom, and according to Basil Mramba (1967, 122, 123), Mtenga's marriage to a man from Rombo, which is the neighbouring ex-chiefdom and constituency, made her local commitment somewhat suspect to the voters. In addition, some voters, women among them, played her down simply because they did not think parliamentary work suitable for a woman. According to Mramba (*ibid.*, 117), in Kilimanjaro the common criteria of success were candidates' past record and character, education, local base, tradition, and effective campaigning including the use of rumour. The voter turnout was high and the parliamentary elections raised a lot of local discussion, whereas the presidential election was not discussed so much (*ibid.*, 125). An overwhelming number of the 24,500 voters said 'Yes' to Nyerere while the number of 'No' votes was only 100.

In Ngorongoro, in the 1970 elections, it was still apparent that in the rural areas many voters did not understand what registration meant. The lack of accurate knowledge slowed registration. (Mbise and Moris 1974, 265–275). Before the presidential elections people had said they were quite satisfied with Nyerere: why should they oppose him? Others – usually older men with memories of the colonial experience – balked at providing the thumbprint required of illiterate voters, because it was rumoured that it meant the introduction of a new *kodi* (tax). In the Loliondo Division, then part of the Masai constituency, there was only one voting centre in Loliondo town, which discouraged people from voting as most Maasai live further away from the town. Even in the 1980 elections, people said that they were not informed about registration and the exact voting day. It seems clear that registration and the conduct of voting were not carried out thoroughly in the Loliondo Division. In 1980, Sokoine, who was then Prime Minister, was returned unopposed. (Bavu 1989, 27.)

In all the constituencies of Kilimanjaro in 1970, education – both the aim of enhancing educational opportunities and the education level of the candidates themselves – was an issue used in the campaigns, and it had a strong impact on voters' choices. In two of the constituencies a woman won. This time Mtenga, who in her campaign had emphasised her higher education and fluent English, won in Vunjo. (Election Study Committee 1974, Constitution Summaries, 395–7.) Interestingly, in the presidential elections, Kilimanjaro was the region with the strongest support (98 per cent) for Nyerere in the whole country (Samoff 1987, 165).

Five years later, for the 1985 elections, the Masai constituency was renamed the Ngorongoro constituency. People said that voter registration was carried out better, but accurate information about the voting day and electoral procedures was still missing.[13] Of the estimated 26,000 eligible voters in Ngorongoro, about half registered and the number of votes cast was only 9,000. The poor turnout was a nationwide phenomenon. Many Maasai were disappointed with Nyerere's exit and had grievances against the government. The coming era of President Mwinyi was generally expected to be worse than that of Nyerere. But in elections without an alternative (an opposing candidate) the results did not really reflect this feeling. The decline of the 'Yes' votes in the presidential elections was only marginal: from 96 per cent in 1980 to less than 92 per cent in 1985 (Samoff 1987, 166).

In Kilimanjaro, in the 1985 parliamentary elections, the former Vunjo constituency was attached to the Moshi rural constituency. In the latter, the number of eligible voters was estimated to be almost 170,000. Even the number of registered voters was close to 95,000. Turnout was as high as 80 per cent. In the elections Mrema won, but only by a narrow margin. He received 53 per cent of the votes. Although Mwinyi's support with 72,000 'Yes' votes in the presidential elections was convincing, the share of the 'Yes' votes was not as overwhelming as in earlier elections. Almost 2,000 'No' votes were cast while the number of spoilt papers was more than 1,500. (Othman *et al.* 1990, Appendix, 219–235.)

According to the Maasai in the Loliondo Division, during the 1990 elections campaigning was more effective than before. This time MP candidates campaigned even in the remote villages. For instance, the former District Commissioner campaigned for the presidential candidate. The campaigners also contributed to the voters' education in general. For the first time people were encouraged to ask candidates important questions. The Maasai themselves have a tradition of questioning and political dialogue at their meetings but one-party rule had not encouraged this tradition in national politics. In 1990, the District Commissioner from the area mobilised the Maasai to attend the campaign rallies and speak their minds there. In Ngorongoro constituency the winning candidate Richard Pawin Koillah polled about 8,000 votes while James Loipukie Mollel received 2,000 votes, which means that although the turnout was still rather low, there was some contest between the candidates.

In the Moshi rural constituency in the 1990 parliamentary elections, Mrema had consolidated his support receiving over 70,000 votes, and his competitor a little less than 4,000 votes (Mukandala and Othman eds. 1994, Appendix III).

---

[13] A new thing in the elections was the use of photographs of the candidates on the ballot papers. Until 1985 the candidates were identified through the symbols of hoe and house.

On the whole, throughout the electoral history, both the Maasai and the Chagga have judged candidates on the grounds of their reputation, education, and their evaluated ability to represent the local interests (see also Cliffe and Puritt 1967, 182, 183; Munishi and Mtengeti-Migiro 1990, 198). In Kilimanjaro, in the 1970s educational issues were already in the forefront of the campaigns. In Arusha, votes were given especially to the candidates for whom people felt a close loyalty, including gender-based qualifications. In Kilimanjaro, women were quite active and some women stood up at candidates early on, while the Ngorongoro Constituency was, and is still, lacking in politically active women. Mbise and Moris (1974, 276) had already noted in the 1970s that women in Arusha did not attend the campaign rallies but rather saw the whole election as an entertainment organised for men.

In spite of a few Maasai politicians, like Sokoine, who were notable also at the national level, the Maasai in general have been marginal *vis-à-vis* the political life of the country. The Maasai have had a stronger tendency to drop out of the election procedure than the Chagga. During past years, the actual number of registered voters has been just above 50 per cent of the eligible voters and it took nearly two decades before the electoral procedures started to reach the whole area. It was not until the 1990s that the campaigns reached far-flung Maasai villages.

Subsequently, the signs and effects of the multi-party politics were seen in the Kilimanjaro area much earlier than in Arusha. While a year before the first general multi-party elections there were hardly any signs of multi-partyism in Loliondo, in Kilimanjaro the opposition campaigning had already begun.

Multi-party politics and elections in Kilimanjaro

The evolving political field in 1994

By 1994, the political campaigning in Kilimanjaro was quite vital, as it was the strongest region of the then promising opposition party, Chadema. Both the Chairman of Chadema, Edwin Mtei, and the CCM's Minister of Home Affairs, Augustine Mrema, were Chagga men, born in areas relatively close to each other. Mrema had been re-elected to Parliament in 1990, and in the beginning of his second term he had entered the cabinet as a Minister. In 1993, he was further appointed to the re-established post of Deputy Prime Minister.[14] Both Chadema and the CCM were forcefully campaigning in the area, with very different profiles, however.

In his campaigning in Kilimanjaro, Mrema concentrated on visiting and giving speeches in the local market places. He had gathered popularity as a defender of petty traders' and women's rights, and as an anti-corruption campaigner. In 1994, there were several recurrent stories in Mayanka of Mrema's efforts to defend the common people. For instance, people were recalling how Mrema, at the end of the 1980s, had been defending the trading women and young boys selling smuggled goods. According to one story, when walking in a market place, Mrema had been observing how the police were trying to tax the petty traders by harsh methods. He had intervened, advising the police to concentrate on catching the real criminals instead of harassing people who were just trying to scrape a daily living. According to the accounts, the police did not recognise Mrema but considered him a quarrelmonger and took him to the police station. There, Mrema showed his identity card and the policemen were allegedly fired. After this incident, the market women had reportedly carried Mrema high on their shoulders through the market place.

According to other accounts, Mrema had been going around in the local courts and jails and had found out that they were full of people imprisoned for about ten years for stealing a minor thing like a radio or for smuggling a few things across the border. Consequently, Mrema had all these minor cases abolished in the courts, reminding the officials that they should catch the really big criminals instead. Mrema was also famous for his interest in arbitrating marital disputes in which he again had a special concern for women's rights. Additionally, he was involved in mediating – in 'achieving reconciliations', as he put it – in civil disputes between creditors and debtors.

---

[14]The post of Deputy Prime Minister had been abolished in 1989 (*Economist Intelligence Unit* 1st quarter 1993, 14).

The researcher observed one public meeting in a market place. Women especially gathered to listen and show their support for Mrema by clapping and waving their hands. The men were fewer, mostly sitting calmly on steps and bars. At the meeting the local leaders thanked Mrema for arranging assistance for the local road building – named Mrema Road – and for a nearby girls' secondary school building. In his speech, Mrema concentrated on promising higher coffee prices, naming South Africa, Korea and China as the countries that had promised to buy the coffee at a certain price. He gave the exact prices that the producer and the government would receive, and it amounted to about double the producer price of the year before.

In these efforts, Mrema presented himself as the spokesman of the 'underdogs' (*walalahoi/ wanyonge*), the market places representing the most natural and likely location for meeting the common people. This appealed – and was meant to appeal – to the petty traders, especially women and young men. The local men, for their part, were touched by Mrema's promises to increase producer prices for coffee, while his criticism of the Asian business community found resonance among the rich Chagga men.

The profile of the competing new opposition party, Chadema, was kept – no doubt deliberately – very different from that of Mrema. The supporters of Chadema on both the local and national level were mostly wealthy people with relatively high education and experience of extensive travelling abroad. The leader of Chadema, Edwin Mtei, was a former Finance Minister and Bank of Tanzania governor. Other senior members were a former Deputy Agriculture Minister and Kilimanjaro regional commissioner, Edward Barango, and president of the Law Society, Bob Makani. Mtei was also the chairman of the Presidential Commission of Enquiry into public revenues, taxation and expenditure, after which he was appointed to the Commission for Parastatal Reform.[15] Partly because of these roles close to the government, Chadema was charged by opponents for being 'CCM number two'.[16]

In Mayanka, the men most active in advertising Chadema were those mainly living in other areas, often Dar es Salaam, and frequently visiting their rural home areas. In one Chadema party that the researcher attended, most of the visitors were highly educated men and women born in the area but living outside in the major towns. The local people attending were less cosmopolitan, yet relatively wealthy by local standards. The gathering was organised by a man who was working for the Chadema office in Dar es Salaam, his area of responsibility being the Moshi rural area. The chairman of Chadema in Mayanka was this man's lineage elder, a well-respected man who was a retired teacher and whose wealth was based on the successful cultivation of coffee and maize on larger than average land plots. The local secretary of Chadema was a bar owner whose bar became a centre for Chadema meetings and was thus called the 'Chadema bar'. The chairman of Chadema of the Moshi town area was known to be very rich; he allegedly owned a hotel chain and numerous cars and houses. The local high-level members of Chadema included also the son of a very famous ex-chief, Petro Marealle.

In Mayanka, among the more ordinary people – that is, civil servants, artisans, employees, petty traders, and business people, aged 30 and over – Chadema raised little interest. Instead they supported the CCM. These people regarded the Chadema people as the former CCM members and were suspicious of what kind of change, if any, they would bring. The fact that they were rich people cruising around in their cars and meeting in 'better' homes and bars made the profile of Chadema very different from that of Mrema. Many of the local people regarded Chadema and multi-party politics in general as something rather foreign, unpredictable and capricious in 1994. For instance, at the beginning of her field work, when the researcher had just arrived in the area, she was frequently asked if she was a 'Chadema person' (*mtu wa Chadema*).[17] The same attitude was revealed by the recurrent local suspicion that some of the richer and somewhat controversial market women were 'Chadema persons' even though they were not. One such relatively wealthy woman, whom some people suspected of being a Chadema supporter, put her political stance in

---

[15]*Economist Intelligence Unit* 4th quarter 1992, 12, 13.

[16]*Economist Intelligence Unit* 1st quarter 1993, 12.

[17]As the focus of the original research was not on politics, the researcher's questions did not in any way encourage or urge these associations. The question indicates the popular association of Chadema with foreignness.

this way: 'Why should I change the party if I would not even change my religion?', saying thus that she was and would remain a member of the CCM. Comparably, the local Chadema candidate in the district council elections was frequently characterised as a 'mentally confused' person (*amechanganykiwa*) who had 'bad spirits' (*majini*). This characterisation was explained by his recurrent changing of mind and overall whimsicality. As proof of that were listed his changing political, religious, and conjugal affiliations. He had retired from the CCM and joined Chadema (by 1997 he had become a member of NCCR-Mageuzi). He had separated from his wife, and changed his religion from Lutheran to Pentecostal (and by 1997 he had become a member of a new sect called Amrec). His walking pace was depicted as another indication of his odd restlessness, allegedly never normal but closer to running. He, like multi-party politics in general, was considered rather unpredictable and strange.

From political apathy to enthusiasm

In general, people in Mayanka in 1994 held rather cynical views about politics and multi-partyism, and considered the administration thoroughly corrupt. Even though people were not satisfied with the CCM, at least they thought they knew what it was. They thought that there was no guarantee that another party or multi-party system would bring about possible change, and if it would be a change for anything better (cf. Booth *et al.* 1993, 91–98). Mrema, as a man of the region, gained support and gathered cheering crowds around him. However, there were numerous people in Mayanka – men as well as women – who considered Mrema's speeches and politics as populist, calculating and biased.

For instance, most of the local market women whom the researcher regularly observed[18] had not paid attention to Mrema giving speeches in the market places or if they had, they had not gone to listen to him, often giving the practical reason of not being willing to leave their business for that length of time. Neither were they very much interested in what he had said.

Political apathy and disillusionment became obvious in October 1994 during the district council elections which were the first multi-party elections but gained very little attention. The registration for the elections was in April but only a few people had registered.[19] Women in particular showed little interest, while some men had registered not only for themselves but also for their wives. One man, an ex-party activist, decided to register for his brother's wife too, as she was not interested in registering nor voting herself. None of the 20 market women whom the researcher observed voted, the common attitude being that the district councillors (DCs) have no importance in their life and do not help people in any way. For instance, one woman whom the researcher asked if she was going to vote in the elections answered by saying: 'Me I just go to Himo [a market place]; I don't care about DCs. Nowadays it is up to each person to make her own life and take care of oneself. The DCs only eat our money.'

In the DC elections, the majority of the votes in Mayanka and Tanzania altogether were cast for the CCM. Each of Mayanka's two wards elected one representative. While the CCM candidate in the other ward was finally elected unopposed – because the Chadema candidate suddenly withdrew – in the other ward the CCM candidate beat the Chadema candidate with 70 per cent of the votes against the latter's 20 per cent.[20]

In Mayanka in 1994, even though Mrema was famous, in general people did not expect that he would gain nationwide prominence. People were already speculating about who would be the next

---

[18]20 market women were regularly observed by the researcher.

[19]Councillors were elected in 2,418 wards. In 1,191 nominees, nearly all from the CCM, ran unopposed. In the remaining 1,227 wards there were 3,000 contestants representing all 13 registered parties. According to the IFES, the elections went smoothly for the most part with only minor delays and disputes (Reeves and Klein eds. 1995, 12). According to the Economist Intelligence Unit report (4th quarter 1994, 11), voter apathy in these local elections was, however, considerable countrywide, with the first campaign of electoral registration being abandoned for lack of voters wishing to be registered.

[20]CCM won over 90 per cent of the posts nationwide (Reeves and Klein eds. 1995, 13). According to informal information in Kilimanjaro as a whole Chadema won only one seat, in Kigoma a few seats and some others in other parts of the country. By the end of January 1995, the election results were still unreleased. According to an independent Danida Survey (cited by *Economist Intelligence Unit* 1st quarter 1995, 10) Chadema had won 20 seats in the whole country. The other opposition party that won seats was CUF.

president, but most of the people in Mayanka did not expect Mrema to be among the candidates. His low level of education was regarded as the worst impediment to such a status, and people did not think he would be popular enough in the CCM to be nominated as a candidate. During 1995, however, crucial changes took place both in the general political field and in people's political enthusiasm in Kilimanjaro. These changes essentially evolved and revolved around Mrema.

In December 1994, President Mwinyi, under pressure from the previous President Nyerere, the donors and the popular discontent in the country, had to dissolve the cabinet. In that connection, the post of Deputy Prime Minister was once more suspended, and Mrema was transferred from the Ministry of the Interior to a less weighty Ministry of Labour, Community Development and Youth in the cabinet formed under the newly-appointed Prime Minister, Cleopa Msuya.[21]

In February 1995, Mrema was forced to resign from the government in connection with the alleged abuse of the former debt-conversion programme by Asian businessman, Vidyadhar Chavda. Debating the issue, Mrema had announced that there was no way he could support the government on that matter – and was fired from the cabinet the following day.[22] A few days later he quit the party and lost his position in Parliament as well.[23]

Ensuing discussions between Mrema and Chadema failed as its chairman, Edwin Mtei, would not step down and give his position to Mrema, which was Mrema's condition for affiliating himself with the party.[24] Consequently, Mrema joined the opposition party NCCR-Mageuzi and was soon elected its chairman and the presidential candidate. The party's membership rocketed fast in the city, as well as in parts of Kilimanjaro and Arusha regions.[25] Before the 1995 elections, wild scenes of celebration took place in and around the Moshi area.[26] With the changed political field and Mrema turned into a nationally celebrated, if controversial, figure in opposition politics, the political atmosphere also became much more agitated in Mayanka.

Election results 1995

In the 1995 parliamentary elections, 12 parties competed in the Kilimanjaro region. The region was divided into 9 constituencies. In 5 of the 6 Chagga-predominated constituencies, NCCR-Mageuzi received the largest share of votes. The only exception was the Rombo constituency where Chadema received most of the votes, followed by the NCCR-Mageuzi. In the other 3 constituencies of the region where the Pare ethnic group predominates, the CCM won the elections. Of all the Kilimanjaro region's votes the NCCR-Mageuzi received 54 per cent, followed by the CCM with 25 per cent, and Chadema with 18 per cent.

In the Vunjo constituency, to which Mayanka belonged, seven parties competed. The NCCR-Mageuzi was more successful in Vunjo than anywhere else in Kilimanjaro and the whole country; it received 84 per cent of the votes. CCM gained less than 10 per cent and Chadema only 4 per cent.

In the presidential elections, Mrema received 78 per cent of the Kilimanjaro region's votes against Mkapa's 20 per cent. In the Vunjo constituency, Mrema received 65,000 votes, and Mkapa 4,000 votes; CUF's Lipumba received less than 300 votes and the UDP's Cheyo less than 150 votes.

Voter opinion

All the people studied in Mayanka had voted for Mrema and the NCCR-Mageuzi[27] and thus represented the vast majority of the constituency's voting behaviour. An important reason for the older

---

[21]*Economist Intelligence Unit* 1st quarter 1995, 6, 7.

[22]*Economist Intelligence Unit* 2nd quarter 1995, 6, 7.

[23]*Uhuru* 4 March 1995.

[24]*Economist Intelligence Unit* 2nd quarter 1995, 7. That was the understanding also in Kilimanjaro. The researcher was told by several people that Mrema had initially wanted to join Chadema but on the condition that he would become its chairman. As Mtei did not want to step down, Mrema joined NCCR-Mageuzi.

[25]*Economist Intelligence Unit* 2nd quarter 1995, 7.

[26]*Economist Intelligence Unit* 3rd quarter 1995, 5.

[27]The attitudes on the 1995 elections and election results were compiled in retrospective discussions with people at Mayanka in the beginning of 1997, and not at the time of voting. In 1997, the same people in Mayanka were visited as in 1994.

people's voting behaviour was their wish and belief that Mrema would increase coffee prices once again. Thanks to Mrema's campaign promises, many believed that he had induced the price increases in 1994, even though in fact the increases were due to the liberalisation of coffee trading, which brought private coffee buyers to Kilimanjaro, and to the increased world market prices after the failure of the Brazilian coffee harvest.

Another commonly-stated reason for voting for Mrema was the fight against corruption to which he was believed to be seriously committed. One market woman said: 'He does not want corners, but instead says things straight and honestly.' Straightness, honesty, and strong action in the face of corruption were the attributes commonly related with Mrema. His fame in this respect had clearly increased in the course of the events in 1995, and in Mayanka people seemed to take his commitment to fight corruption more seriously and less cynically than in 1994.

In Kilimanjaro, the 'Chavda case' was taken as the initial reason for first dropping Mrema from the Labour Ministry and then firing him from the cabinet. According to a local Chagga man, Chavda had borrowed money from the government under the debt conversion programme for buying and restoring sisal plantations in Tanga. Instead he just bought a few run-down tractors and claimed he had used all the money on these. With this pretext he took the money abroad and deposited it in his own name. Mrema made the case public but as Chavda allegedly had friends in the government, Mrema was transferred to the Youth (*vijana*) Ministry.[28] The Chagga man explained that as soon as he heard Mrema comment on the radio, saying that he did not approve of government policy towards Chavda, it was obvious to him that Mrema would soon be fired since such public criticism is not tolerated by the government.

Several people in Mayanka recalled another big case that Mrema had made public in 1991 during his tenure as Interior Minister.[29] He had led the police in a swoop on transit travellers at Dar es Salaam international airport to discover TSh 173 million (US$765,000) in gold, travellers' cheques and foreign currency being carried to Dubai from Zanzibar.[30] Two Chagga men talking about the case said that the exporters of the gold were *vigogo* (that is, 'strong, central roots' of the CCM and government). After the swoop, Mrema had promised to reveal the names of the persons involved, but he did not do so, since he was apparently restrained. The ensuing silence only assured people that 'big people' (*watu wakubwa*) were involved, President Mwinyi's wife being among those suspected.

A third common statement by those who had voted for Mrema was that he knew and cared about the problems of the underdogs (*wanyonge*). Also the fact that Mrema was a Chagga who could bring 'good development' (*maendeleo mazuri*) to his home region was stated as a reason for voting for him.

Without exception, the people studied believed that the number of votes attributed to Mrema in the elections did not reflect his real support. Some admitted and lamented that many of the loud celebrators around Mrema before the elections had turned out to be just drifters (*wahuni*) who did not have any serious stance and who never registered for voting. However, in spite of this people believed, quite unanimously, that the election results were false. They were convinced that in fact Mrema had received more votes but that either part of them were stolen by the CCM or fake votes were added to the CCM's votes. Everybody seemed convinced that Mkapa did not win a fair election. Mkapa's victory was also associated with Nyerere's strong campaigning for him, and was attributed to the continuing political orchestration by Nyerere in the running of the state, rather than to any political strength of Mkapa himself.

While the belief about the falsified presidential election results was widespread in Mayanka, the specific issues and confusion related to the Zanzibar and the Dar es Salaam elections raised very

---

[28]In Kilimanjaro, Mrema's position was always called 'Youth Ministry', not Labour or Development Ministry, although all these three fields were included in the position. This emphasised the perceived low value of the position.

[29]The researcher did not hear this story in 1994, whereas during the 1997 fieldwork several people were recalling and explaining the case to her. Altogether, the 'hero' stories about Mrema were more common in 1997 than in 1994, which indicates the changed attitudes and risen hopes. Moreover, the heroic stories in 1997 concerned national events more, whereas in 1994 the focus was more on Mrema's local level accomplishments.

[30]See also *Economist Intelligence Unit* 3rd quarter 1991, 15.

little interest or discussion, even though the heated Zanzibari situation was recurring front page news at the beginning of 1997.

As for the parliamentary elections, all the people studied in Mayanka said that they had voted primarily for the party and not for the person. Many people said that any person running under the title of NCCR-Mageuzi would have won, and that the winning NCCR-Mageuzi candidate was not elected because of his intelligence or suitability. In fact the CCM candidate was considered by many a better and more intelligent man, but representing the wrong party.

In 1997, there were hardly any signs of Chadema left in Mayanka. The bar that three years earlier had been called the Chadema bar had the NCCR Mageuzi flag flying on its roof as its owner, the ex-secretary of the local Chadema branch, had changed his party. Many private homes had big posters of Mrema on their walls. In one house, Mrema's picture was hanging on the wall beside a poster of Queen Elizabeth. There were Mrema kangas and scarfs in the NCCR blue colour. Some had had clothes made of the Mrema kanga.

The chairman of the local Chadema party had died and the previous Chadema DC candidate of Mayanka had joined NCCR-Mageuzi. In 1997, Mtei was lying ill in a Nairobi hospital. In Mayanka, many people would bluntly say that 'Chadema is dead'. Naturally the comment did not only mean that the central persons of Chadema were literally dead or dying but also that many of the people once associated with Chadema had changed their party to NCCR-Mageuzi. So also had the locally prominent market woman who in 1994 had been suspected of being a 'Chadema person' but who then steadfastly attested to being a devoted CCM member. In 1997, she explained: 'Chadema was a party of young people (*vijana*), they were defeated, and so they joined this party of Mrema.' This statement and the description of the Chadema people as *vijana* emphasised and expressed the weak and fleeting character of the party, something that allegedly never took root in Kilimanjaro. One convert was a wealthy Chagga man living in Dar es Salaam who said that he used to be a Chadema member but left and joined the NCCR-Mageuzi since Chadema was now weak, its chairman Mtei being weary and meek like a pastor when the country needs a severe (*mkali*) man of action like Mrema. When the researcher later repeated this comment to the man's in-law, the in-law replied that he had not listened to the man at that point because he was not interested in his political views. As in 1994, it was a common suspicion that the wealthy Chagga living in Dar es Salaam and other major towns and some local wealthy men and women were still Chadema or CCM members, although there was seldom any clear evidence or knowledge of it. The suspicions concerning Chadema and those considered 'Chadema persons' reveal certain divisions among the Chagga that partly explain Mrema's popularity in Mayanka and among the rural Chagga, as will be dealt with later.

Multi-party politics and elections in Arusha

Compared to Kilimanjaro, the effects of multi-partyism were seen much later in the peripheries of Arusha. The first multi-party elections for the district councillors in 1994 did not bring opposition campaigning to Loliondo. It was only the CCM party chairmen who were mobilising people there and village leaders advised their communities to vote for CCM. By 1995, the effect of multi-partyism was stronger. This time the Maasai said that the competition between rival parties through campaigning was evident in the rallies held even in small Maasai villages.

Election results 1995

The parties that were contesting in the Loliondo District were the CCM, NCCR-Mageuzi and Chadema, and each party had a local candidate who was campaigning in the area. In Ngorongoro constituency, the turnout among the 24,000 registered voters was relatively high: 67 per cent. The CCM presidential candidate won, polling 8,500 votes. However, the NCCR-Mageuzi candidate gained a remarkable 7,000 votes. Ibrahim Lipumba's share was less than 200 votes. In the parliamentary elections also the opposition showed that it was able to mobilise support although the victory of the CCM was very clear. CCM's Matthew Taki Ole Timan won, polling 8,700 votes against NCCR-Mageuzi's Moringe Lazaro Ole Parkipunyi's 4,500 votes and Chadema's Tipilet Ole Saitoti's 2,500 votes.

Voter opinion

In the Maasai community in Loliondo, two different groups could be indicated among the Maasai voters. The first group consisted of those voters who knew the meaning of voting, understood the procedures of voting and were aware of their right to vote. They saw voting as a procedure whereby they could select a person from the political field who could protect and help their society at the local level and bring development there. Voting was seen as a duty (*esiai*-work) that one fulfils every five years. Yet political awareness seemed to lie in the hands of a few men, who already held positions of leadership, like village secretary, ward secretary or spokesmen/leaders. They were the ones who travelled frequently in Tanzania and across the border to the Kenyan side. Some of them had as good relations with prominent Kenyan Maasai politicians as with their fellow politicians in Tanzania.

On the other hand, young Maasai men, who were most actively participating in politics, were emphasising how multi-partyism had introduced more democratic ways for an individual to express himself in local politics. They were referring to the decline of the village leaders' power that in former times had been seen as unjust. They referred to the land clashes that have been common in the area. Nowadays, they said, even an individual can make a protest about land disputes without being directly threatened by the village-level authorities. It seems evident, as is also noted by Mmuya and Chaligha (1994, 160, 165), that for example in legal cases in Tanzania, multi-partyism is slowly influencing government practice.

These young Maasai men also saw different parties as functioning not for the tribes or for an individual only but for all Tanzanians. The freedom to choose one's electoral candidate from a list among many other competitors was seen as a very positive development: *'Dukyua naat enaas'* (a new thing is profitable) meaning that the new parties would lead to change. That is perhaps why some young Maasai voted for an NCCR-Mageuzi candidate as President: to break up the tradition in which one had little chance to say who would be elected as the leader of the country. The Maasai thus interpreted how the one-party system had worked: *'Mtu na kivuli pande nyingine. Hivyo hapakuwa na namna ya kukataa kuchangua mtu badala ya kivuli'* (There was only one person to choose and there was no way to change the habit).

The other group of voters are the ones who do not understand the meaning of voting and do not participate actively in politics. They have only a fair knowledge of politics or electoral procedures. Although, during the past few years, general knowledge of the different parties has become more common, the majority of the Maasai still have difficulties in understanding the meaning of multi-partyism. The Maasai regard Tanganyika African National Union (TANU)/CCM as the major party that has been mobilising people and that therefore is known to everyone, both men and women. For these reasons many people still believe that it is 'safe' to vote for the CCM. Some of these voters are often pushed by the Maasai leaders to register and even forced to vote. Some Maasai even refer to voting as a Swahili activity only, an activity that does not belong to Maasai but to the 'others', the non-Maasai. The majority in this latter group are women. They are often illiterate and do not speak or understand Swahili well. This is an important factor, since most election campaigns are run in Swahili in the media, and interpreters are seldom used. On election day, men might force their wives to vote for their candidate. Politically active women voters said they wanted to elect a person whose face satisfied them. Women also emphasised how in the Maasai community women often cast their vote for the person that the traditional local leader had openly announced he was voting for. Some Maasai women said the meaning of elections was 'to wait for development' to come to their areas.

Another group of Maasai who belong to the group of non-voters are very old Maasai men. In old age, the men mostly remain with their families but distribute their wealth, i.e. livestock, to their sons. Once the inheritance has been distributed, they do not feel obliged to act politically or 'rule over' others any more, and they do not want to influence their sons' political decisions either.

The Maasai's passivity in the national elections cannot only be explained by political marginal-isation or disqualification from the political process but a lot can also be explained by the fact that the very strongly built traditional institutions of Maasai society (i.e. age-set structures) erode the significance of national-level political institutions. In their traditional society, the Maasai enforce certain duties on young men (warriors), choose their own traditional leaders and spokesmen, and hold public meetings on a regular basis.

Besides, the effects of 'modern' national politics are often far beyond the reach of the average Maasai. One village chairman tried to explain why members of the community do not raise some serious local problems and bring them to the knowledge of their MP. He said that politicians are far above their own status, which then constrains the needed dialogue between people and political representatives.[31] Others were emphasising how the complaints (especially concerning land disputes) would not get anywhere and the expected results would not be seen in the area anyway.

In the Loliondo Division, Kenyan politics had had an effect on people's views of multi-partyism. Some Maasai interviewed referred to how multi-partyism had brought disputes and even unexplained killings of opposition leaders to Kenya, together with the growth of corruption and fear in society.

Many Maasai agreed that the elections themselves did not have much importance in their own lives. Neither did they see political rivalry or participating in politics as being very meaningful. The majority of the Maasai tended to describe MPs as the ones who have no traditional role, who do not have enough cattle in addition to other kinds of material wealth, etc. These are the reasons why, in their opinion, for example, a parliamentary candidate enters politics. As one Maasai man indicated: it is only after the elections that the Maasai will see if they have elected a significant candidate for themselves and for their communities.

The strong CCM party loyalty is still very common for many ex-civil servants, ex-policemen and those who were active in politics during the one-party era. The following example describes one old Maasai's party loyalty to the CCM.

The Maasai man from Loliondo, who was about 55 years old, was selected to join the police force at independence. In 1964, he had voted for the first time. It was then that the police force was allowed to participate in politics. Former Maasai leader Edward Moringe Sokoine from Monduli town had told him and other colleagues to vote. So from then onwards he had always voted for TANU/CCM, even in the 1995 multi-party elections. His feelings towards multi-partyism were sceptical, and he emphasised how it was too early to criticise the government. His comment on multi-partyism was: 'If each party seeks or implements its legal objectives without bias and/or individualism, we might hope to earn true democracy and attainable development for all the local communities in Tanzania.' He also said that during the time of CCM politics, there was longer-lasting peace in Tanzania than in the neighbouring countries, Kenya or Uganda. During the time of *Ujamaa* or villagisation, he thought the political system from ten cell leadership at the village level up to the national CCM meeting functioned much better, for example, in cases of mistreatment and conflict. He noted how nowadays multi-partyism has created mistrust, conflicts and other kinds of misunderstanding between families and friends in the name of different political party allegiances.

The NCCR-Mageuzi candidate in the 1995 elections from the Loliondo Division had in the 1980s been the very prominent MP, Moringe Lazaro Ole Parkipunyi. Originally, he did not come from the Ngorongoro Constituency. He was well-known for mobilising the Maasai people and other pastoralists and hunter-gatherers, and therefore he was sometimes seen as a threat to officials in the district. Furthermore through his NGO, KIPOC, he organised when an MP, for example, a tilling programme in some villages together with the Catholic Development Organisation, ADDO. Due to his educational background (MSc from Dar es Salaam University), he was elected to Parliament in 1985. His recent achievements at the local level include a secondary school in the Loliondo Division.[32] In the 1995 elections, Ole Parkipunyi naturally received most of the votes in the areas where he had been influential, but he did not win a parliamentary seat.

In 1995, it was the CCM candidate, Matthew Taki Ole Timan, who won. He comes from the Purko Maasai-dominated Ololosokwan ward in the Loliondo Division. Ole Timan, who is about 45 years old, had been a Catholic priest and later on in life he became a teacher and businessman. He has travelled all over the world and studied in Europe. At the local level, he was known to be prosperous and married to a Kenyan Maasai lady who was herself the owner of the best known tourist lodge in Masai Mara, Kenya.

---

[31]This kind of situation is totally contrary to the traditional Maasai age-set system where everything (respect, dialogue, honour etc.) is based on the warriorhood-elderhood institution.

[32]The school was built in Ololosokwan ward with a pastoralist research centre funded by the Italian government.

In Loliondo, an analysis of the distribution of Maasai votes reveals that the Maasai tend to have political affiliations with members of the same clan and also according to the reputation the person has in the area. Ole Timan, being a Purko Maasai, received most of his votes from Purko-dominated Maasai areas. Some additional votes came from the Ngorongoro District Headquarters, since there were rumours that the Chadema candidate, Ole Saitoti, a prosperous and famous Kisongo Maasai from the area, had advised people to vote, if not for him, then for Ole Timan. Ole Timan also received votes from the Batemi/Sonjo people, because, since the land demarcation project that was carried out in the division by Ole Parkipuny's NGO in the 1980s, many Batemi/Sonjo people felt that they had been mistreated and naturally would not vote for him. On the other hand, Ole Parkipuny may have lost votes because of his personal problems since 1994–95: ongoing rumours concerned cases of fraud in his own NGO, misbehaviour and his drinking habits.

These examples show how personal relations and rumours can affect a candidate's support. After the 1995 elections, many Maasai emphasised how the newly elected MP, Ole Timan, was too ineffective, did not raise his voice during parliamentary sessions, and did not help communities with their grass roots problems.

Post-election views on the different political eras

Economic development

While many people in Loliondo could not yet clearly distinguish between multi-party and one-party politics, the Maasai interviewed, especially the older people, referred openly to the political periods of different leaders, i.e. presidents. The first one, Nyerere's era, was seen by the majority of people as better than the present state of affairs. The Maasai interviewed expressed opinions such as: 'Commodities were cheaper, peace was long-lasting and conflicts were solved better at the local level', which referred to the *Ujamaa*-cell leadership system.

The era of the second president, Mwinyi, was rated worse than the previous one. Many Maasai remember it as the era of land allocation to outsiders according to the policy of liberalisation. Over 200 land allocation applications were given to local authorities in Loliondo. The Maasai felt discriminated against, while the growing corruption often deprived them of any means to protect their land rights.[33] Many people agreed that it was too early to give any definite comments about today's government or the current president, Benjamin Mkapa. Yet it was very much hoped that the ministers and the president himself could pay respect to the Maasai community by visiting their areas and hearing, at the grass roots level, their opinions about, for example, the land issues.

In Mayanka, Kilimanjaro there were different opinions on Mkapa's administration and policies in 1997. The major complaint was the dire economic situation. Business people complained that their business was down, since people did not have any money to buy things. Many traders who had sold second-hand clothes in 1994 had changed into trading food items, especially grains, explaining that people did not have the money to buy clothes. Bars that were filled with people most evenings in 1994, were lacking customers and closing early. People who wanted to sell a cow had difficulties in finding anybody to buy it, and the price of goats was down. Some bus fares had been reduced due to the lack of passengers. Undoubtedly the economic problems were related to the severe drought that Kilimanjaro and other areas were experiencing, but in popular discourse they were more often associated with the political situation. The reason for the generally-felt lack of money was believed to be Mkapa's decision to withdraw 17 billion shillings from the market. There were suspicions among the older people that Mkapa had reduced coffee prices, as well.

---

[33]The biggest land case was in the 1990s, called the Loliondogate scandal, when a large piece of land was allocated from the Loliondo Division for ten years to an outsider, a Brigadier of the United Arab Emirates, as a private hunting block. It was stated that in the Loliondogate scandal the Office of the President, the Ministry of National Resources and Tourism as well as the Attorney General's office were involved. A senior officer in the Attorney General's office acted as a private counsellor and helped the perpetrators to prepare the contracts on Loliondo (Mmuya and Chaligha 1994, 150). Worst of all the land was allocated without first consulting the local Maasai.

Some suspected that Mkapa had imposed a new coffee tax. People who owned a shop or other business were complaining that the gathering of taxes and licences had been intensified and their amounts increased. The general feeling was that the business people, who had been the benefici-aries during the Mwinyi regime, were suffering losses under the administration of Mkapa.

Among the wealthier Chagga, the views on Mkapa were often critical. For instance, a relatively affluent Chagga man, who had served a long time as a high level official in the civil service and was living in Dar es Salaam, criticised Mkapa harshly by saying that 'he's a real dummy' (*mjinga kweli*). According to him, it was a wrong policy to fire people from the government and other jobs. This had been a measure taken by the government with the explanation – fostered by donors – that the wages of the remaining workers would thus be increased and consequently their need to take bribes reduced. The urban Chagga man criticised this policy, saying that firing people from their jobs is equal to leaving people without food (*chakula*).[34]

Not all the people considered the Mkapa administration only in negative terms, however. Many of the petty traders, civil servants and other employed people who had voted for Mrema said that Mkapa's policy was not so bad, that it was better than during Mwinyi's time, and that Mkapa was a 'rational' man. Many of these people said that it was too early to condemn Mkapa. For instance, a teacher said that he had voted for Mrema, and were there a new election, he would vote the same way even though he believed that Mkapa was a sensible leader. He suspected that as a man of fast action and low education, Mrema might make a weaker leader; he would not have the far-sighted intelligence and patience that Mkapa had already shown. However, he considered Mrema a more honest man who dedicatedly fought against corruption. Another young man, a petty trader, said that Mkapa's economic policy was not bad, but that his administration would be really strong had he nominated Mrema as the Internal Minister. He believed, however, that Mkapa was afraid that Mrema would become more popular in that position than himself. Many people said that Mkapa's anti-corruption campaign was adopted from Mrema with the intention of downplaying Mrema's strongest political asset and appeal.

In 1997, Mwinyi's era was described as the 'period of freedom', which distinguished it espe-cially from Nyerere's era. During Mwinyi's administration, the Leadership code of Nyerere's time that forbade other sources of income for civil servants was abolished. Later came the enlargement of political freedoms, which was most clearly shown by the numerous private news-papers, the three new TV channels, and multi-party politics. With all this liberalisation, Mwinyi earned the nickname Mzee Ruksa ('Mr Permit'). Everyone in Mayanka appreciated Mwinyi's time for having brought goods to the empty shop shelves again, and for lifting the ban on importing cars, petrol, and second-hand clothes. Another good and locally meaningful devel-opment of Mwinyi's era was the increase in coffee prices in 1994. As was mentioned above, however, in Mayanka this was, usually seen as the outcome of Mrema's efforts.

'The period of freedom' was also associated with ever escalating corruption. Even though corruption was known to have existed during Nyerere's regime as well, the private and illegal profit-making was clearly seen to have expanded and become permissible and blessed by the administration of Mwinyi. A rural Chagga man, a civil servant, explained that in the 1990s, during the time of Mwinyi, the rich Chagga, especially those living in Dar es Salaam, started to arrange big feasts and ceremonies to increase and compete on prestige (*fahara*), because they had earned money through means that were not proper (*njia hasizofai*) and did not know how else to use all that money.[35] Thus, in addition to the economic and political liberalisation, Mwinyi's regime was also seen as a time when the gap between the rich and the poor increased. In the 1995 elections, the rich were believed – quite apart from what the reality was – to have voted for Chadema or the CCM because they wished to cling to their previous benefits and favoured position.

In sum, in Mayanka the reasons for supporting Mrema and Mkapa were their equalising measures, and the most important mistakes of Mwinyi's time were seen as the increased corruption and socio-economic differences between people. Statements like 'all who have been able to build a modern house are thieves', 'all the rich people are thieves', 'all the business

---

[34]There is a possible–intentional or unintentional–double message in this comment since *chakula* (food) as well as *kula* (to eat) are common euphemisms for bribes and the taking of bribes in Tanzania.
[35]See more in Pietilä 1999, 269–274.

people are thieves' and 'the rich Chagga think only about themselves' constituted an internal criticism of those Chagga who had been able to amass money. This, according to many rural people, increased during the 'crazy years' of the Mwinyi regime, when money was easy and abundant, and often allegedly illegitimately made and spent. These attitudes are reflected in political opinions and voting behaviour: voting for NCCR-Mageuzi was motivated by the long-standing antagonism between the Chagga and the state, but additionally by the internal economic differentiation among the Chagga and more generally between those with direct or indirect access to state power and those who remained on the periphery. Some of the rural Chagga saw themselves as *wanyonge* in comparison to the urban Chagga and the other 'big shots'.

Political development

In Kilimanjaro, the country's political development under the administration of Mkapa raised discussion and some worries. This was due to certain deaths among high-level politicians that in Mayanka were widely interpreted as political murders. These were the deaths of the former Director of Intelligence and Security, Lt General Imran Kombe, in June 1996; the death of the MP for Morogoro; and in March 1997, the death of an MP and the former Chief Secretary of the CCM, Horace Kolimba. All these politicians were believed to have cooperated with Mrema and/or the opposition parties for which they were allegedly killed.

According to many people in Mayanka, Kombe was giving information to Mrema about highly secret security matters of the state. Having found this out, the government called Kombe to a meeting and fired him from his post. When he was asked what post he would like to step into instead, Kombe had asked for some time to consider the matter. He was shot dead by two policemen before giving his answer, however. The policemen claimed to have mistaken him for a car thief.[36] Kolimba, for his part, was called to a hearing in Dodoma after having criticised the CCM in public by saying that it did not have any policy direction.[37] ʼAccording to the national news, Kolimba spoke in front of the meeting from 5 to 7 o'clock, and as soon as he returned to his seat, he suffered a heart attack and was taken to the hospital where he soon died. According to the government media, his death was the result of high blood pressure. People in Kilimanjaro were convinced that he had been killed. There had been rumours of Kolimba planning to join the NCCR-Mageuzi.[38] In Kilimanjaro, many people believed that the CCM leaders had been worried that Kolimba would start gathering votes for NCCR-Mageuzi in the south of Tanzania, while Mrema would gather them in the north. Also the MP for Morogoro was believed to have been murdered by state representatives because he allegedly wanted to break off from the CCM and join NCCR-Mageuzi.

Due to these cases, some people in Mayanka were of the opinion that Mkapa was getting really merciless. Even among those who were hopeful about economic development, political development under the new administration raised some worries, and they were wondering if Tanzania was turning into a new Kenya. Others saw the cases as examples of a hopeless and spasmodic attempt by the 'old CCM men' (Nyerere included) to cling to power and sweep away their opponents.[39] Even so, these cases and the vigorous discussion and criticism that they raised in the independent newspapers and beyond were celebrated as signs of the expanding freedom and public courage to speak out. Indeed, in Mayanka laments of the continuing corruption and worrying political development were frequently related to the approving observation that such problems were, however, more openly and specifically brought into public than ever before.

---

[36]A committee was set up to investigate the killing. The report stated that the government was not involved in any way in the killing, but the full report could not be released until court cases against the police officers involved had been completed (*Tanzanian Affairs* 56, 1997).
[37]*Majira* 25 February 1997.
[38]Some newspapers were speculating about this before Kolimba's death (see e.g. *Majira* 8 March 1997), and after his death about him having had plans to join Chadema (*Majira* 18 March 1997).
[39]Many people in Kilimanjaro were convinced that there had been an attempt to kill Mrema as well (see also the Economist Intelligence Unit reports), but some claimed that Nyerere had forbidden it on the grounds that it would lead the country into civil war. According to other people, Mrema had 'medicine' against killing.

Conclusion

The fact that, on the mainland, Kilimanjaro region and its predominantly Chagga areas formed the strongest opposition area in the first multi-party elections, indicates its continuing uneasy relation to the state. However, regardless of the critical attitudes towards the state administration and the governing party, there were never any radical suggestions, before or after the elections, about separation from or violent resistance against the state in Kilimanjaro. Rather, the quest was for a newly acknowledged legitimacy of the local and regional initiatives and efforts, in the form of higher producer prices for coffee, more school places and the local political and religious institutions. After the decades of the independent government's restrictive measures, multi-partyism had gradually become seen as a possibility to re-elevate the region's position in the state.

Thus, when voting the Chagga did not simply vote against the state, but more properly tried to effect the terms of their relation to the state. It is, however, important to note that this included simultaneously the question of on whose terms; the rural Chagga made distinctions among themselves as well, and in their political support and voting expressed their opinion of who among the Chagga were considered eligible to represent them in the state. In 1994, Chadema and Mrema gathered very different crowds of people around them in rural Kilimanjaro. Mrema's approach, his courting of the 'common' men and women, found more resonance than Chadema's elitist profile.

By the time of the elections, Mrema had succeeded in building and strengthening the image of himself and his party, NCCR-Mageuzi, as the true fighters against corruption, especially that on a high level. After the elections, the popular interpretation of the several deaths of politicians enforced the contrast between, on the one hand, the corrupt state and the 'old administration', and on the other, Mrema and his party as the voice of and hope for a more democratic future and fairer governance. In Mayanka, many hoped that Mrema would become a real, fair 'big man'.[40] Thus, in addition to the regional concerns in regard to the state, it was also the tiredness over corruption and the experienced impoverishment of the rural Chagga that explained their voting behaviour and political opinions; in relation to their urban brothers and the other well-connected people, many of the rural Chagga considered themselves deprived, *wanyonge*.

While the increased wealth differences among the Chagga partly explain the rural people's voting in Kilimanjaro, the generational division was important for the Maasai. Among the Maasai, the most politically active persons were young men getting acquainted with the ideas of opposition parties. For them, NCCR-Mageuzi was the party that would bring changes. It is noticeable that its popularity did not depend so much on Mrema's personality, however. That multi-partyism could balance the village leaders' power was an idea of the young Maasai men, who due to the age-set structure and gender-division of their society were relatively empowered in terms of their political participation.

Even the Maasai women, though rather passive voters, had hopes and aspirations towards political change and development. These aspirations were not necessarily translated into support for the opposition, however. Showing clear disappointment, people said that President Mkapa had promised to come and visit Ngorongoro four times. When he finally arrived at the Ololosokwan village in the Loliondo Division on 10 July 1998 as the first president to tour the Ngorongoro District since independence in 1961,[41] this was respected by many Maasai.

---

[40]It is important to note, however, that Mrema's appeal was not restricted to the Chagga. He got support across ethnic and religious boundaries. This was revealed for example by the rather surprising parliamentary by-election that was held in Temeke, Dar es Salaam, in October 1996. Two candidates (of NCCR-Mageuzi and Chadema), who had been defeated in the 1995 election in Temeke constituency, had filed and won a petition in the High Court. There were allegations that the victorious CCM candidate had lapsed into bribing and subsequently it was confirmed that he had lied about having studied at and graduated from the Dar es Salaam Technical College. Mrema put himself forward in the ensuing by-elections. Few observers believed that he, as a Christian and Chagga, would be able to win in Dar es Salaam, in a predominantly Muslim constituency, where he was standing against the local man, Abdul Cisco Ntiro, representing CCM. Mrema won, however, receiving 59 per cent of the votes, while the CCM candidate got 36 per cent (*Tanzanian Affairs* 56, 1997).

[41]*Daily News* 11 July 1998.

Thus, the young Maasai men saw in multi-partyism hopes for an individual's increased ability to express himself in local politics, even though the continuing marginality of the whole Maasai community in the state explains the general political inactivity there. In Kilimanjaro, by 1997, multi-partyism had become a generally accepted and even celebrated political development. The rather widespread political apathy and disillusionment of 1994 had turned into much more active, hopeful, even agitated attitudes. In 1997, there was a sense of increased freedom of speech and room for both local and national manoeuvring (see also Moore 1993).

All in all, it is in the political liberalisation in general rather than in the electoral competition, where the fruits of multi-partyism are most appreciated. While this is probably true all over Tanzania, opening up the political space is perhaps particularly significant in the borderlands, where people's political identities tend to have dynamics distinct from the national political centres.

12

Contesting Democracy
The 1996 Elections
in Zambia

JEREMY GOULD

> The limitation of the democratic process is that sometimes those in power can use state power and machinery for their own selfish interests. It has been established even in the most successful democracies that ... those in control of the state can use it to concentrate more political power in their own hands and to acquire social wealth too. They may use the state to subordinate the interests of the rest of society to their own (Mwanakatwe 1994, 286).

Introduction

The 1996 Zambian elections were the second (after Benin) in a 'Second Round' of elections following the initial transition to multi-party regimes that swept across Africa in the early nineties. In 1991, the Movement for Multiparty Democracy, led by trade union leader Frederick Chiluba defeated Zambia's founding president Kenneth Kaunda (KK) and his United National Independence Party at the polls, instigating a peaceful transfer of power that was widely touted as a model for democracy in Africa. Many commentators saw in the 1996 elections a test case by which to assess whether an incumbent party would honour newly established rules of democratic process.

For the theoreticians of democratisation, Zambia's 1996 elections provided means to measure the degree of 'consolidation' or 'slippage' in one of the foremost democracies of Africa. The general verdict has fallen on the side of 'slippage.' The leaders of the MMD were found by many analysts to have 'openly manipulate[d] constitutional and electoral rules to trip up their competitors' (Bratton and Posner 1999). Through a number of actions – to be elaborated below – President Chiluba exploited his constitutional control over the legislative branch of government to eliminate the possibility of an effective challenge to MMD hegemony. Critics reasonably questioned the political morality of one political actor exercising such absolute powers over the process of political selection itself.

The analysis of Zambia's 1996 elections has a special role in the discourse on African democracy: as a 'second round' election, it speaks to the issue of consolidation; as a site of boycotts, constitutional politics and legal disputes, it provides grist for the analysis of slippage. The literature on the 1996 elections has revolved around processual issues: the freeness and fairness of the elections has been of central attention in the debate, spawning a residual discussion of how freeness and fairness, and democracy itself, should be defined. These elections – and indeed the overall dispensation of political actors and institutions in Zambia's Third Republic – provide analysts and actors alike with succulent materials for debating these themes, and I will also comment on them. This narrative of slippage, however, has been documented elsewhere.[1]

---

[1] See Committee for a Clean Campaign (no date), 45–48; Zambia Independent Monitoring Team (no date), 13–15; Foundation for Democratic Process (no date), 16–17; Human Rights Watch 1996b, 39–41; Bratton and van de Walle 1997; Bratton and Posner 1999; van Donge 1998b.

Thus, the purpose of this chapter is to move beyond the judgmental assessment of the MMD government's behaviour to an exploration of what might be learned from the 1996 elections about the unfolding dynamic of the politics in Zambia's fledgling pluralist arena.

One election, two contests

In their introduction to this volume, Cowen and Laakso identify two theoretical approaches to the study of elections. One takes the perspective of *voter choice* while the other focuses on the role of elections in *the legitimisation of state authority*. Stretching the analytical brevet of this distinction, one could say that the 1996 presidential and parliamentary elections in Zambia comprised two discrete, yet interwedged contests. One involved the competition for office among parties and personalities characteristic of any ballot. In these general elections, 5 men competed for the nation's presidency, while some 600 individuals from a dozen parties (including 99 Independent candidates) vied for 150 parliamentary seats.

Beyond this race for a grip on the handle of political power, the November 1996 elections constituted the site of a secondary contest over the rules of political process in a multi-party democracy.[2] This latter contest engaged the energies of a smaller group of actors. These comprised the leaderships of the ruling MMD and its main challenger, UNIP; the public media; an assembly of civic associations (human rights organisations and independent monitoring bodies); and a number of foreign actors, including the South African head of state, plus some bilateral aid agencies and international NGOs. The two contests were simultaneous, intermeshed in time and space. Yet each mobilised different participants and involved different stakes. Most significantly, the two contests produced somewhat different outcomes.

The extensive commentary and controversy surrounding Zambia's 1996 elections has tended to conflate these two contests. More precisely, the attention given to the meaning of the election for the democratisation process has eclipsed the substantial implications of the contest between actors and ideas. This may be because the result itself was not particularly dramatic. The elections did not unseat the incumbent President, nor were there significant changes in the composition of Parliament. In terms of politics and policies, the election outcome, which returned the ruling clique with what it termed a 'landslide' majority, communicated continuity with the politics of the previous term of office. The fact that a great many of the commentators found the behaviour of the MMD regime to be damaging to the social welfare and/or of questionable political morality encouraged a dismissive regard of the election results. Ironically, then, the often impassioned debate over the fate of the 'democratisation' process in Zambia has been focused almost exclusively on the actions of the political elite, including powerful international actors. The lynchpin of democracy, the grass roots citizen-voter, has remained largely in the shadows.[3]

The two contests are obviously interdependent. Whoever can determine the 'rules of the game' may have a distinct advantage over their political competitors in gaining access to power. It is possible for the misuse of a democratic mandate to undermine the very foundations of democracy. Zambia's general elections of 1991 were a textbook example of a situation where one actor – KK and UNIP – had monopoly control over the legislature, the media and the public administration with all its grass roots resources. Yet UNIP opted to play (relatively) fair, negotiated a compromise on constitutional reform and electoral procedure with the opposition MMD – and suffered a resounding defeat at the polls. In 1996, MMD backtracked on its rhetoric of accountability, manipulated the Constitution, refused to consult with other political players on procedural issues – and improved its grip on power at the polls. These facts pose questions about voter behaviour that a serious consideration of the future of democratic politics needs to take into account. The central quandary is about the effect of MMD's performance during its first term upon voter behaviour and how Zambian voters assessed their own options.

---

[2] 'Political process' is understood here in a broad sense encompassing all aspects of the negotiation of formal state power. Thus the political process includes but goes beyond the electoral process, involving debates and non-electoral events which determine who controls the state.

[3] See two academic analyses of the elections by Bratton and Posner 1999, and by van Donge 1998b. While each article gives the elections a different normative spin, they share an indifference to the interests and behaviour of the electorate itself.

In attempting to address this quandary, this chapter offers a balanced commentary on the highly polarised and impassioned controversy surrounding the quality of the electoral process, while at the same time delving into the political substance and implications of the ballot. Contrary to the accounts that have portrayed voter response as apathetic,[4] I suggest that most Zambians took these elections seriously. While the outcome did not portend dynamic shifts in policies or personalities, I will argue that an analysis of voting patterns and the micropolitics of specific constituency contests indicates that voters have not been blind nor indifferent to the actions of the ruling elite. On close inspection, it becomes evident that the choices that voters make regarding political ideals and personalities are not distinct from issues of democratic process.

Analytical framework

The two contests discussed above imply distinct demands for political reform. According to this hypothesis, each contest can be distinguished by a civic protest against two inter-related forms of political domination. These are *patrimonialism* and *clientelism*, respectively.[5] In my view, the secondary struggle about the rules of the game should be understood in terms of the critique of patrimonialism, and its specific *presidentialist* variant. Patrimonialism refers, at its theoretical roots, to economic behaviour. In its classical, Weberian, definition patrimonialism refers to the failure of a ruler to distinguish between the *private* assets of his household and those *public* resources that he administers (Weber 1968, 1006 *et seq.*). Critiques of MMD's regression into autocratic politics have been based on a demand for a clearer recognition that the government of Zambia has distinct, national responsibilities which transcend the narrow partisan interests of the ruling party. As we shall see below, this point was made most succinctly in connection with the constitutional amendment process.

The contest for public office, in contrast, did not incorporate an explicit critique of patrimonial politics. Instead, the critical issue at stake in the elections and especially the parliamentary race was that of *clientelism*. Clientelism can be defined, in very general terms, as the exchange of political loyalty for promises of material reward and security. Clientelism, as Mouzelis points out, is both a form of domination by a political elite and a mechanism by which the 'lower' classes such as workers and peasants are integrated into the political structures of the state (Mouzelis 1985). Such patron-client networks are based on vertical ties. Clientelist structures are distinct, both analytically and pragmatically, from integrative mechanisms based on horizontal bonds, for example, in political relationships initiated by self-organised associations of workers or farmers (Fox 1994). Classical accounts of the patron-client relationship emphasise the dialectic of trust and domination, asymmetry and solidarity, which such an exchange implies.[6] Clients voluntarily enter into an asymmetrical relationship based on the expectation of a tangible material benefit in return for awarding political support to their patron. Patrons, therefore, must command resources with which to feed the clientelist networks upon which their political influence is based.

---

[4]According to the Zambia Country Profile of the Economist Intelligence Unit, voter apathy in Zambia is 'widespread' (Economist Intelligence Unit 1996b, 7).

[5]The concepts of patrimonialism and clientelism have become entrenched in the mainstream (judgmentalist) analysis of African politics. They are currently used very loosely, and with strong functionalist overtones, as an independent variable that needs little explanation beyond a vague reference to 'African political culture'. A recent example is P. Chabal and J.-P. Daloz, whose book *Africa Works: Disorder as Political Instrument* (Chabal and Daloz 1999) anchors its paradigm of African political disorder in a rather vague notion of patrimonialism. Seldom is sufficient attention paid to the production and reproduction of these forms of domination, to the needs and circumstances to which they correspond, and to the popular, everyday struggles surrounding the cultural imagery they feed upon. These notions require much more analytical rigour before they can be used to *explain* political processes. My purpose in introducing concepts of this order here is to test their adequacy in fleshing out a more variegated picture of the aims and ideals of empirical actors. The point is to see what a deconstruction of local politics can tell us about the explanatory powers of a notion like clientelism, and not simply to collect anecdotal evidence in support of a patrimonialist 'paradigm' of African politics.

[6]For a comprehensive overview and discussion see Eisenstadt and Roniger 1984, esp. 48 *et seq.*

The severe lack of resources available to Zambian politicians, especially in rural constituencies, has engendered a crisis of clientelism that was strongly evident in the 1996 elections. I will argue that inasmuch as the electorate vented a political protest at the polls, it was a reaction towards the national MMD's attempts to impose its clients in key positions *vis-à-vis* the local political arena. What this implied was a growing assertiveness of local political actors *vis-à-vis* the national elite. This brought with it a concomitant increase in competitiveness within local political arenas that mobilised new political actors and renovated established political roles.

Secondary contest: The 'rules of the game'

The debate over the rules of democratic procedure has brought the critique of patrimonialism to the forefront of Zambian political discourse. The articulation of this critique has gained momentum via three emerging processes in the Zambian political realm. The three tendencies are (a) the fragmentation of the MMD and a concomitant pluralisation of the political arena; (b) the consolidation of election monitoring bodies as non-partisan 'referees' with respect to political controversy; and (c) a focusing of public debate on the contradiction between private and public interests in the practice of national leadership. This section tries to show how these processes have unfolded in the course of the first election cycle following the re-introduction of multi-partyism in 1991.

MMD's first term (1991–96)
There are two mutually contradictory interpretations of the MMD's first term in office. The MMD interpretation has been broadly elaborated via the state-owned media. According to the MMD view, after taking power at the end of 1991 it lived under the continual threat of undemocratic forces based in UNIP. These forces, it is alleged, actively pursued to overthrow the government through conspiracy and violence. Proponents of this view have cited four conspiracies as their main evidence of these intentions.

First is the so-called Zero Option plan. This refers to a clandestine document, purportedly leaked from within UNIP to the MMD in 1993, outlining plans for a UNIP-orchestrated *coup d'état*. Second is the Black Mamba conspiracy, which involves a bomb campaign in Lusaka and Ndola in early 1996. The spate of bombings was linked to a group which identified itself as the 'Black Mamba' and which demanded the withdrawal of the 1996 Constitutional (Amendment) Act from Parliament. This Act, which was legislated in May 1996, effectively disqualified UNIP president Kenneth Kaunda from contesting the presidential elections. The government arrested a number of UNIP leaders on treason charges related to the Black Mamba bombings.

The third evidence of conspiracy against the MMD is a 'defamation campaign' against President Chiluba. Since 1993, the independent press, especially the *Post*, has run especially virulent stories about President Chiluba linking him to such 'crimes' as adultery, graft, dishonesty, drug abuse, and the falsification of his birth certificate.

Last, government apologists have cited an 'election monitoring conspiracy' in reference to the pronouncement by 3 independent monitoring groups (including a coalition of 19 NGOs and semi-political civic organisations) that the 1996 elections did not meet international standards and could not be considered 'free and fair.

The countervailing interpretation of the first years of the Third Republic has portrayed the MMD leadership as paranoiac and authoritarian. MMD's first five years in office have been a retrogressive betrayal of the democratic principles that brought it to office (Human Rights Watch 1997). This view gained wide currency among the domestic monitoring groups (see below), and among many international observers (for example Human Rights Watch 1996b and 1997; Bratton and Posner 1999; Chabal and Daloz 1999). Proponents of this assessment invoke four main points. One, that no tangible evidence was produced to link UNIP and Kaunda to the Zero Option and Black Mamba 'conspiracies.' Many believe that both were contrived by the MMD itself in order to justify the victimisation of the opposition. Second, the government has systematically harassed the independent media, especially the *Post*. Third, critics of the MMD invoke the undemocratic manner in which the MMD has exploited its parliamentary majority to effect far-reaching legislative reform, especially the 1996 Constitutional Amendment Act. Finally, the government's unilateral manipulation of the electoral process, especially its decision to subcontract the voter registration to an unknown Israeli computer company (Nikuv) raised the ire and suspicions of many.[7] All in all, critics were unable to both countenance the government's refusal to consult with other stakeholders and seek a consensus on crucial aspects of the electoral process, including the composition and purview of the Electoral Commission.

Any one of these charges against the government implied a serious contravention of the principles of openness and dialogue to which the MMD had pledged itself in 1991. Despite the harassment of individual journalists, there was virtually no direct censorship of the press, and the facts of the government's actions were well known.[8] The political debate revolved around whether one could accept the government's justifications for its behaviour.

Players and positions

From late 1993, a debate around the rules of democratic procedure gradually came to dominate (urban, élite) public discourse in Zambia. Actors from political parties, foreign agencies and from civil society were mobilised in a contest of actions and arguments of unprecedented dimensions.

As the MMD's hegemonic position began to unravel, numerous opposition parties began to emerge. Many of these, beginning with the formation of the National Party in August 1993, were offshoots from the MMD. Parallel to this, international donor agencies and non-governmental organisations (NGOs) entered into the domestic political debate with great visibility and determination. Donor agencies have long had a tacit role in domestic politics (Abrahamsen 1997). Since the late 1980s, the influence of international creditors on domestic politics had grown in proportion to the government's dependence on donor funds (especially the IMF-sponsored Enhanced Structural Adjustment Facility) to maintain fiscal solvency. As the MMD's actions took on increasingly autocratic features, donors and international NGOs became explicit in their threats to sanction undemocratic behaviour by withholding aid. Since it was generally believed that the MMD could not survive without donor support, the discourse about the rules of the game was increasingly performed for the purpose of satisfying these foreign constituencies.

Domestic civic groups also participated in the political debate. The pluralisation of political life during the 1990s, and increased donor funding to NGOs have given an impetus to the proliferation of civic organisations, especially to those involved in civic education and human rights advocacy. A specific kind of 'referee' – the so-called independent monitoring bodies – has come to play a special role in the domestic political arena.

Independent election monitoring bodies

The Zambian Independent Monitoring Team (ZIMT) and the Zambian Elections Monitoring Coordinating Committee (ZEMCC) were formed to monitor the multi-party elections in 1991. At that time, ZIMT suffered from UNIP infiltration and a lack of trust among the main players, but ZEMCC, which incorporated the Christian Churches Monitoring Group and a broad spectrum of civic organisations, played a key role in promoting the freeness and fairness of the 1991 elections. ZEMCC's efficiency was much enhanced by its close collaboration with the major foreign

---

[7] On the NIKUV controversy see Committee for a Clean Campaign (no date), 45–48; Zambia Independent Monitoring Team (no date), 13–15; Foundation for Democratic Process (no date), 16–17; Human Rights Watch 1996b, 39–41.

[8] Under Section 53 of the Penal Code concerning 'Prohibited Publications', the president has the powers to ban publications in the public interest. Chiluba has invoked these powers only once, in February 1996, when he banned edition 401 of *The Post* newspaper which had run an article claiming that the government planned to hold a referendum to adopt the controversial Constitution at short public notice. A more subtle form of censorship, practised by both UNIP and the MMD, has been to sanction a newspaper by forbidding state agencies from advertising in it. See Banda 1997. Human Rights Watch has systematically documented countless cases of the direct harassment of Zambian media workers. See Human Rights Watch 1996b and 1997.

monitoring effort, Z-Vote (Mushota 1995).[9] After the elections, ZIMT cleansed its reputation and continued to develop its organisation while a new body with a similar social background, the Foundation for Democratic Process (FODEP) superceded ZEMCC.

During the inter-election period, both ZIMT and FODEP were active in the monitoring of by-elections and in voter education. In 1995, ZIMT and FODEP joined seventeen other NGOs to form the Committee for a Clean Campaign (CCC). The CCC incorporated a broad range of vocal political commentators, and rapidly became embroiled in the public assessment of the Government's actions.[10]

The major international monitoring bodies refused to participate in monitoring the 1996 elections due to 'inconsistencies' in the electoral process. Instead, the CCC, FODEP and ZIMT secured substantial donor support to undertake the election monitoring exercise. All three organisations released extensive reports on the election process, finding that the elections had *not* been free and fair. Exactly one month before the elections, a fourth monitoring group emerged as the Patriotic Rescue Monitors (PAREMO). Whereas FODEP and ZIMT were able to post trained monitors in nearly all of the country's 4,610 polling stations, PAREMO's coverage was far less extensive.[11] Of the four main monitoring bodies, only PAREMO declared the elections to have been 'free and fair'.[12]

The negative assessments of the elections by the CCC, ZIMT and FODEP were based above all on procedural issues – the lack of consensus on the constitutional reform and disputes concerning the voter registration exercise. PAREMO's judgment of the elections as free and fair referred solely to lack of problems on election day.[13] In PAREMO's view, the other monitors had 'strayed out of bounds' and its chairman argued that 'monitoring groups had no business commenting on these [procedural] issues' (see Mulikita 1998, 65).

The MMD's conspiracy theories

The MMD government's justification for bending democratic procedures was based on the allegation that international agencies were sponsoring UNIP and allied opposition forces through a series of anti-government conspiracies that threatened national security. The first example of this kind of thinking surfaced in 1993 over the Zero Option plan. When the alleged UNIP coup plot came to light, President Chiluba declared a State of Emergency and proceeded to expel the diplomatic representatives of Iran and Iraq on the grounds that they were funding the operation. A 'foreign threat' was also invoked in connection with the 1996 elections. As the independent monitoring bodies became more vocal about flaws in the electoral process, the state-owned public media launched a campaign against 'unpatriotic' NGOs who were marked as agents of 'malicious' foreign powers. Immediately after the elections – and after CCC, ZIMT and FODEP had declared their negative assessment of the electoral procedures – the state-owned *Times of Zambia* published an 'investigative' feature entitled 'Behind NGOs cash curtain'. Its author, Joe Chilaizya, revealed that 'ZIMT, FODEP and the CCC were paid to declare the elections not free and fair'. In Chilaizya's rendition of government thinking, Sweden, Japan, Britain and the United States emerged as

---

[9]Z-vote was sponsored by the Carter Center of Emory University and the National Democratic Institute for International Affairs, both of the United States.

[10]CCC members included The Catholic Commission for Justice and Peace, the Inter-African Network for Human Rights and Development (Afronet), The National Women's Lobby Group, the University of Zambia Students Union and the Zambia Congress of Trade Unions.

[11]Fodep claims to have covered 98 per cent of the polling stations. The ZIMT report does not specify the extent of its coverage but claims to have fielded '5,000 plus' monitors. Paremo claimed to have sent monitors to all nine provinces. According to ZIMT's Alfred Zulu, Paremo monitors were only seen in Lusaka Province (interview, April 1998).

[12]A few minor organisations came out in favour of the freeness and fairness of the elections. These included the small Rainbow Monitors and the Christian Council of Zambia. The CCZ's declaration was somewhat surprising since its representative has approved the contradictory report of the CCC of which the CCZ was a member. See Committee for a Clean Campaign (no date).

[13]According to PAREMO chairman Sidney Chellah on a ZNBC Round Table discussion of election monitoring (18 November 1996).

the co-conspirators with UNIP and the three monitoring teams. The plot…was to have the three monitoring teams declare the elections not free and fair and then the opposition alliance led by former president Kenneth Kaunda would move in and declare a take-over using the verdicts as its litany of justification.[14]

In harassing the media along the same lines, the MMD government portrayed its arrest, detainment and imprisonment of independent journalists as part of an inevitable war against an 'unpatriotic' enemy. Before the 1996 elections, the government's main target was the *Post* newspaper.[15] The dual between the MMD and the *Post* came to resemble a viscous circle of self-fulfilling paranoia. The more the government harassed editor Fred Mmembe and other *Post* writers, the more intent the *Post* appeared to be on headlining any rumour which was unfavourable to Chiluba and the MMD.

The stakes grew after the elections. In December 1996, a ZIMT ex-Vice-Chairman, Isaac Zimba, claimed that the ZIMT organisation had been paying six Zambia National Broadcasting Company (ZNBC) journalists to present a biased image of the elections. The state-owned media journalists were subsequently suspended by Ministerial decree. Zimba implicated the above-mentioned donor agencies in the attempt to invalidate the elections.[16]

MMD had two opportunities to produce evidence in support of its conspiracy theory since the Zero Option and the Black Mamba incidents each led to High Court trials against the UNIP leadership. In neither case, however, was the Public Prosecutor able to make a case against UNIP. In both cases, the High Court judges, who were Chiluba's appointees, dismissed charges for lack of evidence.[17] Under the circumstances, it is reasonable to conclude that the government's harassment of UNIP and Kaunda is the product of intense paranoia or calculated political manoeuvring.

Zambia's constitution had granted the president sole legal authority over the legislature and the judiciary. President Frederick Chiluba has asserted his constitutional mandate to control the political arena with impunity. In faulting this behaviour, critics have invoked the rhetoric of democracy, transparency and dialogue which MMD used against UNIP when Kaunda was in State House. As political and civic opposition has become more virulent, Chiluba has waxed increasingly intransigent. Like his predecessor, the autocrat Kenneth Kaunda, Chiluba evinces the habitus of a hard-nosed political strategist. Like Kaunda, his main political weapon has been the pre-emptive strike. When, early in his first term, discord arose within the MMD leadership, Chiluba was quick to sack ministers suspected of dissension. At a press conference announcing the removal of four suspect cabinet ministers in April 1993, Chiluba asserted: 'If I know that someone wants to remove me, I will work to remove him. That is politics. That is the game we are in.' (Phiri 1993, 33)

Like his predecessor, Chiluba has been prepared to strike as hard as necessary at potential enemies in order to stay in command. Ironically, the abuses of which Chiluba is accused were part and parcel of Kaunda's political armoury. During the early 1980s, Kaunda imprisoned the then trade union leader Chiluba and several other MMD leaders for resisting UNIP's authority. It is hard to avoid the conclusion that the government's actions have been motivated more by personal vendetta against Kaunda and UNIP than by security considerations or a concern for the fate of Zambian democracy.

All of the foregoing has undermined the political culture of openness and accountability that the majority of Zambians voted for in the 1991 elections. Chiluba's extension of his wrath against Kaunda into the realm of constitutional law was a further blow against the nascent culture of democracy. In doing so, the President overstepped the boundary between bending the rules of

---

[14]*Sunday Times of Zambia* 1 December 1996, 7.
[15]The *Post* appears five days a week (Monday–Friday) and has an effective circulation along the urban line of rail. Like the government newspapers (the *Times of Zambia* and the *Sunday Times*, the *Daily Mail*, the *Sunday Mail* and the *Financial Mail*), the *Post* can also be read via ZAMNET, the Zambian WWW server and thus can be assumed to have a wide international readership.
[16]'Press Statement by Mr I. Zimba', *Times of Zambia* 26 November 1996, 3.
[17]On the Zero option and Black Mamba trials, see Human Rights Watch 1996b, 7–9.

democratic procedure and breaking them in a blatant patrimonial manner. In stooping to fiddle with the constitution, the MMD demonstrated its disregard of the distinction between private and public interests in Zambian politics. Hence, the Constitutional (Amendment) Act of 1996 constitutes the decisive site of the struggle over the rules of the political game during the first five years of the Third Republic.

Constitutional politics

When Kaunda agreed to re-introduce multi-party politics in 1990, he empowered a Commission, headed by Professor Patrick Mvunga, to draft the necessary changes to the Constitution. On the basis of negotiations with the newly formed MMD, the UNIP government adopted, with only minor revisions, the Mvunga Constitutional Review Commission's recommendations in August 1991. This 'constitutional compromise' (Committee for a Clean Campaign, no date, 15) formed the legal basis for the 1991 elections. The Mvunga Constitution, while reinstating the principles of pluralist politics, did not address a number of basic issues that were crucial to the consolidation of democratic institutions in Zambia. According to the London *Economist*, such issues included 'accountable governance, additions to the Bill of Rights and checking the powers of the president' (Human Rights Watch 1996b, 7).

Throughout its 1991 election campaign, the MMD 'pledged to put in place a constitution which would be above partisan considerations and reflect higher goals of national interest' (Committee for a Clean Campaign, no date, 15–16). The MMD promised the citizenry that, when elected, it would instigate a broad public debate concerning constitutional reform. To this end, the new MMD government set up a task force, chaired by the Attorney-General, to review the Constitution. This task force led, in late 1993, to the appointment of a new Constitutional Review Commission chaired by John M. Mwanakatwe, a High Court Advocate, former Minister and State Counsel under UNIP, and from 1992, the Chancellor of the University of Zambia. Among its other terms of reference, the Mwanakatwe Commission was requested to:

> 2. Recommend a system of Government that will ensure that Zambia is governed in a manner that will promote the Democratic principles of Regular and Fair Elections, Transparency and Accountability and that will guard against the re-emergence of a Dictatorship ...
> 5. Examine and recommend the composition and functions of the organs of the state and their manner of operating, with a view of maximising their checks and balances and securing, as much as possible, their independence...
> 9. Recommend on whether the Constitution should be adopted by the National Assembly or by a Constituent Assembly by a National Referendum or by any other method. (Zambia Independent Monitoring Term, no date, 3.)

The Mwanakatwe Commission carried out an extensive review of popular sentiments on constitutional law, travelling to each of the 9 provinces and organising 46 open hearings which attracted a total of 996 citizen petitions (*ibid.*). On the basis of these hearings, in June 1995, the Commission presented a report including a draft constitution. The recommendations of the Commission did little to improve the checks and balances of executive powers.[18] However, the Commission recommended, on the basis of its public consultations, that the new Constitution be adopted by a special Constituent Assembly and that it be put to a National Referendum before being signed into law by the President. In terms of substance, the main innovation in the Mwanakatwe draft was the so-called third generation clause (Article 34 (3)(*b*)) which stipulated that the parents of any presidential candidate must be Zambians 'by birth or descent' (Zambia Independent Monitoring Team, no date, 7).

This clause aroused intense civic controversy. The third-generation stipulation was widely seen as having been specifically designed to disqualify former President Kenneth Kaunda, a son of Malawian missionaries, from contesting the presidency.[19] By selectively targeting the leader of

---

[18]See Economist Intelligence Unit, 1996b, 6.
[19]The draft constitution also stipulated that 'no person who has twice been elected as president shall be eligible for re-election to that office.' Since Kaunda had previously served six terms as president, this article (35) had the same effect.

UNIP, the constitutional reform caused an uproar among the opposition parties and movements, civic rights organisations and donor agencies. The more the MMD harassed Kaunda, the more his cause became a rallying point for the opposition. It is ironic that Kaunda, an infamous patrimonial autocrat, became a martyr of the reformists who demanded a more genuine democracy.

By focusing public attention on Kaunda, the MMD reaped obvious political dividends. In embracing Kaunda's cause, opposition leaders inevitably became associated with UNIP-era politics and policies. By the mid-1990s, Kaunda had become an anachronism for the majority of Zambians. While his achievements as the founding 'father of the nation' were not in dispute, few desired to resubmit to UNIP's inert and authoritarian rule. The Mwanakatwe Commission's report indicates that the rural population felt strongly that Zambia should be ruled by a 'true' Zambian.[20] The obvious national chauvinism of these sentiments notwithstanding, the government would probably have succeeded in securing sufficient support for its proposal through a national referendum, as Mwanakatwe had proposed. Even were this support not forthcoming, MMD had worked hard to convince Zambians that their current problems were the result of UNIP's corrupt and incompetent policies. Chiluba and the MMD had already humiliated Kaunda once at the polls and no doubt could repeat the performance. Despite widespread economic hardship and growing anxiety over MMD's autocratic behaviour, only a miracle could have brought Kaunda back into power via the ballot.[21]

It is my view that in manipulating constitutional law, the MMD élite was behaving in a patrimonial manner. It did not distinguish between the long-term public good of political stability based on consensual rule of law, and its own short-term private interests. These private interests related, first of all, to staying in power. For politicians, holding political office is an end in itself, but one which can be justified in terms of the public good – 'it is in the public interest that I retain my cabinet portfolio to ensure that my superior policies continue to be implemented'. My claim that the MMD conflated public and private interests implies something more than this. For many public leaders in the Third Republic, political position had become an integral part of a strategy of private accumulation. Such claims are difficult to substantiate empirically, but circumstantial evidence abounds of the rent-seeking behaviour of the MMD leaders.[22] Beyond the direct extraction of rents, controlling the reins of government was also the most effective way of obstructing the success of competitors. With politics and business inseparably intertwined, harassing the opposition and the independent media and juggling with the Constitution were means of promoting private interests in the strict sense of the term.

The Constitution of Zambia (Amendment) Act of 1996
In response to the Mwanakatwe Commission's proposals, the MMD Government issued a White Paper (No. 1 of 1995) on constitutional reform. In its White Paper, the government accepted many of the Commission's substantial recommendations – including the third generation clause – and made some additions, including the provision that incumbent traditional leaders would not be eligible to stand for political office (Committee for a Clean Campaign, no date; Foundation for Democratic Process, no date). The government also introduced a number of revisions that weakened the autonomy of the judiciary. The amended constitution, for example, made it possible for Parliament to enact legislation which assumed the status of constitutional law, and which could not be challenged by the judiciary. Furthermore, a new clause allowed the President, subject to parliamentary approval, to remove High Court judges

---

[20]Bobby Bwalya (Electoral Commission), interview, April 1998.
[21]Not all agree on Kaunda's political impotency. Bratton and Posner 1999, for example, suggest that had KK been allowed to run he was likely to have defeated Chiluba. I find it difficult to read this interpretation into the actual results.
[22]Such rent-seeking can occur in both legal and illegal economic activities. The late Minister of Finance Ronald Penza was widely believed to have juggled with tariff regulations to promote his own business interests. Former Foreign Affairs Minister Vernon Mwaanga has been repeatedly linked to drug trafficking (Ihonvbere 1996, 187). Claims of political involvement in illegal and clandestine business have gained impetus in the wake of recent accusations by the Angolan government tying members of the MMD inner circle to a gun-running operation between Zambia and Unita (*The Post,* 11 February 1999).

(Economist Intelligence Unit, 1996b. Most significantly, the MMD government opted to ignore the Commission's procedural design. It rejected the idea of public debate of the new Constitution in a Constituent Assembly and dismissed the proposal to hold a national referendum. Instead, the government offered Zambians 60 days to 'fully discuss, contribute, react and challenge the proposed amendments', before submitting the new Constitution for approval by the National Assembly (Parliament), where the MMD held an 80 per cent majority (Zambia Independent Monitoring Team, no date, 5).

During early 1996, the government submitted its draft of the new Constitution to Parliament in the form of the Constitution of Zambia (Amendment) Act. The government's refusal to negotiate with civic and political groups over both substantive and procedural issues aroused a public furor. Twenty-one NGOs convened a ten-day Citizen's Convention in March 1996 and produced a Citizen's Green Paper, demanding that the new Constitution should be subordinated to the procedures outlined by the Mwanakatwe Commission. Parallel to this, the opposition Zambian Democratic Congress initiated court action to challenge the third generation clause as well as the procedures by which the Parliament could adopt the Constitution. The courts upheld the government's position and the government refused to withdraw the Act. Against the backdrop of the Black Mamba bombings, the new Constitution was approved by Parliament and signed into law by President Chiluba on 28 May 1996.

As FODEP would later remark, 'the use of a transient legislative majority to push through the hotly contested provisions was not the best way of conferring legitimacy on the constitution'. (Foundation for Democratic Process, no date, 14). By the same token, the contested Constitution seriously undermined the legitimacy of the subsequent elections. In protest against these actions and in response to the MMD's refusal to participate in equitable negotiations about the political impasse, UNIP and six small opposition parties decided in October 1996 not to participate in the elections. This boycott further deepened the legitimation crisis and evinced a flurry of protests from international observers. President Mandela of South Africa intervened directly in the conflict, conferred with Chiluba and proceeded to send his personal envoy, Judge Richard Gladstone, to explore the possibility of postponing the elections until consensus could be reached among the major players (Committee for a Clean Campaign, no date, 22–3). None of these manoeuvres affected the government's decision to proceed with the elections.

These were the decisive factors that eventually led the CCC, ZIMT and FODEP to declare the elections neither free nor fair. The government's patrimonial manipulation of the constitution also caused it considerable damage in the eyes of Zambia's external supporters. A number of donors froze the disbursement of their aid funds. These protests were largely symbolic; aid flows were gradually restored during the course of 1997.

Primary contest: The struggle for power

Players and outcomes
The presidential and general elections of October 1991 were the first testing ground of the new post-colonial regime of multi-party politics. The MMD promised to dislodge a centralist, authoritarian regime and implant a liberal normativity in its place:

> MMD believes that economic prosperity for all can best be created by free men and women through free enterprise, by economic and social justice involving all the productive resources – human, material and financial, by liberalising industry, trade and commerce, with the government only creating an enabling environment whereby economic growth must follow as it has done in all the world's successful countries. ('The MMD Campaign Manifesto', no date, 67ff.)

The message was that leaders, politicians and citizens should be judged according to their individual enterprise and that the unconstrained pursuit of opportunity would take Zambia along the path of 'all the world's successful countries'. This libertarian message appealed very strongly to the Zambian electorate in 1991, when the powerful conflation of political *cum* economic liberalisation constituted a utopian horizon for the impending Third Republic.

Table 12.1: Final results of the 1991 presidential elections

Candidate	Party	Votes	%
Chakomboka, Chama M.	MDP	41,471	3.3
Chiluba, Frederick J.T.	MMD	913,770	72.6
Mbikusita-Lewanika, Akashambatwa	AZ	59,250	4.7
Mulemba, Humphrey	NP	83,875	6.7
Mung'omba, Dean M.	ZDC	160,439	12.7
Total		1,258,805	100

Source: Zambia Electoral Commission, as published in Zambia Independent Monitoring Team, no date, Appendix IV.

The MMD scored an overwhelming victory over UNIP in the 1991 elections, capturing 125 of 150 parliamentary seats, as well as the presidency. In the presidential elections, Chiluba won 70 per cent or more of the vote in 8 of Zambia's 9 provinces. After 27 years of political monopoly, UNIP was demoted to the role of a minority, regional party, its only strong base lying in the predominantly agrarian Eastern Province (National Institute for International Affairs 1992, 58–9).

With UNIP boycotting the 1996 elections, Chiluba was the only presidential candidate with strong national support. Table 12.1 shows how Chiluba held on to his 1991 support.

Between 1991 and 1996, roughly 30 new political parties were registered, although most of these existed only in name. Only 4 managed to capture significant electoral support at the 1996 polls. The second largest political force, in terms of votes and successful candidates, was not a political party at all, but the set of Independent candidates running without party backing. This is evident from Table 12.2, which present the outcome of the parliamentary elections.

Table 12.2: Final results of the 1996 parliamentary elections

Party	Candidates	Votes	%	Seats	%
Agenda for Zambia (AZ)	11	18,982	1.5	2	1.3
Independent (IND)	99	127,760	10.2	10	6.7
Liberal Progressive Front (LPF)	1	759	0.1	0	0
Movement for Democratic Process (MDP)	2	632	0.1	0	0
Movement for Multi-Party Democracy (MMD)	150	750,204	60	131	87.3
National Congress (NC)	5	2,313	0.2	0	0
National Lima Party (NLP)	83	81,876	6.5	0	0
National Party (NP)	98	90,823	7.2	5	3.3
Progressive Party (PPP)	1	293	0.02	0	0
Real Democracy Party (RDP)	1	182	0.01	0	0
United National Independence Party (UNIP)	2	477	0.03	0	0
Zambia Democratic Congress (ZDC)	141	175,997	14.2	2	1.3
Total	594	1,250,298	100	150	100

Source: Zambia Electoral Commission, as published in Zambia Independent Monitoring Team, no date, Appendix III.

By the final run-up to the 1996 elections, the following players, listed alphabetically, had accumulated some degree of weight in the political arena:[23]

Agenda for Zambia (AZ)
AZ is the party of MMD founding member and former minister Akashambatwa Mbikusita Lewanika. It was formed little more than a month before the elections, in October 1996. Lewanika (popularly known as 'Aka') was in the avant-garde of the anti-UNIP movement at the end of the Second Republic. Aka was the main organiser of the famous Garden House Conference of 1990 that launched the MMD as an opposition party. He was awarded a minor ministerial post in

---

[23]Unless otherwise noted, this information on Zambian political parties is drawn from Committee for Clean Campaign, no date, 26–30.

Chiluba's first cabinet, but resigned from this post after eight months, disappointed with the 'greed and corruption' among the MMD leadership. Lewanika left the MMD in August 1993 during the first major wave of political desertions which included the group that founded the National Party (see below). He regained his parliamentary status under the NP banner in January 1994 in the Mongu (Western Province) parliamentary by-election.

According to Lewanika, AZ was not a party but a 'front' allied with Zadeco and some Independents in a common endeavour to topple MMD. AZ emerged from the 1996 elections as a minor, regionally based party, fielding eleven candidates and picking up two parliamentary seats, both in Western Province. Lewanika's presidential bid drew nearly 5 per cent of the national vote, predominantly from the West.

Liberal Progressive Front (LPF)
The LPF boycotted the 1996 elections and thus does not appear in the tables of results. It was established by ex-MMD Legal Affairs Minister Roger Chongwe, but soon lost three of its leaders to the National Lima Party. Chongwe spearheaded the formation of an Inter-Party Alliance that pressured MMD for pre-elections dialogue. Chongwe has been one of Kaunda's most out-spoken defenders. He received a wound in the neck from a policeman's firearm at a political demonstration in August 1997 while riding in Kaunda's vehicle. Chongwe left Zambia soon after the shooting incident and has been residing abroad ever since.

Movement for Democratic Process (MDP)
The MDP was formed in 1991. Its main political activity in 1996 was the presidential bid of octogenarian civil servant Chama Chakomboka. Chakomboka ran on a reformist ticket, promising to restore accountability to government if elected. He received a little more than 3 per cent of the national vote. The MDP fielded two parliamentary aspirants on the Copperbelt but neither succeeded, each also accumulating 3 per cent of the vote in their respective constituencies.

Movement for Multi-party Democracy (MMD)
The MMD that campaigned for popular support in 1996 was rather different from the political entity that wrested state power from UNIP in 1991. Formed in July 1991, the young MMD was a 'popular front' movement, a loose alliance of forces united against UNIP. This original multi-party democracy movement comprised radical democrats, domestic businessmen thwarted by UNIP's patrimonial grip on the parastatal economy, as well as spurned, exorcised or lapsed activists and members of UNIP.

The MMD of 1996, on the other hand, was a disciplined party of tightly linked patrons and clients. The radical democrats had long since quit, as had many of the former UNIP activists who had failed to gain access to the inner circle of power and patrimonial benefits. As ministers and MPs deserted the movement to form opposition parties, the MMD mutated from a popular movement dedicated to dialogue and reform to an increasingly jealous and confrontational guardian of its monopoly over state power. Chiluba increasingly drew from the pre-1991 experience of UNIP political strategy, harassing the independent media (something Kaunda had never had to deal with), announcing surprise cabinet shuffles and sporting a penchant for blaming international actors and agents for domestic problems. The MMD in 1996 was a party of powerful, modern-minded men and women who had grown visibly wealthy over their five years in office. Its national leadership mainly comprised businessmen who were ostentatious in their wealth and their power.

MMD's campaign was openly clientelistic. On the eve of the elections, President Chiluba told a crowd in the Eastern Province (where UNIP had held all 20 Parliamentary seats in 1991) 'How can I assist you if you don't support my candidates.'[24] MMD Lusaka parliamentary aspirant Silvia Masebo advised a ZNBC television audience that voting for the winning party was the only way for voters to benefit after the elections. When challenged, MMD stuck by its liberalist policies with less State and more entrepreneurial initiative, even in sectors such as agriculture and health where privatisation policies were not popular. MMD politicians were most at home in urban

---

[24]ZNBC News broadcast, 17 November 1996.

contexts, where they appealed to supporters who identified with the upwardly-mobile style of business entrepreneur that held the reins of power.

National Lima Party (NLP)

The NLP received much media attention during the campaign, despite its being formed only three months before the elections. It was the only one of the 'national' parties that decided not to field a presidential candidate. On the basis of numerous ZNBC television panels, NLP stood out from the other parties in its attempt to run an issues campaign. The cornerstone of its programme was the restoration of agriculture to the centre of Zambia's development policy. The NLP's campaign platform was also the most articulate. Instead of criticising the MMD's policies, the NLP demanded that the government should adhere to them. Guy Scott, the party's main figurehead, was an MMD founder, a co-author of the original MMD Manifesto and Chiluba's first Minister of Agriculture.

NLP representatives often spoke about the possibility of a post-election 'coalition' with the new government, but the party's assessment of its rural popularity was grossly inflated. It captured only 6 per cent of the vote with its best returns in Central and Southern Provinces (where its support reached 12 per cent). The party's poor rural performance, despite its pro-agricultural platform, reflected its lack of resources. NLP lacked the means to get its message out to the agrarian voter. Other factors may have also contributed. Scott's personal campaign in the Chongwe constituency of Lusaka Province was unsuccessful amidst evidence of electoral malpractice (Foundation for Democratic Process, no date, 49).[25] Scott's petitions were rejected by the High Court, however, and the NLP was left without an MP.

National Party (NP)

The NP was the first MMD splinter party, formed when ten MPs left MMD in 1993. At first look, NP promised to be a serious threat to the MMD's hegemony, bringing together politicians from backgrounds that were pregnant with historical and symbolic capital. Among the NP's founding members were Humphrey Mulemba and Arthur Wina, founding members of UNIP whose political origins lay in the anti-colonial struggle. Mulemba held various ministerial positions under UNIP and was a Mines minister in Chiluba's first cabinet. Also present were ex-MMD parliamentarians Baldwin Nkumbula and Chilufya Kapwepwe, the children of Harry Nkumbula and Simon Kapwepwe, respectively, legendary leaders of the original Zambian nationalist movement during the colonial period. Nkumbula's roots were in the Southern Province, while Kapwepwe hailed from the Northern Province. Mulemba's power base was in the North-western Province. Add to this Arthur Wina's and A.M. Lewanika's staunch support from the Western Province and the NP looked particularly threatening to the MMD.

However, the NP was plagued by internal conflicts and leadership problems. Between 1993 and 1996, the party went through three leaders: Interim President Inonge Mbikusita-Lewanika (Aka's sister), Baldwin Nkumbula and finally Humphrey Mulemba, the NP's presidential candidate in the 1996 elections. Wina passed away in 1995; Nkumbula returned to MMD (just days before his death in an automobile crash); and Aka Lewanika withdrew in 1996 to form his own Agenda for Zambia (see above). At the 1996 presidential elections, Mulemba won 35 per cent of the vote in Northwestern Province but less than 7 per cent nationwide. NP nonetheless won four seats in the Northwest, plus one surprise seat in Lusaka, which went to Samuel Chipungu, a professor of history at the University of Zambia.

United National Independence Party (UNIP)

UNIP was formed in 1958 when Kenneth Kaunda broke away from Harry Nkumbula's African National Congress (ANC). UNIP led Zambia to independence from Britain in 1964, and Kaunda led the party to a landslide victory in the 1964 legislative elections, becoming the first African prime minister of colonial Northern Rhodesia and, subsequently, the first President of the new Republic of Zambia (see Rotberg 1995). With Kaunda at its helm, UNIP held onto state power

[25] See also the Supreme Court's 'Petition Judgment on the 1996 Zambia Election and Presidential Eligibility Case' [www.zamnet.zm/zamnet/afronet/other/petition_3.htm].

throughout the multi-party First Republic (1964–72) and the one-party Second Republic (1973–91). UNIP was defeated at the polls in 1991 and Kaunda announced his retirement from politics the following year. Kebby Musokotwante ran the party from 1992 until June 1995, when Kaunda wrested leadership back into his own hands. In protest against the MMD's unilateral Constitutional (Amendment) Act of 1996 which, as mentioned above, disqualified Kaunda from contesting the republican presidency, UNIP declared an election boycott in October 1996. Nevertheless, two candidates unsuccessfully stood for Parliament on the UNIP ticket, one in Eastern Province and one in Luapula.

Zambia National Congress (ZDC, Zadeco)
Dean Mung'omba was a Deputy Minister and Deputy National Secretary of the MMD before being sacked in 1994. He then established Zadeco with another 'Young Turk', Derrick Chitala, in a self-proclaimed bid to restore the original vision of the 1991 anti-Kaunda movement. Zadeco attacked the MMD for corruption and ineffective economic policies. Mung'omba, with the party's parliamentary candidates, promised voters what the MMD had offered them in 1991 – both more democracy and greater prosperity. As Zadeco's presidential candidate, Dean Mung'omba polled the highest number of votes after Chiluba (see Table 12.1).

Zadeco differed from the other MMD splinter parties (such as the AZ and the NP) in that it succeeded in attracting a modicum of even support across the country. Zadeco did best in the old UNIP stronghold of Eastern Province, where it captured a little less than a quarter of the vote. It would appear that Zadeco profited most from the UNIP boycott. Like UNIP before the boycott, Zadeco candidates came out for greater government intervention in the economy and its platform was clearly reminiscent of 'tried and true' UNIP policies: Agricultural subsidies, governmental job creation, better public health, education and roads. Donors were expected to provide the funding for the increased public spending.

Mung'omba was clearly shocked by Zadeco's poor showing at the polls and refused to accept the result. He charged the MMD with rigging the ballot and threatened the government with civil unrest if it refused to nullify the polls. The reports of the independent monitoring groups found that the MMD and Zadeco candidates were as guilty as each other of electoral misdemeanours, but not to such an extent as to systematically skew the result. Some 14 months after the election, Mung'omba was detained by the government, when he was accused of involvement in the botched 'Captain Solo' coup attempt of August 1997.[26]

Independents
Independent candidates secured the second largest block of seats in parliament. A total of 99 Independents contested parliamentary seats, with as many as 3 independents standing in a single constituency. Independents had a variety of reasons for rejecting party affiliation. Many had failed to secure the candidacy within their home parties. Some had side-stepped the Inter-Party Alliance election boycott. A third group was 'clearly non-partisan and were urged by their communities to run for political office' (Committee for a Clean Campaign, no date, 30).

This overview of the political arena indicates the extent to which Zambian politicians embraced multi-partyism. It also suggests how difficult it is to challenge the ruling party in an impoverished economy. As long as accumulation is strongly tied to patrimonial privilege, only the ruling party is able to muster the resources necessary to establish and maintain clientelist networks.

Seen in the aggregate, the Zambian electorate appears to have given staunch support to the MMD's policies as well as to its practice of politics. In the following section, I attempt to qualify this interpretation. I argue that an analysis of parliamentary contests at the constituency level reveals clear elements of voter protest against the MMD. This protest was limited by a number of practical factors, including poor communications, atrocious logistics and a lack of awareness among voters of their political options. Yet despite these conditions, a significant number of voters at the grass roots registered their protest over the clientelist culture of politics which the MMD attempted to cultivate amidst a deteriorating material base.

---

[26]See *Zambia. Misrule of Law: Human rights in a state of emergency.* Amnesty International – Report AFR 63/04/98, March 1998 [www.amnesty.org//ailib/aipub/1889/AFR/16300498.htm].

Within the neo-Weberian tradition, clientelism is theoretically linked to patrimonialism; both are seen as survivals of a 'pre-modern' culture of personalised politics (Médard 1982; recently Chabal and Daloz 1999). The British system of colonial Indirect Rule in Zambia operated via a weak form of clientelism that co-opted traditional authority. After independence, UNIP modernised and consolidated clientelist structures within its own party apparatus. These extended down to the lowest level of political administration (see Bond 1976; Bratton 1980; Gertzel ed. 1984).

Clientelism is generally dependent on political leaders' patrimonial access to public assets. Indeed, the maintenance of clientelist structures or networks demands extensive resources. The fiscal crisis of the state in the Second Republic eventually undermined the financial basis of UNIP patronage. MMD has had to grapple with the same dilemma (see Ihonvbere 1996, 77 *et seq.*). As guardian of a shrinking public sector, and one that is under close debtor scrutiny, the MMD has limited means to maintain a political clientele at the grass roots. International food aid, the residual benefit of repeated droughts in the early 1990s, and a number of balance-of-payment support programmes have provided the government with some financial leeway to consolidate clientelist structures.[27] For the most part, however, the national MMD leadership has not managed to establish a political clientele below the provincial level, where public resources allow it to maintain regional deputy ministerial posts. Below the province, district-level political structures have remained relatively autonomous, and beyond this level, at the constituency and ward levels, MMD is extremely thinly organised.[28] An analysis of the electoral results from one region of Zambia provides the means to examine the clientelist structure in more detail. Politics can be a face-to-face affair, especially in an arena saturated with personalised practices. Political analysis that begins and ends with aggregate patterns misses something essential about the special relationship between parties, politicians, and their constituencies. An aggregated view is not able to confront the particular forms of morality and emotive argument that bind actors together in a political relationship. A generic label, such as clientelism, conveys the intimacy of the political relationship, yet brushes aside the contextualised substance of the 'social emotions', to use Richard Sennet's term (Sennet 1980), through which actors commit themselves to the roles of leader and led.

Anthropologist Wim van Binsbergen has characterised Zambian 'political culture at the grass-roots' as an arena where 'traditional leadership, religious alternatives and local/national relations constitute important dimensions' (van Binsbergen 1995, 21). The case study of Luapula Province that follows represents an attempt to situate the electoral process within this grass roots context in order to provide a basis for alternative readings of the aggregate. Instead of complacency and apathy, close scrutiny of political interaction reveals a commitment to oppose clientelist privilege at the very base of rural politics. A few sketches of particular contests, and contexts, can help to substantiate these tendencies and to anchor electoral politics in the lifeworlds of the actors involved.

Clientelism and protest in Luapula:
Voter interests in the 1996 elections[29]

Luapula Province is hardly representative of the illusory 'Zambia in general'.[30] Given the marked regional specificities that characterised these elections, no one provincial profile could possibly

---

[27]On aid and clientelism in the 1990s, see Polhemus 1997.

[28]This is especially true in rural areas, as discussed in the section below on Luapula, an MMD stronghold. The exception to this are urban constituencies in Lusaka and the Copperbelt and those rural constituencies (such as Mpika and Mbala) where key MMD leaders are MPs.

[29]If not otherwise noted, the data presented in this section derive from first-hand observations and interviews carried out in Luapula in October 1996 and March 1998. Confidentiality and discretion prevents me from citing the source of certain details.

[30]The choice of Luapula stems simply from the fact that it is the part of Zambia that I know best, having lived and worked there off and on over the past 15 years. Even within Luapula, my in-depth knowledge is patchy, concentrated on the southern or 'Aushi' region. My familiarity with the northern, or 'Lunda', part of the Province is far more circumstantial.

convey typical voting patterns. Since 1991, Luapula has enjoyed the political asset of being the President's homeland. Chiluba's precise place of birth is a contested issue[31] but there is no ambiguity about the fact that the President's lineage is rooted in the Lunda kingdom of the Luapula River valley. Luapula has a long history of political militancy. During the late colonial period of the 1950s, Luapulans were staunch supporters of the anti-Federationist African National Congress. Local leaders, both nationalist politicians and traditional authorities, openly confronted colonial rule (Gould 1997a). During the 1960s, the Province earned the reputation of being a militant UNIP power base. The local economy has suffered from poor markets and low productivity, but Luapula has been a perennial source of migrant labour for the adjacent copper fields in the Katanga Province of Zaire (currently Democratic Republic of Congo) and the Zambian Copperbelt. Part of the region's political militancy no doubt stems from the extensive experience of trade union activism and urban media exposure that returning mineworkers brought to their villages. Not unexpectedly, Luapula backed the MMD enthusiastically in 1991, giving Chiluba 90 per cent of the vote, his second highest polling return in the presidential race against Kaunda.

The ensuing five years of MMD rule did not bring any remarkable economic improvement to Luapula. Situated in the Central African high-rainfall belt, Luapula did not experience the full impact of the droughts that ravaged agriculture across the country during the early 1990s. During this period, the government's main attention was directed toward the severely drought-affected regions. Yet, the majority of smallholder farmers were heavily hit by the removal of agricultural subsidies and by the dismantling of the state-sponsored rural credit schemes that were UNIP's main instruments of rural political patronage. Luapulans no doubt expected to benefit handsomely from having a local son in State House and Luapulan politicians indeed received a substantial slice of the patronage pie: by 1997, two of the Province's 14 MPs had risen to full Minister, while four others had been appointed Deputy Ministers in the Chiluba administration.

These political assets did not convert into developmental gains. The government lacked both the resources and the vision to address the province's economic problems. This was partially due to the fact that the MMD had been led by urbanites, and has lacked an agrarian policy.[32] The IMF-sponsored Enhanced Structural Adjustment Facility obliged the government to end the state grain monopsony. This manoeuvre benefited commercially-oriented farmers with ready access to capital and markets, but there were few such entrepreneurs in Luapula. The economic liberalism of the Third Republic promised higher farm-gate prices and new opportunities to rural producers. However, few farmers could afford, or often even find, the fertilisers and improved seed necessary to compete in the booming market enclaves for maize and vegetables. Smallholders, without the possession of collateral, were cut off from the seasonal credit arrangements of the commercial banks. Under these circumstances, the meagre surpluses that marginal farmers managed to produce were insufficient to entice private traders to venture out on deeply rutted or washed-out rural roads to buy the crop of maize and other produce (see Gould 1997b).

Given the historical volatility of Zambian politics, a protest at the polls was not out of the question. Given the distinct lack of 'development' under the MMD, the question was whether Luapulan voters would abandon Chiluba with the same decisiveness that led them to jettison Kaunda in 1991. A quick look at the aggregate results reveals no such rejection: despite a diverse fielding of opposition party and independent candidates, the MMD swept all 14 parliamentary constituencies in the Province. In the presidential race, Chiluba grossed one of the highest shares of the vote in the country.

Three possible reasons could explain the results in Luapula. The elections may have been rigged or the electoral process manipulated to an extent that a free choice was not possible. On the other hand, one could believe that Luapulans were blinded by presidentialist patronage to the extent that it obscured their objective interests. Alternatively, local citizens may have been so intimidated by the MMD machine that they would not consider opposing Chiluba and his network

---

[31]When it became evident that the MMD government planned to adopt the Mwanakatwe Constitutional Review Commission's recommendation that only second generation Zambians be valid presidential candidates, the opposition dug up evidence according to which Chiluba was born in Zaire.

[32]Dr Guy Scott, MMD's first Minister of Agriculture, formulated such a policy, but was relieved of his portfolio after only six months in office.

Table 12.3: Winning candidates in parliamentary elections in Luapula Province, 1991–1996.

Constituency	Year	Winning candidate	Votes received	Percentage of vote	Chiluba's share per cent
56. Kawambwa	1996	MUTALE, Elizabeth	4,219	71	85
	1991	MPUNDU, Joseph	4,267	90	89
57. Mwansabombwe	1996	CHISALA, Josiah C.	3,818	61	84
	1991	MUONGA, Edward	3,864	82	84
58. Pambashe	1996	CHAMA, Alex M.	Unopposed	–	90
	1991	MUSHOTA, Remmy	3,589	86	87
59. Bahati	1996	KAYOPE, Valentine	4,488	55	83
	1991	KAYOPE, Valentine	6,805	84	87
60. Chembe	**1996**	**SOKONTWE, D. M.**	**3,918**	**61**	**86**
	1991	**SOKONTWE, D. M.**	**4,474**	**84**	**85**
61. Mansa	1996	MWITWA, Kelvin	8,230	75	86
	1991	CHISHA, Edward	9,021	80	82
62. Chipili	1996	CHINDOLOMA, Ntondo	1,447	42	86
	1991	CHINDOLOMA, Ntondo	1,228	71	81
63. Mambilima	1996	KALIFUNGWA, Patrick	4,171	73	88
	1991	BANDA, Chisenga	4,216	85	85
64. Mwense	**1996**	**CHIBAMBA, Norman**	**4,947**	**59**	**90**
	1991	**CHIBAMBA, Norman**	**5,723**	**86**	**86**
65. Chienge	1996	KALUMBA, Katele	8,932	85	65
	1991	CHIBWE, Ephraim	7,410	88	89
66. Nchelenge	1996	CHITALU, Ndashi	6,396	67	90
	1991	MUTOBOLA, Daniel	6,386	85	86
67. Bangweulu	1996	PULE, Daniel C.	4,674	47	80
	1991	PULE, Daniel C.	10,303	86	88
68. Chifunabuli	1996	MWANSA, Ernest C.	6,055	61	88
	1991	MWANSA, Ernest C.	10,153	91	92
69. Luapula	1996	MACHUNGWA, Peter	Unopposed	–	88
	1991	MACHUNGWA, Peter	3,140	82	87

Source: Zambian Electoral Commission; as published in Zambia Independent Monitoring Team, no date.

of political cronies for fear of serious reprisal. Clientelism, patronage and intimidation do all play a role in Zambian politics, yet inflating their importance may obscure the real dynamics of local politics. A closer look at the results at the constituency level suggests that the MMD's hegemony is not as watertight as the aggregate pattern suggests. Looking at the local constituency results reveals a set of emerging trends that belies the apathetic and stagnating image of Zambian democracy conveyed by the aggregating view.[33]

Table 12.3 shows the results of the parliamentary race by constituency in 1996 and 1991. In both years all the successful MPs for Luapula came from the MMD. Chiluba obviously remains very popular in Luapula, capturing more than 85 per cent of the valid vote. To determine whether this numerical support might be explained by political manipulation or voter apathy it is necessary to reflect on the quality of the Voter Registry.

The overall voter registration for Luapula Province fell from 203,000 in 1991 to 170,000 in 1996; this decline conforms to the national trend. The 1991 register was compiled by UNIP for the 1987 one-party elections. There is good reason to suspect that accuracy in the voter registry was not a high priority for UNIP. If the 1991 registry was inaccurate, inflated perhaps by deceased and fictional voters, the lower numbers on the newer registry do not necessarily reflect citizen indifference in the electoral process. Nonetheless, compared to the potential electorate – in purely demographic terms – the proportion of registered voters is small. Calculations based on aggregate national figures suggest that fewer than half of eligible Zambians registered to vote during the 1995–6 registration exercise.[34] While one would naturally like to see all citizens exercising their

---

[33]For example, Bratton and Posner (1999, 403) conclude that 'ordinary citizens are unlikely to stand up against the gradual erosion of democracy'.

[34]On the number of eligible voters, see Van Donge 1998b, 82–83.

electoral rights, it is justified to ask what would be considered a *reasonable* level of registration in conditions such as those prevailing in rural Zambia. Registration in 1995–6 required up to four separate visits to the polling station (van Donge 1998b). There were long distances from home to registration site, with travel done predominantly on foot. Communication was another bottleneck. There are no public media that enjoy blanket coverage of the rural areas. That 2.3 million of a potential 4.6 million Zambians did register to vote is hardly ideal, but under the circumstances it might also be deemed an achievement of sorts.

It is also possible that the register was systematically biased in such a way as to prejudice political outcomes. Civic rights monitors and opposition parties protested when the MMD government made a unilateral decision to subcontract the voter registration exercise to an Israeli computer firm called Nikuv. Judged in terms of openness and accountability, criticisms of this arrangement were justified. The government clearly overstepped its mandate by making a unilateral decision in this sensitive area. Yet none of the inquiries or monitoring reports have succeeded in demonstrating that Nikuv systematically falsified the roll. Lacking disaggregated data on the composition of the registry, it is not possible to give a confident verdict on its reliability. Obviously the MMD had more resources at its disposal to mobilise its supporters during voter registration. Yet, as already noted, the MMD lacks a mass grass roots organisation. Its political reach ends at the district level. This would make it difficult for political organisers to differentiate between friends and foes at the level of the polling station. As the results indicate, a relatively large number of voters who supported competing candidates had been registered to vote.

It is evident, on the other hand, that the arduousness of the voter registration process would militate against the participation of the poor, weak, infirm and overburdened. The weak and the marginalised were precisely those sections of the rural population who were most severely hit by the MMD's economic reform measures, including the demise of subsidised seasonal credit facilities. In this respect, the low registration rate may have biased the registry in MMD's favour. Yet, it is hard to conclude that a more complete voters' registry could have negated Chiluba's substantial majority at the polls.

Despite the shrinkage in the volume of the registered electorate, voting activity in Luapula increased noticeably from 1991 to 1996. This is the second cogent point to be drawn from Table 12.3. Voter turnout *rose* from 47 per cent in 1991 to 65 per cent in the more recent ballot. Far from being demobilised by the MMD's poor delivery of developmental goods, Luapulans increased their level of electoral participation.

A third observation is that the MMD's proportion of the parliamentary vote dropped sharply across the board. Chiluba's share of the presidential vote held its own, or increased in nine of the province's 14 constituencies.[35] Yet the share of the vote attracted by MMD parliamentary aspirants was, on the average, more than 20 per cent *less* than it had been in 1991. This points to two theses: first, that voters saw the presidential and parliamentary elections as relatively independent races. Party loyalty, or voter consistency, was far from sacrosanct. Second, parliamentary races were far more competitive than the aggregate outcome indicates. In aggregate terms, MMD candidates captured a respectable 65 per cent of the parliamentary vote, far less than their 84 per cent share of the vote in 1991. Furthermore, 2 MMD candidates squeaked through on less than half of the total ballot. It would seem that here in the rural heartland of Chiluba's power base, the MMD's hegemony was far from self-evident. If the 1996 results were to indicate a linear trend, the MMD could be in serious trouble in 2001.

---

[35]In one constituency, Chiengi in the far north of the Province, the official result shows Chiluba's support falling from 89 per cent to 65 per cent of the total vote. The reason for this is a set of 4,480 votes cast for the Agenda for Zambia candidate, Akashambatwa Mbikusita-Lewanika. While none of the monitoring reports comment on this highly unlikely result, there was clearly something fishy going on. As noted elsewhere, AZ's power base is largely limited to a number of constituencies in the Western Province, some 2,000 km from Chiengi by road. Lewanika's best result in any other Luapula constituency was 146 votes and in the neighbouring constituency of Kaputa (in Northern Province) he amassed 37 votes. A solution to this anomaly suggests itself when one notes that the number of votes cast in the presidential race in Chiengi were 4,141 (39 per cent) more than those cast in the parliamentary contest.

In terms of future prospects, one feature of these returns is especially telling. Parliamentary contests could be divided into two distinct groups: one for which an incumbent MP sought re-election, and another in which the MMD fielded a newcomer. While both categories of candidate performed less well than did MMD candidates in 1991, newcomers did less poorly than incumbents. The incumbents received nearly 30 per cent fewer votes than they had in 1991. When a newcomer contested the seat, the MMD share of the constituency's vote dropped only 15 per cent. The electorate was clearly looking for change.

That this dissatisfaction failed to push through even one opposition candidate can be attributed to several factors. Opposition parties were disorganised and poorly prepared to carry out a demanding and expensive rural campaign. The MMD could, and did, requisition government vehicles to transport its parliamentary candidates. This option was not available to other aspirants, making it difficult for opposition candidates to make themselves known to the electorate. Beyond this, patronage has powerful roots in Luapula. Voters believe that only those constituencies that support the winning side will benefit in the next distribution of budgetary allocations and donor projects.

The factor attributing most to the sharp decline in support for incumbent candidates derived from the relationship between the local and the national party organisations. The relatively poor performance of the incumbents can be seen as a protest of local versus national political interests. As early as 1991, the 'dictatorial' way in which Chiluba imposed his *protégés* on local constituencies raised eyebrows within the MMD.[36] This trend continued in 1996, with politicians appointed by the MMD National Executive Committee in Lusaka generally capturing the local MMD candidacies.[37] The insensitivity of the national MMD heavyweights toward local political dynamics generated serious tensions within the party.[38]

In Luapula, as in the rest of the country, MMD parliamentary candidates were appointed by the National Executive Committee (NEC). Nominated candidates were commonly local sons who, like Chiluba himself, had long since shifted their base of operations to the urban centres of Lusaka and the Copperbelt. Lusaka appointees superseded popular politicians who had a firm local base but weaker connections to the national committee. A number of local politicians who failed to win an MMD candidacy opted to contest their constituency's seat as an independent. Nine independent candidates stood for parliamentary seats in 6 of Luapula's 14 constituencies. Independents grossed 12 per cent of the vote, more than NP and NLP combined, and roughly equal to that of Zadeco. None of the Independents came within striking distance of a parliamentary seat, but their candidacies altered the future of Luapula politics. An examination of 2 such contests provides a glimpse of the internal dynamics of constituency politics in an MMD stronghold.

Chembe constituency

D. M. Sokontwe was one of the Lusaka-based incumbents endorsed by the MMD NEC in 1996. At the time of the elections, Chembe constituency, which Sokontwe represents, covered the rural part of Mansa District, encompassing the palace and most of the subject-lands of Aushi Senior Chief Milambo. Subsequently, largely due to Sokontwe's efforts, much of rural Mansa has been annexed to a newly-established Milenge district. As Table 12.3 shows, Sokontwe's performance in the 1996 elections was well below that of five years before. This 23 per cent drop in Sokontwe's popularity does not necessarily derive from any one factor. Sokontwe's primary asset in Chembe politics was his connection to the royal *benang'ulube* or Red Ant clan. Theoretically he is in line to inherit the junior chieftaincy currently held by his classificatory sister, sub-Chieftainess Sokontwe. (By his own account it is a remote likelihood that he would ever leave his lucrative holdings in Lusaka.) The royal blood that flows in chiefly lineages constitutes important political

---

[36] Economist Intelligence Unit 1996b.

[37] Interview with Fodep Provincial Chairman for Luapula, April 1998.

[38] The most publicised case of this on the national level occurred in Kabwe, an agricultural and mining centre on the line of rail north of Lusaka. Against great local resistance, President Chiluba insisted on the candidacy of Paul Tembo, a member of Chiluba's inner circle, for the Kabwe constituency race. Having lost the candidacy, Capt. A. C. Chewe, the favorite among Kabwe MMD supporters, stood as an independent. Tempers were heated in both camps and violence broke out between supporters of the MMD's Tembo and the independent Chewe, claiming two lives. On election day, Chewe defeated Tembo with a 3:1 margin. See Committee for a Clean Campaign, (no date), 57.

capital in Aushiland. In the 1996 contest, Sokontwe enjoyed both the endorsement of the NEC, and the support of the Aushi royalty.

These were important assets, especially since Sokontwe's reputation in at least part of his constituency was somewhat tarnished. In the populous centre of Milambo, for example, a group of elders I met in October 1996, on the eve of the elections, agreed that their MP was a 'useless fool' who was 'never seen' in his constituency. Sokontwe's alleged invisibility was not fully accurate; minutes of the Lwela Rural Clinic Management Committee revealed that Sokontwe had, in fact, attended several meetings. What the elders meant was that the MP 'never brought them anything' of value. In this respect, the villagers' priority was to exercise demand on the distributive function of the state to obtain development inputs. This implied functioning schools, a rural transport network and the basic infrastructure necessary to make a living out of agriculture in the liberalised market context. Their basic requirements were for passable roads, fertilisers, improved seed and affordable credit schemes.

Discussions with Milambo villagers in October 1996 and again in May 1998 indicated that their candidate of choice was Aaron Kabengele. Kabengele is a small-scale businessman and politician based in the provincial capital of Mansa, who maintains close ties to the Milambo core of *benambushi* (Goat Clan) elders. Kabengele sought the MMD nomination for the Chembe constituency ballot, but like many local politicians in Luapula he was passed over by the NEC. Kabengele was popular in Milambo and its environs because of his frequent visits to the constituency and because of the gifts of fertiliser he distributed in the run-up to the MMD Provincial Party Conference at which candidates were chosen. Political gifts like these were seen to demonstrate a 'real understanding' of the problems of local farmers.

Table 12.4: 1996 Parliamentary election returns, Chembe Constituency

Candidate	Party	Votes	Share of valid votes (%)
Kabengele, Aaron	IND	980	15
Katunasa, Bornface	ZDC	392	7
Mumba, Chrispine	NLP	1,105	17
Sokontwe, Dalton	MMD	3,918	61
Total Votes Cast		6,395	100

Source: Zambian Electoral Commission, as published in Zambia Independent Monitoring Team, no date.

After the NEC nominated Sokontwe as the MMD candidate, Kabengele decided to stand as an independent. However, he lacked the resources to compete effectively with the provincial MMD campaign apparatus. The costs and logistics of running a political campaign in rural Mansa were beyond the means of any but the most affluent individuals. Indeed, without the organisational backing of an entrenched political party, it is difficult to make credible promises to prospective voters. Since Sokontwe, as a member of the MMD, was unable to upgrade the road to his uncle's, Chief Milambo's, palace it was very unlikely that an independent MP would have greater success. These 'facts of life' were driven home by President Chiluba himself in the last-minute crash campaign that he carried out in Luapula on behalf of 'his' candidates.

The results of this election, as revealed in Table 12.4, emphasise the dilemma of opposition candidates in rural areas like Luapula. A persevering opposition candidate may manage to visit communities along the major roadsides. Away from the busier transport arteries, voters had little idea of the alternatives that independents or opposition candidates might have to offer. Hence, a community such as Milambo can give sizeable support to a favourite political son like Kabengele, but elsewhere in the constituency he may well remain completely unknown.

Mwense Constituency
Mwense Constituency is Chiluba's home base in Luapula; his mother and closest lineage kin live in a rural Mwense village. Since 1991, the MP for Mwense, Norman Chibamba, had also functioned as the Provincial Deputy Minister. The Provincial Deputy Minister is a Presidential appointee and the highest-ranking politician in the province. Chibamba and the President are kinsmen. According to

the matrilineal principles of Lunda kinship, Chibamba addresses Chiluba as *bayama* (mother's brother). Within this regime of family relations, the nephew (*mwipwa*) is entitled to inherit the property, spouse, name, and identity of the maternal uncle (Cunnison 1959). Among urban Lunda such as Chiluba and Chibamba, such entitlements are not strictly obeyed, but the tie is still strong. Chibamba has been known to exploit this link with impunity in his dealings with local politicians and civil servants. His willingness to invoke his powerful uncle in order to get his way earned Chibamba much animosity among the people with whom he is expected to work for the good of the province.

Apart from his arrogant demeanour and patrimonial bent, Chibamba's appointment to Deputy Minister would have generated political tension within the province. Endemic to the political dispensation in Luapula is a traditional rivalry between two socio-linguistic groups, the Lunda of the Luapula river valley – the kin of Chiluba and Chibamba – and the Aushi of the plateau region (Gould 1997).[39] This rivalry has deep historical roots, but its modern antecedent derives from colonial politics. Early in this century, British administrators placed the nominal leader of the Lunda, the *Mwata* Kazembe, at the top of an invented 'traditional' hierarchy of Luapula chiefs. Kazembe became a 'Paramount' chief, whereas the Aushi Chief, Milambo, was subordinated to the second tier of 'Senior' chieftancy. This hierarchical relationship hangs in the background of persistent Aushi complaints about the preferential treatment afforded Lundas in the political realm.

Of late, however, these quasi-ethnic tensions have played a backseat role to personal rivalry. During the period immediately before and after the 1996 elections, the focal point of political gossip in Luapula was a serious schism between the MMD Deputy Minister and the Permanent Secretary (the civil servant who heads the Provincial administration) – who both come from the Lunda area. Friction between the party and the civil service has been common throughout the post-colonial period. Before 1991, the repercussions of conflicts between the party and the civil service were contained by UNIP's political hegemony since a civil servant's leeway to challenge party supremacy was negligible. Under the multi-party system, there has been a subtle shift in the relationship between the political and administrative wings of local government. The UNIP-era litany about 'the Party and its Government' is no longer in use, and the civil service appears to have gained a degree of autonomy. The Deputy Minister is still the nominal head of the Province and speaks for the political leadership of the country, but it is no longer politically correct to invoke party discipline when dealing with senior civil servants. In principle, a Permanent Secretary can belong to any party he or she chooses.

In any event, multi-party politics have created space at the grass roots for more elaborate and more open political manoeuvring against unpopular leaders. As shown above, this can happen within the confines of the electoral process, as for the present case of Mwense. An active farmer/businessman named Joseph Chisakula was by far the most popular MMD politician in Mwense. Chisakula began his campaign under the MMD banner, but was predictably rejected by the MMD NEC in favour of the President's nephew. Chisakula stood as an Independent but, as Table 12.5 shows, failed to challenge the MMD candidate.

Table 12.5: 1996 Parliamentary election returns, Mwense Constituency

Candidate	Party	Votes	Share of valid votes (%)
Chibamba, Norman K.M.	MMD	4,947	60
Chisakula, Joseph K.	IND	1,843	22
Chishimba, Vincent	NP	99	1
Mushinka, Bernard	IND	1,409	17
Musonda, Samuel M.	ZDC	–	0
Total Votes Cast		8,397	100

Source: Zambian Electoral Commission, as published in Zambia Independent Monitoring Team, no date.

[39] I use the term 'socio-linguistic group' in preference to the colonial concept of 'tribe' or the culturalist notion of 'ethnic' group. The local language groups in Luapula – such as the Lunda, Aushi, Kabende and Chishinga – have common origin in the Kongo, speak a mutually-comprehensible language (dialects of ciBemba), share a virtually identical kinship and descent system. The main distinction between the groups is of political identity, a construct of colonial policy. This is not to imply that there are no ethnic divisions within Zambia; see the discussion of Lozi ethnicity by Sichone and Simutanya 1996.

News of Chibamba's decisive victory at the 1996 polls was received sceptically in the province. The fiasco surrounding the presidential results in Chiengi indicated that ballot stuffing was possible in Luapula where the MMD has the wherewithal to manipulate an election result.[40] The CCC reported that in adjacent Nchelenge District, Chibamba 'intimidated civil servants not to vote for an opposition candidate' with threats of discipline (Committee for a Clean Campaign, no date, 56). On the other hand, as the President's homeland, Mwense is a constituency where clientelist pressures to stick with the MMD are very intense. Despite all this, Chisakula and a second independent candidate, a local businessman, Bernard Mushinka, made a serious dent in Chibamba's credibility.

The means of challenging political clientelism are hardly limited to electoral procedures. This is evident from two post-election events that stem directly from the Mwense contest. Each illustrates the changing dynamics of grass roots politics during the era of multi-party politics. The first incident concerns the way that local MMD politicians reacted to the clientelism underlining Deputy Minister Chibamba's political trajectory. The MMD held its first post-election Provincial Conference in Luapula during October 1997, to select provincial MMD officers, including the Provincial Chairman. The representatives of local politicians supported a local MMD activist, Davis Chibombwe, for the chairmanship. During the opening session, the national MMD Vice-President, Brigadier-General G. K. Miyanda, was 'riled' by Mansa MP Kelvin Mwitwa, an Aushi from Mansa, who accused National MMD Secretary Michael Sata of promoting Chibamba's candidacy for the chairmanship. Under the patronage of the MMD national leadership, the conference elected Chibamba to the post of Provincial Chairman. As a result, eight of the Luapula MPs, including three cabinet ministers, boycotted the final session chaired by Michael Sata. Sata was reported to have said: 'This is a serious offence and I will have all those who boycotted my closing ceremony punished for insubordination'.[41] According to the government-owned *Daily Mail*, only 'Health Minister Katele Kalumba, Information Deputy Minister Earnest Mwansa and Luapula Province Deputy Minister Norman Chibamba stayed behind to witness the closing ceremony and announcement of resolutions long after the other MPs had left'. None of these three loyal ministers come from Aushiland. The Aushi MP walkout was a direct affront to the powerful and notoriously vindictive Sata (known affectionately as 'King Cobra'), and an indirect criticism of 'uncle' Chiluba. It could thus be read as a critique of the clientelism exercised by the MMD national leadership *vis-à-vis* local party actors.

The second incident arises out of the aforementioned schism between the Provincial Deputy Minister and the Permanent Secretary (PS). Following Chibamba's selection to the MMD Provincial Chairmanship, the Provincial PS launched a new manoeuvre against the Deputy Minister. An innovative element in the PS's campaign was his use of the Aushi chiefs, thus playing on the Aushi-Lunda/Valley-Plateau rivalries that characterised local political relations. In November 1997, 16 Aushi chiefs met to draft a letter to the President demanding the removal of the Deputy Minister on a number of grounds. In their petition, the chiefs accused Chibamba of the following offences:

1. He has no respect for us as Chiefs of the people in Mansa District.
2. He even wants to put some Chiefs in prison for crimes that are not justified.
3. He is ever in conflict with his colleagues. The situation is very bad and can even retard development in the Province.
4. He has developed a bad habit of separating the Lunda Chiefs in the valley from the Aushi Chiefs in Mansa District.[42]

Two Aushi Chiefs reported that, after drafting their petition, it was 'sent to the Permanent Secretary's office for typing'. Vehicles from the PS's office were seen taking the letter around to various chiefs to collect their signatures.[43]

---

[40] Concerning the Chiengi incident, see footnote 35.
[41] 'Three ministers face axe,' *The Daily Mail* (Zambia), 22 October 1997.
[42] Translated from the c'Aushi by Charles Chambula. I have discussed this incident and the changing political role of the Chiefs in greater detail in Gould 1998.
[43] Interviews with chiefs Milambo and Mabumba, April 1998.

A year after the chiefs' petition Norman Chibamba was transferred from the post of Provincial Deputy Minister back to Lusaka as a deputy minister in one of the line ministries.[44] Chiluba replaced him with another hand-culled 'local' politician, MP Alex Chama from Pambashe constituency.[45] It is not clear whether or not the chiefs' petition had any influence on the President's decision to remove Chibamba from Luapula. Nevertheless, this incident points to a dimension of growing importance for multi-party politics in Zambia: the incursion of new categories of 'charismatic' actors into the politics of the modern state.

The role of the chiefs

Chiefs have always seen themselves as political actors, but an overt intervention of the kind mentioned above in the arena of 'modern' party politics is unprecedented. There is a long history, extending back to colonial Indirect Rule, of co-opting traditional leaders into the political projects of the state (Gould 1997a, chapter 5). During the 1980s, for example, President Kaunda made a point of appointing traditional chiefs to the all-powerful UNIP Central Committee. During this same period, the *Mwata* Kazembe of the Luapula Lunda was made a District Governor, the nominal head of the UNIP apparatus at the District level. By transforming chiefs into politicians, their 'traditional' authority was undermined. In drafting a petition to the President, as described above, local chiefs acted politically according to their own volition. There are various indications that a proliferation of actions of this sort, both by chiefs and by other forms of local authority including religious leaders, will become more common.[46]

This incident suggests that the decline in resources, by which political patrons can feed their clientelist networks, promotes an increased competition for loyalty and support in the local political arena. Enhanced political competition has stimulated the mobilisation of a wide range of local actors, including chiefs who, as we have seen, feel they have a legitimate claim on state authority. The events recounted above also indicate how these same circumstances engender the valourisation of local resources, sometimes in new ways, including quasi-ethnic and 'primordial' clan identities within the arena of modern politics (cf. Young 1994). The analysis here suggests that under some circumstances, these new actors, alliances and resources *may* be wielded *against* the kind of clientelism that maintains an authoritarian and patrimonial state apparatus.

Tragic events in the Great Lakes region of central Africa have highlighted the role of the ethnic factor in politics. One should be clear about the fact that the 'ethnicity' invoked in the Luapula context has nothing to do with the constructed identities that have run amok in the Great Lakes region.[47] That such micro-regionalist distinctions can come into play so explicitly in local Zambian politics is an indication of the unanchored, transitory nature of existing political structures. The real issue is not a rise in 'ethnic' tensions, but the fact that the earlier political structures of the UNIP party-state have found no institutional replacement. This lack of a framework for organising grass roots rural politics has created space for new alliances and new forms of political

---

[44]'Chiluba reshuffles deputy ministers,' *The Post* 18 January 1999.

[45]The Chama family hails from the Chishinga socio-linguistic group who live on the plateau region of Luapula province, but are allied with neither the Lunda nor the Aushi. Chama's appointment to the post of Provincial Deputy Minister may thus represent an attempt to defuse the Lunda-Aushi rivalry.

[46]Two trends support this view. One is the growing incidence of demands to review the chiefly hierarchies instated under the colonial administration. I have documented one such dispute in Mansa District between chiefs Milambo and Mabumba over the Aushi senior chieftaincy', see Gould 1998. A similar case has arisen in Northwestern Province over the provincial 'paramountcy', which has taken the form of a dispute between Luvale and Lunda chiefs. See 'Likumba lya Mize ceremony', *The Post*, No. 1068, 25 September 1998.

A second indication of the growing political ambitions of Zambian chiefs emerged in a national workshop for Zambian Traditional Rulers organised by Zambia Independent Monitoring Team, Konrad Adenauer Foundation, Royal Foundation of Zambia and the Ministry of Local Government and Housing, 26–29 June, 1997 in Kabwe. Via the resolutions approved by the workshop, the 50 participating chiefs demanded, among other things, that a House of Chiefs be instated as an 'Upper Legislative Chamber' of the nation. See Zambia Independent Monitoring Team and Konrad Adenauer Foundation 1997, 43.

[47]For a subtle analysis of 'constructed ethnicity' as a political strategy, see Philip Gourevitch's insightful account of the Rwanda genocide (Gourevitch 1998).

manoeuvring. The permeation of the institutional vacuum by an ethic of multi-party competition has opened up inroads for an explosion of various 'politics of identity' in the local arena, including the quasi-ethnic factors cited here.

Van Binsbergen is of the view that chiefs are enemies of patrimonial clientelism. This position is grounded in the view that traditional authority represents a form of democracy that is better suited to the cultural conditions of Africa than is the 'North Atlantic model of formal democracy' which is 'disguised as universal' in the mainstream literature. (Van Binsbergen 1995, 5.) A diametrically opposed view can be found in the work of Mahmood Mamdani who characterises traditional authority in Southern Africa as despotic fiefdoms.[48]

In Zambia, chiefs do personify a notion of local and autonomous community that seems to be gaining currency as neo-liberal policies undermine the material foundations of the post-colonial state. The case of Norman Chibamba testifies to the currency of a notion of accountability among the chiefs which is hostile to the patrimonial politics of the deputy minister. This does not imply that chiefs are automatically the allies of representative democracy. Chiefs are not elected leaders; their authority is grounded in claims to esoteric knowledge and supernatural powers (see Geschiere 1996). Yet they do lay indisputable claim to a spiritual legitimacy, grounded in what van Binsbergen terms 'cosmological' factors – the reverence of ancestors, communion with the spirit world – that has currency in all walks of Zambian society. The entry of chiefs – together with other charismatic leaders[49] – into the political arena can unleash an unpredictable element into the means via which leaders and citizens negotiate what constitutes legitimate authority.

Yet, it would be a mistake to view the mobilisation of traditional authorities, as shown here, as a simple resurgence of primordial powers. What the above narratives provide is a glimpse of a *re*configuration of the arena, that is still in process. The role that any given category of actor has in the consolidation or slippage of Zambian democracy depends on the modalities of the emerging configuration of political forces. The 'threat' that traditional authority poses to democracy in Zambia is not of 'ethnic' conflict. Rather, local politicians can easily incite chiefs to invoke their own undemocratic means of political influence. Either way, the political process is made less transparent and governmental structures become less accountable to citizens.

Conclusions

Two fallacies distort much of the literature about the experiences of multi-party politics in Zambia. According to one view, that espoused by MMD apologists, the practice of politics in Zambia underwent a qualitative transformation on 31 October 1991, the day of Zambia's first multi-party election in 23 years (see Chanda ed., no date). 'Democracy', it is claimed, represented by MMD, vanquished the 'totalitarianism' of UNIP. The second fallacy is the inverse of the first. As espoused by Chiluba's most acidic critics, this view is that nothing of note has changed with the reintroduction of multi-party politics.[50] Much of what has been written about the first five years of the Third Republic has fallen into one of these two perspectives. This chapter contests both views.

The presidentialist patrimonialism that has characterised state governance is the most obvious element of continuity between the Second and Third Republics. One of the ironies of the controversies surrounding the 1996 elections was the thinness of the critique of MMD patrimonialism in the economic realm. For months prior to the elections, civic energies were consumed in the debate about political and procedural issues. As a result, the behaviour of government ministers over the extensive privatisation exercise was pushed into the margins of the public debate. Perhaps this is one explanation for the MMD's penchant for political provocation in the run-up to the elections. It would seem in retrospect that the debate about the rules of the game, centring as they did on the boundaries and status of 'the public,' would have profited from a stronger emphasis on patrimonial economics.

---

[48]Mamdani 1996. See also Neocosmos in this volume.

[49]On the national level, televangelist Nevers Mumba's bid for a political role represents another precedent: the emergence of a religious personality into the politics of the modern state.

[50]For example, Chabal and Daloz (1999) take a view akin to this.

Understood more generally as a conflation of public and private interests, patrimonial privilege has shown itself more clearly via the government's unilateral manipulation of the Constitution. Accounts of colonial elections in Northern Rhodesia have also stressed the importance of constitutional law in the control of electoral procedure. The struggle by which Africans gradually wrested representational rights in the Northern Rhodesian Legislative Council revolved around the procedural issues of eligibility for office and franchise (see, for example, Mulford 1964, 183–188). This continues to be the case, and the terms of citizenship remain a political hot potato. This is largely because of the third generation clause of the 1996 Constitution, which has spawned the proliferation of hyphenated Zambians, such as Malawian-Zambians, Tanzanian-Zambians, Zimbabwean-Zambians, Zaïrean-Zambians (see Lumbwe 1997). That a politically, and constitutionally, condoned political exclusivity has raised its hoary head in Zambian politics runs counter to the post-independence political culture that was grounded in the motif of 'One Zambia, One Nation', and signals a disturbing rupture in the nation's political milieu.

The struggle over the rules of the game revolved around issues of legislative interpretation. It has become commonplace, especially in the independent media, to bemoan the ineffectuality of the under-resourced and over-controlled Zambian judiciary. While the court system certainly suffers from a lack of independence as well as of funds, it is also true that its political weight has become grossly inflated in the Third Republic. In *principle,* the judiciary constitutes a major check on the contravention of democratic procedure. With political pluralism enshrined in the Constitution, political minorities have the right to petition the court to overturn majority decisions they could not influence in the legislature. In *practice*, the judiciary is composed of political appointees who are obliged to resolve political disputes between competing parties. Such a practice underscores the alienation of the political process from the citizenry. As judiciary processes become increasingly politicised, and as political outcomes are increasingly battled out in the courtroom, politics has become dominated by an élite specialisation of political lawyers. The voter is left feeling redundant and politically impotent.

These trends suggest the gradual movement of Zambia towards a society of greater social divisiveness, polarity and ingrained social tension. This *rupture* with the past is a predictable outcome of the greater individual freedoms implied by political and economic liberalisation. It is evident that individual Zambians have more freedom today than they did in the 1980s. One expression of this freedom is the mobilisation of new alliances at the political grass roots discussed above. It is a primary concern of the political élite to contain the expanded freedoms of the citizenry, and to do so in a way that promotes élite interests. If one accepts the hypothesis that the clientelist structures of the past have begun to unravel, the question arises of the forms of political domination and integration that can supersede prevailing patron-client networks.

Following Nicos Mouzelis, one might chart two paths out of clientelism: one towards populism and another toward more legal-rational (bureaucratic) forms of political domination. The populist option, which Mouzelis sees as fully compatible with patrimonial domination, seeks to substitute horizontal linkages based on common local interests for the vertical asymmetries of patron-client relationships. The legal-rational path substitutes the protection of formal political regulation – that is, the rule of law – for the security of political patronage. In relying on electoral accountability and legal rationality, the bureaucratic path is more likely to undermine than to support patrimonial practices.

Zambian politics would seem more likely to pursue a populist path. The strategy of the National Lima Party, for example, was clearly to exploit the dissatisfaction of smallholder farmers towards rural market liberalisation in order to build a power base grounded in peasant communities. The reformation of the NLP was thus of a classical populist bent. It seems evident that this political strategy was informed by an attempt to deconstruct the vertical clientelist networks by which rural Zambians were integrated into the patrimonial state, and replace them with localised horizontal links based on common (agrarian) interests.[51] That the NLP failed at the polls in 1996 does not mean that the strategy itself was misconceived. The NLP entered the electoral race at a very late date and its leadership, headed by a former MMD minister, may not have

---

[51]On the distinction between populist and clientelist integration in the state see Mouzelis 1985.

evoked the fullest confidence of the rural masses. One can expect a great deal more in the way of explicitly populist platforms to emerge at the 2001 elections. The 'charismatic' alternative offered, for example, by televangelist Nevers Mumba falls clearly within this purview. A scenario consistent with the consolidation of democracy in Zambia depends on how, and if, local dissatisfaction with clientelism links up with the criticisms of patrimonial rule.

F.G. Bailey, the anthropologist of the 'political game', points to the critical role of the referee in mediating complex political conflicts (Bailey 1969, 32). It is noteworthy that the emerging network of political referees in the Zambian context, the self-styled independent monitoring bodies, has rallied around a legal-rational template. This approach has permeated the interaction of the monitors with grass roots groups, with whom they deal in the context of 'civic education'. The same pertains to their relations with the political élite, based on a dialogue about the 'international standards' of democratic process.

The monitoring organisations' campaign to maintain formal regulations for the electoral process under the rubric of international standards might be seen as an attempt to contain the excesses of political freedom within a 'rationalising' structure. Electoral standards, encompassing an Electoral Commission, an official voter register, the systematic zoning of polling districts, and procedures to legally petition for a redress of grievances represent the application of a formal bureaucratic logic to ensure that too much freedom does not threaten the fabric of the social order. Pluralisation has decontrolled some aspects of the political system; politicians can be challenged in the media, in the courts and at the polls. At the same time, pluralisation has expanded the scope of competition over the control of public institutions and resources of actors, such as chiefs, who used to be marginal to the political realm.

Multi-party politics have engendered two disparate forces for change in contemporary Zambia. On the one hand, a section of the intelligentsia appears committed to combating patrimonial misbehaviour through the rationalisation of politics. On the other hand, a populist coalition of grass roots politicians and their local allies struggles against clientelist domination and the integration of their horizontal alliances into patrimonial state structures. Each force confronts different aspects of the same adversary – a self-serving national leadership that resorts to increasingly autocratic measures to maintain the crumbling clientelist structures via which it legitimises its monopoly control over public resources. This explanation offers a basis to understand the contests each of the reformist groups lost under the auspices of the 1996 elections, and why their separate struggles failed to link up in a concerted challenge to MMD hegemony.

The 1996 elections cannot be considered fair, nor did they mark the further consolidation of democracy in Zambia. Still, the formal quality of the electoral procedure may not be the full measure of democratisation. In the long run, subtle changes in the culture of politics at the grass roots may be more important than a model performance at one election. The main point of this piece is that, despite the inadequacies of the registration process, ballot manipulation, and the difficulties that opposition and independent candidates had in getting their message out to the electorate, voters quite clearly vented their dissatisfaction with the politics of patrimonial patronage. It would seem that a significant proportion of the Zambian people has taken the promise of democratic representation seriously. Even if the MMD is no longer its primary vehicle, the spirit of 1991 is far from dead.

13

When Elections are Just a Formality
Rural-Urban Dynamics in the Dominant-Party System of Zimbabwe

LIISA LAAKSO

Before the 1995 elections, the *Zimbabwe News*, an official organ of the ruling party Zimbabwe African National Union (Patriotic Front), ZANU(PF), stated in its editorial that '[t]he holding of the elections is a Constitutional necessity but in reality it is just a formality under the present political realities'.[1] Indeed, although Zimbabwe is one of the very few African states that has had a continuous multi-party system since majority rule in 1980, elections there did not threaten the position of the ruling party, until the hotly contested elections of June 2000, but rather confirmed its power in a ritualistic manner.

Elections that are 'just a formality' can either imply obedient support of the ruling party or, alternatively, electoral apathy signifying the lack of real choice. Yet, the post-Cold War wave of popular struggles for political freedom all over the world suggests that such a situation can hardly be taken at face value anywhere. For the ruling party to retain power the mere *possibility* of electoral competition inherent in a multi-party system requires careful and consistent management of the election process throughout its different phases. As much as multi-party elections can be made meaningful, they can also be made meaningless. Thus elections were made 'just a formality' by institutional design, manipulation of the registration process, gerrymandering of the constituency boundaries, government control over the media and by different levels of state coercion. By the same token, elections are an important means to legitimise government power. In this respect the need to represent the electoral process as 'free and fair' is still evident.

However, in order to understand the organisation and the use of state power, one needs to go beyond elections as such. In the case of Zimbabwe, it is the one-party ideology that looms large. As an anecdote, one can quote the then Prime Minister Robert Mugabe's appeal to ZANU's party officials in 1982 to recruit all the people of Zimbabwe, including the members of the Zimbabwe African People's Union (ZAPU), to his party. Mugabe said: 'When all people carried party cards, the present national registration cards would be abolished, because they would serve no purpose. It would also be easier to identify the enemy'.[2] If the constitution of Zimbabwe is a formality for the ruling party, so is citizenship. In its ideal form, being Zimbabwean means being ZANU, and citizenship as an idea that empowers individuals with a range of political and civil rights is replaced by one which arises from membership and loyalty towards one political organisation and, above all, one leader. By the same token, the mere existence of other political organisations would mean that there are still 'enemies' of the people inside Zimbabwe.

It is easy to interpret this kind of thinking as a legacy of the liberation war and the 'commandist' nature of mobilisation it involved (Sithole 1988, 248). This, however, is not the whole story. The country-wide organisation of the ruling party did not occur until after independence and its tasks have been very different from those of a liberation movement.[3] Of course,

---

[1] *Zimbabwe News* 26 (6) 1995, 2
[2] *The Herald* 25 January 1982
[3] The constitution of ZANU vesting extensive powers in its president was accepted by the Congress of the party in August 1984.

the rhetoric emphasising unity and a common struggle made strategic sense as long as South Africa was under minority rule, but this is no longer the case.

As will be shown below, the dominant-party system in contemporary Zimbabwe can also be approached by recognising the fact that already in Southern Rhodesia the representative institutions of the state did not stem from a need to incorporate all citizens who were franchised (i.e. the Europeans) into the decision-making procedures by providing them with a public forum to express and solve their political disputes. As a matter of fact, the more coercive the state's response to the intensified nationalist demands and struggle, the more important it was to present the white minority as politically united.

The argument presented here is that to the same extent that state power in Zimbabwe leans on inherited state institutions, the dominant-party system also represents a continuity from the Rhodesian era. This is not to deny the significance of the rupture brought about by internationally recognised independence of the state and by the ideological and pragmatic decisions constituting rules of the new regime, but it is to note that the instruments that were chosen were largely those inherited from minority rule.

One-party rule in Southern Rhodesia

The first elections for a partially elected Legislative Council in Rhodesia were held in 1899, when Southern Rhodesia was governed by the British South Africa Company (BSAC) with a Resident Commissioner appointed by the British government. The elections marked a first step towards the establishment of responsible self-government for the few thousand European immigrants in the country. Soon the BSAC realised that its expectations of substantial profits from Rhodesia were unrealistic. Therefore, the settlers' responsibility for the government there had to be developed further. In 1907, the number of elected members in the Legislative Council was increased so that for the first time the settlers formed a majority.

The same year Rhodesia saw the emergence of its first, although loose, political organisations, the Rhodesian Constitutional League, promoting representative government under the crown, and the Mashonaland Progressive Association which supported the continuation of company rule. Yet, the general interest in elections was not very impressive. Only 10 candidates stood for the 7 seats and it was not until 1914 that the constitutional future of the country became a political issue. Only one of the 12 elected MPs was not supporting the BSAC rule for the time being. However, by the end of the First World War, the elected members decided that the time was ripe for the establishment of a responsible government. According to Colin Leys, it was this development that led to the formation of the first real political parties propagating their cause in an organised manner. The parties were the Responsible Government Association and the Rhodesia Union Association, which preferred either company rule or, more realistically, incorporation into the Union of South Africa (Leys 1959, 131, 132). The 1920 elections were contested by these two parties. A great majority, 11 of the 13 elected members, were for responsible government. The Unionist Association did not win a single seat. In addition to low electoral competition, the voters' participation remained relatively low: it varied from less than 40 to just over 50 per cent of the registered voters (see Nuscheler 1978, 1670, 1674).

In 1922, a referendum was held on whether company administration should be terminated and the territory incorporated into the Union of South Africa or whether the colony should be accorded a responsible government. The latter option won and Southern Rhodesia was accorded full self-government within the British Empire. Although there were more than 20 parties recorded, Leys' analysis (Leys 1959) shows how Rhodesia was a one-party system. From 1923, the ruling party was the Rhodesian Party, which was a direct successor of the Responsible Government Association. In 1933, it was defeated by the Reform Party. However, a large number of the Reform Party MPs came from the Rhodesian Party and, immediately after its electoral victory, it merged with the Rhodesian Party under the name of the United Party (UP).

In 1953, Southern Rhodesia joined the Central African Federation with Northern Rhodesia and Nyasaland. The Federation was approved in a referendum with an impressive 82 per cent turnout of the almost 50,000 registered voters, including the statistically insignificant 429 African voters (Nuscheler 1978, 1671; Bowman 1973, 20). The Federation was dominated by UP, which changed its name to the United Federal Party (UFP) and ruled until 1962 when it was decimated at the polls by the Rhodesian Front (RF). RF's political asset was to reject UFP's political reform programme leading to majority rule in 15 years – a reform programme that, one can note today, would have been very realistic. RF also recognised that the government was not able to halt independence in the two other parts of the Federation and that this alone jeopardised white rule in Southern Rhodesia (Bowman 1973, 34–36).

Thus the elections in 1962 marked a change in the ruling party, but even then a system where the opposition would have had a balancing role did not emerge. On the contrary, the RF created the strongest party machinery ever known in the country. Because RF's base was the almost complete consensus among the Europeans on the necessity to defy domestic and international pressures for change, the opposition had virtually no chances to challenge it. Leys' analysis of the one-party character of the Rhodesian political system became even more appropriate after the 1965 Unilateral Declaration of Independence (UDI) of the RF regime.

The Constitution accepted in 1961 expanded for the first time the right to vote to a few thousand Africans, but this was done by registering voters on A and B rolls according to income and property. In practice, the number of Africans in the more powerful A roll remained marginal (Palley 1966, 413–24). The next Constitution in 1969 introduced a Senate and increased the number of African representatives in the newly named House of Assembly. Half of the African seats were reserved for the chiefs and the number of elected African MPs was only eight. This figure was to remain fixed until Africans were paying at least 24 per cent of the state revenue raised by direct income tax. After that threshold, African representation could have increased to a maximum of one-half of the parliamentary seats. In 1968, the African population as a whole paid slightly more than 0.2 per cent of the income tax raised. In practice, therefore, Africans had no possibility of increasing their representation in parliament.

In an attempt to end the intensifying liberation war in the country, the government increased African representation to a majority in parliament by the new Constitution of Zimbabwe-Rhodesia, which was agreed upon with moderate African leaders in 1978. This constitution reserved only 28 seats for whites in the 100-seat House of Assembly but ensured that they could veto any constitutional changes. Of the 30 members in the Senate, 10 were elected by the white members of the House of Assembly, 10 by the other 72 members and 10 were African chiefs elected by the Council of Chiefs. Of the white representatives, 20 were elected on a preferential voting system and the remaining 8 representatives on an indirect system, in which the electorate was formed by the 92 directly elected MPs, and 16 candidates were nominated by the white MPs of the previous House of Assembly. After 10 years, or after the second parliament, a special commission was to be nominated to discuss whether to retain these 28 white seats. As Masipula Sithole has noted, the system 'was made deliberately complex' (Sithole 1986, 77).

The Zimbabwe-Rhodesia Constitution also provided a coalition government of national unity so that all parties with at least 5 seats would be represented in the cabinet according to the number of seats they won in the elections. Most importantly, the Constitution introduced a complicated system of commissions to ensure white control over all important appointments in the administration, the judiciary, police and army. Therefore, an African prime minister had only minimal executive power (Hatchard 1993, 13, 14). Nevertheless, the fact that 72 seats were reserved for the Africans and that the collaborating African leaders and their political organisations participated in the elections brought a new 'government party' to the country, that of Bishop Muzorewa's United African National Council (UANC) with 51 seats. A split-off from the liberation movement, Sithole's ZANU, was able to win 12 seats, and a third African party, the United National Federal Party, won 9 seats. In spite of the boycott campaigns of ZANU and ZAPU, the turnout was estimated to have been 60 per cent of eligible African voters (Freedom House 1980, 12). In the white elections, RF won all the 28 seats, with 18 of its candidates being returned unopposed in direct elections.

The Independence Constitution of Zimbabwe that finally ended the war was agreed on at the Lancaster House peace negotiations. It guaranteed 20 of the 100-seat House of Assembly for the whites for at least seven years. The following elections in 1980 again confirmed RF's dominance among the Europeans. It won all 6 contested white seats while as many as 14 of its candidates were returned unopposed. The next and last elections held separately for whites in Zimbabwe in 1985 took place after RF had been renamed the Conservative Alliance of Zimbabwe (CAZ) and more than half of its MPs had split from it and formed the Independent Zimbabwe Group (IZG). In spite of a historical situation in which all the seats were contested, the white elections of 1985 were without any real substance. To the surprise of many, not least Prime Minister Mugabe, CAZ won 15 seats. But for many white voters the only difference between IZG and CAZ was in the style by which white interests were to be safeguarded. Smith's sceptical opinion that his opponents were 'opportunists' was probably widely shared. As noted by Masipula Sithole, many had voted for Smith all their lives and not voting for him in the last white elections would have appeared as a betrayal of past loyalty. An elderly white lady explained to Sithole: 'I have always voted for Mr Ian Smith... He tried his best. God knows he tried... I know he is now finished. Anyway, it's the last time the Europeans are going to vote, I don't think we should forsake good old Smithy. I rather vote for one I have always voted for' (Sithole 1986, 91). Only two years later the white seats were abolished and the history of white parties in the country was over.

The most striking feature of electoral politics in Southern Rhodesia was the restriction of the effective franchise to the Europeans, unmistakably manifest in the complicated constitutional manoeuvring in order to halt the nationalists' cause. But in addition to this, two other phenomena were also important in Rhodesian elections. First, the relationship between the Europeans and the state gave only limited impetus to the formation of interest-based political parties even though – or precisely because – the most important economic interest groups were able to collaborate with the government directly in its sectoral policy on agriculture, trade, industry, commerce and mining (see Skålnes 1995, 46–53, 60–69). Furthermore, the Labour Party did not find an established role in Rhodesian politics, although during the 1930s it was the major challenger of the ruling party and in 1939 held nearly one-third of the seats in the Parliament. According to Colin Leys,

> The chief reason why the Rhodesian Labour Party was eliminated was that it did not represent a permanent political interest... To exclude Africans from membership of the party was to exclude most of the country's labour force, and a section of it for whom socialism (as distinguished from controlled capitalism) would be likely to have more appeal than it had for skilled and semi-skilled European workers whose fear of African competition was quite as strong as their hostility towards capitalists (Leys 1959, 188, 189).

This single factor made the elections in Rhodesia very different from contemporary elections in industrial Western multi-party or two-party systems, Britain included.

Another characteristic was a relatively low voter turnout, the only exceptions being the referenda on the status of the state. Although apathy as such was and is not exceptional in representative democracies, its functionality was. In contrast to the United States for instance, where voters' apathy has been explained as a moderating factor halting extreme politicisation and fanaticism, the same can hardly be said of Ian Smith's Rhodesia. In Southern Rhodesia, voters' apathy was only one aspect of a representative system that played almost no role with regard to the actual political conflicts in the country.

The transition to majority rule has meant that the electorate in contemporary Zimbabwe consists of a far more heterogeneous group than it did in Southern Rhodesia. Although, in Southern Rhodesia, different white interest groups and the conflicts and compromises between these interests were politically significant (Skålnes 1995, 38–45), they seldom affected the electoral competition. In Zimbabwe, different connections between different groups and the state are more likely to be transmitted to electoral politics. In terms of the electorate's voting power, the most obvious divide in Zimbabwe is that between the rural and urban populations. The differences between voting in towns and in the countryside are put into a detailed analysis below. While this implies recognising the fact that elections in Africa, as elsewhere in the world, are about the use and legitimation of state power, it is also to recognise that this power is contested by different interests and rationalities.

Rural and urban voting in Zimbabwe

Majority rule extended effective franchise to about 3 million people. Even when excluding the rather minuscule group of the 100,000 whites who decided to stay in the country, an electorate of this size can hardly be politically monolithic. Hundreds of thousands of African voters could be divided into different political groups mainly according to their regional background. Much has been written about the political divide between the Ndebele and the Shona as well as the Zezuru, Manyika and Karanga subgroups in the latter, and indeed it is difficult to understand politics in Zimbabwe without understanding these divides.[4] Yet the mere recognition of them, like the fact that in 1980 and 1985 the Ndebele voted for Joshua Nkomo and ZAPU and the Shona voted for Robert Mugabe and ZANU, does not imply that voters in Matabeleland would have been different from voters in Mashonaland. Neither does the mere existence of these divides explain why the internal factionalism in the ruling party in 1995 seemed to go along the Zezuru-Karanga-Manyanka divides and affected even the allocation of seats in parliament to the areas dominated by these groups, while the Ndebele-Shona divide probably played no role as far as the delimitation of the constituencies was concerned. The dilemma that ethnic politics poses for any attempt to understand it, is precisely this. If voters vote according to their ethnic identities, they do so because they are similar not because they are different, and explaining ethnic voting by politicised ethnicity explains very little. It is much more critical to firstly understand the actual mobilisation of voters behind these identities and secondly the character of the state power which makes the political competition a zero-sum game so that one-time allies can easily become enemies.

Independence elections of 1980

The elections preceding Zimbabwe's independence were organised by the Rhodesian administration, supervised by the British Governor and monitored by international observers. Although the two liberation movements ZANU and ZAPU had united as the Patriotic Front before the Lancaster House peace negotiations, ZANU decided to contest the independence elections in 1980 alone, apparently in order to solve the question of the country's leadership (see Mnangagwa 1989, 227). All the parties that participated in the elections had strong expectations about the outcome. ZANU's Mugabe, ZAPU's Nkomo and UANC's Muzorewa were all probably quite certain that they could win in free and fair elections, while Smith probably expected that the elections would bring an anti-Mugabe coalition to power, which for him must have appeared a far better solution than losing the war to the Zimbabwe African National Liberation Army (ZANLA), the military wing of ZANU.

To the surprise of many, ZANU won as much as 63 per cent of the votes and 57 seats out of the 80 seats reserved for the Africans, while ZAPU under the name the Patriotic Front (PF) won 24 per cent of the votes and 20 seats. Only three seats went to UANC with 8 per cent support. As expected, ZAPU's stronghold was Matabeleland and it was able to win half of the seats in the Midlands as well. Due to the proportional system[5] it was able to win one seat in Mashonaland, just as ZANU won one seat in Matabeleland North. The decision to count the votes only at the provincial level meant that no information was available on how people voted at the district level. This was intended to safeguard the secrecy of voting. For the same reason, it is not possible to analyse the results according to the urban-rural divide exacerbated by the fact that the big cities, Harare-Chitungwiza area and Bulawayo, were not regarded as separate provinces but included in Mashonaland East and Matabeleland North respectively. On the other hand, both of these provinces showed more political pluralism than the provinces on average. In Matabeleland North, 1 out of 10 seats was won by ZANU; in Mashonaland East, 2 out of 16 seats were won by the UANC.

---

[4]In very general terms and with regard to the rural population that constitutes the overwhelming majority, it can be said that Midlands and Masvingo are the regions of the Karanga ethnic group; Mashonaland is the region of the Zezuru; Manicaland is the region of the Manyika; and Matabeleland is the region of the Ndebele. But even these ethnic groups can be divided into subgroups and even the rural population is often mixed (see Sithole 1988, 222, 223). Definitions of ethnic identities in Zimbabwe as elsewhere in the world seem to be fluid and the object of more or less arbitrary divisions.

[5]Since there was no electoral roll for the African majority, the number of seats in each of the eight provinces, which served as electoral districts, was determined by the estimated number of voters in the province. Thus, the elections were held according to a party list and a proportional system instead of a majoritarian system. The number of seats each party won was to be determined by its share of votes obtained in the whole province.

It is possible to approach the rural-urban difference from another angle, that of intimidation during elections. To a large extent this was about making people believe that their vote was not secret. An old man illustrated this point when he replied to a question on whether he thought the vote would be secret: 'I do not want to die' (New Zealand Election Observation Group 1980, 11). While the secrecy of voting was an issue which was frequently stressed by the authorities, voters in the urban areas generally believed that the ballot was secret, whereas this was not the case in the rural areas (Election Commissioner 1980, 5).

Although intimidation was not restricted to any particular party alone, the British governor concluded that ZANLA activities were the main constraint against peaceful electoral campaigning. He published a map indicating information about intimidation that he had received especially from the Tribal Trustlands[6] in Mashonaland Central, Mashonaland East, Manicaland, Victoria (nowadays Masvingo) and the Midlands. But according to observers, intimidation was also common elsewhere (Commonwealth 1980, 38). There was evidence that thousands of fighters from the Zimbabwe People's Revolutionary Army (ZIPRA), the military wing of ZAPU, campaigned for their party in the Tribal Trustlands outside the assembly points (Freedom House 1980, 6, 7; New Zealand Election Observation Group 1980, 5).[7] Furthermore, a list of inter-faction incidents reported to the police during the campaign period showed that ZIPRA was at least as 'active' in Matabeleland as ZANLA was in Mashonaland (Commonwealth 1980, Annex 27). Although the observers noted that the pressure upon voters extended also into urban areas (Freedom House 1980, 15), most of the intimidation took place in rural areas.

In terms of 'ethnic voting', it is interesting to note that rural areas where people were committed to more than one party, as in Manicaland, Victoria Province and part of the Midlands, and where both liberation parties had a presence, were the areas of the most serious intimidation (Election Commissioner 1980, 18). While much of the intimidation can be regarded as more or less neutral in terms of the final results,[8] according to the observers intimidation influenced the results in Victoria Province (particularly in Gutu district), in Manicaland and in some Tribal Trustlands in the Midlands province (Gregory 1980, 10; Freedom House 1980). Intimidation also partly explained the high turnout. The Election Commissioner noted that in the areas of most intimidation

[t]he massive turnout ... was largely achieved by aggressive 'herding' of voters by party supporters, who escorted voters to the polls, patrolling up and down or insinuating themselves into the queues to ensure support for their party by sounds and gestures backed by threats. Many voters were frightened into voting by threats of death and the aged, infirm and pregnant were denied the opportunity to abstain. Many voters by-passed nearer polling stations in obedience to party instructions, to swamp other polling stations more distant where no doubt their party discipline and control was more rigid. Some voters were so anxious to demonstrate their obedience that they declared orally or by display of their ballot papers (e.g. to be visible at a window in the polling station) that they had voted as instructed. Voting in these areas took place in an atmosphere of fear and under evident compulsion. (Election Commissioner 1980, 18, 19)

About 2.6 million valid votes were cast. Supposing the voter turnout had been 60 per cent in 1979, it had increased to about 90 per cent in 1980. When compared to the 1979 elections, in

---

[6]Tribal Trustlands were after independence renamed Communal Areas. Historically these are the 'reserves' of the Africans who by the Land Apportionment Act of 1930 were denied the right to occupy the best farming land in the country. See for instance Amin 1995.

[7]In addition the British governor's decision to use the Rhodesian Security Forces, including the pro-Muzorewa Auxiliaries to maintain law and order, violated the Lancaster House Agreement, which stated that 'the task of maintaining law and order in the transition period will be the responsibility of the civil police'. See New Zealand Election Observation Group 1980. UANC and ZANU (Sithole) had formed the Auxiliaries after the internal settlement in 1978 as political armies with minimal training to fight 'terrorists' with 'terrorist' tactics. The Auxiliaries, were subsequently affiliated to the regular Security Forces. For many of them the prospect of a ZAPU or ZANU government was tantamount to their punishment.

[8]For instance if the activities of the Auxiliaries made any difference it was only harmful to the support of Muzorewa.

Matabeleland South and North and in Victoria increases in the number of voters were quite impressive, whereas Mashonaland Central and West were areas with no significant changes (see Election Commissioner 1980, 11). While all the parties in these elections campaigned for a high turnout, this had not been the case in 1979, when the liberation movements urged people to boycott the whole exercise. It seems that ZAPU in particular had been successful in demobilising its supporters in 1979.

The guerrilla war had been most effective in the rural areas. The majority of the people were peasants and most of them lived in the eastern ZANLA parts of the country. They regarded Mugabe as a leader who had already proved he could stop the war. As noted by Masipula Sithole, '[t]he people were left without any doubt that peace meant a ZANU(PF) victory' (Sithole 1986, 84). By voting for ZANU the majority of Zimbabweans voted for peace.

Elections in 1985 and the war in Matabeleland

The honeymoon between ZANU and ZAPU did not last very long, and government repression of ZAPU activists and supporters became extensive. In the context of the Southern African regional conflict and a hostile apartheid regime in South Africa, the government regarded itself as justified in keeping the emergency powers in force and the antagonism between the two parties escalated into a war in Matabeleland. Thousands of civilians suffered from atrocities conducted on the one hand by the so-called dissidents and on the other hand by the government security forces. In 1983, Mugabe sent a Fifth Brigade to Matabeleland, composed of ex-ZANLA combatants, who were trained by North Korean military advisers. According to the Africa Watch, 'often they [the Fifth Brigade] visited villages with lists of ZAPU officials and sympathisers, who were singled out and killed. They made little attempt to engage the "dissident" militarily' (Africa Watch 1989, 16).

It has been claimed that the war was just one occasion that showed the extent to which the government had inherited the coercive apparatus of the Rhodesian state.[9] Indeed, it was only in 1997 that a comprehensive study of the human rights violations between 1980 and 1988 was published (Catholic Commission for Justice and Peace in Zimbabwe 1997), although information and critical voices already existed at the time these atrocities were perpetrated.[10] It was only after the death of Joshua Nkomo in July 1999 that the government announced that it would compensate those who suffered during the atrocities. ZANU campaign material claimed that ZAPU was disloyal and divisive and that therefore voting for it was tantamount to making war. Already in 1982, Mugabe had argued that 'dissident activities stemming from ZAPU' had seriously eroded the popularity of ZAPU in Matabeleland. Mugabe predicted that in 1985 the party would get less than 50 per cent of the votes it received in the first elections.[11] ZANU would be the people's choice for peace, he claimed. In addition to this, the ZANU campaign concentrated on the achievements of the party during the first years of independence. In the urban areas, minimum wage and workers' protection legislation were claimed as such achievements. Although the decline in real earnings in the urban areas had already started in 1982 due to the freeze on wages and the reduction of food subsidies imposed by the IMF stabilisation programme (see Amin 1992), the ruling party could still present itself as the protector of the workers' interests.

In the countryside, various development programmes were regarded as a political asset 'to a party unashamed of reciting its success and promising more in the next five years' (Sithole 1986, 91). Interestingly enough, ZAPU refrained from accusing the ruling party of not implementing development programmes in 'its regions' in Matabeleland. But Anthony Lemon has pointed out:

> Although Matabeleland may have received its fair share of development expenditure in proportion to the population, this was not the popular perception, in part because low population densities make infrastructure relatively more expensive and such a dry region needs more dams and boreholes (Lemon 1988, 15).

---

[9]Ronald Weitzer (1990) has shown that there was little difference in the way that Zimbabwe handled the insurgency in Matabeleland during the 1980s and the way that the Rhodesian security forces handled the liberation struggle during the 1970s.

[10]The first report on security force atrocities was published by the Catholic Commission for Justice and Peace in Zimbabwe (CCJP) during April 1983.

[11]*The Herald* 1 September 1982.

In any case, the government had punished the dissident-affected areas during 1983 by deliberately withholding drought relief food, thus indicating to the electorate the power which ZANU possessed. In this respect, it was only logical that ZAPU was reluctant to raise the whole issue of uneven development during its election campaign. Speaking about the possibility that areas supporting it had been punished by not being developed as much as the rest of the country would only have been an asset to the ruling party. ZAPU was not likely to be able to replace the ruling party. Thus, it hardly wanted to remind its supporters of the potentially negative consequences of voting for it.

As will be shown below, questions of the political independence of the institutional framework administering elections became pertinent in the 1990 and 1995 elections. It is useful to look at these institutions firstly with regard to the 1985 elections, as these were the first elections organised by the independent Zimbabwe and were preceded by a massive voters' registration exercise in order to apply the majoritarian first-past-the-post system. The first Delimitation Commission had already been convened in June 1981 and voters' registration started, also in good time, in May 1982. The chairs of the bodies overseeing the conduct of elections, the Election Directorate and the Electoral Supervisory Commission (ESC), were appointed by President Canaan Banana, who, according to the Lancaster House Constitution, held a rather ceremonial post. Thus, the Constitution required consultations with the Speaker of Parliament and the Prime Minister before the ESC appointments and the Electoral Act stipulated that members of the Electoral Directorate, including the Registrar General, were nominated by the Government.[12] In accordance with the Constitution, the President also appointed the chair of the Delimitation Commission, a Supreme Court judge, as well as three other members on the advice of the chair. The choice was Justice Wilson Sandura who later became respected as a very independent-minded person although his loyalty to Mugabe can hardly be questioned.[13]

The first 1985 registration proceeded much more slowly than expected. It had to be extended several times and, finally, the government announced that every citizen above 18 who had an identity document was able to vote even if his or her name did not appear on the voters' roll. Thus, delimitation of the constituencies was executed according to an incomplete registration. When compared to the provincial distribution of the seats in the 1980 elections, Mashonaland East with its growing urban areas won two more seats, while Mashonaland Central and Matabeleland North, which included Bulawayo, lost one seat each.

With 77 per cent of the popular vote, ZANU received 64 seats, ZAPU 19 per cent of the vote and 15 seats, and Sithole's ZANU 1 seat at Chipinge on the eastern border with 1 per cent of the vote. When compared to the 1980 elections, the majoritarian system polarised the political map of the country. All seats in Matabeleland went to ZAPU, which did not win a single seat outside the area, although it won 5 per cent of the vote in the Midlands. Accordingly, ZANU was not able to win a single seat in Matabeleland although it won 14 per cent of the vote there.[14] It is even more important to note that, although ZAPU's support had dropped from the 24 per cent of the vote it received in 1980, this was far from Mugabe's prediction of a 50 per cent drop. The Ndebele population in Matabeleland did not abandon ZAPU irrespective of all the dissident activities and state repression there.

It is possible to look at the rural-urban divide in detail, because the 1985 results were published at the constituency level. Table 13.1 reveals the level of 'one-partyism' along the rural-urban divide, whether for ZANU or the opposition. There was very little electoral competition in the rural areas, while the 'intra-constituency' opposition was marginally stronger in the cities of Harare, Chitungwiza and Bulawayo. Table 13.1 also clearly shows the electoral basis of political power in Zimbabwe. Most MPs were elected from the rural areas and most of the rural

---

[12]According to a common perception, Registrar General Tobaiwa Mudede, appointed for the 1985 elections and still in office, is a relative of Mugabe. As noted by Makumbe and Compagnon, he is subject to no control or direction except by the President (Makumbe and Compagnon, 2000, 52).

[13]In 1989 Sandura chaired a commission of inquiry into the so-called Willowgate corruption scandal that led to the resignation of several ministers, but, as noted by John Makumbe and Daniel Compagnon, did not question the inner circles of Mugabe (Makumbe and Compagnon, 2000, 60).

[14]Calculated from results published in *Sunday Mail* 7 July 1985.

constituencies consisted predominantly of Communal Areas. In Communal Areas the average support for the winning candidate was above 93 per cent, which means that in practice they were one-party constituencies, whether ZANU or ZAPU. While there is no doubt that this one-partyism indicates the ethnic homogeneity of the rural areas when compared to the cities, in many Communal Areas the institution of the chief also played a major role: although the voters were many, in a hierarchical system the choice was made by one person only.

Table 13.1: Rural and urban vote in the 1985 common roll elections[15]

	Contested seats	Winning candidates, per cent of all votes	Turnout, per cent
Cities	13	85	106
Other urban areas	5	92	113
Communal areas	33	93	94
Other rural areas	29	89	94
Total	80	90	98

Source: Calculated from *Sunday Mail* 7 July 1985.

The turnout figures in Table 13.1 are calculated from valid votes[16] and those registered before the delimitation of the constituencies. Because the registration was then incomplete, the turnout in many cases exceeded 100 per cent of those registered. Thus, the national turnout of 98 per cent is not reliable. It is more reliable to estimate the turnout by comparing the numbers of voters, about 2.7 million, to the number of voters in 1980. Taking into consideration the population growth, the turnout can be said to have been about 5 per cent lower than in 1980. If it was about 90 per cent in 1980, then it was now about 85 per cent, which in any case is very high.[17] What is evident in Table 13.1 is that participation in the urban areas was also very high, although it might be that registration was most problematic there. But even if we assume that under-registration diminished the relative voting power of the urban electorate, it is important to note that this was not yet biased in favour of the ruling party, in contrast to what happened in the following elections. In the 1985 elections under-registration was as common in ZAPU areas as it was in ZANU areas.

Elections after Unity in 1990

Politically, the state response to the dissident problem in Matabeleland meant that the ZAPU leadership was left with very few alternatives if it wanted to get a minimal share of state power for itself and if it wanted to safeguard the security of its constituency. Thus the party was forced to join ZANU.

The March 1990 parliamentary elections, together with the first presidential elections in the country, were preceded by significant constitutional amendments. The sequence in which they were proposed was most crucial for their adoption. Firstly in 1987, the white seats were abolished and the white roll was merged with the common roll. This became possible because the provisions

---

[15]The rural-urban-divide of the constituencies in Tables 13.1–13.4 indicates the *dominant* character of each constituency and can thus give only a rough idea of the real situation. Naturally, the constituencies are not delimited according to this kind of categorisation. Yet according to the Constitution, the Delimitation Commission should 'give due consideration' to 'any community of interest' between voters (section 60, 4 d). In reality the constituencies often arbitrarily include both rural and urban areas, which more often than not has played against the voting power of the urban opposition. My categorisation of the constituencies is based on the descriptions and maps produced by the Delimitation Commission (Zimbabwe Inter-Africa News Agency 1985; *The Herald* 4 June 1985; Zimbabwe 1990; and Zimbabwe 1995).

[16]This is due to the technical reason that the number of spoilt papers was not reported for all constituencies. The same applies to the tables below.

[17]The turnout is only from 79 constituencies. Due to the death of the ZANU(PF) candidate in Kariba, Mashonaland West, elections were not held there. Subsequently the seat went to ZANU(PF) unopposed.

of the Lancaster House Constitution – requiring a unanimous decision in the House of Assembly to amend the composition of parliament – expired. The 20 vacant seats in the House of Assembly were elected by the 80 common roll MPs. Because ZANU had a clear majority, all ZANU candidates were successful. Subsequently ZANU held 85 out of 100 seats. This new Parliament soon passed the next constitutional amendment bill which created an executive presidency, which had been on the agenda of the ruling party since independence. In practic, the powers vested in the executive make it possible for the President to run the country without the approval of Parliament or the cabinet (Makumbe and Compagnon 2000, 33–36). These two amendments were introduced just before the politically important Unity Accord between ZANU and ZAPU was publicised. When ZAPU MPs joined ZANU in December, the ruling party's majority rose to 99 out of 100 MPs. This was the parliament that appointed Mugabe as the first Executive President of Zimbabwe on 30 December 1987. The next amendment created the office of the vice-president to be appointed by the President. Before the first national congress of the 'new' united ZANU(PF) in December 1989, Parliament passed an amendment which abolished the Senate and increased the number of MPs to 150, 30 of whom were to be appointed by the President. Appointed MPs included 10 chiefs, 8 provincial governors and 12 'free choices' – all of whom, without doubt, were supporters of the ruling party. The foremost consequence of all these constitutional amendments was the concentration of power in the office of the President. In this respect, Zimbabwe started to resemble a typical African post-colonial state.

The concentration of power in the President also affected the political position of the institutions responsible for the practical arrangements of the elections. The fact that the Delimitation Commission chaired again by Justice Sandura made some last-minute changes to the boundaries of some constituencies favouring the ruling party, caused wide speculation about the impartiality of the Commission. The Chair of the Electoral Supervisory Commission, Walter Kamba, in turn, was not even aware that the Constitution required the ESC to report to Parliament. Instead it gave its report and recommendations to the President only. The composition of the Electoral Directorate also raised questions about its fairness as many of its members were political appointees.

The total number of officially registered voters was as many as 4.8 million, marking an increase of more than 60 per cent of the registration in 1985. This caused obvious misgivings. If about 45 per cent of the population were above 18 years old as the population pyramid in Zimbabwe suggests, then the number of eligible voters among the total of about 9.4 million Zimbabweans would have been about 4.2 million. According to Jonathan Moyo, it was apparent that

the 4.8 million figure was given by the Election Directorate in order to silence critics who had complained about the slow pace of the voter-registration exercise and, arguably, to under-register voters in volatile political areas to ensure a concentration of constituencies in areas which the ruling party considered safe (Moyo 1992, 62).

Proportionally, the increase in seats was largest in Mashonaland West, Mugabe's home province, where the number rose from 7 to 13 seats. Other above-average increases were more plausible, occurring in the big cities: Mashonaland East, with Harare and Chitungwiza, increased its seats from 18 to 28 while the number of seats in Matabeleland North, encompassing Bulawayo, increased from 9 to 16.

In possibly reflecting the responsible authorities' own distrust of the registration exercise, the Election Directorate announced before polling, as in the previous elections, that all Zimbabwean citizens would be allowed to vote by proving their citizenship. That there were still many people who were not registered was evident as there were polling stations where half or even as many as three-quarters of the actual voters had not registered before voting (Electoral Supervisory Commission 1990). Thus the 4.8 million names on the voters roll probably contained hundreds of thousands of erroneous names.

The main theme of these elections was the constitutional possibility for introducing a one-party state. Mugabe stated that:

the united ZANU(PF) has the potential, given the commitment of its leadership and members, to develop into that sole party to which all Zimbabweans can and should lend their membership and support… any attempt to form any new political parties for the future is a long step backwards in the search for greater national unity and the transformation of society in favour of the people and, in particular, the peasants, the urban and farm workers, professionals and intellectuals. (Mugabe 1989, 354, 355.)

However, a new opposition party: the Zimbabwe Unity Movement (ZUM), emerged to be led by a former liberation fighter, Edgar Tekere, who was expelled from ZANU after criticising the government in Parliament. It gained its strength from the disclosure of widespread corruption scandals, the deteriorating economy and increasing unemployment, which mobilised against ZANU the very people Mugabe had proclaimed as favoured by the government, particularly students and trade unions in the urban areas. Thus, the 1990 elections, with ZUM putting up candidates throughout the country, provided people with an opportunity to vote against the ruling party and its plans to establish a one-party state.

The state response to opposition mobilisation was very repressive. Some reported incidents suggested that police partiality was striking. ZUM had to fight against the ruling party on a very uneven playing field and intimidation of its supporters was rampant. The police did very little in order to stop the intimidation which was carried out by the Youth League and the Women's League of ZANU. 'Cooperation' between ZANU youth and the police was common. Most serious was an incident in Gweru where security officials shot and seriously wounded a popular ZUM candidate.

ZUM's attempts to hold public rallies were almost always systematically rejected. Also, Sithole's ZANU(Ndonga) faced difficulties in holding its planned rallies. At the same time not a single ZANU(PF) meeting was forbidden (Masendeke *et al*. 1991, 15, 19). The holding of public rallies had been made difficult for ZUM during earlier 1989 by-elections. Permission was either denied under the state of emergency regulations or eventually given, but then the police claimed that they could not guarantee the security of a rally for technical reasons, thereby preventing rallies from being held. In some cases, however, ZUM was innovative in circumventing the difficulties. For example, it booked the St Michael's Anglican Church for a wedding, but to the surprise of the priest, Tekere then held a political meeting and shared the platform with Ian Smith (Mhlaba 1991, 5).

The allocation of advertising time for government-controlled TV and radio broadcasting was based on the number of parliamentary seats. This formally non-discriminating procedure ensured that in practice the opposition parties received only the minimum of four minutes per day, while the ruling party received half an hour (Makumbe 1991, 2). In any case, the content of electoral coverage was sometimes far from fair. ZANU(PF), for example, ran television commercials saying that to vote for ZANU(PF) was to choose life but to vote for the opposition was a decision to die. One commercial showed the scene of a car crash followed by a threatening voice: 'This is one way to die. Another is to vote for ZUM. Don't commit suicide … vote ZANU(PF)'. Another advertisement showed a coffin and a grave pronouncing: 'AIDS kills, so does ZUM. Vote ZANU(PF)' (Ncube 1991, 7). Furthermore, ZANU(PF) received free media exposure in the form of news and commentaries.

State-owned newspapers, the only dailies in the country, also refused to publish campaign advertisements by opposition candidates or censored them to an extent that they lost all their meaning (Mhlaba 1991, 8). In addition, while the independent newspapers revealed some irregularities in the election campaigns and criticised the government, they did not promote any of the opposition parties by presenting their manifestos (Quantin 1992, 35).

According to John Makumbe, the campaign period was 'one of the most viciously contested' in the country (Makumbe 1991, 1). The urban and communal areas were markedly politicised while the commercial farming areas and the low density areas in the towns, lacking active youth engagement, were less so. In the urban centres of Manicaland, ZUM carried out a special campaign by concentrating on the war in Mozambique: Zimbabwean solders, who were in Mozambique to safeguard the Beira corridor, had become more and more involved in the internal struggle against Renamo, which then affected the security situation along the eastern border of Zimbabwe. The electorate was told by ZUM that if they voted for the party, Zimbabwean soldiers would be withdrawn, thereby saving taxpayers' money and ending Renamo's attacks (Masendeke *et al*. 1991, 14, 26). ZUM nationally concentrated on corruption, increasing commodity prices and transportation problems. In practice, ZUM's political programme, however, was often clouded by Tekere's populism and personal attacks against Mugabe, a new phenomenon for Zimbabwean elections (Quantin 1992, 31).

It has to be noted that, in contrast to previous elections, ZANU had to respond to substantial criticism against its government, including that from outside the opposition parties. According to Patrick Quantin, the very fact that there was a new opposition challenging the ruling party encouraged many interest groups in the country to present their claims, 'more or less openly bargaining their support for the party in power' (Quantin 1992, 30). As Quantin notes, during the campaign period, the president had to face the complaints of the representatives of civil servants, nurses, teachers, churches, farmers and industrialists. After political space was opened up by the Unity Accord, ZUM's existence provided a chance for many of these organisations to express their loyalty to the government and this, although apparently strengthening the position of the ruling party, also meant that a new kind of interest-based and more horizontal political mobili-sation had become possible (see Quantin 1992, 30, 43).

As many as 14 seats were unopposed due to last minute withdrawals of some ZUM candidates and its inability to raise enough funds to pay electoral deposits. It should be noted that the ruling party received substantial funding, through the Ministry of Political Affairs, from the state budget. The independents were a new phenomenon in Zimbabwe. But remembering the Rhodesian 'one-party' era, independent candidates and uncontested seats were a return to the old system. Many of the independents now were former ZAPU members, whose participation was a protest against the merger of the parties (Mhlaba 1991, 8).

ZANU(PF) received 80 per cent of the popular vote and won in 103 of the 106 contested constituencies. Its victory was no surprise. But the fact that most observers expected a better result for ZUM gave rise to many rumours or 'unconfirmed reports' about rigging (Makumbe 1991, 3). Yet, 18 per cent support was quite impressive. It was the majoritarian first-past-the-post electoral system and possible gerrymandering, especially in the urban constituencies, in the delimitation process which proved to be unfair to ZUM. Although its support was often close to 50 per cent in the cities of Harare, Chitungwiza and Bulawayo, it was not able to win a single seat in these constituencies. ZUM's election support, in the two constituencies which it did win, was regionally based. Tekere was elected from Mutare Central, his home area, and Daniel Sithole from Chipinge North, an area that was already prominent in its opposition against the ruling party.

As noted by Lloyd Sachikonye, ZUM's anti-corruption populism fed on the grievances of the working class in the urban areas caused by unemployment, falling incomes, increasing consumer prices, housing and transport crises, while the personal accumulation and wealth of the political leadership had become more obvious. As much as the urban population voted for ZUM, they also voted against ZANU. On the other hand, ZUM was also able to establish at least some structures to mobilise voters in the cities, whereas the lack of organisational infrastructure and access to media constrained its ability to penetrate the rural areas (Sachikonye 1990, 97).

Table 13.2 shows a growing tendency that had been evident in the previous elections. The constituencies in the big cities were most competitively contested, while competition was also considerably higher than average in other urban areas. In the rural constituencies, the support of the winning candidate was notably higher, amounting to almost 90 per cent in the Communal Areas. For 1990, the winning candidates, with the exception of two opposition seats in Chipinge, were all from ZANU(PF).

Table 13.2: Rural and urban vote in the 1990 elections

	Contested seats	Winning candidates, per cent of all votes	Turnout, per cent
Cities	27	69	51
Other urban areas	11	78	62
Communal areas	41	88	47
Other rural areas	24	84	49
Total	103	81	50

Source: Calculated from Moyo 1992.

Official voter turnout was generally higher in urban constituencies than in the rural areas. When compared with the previous turnout, it can be quite safely said that the turnout figures in Table 13.2 are, on average, about 6 per cent too low. Yet, it is difficult to say much about the actual situation in each area. Errors in the electoral register, whether deliberate or accidental, most likely increased the number of fictitious voters in the rural constituencies. In Zvimba, which is Robert Mugabe's home area, Sabina Mugabe won on only a 20 per cent voter turnout, the lowest rate which was officially recorded. This supports Moyo's suggestion of deliberate errors in the registers but not only insofar as under-registration in the volatile areas was concerned. It seems rather that the number of seats was maximised in Mashonaland West by over-registration of voters. Mhondoro, Ngezi and Karoi, also in Mashonaland West, recorded a very low participation, but strong support for ZANU(PF). It can be said quite safely that the above-mentioned proportional increase in the number of seats in Mashonaland West was not based on a corresponding increase in the number of voters.

Another low turnout rate of 24 per cent was recorded in Lobengula, Joshua Nkomo's constituency. Commonly, this was interpreted as a sign of protest against the Unity Accord (see Chan 1992, 186). At the same time, Nkomo's share of votes cast was 84 per cent, the highest of the big cities. In comparison, ZANU's Richard Nyandoro in the Highfield West constituency won with the lowest margin in the cities, receiving 57 per cent of the vote, against ZUM's Isaac Manyemba and UANC's William Chadzukwa, while the turnout there was the highest recorded in the cities: 90 per cent. In the big cities in general, the level of competition seemed to correlate with the level of voters' participation. It was not surprising, however, that in Gokwe West, where ZUM's candidate was hospitalised after the shooting incident, the turnout was exceptionally low, 27 per cent, reflecting a deep frustration with the uneven playing field of the opposition.

However, ZANU's victory did not convince everybody of its legitimacy to be the only political organisation than could rule the country in the future and the party soon abandoned the idea of a one-party state. The decision was first made by the Politburo, where four former ZAPU members opposed it (Sithole 1997, 133, 134). In September, the Central Committee came, after long debate, to the same conclusion without the need to vote on the issue.[18]

Elections without contest in 1995 and 1996

The next general elections were the parliamentary elections in 1995 and the presidential election in 1996, held for the first time as separate elections. In 1995, according to official data, the total number of registered voters was 4.8 million, which was reasonably plausible when compared to the rough estimate of about 4.9 million eligible voters in the country. However, this did not mean that the rolls would have contained fewer errors than in 1990. On the contrary, examples of registered people whose names did not appear on the roll, names that appeared twice and names of people who had died years earlier were numerous (ZimRights 1995, 11, 12). Makumbe and Compagnon were able to check thoroughly the roll of the Harare South constituency and concluded that at least 41 per cent of the names there were not genuine. Although Harare South most probably was an extreme case including deliberate and massive registration of people not eligible to vote in the constituency in order to justify the division of Margaret Dongo's

---

[18]*Parade* November 1990. In principle the Central Committee is the most important organ of the party. The majority of its members are elected by the Congress, which consists of a few thousand party officials and members of the executive bodies at the national and provincial level. Central Committee members also include representatives of the Youth and Women's leagues as well as presidential appointees. In practice the most important organ of the party is its 22-member Politburo. It consists of the party's *presidential commission* elected by the Congress (the President and First Secretary, Robert Mugabe, and Vice Presidents and Second Secretaries Simon Muzenda and Joshua Nkomo) and *the secretaries of the party* appointed by the President. The secretaries are Central Committee members and heads of party commissariats dealing with different policy areas from foreign policy to women's affairs, resembling a state cabinet (see *Constitution of The Zimbabwe African National Union Patriotic Front, ZANU PF.*) It was not until December 1998 that the party reviewed the powers of its president. The annual conference of the party resolved that the members of the Politburo should be elected by the Central Committee (*Zimbabwe Standard Online* 13–19 December 1998). [http://www.samara.co.zw/standard/index.cfm].

constituency, it shows that there were no inbuilt checks in the process to prevent even the most dubious registrations. (Makumbe and Compagnon 2000, 69–70).

Due to the new system of 'voters' blocks', a fresh delimitation was to be carried out. In addition, there were administrative changes that affected the constituency boundaries. Most importantly Harare and Bulawayo officially became provinces in 1992. However, it seems that since the registration did not proceed as expected the Registrar-General decided to amalgamate the old roll and the new one with hazardous results.[19] Among other things, this meant that it was very easy to change the existing constituency boundaries without regard to population changes.[20] At the provincial level, it is striking that Masvingo and Manicaland lost two constituencies each, while Matabeleland South and the Midlands each lost one and Harare, Mashonaland Central and Mashonaland East each gained two. Makumbe and Compagnon have evaluated the real changes in the proportion of voters in these areas by looking at the figures of natural increases and internal migration given by the Central Statistical Office. According to them, the changes in the allocation of seats were politically motivated, particularly in the cases of Masvingo, Manicaland and Mashonaland East which had experienced rather similar demographic trends. This divide coincides with the internal factionalism in the party which will be analysed below and, as noted by Makumbe and Compagnon, is most relevant with regard to the presidential succession struggle:

> What was important for the President was that Mashonaland as a whole gained four constituencies, thus reinforcing the Zezuru MPs within the ZANU(PF) caucus. The loss of seats in Matabeleland, Masvingo and Manicaland may indicate that these are provinces that the president does not trust (Makumbe and Compagnon 2000, 80)

Delimitation also provided an easy way for the government to get rid of its individual critics in Parliament.[21] The most significant case was the division of Margaret Dongo's Sunningdale constituency in Harare. Margaret Dongo withdrew from the contest in the primaries altogether and decided to contest the seat as an independent. The number of independent candidates was larger than for previous elections in Zimbabwe. After a few last-minute withdrawals, 29 independent candidates stood for the 1995 elections.

Independent candidates, however, were not the only opposition. Since the formation of ZUM, new opposition parties had also emerged. ZUM had disintegrated during 1991, when Tekere suspended some of the party leaders, who then formed the Democratic Party (DP). But the playing field seemed very uneven. After much criticism, the Ministry of Political Affairs was abolished in mid-1992 and its function of using state finance to fund the ruling party was replaced by the Political Parties (Finance) Act of 1994. According to this act, parties had to have a minimum of 15 seats in Parliament in order to be entitled to state funding. Although in principal non-discriminatory, in reality it left all opposition parties without public funding. Some of the opposition parties, most importantly ZUM, the Democratic Party, and Bishop Abel Muzorewa's United Parties (one of the attempts to unite the opposition that had failed due to the dispute over the leadership) decided to boycott the elections. As a result, 55 constituencies were not even contested. Because the President had the constitutional right to appoint 30 MPs, the ruling party was guaranteed a majority even before polling started. Thus, Mugabe was confident enough to disparage the opposition leaders by saying that, instead of

---

[19]The names from the old rolls were extracted to the new rolls according to the new block system. This did not prevent the erroneous names of the previous registration being extracted as well. Besides, the registration had to be extended again until the polling in April 1995.

[20]Whether the proportional shares of voters in the 1990 constituencies had changed or not was impossible to verify, because the released figures showed only the number of registered voters in each of the country's 59 administrative districts. Therefore evidence does not support an accusation, in an editorial in *The Herald*, published during the ZANU(PF) primary elections, that losing MPs had not mobilised their supporters to register and therefore could only blame themselves when their old constituencies were redrawn (*The Herald* 21 February 1995).

[21]In Harare, alone, during the ZANU(PF) primaries, four constituencies were contested by two MPs each, while six constituencies had no incumbent MPs contesting the election (*The Herald* 9 March 1995).

politics, 'Muzorewa should stick to his collar and Bible and pray for rain'.[22] The Forum Party's Enoch Dumbutshena, the first Chief Justice of Zimbabwe, in turn, was not a serious leader since his opposition was based on 'homeboy competition' – Mugabe and Dumbutshena were rural area neighbours.[23] The antagonism between Mugabe and ZANU(Ndonga)'s Ndabaningi Sithole, who had returned from his self-imposed exile to the United States in January 1992, was well known. Soon after the elections, Sithole was accused of two assassination attempts against Mugabe – and of urging young men to go into military training for a violent struggle against the regime – and detained.

According to official election results, almost 1.5 million people cast their votes, representing 54 per cent[24] of the registered electorate in the 65 contested constituencies. It was hardly a surprise that ZANU(PF) won more than 82 per cent of the votes and 63 of the 65 contested seats. ZANU(Ndonga) was able to win 2 seats in its traditional base of Chipinge with almost 7 per cent of the national vote and Ndabaningi Sithole was elected to parliament. Forum, which received about 6 per cent of the votes, had more dispersed electoral support and was not able to win a single seat. The independents got 5 per cent of the votes, thus forming the third biggest 'opposition party'. Margaret Dongo, who according to the official results was defeated, appealed for a fresh election due to irregularities in the voters' roll in her constituency, and won her case in the High Court. Subsequently, Dongo was elected to become the third opposition MP.[25]

Table 13.3: Rural and urban votes in the 1995 parliamentary elections

	Contested seats	Winning candidates per cent of all votes	Turnout, per cent
Cities	22	77	51
Other urban areas	8	81	53
Communal areas	13	89	58
Other rural areas	22	84	55
Total	65	83	54

Source: Calculated from *The Herald* 11 and 12 April 1995.

Taking into account the weakness of the opposition in these elections, it is striking that almost a quarter of the voters in the big cities voted against the official candidate of the ruling party, thereby confirming the urban tendency to support the opposition. 'One-partyism' was again most evident in the rural areas, especially in the Communal Areas (see Table 13.3).

Actual turnout rates were difficult to estimate due to irregularities in the voters' roll and the extended period of registration. The lowest official turnout, 33 per cent, was in the troubled Harare South constituency and the highest, 75 per cent, in the Zvishavane communal area. The real turnouts in the rural areas were probably higher than the official figures indicate because of voters' over-registration.

As Table 13.4 shows in the presidential elections that followed a year later in 1996, the tendency of urban frustration and rural obedience was even clearer.[26]

---

[22]*Sunday Mail* 26 March 1995.

[23]*Sunday Mail* 26 March 1995.

[24]If the spoilt papers are included the turnout was 57 per cent.

[25]Dongo is not the only candidate who has successfully applied to the court after losing an election. Since her case, it seems to have become almost a habit for the losing candidates to petition the court to nullify the elections because of irregularities.

[26]The data is incomplete, because the results for Masvingo, Mashonaland West and Matabeleland North provinces were not published. Comparison with the official national level figures, however, suggests that their inclusion would slightly increase the turnout and support of the winning candidates outside the cities thus strengthening the difference shown between the rural and urban areas.

Table 13.4: Rural and urban votes in the 1996 presidential elections

	Mugabe, per cent of all votes	Turnout, per cent
Cities	87	18
Other urban areas	91	22
Communal areas	94	41
Other rural areas	91	35

Source: Calculated from *The Herald* 19 March 1996.

In all three Matabeleland provinces, Mugabe's support was below 90 per cent. The lowest was Bulawayo, where less than 84 per cent of the votes were cast for Mugabe. In the rest of the country, Mugabe won with over 90 per cent support; the highest was Mashonaland Central with a support of 96 per cent. Muzorewa's support was highest in Bulawayo, where he received 14 per cent of the votes. As expected, Ndabaningi Sithole's best result was Manicaland where he won 7 per cent of popular vote.[27] Thus his detention had not reduced his support in Chipinge.

It was most embarrassing for the leadership of the ruling party that the official turnout did not reach even 32 per cent.[28] Although some Communal Areas saw turnouts close to 60 per cent of registered voters, apathy was rampant in the big cities. In Dongo's Harare South, the turnout was only 9 per cent.

Explaining urban apathy and rural obedience

Zimbabwe inherited the state instruments from Southern Rhodesia. In accordance with the ideological premises of the new leadership, these instruments were consciously utilised and shaped during the first decade to facilitate the introduction of a socialist, one-party state. Neither socialism nor one-partyism became realised. Instead, the concentration of state power seemed to provide important means for personal accumulation for the leadership, evident in the recently rampant public revelations of corruption cases. Only ten years ago, the revelation of a corruption scandal shocked the whole political system in the country, today similar stories are told almost weekly. Whether due to material or immaterial gains, state power is as desired as ever and struggle over it is as intensive as ever. Paradoxically, making the elections 'just a formality' is an important element in that struggle.

Urban apathy and rural obedience in contemporary Zimbabwe are two sides of the same coin, guaranteeing landslide electoral victories to rulers whose performance and popularity are no longer so convincing. The Economic Structural Adjustment Programme (ESAP), launched by the government in 1991 and supported by the IMF and World Bank, was popularly known as 'extended suffering for the African people'. Between 1992 and 1996, GDP per capita dropped by about 9 per cent and the share of industry in GNP dropped from 30 per cent to 9 per cent manifest in drastically increased unemployment. Due to the 15 per cent budget deficit in 1995, the IMF and World Bank froze their balance-of-payments support for ESAP, which then made the situation even worse.[29] Cuts in government spending on health care and an intensifying AIDS epidemic eroded the first decade's achievement in popular health care. The introduction of school fees has had a similar impact on popular education.

Constraining civil society
As already mentioned above, it is conventional to interpret political apathy as an aspect of political stability (see Diamond 1993, 103). In Zimbabwe, however, political apathy in the 1990s did not coincide with political stability in the urban areas as the riots and strikes against rising taxes and

---

[27]*The Herald* 20 March 1996.
[28]Makumbe and Compagnon (2000, 292) calculated the turnout to be only 30 per cent.
[29]Consequently the second phase of the reform ZIMPREST, which was planned for the years 1995–2000, could not start before 1998 after the World Bank in December 1997 finally published its support. If there was one reason for the World Bank and IMF to come back to Zimbabwe it was certainly not an improved economic policy but an attempt to prevent the total bankruptcy of the Zimbabwean economy.

consumer prices in late 1997 and early 1998 showed. Rather than people's lack of interest in politics, apathy reflected cynicism and frustration due to the continuous and systematic state repression of any political dissent in the country.

The Unity Accord between ZANU and ZAPU opened up space for civil society and encouraged public criticism of the government, especially towards the establishment of a one-party state. Therefore, as in all the one-party states in Africa which took steps towards multi-party systems, the role of civil society in Zimbabwe was prominent in the defence and support of multi-party democracy. As well as civic organisations like the Zimbabwean human rights organisation (ZimRights) and the Catholic Commission for Justice and Peace in Zimbabwe (CCJP), the media, the universities and the labour unions became focal points for critical discussion about the one-party state. All these institutions were influential in mobilising the urban population.

The state responded to this development as soon as it appeared. As was mentioned above, the 'new' opposition politicians were harassed and prevented from holding meetings. But also the media, universities, and the trade unions were attacked. Critical reporters and journalists in the employ of the government-controlled radio, TV, and the major newspapers, were removed from their posts.[30] Furthermore, even though the independent media had presented a critical voice, it had also learned to be very careful not to sympathise with the political opposition. In the case of such newspapers as the *Financial Gazette* for example, this reluctance indicated the uneasy position of the business community *vis-à-vis* state power. A detailed analysis by Staffan Darnolf of the content of the newspapers during the 1995 elections showed that although the *Financial Gazette* – and the *Sunday Gazette*, another important mouthpiece of the business community – were critical towards the ruling party and did not disparage the opposition in the manner of the government-controlled press, the newspapers did not report on the programmes or views of the opposition parties (Darnolf 1997, 181). In other words, the independent media seemed reluctant to support the political opposition. If the media did promote a political agenda, it was about cynicism and boycotting of elections.[31] It was only before the election in 2000 that this mood changed and independent media were openly campaigning for the opposition.

The position of the Zimbabwe Congress of Trade Unions (ZTCU) was just as difficult. Immediately after independence, the trade unions became more or less co-opted by the ruling party. Towards the end of the 1980s, following a deteriorating economy, the congress became more critical, and, in 1989, the general secretary of ZCTU, Morgan Tsvangirai, was detained and released only after international pressure. At the height of the debate over proposals for a one-party state, the general council of ZCTU stated that it fully supported a multi-party system.

Although emergency regulations were enacted outlawing strikes in essential services, 1990 showed a new kind of confidence on the part of the unions who were now in a position to bargain with the ruling party which was worried that unions might support the opposition. Many Zimbabwean civil servants, teachers, nurses and doctors went on strike during the autumn of 1990 for the first time in their history (Chan 1992, 187). ZCTU increased its independence of the ruling party under the leadership of Tsvangirai but he was warned several times by members of ZANU(PF) not to become 'another Frederick Chiluba' (Deve and Gonçalves 1994).

However, independence from the ruling party also meant 'independence' from opposition parties. In the run up to the 1995 elections, it became clear that ZCTU was not willing to participate in party politics on the grounds that the general election was a non-event and that opposition parties were merely opportunistically trying to get their vote without any deeper interest in workers' problems. After the mass strikes and demonstrations of December 1997, the relationship between the trade unions and the government became tense again; Mugabe was again accusing the congress of becoming another political party.[32] In September 1999, the nightmare of the government came true – a new opposition party, Movement of Democratic Change (MDC), was formed under the leadership of Morgan Tsvangirai.

---

[30]That this habit is still alive became evident in December 1997 when a radio reporter was fired for allowing listeners to phone in live on the day of mass demonstrations. Most of those who called into the radio broadcast criticised the brutality of the police. (*Financial Gazette* 15 January 1998.)

[31]See a column by 'J.M.' in *Financial Gazette* 6 April 1995.

[32]*Financial Gazette* 10 December 1998.

The University of Zimbabwe had started to look like one of the strongholds of the opposition before the 1990 elections. As a result, the government detained student leaders, closed down the university and put it under state control through the University of Zimbabwe Amendment Act. The law gives disciplinary powers to the university authorities appointed by the government in that the vice-chancellor is authorised to ban, suspend or expel any student or lecturer. The students were forbidden to demonstrate outside the campus in town. As a result, the students' discontent took on an increasingly violent tone (see Nkiwane 1998). Instability and riots became rather the norm of university life, and few seriously expected it to become a centre of new political thinking in the country.

The short period of time before the 1990 elections had, in a way, provided a momentum for civil society, including a more horizontal interest-based mobilisation of the workers. Five years later the state repression had already blocked even a potential for serious opposition. There seems to be a general conviction that the political and civil rights of the citizens of Zimbabwe have deteriorated since 1990 (see Makumbe and Compagnon 2000, 4–7). In 1995, the ability of the voters to check the state power through a multi-party system, articulating alternatives to the incumbent regime's policies, was replaced by the formality of multi-party elections. By the same token, the many grievances of the ordinary people had no party-political channel through which to be expressed – hence the electoral apathy. It is not surprising that the deteriorating economic situation at the beginning of 1998 so easily translated into violent riots in Chitungwiza and Harare.

Dependency of the rural community

As was shown above, the real power base of the ruling party lies in the rural areas, especially in the Communal Areas. As far as the one-party character of these areas is concerned, there is no doubt that the institution of chief plays an important role as stated above, and this is true even in the registration of voters. The Registrar-General has admitted that in the Communal Areas he relies on the testimony of the village headmen to define the voters' residences (Makumbe and Compagnon 2000, 70). But while it is possible to claim for Zimbabwe, like other African countries, that structural adjustment policies have not affected the rural areas as badly as the urban areas, and that this would explain the relatively higher rural support for the ruling party, the Communal Areas in Zimbabwe can hardly be described as economically successful.

On independence, half of the productive land was owned by less than 6,000 white commercial farmers. The government promised to resettle 162,000 African families within five years. Since 1980, only 70,000 families have been resettled and 4,000 large-scale farmers remain.[33] Much of the reallocated land has gone to prominent politicians – not to landless peasants. The meagre results of the state's resettlement policy are also due to its cost, not only because of buying land according to the 'willing seller – willing buyer' principle for the first ten years of independence as stipulated in the Lancaster House Constitution, but also because of the economic consequences which would follow from disbanding large-scale production without adequate state investment in agriculture. A further need has been to construct roads, clinics and schools for resettled people moving to new areas. Western donors had not given all the aid they promised in the Lancaster House Agreement on land reform, while the white farmers had also shown little eagerness to surrender their land to the landless.

This is also the background to the government's sudden announcement in autumn 1997 that over 1,500 commercial farms were gazetted for acquisition and to the forceful occupation of more than 1,000 farms by war veterans and ZANU(PF) activists before the elections in 2000. These moves can be seen as an attempt by ZANU(PF) to regain popularity. Yet the resettlement of landless peasants on these farms is most uncertain simply because the government does not have enough funds for this purpose.

Population growth in the Communal Areas alone has made overcrowding a cause of food vulnerability. Many Communal Areas have become dependent on the government for the development of their areas and the supply of fertilisers, seeds and drought relief (Masendeke et al. 1991, 3). Drought relief began during the three years of drought between 1982–84. Paradoxically, dependency on drought relief is explained by the government failure to invest in agriculture and to conduct its land

---

[33]*Africa Confidential* 5 December 1997.

reform programme as intended while also providing an easy asset to the ruling party in mobilising voters. Michael Drinkwater has noted that, after the government resettlement policy lost its credibility, drought relief has become the most important political means of ruling the Communal Areas.

> Across the broad swathes of country where most of the communal area population live, in Manicaland, Masvingo, Midlands and Matabeleland provinces, this drought relief has continued ever since [1984]. At independence the 'big' policy for the rural peoples was supposed to be resettlement, bringing the colonial policy of land apportionment to a final end. This end has not occurred however. (Drinkwater 1994, 5.)

According to the 1992 census, the number of people living in the Communal Areas is almost 5.5 million, above 51 per cent of the population. In the Matabeleland provinces and in Masvingo, more than three-quarters of the population live in the Communal Areas (Zimbabwe 1994b, table 2.2.). According to official figures (Zimbabwe 1994a), the share of those dependent on drought relief has increased most drastically in Mashonaland, although people in Matabeleland seem to be most dependent on it. For instance, in Matabeleland South 42 per cent of the population annually requested drought relief between 1989 and 1993 while the same figure for the whole ten-year period from 1982 to 1993 was 34 per cent. For Mashonaland Central the respective figures were 27 per cent and 14 per cent and for Mashonaland 19 per cent and 9 per cent. According to the same figures, the percentage of those fed from those requesting drought relief during the ten-year period (1982–1993) has ranged from 77 per cent in Mashonaland West to 62 per cent in Matabeleland South.

ZANU presents itself as the source of drought relief, seeds, fertilisers, roads, schools and medical facilities. To vote against the party would mean that 'the angry father may just cut off all rural programmes' (Sylvester 1995, 410). Sylvester quoted the following statement from her discussions with farm workers during the 1990 elections: '[i]n the communal areas you must vote for him [Mugabe] or you don't get government relief food – this has been a bad rainy season' (Sylvester 1990, 399). According to ZANU, voting for ZUM would simply imply 'discontinuation of food relief' (Sachikonye 1990, 98). Similar threats were repeated during the 1995 elections.[34]

In 1995, ZANU(PF) Manicaland chairman Kumbirai Kangai stated in Chipinge that people there should vote for ZANU(PF) 'or there will be no development'.[35] According to Vice-president Muzenda some members of the opposition parties had 'admitted that they cannot influence development while in Parliament because they are too few to do so'.[36] Muzenda appealed to members of ZANU(Ndonga) in Chipinge to join ZANU, saying that it was only through joining hands with other Zimbabweans that people in Chipinge could see development taking place in their area.

Intra-party competition

If obedience and apathy in 1995 seemed to be 'a rational choice' for most of the Zimbabwean electorate, this did not imply a total absence of political and electoral competition. The locus of this competition was inside the ruling party. As argued by Makumbe and Compagnon, these tensions had become more open than before, suggesting that they were not as easily managed by the leadership as they used to be (Makumbe and Compagnon 2000, 2–3, 120–2). Faction cleavages and flaws within the monolithic structure of 'Democratic Centralism'[37] inside the party reflected an intense political struggle and explained also the emergence of the most significant 'opposition' electoral group, that of independents.

Not all party members have been satisfied with the way in which the primaries were conducted, both before the 1990 and the 1995 elections.[38] Allegations of irregularities, vote-buying and rigging have been frequent. In each constituency where the primaries were held, only a few

---

[34]ZimRights 1995, 8–10; see also *The Herald* 23 March 1995.

[35]*The Herald* 25 March 1995.

[36]*The Herald* 3 April 1995.

[37]The resolutions of ZANU's Congress, 8 August 1984 stated that '"Democratic Centralism" shall be the fundamental tenet in the internal functioning and administration of the Party' (Zimbabwe African National Union 1984, 1:5).

[38]There were no primaries in 1985.

hundred ZANU district officials and branch representatives were eligible to vote. This means that attempts to buy votes were possible and that, in many constituencies, the actual choice of an MP was made by only a small fraction of the registered voters there.[39]

By 1995, many primary elections brought unexpected results. Only half of the nominated candidates were sitting MPs. Soon after the primaries, the party's deputy secretary for information and publicity, Chen Chimutengwende, revealed that it was worrying from the point of view of the party leadership that many sitting MPs lost the primary election, since in principle it would then be possible that the party leadership would not be in Parliament. This was not a controllable situation. Totally open primaries could become a 'constitutional problem' for a party such as ZANU. On the other hand, according to Chimutengwende, the idea of primary elections is a useful mechanism for a mass party, because it also provides the executive with the ability to safeguard party interest, when it is endangered by 'members who have just joined to be elected MPs'.[40] In practice, this meant that the Politburo was able to revise the list of aspiring candidates in each constituency.

For a few constituencies, no primary elections were held. Although there would have been enough aspiring candidates, electoral competition was not regarded as appropriate for the status of certain candidates. Thus, the Politburo assured that vice-presidents were the official party candidates for their chosen constituencies and there was more or less general consensus that the other party leaders should also be nominated without primary elections. Nevertheless, even this privilege was not enough for Vice-president Joshua Nkomo, who regarded the requirement to stand for parliamentary elections in one constituency as being below his political position. President Mugabe insisted that he defend his seat since the Constitution required vice-presidents to be MPs. Nkomo, however, wanted to be elected on a national ticket although this would have required a constitutional amendment. Besides, when refusing to be nominated as candidate for the parliamentary elections, he imposed his own candidate upon the Lobengula constituency in Bulawayo. No elections were held in Lobengula, although there were nine other candidates, who had expressed an interest in contesting the constituency if it became vacant. After the general elections, President Mugabe had no choice but to appoint Nkomo as a non-constituency MP.

The other Vice-president, Simon Muzenda, in turn, was nominated as ZANU(PF) candidate for the Gutu-North constituency in Masvingo. Simultaneously, he edged out the retired and respected commander of the Air Force, Josiah Tungamirai, who had wanted to contest the same constituency.[41] Tungamirai then criticised the Politburo for using powers that actually belonged to the Central Committee. In this he was supported by Eddison Zvobgo, the party secretary for legal affairs, while Mugabe explained that decisions made by the Poltburo were also decisions of the Central Committee. As argued by Makumbe and Compagnon, behind this disagreement was the President's concern to ensure the election of Muzenda to represent the Masvingo region in the presidential commission and Zvobgo's interest to challenge that representation.[42] In Masvingo, the whole party appeared to have been divided between the Zvobgo and Muzenda camps. Another province which experienced factional fighting during the primaries was Manicaland. There the cleavage was between Politburo member Didymus Mutasa and Minister Kumbirai Kangai. According to a recent statement by a party member in Manicaland, 'Each faction is always out to discredit the other [in their fight] for political supremacy in the province'.[43]

Although the party had made it clear many times that all those standing as independents would be expelled from the party, the Central Committee after the 1995 parliamentary elections and before the local elections, decided to expel only four members, Dongo among them. Three other members were suspended from the Central Committee for five years but were able to keep their

---

[39]The primary election results published in *The Herald* (between 20 February and 2 March 1995) showed that an average number of votes cast in each constituency was less than 1000.

[40]Chimutengwende spoke on 30 March 1995 in the Monthly Forum of the African Association of Political Science (AAPS) Zimbabwe National Chapter at Monomapata Hotel, in Harare, on the theme 'Are Primary Elections Democratic?'.

[41]*Financial Gazette* 16 February 1995.

[42]That the President appointed Tungamirai as a non-constituency MP showed that it was not Tungamirai but his popularity that was a problem.

[43]*Sunday Standard* 24–30 May 1998.

party cards. It is not surprising that the people's confidence in both the electoral process and the ruling party is deteriorating.

Concluding remarks

During the hundred-year long history of elections in Rhodesia/Zimbabwe, there have been six referenda, 25 legislative elections and two presidential elections. The number of eligible voters in these elections has grown from less than 5,000 to the current 5 million. The state has endured 6 major changes in the constitution. The number of political parties has been probably close to one hundred. At the same time, intense political party competition in these elections has been the exception rather than the rule. As a result, discontent in society seems to call for a facade of a united ruling elite. Hence for most of its history the country has been a *de facto* one-party state.

This chapter has attempted to approach the formality of multi-party competition by looking at the dynamics of rural and urban political mobilisation in Zimbabwe before the 2000 elections. It was hardly surprising that in the rural areas intimidation permeated the very first elections, which effectively ended the liberation war. The same pattern, however, was still present during the 1985 elections, particularly in areas that supported the main opposition party. Power-sharing between the two parties with regional support, and between the two leaders, proved to be impossible and peace was restored to the country only by eliminating the two-party system. Since then, coercion has continued to play a role in the elections and was again very open in 2000. The people's dependency on the state has been used in order to guarantee their vote for the ruling party. In the urban areas, the fact that the Unity Accord between the rival parties coincided with the wider movement towards democratisation all over Africa, apparently encouraged a more horizontal and interest-based mobilisation of the people. The state response, however, was repressive. The state presented itself as having a monopoly over both development in the rural areas and the people's mobilisation in the urban areas. This is not to say that the party would have entirely lost its legitimacy in the eyes of the voters but it is to say that their ability to make an electoral choice was very constrained until the 2000 elections, when the new party MDC posed a serious challenge to the ruling party.

After the 2000 elections, the rural-urban divide in Zimbabwe has become politically more important than ever before. In June 2000, the voters were given an opportunity to vote against the ruling party and urban apathy changed into massive support of the new opposition.[44] However, pre-election intimidation was most severe in the rural areas. Due to the power of the rural vote, ZANU (PF) was able to get a majority, 62 seats, of the 120 contested seats. MDC was able to secure all the urban seats in Harare and Bulawayo. It also got most of the seats in the Matabeleland provinces, reflecting the unpopularity of Mugabe's regime among the Ndebele population as a whole. MDC holds 57 seats in the new parliament and Sithole's ZANU was able to keep one seat at Chipinge.

With regard to future scenarios, the above analysis of the previous elections raises an important point. A reform of the constitution and the electoral legislation is necessary to make competition between the government and the opposition more fair. However, given the level of dependency and intimidation in the rural areas, and the heterogeneous character of the opposition (that includes workers, unemployed people, civic groups, whites and the Matabeleland region), it is possible that these reforms alone would not threaten the position of the ruling party. Both in the rural and urban areas, it is the state–society relation, and in particular the form and content of institutions of the state as a whole, that requires a detailed analysis if people's political behaviour is to be understood.

---

[44]These elections were preceded by a referendum in February 2000 on a new constitution. The government proposal was opposed by civic groups and MDC, which had agitated for more radical reforms especially as far as the limitation of the powers of the president were concerned. The government proposal was rejected by the electorate largely due to the 'No' vote in the urban areas.

APPENDIX

Testing for Political Business Cycles in Africa

MICHAEL COWEN, LIISA LAAKSO & SIMO VIRTANEN
WITH RIINA YRJÖLÄ

A statistical analysis was undertaken, for 12 of the case study countries included in this book, to estimate the impact of elections upon a set of macroeconomic variables.[1] Time series for five macroeconomic aggregates – central government expenditure, government budget deficit, the money aggregates M1 and M2 and domestic credit expansion – were compiled for the period 1967–97.[2] All variables were expressed as ratios of Gross Domestic Product (GDP) at current prices. More specifically, we were interested in whether the variation in the *change* in the mean value of each variable was significantly correlated with an election year and could be explained by the impact of elections both during the 1967–96 period as a whole and for two sub-periods, 1967–89 and 1990–97. This partition of the data set enabled us to see whether multi-party elections of the second period have had a significant impact upon the set of macroeconomic variables included in the analysis of political business cycles. The tables below show the results of two different methods that were employed to test for cycles.

In summary, the results show that multi-party elections have had some impact upon the year-on-year change and the trend of the measured economic variables. Deficit financing for government spending was statistically significant for the multi-party period, according to one of the measures deployed to test for cycles, and the impact of elections for this variable was significantly different from that of the 'one-party' period. However, estimations for the later 1990–97 period tended to be generally more significant than for either the earlier 'one-party' period or that of the full period taken as a whole. Further, the results show some evidence that the governments tended to manipulate money supply aggregates during electoral years for multi-party elections.[3] Although less significant than other measured variables, there is also some evidence that domestic credit expansion, probably through bank lending, was evident for the 1967–97 period as a whole.

---

[1] As we explained in the preface to this volume, the choice of country case studies was entirely dependent upon the association of the contributors with the Institute of Development Studies at the University of Helsinki. Thus, while the contributions may not have been randomly chosen, there was no systematic basis for choosing the countries entering into this analysis. The set of countries that constituted the tests for political business cycles is not to be construed as a statistical sample. This said, and given the range of different countries entering the set, we have no reason to suppose that this set of countries does not represent trends throughout Africa.
Namibia and Guinea Bissau were not included in the analysis due to data problems.
[2] Some time series of particular countries, started before 1967; for others, data for 1996 were incomplete. We are also grateful to Anthony Aubynn, Atta El-Battahani and Michael Neocosmos for obtaining data to fill some gaps in the Ghana, Sudan and Botswana data sets.
[3] It should be noted that the electoral impact upon economic variables, especially money supply aggregates, may follow from indirect manipulation. Governments, as mentioned in some of the chapters in this volume, may not directly manipulate economic aggregates but indirectly do so by taking deliberate actions for electoral purposes that are to be regarded here as having the same impact as if they had engaged in manipulation.

Results from this analysis should be interpreted in context. Most election years in our data set occurred during the one-party period when there was little or no need for state regimes to manipulate macroeconomic aggregates of the economy. Since relatively few elections have been held during the multi-party period, and this period encompasses far fewer years and, therefore, observations, the measured impact of elections upon the evident manipulation of macroeconomic aggregates means that any statistical impact shown below has added political significance. Generally, the results of the analysis for the 1967–97 period taken as a whole show a high degree of year-on-year variation for virtually all dependent variables in the analysis. This variation may be due to structural reasons. For example, when some countries are susceptible to periodic droughts, and/or are dependent upon one or a small number of primary product exports, this impact of output and price fluctuations upon the economic variables tested here can be expected to swamp any variation that might stem from electoral manipulation. Thus, the kind of statistical impact shown here also had added political significance.

The choice of macroeconomic variables for the analysis depended upon our perception of what were thought to be the key *measurable* instruments through which state regimes might manipulate the economy. Impacts of elections upon wage-employment, unemployment and real wages, the key variables which enter into most political business cycle analysis, were not estimated here due to the problem of finding reliable, accessible data across most of the cases under review.

Although the time series was partitioned into two periods, the methods involved in this kind of exercise presuppose that historical time is constant insofar as differences in historical experience over the years of the period as a whole are necessarily reduced to a common unit of time. Thus, this relatively simple statistical analysis presupposes that the political and economic meaning of government spending, and all the other measured variables in relation to the impact of elections, is the same for all years under review. Also, and due to all the foregoing, the exercise also suffers from bias that arises from omitting a host of variables of a political and/or institutional kind that could be correlated with the election variable and influence the dependent economic measures. However, omitted variable bias need not necessarily bias the impact of the election variable itself. Therefore, while the results should also be understood within this more general context and cautiously interpreted, they need not be treated with undue caution.

Methods for the Analysis

Multiple regression is the simplest method that is used to test time series for political business cycles.[4] Normally, one would analyse the *levels* of the dependent macroeconomic variable as a possible effect that can be partly attributed to the periodic holding of elections. Thus, in taking money supply as an example, an election effect would be evident if the average money supply for election years is higher than that in non-election years. However, economic time series of macroeconomic variables have a characteristic, that of serial correlation that precludes the use of simple ordinary least squares regression (OLS) in cyclical analyses. Serial correlation (autocorrelation) means that successive observations of any time series are not independent of each other. Baseline budgeting is another good example: The starting point for the planning of next year's budget is not zero but is often the present year's budget and the procedure is then to make any necessary adjustments to this baseline. This successive dependence of one observation upon another violates the assumptions underlying the OLS method and makes calls upon other estimation methods.[5]

One way to usefully overcome autocorrelation problems is to examine *changes*, rather than levels of each dependent variable. The method used for examining changes in dependent variables is called the first difference method (FD). By differencing the series, the dependence between successive observations can be removed and OLS can then be applied to the differenced series. In taking the first of the above examples, an election effect would then be evident if the average

[4]See, for example, the papers in Willet 1989 and Frey 1997.
[5]See D.N. Gujarati, *Basic Econometrics,* New York: McGraw Hill 1988 (2nd edition), pp. 380ff.

change in money supply for election years is higher than that of money supply in non-election years. In most cases, the FD procedure requires an assumption that the money supply in a given election year changes from the previous year. This is a more stringent criterion than that mentioned above for simple OLS because an election year is then compared with one specific year rather than all non-election years. In addition, in a situation where one election year follows another it would require changes in both of them. FD models are normally estimated *without* a *constant* term. A constant would indicate linear trend in the series.

The FD method assumes that the magnitude of autocorrelation is perfect, namely that it has the value of one.[6] This assumption, however, may not be true for any given series of a particular variable. Therefore, methods that estimate the degree of autocorrelation, along with the usual effect parameters, have been developed. These methods are generally known as estimated generalised least squares (EGLS).[7] As well as providing better estimates for the effects of independent upon dependent variables, EGLS models are easier to interpret than those based upon changes in the estimated variables. The SPSS computer package includes the named procedure, AREG, which we have used here to estimate EGLS models. Unfortunately, EGLS methods are based upon desirable large-sample properties and it is for this reason that we have also reported results of the analysis obtained by using the FD method.

Definitions of variables

M1: Sum of money outside banks and demand deposits other than those of the central government.

M2 (money plus quasi-money): M1 plus sum of time deposits and time and savings deposits comprising time savings and foreign currency deposits of resident sectors other than central government.

Government expenditure: all payments by government for current and capital purposes.

Budget Deficit: Government revenue minus government expenditure where revenue is defined as all receipts other than grants.

Domestic Credit: Sum of claims on central and local government and non-financial public enterprises and private sector and other bank and non-financial institutions.

Data sources:

Basic data set compiled from: *International Financial Statistics Yearbook,* Washington DC: IMF 1996–8; *World Data CD-Rom,* Washington DC: World Bank 1995–8.

---

[6]*Ibid.*; C.W. Ostrom, *Time Series Analysis: Regression techniques,* Newbury Park, CA: Sage 1990 (2nd edition), chs. 1–4.
[7]P. Kennedy, *A Guide to Econometrics,* Cambridge, MA: MIT Press 1985 (2nd edition), pp. 98–110.; Ostrom, *op. cit.*

Results of the analysis
First Difference Method

Table A1: First-Difference estimates of the electoral impact on year-on-year change in selected macro-economic variables

Dependent Variable	Coefficient 1967–97 (t value)	Coefficient 1967–89 (t value)	Coefficient 1990–97 (T value)	Chow test F ratio (probability)
Government	.268	−.158	1.668	1.238
expenditure	(.386)	(−.251)	(.732)	(0.267)
Budget deficit	−.431	.750	−3.580	6.448*
	(−.562)	(.858)	(−2.308)*	(0.012)
Domestic credit	1.508	1.162	2.184	0.189
	(1.358)	(1.218)	(.715)	(0.664)
M1	.0573	−.148	.526	1.203
	(.203)	(−.425)	(1.136)	(0.273)
M2	.625	.533	.830	0.100
	(1.444)	(1.011)	(1.109)	(0.752)

*Significantly different from zero at the 5 per cent risk level (two-sided test).

Each cell in Table A1 represents one model estimating the impact of elections on a dependent variable. Since a *constant* term was not included in the estimation procedure, the average change for non-election years is assumed to be zero or that changes over a period of time cancel each other out. The coefficient in each cell represents the average change for election years. If electoral manipulation is predicted to have taken place then these estimated coefficients should be positive except for that of the budget deficit where they should be negative because it is likely that electoral manipulation will increase the deficit. A Chow test was deployed (last column) to show whether these coefficients for the one- and multi-party periods were statistically significant from each other.[8]

Table A1 shows that multi-party elections, during the 1990–97 period, have had a statistically significant impact on deficit financing for government spending but that the other estimated impacts do not reach the 5 per cent significance level. This table also shows that the coefficient for deficit financing for the multi-party period is significantly different from that of the earlier period at the 5 per cent level. Despite the lack of statistical significance for the other variables, all coefficients for the whole study period (first column) and multi-party period (penultimate column) are in the expected direction. Furthermore, the estimated impacts are *all* stronger for the multi-party period than for the earlier one-party period.

EGLS method
For the purpose of data analysis, election years were regarded as the independent variable and assigned a dummy value. The five macroeconomic aggregates, as mentioned above and all expressed as percentages of GDP at current prices, appear below as the dependent variables. One country, Botswana, represents the base-line reference point for the study as a whole. Botswana appears in the tables below as the variable known as the CONSTANT. The variable named ELECTIONS represents the average impact of all countries taken as a whole. The parameter estimate (or B coefficient) is the difference between election and non-election years for the level in each of the five macroeconomic variables. The AR1 parameter estimates the degree of *autocorrelation* present in the series (dependence between successive observations). This parameter does not have a substantive meaning here but without it the other parameters of interest cannot be estimated reliably.

[8]See Gujarati, *op. cit.*, 443–5.

Example

Take Table A2.1 as an example. The parameter estimate for ELECTIONS is the impact of an election upon the change in government expenditure. For all countries taken as a whole, this coefficient estimates that an election year will increase the average government expenditure spending as a percentage of GDP by 0.71. However, the associated approximate probability (.206) warns us that there is a 21 per cent chance that we will falsely conclude that elections influence the level of government spending.

The CONSTANT parameter estimate represents the average level of government expenditure, as a percentage of GDP, in Botswana during non-election years (35.17). For Botswana, therefore, the average level in election years would be the sum of
CONSTANT+ELECTIONS (35.17 + 0.71 = 35.88).

For all other countries, the following procedure applies. Take Ghana as an example, where the average level in proportionate government expenditure is estimated to be 18.47 *lower* than that of Botswana, the reference point, for both election and non-election years.

For non-election years, the average level in proportionate government expenditure is CONSTANT+GHANA.
Therefore, for Ghana from Table A2.1, the average level in government expenditure is
(35.17)+(−18.47) = 16.70.
For election years, the average level in proportionate government expenditure is
CONSTANT+GHANA+ELECTIONS.
Therefore, for Ghana from Table A2.1, the average level in government expenditure is
(35.17)+(−18.47)+(0.71) = 17.41.

One should note that the country effects are not really of much interest here. Country effects are included only to make sure that the impact of elections could be estimated more reliably, especially by reducing omitted variable bias. A model without these effects would implicitly assume that all countries entering into this analysis have experienced, for example, the same level of government expenditure relative to GDP. We consider this to be an unrealistic assumption.

Interpretation of the results

Tables A2.1 to A6.3 present the results of the EGLS analysis. First, it can be seen that the pattern of the results confirms that for the FD method insofar that (a) estimates for the whole period (1967–97) and multi-party period (1990–97) are always in the right direction and that (b) the estimated impacts are always stronger for the multi-party period. Only one of the five estimates for the one-party period, that of M1, is in the wrong direction.

Second, the conventional 5 per cent significance level for a two-sided test was reached only for M2 during the multi-party period. However, marginally significant results, the risk of less than 10 per cent in obtaining a false prediction, appear for the budget deficit and domestic credit during the whole study period and for M1 during the multi-party period. For a one-sided test, these money supply results are significant at the per cent level. We were not able to run the analysis for a broader measure of money, M3. It is likely that elections may have produced a larger impact upon a broader measure of money.

Table A2.1: Government expenditure as a ratio of GDP at current prices, 1967–97

	B parameter	Standard error	t-Ratio	Approximate probability
AR1	.673744	.0409728	16.443675	.00000000
CONSTANT	35.168004	2.8522206	12.330044	.00000000
ELECTIONS	.710587	.5609233	1.266816	.20620053
ETHIOPIA	−15.514981	3.8504723	−4.029371	.00007089
GHANA	−18.468231	3.9266833	−4.703265	.00000391
KENYA	−10.494316	3.8145413	−2.751134	.00629881
LESOTHO	7.877265	4.0685999	1.936112	.05379001
MALAWI	−9.146544	4.0316454	−2.268688	.02399525
NIGERIA	−19.495490	3.8829868	−5.020746	.00000088
SUDAN	−17.573341	4.4587661	−3.941301	.00010082
SWAZILAND	−5.475800	3.9981780	−1.369574	.17184083
TANZANIA	−13.022839	3.8783060	−3.357868	.00088644
ZAMBIA	−3.620092	3.8048311	−.951446	.34214128
ZIMBABWE	−10.541778	3.8212116	−2.758753	−.00615743

Table A2.2: Government expenditure as a ratio of GDP at current prices, 1967–89[a]

	B parameter	Standard error	t-Ratio	Approximate probability
AR1	.779459	.0387996	20.089355	.00000000
CONSTANT	33.489869	3.8026634	8.806951	.00000000
ELECTIONS	.417349	.5421534	.769798	.44221655
ETHIOPIA	−11.388685	4.8518238	−2.347300	.01976658
GHANA	−16.288543.	4.9912467	−3.263422	.00126977
KENYA	−11.796127	4.8207870	−2.446930	.01516430
LESOTHO	10.835369	5.4326110	1.994505	0.4728783
MALAWI	−7.172688	5.1501441	−1.392716	.16506229
NIGERIA	−19.594464	5.1548356	−3.801181	.00018486
SWAZILAND	−5.550752	5.3786720	−1.031993	.30316879
TANZANIA	−7.395356	4.9805225	−1.484855	.13896336
ZAMBIA	.597497	4.7906190	.124722	.90085332
ZIMBABWE	−11.210001	4.8278437	−2.321948	.02111793

a. Due to data problems, Sudan was excluded from this estimation

Table A2.3: Government expenditure as a ratio of GDP at current prices, 1990–97[a]

	B parameter	Standard error	t-Ratio	Approximate probability
AR1	.202818	.1525844	1.3292213	.19033015
CONSTANT	37.357634	3.7868008	9.8652228	.00000000
ELECTIONS	2.674761	2.2755027	1.1754594	.24585929
ETHIOPIA	−14.063265	5.5716243	−2.5240871	.01511556
GHANA	−21.255682	5.8893723	−3.6091592	.00075523
KENYA	−10.298728	5.5694412	−1.8491493	.07086830
LESOTHO	8.111566	5.1519845	1.5744546	.12223586
MALAWI	−11.596003	8.6988260	−1.3330538	.18907900
NIGERIA	−16.113521	5.3438220	−3.0153551	.00416907
SWAZILAND	−6.818997	5.1614235	−1.3211467	.19298679
TANZANIA	−20.824387	5.1613723	−4.0346609	.00020440
ZAMBIA	−11.230160	5.1613958	−2.1757990	.03474410
ZIMBABWE	−8.959296	5.8991035	−1.5187555	.13566782

a. Due to data problems, Sudan was excluded from this estimation

Table A3.1: Government budget deficit as a ratio of GDP at current prices, 1967–97

	B parameter	Standard error	t-Ratio	Approximate probability
AR1	.548033	.0512009	10.703592	.00000000
CONSTANT	3.525769	2.2201226	1.588097	.11338901
ELECTIONS	−1.144943	.6569817	−1.742733	.08247427
ETHIOPIA	−7.589885	2.9912288	−2.537380	.01170936
GHANA	−6.983161	3.0565780	−2.284634	.02307983
KENYA	−7.812408	3.1962272	−2.444259	.01512982
LESOTHO	−6.099246	3.3310471	−1.831030	.06815491
MALAWI	−10.312356	3.1355203	−3.288882	.00113398
NIGERIA	−6.160938	3.0121169	−2.045385	.04174808
SUDAN	−6.250170	3.6226684	−1.725295	.08557382
SWAZILAND	−4.791765	3.1078114	−1.541845	.12423651
TANZANIA	−9.043688	3.0270495	−2.987625	.00305976
ZAMBIA	−13.980236	2.9967286	−4.665166	.00000478
ZIMBABWE	−10.386221	3.3931064	−3.060977	.00241960

Table A3.2: Government budget deficit as a ratio of GDP at current prices, 1967–89[a]

	B parameter	Standard error	t-Ratio	Approximate probability
AR1	.555936	.0568143	9.7851479	.00000000
CONSTANT	2.588265	2.5123926	1.0301991	.30410724
ELECTIONS	−.794267	.7855077	−1.0111508	.31311342
ETHIOPIA	−6.256533	3.3729530	−1.8549124	.06501715
GHANA	−6.318004	3.3699884	−1.8747852	.06221713
KENYA	−7.581958	3.5858074	−2.1144354	.03566319
LESOTHO	−8.887582	3.9135100	−2.2710001	.02416591
MALAWI	−9.690338	3.3730113	−2.8729041	.00448678
NIGERIA	−4.326034	3.3740514	−1.2821483	.20121097
SWAZILAND	−3.928537	3.5429926	−1.1088189	.26878259
TANZANIA	−9.697857	3.3928102	−2.8583552	.00468949
ZAMBIA	−12.281527	3.3371859	−3.6802046	.00029657
ZIMBABWE	−8.147157	3.8015175	−2.1431328	.03325815

a. Due to data problems, Sudan was excluded from this estimation

Table A3.3: Government budget deficit as a ratio of GDP at current prices, 1990–97[a]

	B parameter	Standard error	t-Ratio	Approximate probability
AR1	.178723	.2598861	.6876969	.49509683
CONSTANT	8.331414	3.0225278	2.7564393	.00834939
ELECTIONS	−2.572920	1.8495085	−1.3911373	.17087618
ETHIOPIA	−14.496036	4.1148106	−3.5228927	.00097675
GHANA	−8.980940	4.7086153	−1.9073420	.06273159
KENYA	−10.662516	4.4465756	−2.3979163	.02060340
LESOTHO	−4.963499	4.1096911	−1.2077547	.23331471
MALAWI	−9.936679	7.0516841	−1.4091214	.16552381
NIGERIA	−15.644338	4.2647702	−3.6682723	.00063218
SWAZILAND	−7.616707	4.1173489	−1.8499058	.07075704
TANZANIA	−10.546149	4.1174588	−2.5613247	.01377131
ZAMBIA	−20.158124	4.3844975	−4.5975904	.00003346
ZIMBABWE	−15.885944	4.7146808	−3.3694633	.00153226

a. Due to data problems, Sudan was excluded from this estimation

Table A4.1: M1 as a ratio of GDP at current prices, 1967–97

	B parameter	Standard error	t-Ratio	Approximate probability
AR1	.8683011	.0254904	34.063809	.00000000
CONSTANT	9.6924536	2.3675933	4.093800	.00005300
ELECTIONS	.1645312	.2182722	.753789	.45149448
ETHIOPIA	9.6915918	2.8663821	3.381123	.00080542
GHANA	8.1548047	2.1161097	3.853678	.00013895
KENYA	4.9938989	3.0090820	1.659609	.09790982
LESOTHO	8.8938671	3.9667627	2.242097	.02559563
MALAWI	.8414547	3.5091448	.239789	.81063741
NIGERIA	1.7448509	3.1278125	.557850	.57731163
SUDAN	9.7352486	3.4624270	2.811683	.00521255
SWAZILAND	.6822627	3.7137430	.183713	.85434752
TANZANIA	8.1018472	3.3539254	2.415631	.01623159
ZAMBIA	5.4776244	3.3457941	1.637167	.10251531
ZIMBABWE	7.4785080	3.4502754	2.167510	.03088550

Table A4.2: M1 as a ratio of GDP at current prices, 1967–89

	B parameter	Standard error	t-Ratio	Approximate probability
AR1	.841299	.0325544	25.842895	.00000000
CONSTANT	12.612716	2.3841716	5.290188	.00000026
ELECTIONS	−.116574	.2643691	−.440952	.65961255
ETHIOPIA	5.900144	2.6766446	2.204306	.02837579
GHANA	6.178050	2.1729221	2.843199	.00481959
KENYA	−1.044441	2.8748577	−.363302	.71667362
LESOTHO	6.602974	4.0636308	1.624895	.10539183
MALAWI	−1.745936	3.4289257	−.509179	.61105713
NIGERIA	−1.632250	3.0580945	−.533747	.59397060
SUDAN	8.444797	3.2843951	2.571188	.01068962
SWAZILAND	−.936824	3.7153411	−.252150	.80112332
TANZANIA	7.438151	3.2532484	2.286377	.02303363
ZAMBIA	5.222904	3.2574168	1.603388	11005838
ZIMBABWF	3.144323	3.3343828	.943000	.34655289

Table A4.3: M1 as a ratio of GDP at current prices, 1990–97

	B parameter	Standard error	t-Ratio	Approximate probability
AR1	.384828	.1156430	3.327721	.00142499
CONSTANT	7.242291	.9701224	7.465337	.00000000
ELECTIONS	.827809	.4327767	1.912785	.06005102
ETHIOPIA	22.665336	1.4150162	16.017722	.00000000
GHANA	4.191008	1.3290956	3.153278	.00241625
KENYA	8.377361	1.3711849	6.109578	.00000006
LESOTHO	10.454707	1.4194563	7.365290	.00000000
MALAWI	3.052747	1.4202123	2.149500	.03520980
NIGERIA	7.702623	1.4566273	5.287985	.00000146
SUDAN	15.796361	1.7393301	9.081865	.00000000
SWAZILAND	.725768	1.4208455	.510800	.61117011
TANZANIA	5.809912	1.4194453	4.093086	.00011676
ZAMBIA	.953000	1.3805331	.690313	.49238173
ZIMBABWE	5.609799	1.4194715	3.952034	.00018906

Table A5.1: M2 as a ratio of GDP at current prices, 1967–97

	B parameter	Standard error	t-Ratio	Approximate probability
AR1	.984260	.008759	112.36905	.00000000
CONSTANT	57.660125	13.477128	4.27837	.00002456
ELECTIONS	.449974	.326176	1.37954	.16864176
ETHIOPIA	-8.396650	6.145258	-1.36636	.17273620
GHANA	-4.105682	3.613580	-1.13618	.25668799
KENYA	-29.405126	7.810050	-3.76504	.00019643
LESOTHO	-28.809925	20.821626	-1.38365	.16738024
MALAWI	-56.555987	19.089983	-2.96260	.00326733
NIGERIA	-61.805720	8.496736	-7.27405	.00000000
SUDAN	-45.927593	18.004373	-2.55091	.01118559
SWAZILAND	-38.167048	14.524849	-2.62771	.00898935
TANZANIA	-39.033367	15.746932	-2.47879	.01367167
ZAMBIA	-47.640904	16.044202	-2.96935	.00319818
ZIMBABWE	-40.387493	17.824649	-2.26582	.02409621

Table A5.2: M2 as a ratio of GDP at current prices, 1967–89

	B parameter	Standard error	t-Ratio	Approximate probability
AR1	.954140	.016803	56.784570	.00000000
CONSTANT	47.696853	7.181790	6.641360	.00000000
ELECTIONS	.082248	.391837	.209904	.83390933
ETHIOPIA	-14.532405	5.014500	-2.898076	.00407985
GHANA	-10.861874	3.636737	-2.986709	.00309353
KENYA	-30.880048	5.973042	-5.169903	.00000047
LESOTHO	-7.928476	12.807937	-.619028	.53644816
MALAWI	-33.917483	11.216688	-3.023841	.00274955
NIGERIA	-44.113323	6.765178	-6.520645	.00000000
SUDAN	-28.448891	10.832352	-2.626289	.00915230
SWAZILAND	-12.911806	10.598455	-1.218273	.22424198
TANZANIA	-18.894768	10.360497	-1.823732	.06935853
ZAMBIA	-24.091977	10.420224	-2.312040	.02156951
ZIMBABWE	-23.282266	10.904098	-2.135185	.03369545

Table A5.3: M2 as a ratio of GDP at current prices, 1990–97

	B parameter	Standard error	t-Ratio	Approximate probability
AR1	.465524	.1087929	4.278991	.00006107
CONSTANT	24.180125	1.7312174	13.967123	.00000000
ELECTIONS	1.569123	.6761558	2.320653	.02335817
ETHIOPIA	20.111762	2.5171562	7.989874	.00000000
GHANA	-8.085975	2.2934969	-3.525610	.00076732
KENYA	14.238310	2.4445050	5.824619	.00000018
LESOTHO	13.734878	2.5385264	5.410571	.00000091
MALAWI	-4.747526	2.5391234	-1.869750	.06588872
NIGERIA	-1.989842	2.5844161	-.769939	.44404252
SUDAN	5.336718	3.0527843	1.748148	.08501926
SWAZILAND	4.273771	2.5388369	1.683358	.09696023
TANZANIA	-2.651056	2.5330697	-1.046579	.29905503
ZAMBIA	-5.232860	2.4529709	-2.133274	.03656819
ZIMBABWE	-2.254273	2.5236609	-.893255	.37491787

Table A6.1: Domestic credit expansion as a ratio of GDP at current prices, 1967–97

	B parameter	Standard error	t-Ratio	Approximate probability
AR1	.974647	.012202	79.875152	.00000000
CONSTANT	−3.446942	25.873776	−.133221	.89410197
ELECTIONS	1.511801	.847142	1.784588	.07527536
ETHIOPIA	54.104668	15.064890	3.591441	.00038050
GHANA	67.812993	8.958466	7.569710	.00000000
KENYA	32.725525	25.584639	1.279108	.20178566
LESOTHO	−43.521477	42.337414	−1.027967	.30474159
MALAWI	−21.166776	39.378647	−.537519	.59128266
NIGERIA	7.308515	26.408871	.276745	.78215480
SUDAN	7.604496	38.141249	.199377	.84209431
SWAZILAND	13.620698	34.637779	.393232	.69440968
TANZANIA	32.314020	35.683372	.905576	.36584142
ZAMBIA	21.584701	36.296234	.594682	.55247660
ZIMBABWE	14.552374	38.189291	.381059	.70341232

Table A6.2: Domestic credit expansion as a ratio of GDP at current prices, 1967–89

	B parameter	Standard error	t-Ratio	Approximate probability
AR1	.921238	.021550	42.749548	.000000000
CONSTANT	−.837630	9.239063	−.090662	.92783724
ELECTIONS	.230529	.706248	.326413	.74439722
ETHIOPIA	28.853820	8.175973	3.529099	.00050001
GHANA	37.913463	6.033090	6.284253	.00000000
KENYA	22.310847	11.974837	1.863144	.06366864
LESOTHO	30.567331	16.215312	1.885090	.06063083
MALAWI	19.903990	14.144131	1.407226	.16065948
NIGERIA	11.894647	12.178695	.976677	.32971679
SUDAN	31.370476	13.710238	2.288106	.02300528
SWAZILAND	20.691717	14.801854	1.397914	.16343497
TANZANIA	40.282447	13.781447	2.922948	.00380006
ZAMBIA	37.806845	13.889803	2.721914	.00696842
ZIMBABWE	31.768652	14.051846	2.260817	.02467069

Table A6.3: Domestic credit expansion as a ratio of GDP at current prices, 1990–97

	B parameter	Standard error	t-Ratio	Approximate probability
AR1	.96196	.033198	28.976409	.0000000
CONSTANT	−81.78039	44.941884	−1.819692	.07327356
ELECTIONS	4.36481	2.913389	1.498189	.13878114
ETHIOPIA	122.40118	26.371036	4.641501	.00001660
GHANA	85.98709	15.624191	5.503459	.00000063
KENYA	109.46206	32.966436	3.320409	.00145738
LESOTHO	50.86292	58.187171	.874126	.38517216
MALAWI	42.02240	56.695896	.741189	.46116862
NIGERIA	88.11437	35.891406	2.455027	.01668984
SUDAN	79.47756	51.561854	1.541402	.12792904
SWAZILAND	58.86855	41.985343	1.402121	.16549521
TANZANIA	76.56872	45.089848	1.698137	.09412214
ZAMBIA	112.06182	47.744354	2.347122	.02188263
ZIMBABWE	82.91565	48.883880	1.696176	.09449473

Bibliography

Abbink, Jon (1995) 'Breaking and Making the State: The Dynamics of Ethnic Democracy in Ethiopia', *Journal of Contemporary African Studies* 13(2): 149–163.

Abrahamsen, Rita (1997) 'The Victory of Popular Forces or Passive Revolution? A Neo-Gramscian Perspective on Democratisation', *Journal of Modern African Studies* 35(1): 129–152.

Abshire, David M. and Samuels, Michael A. (eds.) (1969) *Portuguese Africa: A Handbook*, New York and London: Praeger and Pall Mall Press.

Adekanye, J. Bayo (1981) *Nigeria in Search of Stable Civil-Military Relations*, Aldershot and Boulder, CO: Gower and Westview.

Adekanye, J. Bayo (1993) 'Military Occupation and Social Stratification', inaugural lecture, Ibadan: University of Ibadan Press.

Adekanye, J. Bayo (1995) 'Structural Adjustment, Democratization and Rising Ethnic Tensions in Africa', *Development and Change* 26(2): 355–374.

Africa Watch (1989) *Zimbabwe: A Break with the Past? Human Rights and Political Unity*, New York: The Africa Watch Committee.

African Association of Political Science (1995) 'Democratic Transition in Africa', *Newsletter* 19.

Agbu, Osita (1998) 'Political Opposition and Democratic Transitions in Nigeria, 1985–1996', in Adebayo O. Olukoshi (ed.) *The Politics of Opposition in Contemporary Africa*, Uppsala: Nordiska Afrikainstitutet.

Agnew, John A. (1987) *Place and Politics: The Geographical Mediation of State and Society,* Winchester, MA: Allen & Unwin.

Agnew, John A. and Corbridge, Stuart (1995) *Mastering Space: Hegemony, Territory and International Political Economy,* London: Routledge.

Agnew, John A. and Duncan, James S. (1989) *The Power of Place: Bringing Together Geographical and Sociological Imaginations,* Winchester, MA: Allen & Unwin.

Agovi, K. (1991) 'A King is not Above Insult: The Politics of Good Governance in Nzema Avudwene Festival Songs', *International Journal of Black Oral Tradition and Literary Studies* 3(1).

Aguilar, Renato and Stenman, Åsa (1996) *Guinea-Bissau 1995: Missing the Beat*, Göteborg: University of Göteborg Department of Economics.

Ahluwalia, D. P. (1996) *Post-Colonialism and the Politics of Kenya*, New York: Nova Science Publishers.

Ake, Claude (1993) 'The Unique Case of African Democracy', *International Affairs* 69: 239–244.

Akc, C. (1996) 'The Political Question', in O. Oyediran (ed.) *Governance and Development in Nigeria: Essays in Honour of Professor Billy J. Dudley*, Ibadan: Oyediran International/Agbo Ero Publishers.

Alemayehu, Rahel (1992) 'Women and the Ethiopian Legal System', in *Proceedings from the National Workshop on the Rights and Responsibilities of Ethiopian Women in the Rehabilitation and Reconstruction of the Nation,* Transitional Government of Ethiopia, Office of the Prime Minister.

Al-Hardallo, Adlan (1998) 'Preliminary Observations on Civil Society in Sudan', *Mahawir* 1(1): 52–63.

Ali, Abdelagdir (1992) 'Structural Adjustment Programmes and Poverty Creation: Evidence from Sudan', *East African Social Science Research Review (EASSRR)* 8(1).

Ali, T. M. A. (1989) *The Cultivation of Hunger: State and Agriculture in Sudan*, Khartoum: Khartoum University Press.

Al-Karsani, Awad A. (1997) 'Presidential and National Council Elections for 1996', University of Khartoum Development Studies Research Centre Seminar Paper 105.

Allen, C. (1977) 'Sierra Leone', in J. Dunn (ed.), *West African States: Failure and Promise: A Study in Comparative Politics,* Cambridge: Cambridge University Press.

Al-Mahdi, Sadiq (1996) A Press Speech. Omdurman in the aftermath of the 1996 elections.

Almond, Gabriel A. and Coleman, James (eds) (1960) *The Politics of the Developing Areas*, Princeton, NJ: Princeton University Press.

Amin, Nick (1992) 'State and Peasantry in Zimbabwe since Independence', *The European Journal of Development Research* 4(1): 112–162.

Amnesty International (1995) *Ethiopia, Accountability Past and Present: Human Rights in Transition*, London: Amnesty International.

Amnesty International (1996) *Nigeria: Human Rights Defenders Under Attack*, London: Amnesty International.

Anderson, Benedict (1983) *Imagined Communities: Reflections on the Origin and Spread of Nationalism*, London: Verso.

Angula, Nahas (1998) 'Namibia at the Age of Eight', *The Namibian*, 20 March.

An-Naim, Abdellahi and Kok, Peter Niot (1991) *Fundamentalism and Militarism in Sudan*, Washington, DC: Fund for Peace.

Anyang' Nyong'o, P. (1989) 'State and Society in Kenya: The Disintegration of the Nationalist Coalition and Rise of Presidential Authority in Kenya, 1963–1978', *African Affairs* 88(351).

Apter, David (1955, second edn 1959) *The Gold Coast in Transition*, Princeton, NJ: Princeton, University Press.

Apter, David (1964) 'Some Reflections on the Role of a Political Opposition in New Nations' [published in 1962 *Comparative Studies in Society and History* IV], in William John Hanna (ed.) (1964) *Independent Black Africa: The Politics of Freedom*, Chicago: Rand McNally & Company, pp. 456–471.

Apter, David (1968) *Some Conceptual Approaches to the Study of Modernization*, Englewood Cliffs, NJ: Prentice-Hall.

Ardener, Shirley (1993) [1981] 'Introduction' in S. Ardener (ed.) *Women and Space: Ground Rules and Social Maps*, Oxford: Berg, pp. 1–30.

Ardener, Shirley and Burman, Sandra (1995) (eds.) *Money-Go-Rounds. The Importance of Saving and Credit Associations for Women*, Oxford: Berg, pp. 1–13.

Article 19 (1997) *Nigeria: Abacha's Media Crackdown*, London: Article 19.

Aryee, J. (1996) 'Quo Vadis, Ghana', *The Ghanaian Voice*, 25–27 November.

Aspen, Harald (1995) 'The 1995 National and Regional Elections in Ethiopia: Local Perspectives', University of Trondheim Center for Environment and Development Working Paper 10.

Aubynn, Anthony (1993) 'Structural Adjustment and the "Stagger" Towards Democracy: The Role of Social Movements in Ghana' in Staffan, Lindberg and Arni Svensson (eds), *Social Movements in the Third World*, Conference Proceedings, Vol. 12, Lund University of Lund, Department of Sociology.

Austin, D. (1964) *Politics in Ghana 1946–60*, Oxford: Oxford University Press.

Awad, Mohamed H. (1993) *Social Impact of Economic Liberalization Policies,* Omdurman: National Transitional Council.

Awoonor, K. (1990) *Ghana: A Political History*, Accra: Sedco.

Ayee, J. R. A. (1997) 'The December 1996 General Elections in Ghana', *Electoral Studies* 16(3).

Azam, J.-P. and Daubrée, C. (1997) *Bypassing the State: Economic Growth in Kenya, 1964–90*, Paris: OECD Development Centre.

Bailey, F. G. (1969) *Strategems and Spoils: A Social Anthropology of Politics*, Oxford: Blackwell.

Banda, Ellias N., Nankhuni, Flora S. and Chirwa, Ephraim W. (1998) 'Economy and Democracy: Background, Current Situation and Future Prospects', in K. M. Phiri and K. R. Ross (eds) *Democratization in Malawi: A Stocktaking*, Blantyre: CLAIM.

Banda, Fackson (1997) *Elections and the Press in Zambia: The Case of the 1996 Polls*, Lusaka: Zambia Independent Media Association.

Banda, Jande R. (1998) 'The Constitutional Change Debate of 1993–1995', in K. M. Phiri and K. R. Ross (eds.) *Democratization in Malawi: A Stocktaking*, Blantyre: CLAIM.

Bardill, J. E. and Cobbe, J. H. (1985) *Lesotho: Dilemmas of Dependence in Southern Africa*, Boulder, CO: Westview Press.

Barkan, J. (1976) 'Further Reassessment of "Conventional Wisdom": Political Knowledge and Voting Behaviour in Rural Kenya', *American Political Science Review* 70(2).

Barkan, J. (1979) 'Legislators, Elections, Political Linkage', in J. Barkan and J. J. Okumo (eds.) *Politics and Public Policy in Kenya and Tanzania*, New York: Praeger, pp. 64–91.

Barkan, J. and Chege, M. (1989) 'Decentralizing the State: District Focus and Politics of Reallocation in Kenya', *Journal of Modern African Studies* 27(2).

Barkan, J. and Holmquist, F. (1989) 'Peasant-State Relations and the Social Base of Self-help in Kenya', *World Politics*, 41(3).

Barkan, J. and Ng'ethe, N. (1998) 'Kenya tries again', *Journal of Democracy* 9(2): 32–48.

Barkan, J. and Okumu, J. (eds.) (1979) *Politics and Public Policy in Kenya and Tanzania*, New York: Praeger.

Barnett, Tony and Abdelkarim, Abbas (1988) *Sudan: State, Capital and Transformation*, London: Croom Helm.

Bates, R. (1989) *Beyond the Miracle of the Market: The Political Economy of Agrarian Development in Kenya*, Cambridge: Cambridge University Press.

Bates, Robert H. (1999) 'The Economic Bases of Democratization', in Richard Joseph (ed.) *State, Conflict, and Democracy in Africa*, Boulder, CO: Lynne Rienner, pp. 83–94.

Bavu, Immanuel (1989) 'Election Management and Democracy', in Haroub Othman, Immanuel Bavu, and Michael Okema (eds.) *Tanzania: Democracy in Transition*, Dar es Salaam: Dar es Salaam University Press, pp. 22–36.

Bawumia, M. (1997) 'Understanding the Rural-Urban Voting Patterns in the 1992 Ghanaian Presidential Elections: Closer Look at the Distributional Impact of Ghana's Structural Adjustment Programme', *Journal of Modern African Studies* 36(1): 47–70.

Bayart, J.-F. (1992) 'Introduction', in J.-F. Bayart, A. Mbembe and C. Toulabor (eds) *La politique par le bas en Afrique noire*, Paris: Karthala.

Bayart, J.-F. (1993) *The State in Africa. The Politics of the Belly*, London: Longman.

Bechtold, Peter (1976) *Politics in the Sudan*, New York: Praeger.

Becker, Heike (1993) 'From Anti-colonial Resistance to Reconstruction: Namibian Women's Movement from 1980 to 1992', unpublished PhD dissertation, University of Bremen.

Bennett, G. (1963) *Kenya: A Political History*, London: Oxford University Press.

Bennett, George and Rosberg, Carl G. (1961) *The Kenyatta Election: Kenya, 1960–1961*, London: Oxford University Press.

Berelson, Bernand, Lazarsfeld, Paul and McPhee, William (1954) *Voting: A Study of Opinion Formation in a Presidential Campaign*, Chicago: University of Chicago Press.

Berg-Schlosser, D. (1994) 'Ethnicity, Social Classes and Political Process in Kenya' in W. Oyugi (ed.) *Politics and Administration in East Africa*, Nairobi: East African Education Publishers.

Berman, B. (1990) *Control and Crisis in Colonial Kenya: The Dialectic of Domination*, London: James Currey.

Berman, B. and Lonsdale, J. (1992) *Unhappy Valley: Conflict in Kenya and Africa*, London: James Currey.

Beshir, M. O. (1974) *Nationalism and Revolution in Sudan*, London: Rex Collings.

Bettison, D. G. and Apthorpe, R. J. (1961) 'Authority and Residence in a Peri-urban Social Structure – Ndirande, Nyasaland', *Nyasaland Journal* 14: 7–39.

Boahen, A. (1989) *The Ghanaian Sphinx*, Accra: Ghana Academy of Arts and Sciences.

Boateng, E. A. (1996) *Government and the People: Outlook for Democracy in Ghana*. Accra: Buck.

Bond, George C. (1976) *The Politics of Change in a Zambian Community,* Chicago: University of Chicago Press.

Booth, A. R. (1983) *Swaziland: Tradition and Change in a Southern African Kingdom*, Boulder, CO: Westview Press.

Booth, David, Lugangira, Flora, Masanja, Patrick, Mvungi, Abu, Mwaipopo, Rosemarie, Mwami, Joaquim and Redmayne, Alison (1993) 'Social, Cultural and Economic Change in Contemporary Tanzania. A People-Oriented Focus', report to SIDA, commissioned through Stockholm University Department of Social Anthropology Development Studies Unit.

Botswana Institute for Development Policy Analysis (BIDPA) (1996*) Study of Poverty and Poverty Alleviation in Botswana*, Gaborone: BIDPA.

Bourdieu, Pierre (1990) [1977] *Outline of a Theory of Practice*. Cambridge: Cambridge University Press.

Bowman, Larry W. (1973) *Politics in Rhodesia: White Power in an African State*, Cambridge, MA: Harvard University Press.

Bratton, Michael (1980) *The Local Politics of Rural Development: Peasant and Party-State in Zambia*, Hanover, NE: United Press of New England.

Bratton, Michael and Posner, D. N. (1999) 'A First Look at Second Elections in Africa with Illustrations from Zambia', in R. Joseph (ed.) *State, Conflict and Democracy in Africa*, Boulder, CO: Lynne Rienner.

Bratton, Michael and van de Walle, Nicolas (1997*) Democratic Experiments in Africa. Regime Transitions in Comparative Perspective*, Cambridge: Cambridge University Press.

Brautigam, Deborah (1999) 'The "Mauritius Miracle": Democracy, Institutions, and Economic Policy' in R. Joseph (ed.) *State, Conflict and Democracy in Africa,* Boulder, CO: Lynne Rienner.

Breaking the Wall of Silence Movement (1997) *A Report to the Namibian People: Historical Account of the Swapo Spy Drama*, Windhoek: Breaking the Wall of Silence Movement.

Cabral, Amílcar (1970) 'Sur les lois portugaises de domination coloniale', mimeo, Conakry: PAIGC.

Caetano, Marcello (1970) 'Revision of the Portuguese Constitution', speech delivered by the Prime Minister Marcello Caetano before the National Assembly 2 December 1970, Lisbon: Secretariat of State for Information and Tourism.

Callewaert, Inger (1994) *The Emergence of Kiangiang Ritual Practice within Balanta Form of Life*, Lund: University of Lund Unit of History of Religions.

Callewaert, Inger (1995) 'Fyere Yaabte: um movimento terapêutico de mulheres na sociedade balanta', *Soronda, Revista de Estudos Guineenses* 20: 33–72.

Camps, Nauro F. *et al.* (1997) 'Socio-Political Instability, External Shocks, Institutional Development and Growth in the MENA Countries', a paper presented to a workshop on Institutional Reform and Development in the MENA Region, organised by Economic Research Forum, Dubai, 24–26 November.

Cardoso, Carlos (1995) 'Guineenses contra guineenses? Para um debate sobre a(s) identidade(s) na Guiné-Bissau', *Banobero*, 17 March 1995, p. 9.

Cartwright, John (1970) *Politics in Sierra Leone 1947–1967,* Toronto and Buffalo, NY: University of Toronto Press.

Cartwright, John (1972) 'Party Competition in a Developing Nation', *Journal of Commonwealth Political Studies,* 10(1): 71–90.

Catholic Commission for Justice and Peace in Zimbabwe (CCJP) (1997) *Breaking the Silence, Building True Peace: A Report of the Disturbances in Matabeleland and the Midlands 1980 to 1988,* Harare: CCJP, The Legal Resource Foundation.

Centre for Strategic Studies (1998) *Annual Report,* Khartoum: Centre for Strategic Studies.

Chabal, Patrick (ed.) (1986) *Political Domination in Africa: Reflections on the Limits of Power,* Cambridge: Cambridge University Press.

Chabal, Patrick (1995) 'The (De)construction of the Postcolonial Political Order in Black Africa', *AL Bulletin* 35(35).

Chabal, Patrick and Daloz, Jean-Pascal (1999) *Africa Works: Disorder as Political Instrument,* London: James Currey.

Chan, Stephen with the assistance of Chanda L. J. Chingambo (1992) 'Democracy in Southern Africa: The 1990 Elections in Zimbabwe and 1991 Elections in Zambia', *The Round Table* 322: 183–201.

Chanda, Donald (ed.) (no date) *Democracy in Zambia: Key Speeches of President Chiluba 1991/92,* Lusaka: Africa Press Trust.

Chazan, Naomi (1979) 'A Re-examination of the Role of Elections in African Politics', *Journal of Commonwealth and Comparative Politics* 17(2): 136–159.

Chazan, Naomi (1982) 'The New Politics of Participation in Tropical Africa', *Comparative Politics* 14(2): 169–190.

Chazan, Naomi (1987) 'The Anomalies of Continuity: Perspectives on Ghana Elections Since Independence', in F. Hayward (ed.) *Elections in Independent Africa,* Boulder, CO: Westview.

Chazan, Naomi (1988) 'Ghana: The Problem of Governance and the Emergence of Civil Society,' in L. Diamond, J. Linz and S. Lipset (eds.) *Democracy in Developing Countries, Volume Two Africa,* Boulder, CO: Lynne Rienner.

Chazan, Naomi (1991) 'The Political Transformation of Ghana Under the PNDC', in Donald Rothchild (ed.) *Ghana: The Political Economy of Recovery,* Boulder, CO: Lynne Rienner.

Chazan, Naomi, Mortimer, Robert, Ravenhill, John and Rothchild, Donald (eds) (1988*) Politics and Society in Contemporary Africa,* Boulder, CO: Lynne Rienner.

Chege, M. (1994) 'The Return of Multiparty Politics', in J.D. Barkan (ed*.) Beyond Capitalism vs. Socialism in Kenya and Tanzania,* Boulder CO: Rienner.

Clapham, Christopher (1969) *Haile Selassie's Government,* London and Harlow: Longmans, Green.

Clapham, Christopher (1985) *Third World Politics: An Introduction,* London: Croom Helm.

Clapham, Christopher (1988) *Transformation and Continuity in Revolutionary Ethiopia,* Cambridge: Cambridge University Press.

Cliffe, Lionel (ed.) (1967) *One Party Democracy: The 1965 Tanzania General Elections,* Nairobi: East African Publishing House.

Cliffe, Lionel and Puritt, Paul (1967) 'Arusha, Mixed Rural and Urban Communities', in Lionel Cliffe (ed.) *One Party Democracy: The 1965 Tanzania General Elections,* Nairobi: East African Publishing House, pp. 155–185.

Cluver, A. D. de V. (1991) *Languages in Contact and Conflict in Africa. An Ethnolinguistic Survey of the Languages of Namibia,* Pretoria: University of South Africa Department of Linguistics.

Cohen, Dennis L. (1983) 'Elections and Election Studies in Africa' in Yolamu Barabgo (ed.) *Political Science in Africa: A Critical Review,* London: Zed, pp. 72–93.

Cohen, John and Koehn, Peter (1980) *Ethiopian Provincial and Municipal Government: Imperial Patterns and Postrevolutionary Changes,* Lansing, MI: Michigan State University, African Studies Center.

Cokorinos, L. (1993) 'Diamonds Will Not Last Forever' *Southern Africa Political and Economic Monthly* 6(12).

Colclough, C. and Fallon, P. (1983) 'Rural Poverty in Botswana: Dimensions, Causes and Constraints' in D. Ghai and S. Radman (eds.) *Agrarian Policies and Rural Poverty in Africa,* Geneva: ILO.

Coleman, James (1958) *Nigeria: Background to Nationalism,* Berkeley and Los Angeles: University of California Press.

Coleman, James S. (1960) 'The Politics of Sub-Saharan Africa', in Gabriel A. Almond and James Coleman (eds.) *The Politics of the Developing Areas,* Princeton, NJ: Princeton University Press, pp. 247–368.

Coleman, James and Rosberg, Carl (1964) *Political Parties and National Integration in Tropical Africa,* Berkeley, CA: University of California Press.

Collier, Jane and Yanagisako, Sylvia (1987) 'Introduction', in Jane Collier, and Sylvia Yanagisako (eds.) *Gender and Kinship, Essays Toward a Unified Analysis,* Stanford, CA: Stanford University Press, pp. 1–13.

Collier, Ruth Berins (1982) *Regimes in Tropical Africa: Changing Forms of Supremacy, 1945–1975,* Berkeley, CA: University of California Press.

Comaroff, John (1987) 'Sui genderis: Feminism, Kinship Theory, and Structural "Domains"', in Jane Collier and Sylvia Yanagisako (eds.) *Gender and Kinship, Essays Toward a Unified Analysis*, Stanford, CA: Stanford University Press, pp. 53–85.

Committee for a Clean Campaign (no date) *Presidential and Parliamentary Elections in Zambia, 18 November 1996. A report by the Committee for a Clean Campaign*, Lusaka: Multimedia.

Commonwealth (1980) *Southern Rhodesian Elections: The Report of the Commonwealth Observer Group on Elections Leading to an Independent Zimbabwe*, London: Commonwealth Secretariat.

Commonwealth (1995) *The Presidential and National Assembly Elections in Namibia*, London: Commonwealth Secretariat.

Conférence des Organisations Nationales des Colonies Portugaises (CONCP) (1970) *Guinée et Cap Vert: Libération des colonies portugaises*, Algiers: Information CONCP.

Connel, R. W. (1987) *Gender and Power*, Cambridge: Polity Press.

Connerton, Paul (1989) *How Societies Remember*, Cambridge: Cambridge University Press.

Constantin, Francois and Coulon, Christian (eds.) (1997) *Religion et transition democratique en Afrique*, Paris: Karthala.

Cornia, Giovanni A., Jolly, Richard and Stewart, Frances (eds.) (1988) *Adjustment with a Human Face, Vol. 2*, a study by UNICEF, Oxford: Clarendon.

Cowen, Michael and Kinyanjui, Kabiru (1977) 'Some Problems of Capital and Class in Kenya', University of Nairobi Institute of Development Studies Occasional Paper 26.

Cowen, Michael and Laakso, Liisa (1997a) 'An Overview of Election Studies in Africa', University of Helsinki Institute of Developing Studies Working Paper 1/97.

Cowen, Michael and Laakso, Liisa (1997b) 'An Overview of Election Studies in Africa', *Journal of Modern African Studies* 35: 717–744.

Cowen, Michael and MacWilliam, Scott (1996) *Indigenous Capital in Kenya: The 'Indian' Dimension of Debate*, Helsinki: Interkont Books 8.

Cowen, Michael and Ngunyi, Mutahi (1997) 'Prelude to the 1992 and 1997 Elections in Kenya: Reconciling Reform within a Chain of Events', University of Helsinki Institute of Development Studies Working Paper 10/97.

Cowen, Michael P. and Shenton, Robert. W. (1996) *Doctrines of Development*, London: Routledge.

Cowen, Michael P. and Shenton, Robert W. (1998) 'Agrarian Doctrines of Development. Parts I & II', *Journal of Peasant Studies* 25(2) & 25(3).

Cox, Kevin R. (ed.) (1997) *Spaces of Globalisation: Reasserting the Power of the Local,* New York: Guilford Press.

Crush, J. S. (1987) *The Struggle for Swazi Labour*, Kingston and Montreal: McGill, Queen's University Press.

Cunnison, I. (1959) *The Luapula Peoples of Northern Rhodesia: Customs and History in Tribal Politics*, Manchester: Manchester University Press.

Dahl, Robert (1971) *Polyarchy: Participation and Opposition*, New Haven, CT: Yale University Press.

Dahl, Robert (1982) *Dilemmas of Pluralist Democracy*, New Haven, CT & London: Yale University Press.

Dahl, Robert (1989) *Democracy and its Critics*, New Haven, CT & London: Yale University Press.

Daniel, J. (1985) 'Swaziland: Just Another Bantustan?', paper presented at the Institute of Commonwealth Studies Postgraduate Seminar, London.

Darnolf, Staffan (1997) *Democratic Electioneering in Southern Africa: The Contrasting Cases of Botswana and Zimbabwe*, Göteborg: Göteborg University.

Davies, Robert *et al.* (1985) *The Kingdom of Swaziland: A Profile*, London: Zed.

de Waal, Alex (1993) 'Sudan: Searching for the Origins of Absolutism and Decay', *Development and Change* 24: 177–202.

Dekmejian, R. H. (1980) 'The Anatomy of Islamic Revival: Legitimacy, Crisis, Ethnic Conflict and the Search for Islamic Alternatives', *The Middle East Journal* 34: 1–12.

Deve T. and Gonçalves, J. (1994) 'Whither the Opposition in Zimbabwe', *Southern Africa Political & Economic Monthly* 7(8): 9–11.

Diamond, Larry (1988) 'Nigeria: Pluralism, Statism, and the Struggle for Democracy', in Larry Diamond, Juan. J. Linz and Seymour M. Lipset (eds) *Democracy in Developing Countries, Volume Two, Africa*, Boulder, CO: Lynne Rienner, pp. 33–91.

Diamond, Larry (1992) 'Economic Development and Democracy Reconsidered' in Gary Marks and Larry Diamond (eds), *Reexamining Democracy: Essays in Honour of Seymour Martin Lipset*, Newbury Park: Sage, pp. 93–139.

Diamond, Larry (1993) 'Three Paradoxes of Democracy', in Larry Diamond and Marc F. Plattner (eds.) *The Global Resurgence of Democracy*. Baltimore, MD: Johns Hopkins University Press, pp. 95–107.

Diamond, Larry, Kirk-Greene, Anthony and Oyediran, Oyeleye (eds) (1997) *Transition Without End: Nigerian Politics and Civil Society under Babangida*, Boulder, CO: Lynne Rienner.

Diamond, Larry, Linz, Juan J. and Lipset, Seymour M. (eds) (1988) *Democracy in Developing Countries, Volume Two, Africa*, Boulder, CO: Lynne Rienner.

Diamond, Larry, Plattner, Marc F., Chu, Yun-han and Tien, Hung-mao (eds.) (1997) *Consolidating the Third Wave Democracies*, Baltimore, MD: Johns Hopkins University Press.

Diescho, Joseph (1996) 'Government and Opposition in Post-independence Namibia: Perceptions and Performance', in *Building Democracy: Perceptions on the Performance of Government and Opposition in Namibia*, Windhoek: Namibia Institute of Democracy and Konrad Adenauer Stiftung.

Dlamini, K. and Levin, R. (1997) 'Breaking Tradition: The Struggle for Freedom in Swaziland,' *South African Labour Bulletin*, 21 (3), April.

Dommen, E. and B. (1999) *Mauritius: An Island of Success; A Retrospective Study 1960–1993*, Oxford: James Currey.

'Donor Election Unit's Report' (1995), *The Ethiopian Register*, July: 41–53.

Drinkwater, Michael (1991) *The State and Agrarian Change in Zimbabwe's Communal Areas*, London: Macmillan.

Drinkwater, Michael (1994) 'Beyond Modernization and Liberalism: A Question of Perspective', unpublished paper presented at the workshop of Knowledge, Power, Development – Can Development Studies Make a Difference?, Lammi, Finland.

Dudley, B. J. (1966) 'Federalism and Balance of Political Power in Nigeria', *Journal of Commonwealth Political Studies*, 4(1).

Dudley, B. J. (1972) 'A Coalition Theoretical Analysis of Nigerian Politics, 1950–1966', *The African Review: A Journal of African Politics, Development and International Affairs* 2(4).

Dudley, B.J. (1973) *Instability and Political Order: Politics and Crisis in Nigeria*, Ibadan: Ibadan University Press.

Dudley, B.J. (1982) *An Introduction to Nigerian Government and Politics*, London: Macmillan.

Du Pisani, Andre (1986) *SWA/Namibia. The Politics of Continuity and Change*, Johannesburg: Jonathan Ball Publishers.

Du Pisani, Andre (1996) 'State Power and Social Forces in Namibia', in *Building Democracy: Perceptions on the Performance of Government and Opposition in Namibia*, Windhoek: Namibia Institute of Democracy and Konrad Adenauer Stiftung.

Du Pisani, Andre (1998) 'Namibia: the Pattern of Politics', *The Namibian*, 16 January.

Dzordgo, Dan-Bright (1998) *Ghana In Search of Development: The Challenges of Governance, Economic Management and Institution Building*, Uppsala: Uppsala University, Department of Sociology.

Economist Intelligence Unit (1996a) *Country Profile: Nigeria 1995–1996*, London: Economist Intelligence Unit.

Economist Intelligence Unit (1996b) *Country Profile: Zambia 1996–1997*, London: Economist Intelligence Unit.

Edgar, D. (1988) *Prophets with Honour: A Documentary History of Lekhotla la Bafo*, Johannesburg: Ravan.

Egwu, Samuel (1998) *Structural Adjustment, Agrarian Change and Rural Ethnicity in Nigeria*, Uppsala: Nordiska Afrikainstitutet Research Report 103.

Eisenberg, Andrew (1998) 'Weberian Patrimonialism and Imperial Chinese History', *Theory and Society* 27: 83–102.

Eisenstadt, S. N. and Roniger, L. (1984) *Patrons, Clients and Friends: Interpersonal Relations and the Structure of Trust in Society*, Cambridge: Cambridge University Press.

El-Affendi, Abdelwahab (1991) *Turabi's Revolution: Islam and Power in Sudan*, London: Grey Seal.

El-Affendi, Abdelwahab (1995) *Al-Thawara wa al-Islah al-Siyasi fi al-Soudan* (Revolution and Political Reform in Sudan), London: Montada ibn Rushd.

El-Bashir, Ahmed (1987) 'Whither Sudan? A Moderate, Democratic, Secular Alternative', in Francis Deng and Proseer Gifford (eds) *The Search For Peace and Unity in the Sudan*, Washington, DC: the Wilson Centre Press.

El-Battahani, Atta (1996a) 'Economic Transformation and Political Islam in Sudan', University of Helsinki Institute of Development Studies Working Paper 5/96.

El-Battahani, Atta (1996b) 'Social and Political Impact of Economic Liberalization and Social Welfare in Sudan', University of Helsinki Institute of Development Studies Working Paper 6/96.

El-Battahani, Atta (1996c) 'Economic Liberalization and Civil Society in Sudan: 1989–1995', a paper presented at OSSERIA conference on Political and Economic Transformations and Socio-Economic Development Responses in Africa, Cape Town, South Africa, 4–8 November.

Election Commissioner (1980) 'Common Roll Election 1980 Interim Report by Sir John Boynton, MC, British Election Commissioner', reprinted in Freedom House 1980, Appendix I.

Election Study Committee (1974): *Socialism and Participation – Tanzania's 1970 National Elections*, Dar es Salaam: Tanzania Publishing House.

Electoral Supervisory Commission (1990) 'The Electoral Supervisory Commission's Report', reprinted in Moyo 1992, Appendix 5b.

Englund, Harri (1996) 'Between God and Kamuzu: The Transition to Multiparty Politics in Central Malawi' in R. Werbner and T. Ranger (eds) *Postcolonial Identities in Africa*, London: Zed.

Epstein, A. L. (1958) *Politics in an Urban African Community*, Manchester: Manchester University Press.

Erdmann, G. (1995) 'Guided Democratization: Political Perceptions and Attitudes in Tanzania', University of Bremen Africa Discussion Papers 11.

Ethiopian Human Rights Council (1995) *Democracy, Rule of Law and Human Rights in Ethiopia*, Addis Abeba: Ethiopia Human Rights Council.

Ewusi, K. (1987) *The Impact of Structural Adjustment Programme in a Developing Country. The Case of Ghana's Experience*, Tema: Ghana Publishing Corporation.

Ferguson, J. (1990) *The Anti-Politics Machine: 'Development', Depoliticization and Bureaucratic Power in Lesotho*, Cambridge: Cambridge University Press.

Fernandes, Raúl Mendes (1994a) 'Guinée-Bissau: Transition démocratique?', in *l'Afrique politique 1994. Vue sur la démocratisation à marée basse*, Bordeaux and Paris: Centre d'Étude d'Afrique Noire and Karthala, pp. 81–91. The article is also available in Portuguese in *Soronda, Revista de Estudos Guineenses* 17: 31–43 Fernandes 1994b.

Fisher, Humphrey J. (1969) 'Elections and Coups in Sierra Leone, 1967', *Journal of Modern African Studies*, 7(4): 611–636.

Fortes, Meyer (1969) *Kinship and the Social Order: The Legacy of Lewis Henry Morgan*, Chicago: Aldine.

Fosse, Leif John (1992) 'The Social Construction of Ethnicity and Nationalism in Independent Namibia', University of Namibia, Namibian Institute for Social and Economic Research (NISER) Discussion Paper 14.

Foundation for Democratic Process (no date) *Zambia's 18 November 1996 Presidential and Parliamentary Elections: Final Election Monitoring Report*, Lusaka: Foundation for Democratic Process.

Fox, J. (1994) 'The Difficult Transition from Clientelism to Citzenship: Lessons from Mexico', *World Politics* 46: 151–184.

Fox, R. (1996) 'Bleak Future for Multi-party Elections in Kenya', *Journal of Modern African Studies* 34(4).

Fraser, Lawrence (1996) 'State Disintegration: the Case of Sudan', *Civil Society*, May. [Sudan paper]

Freedom House (1980) *Report of the Freedom House Mission to Observe the Common Roll Election in Southern Rhodesia (Zimbabwe) February 1980*, New York: Freedom House.

Frey, Bruno S. (ed.) (1997) *Political Business Cycles*, Cheltenham & Lyme, NH: Elgar.

Friedmann, Steven (1996) 'From Freedom Fighters to the Seats of Power', in C. Marias, P. H. Katjavivi and A. Wehmhörner (eds.) *Southern Africa after Election: Towards a Culture of Democracy*, Windhoek: Gamsberg Macmillan.

Frochot, Michel (1942) *L'Empire Colonial Portugais: Organisation constitutionnelle, politique et administrative*, Lisbon: Editions SPN.

Funnell, D. C. (1991) *Under the Shadow of Apartheid: Agrarian Transformation in Swaziland*, London: Avery Press.

Gaventa, John (1987) 'Makt och deltagande', in O. Petersson (ed.) *Maktbegreppet*, Stockholm: Carlssons.

Gay, J. *et al.* (1991) *Poverty in Lesotho: A Mapping Exercise*, Maseru: Sechaba Consultants.

General Secretariat for National Congress (1996) *Report on General Elections 1996*, Khartoum: General Secretariat for National Congress.

Gertzel, C. (1970) *The Politics of Independent Kenya*, Nairobi: East African Publishing House.

Gertzel, C. (ed.) (1984) *The Dynamics of the One-Party State in Zambia*, Manchester: Manchester University Press.

Geschiere, P. (1996) 'Sorcellerie et politique: les pièges du rapport élite-village', *Politique Africaine* 63.

Ghai, Y. P. and McAuslan, J. W. P. (1970) *Public Law and Political Change in Kenya: A Study of Legal Framework from the Colonial Times to the Present*, Nairobi: Oxford University Press.

Ghana (1992) *The Constitution of the Republic of Ghana*, Tema: Ghana Publishing Corporation.

Gibbon, P. (1993) '"Civil Society" and Political Change, with Special Reference to "Developmentalist" States', mimeo, Scandinavian Institute of African Studies.

Gibbon, P. *et al.* (eds.) (1992) *Authoritarianism, Democracy and Adiustment: The Politics of Economic Reform in Africa*, Seminar Proceedings 26, Uppsala: Scandinavian Institute of African Studies.

Gifford, Paul (ed.) (1995) *The Christian Churches and the Democratisation of Africa*, Leiden: E. Brill.

Gleijeses, Piero (1997) 'The First Ambassadors: Cuba's Contribution to Guinea-Bissau's War of Independence', *Journal of Latin American Studies* 29(1): 45–88.

Godfrey, M. (1982), 'Kenya: African Capitalism or Simple Dependency?', in M. Bienefeld and M. Godfrey (eds.) *The Struggle for Development: National Strategies in an International Context*, London: John Wiley.

Goldsworthy, D. (1982) *Tom Mboya: The Man Kenya Wanted to Forget*, Nairobi: Heinemann.

Good, K. (1992) 'Interpreting the Exceptionality of Botswana', *Journal of Modern African Studies* 30(1).

Good, K. (1993) 'At the Ends of the Ladder: Radical Inequalities in Botswana', *Journal of Modern African Studies* 31(2).

Good, K. (1996) 'Towards Popular Participation in Botswana', *Journal of Modern African Studies* 34(1).

Good, K. (1997) 'Development and Democracies: Liberal vs. Popular', *Africa Insight* 27(4).

Good, K. and Molutsi, P. (1997) 'The Role of the State in Poverty Alleviation: The Botswana Experience', mimeo, University of Botswana.

Gould, Jeremy (1997a) *Localizing Modernity: Action, Interests and Association in Rural Zambia*, Helsinki: Finnish Anthropological Society.

Gould, Jeremy (1997b) 'Market Liberalization and Smallholder Livelihoods: A Comparative Study of the Domestic Economy in a Rural Zambian Community before and after Economic Reforms (1988–1996),' in *Finnish Development Cooperation in the Rural Sector of Zambia*, Helsinki: Ministry of Foreign Affairs evaluation report 1997:1.

Gould, Jeremy (1998) 'Resurrecting Makumba: Chiefly Powers and the Local State in Zambia's Third Republic', paper presented to the 14th International Congress of Anthropological and Ethnological Sciences, Williamsburg, VA, July 1998.

Gourevitch, Philip (1998) *We Wish to Inform You that Tomorrow We Will Be Killed with Our Families*, New York: Farrar Straus and Giroux.

Green, D. (1995) 'Ghana's Adjusted Democracy', *Review of African Political Economy* 65: 577–583.

Gregory, Martyn (1980) 'From Rhodesia to Zimbabwe: An Analysis of the 1980 Elections and an Assessment of the Prospects', The South African Institute of International Affairs Occasional Paper.

Groth, Siegfried (1995) *Namibia, The Wall of Silence: The Dark Days of the Liberation Struggle*, Wuppertal: Peter Hammer Verlag.

Gustafsson, B. and Makonnen, N. (1991) 'Poverty and Remittances in Lesotho', mimeo.

Gyimah-Boadi, E. (1997) 'The Challenges Ahead: Ghana's Encouraging Elections', *Journal of Democracy* 8(2).

Haile, Daniel (1979) 'Law and the Status of Women in Ethiopia', unpublished study prepared for FAO/UNDP Project ETH 73/003.

Hamid, Malik H. (1990) *Elections in Sudan*, Khartoum: Beit Al-Thaqafa.

Hamid, Mohamed B. (1988) 'Centre-Periphery Relations in the Sudan: The Federal Option', University of Khartoum DSRC Seminar Series 81.

Hanna, William John (ed.) (1964) *Independent Black Africa: The Politics of Freedom*, Chicago: Rand McNally & Company.

Hansom, Dirk and Mupotola-Sibongo, Moonov with the assistance of Daniel Motinga (1998) *Overview of the Namibian Economy*, Windhoek: Namibian Economic Policy Research Unit.

Harbeson, John (1973) *Nation Building in Kenya: The Role of Land Reform*, Evanston, IL: North-Western European Press.

Harbeson, John (1998) 'Elections and Democratization in Post-Mengistu Ethiopia' in K. Kumar (ed.) *Postconflict Elections, Democratization, and International Assistance*, London: Lynne Rienner, pp. 111–131.

Harbeson, John, Rothchild, Donald and Chazan, Naomi (eds) (1994) *Civil Society and the State in Africa*, Boulder, CO: Lynne Rienner.

Harir, Sharif and Tvedt, Terje (1994) *Short-Cut to Decay: The Case of the Sudan*, Uppsala: Nordiska Afrikainstitutet.

Hart, E. (1995) 'African Donors Hindering Democracy', *Network* 1(6).

Hartman, Jeannette (1990) 'A Study of Social Coalitions and their Relationship to the Structural Adjustment Reforms in Tanzania', paper presented for the NRISD/SIAS/CMI Joint Symposium on Social and Political Context of Structural Adjustment in sub-Saharan Africa, Bergen, 17–19 October 1990.

Hastrup, Kirsten (1993) 'The Semantics of Biology: Virginity', in S. Ardener (ed.) *Defining Females, The Nature of Women in Society*, Oxford: Berg, pp. 34–50.

Hatchard, John (1993) *Individual Freedoms & State Security in the African Context: The Case of Zimbabwe*, Harare: Baobab Books.

Haugerud, A. (1995) *The Culture of Politics in Modern Kenya*, Cambridge: Cambridge University Press.

Haynes, Jeff (1995) 'Popular Religion and Politics in sub-Saharan Africa', *Third World Quarterly* 16(1): 89–108.

Hayward, F. M. (1972) 'The Development of a Radical Political Organization in the Bush', *Canadian Journal of African Studies* 6(1): 1–28.

Hayward, Fred M. (ed.) (1987) *Elections in Independent Africa*, Boulder, CO: Westview.

Heard, Kenneth A. (1974) *General Elections in South Africa 1943–1970*, Cape Town: Oxford University Press.

Held, David (1995) *Democracy and the Global Order: From the Modern State to Cosmopolitan Governance*, Cambridge: Polity Press.

Herbst, J. (1993) *The Politics of Reform in Ghana, 1982–1991*, California: University of California Press.

Hermet, Guy, Rose, Richard and Rouquij, Alain (eds.) (1978) *Elections Without Choice*, London: Macmillan.

Hino, H. (1995) 'Kenya: Recent Economic Developments', Washington DC: IMF Staff Country Report 95/133.

Hirschmann, David (1991) 'Women and Political Participation in Africa: Broadening the Scope of Research', *World Development* 19(12): 1679–1694.

Hitchcock, R. K. (1980) 'Tradition, Social Justice and Land Reform in Central Botswana', *Journal of African Law* 24(1).

Hitchcock, R. K. (1985) 'Water, Land and Livestock: the Evolution of Tenure and Administration Patterns in the Grazing Areas of Botswana', in L. A. Picard (ed.) *The Evolution of Modern Botswana*, Lincoln, NE: University of Nebraska Press.

Hitchcock, R. K. and Holm, J. D. (1993) 'Bureaucratic Domination of Hunter-gatherer Societies: A Study of the San in Botswana', *Development and Change* 24.

Hobsbawm, E. J. and Ranger, T. (eds.) (1991) *The Invention of Tradition*, Cambridge: Cambridge University Press.

Hodgkin, Thomas (1961) *African Political Parties*, Harmondsworth: Penguin.

Holm, John D. (1974) *Dimension of Mass Involvement in Botswana Politics: A Test of Alternative Theories*, Beverly Hills, CA: Sage.

Holm, John D. (1982) 'Liberal Democracy and Rural Development in Botswana', *African Studies Review* 25(1).

Holm, John D. (1986) 'Elections in Botswana: Institutionalization of a New System of Legitimacy', in Fred Hayward (ed.) *Elections in Independent Africa*, Boulder, CO: Westview.

Holm, John D. (1988) 'Botswana: A Paternalistic Democracy', in Larry Diamond, Juan J. Linz and Seymour Martin Lipset (eds) (1988) *Democracy in Developing Countries, Volume Two, Africa,* Boulder, CO: Lynne Rienner.

Holt, Peter M. (1961) *A Modern History of the Sudan,* London: Weidenfeld and Nicholson.

Hornsby, C. and Throup, D. (1992) 'Elections and Political Change in Kenya', *Journal of Commonwealth and Comparative Politics* 30(2).

Human Rights Watch (1994) 'Ethiopia, Reckoning under the Law', *Human Rights Watch/Africa* December. No. 11.

Human Rights Watch (1996a) 'Nigeria: Permanent Transition', *Human Rights Watch/Africa* 8(3A).

Human Rights Watch (1996b) 'Zambia: Elections and Human Rights in the Third Republic', *Human Rights Watch/Africa* 8(4A).

Human Rights Watch (1997) 'Zambia: The Reality amidst Contradictions: Human Rights since the 1996 Elections', *Human Rights Watch/Africa* 9(3A).

Huntington, Samuel P. (1965) 'Political Development and Political Decay', *World Politics* 17(3): 386–430.

Huntington, Samuel P. (1971) 'The Change to Change' *Comparative Politics* 3(2): 283–322.

Huntington, Samuel (1991) *The Third Wave. Democratization in the Late Twentieth Century*, Norman, OK & London: University of Oklahoma Press.

Hutchful, E. (1995) 'Structural Adjustment in Ghana: 1983–1994', in P. Engberg, P. Gibbon, P. Raikes and L. Udsholt (eds) *Limit of Adjustment in Africa*, Oxford: James Currey.

Hydén, Göran and Leys, Colin (1972) 'Elections and Politics in Single-party Systems: The Case of Kenya and Tanzania', *British Journal of Political Science* 2(4).

Ihonvbere, Julius (1996) *Economic Crisis, Civil Society, and Democratization: The Case of Zambia,* Trenton, NJ: Africa World Press.

Imbali, Faustino (ed.) (1993) *Os efeitos sócio-económicos do programa de ajustamento estrutural na Guiné-Bissau*, Bissau: INEP.

Institute for Education in Democracy (IED) (1997) *National Elections Data Book: Kenya 1963–1997*, Nairobi: IED.

Institute for Education in Democracy (1998) *Understanding Elections in Kenya: A Constituency Profile Approach,* Nairobi: IED.

Institute of Statistical, Social and Economic Research (1992–1996) *The State of the Ghanaian Economy*, Legon: University of Ghana Press.

Jamal, Abbasher (1991) 'Funding Fundamentalism: the Political Economy of an Islamist State', *Middle East Report* 21(5).

Jefferis, K. (1997) 'Poverty in Botswana', in J. S. Salkin *et al. Aspects of the Botswana Economy: Selected Papers*, Gaborone and Oxford: Lentswe La Lesedi and James Currey.

Jeffries, R. (1980) 'The Ghanaian Elections of 1979', *African Affairs* 79(316).

Jeffries, R. (1991) 'Leadership Commitment and Political Opposition to Structural Adjustment in Ghana,' in D. Rothchild (ed.) *Ghana: The Political Economy of Recovery*, Boulder, CO: Lynne Rienner.

Jeffries, R. (1998) 'The Ghanaian Elections of 1996: Towards the Consolidation of Democracy?', *African Affairs* 97(387).

Jeffries, R. and Thomas, C. (1993) 'The Ghanaian Election of 1992', *African Affairs* 92(368).

Johnston, D. (1996) 'The State and Development: An Analysis of Agricultural Policies in Lesotho, 1970–1993', *Journal of Southern African Studies* 22(1).

Jones, Kathleen (1988) 'Towards the revision of politics', in K. Jones and A. Jónasdóttir (eds) *The Political Interests of Gender. Developing Theory and Research with a Feminist Face*, London: Sage.

Joseph, Richard (1997) 'Democratization in Africa after 1989: Comparative and Theoretical Perspectives', *Comparative Politics,* 29(4): 363–382.

Joseph, Richard (ed.) (1999) *State, Conflict, and Democracy in Africa*, Boulder, CO: Lynne Rienner.

Kalecki, Michael (1943) 'Political Aspects of Full Employment', *Political Quarterly* 14(3): 322–331.

Kanyinga, K. (1994) 'Ethnicity, Patronage and Class in a Local Arena: "High" and "Low" Politics in Kiambu, Kenya, 1982–1992', in P. Gibbon (ed.) *The New Local Level Politics in East Africa*, Uppsala: Nordic Africa Institute Research Report 95.

Kanyinga, K. (1996) 'Struggles of Access to Land: The Land Question, Accumulation and Changing Politics in Kenya', University of Nairobi Institute of Development Studies Working Paper 504.

Kanyinga, K. (1998a) 'The Land Question in Kenya: Struggles, Accumulation and Changing Politics', unpublished PhD dissertation, Roskilde University International Development Studies.

Kanyinga, K. (1998b) 'Contestation over Political Space: The State and Demobilization of Opposition Politics in Kenya', in Adebayo O. Olukoshi (ed.) *The Politics of Opposition in Contemporary Africa*, Uppsala: Nordic Africa Institute.

Kanyongolo, Fidelis E. (1998) 'The Limits of Liberal Democratic Constitutionalism in Malawi', in K. M. Phiri and K. R. Ross (eds.) *Democratization in Malawi: A Stocktaking*, Blantyre: CLAIM.

Karanko, Kari (1995) 'Report of the Coordinator of the Joint International Observer Group of the Zanzibar Elections on 22 October and Union Elections in Zanzibar on 29 October 1995', unpublished report, United Nations Election Observation, November.

Karar, Jaafar (1986) 'The Meaning of the Results in the Graduate Constituencies in 1986 Elections', University of Khartoum DSRC Seminar Paper 71.

Karar, Mohammed M. A. (1989) *Elections and Parliaments of Sudan*, Khartoum: Institute of Research and Social Studies.

Karimi, J. and Ochieng, P. (1980) *The Kenyatta Succession*, Nairobi: TransAfrica.

Karlström, Mikael (1996) 'Imagining Democracy: Political Culture and Democratisation in Buganda', *Africa* 66: 485–505.

Kaspin, Deborah (1995) 'The Politics of Ethnicity in Malawi's Democratic Transition', *Journal of Modern African Studies* 33: 595–620.

Keller, Edmond (1988) *Revolutionary Ethiopia: From Empire to People's Republic*, Bloomington, IN: Indiana University Press.

Kenya (1997a) *District Development Plan, Nyambene, 1997/2000*, Nairobi: Government Printers.

Kenya (1997b) *Economic Survey 1997*, Nairobi: Central Bureau of Statistics.

Kershaw, G. (1997) *Mau Mau from Below*, Oxford: James Currey.

Keulder, Christiaan (1997) *Traditional Authorities and Regional Councils in Southern Africa*, Windhoek: Friedrich Ebert Stiftung.

Keulder, Christiaan (1998) 'Political Views, Attitudes and Opinions of Namibian Students', unpublished report to the National Democratic Institute, Windhoek.

Khaketla, B. M. (1971) *Lesotho 1970: An African Coup Under the Microscope*, London: C. Hurst & Co.

Khalid, Mansour (1986) *Al-Fagr Al-Kazib* (The Mistaken Dawn), Cairo: Dar Al-Hilal.

Khalid, Mansour (1993) *Al-Nukhaba Al-Soudaniyya wa Idman Al-Fashal* (Sudanese Elites Addiction to Failure), Cairo: Dar Al-Amin.

Kilson, Martin (1966) *Political Change in a West African State: A Study of the Modernization Process in Sierra Leone*, Cambridge, MA: Harvard University Press.

Kimble, David (1953) *The Machinery of Self-Government*, London: Penguin.

Kimble, David (1963) *A Political History of Ghana, Vol I, The Rise of Gold Coast Nationalism, 1850–1928*, Oxford: Clarendon.

Kipkorir, B. E. and Welbourn, F. B. (1973) *The Marakwet of Kenya: A Preliminary Study*, Nairobi: East African Publishing House.

Kowet, D. K. (1978) *Land, Labour Migration and Politics in Southern Africa: Botswana, Lesotho and Swaziland*, Uppsala: SIAS.

Kumado, K. (1993) 'Legislation on Political Parties', in K. Ninsin and F. Drah (eds.) *Political Parties and Democracy in Ghana's Fourth Republic*, Accra: Woeli Publishing Services.

Kumar, Krishna (1998) *Postconflict Elections, Democratization & International Assistance*, Boulder, CO: Lynne Rienner.

Kursani, Awad Al-Sid (1997) 'The Presidential and National Council Elections of 1996', *Afkar Jadida* 2: 89–96.

Kössler, Reinhart (1992) 'Towards Greater Participation and Equality? Some Findings on the 1992 Regional and Local Elections in Namibia', Namibia Economic Policy Research Unit working paper 27.

Laakso, Liisa (1997a) 'Afrikka ja politiikan kriisi', *Kosmopolis* 27(1): 5–22.

Laakso, Liisa (1997b) 'Why Are Elections not Democratic in Africa? Comparisons between the Recent Multiparty Elections in Zimbabwe and Tanzania', *Nordic Journal of African Studies* 6(1): 18–35.

Langa Commission (1998) 'The Langa Commissions Findings on Lesotho's Elections of 1998 (the Langa report)', *Public Eye* 14, 4–18 October.

Leftwich, Adrian (1993) 'Governance, Democracy and Development in the Third World', *Third World Quarterly* 14(3): 605–624.

Legum, Colin (1995) 'Ethiopia: The Triumph of Democratic Elections', *Third World Reports*, 24 May 1995.

Leith, J. (1996) *Ghana: Structural Adjustment Experience,* San Francisco, CA: International Centre for Economic Growth.

Lemarchand, René (1992) 'Uncivil States and Civil Societies: How Illusion Became Reality', *Journal of Modern African Studies* 30: 177–191.

Lemon, Anthony (1988) 'The Zimbabwe General Election of 1985', *Journal of Commonwealth & Comparative Politics*, 26(1): 3–21.

Lesotho Highlands Water Revenue Fund (1996) 'Lesotho Highlands Water Development Fund: A Review of Current Operations, Plan of Action and Agenda for Integrated Donor Support', World Bank Macro Industry and Finance Division, Southern Africa Department, Africa region.

Levin, R. (1986) 'Uneven Development in Swaziland: Tibiyo, Sugar Production and Rural Development Strategy', *Geoforum* 17(2).

Levin, R. (1993) 'When the Sleeping Grass Awakens: Land, Power and Hegemony in Swaziland, unpublished manuscript. Published by Witwatersrand University Press 1998.

Lewis-Beck, Michael S. (1990) *Economics and Elections: The Major Western Democracies*, Ann Arbor, MI: University of Michigan Press.

Leys, Colin (1959) *European Politics in Southern Rhodesia*, Oxford: Oxford University Press.

Leys, Colin (1969) 'Introduction', in Colin Leys (ed.) *Politics and Change in Developing Countries: Studies in the Theory and Practice of Development*, Cambridge: Cambridge University Press.

Leys, Colin (1975) *Underdevelopment in Kenya: The Political Economy of Neo-colonialism, 1964–1971*, London: Heinemann.

Leys, Colin and Saul, John S. (1994) 'Liberation without Democracy?', *Journal of Southern African Studies*, 20(1): 123–147.

Leys, Colin and Saul, John S. (eds.) (1995) *Namibia's Liberation Struggle: The Two-edged Sword*, London: James Currey and Athens: Ohio University Press.

Lindeke, William, Wanzala, Winnie and Tonchi, Victor (1992) 'Namibia's Election Revisited', *Politikon* 18(2).

Lipset, Seymor M. (1959) 'Some Social Requisites of Democracy: Economic Development and Political Legitimacy' *American Political Science Review* 53: 69–105.

Lopes, Carlos (1997) *Compasso de Espera: O fundamental e o acesório na crise africana*, Lisbon: Edições Afrontamento.

Luanda, N. N. (1994) 'Parliamentary Elections: Continuity and Change' in Rwekeza Mukandala, and Othman Haroub (eds.) *Liberalization and Politics. The 1990 Elections in Tanzania*, Dar es Salaam: Dar es Salaam University press, pp. 257–264.

Lumbwe, Chitalu (1997) '"Tribalism" and development in Zambia', paper presented at KEPA Zambia, Lusaka, 12 December 1997.

Lundhal, M. and Petersson, L. (1991) *The Dependent Economy: Lesotho and the Southern African Customs Union*, Boulder, CO: Westview.

Lwanda, John Lloyd Chipembere (1996) *Promises, Power, Politics and Poverty: Democratic Transition in Malawi (1961–1999)*, Glasgow: Dudu Nsomba.

MacKenzie, W. J. M. and Robinson, K. (1960) *Five Elections in Africa*, Oxford: Clarendon.

Mahmoud, Fatima (1984) *The Sudanese Bourgeoisie: Vanguard of Development*, London: Zed.

Mahmoud, Fatima (1986) 'On 1986 Elections', *Development and Business Digest*, May–June. [Sudan paper]

Mair, Lucy (1962) *The Nyasaland Elections of 1961*, London: Athlone.

Makumbe, John (1991) 'Zimbabwe Elections 1990: An Overview', University of Zimbabwe Department of Political and Administrative Studies, Election Studies Project Occasional Paper 1(3).

Makumbe, John and Compagnon, Daniel (2000) *Behind the Smokescreen: The Politics of Zimbabwe's 1995 General Elections*, Harare: University of Zimbabwe Publication Department.

Mamdani, Mahmood (1996) *Citizen and Subject: Contemporary Africa and the Legacy of Late Colonialism*, Princeton, NJ: Princeton University Press.

Mandaza, Ibbo and Sachikonye, Lloyd M. (eds.) (1991) *The One-Party State and Democracy*, Harare: SAPES Books.

Marias C., Katjavivi P. H. and Wehmhörner A. (eds.) (1996) *Southern Africa after Election: Towards a Culture of Democracy*, Windhoek: Gamsberg Macmillan.

Markakis, John (1975) *Ethiopia, Anatomy of a Traditional Polity*, Addis Abeba: Oxford University Press.

Masendeke, Anthony F., Mafico, Muriel U. and Citopo, Patson T. (1991) 'Report on the 1990 General and Presidential Elections: Masvingo and Manicaland Provinces', University of Zimbabwe Department of Political and Administrative Studies, Election Studies Project Occasional Paper 1(3).

Matlosa, K. (1995) 'The Military After the Elections: Confronting the New Democracy', in R. Southall and T. Petlane (eds.) *Democratisation and Demilitarisation in Lesotho: the General Election of 1993 and its Aftermath*, Pretoria: Africa Institute of South Africa.

Mayer, Philip and Mayer, Iona (1961) *Townsmen or Tribesmen: Conservatism and the Process of Urbanization in a South African City*, London: Oxford University Press.

Mazoub Abdoun, Laila (1988) 'The Graduate Elections of 1965 and 1986', unpublished BSc dissertation in political science, University of Khartoum Faculty of Economics.

Mazula, Brazão (ed.) (1996) *Mozambique: Elections, Democracy and Development*, Maputo: Inter-Africa Group.

Mbise, Ismael R. and Moris, Jon R. (1974) 'A Study in Contrast: the Election in Arusha and Meru', in Election Study Committee: *Socialism and Participation – Tanzania's 1970 National Elections*, Dar es Salaam: Tanzania Publishing House, pp. 255–277.

McCracken, John (1998) 'Blantyre Transformed: Class, Conflict and Nationalism in Urban Malawi', *Journal of African History* 39: 247–269.

Médard, J.-F. (1982) 'The Underdeveloped State in Tropical Africa: Political Clientelism or Neo-Patrimonialism?', in C. Clapham (ed.): *Private Patronage and Public Power: Political Clientelism in the Modern State,* London: Francis Pinter.

Mhlaba, Luke (1991) 'Report on the 1990 General and Presidential Elections: Mashonaland Central, Mashonaland East, Midlands, Matabeleland North and Matabeleland South Provinces', University of Zimbabwe, Department of Political and Administrative Studies, Election Studies Project Occasional Paper 1(1).

Mhone, G. (ed.) (1992) *Malawi at the Crossroads: The Post-Colonial Political Economy*, Harare: SAPES.

Mhone, G. (1993) 'Botswana: Debunking the Myth of Africa's Economic Cinderella', *Southern Africa Political and Economic Monthly* 6(12).

Miers, S. and Crowder, M. (1988) 'The Politics of Slavery in Bechuanaland: Power Struggles and the Plight of the Basarwa in the Bamangwato Reserve, 1926–1940', in S. Miers and R. Roberts (eds) *The End of Slavery in Africa*, Madison, WI: University of Wisconsin Press.

Mikell, G. (1989) 'Peasant Politicisation and Economic Recuperation in Ghana: Local and National Dilemmas', *Journal of Modern African Studies* 27(3): 455–478.

Mitchell, J. C. (1956) *The Kalela Dance: Aspects of Social Relationships among Urban Africans in Northern Rhodesia*, Manchester: Manchester University Press (Rhodes-Livingstone Institute Papers 27).

Mkandawire, T. (1996) 'Economic Policy-Making and the Consolidation of Democratic Institutions in Africa', in K. Havnevik and B. van Arkadie (eds) *Domination or Dialogue: Experiences and Prospects for African Development Cooperation*, Uppsala: Nordiska Afrikainstitutet.

'The MMD Campaign Manifesto', (no date) in Donald Chanda (ed.) *Democracy in Zambia: Key Speeches of President Chiluba 1991/92*, Lusaka: African Press Trust.

Mmuya, Max (1994) 'Floods and elections in Mtwara', in Rwekaza Mukandala and Haroub Othman (eds.) *Liberalization and Politics – The 1990 Elections in Tanzania*, Dar es Salaam: Dar es Salaam University Press, pp. 233–256.

Mmuya, Max (n.d.) *Government and Political Parties in Tanzania (After the 1995 General Elections), Facts and Figures*, printed with the support of the Friedrich Ebert Stiftung.

Mmuya, Max and Chaligha, Amon (1994) *Political Parties and Democracy in Tanzania*, Dar es Salaam: Dar es Salaam University Press.

Mnangagwa, Emmerson D. (1989) 'Post-independence Zimbabwe (1980–1987)', in Canaan S. Banana (ed.) *Turmoil and Tenacity: Zimbabwe 1890–1990*, Harare: The College Press, pp. 225–241.

Moamogwe, B. V. (1982) 'Rural Conservatism vs. Nationalism in Pre-Independent Botswana: The Bechuanaland People's Party 1960–1966', undergraduate BA Research Essay in History, University College of Botswana.

Molomo, M. G. (1991) 'Botswana's Political Process', in M.G. Molomo and B. T. Makopakgosi (eds) *Multi-party Democracy in Botswana*, Harare: SAPES Books.

Molutsi, P. (1989) 'The Ruling Class and Democracy in Botswana', in J. Holm and P. Molutsi (eds.) *Democracy in Botswana*, Gaborone: Macmillan.

Molutsi, P. (1993) 'Botswana's Democracy: Myth or Reality?', *Southern Africa Political and Economic Monthly* 6(12).

Molutsi, P. (1998) 'Elections and Electoral Experience in Botswana', in W. A. Edgev and M. H. Lekorwe (eds.) *Botswana: Politics and Society*, Pretoria: Van Schaik.

Monga, Celestin (1996) *The Anthropology of Anger: Civil Society and Democracy in Africa*, Boulder, CO: Lynne Rienner.

Moore, David (1996) 'Reading Americans on Democracy in Africa: From the CIA to "Good Governance"', *European Journal of Development Research* 8(1): 123–145.

Moore, Sally Falk (1993) 'Post-socialist Micro-politics: Kilimanjaro, 1993', *Africa* 66(4): 587–605.

Morgenthau, Ruth (1964) 'Single-Party Systems in West Africa', in William John Hanna (ed.) *Independent Black Africa: The Politics of Freedom*, Chicago: Rand McNally & Company, pp. 419–443.

Mouzelis, Nicos (1985) 'On the Concept of Populism: Populist and Clientelist Modes of Incorporation in Semiperipheral Polities', *Politics and Society* 14(3).

Moyo, Jonathan (1992) *Voting for Democracy: A Study of Electoral Politics in Zimbabwe,* Harare: University of Zimbabwe Publications.

Mramba, Basil (1967) 'Kilimanjaro: Localism and Nationalism', in Lionel Cliffe (ed.) *One Party Democracy: The 1965 Tanzania General Elections,* Nairobi: East African Publishing House, pp. 105–127.

Mueller, S. D. (1984) 'Government and Opposition in Kenya, 1966–9', *Journal of Modern African Studies* 22(3).

Mugabe, Robert G. (1989) 'The Unity Accord: Its Promise for the Future', in Canaan S. Banana (ed.) *Turmoil and Tenacity: Zimbabwe 1890–1990,* Harare: The College Press, pp. 336–359.

Mukandala, Rwekaza (1994) 'Whither Ujamaa: Ideological Premises of the 1990 Elections', in Rwekaza Mukandala and Haroub Othman (eds) *Liberalization and Politics – The 1990 Elections in Tanzania,* Dar es Salaam: Dar es Salaam University Press, pp. 54–65.

Mukandala, Rwekaza and Othman, Haroub (eds) (1994*) Liberalization and Politics: The 1990 Election in Tanzania,* Dar es Salaam: Dar es Salaam University Press.

Mulford, David C. (1964) *The Northern Rhodesia General Election of 1962,* Nairobi: Oxford University Press.

Mulikita, Njunga (1998) 'The Role of Election Monitors: A Study of the 1996 Zambian Elections', mimeo, Lusaka: University of Zambia.

Munishi, Gasper and Mtengeti-Migiro, Asha Rose (1990) 'Rombo: the Dynamics of Election Organization in a One-party Democracy', in Haroub Othman, Immanuel K. Bavu and Michael Okema (eds) *Tanzania: Democracy in Transition,* Dar es Salaam: Dar es Salaam University Press, pp. 182–201.

Murray, C. (1981) *Families Divided: the Impact of Migrant Labour in Lesotho,* Johannesburg: Ravan.

Mushota, Robert T. (1995) 'Electoral Reforms and Democratization', in L. C. W. Kaela *et al.* 'Transition to Democracy in Africa. Case Study: Zambia', main report to the Global Coalition for Africa and Africa Leadership Forum', mimeo, November.

Mustapha, A. R. (1986) 'The National Question and Radical Politics in Nigeria', *Review of African Political Economy* 37.

Mustapha, A. R. (1999) 'The Nigerian Transition: Third Time Lucky or More of the Same?', mimeo, Oxford.

Mutharika, A. Peter (1996) 'The 1995 Democratic Constitution of Malawi', *Journal of African Law* 40: 205–220.

Mwanakatwe, J. M. (1994) *End of Kaunda Era,* Lusaka: Multimedia.

Namibia (1996) *Decentralisation, Development and Democracy: Decentralisation Policy for Namibia,* Windhoek: Ministry of Regional and Local Government and Housing.

Namibia (1997) *Integrated Poverty Reduction Strategy for Namibia: A Discussion Document.* National Planning Commission, November.

Namibia Institute for Democracy and Konrad Adenauer Stiftung (1996a) *Accountability and Corruption in Namibia: Challenges for 1997,* Windhoek: Namibia Institute for Democracy and Konrad Adenauer Stiftung.

Namibia Institute of Democracy and Konrad Adenauer Stiftung (1996b) *Building Democracy: Perceptions and Performance of Government and Opposition in Namibia,* Windhoek: Namibia Institute of Democracy and Konrad Adenauer Stiftung.

Namibian Economic Policy Research Unit (NEPRU) (1997) 'Seven Years Independence: Current Developments and Future Prospects in Namibia – Some Topical Highlights', Windhoek: NEPRU Working Paper 54.

Namibian Parliamentary Directory 1996/97 (1996), Windhoek: New Namibia Books.

National Commission for Democracy (NCD) (1991) *Evolving a True Democracy,* Accra: NCD.

National Democratic Institute for International Affairs [USA] (1996) *Report on Focus Group Research in Namibia: Popular Perceptions of Political Institutions,* no place of publication.

National Election Commission (1994a) 'Report from the National Election Commission, on the July 3 1994 elections', unofficial translation into English, stamped '1994–07–21'', Embassy of Sweden, Bissau.

National Election Commission (1994b) 'Reports from the National Election Commission, on the elections of 1994' (1994) unpublished, not available to the general public, Bissau.

National Electoral Board of Ethiopia (no date) 'Information for International Community in View of the Election', unpublished.

National Institute for International Affairs (1992) *The October 31, 1991 National Elections in Zambia,* Washington D.C.: National Institute for International Affairs.

National Society for Human Rights (1997) *Namibia: Human Rights Report 1996,* Windhoek: National Society for Human Rights.

Ncube, Welshman (1991) 'Report on the 1990 General and Presidential Elections: Midlands, Mashonaland West and Mashonaland East Provinces', University of Zimbabwe Department of Political and Administrative Studies, Election Studies Project Occasional Paper 1(2).

Neocosmos, M. (1987) 'The Agrarian Question in Swaziland: Some Considerations on Historical Commoditisation and the Post-colonial State', in M. Neocosmos (ed.) *Social Relations in Rural Swaziland: Critical Analyses,* University of Swaziland Social Science Research Unit.

Neocosmos, M. (1993) 'Towards a Political Economy of Adjustment in a Labour Reserve Economy', in P. Gibbon (ed.) *Social Change and Economic Reform in Africa,* Uppsala: Nordic Africa Institute.

Neocosmos, M. (1997) 'Elections, State Power and Rural-Urban Differences: A Comparative Study of Botswana, Lesotho and Swaziland', University of Helsinki Institute of Development Studies Working Paper 2/97.

Neocosmos, M. (1998) 'From People's Politics to State Politics: Aspects of National Liberation in South Africa', in A. Olukoshi (ed.) *The Politics of Opposition in Contemporary Africa*, Uppsala: Nordic Africa Institute.

Neocosmos, M. and Selinyane, N. (1998) 'State-Civil Society Relations in Southern African "One-Dominant-Party-Democracies": The Cases of South Africa and Lesotho', paper presented to the NAI conference on Youth and Urban Political Identities in Contemporary Africa, Gaborone, January 1998.

New Patriotic Party (1993) *The Stolen Verdict*, Accra: Ghana Publishing Corporation.

New Zealand Election Observation Group (1980) *Rhodesia Elections February–March 1980*, presented to the House of Representatives by Leave, Wellington: P. D. Hasselberg, Government Printer.

Ngasongwa, Juma (1992) 'Tanzania Introduces a Multi-Party System', *Review of African Political Economy* 54: 112–116.

Ng'ethe, N. and Musambayi K. (1997) 'A Comparative Study on the Constitution Making Process in Kenya, Uganda, South Africa and Ethiopia', mimeo, Nairobi: Institute of Policy Analysis and Research.

Ngunyi, M. (1995) 'The State, Elite Politics and Crisis of Opposition in Kenya', unpublished paper, Nordic Africa Institute and University of Accra Department of Politics.

Niblock, T. (1987) *Class and Power in Sudan*, London: Macmillan.

Nigussie, Sinidu (1998) 'Women's Affairs Office and its Role in Empowering Women', unpublished manuscript presented at Uppsala University.

Ninsin, K. (1991) 'The PNDC and the Problem of Legitimacy,' in D. Rothchild (ed.) *The Political Transformation of Ghana under the PNDC*, Boulder, CO: Lynne Rienner.

Nkiwane, Tandeka (1998) 'The Youth in Urban Zimbabwe: University of Zimbabwe Revisited', paper presented at the conference on Youth and Urban Popular Identities During the Era of Economic Crisis, Structural Adjustment, and Political Transition, organised by the Nordic Africa Institute in collaboration with the Faculty of Social Sciences, University of Botswana, Gaborone, 23–25 January 1998.

Nnoli, O. (1980) *Ethnic Politics in Nigeria*, Enugu: Fourth Dimension.

Nordhaus, W. (1975) 'The Political Business Cycle', *Review of Economic Studies* 42: 169–190.

Norwegian Observer Group (1992) 'Local and Regional Elections in Ethiopia 21 June 1992', *Human Rights Report* 1 August 1992.

Nour, El-Tahir, M. (1995) 'Poverty in Sudan with and without Coping Practices', mimeo.

Nujoma, Sam (1998) 'Statement by the Comrade Sam Nujoma President of the Republic of Namibia and President of Swapo Party at the Katima Mulilo Local Authority Election Rally', unpublished statement, 14 February 1998.

Nuscheler, Franz (1978) 'Rhodesien', in Franz Nuscheler and Klaus Ziemer (eds.) *Politische Organisation und Repräsentation in Afrika, tome 2, Afrika*, of Dolf Sternberger, Bernhard Vogel, Dieter Nohlen and Klaus Landfried (eds), *Die Wahl der Parlamente und anderer Staatsorgane. Ein Handbuch*, Berlin and New York: Walter de Gruyter, pp. 1627–1689.

Nuscheler, Franz (1978) 'Äthiopien', in Franz Nuscheler and Klaus Ziemer (eds.) *Politische Organisation und Representation in Afrika, tome 2, Afrika*, of Dolf Sternberger, Bernhard Vogel, Dieter Nohlen and Klaus Landfried (eds), *Die Wahl der Parlamente und anderer Staatsorgane. Ein Handbuch*, Berlin and New York: Walter de Gruyter.

Nuscheler, Franz and Ziemer, Klaus (1978) *Politische Organisation und Representation in Afrika*, tome 2, *Afrika*, of Dolf Sternberger, Bernhard Vogel, Dieter Nohlen and Klaus Landfried (eds), *Die Wahl der Parlamente und anderer Staatsorgane. Ein Handbuch*, Berlin and New York: Walter de Gruyter.

Nussey, W. (1978) 'The Future of Ethnicity in Southern Africa', In B. M. Du Toit (ed.) *Ethnicity in Modern Africa*. Boulder CO: Westview Press.

O'Brien, Donal Cruise (1978) 'Senegal', in John Dunn (ed.) *West African States: Failure and Promise*, Cambridge: Cambridge University Press.

Ogot, B.A. and Ochieng', W.R. (eds.) (1995) *Decolonisation and Independence in Kenya 1940–1993*, London: James Currey.

Olagunju, T. *et al.* (1993) *Transition to Democracy in Nigeria, 1993–1995*, Ibadan: Safari Books.

Olukoshi, Adebayo (1997) 'Associational Life', in L. Diamond *et al.* (eds.) *Transition Without End*, Boulder, CO: Lynne Rienner.

Olukoshi, Adebayo (ed.) (1998) *The Politics of Opposition in Contemporary Africa*, Uppsala: Nordiska Afrikainstitutet.

Olukoshi, Adebayo and Osita Agbu (1996), 'The Deepening Crisis of Nigerian Federalism', in A. O. Olukoshi and L. Laakso (eds) *Challenges to the Nation-State in Africa*, Uppsala: Nordiska Afrikainstitutet.

Omusule, M. (1989) 'Kalenjin: the Emergence of a Corporate Name for the Nandi Speaking "Tribes" of East Africa', *Genève – Afrique* 27(1).

Opschoor, H. (1980) 'Institutional Changes and Environmental Impacts in Semi-arid Regions: The Case of Botswana', paper presented to the workshop on Problems and Prospects of Semi-arid Areas, Nazareth, Ethiopia, 9–13 April 1980.

Oquaye, M. (1995) 'The Ghanaian Elections of 1992: A Dissenting View', *African Affairs* 94: 375.

Organisation for Economic Cooperation and Development (OECD) (1995) *Participatory Development and Good Governance*, Paris: OECD.

Ortner, Sherry (1974) 'Is Female to Male as Nature Is to Culture?', in M. Z. Rosaldo and L. Lamphere (eds) *Woman, Culture and Society*, Stanford, CA: Stanford University Press.

Ortner, Sherry and Whitehead, Helen (1981) *Sexual Meanings: The Cultural Construction of Gender and Sexuality*, Cambridge: Cambridge University Press.

Osaghae, E. (1996) *Structural Adjustment and Ethnicity in Nigeria*, Uppsala: Nordiska Afrikainstitutet.

Osaghae, E. (1998) *Crippled Giant: Nigeria Since Independence*, London: Charles Hurst.

Othman, Haroub, Bavu, Immanuel and Okema, Michael (eds) (1990) *Tanzania: Democracy in Transition*, Dar es Salaam: Dar es Salaam University press.

Otite, O. (1996) *Ethnic Pluralism and Ethnicity in Nigeria*, Ibadan: Spectrum Books

Ottaway, Marina (1993) 'Should Elections Be the Criterion of Democratization in Africa?', *CSIS Africa Notes* 145.

Ottaway, Marina (1994) *Democratization and Ethnic Nationalism: African and Eastern Experiences*, Washington: ODC (Policy Essay No. 14).

Ottaway, Marina (1995) 'African Democratization: An Update', *CSIS Africa Notes* 171.

Ottaway, Marina (ed.) (1997) *Democracy in Africa: The Hard Road Ahead*, Boulder, CO: Lynne Rienner.

Oyediran, O. (ed.) (1996) *Governance and Development in Nigeria: Essays in Honour of Professor Billy J. Dudley*, Ibadan: Oyediran International, Agbo Ero Publishers.

Oyugi, W. (1995) 'Ethnic Politics in Kenya' in O. Nnoli (ed.) *Ethnic Conflict in Africa*, Dakar: CODESRIA.

PAIGC (1973a) 'Constituição da República da Guiné-Bissau (Projecto)', mimeo, Conakry.

PAIGC (1973b) 'Sur la création de l'Assemblée Nationale Populaire en Guinée (Bissau): Résultats et bases des élections générales réalisées dans les régions libérées en 1972', mimeo, Conakry.

PAIGC (1973c) 'Proclamação do Estado da Guiné-Bissau', adopted by the National Assembly of the People meeting in the region of Boé, 24.9.1973, mimeo, Conakry.

PAIGC (1984) *A nossa constituição estabelece a República da Guiné-Bissau como um estado de direito*, Bissau: PAIGC Department of Information, Propaganda and Culture.

Palley, Claire (1966) *The Constitutional History and Law of Southern Rhodesia 1888–1965 – with Special Reference to Imperial Control*, Oxford: Clarendon Press.

Parson, J. (1984) *Botswana: Liberal Democracy and the Labour Reserve in Southern Africa*, Boulder, CO: Westview Press.

Parson, J. (1975) *Aspects of Political Culture in Botswana: results of an exploratory survey*, Gaborone: University of Botswana, Lesotho and Swaziland.

Parsons, N. (1977) 'The Economic History of Khama's Country in Botswana, 1844–1930', in R. Palmer and N. Parsons (eds) *The Roots of Rural Poverty in Central and Southern Africa*, Berkeley and Los Angeles: University of California Press.

Paul, James and Clapham, Christopher (1972) *Ethiopian Constitutional Development, A Sourcebook*, Addis Abeba: Oxford University Press.

Pausewang, Siegfried (1994) *The 1994 Election and Democracy in Ethiopia*, Norwegian Institute of Human Rights Human Rights Report 4.

Pempel, T. J. (ed.) (1990) *Uncommon Democracies*, Ithaca, NY: Cornell University Press.

Pendleton, Wade, Shiimbi, Toivo, Tonchi, Victor and Wanzala, Winnie (eds.) (1993) *A Study of Voting Behavior in the 1992 Namibian Regional and Local Government Elections plus Elections Statistics*, Windhoek: University of Namibia, UNESCO and Friedrich Ebert Foundation.

Perry, J. A. G. (1983) 'Land and Politics in Lesotho', *African Studies* 42(1).

Petersson, L. (1991) 'Lesotho's Structural Adjustment Programmes and Economic Performance, mimeo, Lund University.

Phillips, Anne (1993) *Democracy and Difference*, Cambridge: Polity Press.

Phiri, Kings M. and Ross, Kenneth R. (eds.) (1998) *Democratization in Malawi: A Stocktaking*, Blantyre: CLAIM.

Phiri, Sam (1993) 'More Rotten Eggs', *Africa Events*, May.

Pietilä, Tuulikki (1999) *Gossip, Market and Gender: The Dialogical Construction of Morality in Kilimanjaro*, University of Helsinki Department of Sociology Research Reports 233.

Polhemus, James H. (1983) 'Botswana Votes: Parties and Elections in an African Democracy', *Journal of Modern African Studies,* 21(3): 397–430.

Polhemus, James (1997) 'Democracy Betrayed, Zambia's Third Republic', a paper presented at the annual meeting of the African Studies Assocation of Australia and the Pacific, Canberra, 25–27 September 1997.

Poluha, Eva (1989) *Central Planning and Local Reality – The Case of a Producers Cooperative in Ethiopia*, Stockholm: University of Stockholm Studies in Social Anthropology 23.

Poluha, Eva (1994) 'Publicity and the Wielding of Power – A Case from Gojjam, Ethiopia', in H. G. Marcus (ed.) *New Trends in Ethiopian Studies, Vol II*, Lawrenceville, NJ: Red Sea Press, pp. 954–965.

Poluha, Eva (1995) 'Democracy in Africa – Interpretations of Priorities', *African Anthropology* 2(1): 17–44.
Poluha, Eva (1997) 'Conceptualizing Democracy – Elections in the Ethiopian Countryside', University of Helsinki Institute of Development Studies Working Paper 7/97.
Poluha, Eva (forthcoming) 'Learning Political Behaviour: Peasant-State relations in Ethiopia', in Eva Poluha and Mona Rosendahl (eds) *Contesting 'Good' Governance*, Surrey: Curzon.
Portugal (1963) 'Statut Politico-Administratif de la Province de Guinée', decree no. 45371, Lisbon, 22 November 1963 (official French translation).
Portugal (1972): 'Loi Organique des Provinces Portugaises d'Outre-Mer', law no. 5/72, Lisbon, June 1972 (official French translation).
Portuguese Guinea/Portugal (1972) 'Estatuto Político-Administrativo da Província da Guiné', decree no. 542/72, 22 December 1972, Lisbon.
Post, K. W. J. (1963) *The Nigerian Federal Election of 1959: Politics and Administration in a Developing Political System*, London: Oxford University Press.
Potgieter, P.J.J.S. (1991) 'The Resolution 435 Election in Namibia', *Politikon* 18(2).
Power, Joey (1995) 'Eating the Property: Gender Roles and Economic Change in Urban Malawi, Blantyre-Limbe, 1907–1953', *Canadian Journal of African Studies* 29: 79–107.
Przeworski, Adam (1985) *Capitalism and Democracy*, Cambridge: Cambridge University Press.
Przeworski, Adam (1988) 'Democracy as a Contingent Outcome of Conflict', in Jon Elster and Rune Slagstad (eds) *Constitutionalism and Democracy*, Cambridge: Cambridge University Press.
Pütz, Joachim, Von Egidy, Heidi and Caplan, Perri (1990) *Namibia Handbook and Political Who's Who: Post-Election Edition*. Magus.
Quantin, Patrick (1992) 'The 1990 General Elections in Zimbabwe: Step Towards a One-Party State?', in Simon Baynham (ed.) *Zimbabwe in Transition*. Stockholm: Almqvist & Wiksell, pp. 24–44.
Reeves, Pamela and Klein, Keith (eds.) (1995) *Elections in Tanzania and Zanzibar, December 1995: Republic in Transition*, International Federation of Election Studies (IFES) Observation Report, Washington, DC: IFES.
Remmer, K. (1991) 'Democracy and Economic Crises: The Latin American Experience', *World Politics* 52(3).
Remmer, K. (1996) 'The Sustainability of Political Democracy', *Comparative Political Studies* 29(6).
Résau Africain pour le Développement Intégré (RADI) (no date) *Le RADI: Ce qu'il est et ce qu'il veut*, Dakar: RADI.
Roberts, D. (1996) 'Campaign '96: An Uneven Battle', *Public Agenda* 12–22 December.
Robinson, Pearl T. (1994) 'Democratization: Understanding the Relationship between Regime Change and the Culture of Politics', *African Studies Review* 37: 39–67.
Robson, Colin (1995) *Real World Research. A Resource for Social Scientists and Practioner-Researchers*. Oxford: Blackwell.
Rodney, Walter (1970) *A History of the Upper Guinea Coast 1545–1800*, Oxford: Oxford University Press.
Rosaldo, M. (1974) 'Woman, Culture and Society: A Theoretical Overview', in M. Rosaldo and L. Lamphere (eds.) *Woman, Culture and Society*, Stanford, CA: Stanford University Press.
Rosander, Eva Evers (1997) 'Introduction', in Eva Evers Rosander, (ed.) *Transforming Female Identities: Women's Organizational Forms in West Africa*, Uppsala: Nordiska Afrikainstitutet Seminar Proceedings 31.
Rosberg, C. G. and Nottingham, J. (1966) *The Myth of Mau Mau: Nationalism in Kenya*, New York: Praeger.
Rose, R. and McAllister, I. (1990) *The Loyalties of Voters: A Lifetime Learning Model*, London & Newbury Park, CA: Sage.
Ross, Kenneth R. (ed.) (1996) *God, People and Power in Malawi: Democratisation in Theological Perspective*, Blantyre: CLAIM.
Rotberg, Robert I. (1965) *The Rise of Nationalism in Central Africa: The Making of Malawi and Zambia 1873–1964*, London: Oxford University Press.
Rothchild, D. S. (1973) *Racial Bargaining in Independent Kenya: A Study of Minorities and Decolonization*, London: Oxford University Press.
Rowlands, Michael (1995) 'Inconsistent Temporalities in a Nation-space', in D. Miller (ed.) *Worlds Apart: Modernity Through the Prism of the Local*, London: Routledge.
Rudebeck, Lars (1974) *Guinea-Bissau: A Study of Political Mobilization*, Uppsala: Scandinavian Institute of African Studies.
Rudebeck, Lars (1977) *Guinea-Bissau: Folket, partiet och staten*, Uppsala: Nordiska Afrikainstitutet.
Rudebeck, Lars (1979) 'Socialist-oriented development in Guinea-Bissau', in Carl G. Rosberg and Thomas M. Callaghy (eds) *Socialism in Sub-Saharan Africa: A New Assessment*, Berkeley, CA: University of California Institute of International Studies, pp. 322–344.
Rudebeck, Lars (1982) 'Problèmes de pouvoir populaire et du développement', Uppsala: Scandinavian Institute of African Studies Research Report 63.
Rudebeck, Lars (1986) 'Some Facts and Observations on Relations between the Nordic Countries and the Officially Portuguese-Speaking Countries of Africa', in Bernhard Weimer (ed.) *Die Afrikanischen Staaten*

Portugiesischer Sprache: Interne Entwicklungsdynamik und Internationale Beziehungen, Ebenhausen: Stiftung Wissenschaft und Politik.

Rudebeck, Lars (1988) 'Kandjadja, Guiné-Bissau, 1976–1986. Observaçòes sobre a economia politica de uma aldeia africana', *Soronda, Revista de Estudos Guineenses* 5: 61–82.

Rudebeck, Lars (1991) 'Conditions of People's Development in Postcolonial Africa', in Rosemary E. Galli, *Rethinking the Third World: Contributions toward a New Conceptualization*, New York & London: Crane Russak, pp. 29–87.

Rudebeck, Lars (ed.) (1992) *When Democracy Makes Sense*, Uppsala: AKUT.

Rudebeck, Lars (1992) 'Politics and Structural Adjustment in a West-African Village", in Lars Rudebeck (ed.), (1992) *When Democracy Makes Sense,* Uppsala: AKUT pp. 266–284.

Rudebeck, Lars (1996a & 1998a) 'Popular Sovereignty and Constitutionalism. A Historical and Comparative Perspective', in Lars Rudebeck, Olle Törnquist and Virgilio Rojas (eds.) (1996), *Democratisation in the Third World: Concrete Cases in Comparative and Theoretical Perspective*, Uppsala: Uppsala University Seminar for Development Studies, pp. 219–229. Second, revised edition by Macmillan Press, London 1998, pp. 209–221.

Rudebeck, Lars (1996b & 1997a) *Demokratisering i Guinea-Bissau: "Att söka lyckan"*, Stockholm: Sida and Uppsala: Uppsala University Seminar for Development Studies 1996. Available also in Portuguese as *"Buscar a felicidade": Democratização na Guiné-Bissau*, Bissau: INEP 1997.

Rudebeck, Lars (1997b) '"To Seek Happiness": Development in a West-African Village in the Era of Democratisation', *Review of African Political Economy* 71: 75–86.

Rudebeck, Lars (1998b) 'Guinea-Bissau 1998. Democratic legality versus democratic legitimacy,' *Lusotopie*, pp. 25–30; 'Résumé, Resumo, Abstract,' pp. 605–606.

Rudebeck, Lars (2000) 'Beyond Democratic Constitutionalism: On the Twofold Meaning of Democracy and Democratization', in Gavin Williams (ed.) *Democracy, Labour and Politics in Africa and Asia*, Basingstoke: Macmillan.

Rueschmeyer, Dietrich, Stephens, Evelyne Huber and Stephens, John D. (1992) *Capitalist Development and Democracy*, Cambridge: Polity Press.

Rugege, S. (1993) 'The Chieftaincy and Society in Lesotho: A Study in the Political Economy of the Basotho Chieftaincy from Pre-colonial Times to the Present', unpublished PhD dissertation, St Peter's College, Oxford.

Sachikonye, Lloyd (1990) 'The 1990 Zimbabwe Elections: A Post-Mortem', *Review of African Political Economy* 48: 92–99.

Samoff, Joel (1987) 'Single-Party Competitive Elections in Tanzania', in Fred Hayward (ed.) *Elections in Independent Africa*, Boulder, CO and London: Westview Press, pp. 149–186.

Sandbrook, Richard (1996) 'Transitions Without Consolidation: Democratization in Six African Countries', *Third World Quarterly* 17(1): 69–87.

Saul, John S. (1997) 'Liberal Democracy vs. Popular Democracy in Southern Africa', *Review of African Political Economy* 72: 219–236.

Schuknecht, Ludger (1994) 'Political Business Cycles and Expenditure Policies in Developing Countries', IMF Working Paper WP/94/121, Washington, DC: IMF.

Schumacher, Edward J. (1975) *Politics, Bureaucracy, and Rural Development in Senegal*, Berkeley and Los Angeles: University of California Press.

Selinyane, N. (1993) 'Structural Adjustment in Agriculture and the Challenges of Democratisation in Lesotho', unpublished MA Dissertation, University of London, SOAS Centre for Development Studies.

Selinyane, N. (no date) 'Continuity and Change in State Society Relations in Rural Lesotho: A Critical Historical Analysis', mimeo, National University of Lesotho.

Sen, Amartya (1981) *Poverty and Famines. An Essay on Entitlement and Deprivation*, Oxford: Clarendon Press.

Sennet, Richard (1980) *Authority*, New York: Knopf.

Shellington, K. (1992) *Ghana and the Rawlings Factor*, London: Macmillan.

Sichone, Owen and Simutanyi, Neo (1996) 'The Ethnic and Regional Questions, Ethnic Nationalism and the State in Zambia: The case of Bulozi, 1964–1994', in O. Sichone and B. Chikulo (eds): *Democracy in Zambia: Challenges for the Third Republic,* Harare: SAPES Books.

Sithole, Masipula (1986) 'The General Elections 1979–1985', in Ibbo Mandaza (ed.) *Zimbabwe, the Political Economy of Transition 1980–1986*, Dakar: CODESRIA.

Sithole, Masipula (1988) 'Zimbabwe: In Search of a Stable Democracy', in Larry Diamond, Juan J. Linz and Seymour Martin Lipset (eds) *Democracy in Developing Countries, vol. 2: Africa*, London: Adamantine, pp. 217–257.

Sithole Masipula (1997) 'Zimbabwe's Eroding Authoritarianism', *Journal of Democracy*, 8(1): 127–141.

Sjørslev, Inger (1998) 'Women, Gender Studies and the International Indigenous Movement', in Diana Vinding (ed.) *Indigenous Women: The Right to a Voice*, Copenhagen: IWGIA (Document 88, pp. 296–314.

Skålnes, Tor (1995) *The Politics of Economic Reform in Zimbabwe, Continuity and Change in Development*, London: Macmillan.

Sklar, R. (1989) 'On Democracy and Development in Botswana', in J. Holm and P. Molutsi (eds) *Democracy in Botswana*, Gaborone: Macmillan.

Soiri, Iina (1996) *The Radical Motherhood: Namibian Women's Independence Struggle*, Uppsala: Nordic Africa Institute Research Report 99.

Soiri, Iina (1998) 'Why the 1997 Local Authority Elections in Namibia Were Postponed', University of Helsinki Institute of Development Studies Working Paper 1/98.

Solway, J. S. (1994) 'Drought as "Revelatory Crisis": An Exploration of Shifting Entitlements and Hierarchies in the Kalahari, Botswana', *Development and Change* 25(3).

Southall, R. (1995) 'Lesotho's Transition and the 1993 Elections', in R. Southall and T. Petlane (eds) *Democratisation and Demilitarisation in Lesotho: the General Election of 1993 and its Aftermath*, Pretoria: Africa Institute of South Africa.

Staudt, Kathleen (1986) 'Stratification: Implications for Women's Politics', in C. Robertson and I. Berger (eds) *Women and Class in Africa*, New York: Africana Publishing Company.

Steeves, J. S. (1997) 'Re-democratisation in Kenya: "Unbounded politics" and the Political Trajectory towards National Elections', *Journal of Commonwealth and Comparative Politics* 35(3). Reprinted in D. Pal Ahluwalia and P. Nursey-Bray (eds.) (1997) *The Post-Colonial Condition: Contemporary Politics in Africa*, Commack NY: Nova Science Publishers.

Stevens, C. and Speed, J. (1977) 'Multi-partyism in Africa: the Case of Botswana Revisited', *African Affairs* 71: 304.

Sudan (1967) *General Elections Final Report*, Khartoum: Constituent Assembly Electoral Committee.

Sudan (1978) *1978 Elections Reports*, Khartoum: National Election Committee.

Sudan (1986) *General Elections: Final Report*, Khartoum: National Election Committee.

Sudan (1995) *Rules for General Elections for 1995*, Khartoum: National Electoral Commission.

Sudan (1996) *Presidential and National Council Elections: Final Report*, Khartoum: National Electoral Commission.

Sundet, Geir (ed.) (1996) *Democracy in Transition, The 1995 Elections in Tanzania*, Oslo: Norwegian Institute of Human Rights Human Rights Report 8.

Sweden (1990) 'Report from the Swedish Embassy in Bissau', signed Lars Tengroth, 17 August 1990.

Sweden (no date, probably 1993) 'Report from the Swedish Embassy in Bissau'.

Sylvester, Christine (1990) 'Unities and Disunities in Zimbabwe's 1990 Election', *Journal of Modern African Studies* 28(3): 375–400.

Sylvester, Christine (1995) 'Whither Opposition in Zimbabwe?', *Journal of Modern African Studies* 33(3): 403–423.

Tabatabai, H. (1986) 'Economic Stabilisation and Structural Adjustment in Ghana, 1983–1986', *Labour and Society* 11(7).

Tahir, Mohamed I. (1986) *History of Parliamentary Elections*, Khartoum: Sudanese Data Bank.

Tangri, R. (1993) 'Foreign Business and Political Unrest in Lesotho', *African Affairs* 92.

Tanzania (1988) *Population Census*, Dar es Salaam: Ministry of Finance, Economic Affairs and Planning, Bureau of Statistics.

Taylor, Peter J. (1994) 'The State as Container: Territoriality in the Modern World-System', *Progress in Human Geography* 18(2).

Taylor, Scott D. (1999) 'Race, Class, and Neopatrimonialism in Zimbabwe', in Richard Joseph (ed.) *State, Conflict, and Democracy in Africa*, Boulder, CO: Lynne Rienner.

Thiro-Beukes, Erica, Beukes, Attie and Beukes, Hewat S. J. (1986) *Namibia: A Struggle Betrayed*, Rehoboth: Acasia Drukkery.

Throup, D. (1987) 'The Construction and Destruction of the Kenyatta State' in M.G. Schatzberg (ed.) *The Political Economy of Kenya*, New York: Praeger.

Throup, D. (1995) '"Render unto Caesar the Things that Are Caesar's": The Politics of Church-State Conflict in Kenya 1978–1990', in H. B. Hansen and M. Twaddle (eds) *Religion and Politics in East Africa: The Period since Independence*, London: James Currey.

Throup, D. and Hornsby, C. (1998) *Multi-Party Politics in Kenya: The Kenyatta and Moi States and the Triumph of the System in the 1992 Election*, Oxford: James Currey.

Tingsten, Herbert (1963) [1937] *Political Behaviour: Studies in Election Statistics*, Totowa, NJ: Bedminster.

Titmus, Colin and Steele, Tom (1995) *Adult Education for Independence: The Introduction of University Extra-mural Work into British Tropical Africa*, Leeds: University of Leeds School of Education Study of Continuing Education Unit.

Tostensen, A., Andreassen, B.-A. and Tronvoll, K. (1998) *Kenya's Hobbled Democracy Revisited: The 1997 General Elections in Retrospect and Prospect*, Oslo: University of Oslo, Norwegian Institute of Human Rights, Human Rights Report 2/1998.

Tötemeyer, G. K. H., Wehmhörner A. and Weiland, H. (1996) *Elections in Namibia,* Windhoek: Gamsberg Macmillan.

Tötemeyer, Gerhard, Tonchi, Victor and Du Pisani, Andre (eds.) (1997) *Namibia Regional Resources Manual,* second edition, Windhoek: Friedrich Ebert Stiftung.

'Transitional Period Charter of Ethiopia' (1991), *Negarit Gazeta*, July.

Tripp, Aili (1994) 'Gender, Political Participation and the Transformation of Associational Life in Uganda and Tanzania', *African Studies Review* 37(1): 107–133.

Tronvoll, Kjetil and Aadland, Öyvind (1995) *The Process of Democratisation in Ethiopia – an Expression of Popular Participation or Political Resistance?*, Oslo: Norwegian Institute of Human Rights Human Rights Report 5.

Tsie, Balefi (1993) 'The Political Context of Botswana's Economic Performance', *Southern Africa Political and Economic Monthly* 6(12).

Tsie, Balefi (1996) 'Constitutionalism and Citizenship in Botswana', unpublished paper presented at the conference 'Constitutionalism and Citizenship in Contemporary Africa' conference organized by Nordic Africa Institute and University of Nairobi, Naivasha, Kenya, 13–15 December 1996.

Tufte, E. (1978) *Political Control of the Economy,* Princeton, NJ: Princeton University Press.

Umbadda, Sidig (1989) 'Education, Mismanagement and the Sudanese Economy', University of Khartoum DSRC Discussion Paper.

Umbadda. Sidig (1990) 'Education and the Mismanagement of the Sudanese Economy and Society 1956–1989', University of Khartoum DSRC Seminar Paper 88.

UNDP Election Coordinator (1994) 'Written statement on the 3 July 1994 elections', Bissau, 21 July 1994.

UNESCO (1958) *World Survey of Education, II, 1958, Primary Education*, Paris: UNESCO.

UNICEF (1988) 'Analyse de la situation des enfants et des femmes en Guinée-Bissau', second version (preliminary) of UNICEF-report to the government of Guinea-Bissau.

United Nations (1963) *United Nations Statistical Yearbook 1963*, New York: United Nations.

United States of America (1996) 'Annual Report', US Agency for Arms Control. [Sudan paper]

van Binsbergen, Wim (1995) 'Aspects of Democracy and Democratisation in Zambia and Botswana: Exploring African Political Culture at the Grassroots', *Journal of Contemporary African Studies* 13(1): 3–33.

van Donge, Jan Kees (1995) 'Kamuzu's Legacy: The Democratization of Malawi', *African Affairs* 94: 227–257.

van Donge, Jan Kees (1998a) 'The Mwanza Trial as a Search for a Usable Malawian Past', *African Affairs* 97: 91–118.

van Donge, Jan Kees (1998b) 'Reflections on Donors, Opposition and Popular Will in the 1996 Zambian General Elections', *Journal of Modern African Studies* 36(1).

Vanhanen, Tatu (1984) *Emergence of Democracy*, Helsinki: Finnish Society of Arts and Letters.

Vesa, Unto, Konstari, Timo, Ojalammi-Wamai, Sanna and Rwebangira, Magdalena (1997) 'Finnish Support for Democratic Development in Tanzania', report of the identification mission, 16 June 1997, Helsinki: FINNIDA.

Wallerstein, Immanuel (1961) *Africa: The Politics of Independence*, New York: Vintage.

Wamba-Dia-Wamba, E. (1994) 'Africa in Search of a New Mode of Politics', in H. Himmelstrand (ed.) *African Perspectives on Development*, London: James Currey.

Watson, W. (1958) *Tribal Cohesion in a Money Economy: A Study of the Mambwe People of Zambia,* Manchester: Manchester University Press.

Weber, Max (1968) *Economy and Society: An Outline of Interpretative Sociology,* vol. 2, edited by G. Roth and C. Wittich, Berkeley, CA: University of California Press.

Weiland, Heribert (1996) 'A Political Analysis of the 1994 Presidential and National Assembly Elections', in G. K. H. Tötemeyer, A. Wehmhörner and H. Weiland (1996) *Elections in Namibia*, Windhoek: Gamsberg Macmillan.

Weitzer, Ronald (1990) *Transforming Settler States: Communal Conflict and Internal Security in Northern Ireland and Zimbabwe*, Berkeley, CA: University of California Press.

Werbner, Richard (1995) 'Human Rights and Moral Knowledge: Arguments of Accountability in Zimbabwe', in M. Strathern (ed) *Shifting Contexts: Transformations in Anthropological Knowledge*, London: Routledge.

White, Gordon, (1993) 'Towards a Political Analysis of Markets', *IDS Bulletin* 24(3).

Widner, J. (1992) *The Rise of a Party State in Kenya*, Berkeley, CA: University of California Press.

Wight, Martin (1946) *The Gold Coast Legislative Council*, London: Faber & Faber.

Willett, T. (ed.) (1989) *Political Business Cycles: The Political Economy of Money, Inflation and Unemployment,* Durham: Duke University Press.

Williams, David (1993) 'Liberalism and "Development Discourse"', *Africa* 63: 419–429.

Williams, David and Young, Tom (1994) 'Governance, the World Bank and Liberal Theory', *Political Studies* 42: 84–100.

Williams, Trevor D. (1978) *Malawi: The Politics of Despair*, Ithaca, NY: Cornell University Press.

Wilmsen, E. N. (1989) *Land Filled With Flies: A Political Economy of the Kalahari*, Chicago: University of Chicago Press.

Wiseman J. A. (1992) 'Early Post-redemocratization Elections in Africa' *Electoral Studies* 11(4): 279–291.

Wiseman, J. A. (1996) *The New Struggle for Democracy in Africa*, Aldershot: Avebury.

Wiseman, J. A. and Charlton, R. (1995) 'The October 1994 Elections in Botswana', Electoral Studies 14(3).

Woodward, Peter (1994) 'Constitutional Framework for peace and Stability', in Sharif Harir and Terje Tvedt (eds) *Short-Cut to Decay: The Case of the Sudan,* Uppsala: Nordiska Afrikainstitutet.

World Bank (1989) *Sub-Saharan Africa. From Crisis to Sustainable Growth. A Long-term Perspective Study*, Washington DC: World Bank.

World Bank (1991) *Social Indicators of Development 1990*, Baltimore, MD and London: Johns Hopkins University Press.

World Bank (1993) *Ghana 2000 and Beyond: Setting the Stage for Accelerated Growth and Poverty Reduction*, Washington, DC: World Bank.

World Bank (1995) *Trends in Developing Countries 1995*, Washington, DC: World Bank.

World Bank (1997) *World Development Report 1997: The State in a Changing World*, Oxford: Oxford University Press.

World Factbook (1995) *Washington Post Homepage*
[http://www.washingpost.com/wps/longterm/worlderf/cia/ghana.html]

Young, Crawford (1988) 'The African Colonial State and Its Political Legacy', in D. Rothchild and N. Chazan (eds.) *The Precarious Balance: State and Society in Africa*, Boulder, CO: Westview.

Young, Crawford (1994) 'Evolving Modes of Consciousness and Ideology: Nationalism and Ethnicity' in D. E. Apter and C.G.Rosberg (eds.) *Political Development and the New Realism in Sub-Saharan Africa*, Charlottesville, VA and London: University Press of Virginia.

Young, Crawford (1999) 'The Third Wave of Democratization in Africa: Ambiguities and Contradictions', in Richard Joseph (ed.) (1999) *State, Conflict, and Democracy in Africa,* Boulder, CO: Lynne Rienner.

Young, Iris (1989) 'Polity and Group Difference: A Critique of the Ideal of Universal Citizenship', *Ethics* 99.

Young, Tom (1993) 'Elections and Electoral Politics in Africa', *Africa* 63(3): 299–312.

Young, Tom (ed.) (1991) 'Elections in Africa', unpublished conference proceedings, London: School of Oriental and African Studies.

Young, Tom (ed.) (1993) 'Understanding Elections in Africa: Special Issue', *Africa* 63(3): 299–418.

Zakaria, F. (1997) 'The Rise of Illiberal Democracy', *Foreign Affairs* 76(6): 22–43.

Zambia Independent Monitoring Team (no date) *Presidential and Parliamentary Elections in Zambia 18 November 1996*, Lusaka: Zambia Independent Monitoring Team.

Zambia Independent Monitoring Team and Konrad Adenauer Foundation (1997) *Traditional Leadership and Democracy in Zambia: Report on the National Workshop for Zambian Traditional Rulers,* Lusaka: ZIMT and KAF.

Zimbabwe (1990) *Report of the 1989 Delimitation Commission*, Harare: Government Printer.

Zimbabwe (1994a) *Drought Relief Program,* Government of Zimbabwe Ministry of Public Service, Labour and Social Welfare Department of Social Welfare and the US Agency for International Development's Famine Early Warning System Project, 20 March.

Zimbabwe (1994b) *Zimbabwe National Report, Census 1992*, Central Statistical Office, Harare: Government Printer.

Zimbabwe (1995) *1994 Delimitation Commission Report*, Harare: Government Printer.

Zimbabwe African National Union (1984) *Zimbabwe African National Union Resolutions: Second Congress*, Harare, 8 August 1984.

Zimbabwe Inter-Africa News Agency (ZIANA) (1985) *Election Handbook: A Guide to the General Election of July 1985*, Harare: ZIANA.

ZimRights (1995) *Election Monitoring Report, Parliamentary Elections, 1995*, Harare: ZimRights Information Department, 20 May.

Zolberg, Aristide R. (1966) *Creating Political Order: The Party-States of West Africa*, Chicago: The University of Chicago Press.

Zuccarelli, François (1970) *Un parti politique africain: L'Union Progressiste Sénégalaise*, Paris: Libraire Générale de Droit et Jurisprudence.

Newspapers and Magazines

Addis Tribune, Addis Ababa
Africa Confidential, London
Africa Research Bulletin, Devon
Akhabar Al-Youm, Khartoum
Allgemeine Zeitung, Windhoek
Al-Rai Al-Am, Khartoum
Asharq Al-Awsat, London
Banobero, Bissau
Boletim Oficial, official journal of the Republic of
   Guinea-Bissau
Botswana Guardian, Botswana
The Botswana Gazette, Botswana
Business Day, South Africa
Correio Guiné-Bissau, Bissau
Daily Graphic, Accra
Daily Mail, Zambia
Daily Nation, Nairobi
Daily News, Dar es Salaam
Daily Times, Blantyre
Daily Times, Lagos
The Diet, Ibadan
East African, Dar es Salaam
Economist Intelligence Unit Quarterly Reports:
   Tanzania and Comoros, London
Economist Intelligence Unit Quarterly Reports:
   Botswana, Lesotho and Swaziland, London
Economist Intelligence Unit Quarterly Reports:
   Nigeria, London
Facts and Reports, Amsterdam
Financial Gazette, Harare
Financial Mail, Zambia
Ghanaian Times, Accra
The Guardian, Lagos
The Guardian, London
The Herald, Harare
The Independent, Lagos
Leselinyana, Lesotho
Lesotho Today, Lesotho
Mail and Guardian, South Africa
Majira, Dar es Salaam
Marchés Tropicaux, Paris
The Midweek Sun, Botswana
Miners Speak, Windhoek
The Mirror, Lesotho
Mmegi, Botswana
Mphatlalatsane, Lesotho

Namibia Economist, Windhoek
Namibia Plus, Windhoek
The Namibian, Windhoek
The Nation, Blantyre
National Concord, Lagos
New Africa, Dar es Salaam
New Era, Windhoek
The News, Lagos
Newswatch, Lagos
Nigeria Now. London
Nô Pintcha, Bissau
Parade, Harare
The Post, Lusaka
Post Express, Lagos
Public Eye, Lesotho
O Público, Lisbon, June–September 1998
   [www.publico.pt]
The Punch, Lagos
Republikein, Windhoek
The Standard, Nairobi
The Star, Blantyre
Sudan Focus, London
Sunday Mail, Harare
Sunday Mail, Zambia
Sunday News, Dar es Salaam
Sunday Standard, Harare
   [http://www.samara.co.zw/standard/index.html]
Sunday Times, Lagos
Sunday Times, South Africa
Sunday Times, Swaziland
Swazi News, Swaziland
The Swazi Observer, Swaziland
Tanzanian Affairs, London
Thisday, Lagos
The Times, London
The Times of Swaziland, Swaziland
The Times of Zambia, Zambia
Tribune, Ibadan
Uhuru, Dar es Salaam
Voz de Bissau, Bissau
Weekly Review, Nairobi
West Africa, London
Zimbabwe News, Harare
Zimbabwe Standard, Harare
ZimRights News, Harare

Index

Aadland, Oyvind 64–5
Abacha, Gen. Sani 220–9, 233–46, 250; for President 239–46
Abbink, Jon 64
Abboud, General 253, 263, 275
Abdelrahman, Sheikh Ali 253
Abiola, M.K.O. 221, 223, 232–5 *passim*, 235, 237, 246–7
Abrahamsen, Rita 303
Abshire, David M. 107
Abubakar, Gen. Abdulsalam 220, 246–7, 250
accountability 1, 4, 71, 78, 80, 129, 172, 191, 212, 300, 322, 323
Acheampong, Col. I.K. 79
Adekanye, J. Bayo 219, 227, 231
adjustment, structural 8, 19, 20, 38, 44, 77, 93–5, 106, 111–13, 123, 177, 229–31, 340, 342
administration 128, 189–91, 197, 332, 334, 336, 338
Afari-Gyan, Dr Kwadwo 81, 82
Agbu, Osita 228, 229, 231, 232
agriculture 39, 54, 131, 132, 136, 162, 166, 311, 314, 342
Agovi, Kofi 78
Aguilar, Renato 113
Agyman-Rawlings, Nana Konadu 84, 94
Ahluwalia, D.P. 156
Ahwoi, Kwamena 87
aid 19, 25, 41, 110, 111, 300, 303, 308, 313, 342; conditionality 20, 24, 25, 81; food 47, 313
Ake, C. 212, 219
al-Bashir, President Omer 273
Alemayehu, Rahel 66, 67
Alhardallo, Adlan 253
Ali, Major-Gen. Mohammed Chris 223
Ali, T.M.A. 256, 269
al-Khalifa, Sir al-Khatim 257
Allen, C. 10

Al-Mahdi, Mohammed Ahmed 256
Al-Mahdi, Sadiq 262, 269; Sarra 262
Almond, Gabriel 6
Al-Mustapha, Major Hamza 224
Amin, Nick 331
Amnesty International 223
Amour, Salmin 281
Angaine, Jackson 157, 158
Angula, Nahas 212
Annan, D.F. 80
anti-colonial movement 105; struggle 116, 279, 311; *see also* independence movement/struggle and liberation movement/struggle
apathy 2, 14–16, 23–5 *passim*, 27–8, 140, 182, 204–6, 212, 214, 288, 315, 325, 328, 340–1
Apter, David 6, 7
Ardener, Shirley 60, 70, 72
Arkaah, K.N. 84, 85
Aryee, J. 101
Asamoah, Obed 84
Asia, East 16, 171
Aspen, Harald 65
Atta-Mills, John 85
Aubynn, Anthony Kwesi 2, 75–103
Austin, Denis 6, 78–80 *passim*, 100
autonomy 104, 105, 109, 112, 114, 115, 126, 127
Awoonor, K. 79, 80, 84

Babandinga, General 221, 222, 228–35, 250
Baffuor, Kwabena 87
Bailey, F.G. 324
ballot boxes, transparent 75, 82–3, 102
Banana, President Canaan 332
Banda, Asuma 85
Banda, Elias Ngalande 176
Banda, Dr Hastings Kamuzu 173–5 *passim*, 180

377